FEMINIST FRAMEWORKS

ALTERNATIVE THEORETICAL ACCOUNTS OF THE RELATIONS BETWEEN WOMEN AND MEN

SECOND EDITION

Alison M. Jaggar

Professor of Philosophy
University of Cincinnati

Paula S. Rothenberg

Associate Professor of Philosophy
The William Paterson College
of New Jersey

W9-COL-911

McGRAW-HILL BOOK COMPANY

New York St. Louis San Francisco Auckland Bogotá
Hamburg Johannesburg London Madrid Mexico Montreal New Delhi
Panama Paris São Paulo Singapore Sydney Tokyo Toronto

This book was set in Times Roman by Black Dot, Inc. (ECU).
The editors were Anne Murphy and Susan Gamer;
the production supervisor was Diane Renda.
The cover was designed by Maxine Davidowitz.
The cover illustration was done by Jeanne Fisher.
Halliday Lithograph Corporation was printer and binder.

FEMINIST FRAMEWORKS

Alternative Theoretical Accounts
of the Relations between Women and Men

4567890 HALHAL 89876

ISBN 0-07-032251-1

See Acknowledgments on pages 439–442.
Copyrights included on this page by reference.

Library of Congress Cataloging in Publication Data

Jaggar, Alison M.
  Feminist frameworks.

  Includes bibliographies and index.
  1. Feminism—United States—Addresses, essays,
lectures. 2. Sexism—Addresses, essays, lectures.
3. Social institutions—Addresses, essays, lectures.
4. Women's rights—Addresses, essays, lectures.
5. Social change—Addresses, essays, lectures.
I. Rothenberg, Paula S., date   . II. Title.
HQ1426.J325 1984   305.4'2   83-17518
ISBN 0-07-032251-1

CONTENTS

PART 2   ALTERNATIVE FEMINIST FRAMEWORKS

INTRODUCTION
FEMINIST THEORY AND FEMINIST PRACTICE

The first edition of *Feminist Frameworks* was conceived in the mid-1970s. The years immediately preceding its publication were full of excitement and controversy as millions of women in the industrialized nations of the world came to see themselves as oppressed and moved into action against that oppression. Every modern institution was exposed to critical scrutiny by the new feminists of the late 1960s and early 1970s. Like their predecessors of the late nineteenth and early twentieth centuries, these feminists criticized male dominance in education, religion, government, and the economy. What especially distinguished them from earlier feminists, however, was their challenge to the organization of so-called personal life: marriage, family, sexuality, and even childhood as an institution. Those who were unsympathetic to the new feminism felt that the whole structure of society was under attack—as indeed it was. Conservatives responded with a variety of arguments designed to prove that traditional standards of appropriate behavior for men and women were grounded on biological predispositions that were different for each sex. On this basis, conservatives argued that women's subordination was in some sense natural. According to their analysis, much of the dissatisfaction and misery that pervaded so many aspects of contemporary society was a consequence less of rigid and irrational gender norms than of the prevailing social disregard for biological imperatives.

The first edition of *Feminist Frameworks* reflected the excitement and controversy of the time. It included women's reports of their own experience of oppression and various feminist attempts to analyse the nature and causes of that oppression. Some of the feminist analyses were more than a century old; others constituted new theoretical beginnings, formulating new categories to understand areas of social life that had been ignored hitherto by social theory. The first edition of *Feminist Frameworks* also included some of the new forms of biological determinism that purported to explain and thus justify women's oppression.

The years since the original publication of *Feminist Frameworks* have seen rapid changes, both social and theoretical. The situation of many women has been conspicuously altered, partly as a result of feminist struggles but more fundamentally in response to the changing economic situation. Moreover, the theoretical debate over women's situation has moved to a higher level. On the one hand, the more sophisticated biological determinism of sociobiology has superseded some of the cruder biological determinist theories of ten years ago. On the other hand, feminist theorists have made visible aspects of women's oppression that were previously obscured and have refined the conceptual apparatus needed for a more adequate understanding of women's situation. The insistence by women of color that we pay special attention to the way in which race and gender interact to create special kinds of oppression has contributed greatly to these theoretical achievements.

The first edition of *Feminist Frameworks* sprang out of our concerns as feminists, as philosophers, and as activists. In our introduction to the first edition, we stated that the book was motivated by our deep belief, as feminists, that changes were urgently required in the position of women; that it issued also from our conviction, as philosophers, that the presuppositions and implications of any proposed changes needed to be explored very carefully; and that, finally, it came from our recognition, as activists, that not only must our political activity be guided by theory but our theory must be evaluated by its success in practice.

Today, almost a decade later, our concerns are unchanged. We do not believe that changes in women's situation have rendered feminist social criticism obsolete. On the contrary, we think that, while there have been striking transformations in the life experience and prospects of a few token women, the situation and prospects of most women may have worsened since the original publication of *Feminist Frameworks*. In consequence, we think an improvement in women's situation may be needed even more urgently than it was in the mid-1970s.

Just as in the mid-1970s, however, we believe that the feminist struggle must be guided by feminist theory, by a systematic analysis of the underlying nature and causes of women's oppression. Since the mid-1970s, feminist theory has changed considerably—partly in response to the changing situation of women, partly as a result of increasing theoretical sophistication. Because of the growing maturity of feminist theorizing, we think it is time to update the older analyses. In this second edition of *Feminist Frameworks*, we reprint older feminist theories that continue to attract adherents, but we also present a number of new and insightful analyses. These new theoretical developments result primarily from work by radical feminists, socialist feminists, and feminists of color.

WHAT DO WE MEAN BY A FEMINIST FRAMEWORK?

Feminists are people who demonstrate a commitment to improving women's position in society. Feminist frameworks are systems of ideas, conceptual structures that feminists can use in explaining, justifying, and guiding their actions. Typically, a feminist framework is a comprehensive analysis of the nature and causes of women's oppression and a correlated set of proposals for ending it. It is an integrated theory of women's place both in contemporary society and in the new society that feminists are struggling to build.

Although *Feminist Frameworks* is the title of this book, the positions presented within it vary both in their commitment to feminism and in their degree of cohesiveness, comprehensiveness, and integration—in how closely they approximate a systematic framework. The position that we identify as conservatism, for example, is far from feminist: rather than providing a critique of women's subordination, it provides a justification for it. In addition, some of the more recent versions of feminism were—and remain—more or less fragmentary, not yet constituting entirely unified theoretical structures. This introduction is a good place to explain our reasons for including positions whose feminism or whose status as frameworks may be questionable.

For this second edition of *Feminist Frameworks*, we seriously debated the inclusion of what we call the "conservative" framework. Conservatism is inconsistent with our title; in addition, we wondered whether it was a waste of space to reprint views that have already been circulated too widely. We considered devoting all the space we had available to the exposition of feminist views that are still too little known. In the end, however, we decided that it was necessary to include some representative statements of biological determinism—although we have certainly not given "equal time" to conservatives, since a conservative stance with respect to women can be based on many grounds other than biology. We made this decision because, in our view, the influence of the various forms of biological determinism is so pervasive that we felt it needed to be confronted squarely in its most popular and sophisticated versions. We thought it was vital to demonstrate the arguments that must be answered by an adequate feminist framework.

We had no doubts about including liberal feminism or traditional Marxism as distinct feminist frameworks: each of these positions issues from a well-established political tradition whose conceptual foundations are relatively well-defined. In the past, radical feminism and social feminism were more problematic. At the time of our first edition, radical feminists were still exploring the implications of their new perspective on reality; radical feminism did not yet constitute a unified theory but instead, as our first edition showed, included several diverse strands of thinking. Similarly, at the time of the first edition, socialist feminism had not succeeded in distinguishing itself clearly from the traditional Marxism. Since the mid-1970s, however, both radical and socialist feminism have undergone considerable theoretical development. Radical feminism, which is not the inheritor of a long philosophical tradition (and whose strength may lie precisely in that fact), still does not constitute an entirely unified conceptual framework; nevertheless, its theorists have pressed further their analysis of women's oppression in terms of male control of women's bodies, particularly women's sexuality. This second edition of *Feminist Frameworks* reprints some of the new analyses and so makes clearer the distinctive theoretical contribution of radical feminism. Socialist feminists, too have deepened and sharpened their analyses so that the contrast between socialist feminism and traditional Marxism is now more clearly visible.

The most obvious change between the first and second editions of *Feminist*

Frameworks is the addition of the sections entitled "Feminism and Women of Color." Within the industrial nations, where so far feminists have been most vocal, women of color have always contributed to feminist discourse; however, their voices have not always been heard. In this edition of *Feminist Frameworks*, we wanted to ensure that their contribution was no longer neglected, and we debated how best to include it. Like white women, women of color have undergone a variety of experiences and have used a variety of conceptual structures for interpreting and organizing their experience. Consequently, we first considered integrating work by women of color into our existing frameworks. In some cases, such work fit comfortably; but in others it did not. Ultimately, our reason for rejecting this approach was our concern that the unique aspects of the oppression experienced by women of color not be subsumed (and possibly lost or diluted) under a general feminist heading. At this point in our history, the sad reality is that a separation continues to exist between the white feminist movement on the one hand and feminists of color on the other. Women of color realize that they are never oppressed simply as women but always as women who are not white. Consequently, they regard racism as an enemy that is at least as powerful as male dominance and ultimately inseparable from it.

We have chosen to place in a separate section writing that focuses specifically on the experience of women of color. We made this decision because we believe that this structure best reflects the importance of the insights offered by women of color. We do not think that the papers we have placed in this section were designed to present a comprehensive analysis of women's oppression or a complete set of proposals for ending it. In other words, we do not think that their writers necessarily intended them to constitute a new feminist framework. Nevertheless, we do think that while the experience of women of color has been varied, it has also been grounded on enough basic similarities to have generated a distinctive perspective on social reality. At the present stage of development of feminist theorizing, we do not believe that it is possible to do justice to this perspective without giving it separate consideration. We do not know whether the insights generated by this perspective will one day be elaborated into a systematic framework or whether they will simply be integrated into one of the existing feminist frameworks, perhaps socialist feminism. We do believe that these insights already provide a test for the adequacy of existing feminist frameworks. If feminist frameworks do not take account of the experience of women of color, then they are not only incomplete; they are racially biased.

WHY ARE FRAMEWORKS NECESSARY?

All feminists are united by a commitment to improving the situation of women. Contemporary feminists, moreover, share certain basic assumptions about what would count as an improvement in women's situation. All agree that it is necessary to end sexual harassment, rape, and physical abuse of women; most agree that women should have sexual and reproductive freedom to the extent of having access to contraception and abortion and should be able to choose a sexual partner of either sex; and all contemporary feminists agree that women should have the opportunity to participate fully in so-called public life. Beyond these basic agreements, however, sharp differences between feminists emerge. Does feminism require lesbianism? Does it call for the abolition of marriage? Does it even require the end of the capitalist system?

Feminist disagreement on these and similar issues is grounded partly on women's differences in experience and information, partly on differences in their values, and partly on differences in how they conceptualize and interpret the information available to them. Often these factors are not separable from each other: differences in experience may generate differences in values which in turn generate different ways of interpreting reality; conversely, the way in which we conceptualize reality affects our actual experience of it. In other words, differences in experience, values, and modes of understanding are often bound together in an integrated and systematic theory of society. Such a social theory is what we call a "feminist theory" or a "feminist framework." One of our aims in this book is to show how feminist disagreement over specific issues is often a result of much deeper theoretical differences over the appropriate conceptual framework for feminists to use.

Disagreements on this deep level are really philosophical disagreements; they are fundamental differences over how to characterize social reality. Most people recognize that any recommendations for social change rest on certain philosophical beliefs about such values as social freedom, legitimate authority, and human fulfillment. Fewer people realize, however, that even apparently straightforward descriptions of a social situation also tend to reflect certain values. For instance, to say that a woman has been physically abused is to presuppose a certain standard of appropriate behavior toward women; to say that a woman has suffered job discrimination presupposes certain procedures as appropriate for the assignment of jobs; to say that a woman has been harassed or raped presupposes a certain concept of freedom and coercion. Because there is always some choice over which features of a situation should be emphasized and over which categories or concepts best display those features, some philosophers claim that every description of social reality reflects a set of values.

The evaluative and theoretical presuppositions of our ordinary ways of thinking and speaking are not always conscious. One way in which feminists have challenged traditional views about the status of women has been to uncover the presuppositions of those who deny the need for change. Sometimes popular pressure for change has been intensified simply by a demonstration of the inconsistent nature of those presuppositions or of their conflict with values that are widely accepted. But even if the need for change is acknowledged, there remains the question precisely what changes should be made. It is in answering this question that feminists most immediately have felt the need for a systematic conceptual framework in which to locate both our critique of the contemporary position of women and our recommendations for how that position should be improved.

A comprehensive theory of women's position in contemporary society is necessary primarily for feminists to ensure that our critiques of oppression, our ideals of liberation, and our strategies for change are all consistent with each other. Most obviously, feminists need an alternative to the views that we criticize; indeed, if what we have said earlier is correct, the outline of an alternative will necessarily be presupposed in any social criticism. But it is important that the feminist alternative be carefully worked out and its implications for all women thoroughly explored. Only by doing this can we ensure that our recommendations for change in one area are consistent with our recommendations in another area, and that both are consistent with our deeper beliefs about freedom, justice, and human fulfillment.

In addition to thinking systematically about the future, we need a thorough analysis of our present situation: its benefits, its costs, its reasons for being. We need to know what underlying social forces perpetuate women's subordination and how these can best be challenged. An incomplete understanding of women's contemporary situation may prompt us to direct our energies wrongly, so that, no matter how hard we struggle, we shall make little or no progress. Perhaps we shall end up proposing piecemeal solutions to a problem that requires systematic revision. If a problem pervades the entire system, attempts to improve the situation for some women may make things worse for others; for instance, feminist insistence on the right to paid work for some women may force other women out of the home and into low-paying menial jobs. By failing to develop a complete analysis of the situation, we may well mistake a symptom of the illness for its cause, and we may "cure" the patient's fever only to have her succumb to a massive infection that goes undiagnosed.

HOW SHOULD WE CHOOSE A FRAMEWORK?

Feminist theories are designed for a practical purpose: they are tools for improving women's condition. But which tools are best adapted for that purpose? Which account of women's situation is most illuminating? Which proposals for social change are most conducive to human well-being and fulfillment?

In our view, these questions can be answered only in the context of the feminist struggle. We believe that the adequacy of each of the theories presented will be tested in the process of building a better society. We do not find it useful to view each feminist theory as setting up a blueprint for the position of women in some future utopia; instead, we find it more helpful to view feminist theorizing as a search for the conditions under which women will be able to exercise significantly free choice about our own future position in society. In our view, liberation is not a clearly defined end state; instead, it is a continual process. To look at feminist theories in this way helps to avoid very abstract speculations about the ultimate nature of liberation and encourages us to focus instead on the specific institutions that limit our choices. We may then evaluate feminist frameworks according to their success in identifying the conditions that prevent us from freely choosing which of our potentialities we wish to fulfill.

THE STRUCTURE OF THIS BOOK

Apart from adding the sections on women of color, the second edition of *Feminist Frameworks* retains the structure of the first edition. As before, this structure is designed to facilitate an understanding of the interconnection between specific recommendations for social change and their theoretical presuppositions.

Part One is a collection of readings designed to illustrate many ways in which contemporary social arrangements fail to promote personal happiness and fulfillment, especially for women. In constructing this section, we have drawn upon the experience of people of all ages and ethnic backgrounds and of both sexes, although mostly we have focused on women's experiences. We have been particularly concerned to show that there are problems in the areas of paid labor, the family, and sexuality, since those are the areas through which we shall examine the feminist frameworks that we present.

Part Two of the book presents the major theoretical frameworks within which the problems are examined. The frameworks are presented through the use of selections from classic statements by major proponents of the views.

Finally, in Part Three the frameworks identified are used to conceptualize the problem areas emphasized at the outset of the book, thus demonstrating the alternative solutions generated by different theoretical frameworks. This organization is intended to show the reader how theoretical presuppositions are connected with specific and concrete issues and to demonstrate the striking differences among the frameworks when they are employed as guides in solving specific problems of daily life. In the past, this structure has helped readers to avoid treating either the theories or the solutions they generate in isolation from each other.

Each of the feminist frameworks that we present here is still current; each still has its adherents. Nevertheless, the order in which we have presented the theories reflects the historical order of their articulation: biological determinism is perhaps the oldest account of women's subordination; women of color are the most recent group of feminists to insist on a reevaluation of their social position. Presenting the theories in chronological order suggests that feminist "theory building" is an ongoing historical dialog, each theory constructed in order to remedy apparent defects in earlier accounts. We think that a fuller understanding of each theory can be gained when each is seen in a historical context.

As we stated in our introduction to the first edition, we ourselves are not neutral. Both of us still believe that socialist feminism is the most adequate of the feminist frameworks developed so far. Neither of us believes, however, that socialist feminism has all the answers; one notable gap is its inability so far to achieve a theoretical integration of the concerns of women of color. Our purpose in this book, therefore, is not to "prove" one version of feminism and refute the rest. We do not want to be sectarian or to deepen divisions within feminism. We believe that every position represented in our book has made a unique contribution to feminist theory, and we have endeavoured to display that contribution. We also believe that every position represented in our book has flaws. By presenting the major feminist frameworks in a manner that shows clearly the contrasts among them, we intend to inspire a critical evaluation of both the strengths and the weaknesses of each theory. In this way, we hope that our book will be a contribution to the construction of a more fully adequate feminist framework—and ultimately of a more fully adequate world.

IN ACKNOWLEDGMENT

Many people have contributed to this book. First among them, of course, are the authors whose writing is included; we are extremely grateful to them for allowing us to reprint their work. In addition, a great many people gave us comments on the first edition of *Feminist Frameworks* that were helpful in preparing this new edition. Although we cannot thank each one by name, we would like them to know how much we appreciated all the suggestions we received. We are especially grateful to the following people for their help: Sandra L. Bartky, Barbara Corrado Pope, Susan G. Radner and Evelyn Rosskamm Shalom. A number of people prepared comprehensive reviews of *Feminist Frameworks* which were enormously useful to us in planning the second edition. Our thanks go to: Meredith Gould, State University of New Jersey, Rutgers; Sandra Harding, University of Delaware; Nancy Henley, University of California, Los Angeles; and Beth Mintz, University of Vermont. While many friends and comrades spent time offering us suggestions on this revision, two in particular were instrumental in helping us clarify structural concerns and conceptualize the entire volume. We are grateful indeed to Ann Ferguson and Francine Rainone for their help and friendship. Our thanks go as well to the people at McGraw-Hill who have worked on this book; they include Susan Gamer, Anne Murphy, Kaye Pace, and Dianne Jordan. We are also grateful to Irene Diehl and Mary Von Nida for their prompt and generous typing assistance; to Helga Slessarev and Vicky Spelman; and to Barbara Zimmerman, permissions editor. Finally, Alison wants to express her appreciation to her family, who provided occasional interruption and distraction but also endless understanding, support, and encouragement. Paula would like to thank Greg Mantsios for his unfailing support and Alexi and Andrea for not mixing up the pages.

Alison M. Jaggar
Paula S. Rothenberg

ONE

THE PROBLEM

THE NEED
FOR LIBERATION

Sex prejudice has been the chief hindrance in the rapid advance of the woman's rights movement to its present status, and it is still a stupendous obstacle to be overcome.

This world taught woman nothing skillful and then said her work was valueless. It permitted her no opinions and said she did not know how to think. It forbade her to speak in public, and said the sex had no orators. It denied her the schools, and said the sex had no genius. It robbed her of every vestige of responsibility and then called her weak. It taught her that every pleasure must come as a favor from men, and when to gain it she decked herself in paint and fine feathers, as she had been taught to do, it called her vain.

Carrie Chapman Catt, 1902

Many women entering college today believe that sexism has little to do with them. Of course they have heard stories about unequal educational opportunities, unequal pay, unequal marriages, stories about promotion discrimination and sexual harassment. They believe, however, that these stories refer to a time that is past, to the time before the women's movement changed things. They treat women's oppression as a problem of historical rather than contemporary interest. Whereas many students entering college in the seventies brought with them an intense desire to restructure social institutions and personal relationships, many students of the eighties seem convinced that unlimited possibilities for career achievement and personal fulfillment await them, possibilities that will not be limited either by gender or race. Does this change in attitude and expectation reflect the gains that the women's movement has made in restructuring our society or does it reflect the power of the media and other institutions to shape our consciousness in a way that distorts our perceptions of reality?

The reality is that most women continue to earn a fraction of what men make for the same or comparable jobs; secretaries still earn less than truckdrivers and only 2 percent of the women in the paid labor force earn $25,000 or more a year. The FBI Uniform Crime Reports issued in 1981 tell us that a woman is raped every eight minutes in the United States, while statistics released by women's groups put the figure at one rape every two minutes. By the end of the seventies, black families were 4 times as likely as white families to be living in poverty and 3½ times as likely to be headed by women. For Christmas 1982 you could buy a home video game called "Custer's Revenge," which featured the rape of an Indian woman. During the spring of 1983, heralding a nationwide trend in fashion, a major New York department store opened a shop called "Remembering Marilyn"; according to its ads, this shop features "not so innocent clothes that snuggle the waist, hug the hips and do nothing to stop a head from turning."

That women are now so widely perceived to be "liberated" demonstrates the tremendous power of ideology, both conscious and unconscious, to conceal and mystify the continuing reality of women's oppression. Such an ideology, which in fact perpetuates male dominance, is created and reinforced by all the major social institutions and especially by the mass media. In order to see how this occurs, we must try to understand the forces that shape our sense of self as well as structure our understanding of society.

We are born into the world as females and males, and then we learn to be women and men. Each society defines what it means to be a woman or a man, and these definitions are subject to wide cross-cultural variation. Even within a given society, social conceptions of femininity and masculinity vary according to class and race. They also change greatly from one period to another, depending upon the economic and political realities of the times. For example, during World War II "Rosie the Riveter" replaced the flapper of the twenties as the ideal woman of the United States. As the war(s) ended and the men came home, a new version of the feminine mystique sent women back to their homes to cook and care for their men, breastfeed their babies—and make Rosie's job on the assembly line available once again to male workers,

What we are taught about masculinity and femininity depends on changing historical circumstances, but those circumstances have different effects on different groups within our society. The lessons of gender are learned within the context of race and class. In other words, the experiences we have and the models with which we are presented depend first upon whether we are male or female but in addition will also be shaped by our color or ethnic background and by the way in which our parents and later ourselves earn our living. Other factors, such as our perceived physical normality or whether we live in the city or the country, will also make a difference.

The articles that appear in Part One were chosen to focus our attention on experiences we have living in contemporary American society. In addition they can help us remember some of the lessons we learned both in and out of school while we were growing up. What kinds of things were we encouraged to believe about ourselves and each other? Why did we accept these beliefs? What effect do they have on how we treat others and how we expect to be treated? What is the relation between the treatment we receive, the beliefs and values we are taught, and the expectations we form with respect to our futures? These questions are really questions about the effect of ideology. In Part One, Sandra and Daryl Bem explain ideology by talking about the fish who, being entirely submerged in water, never realizes that she is wet. Because we take so much of what happens to us for granted, because the way things are seems so "natural," we may be very much like that fish—all wet without even knowing it.

Within every society, there exists a prevailing ideology. That ideology is a relatively coherent system of beliefs and values about human nature and social life. In some societies, the prevailing ideology interprets the world in terms of a set of religious beliefs; in modern society, reality is more likely to be interpreted through theories that claim the prestige of science. When we look at the science of the past, it is often easy to pick out ways in which its methods and assumptions were shaped by values that reflected the interests of the dominant social groups. It is not so easy to pick out the social values that are implicit in contemporary scientific theories, still less in those day-to-day assumptions that seem to be "common sense." The system of beliefs and values that prevails in our society is so generally accepted and so familiar that it may seem to be entirely natural or objective, to simply reflect and illuminate the way things are. As we have begun to see already, however, and as will become much clearer later, prevailing common sense and prevailing science are both often formulated in such a way as to demean the abilities and work of women, especially working-class women and women of color. What passes both for common sense and for science may thus be a way of justifying and so reinforcing existing inequalities in wealth, power, and privilege.

One important function of the prevailing ideology is to rationalize differences in the opportunities and rewards available to people of different classes, races, and sexes, to make these differences appear to be rational and just rather than arbitrary and unjust. For example, women in our society routinely are paid less than men and this is justified by defining women's "real" work as maintaining home and family. Women's paid labor is portrayed as secondary and perhaps temporary, something they are doing to purchase "extras" or pay off debts. Insofar as women believe this myth they are less likely to protest poor wages and lack of benefits than are other workers, namely men, "who take their jobs seriously." In addition, because both husband and wife devalue the woman's paid labor and define her real job in terms of homemaking, the myth makes it possible for women to work outside the home without undermining the husband's position as breadwinner and head of the family. In this way, the ideological definition of women's "real" work keeps wages low and profits high at the same time that it protects the male position as head of household and obscures the obvious justice of redefining household responsibilities in light of both partners' participation in the paid labor force. A number of articles in this section expose different versions of the mythology that has been responsible for encouraging women to lower their expectations and to accept the naturalness or inevitability of economic as well as other forms of discrimination. In addition, these articles explore the unique aspects of oppression experienced by women by virtue of their particular class, race, age, or other arbitrary factors.

At the same time as the male-dominant ideology devalues women's paid labor, it places unduly heavy burdens on men's work. If our society evaluates a woman's success in terms of the man or men she attracts, it evaluates the man's success in terms of his ability to make money. The result is summed up in the title of one of the essays that appears in Part One, "Measuring Masculinity by the Size of the Pay Check." This piece focuses on the special pressures men experience because of gender stereotyping. Sex roles are reciprocal. Men pay a price in their own lives for the way society teaches them and us to define femininity.

Many college students find it hard to accept that sexual stereotyping will have an enormous impact on their own lives. This is not surprising when we realize that, during their college years, these students are experiencing the greatest sense of personal freedom and independence they are ever likely to encounter. In addition to having a highly exaggerated conception of the career possibilities open to them, many individuals are probably enjoying the most equal and least gender-defined relations they will ever have.

Once off the college campus, however, the situation is radically different. For instance, even if young women are able to integrate the relatively egalitarian relationships of college into the early period of married life, most of them discover that the birth of children forces them and their partners to revert to older definitions of gender. The lack of adequate child care facilities, together with the fact that the average full-time woman worker earns little more than half the wage of the average full-time male worker makes it almost inevitable that the woman will assume full parenting responsibilities while the children are very young and will work outside the home only part time or not at all. Meanwhile, the father's parenting responsibility is once more defined primarily in terms of financial support.

This sexual division of labor creates problems both for the individuals concerned and for their relationship. For women, one of the most serious consequences of this division of labor is that they suffer extreme economic vulnerability. Studies have shown that one of the major factors keeping women in unsatisfactory or even physically abusive marriages is their realistic anxiety that they and their children will be unable to survive without the male wage. An awareness of the difficulties involved in raising children in this society is leading some young women to question having children at all. Nonetheless, the mystique attached to motherhood remains enormously powerful, so powerful that one may well wonder whether it allows even the possibility of a genuinely free choice over whether or not to have children.

A new way in which contemporary women are being victimized is by a refurbished version of the feminine mystique. This is the myth of the superwoman, a myth that encourages young women to believe that they should be able to do everything without any difficulty—be successful career women, gourmet cooks, cookie-baking mothers and seductive mistresses to their husbands while keeping the floors waxed and the car in perfect running order. Whereas women in the first wave of the contemporary women's movement were presented with a choice between career and family—and bitterly resented having to make that choice—women are now being misled into believing that they can do it all without *any* restructuring of family or paid work. A recent study carried out by seven Ivy League institutions indicated that many women students had lofty goals upon which they were unwilling to compromise, while at the same time, they expressed a desire to have children and remain at home while the children were young. In the past, deferring a career or taking time out to raise children usually had a negative impact on women's chances of future employment. The myth of the superwoman encourages women to believe they can avoid these consequences. But until employers, social services, government agencies, and men accept structural changes that facilitate such multifaceted lives for women, the reality is that many of these goals and responsibilities will inevitably come into conflict. One possible and dangerous consequence of the ideology we have been examining is that women who internalize the superwoman myth but find it impossible to put into practice will regard that failure as a measure of their own inadequacy rather than an indictment of the way that society is organized and an indictment of the myth itself. Whether this conflict serves as the basis for a new feminist critique of society or whether it leads to self-detraction and despondency will depend largely on the ability of the women's movement to encourage large numbers of women to adopt a feminist perspective on their experience.

Although almost two-thirds of all married women with children over six work in the paid labor force, most of them do not face the problem of juggling high-powered careers and family life. The majority of women, married or not, work at *jobs* rather than have *careers.* They work in the home before and after they perform their paid labor. While the hours of their paid labor are clearly demarcated, the hours of their second shift are not. Housework is never done. The demands of children often continue throughout a twenty-four hour day. And there are no paid sick leaves, vacation days, or retirement benefits available to women for the work they do in maintaining their family. At the same time, increasing numbers of women are shouldering these burdens without either the financial help or emotional support of a husband or partner. More than 9 million families in the United States are supported by women alone, and one-third of them subsist below the poverty level.

One lesson that feminists have been learning over the past two decades is that the same issue can have a very different meaning for women of different classes and races. The issue of reproductive freedom is one case in point. The women's movement of the 1970s counted among its victories the right of women to choose whether or not to bear children. Legalizing abortion in the United States meant that women gained control of their bodies in a fundamental way. It meant the end of trips up back stairs to rooms where men wearing stockings over their faces performed hasty, unsafe abortions for exorbitant fees. Aside from the emotional trauma induced by the humiliation and pain, these procedures resulted in the unnecessary deaths of many women, while medical complications left others unable ever to bear children. Although regaining control over their bodies and their reproductive freedom has meant the right to abortion for some, countless other women look forward to the day when they can choose to bring children into this world with dignity. One moving statement from this perspective is Colleen McNamara's article, "I Just Don't Know If I Can Make It." Reproductive freedom requires that pregnant women and nursing mothers be guaranteed adequate diet and health care throughout that period in their lives and that they be assured their children will not lack basic necessities once they are born. The day when all women can be said to possess the freedom to make basic decisions about how, whether, and when to bear children is still a long way off. The article "Sterilizing the Poor" emphasizes just how distant it is. This article shows another aspect of the oppression of poor women, especially women of color, in a society where the treatment we receive from doctors and hospitals is often determined not so much by our needs or our conscious decisions about our bodies as by our class, race, and gender.

Differences in class and race notwithstanding, all women continue to be under enormous pressure to conform to prevailing standards of feminine beauty. College students who shudder in horror when they learn about the practice of footbinding in ancient China are less quick to recognize contemporary fashions that are similarly abusive to women's bodies. Chinese women whose feet were bound were left with tiny, deformed stubs that enhanced their beauty and desirability according to their society's standards but left them crippled for life. Feminists in this society have long pointed out that so-called feminine fashions in shoes and clothing restrict women's ability to move easily and confidently and abuse their bodies in other subtle but equally serious ways.

The cosmetics industry, which reaps enormous profits from making women feel insecure about how they look and smell, encourages women to use paint and powders to define their beauty and obtain their sense of self. Feminists who offer a critique of makeup are often met by the question "What's wrong with wanting to look good?" The answer, of course, is that there's nothing wrong with "looking good," to look good is a normal human desire. But the important question is: "Who and what defines what it means for women to look good?" Feminists maintain that the dominant ideology defines female attractiveness in ways that increase profits and reinforce male dominance while' undermining and degrading women's sense of self rather than enhancing it.

What is the effect of this ideology on the way that women relate to their bodies? The models in *Playboy* centerfolds get thinner every year. The market is flooded with diet books, pills, candies, and liquid means guaranteed to help us lose weight quickly. In the United States today it is unusual to find a young woman of fourteen or fifteen who has not already begun to diet. Most women spend their lives preoccupied with feelings of inadequacy about their bodies and advertising uses all its power to deepen their feelings in order to get us to buy products that promise to make us beautiful. Carried to its logical conclusion, prevailing conceptions of female beauty can in fact be deadly. Millions of American women now suffer from anorexia nervosa, a devastating disease that causes women to starve themselves, sometimes even to death. Women suffering from anorexia always perceive themselves as overweight and unattractive and try to shed pounds through large doses of laxatives and self-induced vomiting, even when they are already desperately thin. What's wrong with wanting to look good? Absolutely nothing. Unless the standard of beauty you've been sold has deadly implications.

Whether or not they choose to adopt the currently fashionable image of femininity, whether or not they are comfortable with their sexuality, women find out early in their adolescence that their bodies are considered public property. Most women have experienced the pain and humiliation, as well as the terror, that is produced by men in the street who call out comments on their bodies in the most intimate terms. The harassment examined in "The Man in the Street: Why He Harasses" is part of a gender-defined package that includes the right to have the door opened, to wear lipstick, nail polish and blush-on, and to be raped and beaten.

We are what we earn. We are what we buy. We are what we spend. We are our bodies objectified and packaged according to the sexual stereotype. In allowing stereotypes to run our lives, we destroy rather than enhance our health and our happiness. Relationships occur between socially defined roles rather than between complete and mature adult human beings. The roles defined by contemporary society create the kind of financial, emotional, and sexual dependency that makes really satisfying relationships between men and women difficult if not impossible. For instance, contemporary standards of masculinity create men without a real capacity for intimacy or tenderness and produce the kind of failure of communication that is examined in "The Politics of Talking in Couples." These ideological sex stereotypes encourage us to judge ourselves and evaluate each other by irrational criteria and then live out our lives in ways that leave us feeling empty and frustrated. The question is: Why?

Although the force of ideology is overwhelming and the mass media are among the most powerful instruments for its perpetuation, it would be a mistake to think that the main problem is ideological. Stereotypes that degrade and oppress women are themselves symptoms of a deeper problem. In the next section we shall begin exploring various diagnoses of this deeper problem by placing the daily experience of all of us within the context of systematic feminist theories. These theories offer deeper explanations of the ways in which society defines what it means to be a woman and what it means to be a man. Once we understand in whose interests it is that we define ourselves in this way, we shall know something about how to change these stereotypes.

Homogenizing the American Woman: The Power of an Unconscious Ideology

Sandra L. Bem
Daryl J. Bem

When a baby boy is born, it is difficult to predict what he will be doing 25 years later. We can't say whether he will be an artist, a doctor, a lawyer, a college professor, or a bricklayer, because he will be permitted to develop and fulfill his own unique potential—particularly, of course, if he happens to be white and middle class. But if that same newborn child happens to be a girl, we can predict with almost complete confidence how she is likely to be spending her time some 25 years later. Why can we do that? Because her individuality doesn't have to be considered. Her individuality is irrelevant. Time studies have shown that she will spend the equivalent of a full working day, 7.1 hours, in preparing meals, cleaning house, laundering, mending, shopping and doing other household tasks. In other words, 43 percent of her waking time will be spent in activity that would command an hourly wage on the open market well below the federally set minimum for menial industrial work.

Of course, the point really is not how little she would earn if she did these things in someone else's home. She will be doing them in her own home for free. The point is that this use of time is virtually the same for homemakers with college degrees and for homemakers with less than a grade-school education, for women married to professional men, and for women married to blue-collar workers. Actually, that's understating it slightly. What the time study really showed was that college-educated women spend slightly *more* time cleaning their houses than their less-educated counterparts!

Of course, it is not simply the full-time homemaker whose unique identity has been rendered largely irrelevant. Of the 31 million women who work outside the home in our society, 78 percent end up in dead-end jobs as clerical workers, service workers, factory workers, or sales clerks, compared to a comparable figure of 40 percent for men. Only 15 percent of all women workers in our society are classified by the Labor Department as professional and technical workers, and even this figure is misleading—for the single, poorly-paid occupation of non-college teacher absorbs half of these women, and the occupation of nurse absorbs an additional quarter. In other words, the two jobs of teacher and nurse absorb three-quarters of all women classified in our society as technical or professional. That means, then, that fewer than 5 percent of all professional women—fewer than 1 percent of all women workers—fill those positions which to most Americans connote "professional" physician, lawyer, engineer, scientist, college professor, journalist, writer, and so forth.

Even an I.Q. in the genius range does not guarantee that a woman's unique potential will find expression. There was a famous study of over 1,300 boys and girls whose I.Q.'s averaged 151.[1] When the study began in the early 1900s, these highly gifted youngsters were only ten years old, and their careers have been followed ever since. What are they today? 86 percent of the men have now achieved prominence in professional and managerial occupations. In contrast, only a minority of the women were even employed. Of those who were, 37 percent were nurses, librarians, social workers, and non-college teachers. An additional 26 percent were secretaries, stenographers, bookkeepers, and office workers! Only 11 percent entered the higher professions of law, medicine, college teaching, engineering, science, economics, and the like. And even at age 44, well after all their children had gone to school, 61 percent of these highly gifted women remained full-time homemakers. Talent, education, ability, interests, motivations: all irrelevant. In our society, being female uniquely qualifies an individual for domestic work—either by itself or in conjunction with typing, teaching, nursing, or (most often) unskilled labor. It is this homogenization of America's women which is the major consequence of our society's sex-role ideology.

It is true, of course, that most women have several hours of leisure time every day And it is here we are often told, that each woman can express her unique identity. Thus, politically interested women can join the League of Women Voters. Women with humane interests can become part-time Gray Ladies. Women who love music can raise money for the symphony. Protestant women play canasta; Jewish woman play mah-jongg; brighter women of all denominations and faculty wives play bridge.

But politically interested *men* serve in legislatures. *Men* with humane interests become physicians or clinical psychologists. *Men* who love music play in the symphony. In other words, why should a woman's unique identity determine only the periphery of her life rather than its central core?

Why? Why nurse rather than physician, secretary rather than executive, stewardess rather than pilot? Why faculty wife rather than faculty? Why doctor's mother rather than doctor? There are three basic answers to this question: (1) discrimination; (2) sex-role conditioning; and (3) the presumed incompatibility of family and career. . . .

Many Americans assume that the recent drive for equality between the sexes is primarily for the benefit of the middle-class woman who wants to seek self-fulfillment in a professional career. But in many ways, it is the woman in more modest circumstances, the woman who *must* work for economic reasons, who stands to benefit most from the removal of discriminatory barriers. It is *she* who is hardest hit by unequal pay; it is *she* who so desperately needs adequate day-care facilities; it is *her* job which is often dead-ended while her male colleagues in the factory get trained and promoted into the skilled craft jobs. And if both she and her husband work at unfulfilling jobs eight hours a day just

---

[1]L. M. Terman and M. H. Oden, *The Gifted Group at Mid-Life: Thirty-Five Years' Follow-up of the Superior Child*, Genetic Studies of Genius, V (Stanford, Calif.: Stanford University Press, 1959).

to make an adequate income, it is still *she* who carries the additional burden of domestic chores when they return home.

We think it is important to emphasize these points at the outset, for we have chosen to focus our remarks in this particular paper on those fortunate men and women who can afford the luxury of pursuing self-fulfillment through the world of work and career. But every societal reform advocated by the new feminist movement, whether it be the Equal Rights Amendment, the establishment of child-care centers, or basic changes in America's sex-role ideology, will affect the lives of men and women in every economic circumstance. Nevertheless, it is still economic discrimination which hits hardest at the largest group of women, and it is here that the drive for equality can be most successfully launched with legislative and judicial tools.

SEX-ROLE CONDITIONING

Even if all discrimination were to end tomorrow, nothing very drastic would change. For job discrimination is only part of the problem. It does impede women who choose to become lawyers or managers or physicians. But it does not, by itself, help us to understand why so many women "choose" to be secretaries or nurses rather than executives or physicians; why only 3 percent of ninth-grade girls as compared to 25 percent of the boys "choose" careers in science or engineering; or why 63 percent of America's married women "choose" not to work at all. It certainly doesn't explain those young women whose vision of the future includes only marriage, children, and living happily ever after; who may, at some point, "choose" to take a job, but who almost never "choose" to pursue a career. Discrimination frustrates choices already made. Something more pernicious perverts the motivation to choose.

That "something" is an unconscious ideology about the nature of the female sex, an ideology which constricts the emerging self-image of the female child and the nature of her aspirations from the very beginning; an ideology which leads even those Americans who agree that a black skin should not uniquely qualify *its* owner for a janitorial or domestic service to act as if the possession of a uterus uniquely qualifies *its* owner for precisely such service.

Consider, for example, the 1968 student rebellion at Columbia University. Students from the radical Left took over some administration buildings in the name of equalitarian ideals which they accused the university of flouting. Here were the most militant spokesmen one could hope to find in the cause of equalitarian ideals. But no sooner had they occupied the buildings than the male militants blandly turned to their sisters-in-arms and assigned them the task of preparing the food, while they—the menfolk—would presumably plan future strategy. The reply these males received was the reply that they deserved—we will leave that to your imagination—and the fact that domestic tasks behind the barricades were desegregated across the sex line that day is an everlasting tribute to the class consciousness of these ladies of the Left. And it was really on that day that the campus women's liberation movement got its start—when radical women finally realized that they were never going to get to make revolution, only coffee.

But these conscious co-eds are not typical, for the unconscious assumptions about a woman's "natural" talents (or lack of them) are at least as prevalent among women as they are among men. A psychologist named Phillip Goldberg demonstrated this by asking female college students to rate a number of professional articles from each of six fields.[2] The articles were collated into two equal sets of booklets, and the names of the authors were changed so that the identical article was attributed to a male author (e.g., John T. McKay) in one booklet and to a female author (e.g., Joan T. McKay) in the other booklet. Each student was asked to read the articles in her booklet and to rate them for value, competence, persuasiveness, writing style, and so forth.

As he had anticipated, Goldberg found that the identical article received significantly lower ratings when it was attributed to a female author than when it was attributed to a male author. He had predicted this result for articles from professional fields generally considered the province of men, like law or city planning, but to his surprise, these women also downgraded articles from the fields of dietetics and elementary-school education when they were attributed to female authors. In other words, these students rated the male authors as better at everything, agreeing with Aristotle that "we should regard the female nature as afflicted with a natural defectiveness." Such is the nature of America's unconscious ideology about women.

When does this ideology begin to affect the life of a young girl? Research now tells us that from the day a newborn child is dressed in pink, she is given "special" treatment. Perhaps because they are thought to be more fragile, six-month-old infant girls are actually touched, spoken to, and hovered over more by their mothers while they are playing than are infant boys.[3] One study even showed that when mothers and babies are still in the hospital, mothers smile at, talk to, and touch their female infants more than their male infants at two days of age.[4] Differential treatment can't begin much earlier than that.

As children begin to read, the storybook characters become the images and the models that little boys and little girls aspire to become. What kind of role does the female play in the world of children's literature? The fact is that there aren't even very many females in that world. One survey[5] found that five times as many males as females appear in the titles of children's books; the fantasy world of Doctor Seuss is almost entirely male; and even animals and machines are represented as male. When females do appear, they are noteworthy

---

[2] Phillip Goldberg, "Are Women Prejudiced Against Women?" *Transaction* 5 (April 1968), 28–30.

[3] S. Goldberg and M. Lewis, "Play Behavior in the Year-old Infant: Early Sex Differences," *Child Development* 40 (1969), 21–31.

[4] E. B. Thoman, P. H. Leiderman, and J. P. Olson, "Neonate-Mother Interaction during Breast Feeding," *Developmental Psychology* 6 (1972), 110–118.

[5] E. Fisher, "The Second Sex, Junior Division," *The New York Times Book Review,* May 1970.

primarily for what they do *not* do. They do not drive cars, and they seldom even ride bicycles. In one story in which a girl does ride a bicycle, it's a two-seater. Guess where the girl is seated! Boys in these stories climb trees and fish and roll in the leaves and skate. Girls watch, fall down, and get dizzy. Girls are never doctors, and although they may be nurses or librarians or teachers, they are never principals. There seemed to be only one children's book about mothers who work, and it concludes that what mothers love "best of all" is "being your very own Mommy and coming home to you." And although this is no doubt true of many daddies as well, no book about working fathers has ever found it necessary to apologize for working in quite the same way.

As children grow older, more explicit sex-role training is introduced. Boys are encouraged to take more of an interest in mathematics and science. Boys, not girls, are usually given chemistry sets and microscopes for Christmas. Moreover, all children quickly learn that mommy is proud to be a moron when it comes to math and science, whereas daddy is a little ashamed if he doesn't know all about such things. When a young boy returns from school all excited about biology, he is almost certain to be encouraged to think of becoming a physician. A girl with similar enthusiasm is usually told that she might want to consider nurse's training later on, so she can have "an interesting job to fall back upon in case—God forbid—she ever needs to support herself." A very different kind of encouragement. And any girl who doggedly persists in her enthusiasm for science is likely to find her parents as horrified by the prospect of a permanent love affair with physics as they would be either by the prospect of an interracial marriage or, horror of horrors, no marriage at all. Indeed, our graduate women report that their families seem convinced that the menopause must come at age 23.

These socialization practices take their toll. When they apply for college, boys and girls are about equal on verbal aptitude tests, but boys score significantly higher on mathematical aptitude tests—about 60 points higher on the College Board Exams.[6] Moreover, for those who are convinced that this is due to female hormones, it is relevant to know that girls improve their mathematical performance if the problems are simply reworded so that they deal with cooking and gardening, even though the abstract reasoning required for solution remains exactly the same.[7] That's not hormones! Clearly, what has been undermined is not a woman's mathematical ability, but rather her confidence in that ability.

But these effects in mathematics and science are only part of the story. The most conspicuous outcome of all is that the majority of America's women become full-time homemakers. And of those who do work, nearly 80 percent end up in dead-end jobs as clerical workers, service workers, factory workers, or sales clerks. Again, it is this "homogenization" of America's women which is the major consequence of America's sex-role ideology.

The important point is not that the role of homemaker is necessarily inferior,

[6]For example, R. Brown, *Social Psychology* (New York: Free Press, 1965).

[7]G. A. Milton, "Sex Differences in Problem Solving as a Function of Role Appropriateness of the Problem Content," *Psychological Reports* 5 (1959), 705–708.

but rather that our society is managing to consign a large segment of its population to the role of homemaker—either with or without a dead-end job—solely on the basis of sex just as inexorably as it has in the past consigned the individual with a black skin to the role of janitor or domestic. The important point is that in spite of their unique identities, the majority of American women end up in virtually the *same* role.

The socialization of the American male has closed off certain options for him, too. Men are discouraged from developing certain desirable traits such as tenderness and sensitivity, just as surely as women are discouraged from being assertive and, alas, "too bright." Young boys are encouraged to be incompetent at cooking and certainly child care, just as surely as young girls are urged to be incompetent at math and science. The elimination of sex-role stereotyping implies that each individual would be encouraged to "do his own thing." Men and women would no longer be stereotyped by society's definitions of masculine and feminine. If sensitivity, emotionality, and warmth are desirable *human* characteristics, then they are desirable for men as well as for women. If independence, assertiveness, and serious intellectual commitment are desirable *human* characteristics, then they are desirable for women as well as for men. Thus, we are not implying that men have all the goodies and that women can obtain self-fulfillment by acting like men. That is hardly the utopia implied by today's feminist movement. Rather, we envision a society which raises its children so flexibly and with sufficient respect for the integrity of individual uniqueness that some men might emerge with the motivation, the ability, and the opportunity to stay home and raise children without bearing the stigma of being peculiar. Indeed, if homemaking is as glamorous as women's magazines and television commercials would have us believe, then men, too, should have that option. And even if homemaking isn't all that glamorous, it would probably still be more fulfilling for some men than the jobs in which they now find themselves forced because of their role as breadwinner. Thus, it is true that a man's options are also limited by our society's sex-role ideology, but as the "predictability test" reveals, it is still the woman in our society whose identity is rendered irrelevant by America's socialization practices.

FURTHER PSYCHOLOGICAL BARRIERS

But what of the woman who arrives at age 21 still motivated to be challenged and fulfilled by a growing career? Is she free to choose a career if she cares to do so? Or is there something standing even in her way?

There is. Even the woman who has managed to finesse society's attempt to rob her of her career motivations is likely to find herself blocked by society's trump card: the feeling that one cannot have a career and be a successful woman simultaneously. A competent and motivated woman is thus caught in a doublebind which few men have ever faced. She must worry not only about failure, but also about success.

This conflict was strikingly revealed in a study which required college women to complete the following story: "After first-term finals, Anne finds herself at the top of her medical-school class."[8] The stories were then examined for concern about the negative consequences of success. The women in this study all had high intellectual ability and histories of academic success. They were the very women who could have successful careers. And yet, over two-thirds of their stories revealed a clear-cut inability to cope with the concept of a feminine, yet career-oriented, woman.

The most common "fear-of-success" stories showed fears of social rejection as a result of success. The women in this group showed anxiety about becoming unpopular, unmarriageable, and lonely:

> Anne starts proclaiming her surprise and joy. Her fellow classmates are so disgusted with her behavior that they jump on her in a body and beat her. She is maimed for life.

> Anne is an acne-faced bookworm. . . . She studies twelve hours a day, and lives at home to save money. "Well, it certainly paid off. All the Friday and Saturday nights without dates, fun—I'll be the best woman doctor alive." And yet a twinge of sadness comes through—she wonders what she really has. . . .

> Anne doesn't want to be number one in her class. . . . She feels she shouldn't rank so high because of social reasons. She drops to ninth and then marries the boy who graduates number one.

In the second "fear-of-success" category were stories in which the women seemed concerned about definitions of womanhood. These stories expressed guilt and despair over success and doubts about their femininity and normality:

> Unfortunately Anne no longer feels so certain that she really wants to be a doctor. She is worried about herself and wonders if perhaps she is not normal. . . . Anne decides not to continue with her medical work but to take courses that have a deeper personal meaning for her.

> Anne feels guilty. . . . She will finally have a nervous breakdown and quit medical school and marry a successful young doctor.

A third group of stories could not even face up to the conflict between having a career and being a woman. These stories simply denied the possibility that any woman could be so successful:

> Anne is a code name for a nonexistent person created by a group of med students. They take turns writing for Anne. . . .

> Anne is really happy she's on top, though Tom is higher than she—though that's as it should be. Anne doesn't mind Tom winning.

> Anne is talking to her counselor. Counselor says she will make a fine nurse.

[8]M. S. Horner, "Fail: Bright Women," *Psychology Today,* November 1969.

By way of contrast, here is a typical story written not about Anne, but about John:

> John has worked very hard and his long hours of study have paid off. . . . He is thinking about his girl, Cheri, whom he will marry at the end of med school. He realizes he can give her all the things she desires after he becomes established. He will go on in med school and be successful in the long run.

Nevertheless, there were a few women in the study who welcomed the prospect of success:

> Anne is quite a lady—not only is she top academically, but she is liked and admired by her fellow students—quite a trick in a man-dominated field. She is brilliant—but she is also a woman. She will continue to be at or near the top. And . . . always a lady.

Hopefully the day is approaching when as many "Anne" stories as "John" stories will have happy endings. But notice that even this story finds it necessary to affirm repeatedly that femininity is not necessarily destroyed by accomplishment. One would never encounter a comparable story written about John who, although brilliant and at the top of his class, is "still a man, still a man, still a man."

It seems unlikely that anyone in our society would view these "fear-of-success" stories as portraits of mental health. But even our concept of mental health has been distorted by America's sex-role stereotypes. Here we must indict our own profession of psychology. A recent survey of seventy-nine clinically-trained psychologists, psychiatrists, and social workers, both male and female, revealed a double standard of mental health.[9] That is, even professional clinicians have two different concepts of mental health, one for men and one for women; and these concepts parallel the sex-role stereotypes prevalent in our society. Thus, according to these clinicians, a woman is to be regarded as healthier and more mature if she is: more submissive, less independent, less adventurous, more easily influenced, less aggressive, less competitive, more excitable in minor crises, more susceptible to hurt feelings, more emotional, more conceited about her appearance, less objective, and more antagonistic toward math and science! But this was the very same description which these clinicians used to characterize an unhealthy, immature man or an unhealthy, immature adult (sex unspecified)! The equation is clear: Mature woman equals immature adult.

Given this concept of a mature woman, is it any wonder that few women ever aspire toward challenging and fulfilling careers? In order to have a career, a woman will probably need to become relatively more dominant, independent, adventurous, aggressive, competitive, and objective, and relatively less excitable, emotional and conceited than our ideal of femininity requires. If she were a man (or an adult, sex unspecified), these would all be considered positive traits.

---

[9]I. K. Broverman et al., "Sex-Role Stereotypes and Clinical Judgments of Mental Health," *Journal of Consulting and Clinical Psychology* 34 (1970), 1–7.

But because she is a woman, these same traits will bring her disapproval. She must then either be strong enough to have her "femininity" questioned; or she must behave in the prescribed feminine manner and accept second-class status, as an adult and as a professional.

And, of course, should a woman faced with this conflict seek professional help, hoping to summon the strength she will need to pursue her career goals, the advice she is likely to receive will be of virtually no use. For, as this study reveals, even professional counselors have been contaminated by the sex-role ideology.

It is frequently argued that a 21-year-old woman is perfectly free to choose a career if she cares to do so. No one is standing in her way. But this argument conveniently overlooks the fact that our society has spent 20 years carefully marking the woman's ballot for her, and so it has nothing to lose in that 21st year by pretending to let her cast it for the alternative of her choice. Society has controlled not her alternatives (although discrimination does do that), but more importantly, it has controlled her motivation to choose any but one of those alternatives. The so-called freedom-to-choose is illusory, and it cannot be invoked to justify a society which controls the woman's motivation to choose. . . .

THE WOMAN AS WIFE

The traditional conception of the husband-wife relationship is now being challenged, not so much because of widespread discontent among older, married women, but because it violates two of the most basic values of today's college generation. These values concern personal growth, on the one hand, and interpersonal relationships on the other. The first of these emphasizes individuality and self-fulfillment; the second stresses openness, honesty, and equality in all human relationships.

Because they see the traditional male-female relationship as incompatible with these basic values, today's young people are experimenting with alternatives to the traditional marriage pattern. Although a few are testing out ideas like communal living, most seem to be searching for satisfactory modifications of the husband-wife relationship, either in or out of the context of marriage. An increasing number of young people claim to be seeking fully equalitarian relationships and they cite examples like the following:

> Both my wife and I earned college degrees in our respective disciplines. I turned down a superior job offer in Oregon and accepted a slightly less desirable position in New York where my wife would have more opportunities for part-time work in her specialty. Although I would have preferred to live in a suburb, we purchased a home near my wife's job so that she could have an office at home where she would be when the children returned from school. Because my wife earns a good salary, she can easily afford to pay a housekeeper to do her major household chores. My wife and I share all other tasks around the house equally. For example, she cooks the meals, but I do the laundry for her and help her with many of her other household tasks.

Without questioning the basic happiness of such a marriage or its appropriateness for many couples, we can legitimately ask if such a marriage is, in fact, an instance of interpersonal equality. Have all the hidden assumptions about the woman's "natural" role really been eliminated? Have our visionary students really exorcised the traditional ideology as they claim? There is a very simple test. If the marriage is truly equalitarian, then its description should retain the same flavor and tone even if the roles of the husband and wife were to be reversed:

> Both my husband and I earned college degrees in our respective disciplines. I turned down a superior job offer in Oregon and accepted a slightly less desirable position in New York where my husband would have more opportunities for part-time work in his specialty. Although I would have preferred to live in a suburb, we purchased a home near my husband's job so that he could have an office at home where he would be when the children returned from school. Because my husband earns a good salary, he can easily afford to pay a housekeeper to do his major household chores. My husband and I share all other tasks around the house equally. For example, he cooks the meals, but I do the laundry for him and help him with many of his other household tasks.

Somehow it sounds different, and yet only the pronouns have been changed to protect the powerful! Certainly no one would ever mistake the marriage *just* described as equalitarian or even very desirable, and thus it becomes apparent that the ideology about the woman's "natural" place unconsciously permeates the entire fabric of such "pseudo-equalitarian" marriages. It is true the wife gains some measure of equality when she can have a career rather than have a job and when her career can influence the final place of residence. But why is it the unquestioned assumption that the husband's career solely determines the initial set of alternatives that are to be considered? Why is it the wife who automatically seeks the part-time position? Why is it *her* housekeeper rather than *their* housekeeper? Why *her* household tasks? And so forth throughout the entire relationship.

The important point is not that such marriages are bad or that their basic assumptions of inequality produce unhappy, frustrated women. Quite the contrary. It is the very happiness of the wives in such marriages that reveals society's smashing success in socializing its women. It is a measure of the distance our society must yet traverse toward the goal of full equality that such marriages are widely characterized as utopian and fully equalitarian. It is a mark of how well the woman has been kept in her place that the husband in such a marriage is almost always idolized by women, including his wife. Why? Because he "permits her" to squeeze a career into the interstices of their marriage as long as his own career is not unduly inconvenienced. Thus is the white man blessed for exercising his power benignly while his "natural" right to that power forever remains unquestioned. Such is the subtlety of America's ideology about women. . . .

THE WOMAN AS MOTHER

In all marriages, whether traditional, pseudo-equalitarian or fully equalitarian, the real question surrounding a mother's career will probably continue to be the well-being of the children. All parents want to be certain that they are doing the very best for their children and that they are not depriving them in any important way, either materially or psychologically. What this has meant recently in most families that could afford it was that mother would devote herself to the children on a full-time basis. Women have been convinced—by their mothers and by the so-called experts—that there is something wrong with them if they even want to do otherwise.

For example, according to Dr. Spock, any woman who finds full-time motherhood unfulfilling is showing "a residue of difficult relationships in her own childhood."[10] If a vacation doesn't solve the problem, then she is probably having emotional problems which can be relieved "through regular counseling in a family social agency or if severe, through psychiatric treatment. . . . Any mother of a pre-school child who is considering a job should discuss the issues with a social-worker before making her decision." The message is clear: If you don't feel that your two-year-old is a stimulating, full-time, companion, then you are probably neurotic.

In fact, research does not support the view that children suffer in any way when mother works. Although it came as a surprise to most researchers in the area, maternal employment in and of itself does not seem to have any negative effects on the children; and part-time work actually seems to benefit the children. Children of working mothers are no more likely than children of non-working mothers to be delinquent or nervous or withdrawn or antisocial; they are no more likely to show neurotic symptoms; they are no more likely to perform poorly in school; and they are no more likely to feel deprived of their mothers' love. Daughters of working mothers are more likely to want to work themselves, and, when asked to name the one woman in the world that they most admire, daughters of working mothers are more likely to name their own mothers![11] This is one finding that we wish every working woman in America could hear because the other thing that is true of almost every working mother is that she *thinks* she is hurting her children and she feels guilty. In fact, research has shown that the worst mothers are those who would like to work, but who stay home out of a sense of duty.[12] The major conclusion from all the research is really this: What matters is the quality of a mother's relationship with her children, not the time of day it happens to be administered. This conclusion should come as no surprise; successful fathers have been demonstrating it for

---

[10]B. Spock, "Should Mothers Work?" *Ladies' Home Journal,* February 1963.

[11]F. I. Nye and L. W. Hoffman, *The Employed Mother in America* (Chicago: Rand McNally, 1963).

[12]M. R. Yarrow et al., "Child-rearing in Families of Working and Non-Working Mothers," *Sociometry* 25 (1958).

years. Some fathers are great, some fathers stink, and they're all at work at least eight hours a day.

Similarly, it is true that the quality of substitute care that children receive while their parents are at work also matters. Young children do need security, and research has shown that it is not good to have a constant turnover of parent-substitutes, a rapid succession of changing baby-sitters or housekeepers.[13] Clearly, this is why the establishment of child-care centers is vitally important at the moment. This is why virtually every woman's group in the country, no matter how conservative or how radical, is in agreement on this one issue: that child-care centers ought to be available to those who need them.

Once again, it is relevant to emphasize that child-care centers, like the other reforms advocated, are not merely for the benefit of middle-class women who wish to pursue professional careers. Of the 31 million women in the labor force, nearly 40 percent of them are working mothers. In 1960, mothers constituted more than one-third of the total woman labor force. In March 1971, more than 1 out of 3 working mothers (4.3 million of them) had children under 6 years of age, and about half of these had children under 3 years of age. And most of these women in the labor force—like most men—work because they cannot afford to do otherwise. Moreover, they cannot currently deduct the full costs of child care as a business expense as the executive can often deduct an expensive car. At the moment, the majority of these working women must simply "make do" with whatever child-care arrangements they can manage. Only 6 percent of their children under 6 years of age currently receive group care in child-care centers. *This* is why child-care centers are a central issue of the new feminist movement. This is why they are not just an additional luxury for the middle-class family with a woman who wants to pursue a professional career.

But even the woman who is educationally and economically in a position to pursue a career must feel free to utilize these alternative arrangements for child care. For once again, America's sex-role ideology intrudes. Many people still assume that if a woman wants a full-time career, then children must be unimportant to her. But of course, no one makes this assumption about her husband. No one assumes that a father's interest in his career necessarily precludes a deep and abiding affection for his children or a vital interest in their development. Once again, America applies a double standard of judgment. Suppose that a father of small children suddenly lost his wife. No matter how much he loved his children, no one would expect him to sacrifice his career in order to stay home with them on a full-time basis—even if he had an independent source of income. No one would charge him with selfishness or lack of parental feeling if he sought professional care for his children during the day.

It is here that full equality between husband and wife assumes its ultimate importance. The fully equalitarian marriage abolishes this double standard and

---

[13]E. E. Maccoby, "Effects upon Children of Their Mothers' Outside Employment," in *Work in the Lives of Married Women* (New York: Columbia University Press, 1958).

extends the same freedom to the mother. The equalitarian marriage provides the framework for both husband and wife to pursue careers which are challenging and fulfilling and, at the same time, to participate equally in the pleasures and responsibilities of child-rearing. Indeed, it is the equalitarian marriage which has the potential for giving children the love and concern of two parents rather than one. And it is the equalitarian marriage which has the most potential for giving parents the challenge and fulfillment of two worlds—family and career—rather than one.

In addition to providing this potential for equalized child care, a truly equalitarian marriage embraces a more general division of labor which satisfies what we like to call "the roommate test." That is, the labor is divided just as it is when two men or two women room together in college or set up a bachelor apartment together. Errands and domestic chores are assigned by preference, agreement, flipping a coin, alternated, given to hired help, or—perhaps most often the case—left undone.

It is significant that today's young people, so many of whom live precisely this way prior to marriage, find this kind of arrangement within marriage so foreign to their thinking. Consider an analogy. Suppose that a white male college student decided to room or set up a bachelor apartment with a black male friend. Surely the typical white student would not blithely assume that his black roommate was to handle all the domestic chores. Nor would his conscience allow him to do so even in the unlikely event that his roommate would say: "No, that's okay. I like doing housework. I'd be happy to do it." We suspect that the typical white student would still not be comfortable if he took advantage of this offer because he and America have finally realized that he would be taking advantage of the fact that such a roommate had been socialized by our society to be "happy" with such obvious inequity. But change this hypothetical black roommate to a female marriage partner, and somehow the student's conscience goes to sleep. At most it is quickly tranquilized by the comforting thought that "she is happiest when she is ironing for her loved one." Such is the power of an unconscious ideology.

Of course, it may well be that she *is* happiest when she is ironing for her loved one.

Such, indeed, is the power of an unconscious ideology.

Native Women Today:
Sexism and the Indian Woman

Shirley Hill Witt

The stereotypes concerning Native Americans popular among the descendants of the European pioneers—whether in legend or on television—nonetheless depict *male* Natives. A different set of stereotypes materializes when one says "an Indian woman" or, so demeaningly, a "squaw." In fact, it takes some effort to conjure up an impression of that invisible Native woman.

On a time line of New World history, one might locate Malinche of Aztec Mexico, Pocahontas of Virginia, and Sacajawea of the Northwest. They are probably the only female "personalities" that come to mind out of the great faceless sea of all the Native women who were born, lived, and died in this hemisphere.

And ironically, these three Native women are not now Native heroines, if they ever were. In Mexico, the term "malinchismo" refers to selling out one's people to the enemy. Malinche, Pocahontas, and Sacajawea aided—perhaps unwittingly—in the downfall of their own people.

Another stereotype, the personality-less squaw, is regarded as a brown lump of a drudge, chewing buffalo hide, putting that tipi up and down again and again, carrying heavy burdens along with the dogs while the tribe moves ever onward, away from the pursuing cavalry.

The term "squaw" began as a perfectly acceptable Algonkian term meaning "woman." In time, it became synonymous with "drudge" and, in some areas, "prostitute." The ugliest epithet a frontiersman could receive was to be called a "squawman"—the lowliest of the low.

Very much rarer is the image of a bronze nubile naked "princess," a child of nature or beloved concoction of Hollywood producers. This version is often compounded with the Pocahontas legend. As the story goes, she dies in self-sacrifice, saving the life of the white man for whom she bears an unrequited love, so that he may live happily ever after with a voluptuous but high-buttoned blonde.

Since all stereotypes are unsatisfactory and do not replicate real people, the myths of Native women of the past ought also to be retired to the graveyard of stereotypes. But what about stereotypes of modern Native women—are there any to be laid to rest? Present stereotypes are also male, are they not? The drunken Indian, the Cadillac Indian, Lonesome Polecat—facelessness still characterizes Native American women.

In this third quarter of the century, Native Americans yet remain the faceless minority despite a few "uprisings" such as Alcatraz, the Trail of Broken Treaties, and the Second Wounded Knee. That these "uprisings" were of definitive importance to the Indian world only underscores its basic invisibility to most Americans, many of whom pass off those protests as trivial and, naturally, futile—much ado about nothing.

And if a million Native Americans reside below national consciousness, certainly that fifty-or-so percent of them that are female are all the more nonentities.

BEFORE COLUMBUS

As many as 280 distinct aboriginal societies existed in North America prior to Columbus. In several, the roles of Native women stand in stark contrast to those of Europeans. These societies were matriarchal, matrilineal, and matrilocal—which is to say that women largely controlled family matters, inheritance passed through the female line, and upon marriage the bride usually brought her groom into her mother's household.

In a matrilocal society all the women were blood relatives and all the males were outsiders. This sort of residence pattern was frequently seen among agricultural societies in which women bore the responsibility for farming. It guaranteed a close-knit working force of women who had grown up with each other and the land.

Somewhat similar was the style of acquiring a spouse called "bride service" or "suitor service." In this case, the prospective husband went to live and work in his future bride's home for a period of time, proving his ability to manage a family of his own. This essentially resulted in temporary matrilocal residence. After the birth of the first child, the husband usually took his new family with him to live among his own kin.

In matrilineal, matrilocal society, a woman forever remained part of her original household, her family of orientation. All the women she grew up with stayed nearby, although she "lost" her brothers to other households. All the husbands were outsiders brought into the family at the time of marriage.

In such societies, usually agricultural, the economy was maintained largely by females. The fields and harvests were the property of women. Daughters inherited rights to fields and the like through their mothers—fields which they had worked in all their lives in one capacity or another, from chasing away the crows as a child to tilling the soil as an adult.

Women working together certainly characterized aboriginal economy. This life-style was roughly similar in such widespread groups as the Iroquois, the Mandan, the Hopi and Zuni, and various Eastern Pueblos. Among the Hopi and the Zuni the husband joined the bride's household upon marriage. The fields were owned by the women, as were their products, the house, and related implements. However, the men labored in the gardens and were (with the unmarried brothers) responsible for much or most of the work.

The strong and influential position of women in Navajo society extended beyond social and economic life. Navajo women also controlled a large share of the political and religious life of the people, called the Dinè. Hogans, herds, and equipment were passed down through the female line, from mother to daughters. Like the Iroquois, women were integral to the religious cycle. The Navajo female puberty ceremony ranked among the most important of Dinè activities.

Although the lives of Native American women differed greatly from tribe to tribe, their life-styles exhibited a great deal more independence and security than those of the European women who came to these shores. Indian women had individual freedom within tribal life that women in more "advanced" societies were not to experience for several generations. Furthermore—and in contrast—Native women increased in value in the estimation of their society as they grew older. Their cumulative wisdom was considered one of society's most valuable resources.

TODAY

What do we know about Native American women today? Inclusive statements such as the following refer to both sexes:

- Only 13.4 percent of the U.S. Indian population had completed eight years of school by 1970.
- The average educational level of all Indians under federal supervision is five school years.
- Dropout rates for Indians are twice the national average.
- Only 18 percent of the students in federal Indian schools go to college; the national average is 50 percent.
- Only 3 percent of the Indian students who enroll in college graduate; the national average is 32 percent.
- Indians suffer from unemployment and underemployment—up to 90 percent unemployment on some reservations in winter months.
- Indians have a high birth rate, a high infant mortality rate, and a short life expectancy.

But there are differences in how these facts relate to Native American women as opposed to men. There has not been equal treatment of Native males and females any more than there has been equal treatrent of the two sexes among non-Natives. We can look at this by considering a few major institutions affecting all our lives—education, employment, and health.

Education

For over a century the federal government has assumed the responsibility for educating Native Americans to the standards of the general population. Nearly every treaty contained provisions for education—a teacher, a school, etc.—as partial payment for lands and rights surrendered.

Until recent years, the U.S. Bureau of Indian Affairs educational system relied upon the boarding school as the cornerstone of Native education, the foundation for indoctrination. Generation after generation of Native children were processed through boarding schools, from the time they were five or six years old until departure or graduation, whichever came first. They lived away from their homes from four to twelve years except during summer (and in some cases, even then). They became divorced from their cultures in line with the government's master plan for the ultimate solution to the "Indian Problem": assimilation.

And so generation after generation of Native women have been processed through a system clearly goal-oriented. That is to say, the government's master plan for women has been to generate an endless stream of domestics and, to a lesser extent, secretaries. The vocational choices for Native children in boarding schools have always been exceedingly narrow and sexist. Boys do woodworking, car repair, house painting, or farm work, while girls do domestic or secretarial work.

Writing about Stewart Indian School in their book *To Live on This Earth*, Estelle Fuchs and Robert J. Havighurst report:

> The girls may choose from only two fields: general and home service (domestic work) or "hospital ward attendant" training, which the girls consider a degrading farce, a euphemism (they say) for more domestic work.

Thus young women are even more suppressed in working toward their aspirations than are boys. Furthermore, just as the males will more than likely find they must move away from their communities to practice their crafts, females cannot exercise their learned domestic crafts in the reservation setting either. A woman cannot even play out the role of a domestic, or the average American housewife and mother (as portrayed by the BIA), in the reservation atmosphere. As one author explains the Navajo woman's dilemma:

> Reservation life . . . cannot support the picture of the average American homemaker. The starched and relatively expensive advertised clothes are out of place and unobtainable. The polished floors and picture windows which generated her envious school dreams are so removed from the hogan or log cabin as to become unreal. The many convenient appliances are too expensive and would not run without electricity. The clean and smiling children require more water than the Navajo family can afford the time to haul. Parent Teacher Association meetings, of which she may have read, are the product of tax-supported schools with the parent in the ultimate role of employer. On the reservation the government-appointed teacher is viewed more as an authority figure than a public servant.

Off-reservation, given the prevalence of Indian poverty, the all-American homemaker role still is thwarted, although hiring out as a domestic servant is possible.

Statistics about the educational attainment of Indians, Eskimos, and Aleuts are not hard to come by, but it is very difficult to obtain figures by sex. The exhaustive Havighurst report does not provide separate tabulations by sex in its summary volume *To Live on This Earth*. A U.S. Civil Rights Commission staff report found that 5.8 percent of the Indian males and 6.2 percent of the Indian females in a recent Southwest study had completed eight years of school. (The rate for all U.S. Indians in 1970 was 13.4 percent.)

The impression left from scanning available surveys is that in recent years females attain more years of formal education than do males, although some fifty years ago probably the reverse was true. This impression sits uneasily with study after study indicating that Native women are dramatically less acculturated than males.

Much data suggests that the BIA educational system is less effective for females than it is for males in creating successful mainstream prototypes—although young males have an alarming suicide rate that is far higher than that of females.

An investigation by Harry W. Martin, *et al.,* showed that of 411 Indian women at two Oklahoma Public Health Service medical out-patient clinics, 59.4 percent were classified as mildly or severely neurotic, compared to 50 percent of the males.

For the severely neurotic category alone, 31.7 percent of the Indian females were found to be severely impaired. This was almost one third more than the males, who rated 23.7 percent. No clear relationship seemed to exist between the ages of the women and the incidence of impairment. (Men, on the other hand, tended to show neurotic symptoms more often in the fifty to fifty-nine age bracket.)

When scores and level of education were correlated, it appeared that males with less education suffered more psychiatric problems than high school graduates, although the rates rose again with post–high school attainment. For females, a similar set of rates prevailed, but—as with suicide—their rate was not as acute as the male rate.

Such evidence suggests that amid the general failure of the federal system to educate Native Americans in school curricula, the system also acculturates native females to a lesser degree than males. It cannot even transform women from native homemakers into mainstream homemakers. The neurotic response seems to tell us of widespread female disorganization and unhappiness.

The suicide statistics for young males who rate as more acculturated than females simply point up the shallowness of the assimilationist mentality of the BIA educational system. Is it not ironic that after more than a century of perfecting a federal indoctrination system, their best product—the more acculturated males—so often seek self-destruction, while nearly one third of the females abide in a state of neuroticism?

Employment

Employment of Native women is as one might expect, considering the level and quality of their educational background. Most employed women are domestics, whether in private homes, in janitorial positions, or in hospitals. The *Navajo Times* newspaper regularly carries want ads such as:

> WANTED   strong young woman for live-in babysitter and mother's helper. No smoking or drinking. Call collect: San Diego, California.

As one young woman commented, "They must have run out of black maids."

Perhaps the economic reality is that blacks are no longer at the bottom of the pile. Indians who have or will go to the cities are taking their place.

Federal employment for Native Americans essentially means employment in the BIA or the Indian Health Service. Native women in the BIA provide a veritable army of clerks and secretaries. They are concentrated, of course, in lower GS ratings, powerless and vulnerable. The U.S. Civil Rights Commission's *Southwest Indian Report* disclosed that in Arizona, Indians comprised 81.2 percent of all the personnel in grades 1 (lowest) through 5, but white personnel constituted only 7.3 percent of employees in these grades.

The figure for Natives includes both male and female employees, but it might not be unreasonable to suggest that females outnumber males among Natives employed as GS white collar employees. And although men most likely outnumber women in the blue collar jobs, the large numbers of native women in BIA and IHS domestic jobs (for example, hospital ward attendant) should not be overlooked. In general, the *Southwest Indian Report* concluded that although Indians constitute the majority of BIA employees in Arizona and New Mexico, they are disproportionately concentrated in the lower wage, nonprofessional jobs.

In the Commission report, Ms. Julia Porter, a retired Indian nurse who also testified about Indian employment in the IHS, noted that "most of the supervisors are Anglos. You never see an Indian head nurse or a supervisor. You see a lot of janitors. You see a lot of low-grade employees over there." Ms. Ella Rumley, of the Tucson Indian Center, reported that Indians who have jobs in that area are employed only in menial positions. There are no Indian retail clerks, tellers, or secretaries, to her knowledge. The Arizona State Employment Service reported that domestic employment placement averaged out to "approximately 34 percent of the job placements available for Indians in the years 1969 and 1970."

Moreover, given the wage disparity between the sexes in salary in the general population, it comes as no surprise that Native women in clerical and domestic work far often receive only pittances for their labor. The reasons for absenteeism and short-term employment which may to some degree characterize Native as well as Anglo female employment are similar: responsibility for the survival of home and family. Outside employment and familial duties conflict for all women. In addition, discrimination and prejudice produce low employee morale, inhibiting commitment to a job. Native women and men are passed over in promotions, as shown in the congressional staff report *No Room at the Top*—meaning "no Natives need apply."

Sadly, even in the brief but brilliant days of the BIA New Team under former Commissioner Louis R. Bruce, an Iroquois-Sioux, Native females in the upper echelons were scarce. One doesn't need to be an Anglo to be a male chauvinist! The common complaint is, of course, that no "qualified" Native women are available. This brings to mind the statement of U.S. Civil Rights Commissioner Frankie M. Freeman.

I have been on this Commission . . . for about 8½ years. And I remember back in February of 1965 when the Commission held hearings in Jackson, Mississippi (and was told) "We can't find any qualified . . . blacks.". . . And then in December of 1968 we went to San Antonio, Texas (and, we were told) they could not find any "qualified" Mexican Americans or Chicanos! And in February of this year we were in New York, and they couldn't find any "qualified" Puerto Ricans! And today you can't find any "qualified" Indians! What disturbs me is that the word "qualified" only gets put in front of a member of a minority or an ethnic. The assumption seems to be that all whites are qualified. You never hear about anybody looking for a "qualified white person.". . . It seems that the word "qualified" sort of dangles as an excuse for discriminating against minorities. In this sense, clearly *all* women must be included as minority members, but to be a woman *and* a minority member can be all the more difficult.

Health

President Johnson observed that "the health level of the American Indian is the lowest of any major population group in the United States." The situation has not improved, as the *Southwest Indian Report* demonstrates. It is inexplicable that the federal government provides the best health service anywhere in the world to its astronauts, military, and veterans, while its service to Native Americans is hopelessly inadequate. The obligation of the federal government to provide health services to Native Americans derives also from treaty obligations, and appears to be administered in as incompetent a fashion as are the educational services.

The symptom-oriented practice of the IHS makes preventive medicine a secondary effort. Social as well as biologic pathologies are not being attacked at their source, but rather at the stage of acute disability.

Not long ago, Dr. Sophie D. Aberle, a Ph.D. anthropologist and an M.D. advised against following her two-degree pattern:

No [she said], don't go after the M.D. now that you have your Ph.D. in anthropology, for two reasons: one, because you wouldn't want to spend the rest of your life interacting with doctors—they're so shallow! And two, as a doctor I can cure gross symptoms perhaps, but I have to send [people] back into the environment in which they got sick in the first place. Cure the social ills and we're a long way down the road to curing the symptoms.

As it relates to women, the major "preventive" effort has been in the area of birth control and family planning. One gets the impression that it is the sole program concerned with before-the-fact care. But Native Americans on the whole reject the concept of birth control. In an impoverished environment, whether rural or city slum, infant mortality is extremely high. As Robert L. Kane and Rosalie A. Kane describe the rationale for unimpeded reproduction in their book *Federal Health Care (with Reservations!)*:

In earlier years, population growth was crucial to survival of the tribe and its people.

In many agrarian societies, children are a form of economic protection. They guarantee a pool of manpower for maintaining and enlarging one's holdings; they are a source of protection and support when the parents can no longer work. With high rates of infant mortality, large numbers of offspring are needed to ensure that several will survive to adulthood.

When the standard of living is raised above the subsistence level, Third World nations usually experience a diminution of the birth rate. The Native American population so far does not seem to have taken a downward swing. In fact, birth rates for some Native groups may be the highest ever recorded anywhere.

Birth control is a topic laden with tension for many groups, particularly for nonwhites in this country. Federal birth control programs began with nonwhites: Puerto Ricans, Navajos, and blacks. It is not too difficult to understand how some may view this first effort as an attempt to pinch off nonwhite birth production. It is hard not to draw such a conclusion.

Among Native Americans, the memory of genocide and tribal extinction is a raw unhealing wound. Fear persists that the desire for the "ultimate solution to the Indian Problem"—the extinguishment of Native Americans—still lives. Kane and Kane say of birth control:

> It is associated with extinction as a people, [with] genocide. The tension runs close to the surface when Navajos discuss this issue. Many interpret efforts along the family planning line as an attempt to breed the race into oblivion. Other Indian tribes have virtually disappeared because of declining birth rates in the face of captivity and inhospitable government reservations.

Native intractability can be sensed in the statement made at a community discussion with IHS officials about family planning. A Navajo woman concluded "As long as there are big Navajos, there will be little Navajos." And then the meeting broke up.

An exceedingly interesting set of investigations by two Egyptian female scientists, Laila Hamamsy and Hind Khattah, seems to cast in a new light the accelerating birth rates among some Navajo groups. Their thesis suggests that white American males are the cause, and in a wholly unexpected way.

First, Navajos are traditionally matriarchal, matrilineal, and matrilocal. From such a position of strength, Navajo women performed a wide array of roles necessary for the survival and success of the extended family.

However, as the thesis goes, white Anglo males from a rigidly paternalistic, male-dominated society refused to recognize and deal with the fact of Navajo matriarchy. Instead, they dealt only with Navajo males on all matters where the two cultures touched. As a result, more and more of the women's roles were supplanted by male actors and then male takeover.

There seems to be a statistical correlation between the period in which Anglo ascendancy impinged on female roles, and the onset and acceleration of the birth rate around the peripheral Navajo communities where most cultural interaction takes place. Anglo culture as practiced by white males brought about the loss of nearly all Navajo women's roles save that of childbearer. When producing offspring is one's only vehicle for gaining prestige and ego satisfaction, then we can expect the birthrate to ascend.

To what extent this thesis can apply to other minority groups—and also to middle-class white American females who are now the biggest producers of offspring—is not yet answerable. But the thesis is appealing, in any event.

Other preventive programs are virtually nonexistent. Among some of the Northern Pueblo groups and elsewhere, prenatal care clinics are held sporadically and with a minimum of success. This is the fault of both lack of funds and lack of commitment on the part of the IHS and the general lack of information available to potential users about such programs.

That preventive programs can and do succeed where there is commitment is seen in the fine example set by Dr. Annie Wauneka. She received the National Peace Medal for bringing to her Navajo people information and procedures they could use to combat tuberculosis ravaging on the reservation at that time.

Charges that Native Americans are locked into superstition and therefore hostile to modern medicine just are not factual. Preventive programs properly couched would no doubt be welcome. But, as the Citizen's Advocate Center reports in *Our Brother's Keeper:*

> "The Public Health Service has no outreach system or delivery system, no systematic preventive care program, no early detection system. Thus . . . (it) is not structured to cope at the right point and on the proper scale with the underlying causes of poor health."

SOME COMMENTS

In the briefest way, this article has touched upon a few of the major institutions of life—education, employment, and health—as they are experienced by Native American women.

The next step in understanding among women and between peoples is mutual identification of needs. Many of life's difficulties for Native women are no different than those of other minority women—blacks, Chicanas, or the Appalachian poor. And then when the commonalities between minority and majority women are recognized—if not on a socioeconomic level, at least on a philosophic level—we may expect to witness a national movement for the equality of peoples and sexes.

The Myth of the Strong Black Woman

Marcia Ann Gillespie

I was a child when I first heard someone say, "Men work from sun to sun, but women's work is never done." For years I thought it proof that women, rather than being the "weaker" sex, were if anything superior to, stronger than men. I was a woman, very much grown, before I realized how heavy those words can weigh—the reality, the burden.

Black women *work!* Yet the gruesome truth is that "women's work" is often dismissed, taken for granted or devalued. It's almost as if never-ending hard work and bearing burdens is what we were born to. Our plates are piled high with things we have to do or are expected to do or want to do or are pushed to do, and with each step forward there are increasing additions. Single or married, living with someone or alone, mothers or not, we're all ripping and running and panting and juggling—time, priorities and people. No matter that styles have changed or that new opportunities exist or that we are often doing things beyond our mama's wildest dreams—we are all still doing and expected to do all the "women's work," live up to all the same standards and be tied by the same myths our grandmothers and mothers were. Only this time it's with less backup and more stress.

The pressures we women are under are intense. We are bombarded from all sides with all manner of things we gotta do: Gotta make ways for lasting meaningful social, economic and political change. Gotta stop analyzing and amening and get to practical solutions, then make 'em happen. Gotta do well on our jobs, gotta keep 'em or get better ones or make the ones we have pay off. Gotta keep our relationships thriving or get some going. Gotta look good and stay healthy. Told that we gotta be in control of our lives and our destinies. Gotta be past, present and future women all at the same time. Gotta keep our spirits and our sanity. Most important, or so it often seems, is that we Black women gotta be good women, gotta be strong.

What's a good or a strong Black woman anyway? What's the myth, the prevailing image? The myth is that we have to give up our softness in order to be strong, that we're required to be female Atlases. If we give up our joy or begin to believe that being strong won't get our jelly rolled, we're letting myth make our reality. The myth penalizes us. It seems that being a good woman has come to mean that we be all things to all people, be women other people feel free to bring their troubles to. Hard work—shucks, that ain't nothing. Complain and you get labeled evil (shades of the Sapphire syndrome), so good women don't; we smile a lot or pray a lot. We may complain to our friends about keeping up the front, but we find it difficult to admit that we can't cope.

Good women may at times react or respond, but they don't make waves. They usually settle for less—in relationships, in the workplace, in social involvements and in what they accept and demand as their political rights. It's fine if a good woman sparks change, like Rosa Parks did, as long as she acts like a lady and steps back and lets the menfolk carry the torch. So good women wait and look for men to lead them and then work endlessly behind the scenes propping them up. A good woman accepts the assumption that women's work is never done and she's only too willing to let others add to the pile.

Mama passed this message on to us; she got it from hers. Things like the notion that the kitchen was solely our domain and responsibility; that men came to sit and be served, never to cook or clean up; that men were to be catered and deferred to and humored; that male sexuality was praiseworthy while we were to keep ours in check. That good women kept their ankles crossed and their skirts down. We were taught that a good woman marries early, has children for whom she assumes primary responsibility and keeps her marriage going. She must be prepared to make the sacrifices in any situation.

Of course she is a person fashioned by the patriarchy; the rules were imposed on her as part and parcel of the tradition and women were trained to pass it on. Sacrifice, hard work and silence are part of our heritage. It came with us out of Africa, where good women toiled, were expected to produce many children (especially sons), defer to men and cultivate silence. In slavery we learned how to bear humiliation, pain and cruelty, to be chattel of both men and the system and yet to mask our pain, our needs and our rage. Even today when we extol the virtues of our mamas, most often it's a litany of hard work, of what she did without and what she gave—never what she took or expected or demanded as her due.

If good women work endlessly, strive to look pretty and keep silent while serving, the strong Black woman (SBW), the ultimate heroine, is expected to bear increasingly heavy burdens while holding herself and our world up no matter the sacrifice. Being a strong Black woman leaves no room for frivolity. She never giggles and really shouldn't laugh—the last thing a strong Black woman should have is a good time. Think about it: how many times have you heard the term applied to a woman whose life no rational person would choose in a million years? Some sister, struggling under an impossible load, who'd love to be able to shrug her shoulders or at least have a few other shoulders to share the burden with. "That's a strong Black woman," someone will say in a solemn, near-reverent tone that is usually followed by a moment of silence. It's almost as if one were judging a performance instead of empathizing with her life. As a result, her complexities, pain and struggle are somehow made mythic, and she who so desperately needs our support is placed on a pedestal to be admired rather than helped.

It would seem that in order to qualify as heroine or leader, a Black woman's life must be one of personal loss, denial and sacrifice. While our great men are supposed to have good women helpmates, great women are expected to go it alone. Who was Mr. Bethune? Who ever thinks of Harriet or Sojourner as people who needed or wanted emotional backup? We expect great men to be whole people who champion life and also enjoy theirs fully. We applaud their sexuality, yet it's almost heretical to think of a SBW as a person who enjoys snuggling in bed or as a woman who writhes in sexual joy and release. Remember that Sojourner moved to bare her breasts while declaring "Ain't I a woman!" to those who doubted that she was. And yet it is her womanhood that today we too often forget. A SBW is automatically a neuter. She's supposed to be above and beyond the earthly pleasures, to do without or sublimate much of her femininity and her womanhood while accomplishing incredible feats. After all, is there anything that a SBW *can't* bear?

No matter our goodness or our strength—we all face the grim realities of Afro-America summer 1982. We are hard pressed. Most of us who work do so out of necessity, not choice, and praise God that we have jobs to go to. The overwhelming majority of us don't control the source of our income. We're job-dependent, paycheck junkies—living from one payday to another, lost without our plastic cards and in debt up to our eyebrows. We're still working for less money than our white counterparts and *all* men. More than 40 percent of us are heading single-parent households and 36 percent of us have fallen below the poverty line. Everyone knows that we're on the front lines, first to fall victim to a sick economy and federal budget cuts in child care, education, health care, housing—all things we still need the most.

Like our Depression-generation kin, we're forced to come up with endless miracles, wringing every penny out of that dollar and then making each one kiss its behind. Yet our survival skills seem to have gotten rusty. Our support systems, unlike those of our Depression-era kin, have become tenuous and fragmented. We're taking care of number one, which often leads to "I" taking the place of "we."

There's an ugly' acute depression in Black America and, what's worse, it's turning our people into animals who devour their own. Crime blights our communities—rape, robbery, mugging, assault, child abuse, homicide and suicide stalk us. We don't pay the rent or we beat each other over the head to get it. We drink and dope the pain away or sleep in doorways and gutters. Yet the realities are plain, and we know what the stakes are. We must find some way to keep ourselves and our people together, fearing that if we go down this time, there may be no coming back.

Women are the primary victims of Black America's pain. We're locked into poverty, heading households where children are inadequately educated, can't find work and too often turn to crime. Our daughters and sisters are the ones who become mothers at 14; we're the people on welfare unto the fifth generation, needing some means to get out from under. We live longer than our men, so we are the Black aged who suffer from inadequate social security and the lack of pensions. Every time a woman can't find work, goes on welfare, slips into poverty or can't get out, another generation is trapped with her.

Given this bleak landscape, our continuing acceptance of the myths and our striving to achieve the idealized standards of Black American womanhood only compound the problems we face. We women for too long have taken the weight and thought it our due. We make the mistake of thinking that our legendary strength is automatically synonymous with power. And so we call women who are activists or who seem to have achieved some measure of success "strong." Then we subliminally distance ourselves from them or come to believe that they have muscles that should carry but not flex. And because we come from a long line of women who suffered all in a silence that none but Jesus could hear, we feel guilty if we speak out, say no or move to throw it back in someone's face. Or if we rise up to fight for our hard-won rights or move to define and secure others, we worry that we may be thought of as presumptuous or threatening. So the silence is compounded, or else we speak but not loudly enough or forcefully enough or thoughtfully enough or consistently enough to begin to force the issues or to structure mechanisms for meaningful change.

Our strength, our silence and our goodness have helped to push us below the poverty line or to the brink because we haven't pushed to make the problems women face, the pressures we bear, top priorities. Thus never has a major civil-rights organization moved to address what are often written off as "women's issues"—child care, welfare rights, reproductive freedom, full employment for women, the ERA, female-headed households, the victimization of women. . . . Occasionally we women are given a special program that's supposed to appease us, but the matter is never given the full-scale attention it deserves.

Isn't it time we moved from myth to reality? Time we stopped allowing ourselves to be seduced into believing that silent suffering, bearing all burdens and being round-the-clock workers is something to be so proud of that we end up deifying—rather than moving to change—our condition? Time we stopped being good women or women who are victimized by our strength and started seeing and describing and developing images of ourselves that reflect us as self-defined women, as women with *power?* Time that we started demanding recognition of our true condition and the means to change it? Time we became women who can and do move to take charge of our lives and situations, women who move from being those who react or accept and instead become women others must react and respond to? Powerful rather than somebody else's notion of what being a good, strong Black woman is?

It's time we moved to make our institutions and organizations aware of and truly responsive to the issues that affect us. Time that we made women's work pay off. Our hard labor made the churches, now we need to make them work for us. How we use them, what missions we establish can make a difference in our condition. We're needy and our churches must move to provide aid, succor and practical support to our afflicted, our unemployed, our homeless and those who are striving to keep it all together. They must help us love our children by opening their doors after school so that our children don't wander the streets with keys around their necks and risk a repeat of Atlanta.

We know we need child-care facilities that aren't subject to governmental whim. The church is there and we must use it while we press to ensure governmental support. To that end we need to start demanding that our tax dollars be properly spent for child care and education. We need to write letters that pressure Congress and make it clear we intend to be reckoned with. We women need to mobilize our women's organizations, give the call and march to the state houses and to Washington and force them to get their priorities straight.

None of us were born with silver spoons in our mouths, so work is what we must do. In this age of high technology and tight job markets, nonexistent, marginal or dated skills put us at the end of the employment line or lock us into low wages. Those of us who don't move to develop new skills will find we're bearing more, falling behind or being phased out. Women who are about taking power will make skills training part of their ongoing plan. And women's groups must become real skills exchanges. We need "how-to" sessions more than we need chicken luncheons. Us teaching us, sharing what we know on an easy woman-to-woman basis, where the price of a ticket doesn't close out women in need.

Women's work pays off for us when we actively air our definitions, come up with new ones that fit current, real-life situations and do some questioning and demanding. When we move to free women's work from gender identification and therefore free it and ourselves from devaluation. When we move to talk openly and consistently to one another and our men about the problems we face, the pressures we feel. When we move to balance and better share responsibilities.

We take control when we establish our own woman images and begin to force ourselves and others to give up these unrealistic ideals or myths for obtainable, comfortable, flexible goals. When we trade in being strong Black women for being women who are admired for our strengths as we define them, our emotion, our power and our logic. When we realize we need applause and shoulders to lean on sometimes too. When we see ourselves, develop and project images that show us actively, fully engaged in the struggle for our collective strength, survival and freedom and refuse to accept suffering as our birthright or lot. It's time we stopped being the mules of the world and started making the world truly recognize us and move to our beat. It's time for Black women to move and be moved beyond myth to power!

Still . . . Small Change for Black Women

Alexis M. Herman

There is a lot of speculation about the uniqueness of black women's economic progress. It has been said that black women have benefited doubly, both as blacks and as women; that we have outpaced black men in obtaining the

TABLE 1
CIVILIAN LABOR FORCE PARTICIPATION RATES

| | Percentage | |
	March 1970	March 1978
Black women	49.1	52.7
White women	41.9	48.6

Source: U.S. Department of Labor, Bureau of Labor Statistics

available jobs; that we earn more than other women; and that our economic position is to be envied rather than deplored.

These popular myths do not consider the statistical evidence: black women are still economically disadvantaged. While there have been singular outstanding achievements, they are the exception. The yardstick for measuring how far black women as a group actually have come must be applied to their employment and unemployment status, occupational distribution, earnings, education, and incidence of poverty. If we examine changes that have taken place in the 1970s, when efforts resulting from legislation to help eliminate sex and race bias were under way, we see that black women wage earners still are relatively low on the economic yardstick, and this status penalizes not only black women, but their families and in fact, the entire black community.[1]

To determine black women's access to employment as well as to specific kinds of jobs, we need to explore the levels of employment and typical job patterns for black women. Although, recently, white women show the greatest proportional increase in labor force participation, black women still maintain their historically higher rates of participation. [Table 1.]

Yet black women continue to suffer high rates of unemployment: higher among black women than even among black men, for example. In fact, teenage black women (ages 16 to 19) have the highest unemployment rate, while the lowest rate is among adult white men. [Table 2.]

Despite the high unemployment rates of black women, some progress—in terms of upward mobility in job categories—can be shown for all women who are employed. (See [Table 3.], "Occupational Distribution of Women, 1977 and 1970.") The most common job categories for black women are clerical work and service work outside the home, although there has been some dispersion into certain higher-paying occupational categories such as professional, technical, and management. A most significant positive trend is that the proportion of black women in private household work, a generally low-paying occupation, declined by one half over the seven-year period. White women also moved into

[1] Much of the data on black women in this article includes blacks and other minorities. The data are highly representative of black women, however, since they comprise approximately 89 percent of the group.

TABLE 2
UNEMPLOYMENT RATES, SEPTEMBER 1978

	Percentage
Black teenage women	41.2
Black teenage men	35.5
White teenage women	15.9
White teenage men	12.8
Black adult women	11.3
Black adult men	7.2
White adult women	5.6
White adult men	3.1

Source: U.S. Department of Labor, Bureau of Labor Statistics

TABLE 3
OCCUPATIONAL DISTRIBUTION OF WOMEN, 1977 AND 1970

	Percentage			
	Black women		**White women**	
	1977	**1970**	**1977**	**1970**
Total	100.0	100.0	100.0	100.0
Professional and technical workers	14.3	10.8	16.1	15.0
Managers and administrators	2.9	1.9	6.3	4.8
Clerical workers	26.0	20.8	35.9	36.4
Sales workers	2.6	2.5	7.3	7.7
Craft and kindred workers	1.3	.8	1.7	1.2
Operatives	15.9	17.6	11.3	14.1
Nonfarm laborers	1.2	.7	1.1	.4
Private household workers	8.9	17.5	2.2	3.4
Service workers, (except private household)	26.0	25.6	16.7	15.3
Farmers and farm managers	1/	.8	.3	.3
Farm laborers and supervisors	.9	1.5	1.1	1.5

1/ Less than 0.05 percent
Source: U.S. Department of Labor, Bureau of Labor Statistics

higher-paying jobs and have progressed more into the professional and technical category than black women. Yet both groups are still concentrated in traditionally "female" occupations. (See "The Pink Collar Ghetto," *Ms.*, March, 1977.)

Recent statistics show that the gap between the earnings of black women and white women is closing, but this surprising trend does not necessarily indicate progress for black women. Both groups generally are still crowded into the same low-paying traditional jobs, and this crowding contributes to the continuing earnings gap between full-time year-round women and men workers: the gap has remained at about 60 percent for more than a decade. Furthermore, black women are more likely to be supporting children and contributing proportionately more to their household income—and even so, that income is generally still lower than that of the counterpart white household.

The substantial income disparity between men and women in general is evident when we compare the median usual weekly earnings of workers 16 and over in May, 1970, and in May, 1978 [Table 4].

Educational attainment of workers is now virtually the same between the races and sexes, yet great disparities in median incomes continue [Table 5]. Black women who have attended high school have less income than white men and black men who have attended only elementary school—and the same is true for high-school-educated white women.

Probably the most underreported economic fact is the increasing number of black women who live in poverty today. (The officially defined poverty level for nonfarm families in 1977 was about $6,200 and $7,300 for families of four and five persons, respectively.) Of the 57.2 million families living in poverty in March, 1978, 10 percent were black. Black families were four times as likely as white families to be living in poverty, and three and one half times as likely to be headed by a woman. Approximately 40 percent of all black families were headed by women in 1978, with slightly more than half of these female-headed families

TABLE 4
MEDIAN WEEKLY EARNINGS

	May 1970	May 1978
White men	$157	$279
Black men	113	218
White women	95	167
Black women	81	158

Source: U.S. Department of Labor, Bureau of Labor Statistics

TABLE 5
MEDIAN PERSONAL INCOME BY EDUCATIONAL ATTAINMENT FOR FULL-TIME WORKERS, MARCH, 1976

	Women		Men	
	Black	White	Black	White
Attended elementary school	$5,404	$6,114	$8,258	$10,342
Attended high school	7,267	7,748	9,932	13,193
Attended college	10,080	10,218	13,100	16,906

Source: U.S. Department of Commerce, Bureau of the Census

living in poverty. About 11 percent of white families were headed by women and about one fourth of these were poor.

In general, black women support more children than white women. Nearly half of the black families headed by women had four or more persons, compared with one fourth of white families. Of the more than 9 million children in black families, 40 percent were in families living in poverty. Of all black children living in poverty, 75 percent were supported by black women alone in 1977, up from 60 percent in 1970.

While the gains made by black women in education and employment cannot be discounted, the fact remains that they and their children bear an increasing burden of poverty. Efforts that have been made to date have not managed to erase the uniqueness of black women's disadvantaged status. The black community is not only paying a large price for race discrimination, but it is suffering serious consequences from the effects of sex discrimination as well.

Black Women and the Market

Michelle Russell
Mary Jane Lupton

"She picked very fast and very clean, and with an air of scorn, as if she despised both the work and the disgrace and humiliation of the circumstances in which she was placed." The worker is Cassy, the defiant mistress of Simon Legree, who has come down to the cotton fields to get away from the master's house and from the other two jobs black women were forced to do under slavery: domestic work and prostitution.

Uncle Tom's Cabin was written in 1852, nine years before the outbreak of the war between the North and the South over who would continue to control the destiny of black people in America. The victory of the North ended slavery as an institution but left black women far from free.

If the historic life rhythm of the masses of black men takes shape from the beat of sledge hammers in construction gangs and work camps and the pounding of machines in factories, the beat of black women's special oppression rises in the time they have been forced to do on the production line as breeders for the domestic slave market, as the sexual prey of white men, and in the washboard grind of cleaning their bosses dirty linen and nourishing their future oppressors at their breasts. Before the Civil War "the field woman was a laborer beside her man, a begetter of children . . . If she rose in social status then she became a mammy to the white children." (See Pat Robinson's article in *Black Women.*)

The passage of the thirteenth amendment simply expanded the social contexts in which the same kind of female slave-labor could be extracted from black women. Many of the house and field functions merged, so that the paid domestic tended the crops as well as the children. If a woman's "paid" job was that of wetnurse to white babies, then she had to be constantly pregnant just as under slavery she was perpetually employed in producing more "chattel."

The migration of blacks to the northern urban areas during the periods of the two world wars changed little for the black woman. She remained MEAT FOR SALE. Before hiring black women as salesgirls, managers would circulate questionnaires to their white clientele to see if such a move would lose valuable customers. Women were allowed into the factories as blue-collar semi-skilled workers when there were labor shortages; but their desperation was used to pay them the least and to keep black and non-black males from demanding higher wages for the same work. And, of course, in domestic work, where the majority of employed black women find themselves, there is no minimum wage requirement employers have to meet, no benefits such as health insurance, overtime, or vacation coverage demanded by law. As under slavery, all the rules are set by the missus or the master of the house. And there is no way these rules can be anything but degrading.

The tale most often passed on from mother to daughter in black communities, to teach the child what to expect from life, deals with rape by white men. The "normal" circumstances in which this occurs are dramatized by Richard Wright in a story called "Man of All Work." It is about a typical black family. The husband, Carl, is out of work; his wife, Lucy, is recovering from having her second child. They need money desperately and Carl, who is a cook, can only find cook's work in the "Female Help Wanted" column, where there is a "Cook-Housekeeper Job." The job sounds simple, so, much to Lucy's objection, Carl puts on one of her dresses and answers the ad. The employers, the Fairchilds, take "Lucy" at face value. First, Mrs. Fairchild gets "Lucy" to help her with her bath. Then home comes David, who tries to seduce the new maid like he's done successfully in the past. This time the "colored girl" puts up such a fight she nearly breaks Mr. Fairchild's arm. The wife comes home and, in jealousy, shoots the maid. A doctor, a friend of the family, comes to examine the patient. The truth is learned and "Lucy" is paid $200 to keep his mouth shut. Carl goes home. ". . . Carl, promise me you'll never do anything like that again." ". . . Ha, ha, Lucy, you don't have to ask. I was a woman for almost six hours and it almost killed me. Two hours after I put that dress on I thought I was going crazy. I don't know how you women manage it." Their immediate predicament is solved. But the real Lucy, as soon as she's strong, will wear that dress again. And she will have to manage.

To keep pushing is hard. Frances Beal points out in her well-known essay, "Double Jeopardy: To Be Black and Female," that wage scale has always been lower for black women than any other group in the work force. In 1967, yearly median wages looked like this: White Males—$6704; Non-White Males—$4277; White Females—$3991; Non-White Females—$2861. And this is only if she is "lucky" enough to find a job. Unemployment is also higher among black women than for any other group. Black women work. All black women work. They work hard long hours under wretched conditions—in the home, on the street—

to keep body and soul together, raise their own and other's children, and make communities of ghettoes. But they don't get wages for work done.

The only material asset black women have to offer the labor market is themselves. As blues singer Bessie Jackson testified in the 1920's:

I need shoes on my feet, clothes on my back
That's why I'm walkin these streets all dressed in black
I got to make my livin', don't care where I go
They got a store on the corner where they're sellin' stuff cheap
I got a market 'cross the street where I sell my meat
But Tricks ain't walkin', Tricks ain't walkin' no more.

If they resort to selling their bodies for food, they are called prostitutes. If they use the fruit of their wombs, their children, as a claim on the State to help them survive, they are called culturally deprived parasites. The only way their participation in the economy is sanctioned is as consumers; the only official recognition of their existence comes in the form of the welfare system. Trapped in ghettoes, still a domestic, the welfare mother is paid below minimum wages for her labor, refused ADC benefits if she has too many children for the system to control. But her historic role—providing much of the labor which built the system in the first place—is denied. When she has organized against her colonizers, forming groups such as NWRO, demanding a guaranteed income, fighting for legitimacy as a raiser of children through community control of the school struggles, the system has tried to "retrain" her to think of herself as a "para-professional" instead of a mammy, maid, or prostitute. But how significant is this change?

In the New York City schools alone there are over 15,000 para-professionals, perhaps 95% of them Black or Puerto Rican. Most of them only earn between $1800 and $2400 a year. "Ironically, these jobs were first opened up to give the poor a chance to lift themselves out of poverty and also to help them get off welfare. But four years later, the para-professionals are still earning the same hourly rate and are still working under the same conditions." (Dulce Garcia in *Up From Under*, August, 1970).

The consciousness of black women who are placed in para-professional programs is not dulled or blunted by the system's mystification. If anything, their appreciation of their exploitation is sharpened. Recently, a class of women in training to become elementary teacher's aides was asked what the term "para-professional" meant to them. Here are a few of their answers: "Second best; Off the street; Next to nothing; Teacher's maid, not teacher's aide."

A more extensive political analysis of the black woman's position as a para-professional is offered by Cleo Silvers (*Up from Under*, August 1970). She writes: "Our job would be to act as representatives of the community inside their agencies, to interpret things about our people and our community that the professionals did not understand . . . We would gather data that they would never be able to get from our people . . . We were supposed to learn to do the tedious paperwork which the professionals did not want to do . . . Most important, we would act as buffers between our people, who are angry and absolutely disgusted with having exploiters in their midst." These experiences comprise a brutal and stark reality. They epitomize what it means to be simultaneously female in a feudal setting, black in a white racist environment, a colonial tool, and a worker under capitalism.

Employment alone will not change the colonial relationship of black people to Anglo-American society. The struggle is for control—a control that will only come through revolution. For the black woman, control of her body, the social production it engages in, and the ends to which that production is put is what the battle has been and continues to be about. It is the same fight that all black people must wage: for the annihilation of slavery in all its forms and the initiation of a new rhythm of life.

Women Bear the Brunt of Economic Crises

Linda London

Women have only token power in our society—power that can be given or taken away as the economy rises and ebbs. The economic decline of the late 1970s has demonstrated how quickly women's gains in employment, child care, and social programs could be eroded.

From 1970 to 1980, the number of families falling below the poverty line increased by 957,000.[1] Virtually all of that increase involved what the Census Bureau calls "female householders, no husband present."

But women bear the brunt of economic crises in yet another way. While all violent crime increased 58.3% between 1972 and 1982, rape and domestic abuse were the fastest rising crimes.[2] We live in a society that measures a man's power and virility by the size of his paycheck. As rising unemployment leaves men jobless, they suffer a harsh blow to their self-esteem. Many men seek to regain their sense of power by dominating others. With our media sensationalizing sexual aggression and idealizing macho behavior and female submissiveness, women become "natural" targets of male domination.

While 81,536 forcible rapes[3] came to the attention of law enforcement officials in 1981 rape is still recognized as the most underreported crime. The FBI believes that as few as one incident in five is reported. In addition, the U.S.

[1]U.S. Census Bureau Report, 1980.

[2]U.S. Department of Justice, *FBI Uniform Crime Reports* (Washington, D.C., August, 1982). FBI statistics are cited unless otherwise noted.

[3]Forcible rape, as defined by the Uniform Crime Reports, is carnal knowledge of a female forcibly and against her will. Assaults or attempts to commit rape by force or threat of force are included; however, statutory rape (without force) and other sex offenses are not. Nor do the statistics include marital rape, male rape, or the widespread sexual abuse of children.

Human Rights Commission estimates that there are well over one million battered wives in this country. Other nationwide surveys have indicated that over two million American women are beaten in their homes *each* year.[4]

According to the FBI, a woman is raped every 8 minutes in the United States; a woman is beaten by her husband every 18 seconds. One woman in four will suffer sexual assault in her lifetime; one household in four endures on-going domestic violence.

Feminist theorists may disagree on the fundamental causes of violence against women, but statistics demonstrate a direct relationship to economic crises. Unfortunately violence, triggered by financial hardship, becomes a habitual way of coping for many people. The abuser's attacks become more frequent and severe; the rapist repeats his crime. Of those men arrested for rape, 73% are arrested again for the same offense within four years.

Women face harsh alternatives to domestic abuse. Breaking the emotional bonds of a relationship (even a violent one) can be difficult, but the economic ties to a man may be a woman's only safeguard against poverty. Women earn only 59 cents to the male dollar. In families that have struggled to meet their expenses with two salaries, the wife may recognize the impending difficulty of living on one—especially the lower one. Women without paid jobs face an even more ominous future when they leave their partners.

Still, many women do choose to leave abusive relationships. When they do, it is not surprising that the husband fares far better economically. A recent study by Stanford University showed that in the first year after separation, the former husbands improved their standard of living 42% while their former wives and children saw theirs plunge 73%.[5] The researchers found that although men often received salary increases after the divorce, alimony and child support payments remained the same or were reduced. According to Los Angeles court statistics from 1977, the average family received about $195 a month in child-support payments regardless of the number of children.[6] Thus, a battered woman suffers beatings if she stays and often extreme economic hardships if she leaves a violent home.

The woman who is raped is also a double victim. She is brutalized during the assault and then incriminated by public attitudes that blame the victim.

The popular image of rape as an act of sudden passion by a stranger jumping out of a dark alley to "seduce" a promiscuous woman contrasts sharply with the facts:

• Nearly two-thirds of all rapes are preceded by casual, even friendly interaction.

[4]Murray A. Straus, "Wife Beating: How Common and Why," *Victimology: An International Journal,* 2:77 nos. 3–4, 445.

[5]Sheila Caudle, "Divorce Major Reason for Poverty of Women," *The Cincinnati Enquirer* (August 15, 1982), p. A-6.

[6]Ibid.

• Over one-half of reported rapes are committed by forced entry into the victim's home; 67% occur in a residence.[7]

• In nine out of ten cases, the rapist carries a weapon or threatens physical harm.

• There is no "typical" rape victim. Victims can be infants or elderly, thin or obese, beautiful or unattractive . . . even male.

• Men do not rape out of passion. Rape is an expression of power and anger. Prison rape, for example, has nothing to do with sexual feelings. The offenders know that rape is dehumanizing and degrading.

Although feminist efforts have publicized these facts and the high incidence of violent crimes against women, the judicial system has responded weakly. There is no federal legislation on family violence. In the nation's capital in 1974, only 18% of the arrests for aggravated assault in families resulted in conviction.[8] Nationwide, only 38% of known forcible rapes were cleared by arrest in 1980 and a mere 7% resulted in convictions.

Rape and battering were the earliest issues that feminists addressed. Feminists drew public attention to the problems and founded counseling centers and shelters that have provided some relief for victims. These services have traditionally subsisted on meager funding; yet, social service budget cuts threaten even their limited allocations.

After fifteen years of feminist activity, rape and battering remain urgent concerns—in fact these crimes are on the increase. While victim support services remain essential, ultimately feminists must abolish the conditions that both create and perpetuate violence against women.

Older Working Women

Joyce Maupin

Women live too long. We live past the age where we can find employment, we receive meager pensions or none at all, we survive without the companionship, housing, food or medical care which make a long life satisfying.

At forty we grow old in the job market, but we continue living and working. The Women's Bureau Handbook on Women Workers states that women 45 to 64

---

[7]Menachem Amir, *Patterns in Forcible Rape* (Chicago, University of Chicago Press, 1971), p. 145.

[8]Parnas, "Police Discretion and Diversion of Incidents of Family Violence" 36 *Law and Contemporary Problems* (1971).

are "most likely" to work year round. The unemployment rate for this age group is low but of 263,000 reported unemployed ("reported unemployed" means that you qualify for unemployment insurance) many have been looking for work for more than six months and "many more thousands may have given up."

UNEMPLOYMENT

The Senate Special Committee on Aging reports that in the last four years there has been a 22 per cent rise in the unemployment rate of persons over 45. This figure does not reflect the involuntary dropouts who don't qualify for benefits and are not counted, or others who "may have given up." The hidden unemployment of women over 45 is estimated at three times the official rate.

What happens to the involuntary dropouts? They find a little work—Christmas sales, baby sitting, cleaning—you are never too old for housework, 10 per cent of women earning a living at housework are over 65 years of age. Somehow these women hang on until, at age 62, they qualify for social security benefits—a benefit which will be 20 per cent lower than the one they would get if they could wait until age 65.

A lucky 10 per cent of working women qualify for a payment under some type of private pension plan, but these payments are usually small. Private pension plans resemble lotteries—there are only a few winners.

These plans are built on the assumption that most workers will quit or get laid off long before they reach 65. Pension plans are not portable, benefits cannot be carried from one job to another.

Pension funds are not put in a safe place. They may disappear in bad investments, or they may in any case be insufficient to pay promised benefits. The amount of the pension, if you get one, depends upon length of service. Women, due to periods of voluntary or involuntary dropout, rarely have enough tenure to qualify. When they do get a pension, payments average less than half of those received by men.

The meager amount of social security benefits, averaging $140 a month for single women, may explain why a large number of women over 65, and even over 70, are still in the work force.

BE ADAPTABLE

Age discrimination is less evident in unskilled jobs which pay the minimum—or less. Older women are rarely employed, even if they are qualified, in skilled jobs which pay better wages.

The Handbook on Women Workers suggests that women be "adaptable and flexible in their attitudes—willing to learn and make necessary changes . . . alert to new job opportunities and new training programs. Only if they are fully prepared by education, training, and the willingness to learn anew, will they be ready for the challenges and demands of tomorrow's society." This advice will not help the woman past 45, who rarely is offered an interview or even an application form.

Mature women, or senior citizens (it's not nice to say old), evidently do adapt because they continue to survive. As long as they can still get around they survive in little cubicles in rooming houses or rundown hotels, preparing a single meal on an illegal hot plate. They survive their husbands but in very few instances (about 2 per cent) do they receive any part of the husband's pension benefit.

Measuring Masculinity by the Size of a Paycheck

Robert E. Gould, M.D.

Is Bobby Murcer a $100,000 ballplayer? Did Tom Seaver earn a raise above his $120,000 off his 21–12 record? How much is rookie Jon Matlack worth on the open market?

Lead paragraph from a *New York Post* news story, January 10, 1973

In our culture money equals success. Does it also equal masculinity? Yes—to the extent that a man is too often measured by his money, by what he is "worth." Not by his worth as a human being, but by what he is able to earn, how much he can command on the "open market."

In my psychiatric practice I have seen a number of male patients through the years, of all ages, who have equated moneymaking with a sense of masculinity. Peter G., for example. He was 23 years old, very inhibited, and socially inept. Raised in a strict, religious home, he had had very little contact with girls and virtually no dating experience until his second year of college. He was sure that no woman would find him attractive unless he was making good money. In analysis it became evident that he was painfully insecure and unsure of his abilities in *any* area. Money was his "cover": if he flashed a roll of bills, no one would see how little else there was to him. He needed expensive clothes, a big sporty car, and a thick wallet; all these were extensions of his penis. Money would show women he could give them what they needed, and thereby get him what he thought he needed, "a beautiful girl with big boobs." His idea that women were essentially passive and looking to be taken care of by a big, strong male demanded that he "make" good money before he could "make" the woman of his dreams.

This kind of thinking is often reinforced by both men and women who have bought the myth that endows a moneymaking man with sexiness and virility, and is based on man's dominance, strength, and ability to provide for and care for "his" woman. We have many cultural models of this unrealistic and frequently self-defeating image of masculinity. Hollywood has gone a long way to reflect and glorify it in such figures as the John Wayne-style cowboy, the private eye, war hero, foreign correspondent, lone adventurer—all "he-men" (a phrase that in its redundancy seems to "protest too much") who use physical strength, courage, and masculine wiles to conquer their worlds, their villainous rivals, and their women. *Money* rarely has anything to do with it.

But in real life in the 1970s, few women have much concern about men like that. After all, there are few frontiers to conquer, or international spy rings to crack, or glorious wars to wage. All that is left for the real-life, middle-class man is the battle for the bulging wallet.

This measure of one's "masculinity quotient" becomes a convenient fallback to those who have a weak sense of self and who doubt their innate ability to attract women. Because it is hard for these men to face their inadequacies and the anxieties that would follow, they strive for money as a panacea for all their personal ills.

For them, money alone separates the men from the boys. I have even seen youngsters drop out of school to make money, just to prove their manhood.

For their part, women have been taught that men who achieve success are the best "catches" in the marriage market. Women have also been taught that the right motives for marriage are love and sexual attraction. Thus, if a woman wants to marry a man with money, she has to believe she loves him; that he is sexually appealing—even if the real appeal is his money. She has to convince herself—and him—that it's the man behind the money that turns her on. Many women *learn* to make this emotional jump: to feel genuinely attracted to the man who makes it big, and to accept the equation of moneymaking power with sexual power.

There are many phenomenally wealthy men in the public eye who are physically unattractive by traditional criteria; yet they are surrounded by beautiful women and an aura of sexiness and virility. A woman in the same financial position loses in attractiveness (at least if she is *earning* the money rather than spending an inheritance); she poses a threat to a man's sense of masculinity. As I once heard a sociologist say: men are unsexed by failure, women by success.

Yet why is it that many men who have met the moneymaking standards are still not sure of their masculinity? Quite simply because money is—and always was—a pretty insecure peg on which to hang a masculine image.

Take Jerry L., a stockbroker. He lost most of his money three years ago during a very bad spell in the market. Distraught as he was over the financial loss, he was devastated over the sexual impotence which followed in its wake. This direct one-to-one relationship may seem awfully pat, but its validity can be attested to by many men (and "their" women) who have gone through serious financial setbacks. Even a temporary inability to provide properly for his family and to justify himself with his checkbook makes such a man feel totally "worthless."

When Jerry L. recouped most of his losses in the course of the next two years, he did *not* regain his previous sexual potency. The experience had made it impossible for him ever again to rely *solely* on money as proof of his masculinity.

The most extreme and dramatic reaction to personal financial loss is suicide. I have seen several men to whom great losses of money represented such a great loss of self, of ego, and ultimately of masculine image, that life no longer seemed worth living.

The situation becomes even more complicated when "the head of the house" is competing against his wife's paycheck as well as his own expectations. Recently, economic realities have made the two-paycheck family respectable. This is tolerable to Jack as long as he can provide for his family and Jill only earns enough to make all the "little extras" possible.

Given current salary inequities, it is unlikely that she will threaten his place as number-one breadwinner. But if she does, if she can make *real money,* she is co-opting the man's passport to masculinity (thus the stereotype of the successful woman being too masculine, too competitive, too unfeminine), and he is effectively castrated.

Thus it is vital that the woman be "kept in her place," which is classically "in the home," so that her second-class status assures him of his first place. Many divorces and breakups that are blamed on "conflict of careers" often mean nothing more than a wife who would not give up her career (and earning ability) in deference to her husband's.

I know plenty of men who are sufficiently "enlightened" intellectually to accept the idea that a woman has as much right (and power) to make money as a man does. But in practice emotionally—when it comes to *their* wives—these men often feel threatened and emasculated. Because he is unable to see this in himself, such a man expresses his anxiety by forcing a "conflict" with the woman in some other area of their relationship, like dealing with in-laws or running the house, where there is, in fact, no conflict. In this way he deflects attention from his problem but also precludes adequate resolution of it in their relationship.

There is no other common male defense against the income-producing woman. No matter how much she makes, he still maintains she doesn't "understand" money, calling upon the stereotyped image of the cute little wife who can't balance the checkbook. He doesn't have to look further for reassurance than the insurance company, for example, that appeals to a husband's protector-provider definition of himself with pictures of helpless widows and children, and the caption "What will happen to them after you're gone?"

Marty B. was caught in this bind. A successful doctor, he divided his time between research, which he found enjoyable but not very rewarding financially, and the practice of internal medicine, which was more lucrative but not so enjoyable. Marty felt it a strain to deal with many diverse people; he was more comfortable with animal research, which also fulfilled his creative talents and led to his writing a number of solid scientific papers. So far, so good. But then Marty's wife, Janet, an actress who had had only middling success, became an actors' agent and clicked right away.

Soon, Janet began to earn more money than Marty. At first he joked about it with her and even with close friends, but, as it turned out later, the joking was uneasy, and laden with anxiety. Marty decided to increase his patient practice at the expense of his research. He forced himself to make more money—when he actually needed less, thanks to Janet's high income.

They began quarreling about many small things—arguments without resolutions because they had nothing to do with the real issue: that her new money-making powers were a threat to his masculinity.

Marty and Janet came to see me because they were considering separating after eight years of a happy marriage. After a number of sessions, it became clear that Marty felt that Janet's success meant she didn't need him any more; that he had been diminished as "the man of the house." This was not easy for Marty to admit; he had always claimed he was happy to see Janet doing what she wanted professionally. But this was the first time he had to face her actually succeeding at it. Marty agreed, with some ambivalence, to go into psychoanalytic therapy. As therapy evolved, his problem with "masculinity" emerged even more clearly. He had never felt comfortable competing with men; this was a contributing factor to his going into animal research He really received very little gratification from his medical practice, but he needed to make a lot of money to feel competent as a man He resented Janet's success but since he was not aware that his manhood was threatened, he found "other" things to complain and argue about. After three years of therapy and six months of trial separation, Marty worked through his problems. Their marriage and Janet's success both survived.

There are many marriages with similar tension that don't survive. Often neither husband nor wife is aware of how profoundly money and masculinity are equated, or of how much a husband's financial security may depend on having a dependent wife.

But are the old rules working as they once did? Increasing numbers of men making good money are not feeling the strong sense of masculinity it used to provide. A man can buy an expensive car and still get stalled in traffic; how powerful does he feel then? Money seems in danger of losing its omnipotence. In a complicated world, the formerly "almighty" dollar has all too few magical properties.

As a result, we may have to begin dealing with the fact that money has been an artificial symbol of masculinity all along, that we invested it with power and that, like brute strength, it can no longer get us where we want to go.

I suspect we will have to give up the whole idea of "masculinity" and start trying to find out about the real male person. We may find that masculinity has more to do with man's sensitivity, with the nature of his emotional capacity to respond to others, than it has to do with dominance, strength, or ability to "provide for" a woman materially—especially if she isn't pretending to be helpless any more.

Some day soon virility may be the measure of how well a man relates to a woman as an equal, and masculinity will be equated not with moneymaking prowess but with a man's power to feel, express, and give love. That might just possibly be worth much more than money.

The Politics of Housework

Pat Mainardi

Though women do not complain of the power of husbands, each complains of her own husband, or of the husbands of her friends. It is the same in all other cases of servitude; at least in the commencement of the emancipatory movement. The serfs did not at first complain of the power of the lords, but only of their tyranny.

John Stuart Mill
On the Subjection of Women

Liberated women—very different from women's liberation! The first signals all kinds of goodies, to warm the hearts (not to mention other parts) of the most radical men. The other signals—*housework*. The first brings sex without marriage, sex before marriage, cozy housekeeping arrangements ("You see, I'm living with this chick") and the self-content of knowing that you're not the kind of man who wants a doormat instead of a woman. That will come later. After all, who wants that old commodity anymore, the Standard American Housewife, all husband, home and kids. The New Commodity, the Liberated Woman, has sex a lot and has a Career, preferably something that can be fitted in with the household chores—like dancing, pottery, or painting.

On the other hand is women's liberation—and housework. What? You say this is all trivial? Wonderful! That's what I thought. It seemed perfectly reasonable. We both had careers, both had to work a couple of days a week to earn enough to live on, so why shouldn't we share the housework? So I suggested it to my mate and he agreed—most men are too hip to turn you down flat. "You're right," he said. "It's only fair."

Then an interesting thing happened. I can only explain it by stating that we women have been brainwashed more than even we can imagine. Probably too many years of seeing television women in ecstasy over their shiny waxed floors or breaking down over their dirty shirt collars. Men have no such conditioning. They recognize the essential fact of housework right from the very beginning. Which is that it stinks. Here's my list of dirty chores: buying groceries, carting them home and putting them away; cooking meals and washing dishes and pots;

doing the laundry, digging out the place when things get out of control; washing floors. The list could go on but the sheer necessities are bad enough. All of us have to do these things, or get some one else to do them for us. The longer my husband contemplated these chores, the more repulsed he became, and so proceeded the change from the normally sweet considerate Dr. Jekyll into the crafty Mr. Hyde who would stop at nothing to avoid the horrors of—*housework*. As he felt himself backed into a corner laden with dirty dishes, brooms, mops, and reeking garbage his front teeth grew longer and pointier, his fingernails haggled and his eyes grew wild. Housework trivial? Not on your life! Just try to share the burden.

So ensued a dialogue that's been going on for several years. Here are some of the high points:

"I don't mind sharing the housework, but I don't do it very well. We should each do the things we're best at."

Meaning: Unfortunately I'm no good at things like washing dishes or cooking. What I do best is a little light carpentry, changing light bulbs, moving furniture *(how often do you move furniture?)*.

Also meaning: Historically the lower classes (black men and us) have had hundreds of years experience doing menial jobs. It would be a waste of manpower to train someone else to do them now.

Also meaning: I don't like the dull stupid boring jobs, so you should do them.

"I don't mind sharing the work, but you'll have to show me how to do it."

Meaning: I ask a lot of questions and you'll have to show me everything everytime I do it because I don't remember so good. Also don't try to sit down and read while I'm doing my jobs because I'm going to annoy hell out of you until it's easier to do them yourself.

"We used to be so happy!" (Said whenever it was his turn to do something.)

Meaning: I used to be so happy.

Meaning: Life without housework is bliss. *(No quarrel here. Perfect agreement.)*

"We have different standards, and why should I have to work to your standards. That's unfair."

Meaning: If I begin to get bugged by the dirt and crap I will say "This place sure is a sty" or "How can anyone live like this?" and wait for your reaction. I know that all women have a sore called "Guilt over a messy house" or "Household work is ultimately my responsibility." I know that men have caused that sore—if anyone visits and the place *is* a sty, they're not going to leave and say, "He sure is a lousy housekeeper." You'll take the rap in any case. I can outwait you.

Also meaning: I can provoke innumerable scenes over the housework issue. Eventually doing all the housework yourself will be less painful to you than trying to get me to do half. Or I'll suggest we get a maid. She will do my share of the work. You will do yours. It's women's work.

"I've got nothing against sharing the housework, but you can't make me do it on your schedule."
Meaning: Passive resistance. I'll do it when I damned well please, if at all. If my job is doing dishes, it's easier to do them once a week. If taking out laundry, once a month. If washing the floors, once a year. If you don't like it, do it yourself oftener, and then I won't do it at all.

"I *hate* it more than you. You don't mind it so much."
Meaning: Housework is garbage work. It's the worst crap I've ever done. It's degrading and humiliating for someone of *my* intelligence to do it. But for someone of *your* intelligence . . .

"Housework is too trivial to even talk about."
Meaning: It's even more trivial to do. Housework is beneath my status. My purpose in life is to deal with matters of significance. Yours is to deal with matters of insignificance. You should do the housework.

"This problem of housework is not a man-woman problem! In any relationship between two people one is going to have a stronger personality and dominate."
Meaning: That stronger personality had better be *me.*

"In animal societies, wolves, for example, the top animal is usually a male even where he is not chosen for brute strength but on the basis of cunning and intelligence. Isn't that interesting?"
Meaning: I have historical, psychological, anthropological, and biological justification for keeping you down. How can you ask the top wolf to be equal?

"Women's liberation isn't really a political movement."
Meaning: The Revolution is coming too close to home.
Also meaning: I am only interested in how I am oppressed, not how I oppress others. Therefore the war, the draft, and the university are political. Women's liberation is not.

"Man's accomplishments have always depended on getting help from other people, mostly women. What great man would have accomplished what he did if he had to do his own housework?
Meaning: Oppression is built into the System and I, as the white American male receive the benefits of this System. I don't want to give them up.

POSTSCRIPT

Participatory democracy begins at home. If you are planning to implement your politics, there are certain things to remember.

1 He *is* feeling it more than you. He's losing some leisure and you're gaining it. The measure of your oppression is his resistance.

2 A great many American men are not accustomed to doing monotonous repetitive work which never ushers in any lasting let alone important achievement. This is why they would rather repair a cabinet than wash dishes. If human endeavors are like a pyramid with man's highest achievements at the top, then keeping oneself alive is at the bottom. Men have always had servants (us) to take care of this bottom strata of life while they have confined their efforts to the rarefied upper regions. It is thus ironic when they ask of women—where are your great painters, statesmen, etc? Mme. Matisse ran a millinery shop so he could paint. Mrs. Martin Luther King kept his house and raised his babies.

3 It is a traumatizing experience for someone who has always thought of himself as being against any oppression or exploitation of one human being by another to realize that in his daily life he has been accepting and implementing (and benefiting from) this exploitation; that his rationalization is little different from that of the racist who says "Black people don't feel pain" (women don't mind doing the shitwork); and that the oldest form of oppression in history has been the oppression of 50 percent of the population by the other 50 percent.

4 Arm yourself with some knowledge of the psychology of oppressed peoples everywhere, and a few facts about the animal kingdom. I admit playing top wolf or who runs the gorillas is silly but as a last resort men bring it up all the time. Talk about bees. If you feel really hostile bring up the sex life of spiders. They have sex. She bites off his head.

The psychology of oppressed people is not silly. Jews, immigrants, black men, and all women have employed the same psychological mechanisms to survive: admiring the oppressor, glorifying the oppressor, wanting to be like the oppressor, wanting the oppressor to like them, mostly because the oppressor held all the power.

5 In a sense, all men everywhere are slightly schizoid—divorced from the reality of maintaining life. This makes it easier for them to play games with it. It is almost a cliché that women feel greater grief at sending a son off to war or losing him to that war because they bore him, suckled him, and raised him. The men who foment those wars did none of those things and have a more superficial estimate of the worth of human life. One hour a day is a low estimate of the amount of time one has to spend "keeping" oneself. By foisting this off on others, man gains seven hours a week—one working day more to play with his mind and not his human needs. Over the course of generations it is easy to see whence evolved the horrifying abstractions of modern life.

6 With the death of each form of oppression, life changes and new forms evolve. English aristocrats at the turn of the century were horrified at the idea of enfranchising working men—were sure that it signaled the death of civilization and a return to barbarism. Some working men were even deceived by this line. Similarly with the minimum wage, abolition of slavery, and female suffrage. Life changes but it goes on. Don't fall for any line about the death of everything if men take a turn at the dishes. They will imply that you are holding back the Revolution (their Revolution). But you are advancing it (your Revolution).

7 Keep checking up. Periodically consider who's actually *doing* the jobs. These things have a way of backsliding so that a year later once again the woman is doing everything. After a year make a list of jobs the man has rarely if ever done. You will find cleaning pots, toilets, refrigerators and ovens high on the list. Use time sheets if necessary. He will accuse you of being petty. He is above that sort of thing—(housework). Bear in mind what the worst jobs are, namely the ones that have to be done every day or several times a day. Also the ones that are dirty—it's more pleasant to pick up books, newspapers, etc. than to wash dishes. Alternate the bad jobs. It's the daily grind that gets you down. Also make sure that you don't have the responsibility for the housework with occasional help from him. "I'll cook dinner for you tonight" implies it's really your job and isn't he a nice guy to do some of it for you.

8 Most men had a rich and rewarding bachelor life during which they did not starve or become encrusted with crud or buried under the litter. There is a taboo that says that women mustn't strain themselves in the presence of men: we haul around 50 pounds of groceries if we have to but aren't allowed to open a jar if there is someone around to do it for us. The reverse side of the coin is that men aren't supposed to be able to take care of themselves without a woman. Both are excuses for making women do the housework.

9 Beware of the double whammy. He won't do the little things he always did because you're now a "Liberated Women," right? Of course he won't do anything else either . . .

I was just finishing this when my husband came in and asked what I was doing. Writing a paper on housework. Housework? he said. *Housework?* Oh my god how trivial can you get. A paper on housework.

LITTLE POLITICS OF HOUSEWORK QUIZ

The lowest job in the army, used as punishment is: (a) working 9–5; (b) kitchen duty (K.P.).

When a man lives with his family, his: (a) father (b) mother does his housework.

When he lives with a woman, (a) he (b) she does the housework.

(A) his son (b) his daughter learns in preschool how much fun it is to iron daddy's handkerchief.

From the *New York Times*, 9/21/69: "Former Greek Official George Mylonas pays the penalty for differing with the ruling junta in Athens by performing household chores on the island of Amorgos where he lives in forced exile" (with hilarious photo of a miserable Mylonas carrying his own water). What the *Times* means is that he ought to have (a) indoor plumbing (b) a maid.

Dr. Spock said (*Redbook* 3/69): "Biologically and temperamentally I believe, women were made to be concerned first and foremost with child care, husband care, and home care." Think about: (a) *who* made us (b) why? (c) what is the effect on their lives (d) what is the effect on our lives?

From *Time* 1/5/70, "Like their American counterparts, many housing project housewives are said to suffer from neurosis. And for the first time in Japanese history, many young husbands today complain of being henpecked. Their wives are beginning to demand detailed explanations when they don't come home straight from work and some Japanese males nowadays are even compelled to do housework." According to *Time,* women become neurotic: (a) when they are forced to do the maintenance work for the male caste all day every day of their lives or (b) when they no longer want to do the maintenance work for the male caste all day every day of their lives.

I Just Don't Know If I Can Make It

Colleen McNamara

. . . That's what I find myself saying almost every night before I fall asleep. I'm a woman alone with an infant son, trying to exist on welfare. Before the baby was born I used to find myself crying a lot because I just couldn't get the money together to buy things, like a crib and clothes, that the baby would need. I guess like any mother I wanted the best for my child, but now my tears are being shed for things much more serious. I'm 21 years old and my background was far from comfortable and stable. I was raised in a small apartment over a liquor warehouse in New York. We couldn't afford hot running water because my Mom paid the utilities and she had to think of every little way to save. She would turn the hot water heater on once a week and we would all have baths. The rest of the week we'd heat water on the stove. At night we'd all have to stay in one room to save electricity. Our food was always simple and our clothes usually made-over hand-outs.

My parents broke up when I was small because my Dad was slowly turning to drinking as a way of life. I guess it was hard for him to watch his family have to live like that even though he was working. He was a high-school dropout and an unskilled laborer, so the jobs he could find didn't pay enough to raise a family on. When Dad left, Mom started working full time as a nurse's aide at night, and by the time I was a teenager I was practically on my own. We didn't see much of her and the temptations of being on my own started getting me in trouble.

Through those years I met many a social worker and parole officer through the juvenile authorities. At 15 I had a job as a nurse's aide after school and on weekends. I've always worked and worked hard; that illusion that welfare recipients are lazy can't be proved by me.

The reason I told you about my background was to let you see that being poor and not having everything I want is not new to me. And yet the way I live now is like a constant nightmare. As I started to say earlier, I used to cry a lot before the baby was born because I couldn't get him the best of everything; now I'm happy if he's got p.j.'s to keep him warm, no matter what they look like. Now my tears are shed for a much more urgent need—food. According to the county, I'm allowed $14 worth of food stamps for two weeks—that's $7.00 a week, $1.00 a day. Last week when I got my food stamps I bought all the baby's food for the two weeks. That way when the money runs out at least the baby will have food. The other foods I bought were rice, beans, bread, catsup, potatoes, four pork chops, two quarts of milk, one box of cereal and two cans of soup. My bill was $11.00. That means I'm left with $3.00 worth of stamps for the other thirteen days. That $3.00 will have to pay for milk, bread, and butter as they're needed. Right now my baby's only on vegetables, cereal, and formula. God only knows what I'm going to do when he starts eating meat, fruit, and fruit juice.

Please understand that I want to get back to a job as soon as I can, but it's impossible to get employment and the government cut its funds for training programs. I feel like I'm on a dead-end street. I'm cursed for being on welfare and yet the very people who condemn me won't hire me so I can get on my feet again. Is it so hard to understand why the urge to steal is becoming stronger and stronger? I receive $148 a month from welfare to pay for rent, food, clothes, transportation, telephone, and other things, such as soap, Purex, laundromat fees, deodorant, toothpaste, and toilet paper. Maybe a lot of you people take these things for granted, but when you're making a budget out of $148, there's many a time when newspaper or gift box tissue paper is used as toilet paper until the real thing can be afforded.

Many people, especially middle-class liberals, condemn poor people for being apathetic about what's happening in the country. But many of us cannot afford TV's and even a dime for the newspaper is sometimes more than we can spare. Is it any wonder that many a time we don't know what's happening in Washington and in other parts of the world? But just ask us about the things that are happening around us and we could fill a book. Ask us about that tragic battle that roars within us as we desperately try to save our faith in God while all the world is turning into a hell for us and we are being made involuntary martyrs to a country we no longer believe in. Ask us about the cops in our neighborhoods and about the schools. For God's sake, America, put down your newspapers and look around you. ,

Is it any wonder that the health of poor people is so bad? We can't afford balanced meals three times a day and our nerves are shot from being under so much mental strain. My body is so choked up with fear for me and my son's futures and the future of all other people like us that I can hardly breathe. And now we are burdened with the additional threat of the medical program being stopped. Many old people have already died because they were told they could no longer stay in nursing homes when the government cut their funds. They had no families and no place else to go, so they just died. If things keep up this way, soon America will have a mortality rate as high as the so-called uncivilized, underdeveloped parts of the world.

Of all the institutions in America, the institution of poverty is the only one that knows no prejudices. Poor people of all races, creeds, colors, and age groups are slowly being wasted away. I am white, but as the times get worse and worse, my existence seems to be threatened as much as any minority group, not because I'm white, but solely because I'm poor. All we want is for someone to help us help ourselves. I believe people working for change can help all of us. At least I pray you can, because you're our last hope. Otherwise, I just don't know if I can make it.

Sterilizing the Poor

Claudia Dreifus

They sit quietly on her lap as she weeps: the two living children of Guadalupe Acosta, two little girls with coffee-tone skin and classic Indian faces. Clean and pretty in their starched dresses, the girls are with their mother as we meet in the East Los Angeles offices of her attorney, Antonia Hernandez of the Model Cities Law Center.

Mrs. Acosta, a large, somber-looking woman of thirty-five, has taken the morning off to talk with me. The children have been brought because, well . . . baby sitters are expensive. And also because Lupe Acosta finds it hard to be away from them for any sustained period of time. Though Mrs. Acosta has given birth to four infants, it is only these two children—the middle ones—that she has been able to nurture and raise. There was a first baby, born out of wedlock in Mexico, who was taken from her and given to a relative for adoption. The fourth child died shortly after birth at L. A. County General Hospital on August 21, 1973. And it was after that delivery that doctors at L. A. County sterilized her. Without her knowledge. Without her informed consent. And it is because of this sterilization that Lupe Acosta's common-law husband abandoned her. The operation is the reason she cries throughout our interview, the reason she holds her two daughters to her body *so tightly.*

"I didn't want to go to L. A. County Hospital," she begins. "I heard they didn't treat you right there and that they made the women suffer. I had a private doctor. When I was nine months pregnant he told me that the baby's head was too big and I would have to go to the County Hospital because they had better equipment."

The child's head was more than just too big; it was severely malformed— anencephalic, it had no brain. Because of the abnormality, the pregnancy lasted eleven months. For the last month of term, Mrs. Acosta attended weekly prenatal clinic sessions at County—where, not once, was she counseled about sterilization.

However, on August 20, 1973, eleven months and eleven days pregnant, Lupe Acosta entered L. A. County in the final stages of labor. "When I was being examined, they pushed very hard on the stomach," she recalls. "Very, very hard. With their hands. One doctor would have one leg open. The other doctor would have the other leg open. And then, there were two doctors just pushing down on my stomach and I couldn't . . . I couldn't stand it. I pushed one doctor because I couldn't stand the pain. When he came back, he hit me in the stomach and said, 'Now lady, let us do what we have to.' I felt very sick. I was sweat all over, *sweat*. I kept telling them to do something to bring the baby. . . . They kept me in that condition from six o'clock in the evening till three o'clock in the morning. That was the last time I saw the clock—the last time I remember anything."

A question to Mrs. Acosta from her lawyer: "Do you remember signing a consent form?"

"No," she answers. "I don't remember signing anything. Only when I left the hospital—perhaps an exit paper?"

The day after Mrs. Acosta's caesarean delivery, her common-law husband came to her bedside. "He told me the baby was alive and in an incubator," she says, weeping at the mere recollection. "Seven days later the doctor came round to take out the stitches and I asked him how my baby was. 'What baby?' he asked. 'Your baby died when it was born.'" That's how Acosta learned the fate of her fourth child.

But more was to come. A month after delivery, she arrived at County for the standard postnatal check-up. "My common-law husband, he told me to get the Pill at the hospital," she recounts. "When I asked the woman doctor, she asked me if I knew what had happened to me. I said, 'No.' And then the doctor told me, 'Well, you won't need the Pill because they tied your tubes.' I said that I didn't sign anything. She said, 'Your husband did.' And then I told them he wasn't my husband."

When Lupe Acosta got home that night, she was alternating between fury and hysteria. "I became very angry," she says, "and I asked him why he had done that—he had no right. He told me that he didn't sign anything except for a paper for a caesarean. He said, 'If I had signed the paper, would I have sent you for the Pill?'"

The relationship between Guadalupe Acosta and her common-law husband of eight years quickly deteriorated. Built into Mexican culture is the idea of *machismo*, a value that says a man's masculinity is measured by the number of children his wife produces. Given the reality of *machismo*, a sterile woman is considered worthless—useless. On a smoggy day last autumn, Lupe Acosta's man abandoned her and the two children. She was, as a result, forced on welfare. Then the tubal ligation hemorrhaged and she was hospitalized. Nothing has gone right in her life since August 1973. Sometimes she gets pains from the tubal ligation. "And my nerves and my head are in great pain," she complains. "Ever since the operation, I am very inattentive. Not forgetful, inattentive. People sometimes have to tell me things twice. It's not that I don't understand them, it's that I'm not there."

It was a different story for Maria Diaz (not her real name). In 1972, Mrs. Diaz, pregnant with a third child, was living with her family in Hermosillo, Mexico. Because Mrs. Diaz, then thirty-two years old, was a legally immigrated resident of the United States and because her husband had not yet attained that status, it was decided she should journey to Los Angeles alone for the infant's birth. "My brother-in-law told me it would be better for the baby to be born in the United States," she recalls.

Mrs. Diaz explains all this as she pours coffee for me and her lawyer, Antonia Hernandez. It is a warm July afternoon The three of us are sitting in the living room of her spotlessly clean cottage in Glendale, California. On the walls hang dimestore prints of John F. Kennedy and Emiliano Zapata—as well as lovingly mounted crayon scribblings by the children. "Yes, I went there because I thought it would be better," explains Mrs. Diaz who, like her husband, works as a baker. "I could cross the border freely and my husband could not—so I went alone."

On April 6, 1972, Maria Diaz and her brother-in-law arrived at L. A. County Women's Hospital; she was in labor. For three-and-a-half hours they sat in the waiting room until the hospital would admit her. Then, after several more hours of labor, she was informed that the child would be born by caesarean section. "I told them I could not accept the caesarean operation because my husband was not there and I could not do as I pleased. . . . When they were talking about she caesarean, I heard the doctors use the word 'tubes.' The doctors said they were going to tie my tubes because it would be dangerous for me to have more children. I told them I could not accept that. I kept saying no and the doctors kept telling me that this was for my own good,"

Maria Diaz was approached repeatedly during the final stages of her labor. A tube was pushed into her vagina. She was crying with pain. Nevertheless, the attending staff continued pressing her for sterilization. She was drugged and "they had already given me anesthesia when I signed the consent form for the caesarean and they were still insisting that I would accept the tubal operation and I was still saying, 'No, no, no.' "

Finally, Mrs. Diaz broke down. "I was in great pain," she tells us. "I thought I was going to die. The two other children, the pain was nothing like this. I got angry and I cried, 'If you're going to do *anything,* do it, but let me have my baby now because I feel I am going to die.' I remember very little after that because it was like a dream and I was in great pain."

"Did you sign a paper for the caesarean?" I ask.

"For the caesarean, yes," Maria Diaz answers "but for the tubal—no."

"Is it possible that you told them verbally to go ahead?" I inquire.

"I *know* that I didn't because there was a nurse or a receptionist at the hospital who showed me the chart and there was no indication that I approved. The chart said I rejected all their efforts for sterilization, but I don't remember everything. It's possible in the pain . . . but I don't remember doing that."

Mrs. Diaz discovered she was sterile some weeks later during her postnatal clinic visit. "When I heard that, I started to cry " she recalls. "The doctor said,

'Don't cry. It's best for you that you not have any more children. In Mexico, the people are very, very poor and it's best that you not have more children. At that moment, I thought—but I didn't say it, 'What is it to you? You're not my husband.' "

When Mrs. Diaz wrote her spouse of the operation, he sent back a letter saying he didn't understand what she was talking about. "To this day," she says—speaking in a low voice, so that her husband, who sits outside, will not hear, "he is very angry. There are constant problems. Fighting. He says, 'Surely we will part. You never lacked home. You never lacked food. Why did you let them do this to you?' "

Since the operation, Maria Diaz says, she has become nervous, *rare*. That's the word she uses: *rare*. "Now the child is three years old and I think I should be pregnant now, according to the pattern I'd established, but I can't. I go to the doctor every month for the nerves. For a year, I was sick with the wound—the scar that did not close. . . . I feel very bad and I want more people to know this so it won't happen to someone else."

"She's a brave woman," Antonia Hernandez tells me later. "It's dangerous for her to speak up with her husband not yet fully immigrated. We could have had many, many more plaintiffs on the lawsuit, but the women were afraid of the Immigration and Naturalization Service. . . ."

About the lawsuit: Mrs. Diaz, Mrs. Acosta, and nine other Los Angeles area Chicanos are suing USC-L.A. County Medical Center, certain John Doe doctors (the women do not know the names of their sterilizers), the State of California, and the U. S. Department of Health, Education and Welfare. These women, with one exception, were all sterilized at County; they claim the practice of pushing these operations on the poor is a part of a national sterilization epidemic they want stopped. The plaintiffs demand a new set of self-enforcing federal guidelines that will make coercion more difficult; consent forms in English and Spanish; consent forms written on a reading-level comprehensible to all women; conformity by California with the 1974 federal ban on sterilization of women under the age of twenty-one—the California limit is eighteen. What's more, the women are suing for financial damages. "We are asking for money," explains Antonia Hernandez, "because money is the only thing that doctors understand."

To prove her point, Hernandez hands me the legal documents of *Dolores Madrigal et al.* v. *E. J. Quilligan, Director Obstetrics at USC-L. A. County et al.* These documents are so filled with pain that even the cold, objective tone of legalese cannot blunt the suffering that has obviously occurred:

Maria Hustado: "I do not remember the doctor telling me anything about tubalization. All that I remember is after the doctor injected my dorsal, spinal cord, he told me, 'Mama sign here. No more babies. Sign here.' "

Maria E. Figueroa: ". . . A doctor asked me if I wanted to have a tubal ligation. . . . I told the doctor that I did not want to be sterilized since my husband and I planned to have another child. . . . I was groggy from the drugs, exhausted from the labor, as well as from the doctor's constant pressuring. Finally, I told the doctor, 'Okay, if it's a boy, go ahead and do it. . . . My daughter Elizabeth was born by caesarean operation. While my husband was visiting me in the medical center, the doctor came to my bed and informed me that he had performed a tubal ligation on me.''

Reading through the papers, one begins to perceive a pattern. Few of the plaintiffs spoke more than minimal English; they were Mexican and poor. The women were pressured into the procedure during the stress and agony of childbirth—a time when they could not possibly make an informed decision about an irreversible operation. *Even* if they had spoken the language. *Even* if they had been given all the facts.

A few unadvertised, unpleasant bits of information about tubal ligation: the death rate is significantly higher than for long term use of the IUD or the Pill. According to the Health Research Group study on "Surgical Sterilization: Present Abuses and Proper Regulation," the death rate on hysterectomy (often improperly used for sterilization) is 1,000 deaths per million; for tubal ligation, 1,000 per million; for laparoscopic tubals, the mortality rate goes down to 300 per million. According to that same study, the death rate for IUD is nine per million women; for pills, it is thirty-one per million. It should be said, however, that we still do not know all the long-term effects of use of the birth-control pill. There has yet to be a full generation of women who have used oral contraception for their full fertility-life. It is possible that ten or twenty years from now we may see a cancer epidemic among Pill users; the evidence still isn't in. But the point is this: based on what we *now* know, as dangerous as the Pill is, it seems to be safer than sterilization.

Once a woman has had a tubal, she must consider herself permanently, irrevocably sterile. Legal remedies for coercion are rare, expensive, and generally unavailable to the poor. Besides—no judicial award can ever compensate a woman for her stolen fertility; a woman involuntarily sterilized suffers many of the permanent psychological impairments of a rape victim. Between 10 and 30 percent of all women who voluntarily agree to it later regret the operation. Though a costly operation for reversal exists, it is successful in only 10 to 20 percent of all cases.

But the doctors told the women little of this. Consent forms were pushed at women in the throes of labor—women who were drugged, women who were under anesthesia. Sometimes, the physicians even disposed of the minimum legal nicety of a signed consent form; they simply cut without permission. And, if one is to believe the sworn affidavits of eleven women, the L. A. County obstetrics staff, in its zeal to sterilize, was dispensing medical misinformation as if it were aspirin. Though tubal ligation is one of the few operations that is 99 percent elective, an unusual number of Chicanas were told that they would die if they did not submit. Some patients were misled into thinking their tubes could be "untied" at some time in the future. Others were told that there were legal or medical limits on the number of caesareans that patients were permitted—an untruth to say the least. As the late Dr. Alan F. Guttmacher, a leading American authority on contraception, explained: "By tradition the American obstetrician is prepared to sterilize any patient who desires it at the time of the third caesarean section. How magic number three was derived is unknown to me."

"It would be a mistake to think of the situation at L.A. County as an isolated fluke. This is happening all over the country," asserts Dr. Bernard "Buddy" Rosenfeld, the thirty-three-year-old co-author of the Ralph Nader-sponsored Health Research Group study on forced sterilization. To prove his point, the two of us sneak our way past security at USC—L.A. County's dormitory for house staff. Rosenfeld wears his medical whites—he is an MD; I wear a most unjournalistic pair of dungarees. We knock on doors, introduce ourselves as researchers doing a "rough study" on informed consent practices, and ask interns and residents to tell us what they have witnessed at *other* institutions where they have trained. None of the physicians we speak with know that I am a reporter, that I am making careful notes after each interview, that their comments will see print.

Rosenfeld and I are looking for two things: we want to know whether the L. A. County house staff, recent arrivals from some of the ranking medical schools around the country, have seen abuses similar to those that have occurred here. We also want to know whether the 1974 federal guidelines against coercive sterilization are being enforced. Those regulations specifically ban sterilizations on women under twenty-one; prohibit operations on women less than seventy-two hours after they have signed consent forms; require a careful counseling procedure so that patients truly learn that the operation is permanent and that there are other birth-control choices. . . .

Judging from our "rough study" interviews, forced sterilization is a part of academic training at more than a few major teaching hospitals around the nation. The doctors we interview seem to accept coercion as an everyday fact of medical life—few of them are even aware of the moral significance of what they have witnessed. For instance, a friendly intern who has just completed studies at Wayne State Medical School in Detroit, recounts the most remarkable things in perfect innocence:

"Most of our patient population was black, inner city " he explains. "We had a lot of young girls come in . . . thirteen and sixteen and they'd have two or three children. In those cases we'd ask 'em, often when they were in labor, if they wanted tubal ligations. There were *so many* young girls and most of them had a real low mentality. We'd tell them about birth control and they wouldn't take it. It would get some of the residents really mad.

"With sixteen year olds, you needed the parents' permission. *That* usually wasn't hard to get. The parents weren't in labor. Some of the parents said, 'No.' They liked having the babies around. Sterilization was offered to women in labor no matter what their age. Those over eighteen you didn't need the parents' permission. . . ."

"You mean you sterilized *sixteen year olds?*" asks an incredulous intern from Milwaukee, who has been sitting on the side, taking the discussion in.

"Well, yeah . . . if they had two kids. But we didn't do many abortions, though. The residents didn't like to do them. You know, you look at a fetus and you see it is a formed human being, so we didn't do many. There was beginning to be a whole lot of trouble. Detroit's blacks, they're really very anti-white. They were having all these meetings about 'genocide.' "

A similarly pleasant doctor up the hallway claimed his training institution, Jefferson Davis Hospital—Baylor Medical School in Houston, Texas, was a good deal less discriminating:

"Our patient population was 80 percent black, 15 percent Chicano and 5 percent what you'd call poor white trash," he twangs in a voice of pure honey. "There wasn't any racism there. No more than here. If a resident wanted to practice doing a laparoscopic [tubal ligation], he'd push it, sure. There was a basic social pressure that three children were enough. If a woman came in with two children and wanted a tubal, we would try to talk her out of it. But if a woman came in with five children, we'd sell the operation—sure. Women were approached in clinic and sometimes during labor, sure. We'd ask a woman in labor, if her chart wasn't available. . . ."

An intern who had done his medical school rounds at UCLA—Cedars of Lebanon Hospital in Los Angeles: "I did see instances of women in labor being asked. I didn't see any prejudice against Mexicans or blacks *per se* but the ward patients weren't given as much information on sterilization as the private patients. Often an intern would say, 'I want to do a tubal.' That was a big influence in prompting them to do it—they wanted to get another tubal under their belt."

"Why are women approached about sterilization during labor?" I inquire. "It seems so unfair."

"It's expedient," the intern explains. "Although it's like asking a drowning person, do they want to get out of the water."

A female intern in a nearby room had recently completed obstetrics rounds at Riverside General Hospital in nearby Orange County. The patients there were also Mexican. "I didn't see any *real* pushing but it was often suggested after labor," she commented dryly. "The doctors would say, 'Do you want to go through this again?' Mostly, the doctor's individual philosophy towards sterilization had a lot to do with whether or not a patient was approached."

"You don't consider asking a woman about the procedure after labor, pushing?" Rosenfeld asks.

"Not really," she replies. "Now when I was down in Nicaragua, *there* we pushed. People would come in with nine children and they didn't have food and we pushed them."

A pediatric intern, formerly at New York's Bellevue Hospital: "There was a large Puerto Rican population and I think a lot of women didn't know the full consequences of what was happening to them. There was a language problem. Many of the women thought their tubes could be untied."

A former medical student from the University of Chicago, where the patient population is primarily black: "No one ever said to a woman, 'We don't trust you with taking the Pill,' it would be presented very *positively.* 'This is the best thing for you. This will be the easiest thing for us.' Mostly, we'd approach women with large families and we'd tell them this was the best solution. We would explain the world population problem."

An intern previously at Barnes Hospital, St. Louis: "Whether or not a patient was approached positively about sterilization depended on the doctor's own approach. A woman on welfare with a large family was more likely to be approached earlier than a woman not on welfare. No one was pushed, though."

Another intern, formerly at UCSF—San Francisco General Hospital: "It was always explained—*if* the patient asked, yes, she'd be told it was permanent. If there was a big rush, the staff wouldn't bother. There was concern by some of the students that minority groups were getting pushed, so the hospital became very careful. They're slick now. Although official policy has changed, the attitudes of the doctors didn't. They became slicker at talking patients into tubals. Tubals are way up and the birthrate is way down. . . ."

It can't happen here. That is the defensive response most people have when I tell them the L. A. county story. Interestingly, USC–L.A. County Medical Center seems now to be one of the few institutions in the United States actually conforming to law. According to a study made by Elissa Krauss for the American Civil Liberties Union, few major teaching hospitals are following the 1974 HEW orders. In November 1974, when the guidelines were nearly half a year old, Krauss sent questionnaires to the heads of OB–GYN departments of 154 ranking teaching hospitals. Less than a third of the queried chairmen granted the ACLU the courtesy of a reply. And of the fifty-one respondents who did answer the poll, one in three gave replies that showed conformity with the letter and spirit of the Federal guidelines. "Thirty-six major teaching hospitals are in non-compliance with Federal regulations on sterilization," said the ACLU report. "These institutions—plus another twelve hospitals responding to this questionnaire—should be subject to immediate withdrawal of funding because they are in complete non-compliance. . . ." But will those hospitals lose their federal monies? Not likely. The Department of Health, Education, and Welfare has yet to move against a single institution named by the ACLU.

It can't happen to me. That is the response of educated middle-class women when they hear about forced sterilization. Not true. Doctors who learn to push sterilization on indigent patients during training will do the same in private practice. There is profit in it. A gynecologist earns nothing for dispensing condoms or the birth-control pill. The bill for an IUD insertion is rarely more than $100. However, average fees for a tubal ligation begin at $300. Elective hysterectomy is $600—plus. I remember that honey-voiced gynecologist-to-be from Houston whom we spoke with one summer evening in the L. A. County dorm. His eyes gleamed when he spoke of hysterectomy: "In Houston, a lot of well-to-do women would come in and they'd want hysterectomies because their friends had them. Maybe the indications weren't so strong, but why shouldn't we take her womb if it makes her feel better?" Several of my friends have recently submitted to tubal ligations; the doctors call it "Band-Aid surgery." Yet, one study showed 1,594 serious complications and nineteen deaths out of 63,845 operations surveyed.[1] My friends are middle-class and well educated. Nevertheless, the same medical practice that sells tubals to the poor under the stress of labor, sells my affluent friends the lie of Band-Aid simplicity for a dangerous operation.

Ultimately, we are all, as Guadalupe Acosta understood, helpless in the face of a medical system that has little accountability. It was Mrs. Acosta, of all the protagonists, who had the sharpest focus on what had happened. I once asked her if she thought the physicians at L. A. County were racist. "I don't know about things like that," she replied, clutching at her two babies. "You go to the hospital so sick, so dependent. One doesn't ask questions."

Few of us do.

It Hurts to Be Alive and Obsolete:
The Ageing Woman

Zoe Moss

What, fat, forty-three, and I dare to think I'm still a person? No, I am an invisible lump. I belong in a category labelled *a priori* without interest to anyone. I am not even expected to interest myself. A middle-aged woman is comic by definition.

In this commodity culture, we are urged and coerced into defining ourselves by buying objects that demonstrate that we are, or which tell us that they will make us feel, young, affluent, fashionable. Imagine a coffee table with the bestsellers of five years ago carefully displayed. You giggle. A magazine that is old enough—say, a *New Yorker* from 1944 with the models looking healthy and almost buxom in their padded jackets—or a dress that is far enough gone not to give the impression that perhaps you had not noticed fashions had changed, can become campy and delightful. But an out-of-date woman is only embarrassing.

The mass media tell us all day and all evening long that we are inadequate, mindless, ugly, disgusting in ourselves. We must try to resemble perfect plastic objects, so that no one will notice what we really are. In ourselves we smell bad, shed dandruff, our breath has an odor, our hair stands up or falls out, we sag or stick out where we shouldn't. We can only fool people into liking us by using magic products that make us products, too.

---

[1]As more laparoscopic tubals are done by doctors, the safer they'll become. The danger is going to a physician who has little experience with the procedure. But even when safety isn't a factor, there are many harmful side-effects to this "Band-Aid" operation.

Women, especially, are commodities. There is always a perfect plastic woman. Girls are always curling their hair or ironing it, binding their breasts or padding them. Think of the girls with straight hips and long legs skulking through the 1890's with its women defined as having breasts the size of pillows and hips like divans. Think of the Rubens woman today forever starving and dieting and crawling into rubber compression chambers that mark her flesh with livid lines and squeeze her organs into knots.

If a girl were to walk into a party in the clothes of just five or six years past, in the make-up and hairstyle of just that slight gap of time, no one would want to talk to her, no man would want to dance with her. Yet what has all that to do with even a man and a woman in bed? This is not only the middle class I am talking about. I have seen hippies react the same way to somebody wearing old straight clothes.

It is a joke, but a morbid one. My daughter has a girlfriend who always laughs with her hand up to her mouth because she is persuaded her teeth are yellow, and that yellow teeth are hideous. She seems somber and never will she enjoy a natural belly laugh. Most young girls walk around with the conviction that some small part of their anatomy (nose, breasts, knees, chin) is so large or so small or so misshapen that their whole body appears to be built around that part, and all of their activities must camouflage it.

My daughter is a senior in college. She already talks about her "youth" with a sad nostalgia. She is worried because she is not married. That she has not met anyone that she wants to live that close to, does not seem to figure in her anxiety. Everything confirms in her a sense of time passing, that she will be left behind, unsold on the shelf. She already peers in the mirror for wrinkles and buys creams and jellies to rub into her skin. Her fear angers me but leaves me helpless. She is alienated from her body because her breasts are big and do not stand out like the breasts of store mannequins. She looks twenty-one. I look forty-three.

I want to beg her not to begin worrying, not to let in the dreadful daily gnawing already. Everyone born grows up, grows older. and ages every day until he dies. But every day in seventy thousand ways this society tells a woman that it is her sin and her guilt that she has a real living body. How can a woman respect herself when every day she stands before her mirror and accuses her face of betraying her, because every day she is, indeed a day older.

Everything she reads, every comic strip, every song, every cartoon, every advertisement, every book and movie tells her that a woman over thirty is ugly and disgusting. She is a bag. She is to be escaped from. She is no longer an object of prestige consumption. For her to have real living sexual desires is obscene. Her touch is thought to contaminate. No man "seduces" a woman older than him: there is no conquest. It is understood she would be "glad for a touch of it." Since she would be glad, there can be no pleasure in the act. Either this society is mad or I am mad. It is considered incredible that a woman might have had experiences that are valuable or interesting and that have enriched her as a person. No, men may mature, but women just obsolesce.

All right, says the woman, don't punish me! I won't do wrong! I won't older! Now, if a woman has at least an upper-middle-class income, no strong commitments such as a real career or a real interest in religion or art or politics; if she has a small family and hired help; if she has certain minimal genetic luck; if she has the ability to be infinitely fascinated by her own features and body, she may continue to present a youthful image. She can prolong her career as sexual object, lying about her age, rewriting her past to keep the chronology updated, and devoting herself to the cultivation of her image. Society will reward her greatly. Women in the entertainment industry are allowed to remain sexual objects (objects that are prestigeful to use or own—like Cadillacs) for much of their lives.

To be told when you have half your years still to wade through and when you don't feel inside much different than you did at twenty (you are still you!—you know that!), to be told then that you are cut off from expressing yourself sexually and often even in friendship, drives many women crazy—often literally so.

Don't tell me that it is human nature for women to cease to be attractive early. In primitive society a woman who is still useful—in that by all means far more humane definition than ours—will find a mate, whom she may share as she shares the work with his other wives. Black women are more oppressed on the job and in almost every other way in this society than white women, but at least in the ghetto men go on assuming a woman is sexual as long as she thinks so too.

Earlier mythology in which "the widow" is a big sex figure, French novels in which the first mistress is always an older woman, the Wife of Bath, all reinforce my sense that there is nothing natural about women's obsolescence.

I was divorced five years ago. Don't tell me I should have "held on to my husband." We let go with great relief. Recently he has married a woman in her late twenties. It is not surprising he should marry someone younger: most people in this society are younger than my ex-husband. In my job, most of the people I meet are younger than I am, and the same is true of people who share my interests, from skiing to resistance to the war against Vietnam.

When my daughter was little I stayed home, but luckily for me I returned to work when she entered school. I say luckily, because while I believe my ex-husband has an obligation to help our daughter, I would never accept alimony. I can get quite cold and frightened imagining what would have happened if I had stayed home until my divorce, and then, at thirty-eight, tried to find work. I used to eat sometimes at a lunchroom where the rushed and overworked waitress was in her late forties. She had to cover the whole room, and I used to leave her larger tips than I would give someone else because to watch her made me conscious of women's economic vulnerability. She was gone one day and I asked the manager at the cash register about her. "Oh, the customers didn't like her. Men come in here, they want to see a pretty face."

I have insisted on using a pseudonym in writing this article, because the cost of insisting I am not a cipher would be fatal. If I lost my job, I would have an incredible time finding another. I know I will never "get ahead." Women don't move up through the shelves of a business automatically or by keeping their mouths shut. I could be mocked into an agony of shame for writing this—but beyond that, I could so easily be let go.

I am gregarious, interested in others, and I think, intelligent. All I ask is to get to know people and to have them interested in knowing me. I doubt whether I would marry again and live that close to another individual. But I remain invisible. I think stripped down I look more attractive on some abstract scale (a bisexual Martian judging) than my ex-husband, but I am sexually and socially obsolete, and he is not. Like most healthy women my face has aged more rapidly than my body, and I look better with my clothes off. When I was young, my anxiety about myself and what was to become of me colored all my relationships with men, and I was about as sensual as a clotheshanger. I have a capacity now for taking people as they are, which I lacked at twenty; I reach orgasm in half the time and I know how to please. Yet I do not even dare show a man that I find him attractive. If I do so, he may react as if I had insulted him: with shock, with disgust. I am not even allowed to be affectionate. I am supposed to fulfill my small functions and vanish.

Often when men are attracted to me, they feel ashamed and conceal it. They act as if it were ridiculous. If they do become involved, they are still ashamed and may refuse to appear publicly with me. Their fear of mockery is enormous. There is no prestige attached to having sex with me.

Since we are all far more various sexually than we are supposed to be, often, in fact, younger men become aware of me sexually. Their response is similar to what it is when they find themselves feeling attracted to a homosexual: they turn those feelings into hostility and put me down.

Listen to me! Think what it is like to have most of your life ahead and be told you are obsolete! Think what it is like to feel attraction, desire, affection toward others, to want to tell them about yourself, to feel that assumption on which self-respect is based, that you are worth something, and that if you like someone, surely he will be pleased to know that. To be, in other words, still a living woman, and to be told every day that you are not a woman but a tired object that should disappear. That you are not a person but a joke. Well, I am a bitter joke. I am bitter and frustrated and wasted, but don't you pretend for a minute as you look at me, forty-three, fat, and looking exactly my age, that I am not as alive as you are and that I do not suffer from the category into which you are forcing me.

The Man in the Street: Why He Harasses

Cheryl Benard
Edit Schlaffer

It is a violation of my natural external freedom, not to be able to go where I please. . . . My personality is wounded by such experiences, because my most immediate identity rests in my body.

Hegel
Texte Zur Philosophishcen
Propaedeutik

I am standing at Wittenbergplatz waiting for the light to turn green . . . behind me I sense the approach of two men and turn my head, at that moment the man on my left reaches for my hair; he runs his fingers through it experimentally and says to his friend: "Great hair." . . . An ordinary everyday experience for the colonized in a city of the First World.

Verena Stefan
Haetungen

What kinds of men harass women, what do they think they are doing? On the whole, the behavior of the "man in the street" has received little attention, and that is odd because it captures in quintessential, almost primordial form the combination of the oppressive and the bizarre that we have learned to regard as normal. The language clearly reflects this. The "man in the street," a phrase dear to the media and politicians, is a synonym for the citizen, the voter, the average person, and at the same time the male. There is no "woman in the street" in our language; only a streetwalker, or an intruder who can be treated like one.

Stamped as trivial, the harassment of women has received no attention from sociology, and cities that regulate almost everything from bicycles to dogs and the use of roller skates in order to keep the traffic moving have no ordinances or rules to guarantee women the right to free passage. Men, yes; the solicitations of prostitutes are carefully restricted in order not to offend them. The language itself puts women at a disadvantage; it is hard to exchange serious insults without using sexual put-downs that invariably go against women. And passersby will shed their indifference to disapprove of feminine vulgarity.

Explanations of harassment, where they are attempted at all, often try to minimize the universality: it's the Mediterranean cultures, one school of thought believes; or the United States cities, with their extremes of female fashion and their sexual liberalism; or the Arab societies, full of repressed male libidos ready to explode at the sight of a Western female tourist. However, this form of male behavior is quite independent of continent, race, generation, and degree of individual frustration.

In adolescence, experiences of this kind are particularly disconcerting and reinforce the awareness that hostility and sexuality seem to go together.

"When I was about sixteen," one Western woman remembered, "I had real moments of anxiety. In elevators and on the subway men would sometimes look me over with a sort of aggressive, superior little smile. I would always try to stand in quiet corners or look for a family and then stand with them as if I were one of their kids."

Women who are often in public places learn to get used to harassment and develop their own strategies for avoiding or responding to it. A sociology student and feminist reported: "For a while I used to talk back to *all* of these guys. I tried to educate them then just to put them down. I got pretty good at it, but it took up a lot of my time. I used to mind it a lot less, because they just seemed so ridiculous. But now it makes me angry."

What *is* going on in the minds of the men who do this? Not much judging from their difficulties in articulating their intentions. We interviewed 60 men, choosing a range of age groups out of those who addressed us on the street. (Incidentally, this was the only female response we found that genuinely and predictably disarms the harassing male, so if you want to transform a lewdly smirking man into a politely confused one within a matter of seconds, you need only pull a mimeographed questionnaire out of your bag and inform him that he is part of a research project. This method has the disadvantage of being rather time-consuming.)

Pressed for an explanation of their behavior, most of the men initially were at a loss. It alleviates boredom, it gives them a feeling of youthful camaraderie when they discuss women with other men; it's "fun" and it "doesn't hurt anybody," they often added a little defensively. The notion that women dislike this was a novel idea for most men, not because they had another image of the woman's response but because they had never given it any thought at all. Only a minority, around 15 percent, explicitly set out to anger or humiliate their victims. This is the same group that employs graphic commentary and threats.

As is the case with rape, other causes of antagonism become mixed up with the sexual, especially race and class. Some migrant laborers or construction workers, selecting a well-dressed, middle-class woman, insult not so much the woman as the snobbish privileged class she symbolizes to them. Another minority of men believes with firm conviction that women enjoy receiving their attention. One 45-year-old construction worker portrayed himself as a kind of benefactor to womanhood and claimed to specialize in older and less attractive women to whom, he was sure, his display of sexual interest was certain to be the highlight in an otherwise drab existence. A significant group of men, around 20 percent, said that they would not engage in this behavior when alone, but only in the company of male friends. This supports the explanation that the harassment of women is a form of male bonding, of demonstrating solidarity and joint power.

The symbolic nature of the behavior is its most important attribute. A surprising finding was that harassment declines in the late evening and during the night, and that men are then more likely to display the kind of behavior typical of the avoidance usually shown to strangers in public or crowded situations: averting one's eyes, accelerating the pace of walking to keep a distance, and so on. It would seem that harassment would be even more effective at night, even more intimidating to the woman. Probably this is precisely the reason it declines: during the night on a deserted street, it would be *too* effective. The woman, not merely annoyed or unnerved but genuinely alarmed, may well be driven to an "extreme" response (such as calling for help) that the good citizen would not like to have to explain. In the daytime, he takes no such risk.

The age, education and income of the men make little difference; in their street behavior, they revert to a primordially uniform condition across the lines of class and generation. Younger men tend to be more aggressive, and older men to lower their voices and whisper hastily as they pass you. Some areas are exempt altogether: small villages, where all the inhabitants know each other, and residential suburban areas. The genuinely *public* world is the main arena for harassment. The street, as a place where strangers encounter each other is also the place where societies have always taken care to clearly mark the lines of order and status. It is on the streets that members of subordinate groups wear special clothing, uniforms, or identifying marks, that they must salute, take off their hats, or show symbolic deference to members of the superior group. Harassment is a way of ensuring that women will not feel at ease, that they will remember their role as sexual beings available to men and not consider themselves equal citizens participating in public life. But the ritual of harassment does more than that. By its seeming harmlessness, it blurs the borders of women's right to personal integrity, and encourages men who would never commit a violent crime against a strange woman to engage in minor transgressions against her right to move freely, to choose which interaction to participate in and which people to communicate with. By making the average "man in the street" a minor sex-offender, it also makes him an accomplice in the more massive forms of violence against women.

The Politics of Talking in Couples:
Conversus Interruptus and Other Disorders

Barbara Ehrenreich

Not too long ago, this magazine carried an article on how to talk to a man in bed.[1] My only disappointment was that it was not followed up by a series of articles on how to talk to a man in other settings and on other items of furniture: "Talking in Living Rooms," for example, "Talking in Dinettes," and "Talking on Straight-Backed Chairs." For it is my conviction, based on years of what sociologists call participant observation, that far more male-female relationships die in the dining room than in the bedroom. And the problem is not the cuisine, it's the conversation.

The fact is that we are going through a profound Crisis in Intersex Conversation, and that this crisis has been the subject of a vast systematic cover-up. I am not referring to the well-known difficulty of maintaining equity in public discourse—meetings, cocktail parties, seminars, and the like—a problem amply documented by our feminist foresisters in the late sixties. I am referring to the much more insidious problem of intimate conversation between consenting adults of different sexes. Television evangelists alert us daily to new threats to the family, ranging from sex education to secular humanism. No one, however, mentions the crisis in conversation, which is far more serious. It threatens not only the family, but also the casual affair, the illicit liaison, and possibly the entire institution of heterosexuality.

I can understand that there are solid artistic and commercial reasons for the cover-up. If art were forced to conform to conversational reality, "A Man and a Woman" would have been done as a silent film, and the Broadway hit *The Lunch Hour* would have been condensed, quite adequately, into *The Coffee Break*. Imagine, for example, what would happen if the current spate of Gothic novels were required to meet truth-in-conversation standards:

She: Now that we are alone there is so much to talk about! I am filled with such confusion, for I have never told you the secret of my origins. . . .
He: Hmmm.
She: The truth about my identity and my true relationship to the Earl of D'Arcy, not to mention the real reason why the uppermost room in the far turret of Weathermore Manor has been sealed for thirty years!
He: Uh-huh.
She: You know the room at the top of the spiral staircase over the stables? Well, there's something so terrifying, so abominable, so *evil* . . .
He: Hey, will you look at that? It stopped raining.

Nevertheless, the truth about male-female conversations has been leaking

---

[1] See "Talking in Bed—Now That We Know What We Want, How Do We Say It?" by Lonnie Barbach and Linda Levine (January, 1981).

out. In her book, *On Loving Men* (Dial Press), Jane Lazarre recounts a particularly disastrous conversational attempt with one of the objects of her love. Jane has just spent a long phone call consoling her recently widowed mother-in-law, who is hysterical with grief. She tells her husband about the call (after all, it was *his* mother), "after which we both lie there quietly." But she is still—understandably—shaken, and begins to fantasize losing her own husband:

> Crying by now, due to the reality of my fantasy as well as the full comprehension of my mother-in-law's pain, I turn to James, then intrude upon his perpetual silence and ask, "What are you thinking?" hoping for once to be answered from some vulnerable depth. . . . And he admitted (it was an admission because he was incredulous himself at the fact): "I was thinking about the Knicks. Wondering if they were going to trade Frazier."

Jane Lazarre attributes her husband's talent for aborting conversations to some "quality of character" peculiar to him and, in the book, goes off in search of more verbose companionship. Thousands of other women have also concluded that theirs was an individual problem: "*He* just doesn't listen to me," "I just can't talk to him," and so forth. This, however, is a mistake. We are not dealing with individual problems—unfortunate conversational mismatches—but with a crisis of genderwide proportions.

Much of the credit for uncovering the crisis must go to a few stealthy sociologists who have devoted themselves to listening in on male-female conversations. Pamela Fishman planted tape recorders in the homes of three couples and recorded (with their permission) more than 50 hours of real-life chitchat. The picture that emerges from Fishman's work is that of women engaged in a more or less solitary battle to keep the conversational ball rolling. Women nurture infant conversations—throwing out little hookers like "you know?" in order to enlist some help from their companions. Meanwhile, the men are often working at cross-purposes, dousing conversations with "ummms," non sequiturs, and unaccountable pauses. And, in case you're wondering, the subjects that Fishman's women nourished and men killed were neither boringly trivial nor threateningly intimate: they were frequently about current events, articles read, work in progress. Furthermore, the subjects of Fishman's research were couples who described themselves as "liberated" from sex roles. One can only wonder what she might have found by leaving her tape recorder in the average Levittown breakfast nook.

The problem is not that men are so taken with the strong, silent look that they *can't* talk. Sociologists Candace West and Donald Zimmerman did some extensive eavesdropping at various sites around the University of California campus at Santa Barbara and found that men interrupt women much more often than they interrupt other men and that they do so more often than women interrupt either men or other women. In analyzing her tapes of men and women who live together, Pamela Fishman found that topics introduced by men "succeeded" conversationally 96 percent of the time, while those introduced by women succeeded only 36 percent of the time and fell flat the rest of the time. Men can and will talk—if they can set the terms.

There are all kinds of explanations for the conversational mismatch between the sexes, none of which require more than a rudimentary feminist analysis. First, there's the fact that men are more powerful as a class of people, and expect to dominate in day-to-day interactions, verbal or otherwise. Take any intersex gathering and—unless a determined countereffort is undertaken—the basses and tenors quickly overpower the altos and sopranos.

For most men, public discourse is a competitive sport, in which points are scored with decisive finger jabs and conclusive table poundings, while adversaries are blocked with shoulder thrusts or tackled with sudden interruptions. This style does not, of course, carry over well to the conversational private sector. As one male informant admitted to me, albeit under mild duress, "If you're just with a woman there's no real competition. What's the point of talking?"

Male dominance is not the only problem. There's also male insecurity. When men have talked honestly about talking (or about not talking), either under psychiatric pressure or the lure of royalties, they tell us they are *afraid* to talk to women. Marc Feigen Fasteau confessed in *The Male Machine* (McGraw-Hill) that a "familiar blankness" overcame him in conversations with his wife, resulting from an "imagined fear that spontaneous talk will reveal unacceptable feelings—almost anything that would show vulnerability or indicate that the speaker doesn't 'measure up' to the masculine ideal."

Given the cultural barriers to intersex conversation, the amazing thing is that we would even expect women and men to have anything to say to each other for more than 10 minutes at a stretch. The barriers are ancient—perhaps rooted, as some up-and-coming paleontologist may soon discover, in the contrast between the occasional guttural utterances exchanged in male hunting bands and the extended discussions characteristic of female food-gathering groups. History does offer a scattering of successful mixed-sex conversational duos—Voltaire and Madame Du Châtelet, Marie and Pierre Curie—but the mass expectation that ordinary men and women should engage in conversation as a *routine* activity probably dates back no further than the 1950s and the era of "togetherness." Until then, male-female conversation had served principally as an element of courtship, sustained by sexual tension and easily abandoned after the nuptials. After suburbanization threw millions of couples alone together in tiny tract houses for whole weekends at a stretch, however, media pundits decided that conversation was not only a healthy but a necessary marital activity, even if the topic never rose above the level of septic tanks and aluminum siding. While I have no direct evidence, the success of these early mixed-sex conversational endeavors may perhaps be gauged by the mass influx of women into the work force and the explosive spread of feminism in the 1960s and 1970s.

It was feminism, of course, that raised women's conversational expectations. In consciousness-raising groups and National Organization for Women chapters, women's centers and caucuses, women discovered (or rediscovered) the possibilities of conversation as an act of collective creativity: the intimate sharing of personal experience, the weaving of the personal into the general and political, the adventure of freewheeling speculation unrestrained by academic rules or boundaries.

As men became aware of the heightened demands being placed upon them, their intellectual spokesmen quickly displaced the problem into the realm of sexuality. Thus Christopher Lasch, in discussing men's response to feminism, never even touches upon the conversational crisis, but tells us that "women's sexual demands terrify men," evoking images of "the vagina which threatens to eat them alive." But we could just as well invert this florid Freudiana and conclude that it is women's verbal demands that terrify men and that the dread *vagina dentata* (devouring, toothed vagina) of male fantasy is in fact a *mouth* symbol, all set to voice some conversational overture such as "Don't you think it's interesting that . . .?"

Now that the crisis is out in the open, what do we do about it? Is there any way to teach a grown man, or short of that, a little one, how to converse in a manner that is stimulating, interesting, and satisfying to women? One approach might be to work through the educational system, introducing required mixed-gender courses in English Conversation. Or we might take a clinical approach, setting up therapeutic centers to treat Male Conversational Dysfunction. Various diagnostic categories leap to mind: "Conversational Impotence" (total inability to get a subject off the ground); "Premature Ejaculation" (having the answer to everything, before anybody else gets a chance to utter a sentence); "Conversus Interruptus"; and so forth. It may even be necessary, in extreme cases, to provide specially trained female Conversational Surrogates.

My own intuition is that the conversational crisis will be solved only when women and men—not just women—together realize their common need for both social and personal change. After all, women have discovered each other and the joy of cooperative discourse through a common political project—the feminist movement. So struck was I with this possibility that I tried it out loud on a male companion: "Can you imagine women and men together in a movement that demands both social and personal transformation?" There was a long, and I hoped pregnant, pause. Then he said, "Hmmmmm."

SUGGESTIONS FOR FURTHER READING:
Part One

The following is a list of books, mainly anthologies and some of them already classics themselves, that provide an introduction to various aspects of women's oppression. Most of these volumes contain comprehensive bibliographies that can be used to supplement the suggested readings mentioned in this book.

Cade, Toni (ed.): *The Black Woman: An Anthology,* Signet, New York, 1970.

Carroll, Berenice A. (ed.): *Liberating Women's History: Theoretical and Critical Essays,* University of Illinois Press, Urbana, Ill., 1976.

Chesler, Phyllis: *Women and Madness,* Doubleday, New York, 1972.

Deckard, Barbara: *The Women's Movement: Political, Socioeconomic, and Psychological Issues,* Harper & Row, New York, 1975.

Dworkin, Andrea: *Woman Hating,* Dutton, New York, 1974.

Ehrenreich, Barbara, and Deirdre English: *For Her Own Good: 150 Years of the Experts' Advice to Women,* Anchor, New York, 1979.

Gornick, Vivian, and Barbara K. Moran (eds.): *Women in Sexist Society,* Signet, New York, 1972.

Hammer, Signe (ed.): *Women Body and Culture,* Harper & Row, New York, 1975.

Lerna, Gerda (ed.): *Black Women in White America: A Documentary History,* Vintage, New York, 1973.

Liberation Now!, Dell, New York, 1971.

Miller, Jean Baker (ed.): *Psychoanalysis and Women,* Penguin, Baltimore, 1973.

Millett, Kate: *Sexual Politics,* Avon, New York, 1971.

Morgan, Robin (ed.): *Sisterhood is Powerful,* Vintage, New York, 1970.

Roszak, Betty, and Theodore Roszak (eds.): *Masculine/Feminine,* Harper & Row, New York, 1969.

Salper, Roberta (ed.): *Female Liberation,* Knopf, New York, 1972.

Schecter, Susan: *Women and Male Violence,* South End, Boston, 1982.

Spender, Dale: *Man Made Language,* Routledge & Kegan Paul, London and Boston, 1980.

Stacy, Judith, Susan Bereaud, and Joan Daniels (eds.): *And Jill Came Tumbling After: Sexism in American Education,* Dell, New York, 1974.

Vetterling-Braggin, Mary: *Sexist Language: A Modern Philosophical Analysis,* Littlefield Adams, Totowa, N.J., 1981.

Wilson, Carolyn F.: *Violence Against Women: An Annotated Bibliography,* G. K. Hall, Boston, 1981.

TWO

ALTERNATIVE FEMINIST FRAMEWORKS

THEORIES OF
WOMEN'S OPPRESSION

It is a general law that naturally dominant elements and naturally dominated elements exist . . . the rule of free man over the slave is one type of domination; that of man over woman is another.

Aristotle

God almighty made the women and the Rockefeller gang of thieves made the ladies.

Mother Jones

Talk not to us of chivalry, that died long ago. . . . In social life, true, a man in love will jump to pick up a glove or bouquet for a silly girl of sixteen, whilst at home he will permit his aged mother to carry pails of water and armfuls of wood, or permit his wife to lug a twenty-pound baby, hour after hour, without ever offering to relieve her.

Elizabeth Cady Stanton, 1855

For me, women are only amusing, a hobby. No one spends too much time on a hobby.

Henry Kissinger
In an interview with Oriana Fallaci, 1973

For if the phrase biology is destiny *has any meaning for a woman right now it has to be the urgent project of woman reclaiming herself, her own biology in her own image, and this is why the lesbian is the revolutionary feminist and every other feminist is a woman who wants a better deal from her old man.*

Jill Johnston

Feminism is the theory and lesbianism is the practice.

Ti-Grace Atkinson

The work: To make the revolution irresistible.

Toni Cade Bambara

THE ROOTS OF OPPRESSION

Part One of this book showed that both women and men in our society are dissatisfied with central areas of their lives. In the late 1960s, the women's movement forcefully articulated these problems, making many people aware for the first time that their misery was generally shared. This realization led to a recognition that women's problems did not result from individual failures to cope but that they were rooted rather in the structure of the existing society. It followed that the resolution of women's problems required changes in that society. Part Two of this anthology presents several attempts by feminists to state in the most general terms the kinds of social changes that are required.

Most of the theories we shall present here contain some speculation about the historical origins of women's oppression. That is to say, they attempt to uncover its *historical* roots. A reader encountering such speculations for the first time may well wonder why contemporary feminists devote so much energy to an enterprise whose conclusions can never be more than tentative and which may not appear directly relevant to the situation of women and men today.

Perhaps the easiest way to explain the feminists' interest in the historical origins of women's oppression is to remind the reader how much easier it is to understand our friends when we know their past, especially when we learn the circumstances in which they grew up. Seemingly irrational quirks or preferences may become quite intelligible when seen in the context of a person's past life. In the same way, present social phenomena are likely to become more intelligible when viewed as the unfolding of the past.

To uncover the historical origins of women's oppression is not, of course, to assume that those causes are still effective in perpetuating that oppression. Nor is it to assume that they are not. One task of a theory is to determine the relevance of "origins" to the present-day situation. To the extent that the original causes are still operative, a discovery of the historical roots can show us where to focus our energy in order to change the situation. If those original causes are not relevant to the contemporary situation, a theory that demonstrates this fact may refute an old explanation for women's oppression.

This latter point brings out the fact that talk of roots or origins should not be understood only in a historical way. "The roots of women's oppression" may also refer to those conditions, biological or social, that are the most important in continuing women's subordination today. That is to say, to uncover the root causes of women's oppression, in this nonhistorical sense, is to discover not only which biological facts or which social institutions operate to limit women's choices but also which facts or institutions must be changed in order to effect a significant and permanent increase in women's capacity to choose. Obviously, to do this requires a comprehensive analysis of the relations between our biology and our major social institutions. Such an analysis will have to indicate specific changes that must be made (see Part Three), and its truth will be tested, in large part, by the effectiveness of the changes that it indicates.

CONSERVATISM

As their name implies, conservatives are always concerned with conservation: they wish to carry certain aspects of the past or present forward into the future. Typically, conservatives seek to justify existing privileges or inequalities. Sexual conservatives wish to continue what they view as traditional gender arrangements; they want to preserve traditional conceptions of the proper place of women relative to men. Within the context of contemporary society, sexual conservatives claim that men should dominate in the so-called public world of government, industry, trade, and education and that women should have primary responsibility for the nurturing, sexual servicing, and personal maintenance that is supposed to occur in the so-called private world of the home.

Conservative claims can be argued for in a variety of ways. We have chosen to present several conservative variations on a single theme, namely, the theme of biology. All the conservatives represented in this book argue that certain features of human biology make traditional gender arrangements either inevitable or, at least, preferable. On their view, departures from these arrangements, departures such as feminists recommend, impose high costs of social inefficiency and human unhappiness.

During the first half of the twentieth century, Freudian theory was probably the single most powerful rationale for women's subordination. Today it is still often used for this purpose, even though some theorists are trying to reclaim Freudian theory for feminist purposes, as we shall see later in the book. We have chosen to reprint some of Freud's more notorious reflections on women, partly for their historical importance and partly to provide a basis for understanding later feminist efforts to reappropriate Freud.

Sociobiology is the other version of conservatism that we present in this section. Sociobiology is a very recent approach to understanding biological phenomena; it emerged in 1975 with the publication of Edward O. Wilson's groundbreaking book, *Sociobiology: The New Synthesis*. Although most of this massive work was devoted to studies of insects, it was the last chapter, dealing with the implications of Wilson's theory for human beings, that aroused the most controversy. Wilson later elaborated his reflections on this topic in the popular paperback *On Human Nature* (1978), from which the extract here is taken. Like Freud, Wilson does not argue that a change in traditional gender arrangements is impossible, but he believes that a radical transformation is contrary to biological predispositions within each sex, predispositions that had some originally evolutionary advantage. Thwarting these predispositions will impose a social cost that may be too high to offset the intended benefits.

As we shall see, considerations relevant to both these biologically based forms of conservatism will be found in all the subsequent sections of Part Two.

LIBERAL FEMINISM

Liberal feminism has its origins in the social contract theories of the sixteenth and seventeenth centuries. These theories were distinguished from previous political theories by their insistence that any form of social hierarchy or authority required justification. Early liberal theorists postulated the fundamental equality of all men, based on men's allegedly equal potential for rationality. The new social ideals were liberty and equality.

Within the liberal tradition, liberty was construed as freedom from interference, especially interference from the government. The demand for liberty did not require the abolition of government authority, but it recognized that authority as legitimate only if it was grounded on the consent of the governed. Moreover, the sphere of legitimate governmental authority was sharply delimited: government might regulate the so-called public area of human life but it had no authority to intervene within the so-called private sphere. Since the sixteenth and seventeenth centuries, liberals have often redrawn the line between the public and private spheres, but the distinction between public and private remains central to their political theory and is still used in argument by contemporary liberal feminists.

Just as liberals did not take the ideal of liberty to require the abolition of government, neither did they take the ideal of equality to require the abolition of inequalities in wealth and power. Just as "legitimate" authority was acknowledged, so were "legitimate" inequalities. Inequalities were seen as legitimate if they were based or distributed on relevant grounds. Clearly, there is much room for controversy in determining what constitutes a relevant ground for social inequalities, but in general liberals argue against the relevance of inherited characteristics such as family or race. They propose that each individual should be able to rise in society just as far as his or her talents permit, unhindered by restraints of law or custom. What qualities should count as talents and how they should be rewarded is to be determined by the supply of and demand for those talents within a market economy. In order to guarantee that the most genuinely talented individuals are identified, it is necessary to ensure that everyone has an equal opportunity to develop his or her talents. Within the liberal tradition, therefore, equality has come to be construed as equality of opportunity.

Almost as soon as the new ideals of liberty and equality were formulated, women began to demand that these ideals should be applied to them. The first sustained feminist tract was Mary Wollstonecraft's *A Vindication of the Rights of Women,* published in 1792. Wollstonecraft set the direction for later liberal feminism by arguing that physical sex alone was not a relevant ground for denying equal rights to women. As the possession of rationality was then considered the proper basis for the attribution of rights, Wollstonecraft argued that women's capacity to reason was equal with that of men. She claimed that the apparent inferiority of women's intellects was due to women's inferior education; women's apparent inferiority thus should be interpreted as the *result* of women's unequal opportunities rather than as a *justification* for them.

Wollstonecraft's theme has been continued by liberal feminists, such as Taylor and Mill in the nineteenth century, right up to the present day. The stress is always on equality of opportunity. Thus, Taylor and Mill argue that women's legal rights should be the same as those of men and that women should receive the same educational opportunities. Many of the best-known contemporary feminists who protest against contemporary sexist discrimination are making essentially the same point.

The liberal feminist challenge to the conservative theory of human nature is not directed against conservatism's conclusions of innate inequality so much as it is directed against the process of inference through which conservatism derives its conclusions. As we have seen already, liberal feminists have always denied that the undisputed physiological differences between the sexes constitute relevant grounds for closing certain opportunities to women. They admit that psychological sex differences may have social and political relevance, but they deny that there are good grounds for the conservative assumption that these differences are innate and unchangeable. Liberals argue that the current inequalities in the opportunities and education available to women provide strong evidence in favor of the claim that psychological differences between the sexes are socially imposed rather than biologically determined. Liberals such as Mill concede that there may indeed be innate psychological differences between the sexes, but they contend that we cannot be certain either way until educational opportunities are equalized for women and men.

Even if it were to turn out that psychological differences between the sexes were indeed determined biologically, liberal feminists deny the conservative inference that such differences justify providing men and women with different and unequal opportunities. Both J. S. Mill and Joyce Trebilcot argue that atypical individuals should not be forced to conform to the psychological configurations characteristic of most of their sex. Moreover both argue, in different ways, that the social advantages of providing both sexes with equal opportunities far outweigh the possible social costs.

For the liberal feminist, then, the roots of women's oppression lie in women's lack of equal civil rights and equal educational opportunities. There is little attempt at historical speculation as to why such a lack should exist. Because the roots are so easily visible, women's oppression can be tackled immediately by a direct attack on sexist discrimination. When this discrimination has been eliminated, women will have been liberated.

TRADITIONAL MARXISM

Contrary to the conservative, the Marxist rejects explicitly the notion of an essential and biologically determined human nature. Marx saw that, throughout the course of history, human beings in different places and in different times have had recourse to many different techniques in order to feed, clothe, shelter, and reproduce themselves. These different techniques of survival have required many different forms of social organization and hence have shaped many different kinds of social relations between persons. For the Marxist, what persons are like—their motivations, interests, abilities, and even their needs—is very largely a function of the form of society in which they live and of their place in that society. Yet, insofar as human beings create forms of social organization, persons are not seen as totally passive beings at the mercy of their environment; rather, as they create their society, they are the ultimate and active creators of their own nature.

In addition to rejecting the biologism of conservatives, Marxists reject the liberal's belief that it is possible for people to have genuine equality of opportunity for the development of their potential while they remain within a class society where the many produce the wealth but the wealth and power end up in the hands of a few. In such a society, the pursuit of profit by the ruling class determines all aspects of life—the conditions under which people work and the education they receive, for example—and even the quality of personal relations is shaped by the profit motive, which Marxists see as degrading human existence.

From this brief sketch of Marxist theory, it is plain that the Marxist will locate the origins of women's oppression not in biology but rather in a particular system of social organization. In fact, the traditional Marxist sees women's oppression as originating with the introduction of private property. Private ownership of the means of production by relatively few persons, and those all male, instituted a class system. Contemporary corporate capitalism and imperialism are but the latest phase of this development and the root cause of most of the inequality and misery in the world today.

Marxists claim that recognizing the irreconcilable conflict between economic classes is the most important key to understanding the shape of contemporary society and the direction of social change. Women's oppression, in their view, is a secondary phenomenon, a symptom of a more fundamental form of oppression. Ultimately, women are oppressed, not by "sexism," not by men, but by capitalism. If change in women's situation is to go beyond the extension of male privileges to a few token women—in other words, if all women are to be liberated—the capitalist system must be overthrown and replaced by a socialist system. Within socialism, the means of production would belong once again to society as a whole, women as well as men. Women's economic dependence on men would be abolished and this abolition would eliminate the material basis of women's subordination.

Once women become economically independent of the men in their families, traditional Marxists of the past assumed that remnants of the ancient prejudice against women would lose their plausibility and eventually disappear. More recently, Marxists have recognized the necessity for what the Chinese called a "cultural revolution" in order to eliminate remaining attitudes and practices that oppress women. In either case, however, Marxists traditionally have conceived dominance as an ideological or "superstructural" phenomenon rather than as a fundamental feature of the economic foundation of society.

RADICAL FEMINISM

Liberal feminism and traditional Marxism draw on long philosophical traditions. Radical feminism, by contrast, is a very recent political theory and is still in the process of development. For this reason, there is considerable variety among the views that are characterized as radical feminist. In our selections we have tried to illustrate this variety, but in this introduction we identify the basic assumptions that we see as common to all versions of radical feminism.

In our view, what distinguishes radical feminiism from all other feminist theories is its insistence that the oppression of women is fundamental. This claim can be interpreted in several different ways. It may mean:

1 That women were, historically, the first oppressed group
2 That women's oppression is the most widespread, existing in virtually every known society
3 That women's oppression is the deepest in that it is the hardest form of oppression to eradicate and cannot be removed by other social changes such as the abolition of class society
4 That women's oppression causes the most suffering to its victims, qualitatively as well as quantitatively, although this suffering may often go unrecognized because of the sexist prejudices of both the oppressors and the victims
5 That women's oppression, as Firestone claims, provides a conceptual model for understanding all other forms of oppression

Different radical feminists emphasize different aspects of the fundamental nature of women's oppression but all agree at least on the first three claims listed above.

Shulamith Firestone's *The Dialectic of Sex,* published in 1970, was one of the earliest radical feminist attempts to provide a systematic analysis of women's oppression and an explanation of its roots. Firestone's analysis is especially interesting because she contradicts the usual feminist denial that women's subordination is biologically rooted. In contrast to most contemporary feminists, Firestone argues that women's subordination is rooted in certain universal facts of human biology: the long period of infant immaturity, which requires that infants depend on adults and especially on women's milk for survival; and women's physical weakness, associated with childbearing, which requires that women depend on men for survival. Firestone infers that women's liberation requires what she calls a "biological revolution," a series of technological developments that would permit not only bottlefeeding but the extrauterine reproduction of children and that would thus eliminate the physical dependence of women on men, which Firestone sees as the basis of women's subordination. Firestone's theory of human nature at first sight appears conservative in so far as she seems to postulate a version of biological determinism. Because she believes that biology can be conquered by technology, however, Firestone's conclusions are far from conservative.

Most of the rest of Firestone's book consists of a detailed demonstration of the radical feminist claim that oppression on the basis of sex provides the conceptual model for understanding other forms of oppression, such as racism and class society. Firestone also outlines her recommendations for the future of work, sexuality, the family, and child rearing. Despite some flaws, her book is provocative and insightful and is enthusiastically recommended.

Charlotte Bunch's account of the roots of women's oppression does not contain the biological determinist elements that are present in Firestone. Instead, Bunch leaves the origins of women's subordination causally unexplained. However Bunch does believe that women's subjugation was the first form of oppression and that it remains the deepest. Because women are oppressed primarily by male dominance and only secondarily by racism and class society, Bunch argues, contrary to traditional Marxists, that women's struggles must be directed immediately against male dominance. In order to do this, she believes that women must forsake heterosexuality, which divides women from each other and ties them to their oppressors.

Bunch's article makes explicit an idea that was only implicit in Firestone's book. This is the characteristically radical feminist insight that the personal is political. Within the so-called personal sphere, women are oppressed as much as, or even more than, they are within the so-called political realm. To label a certain area of human life as personal is to trivialize and conceal the systematic domination of women that pervades that realm and delegitimizes women's struggle against those forms of domination. Male dominance infects every area of life and must be fought against in every sphere, including the arenas of home and sexuality. For Bunch, lesbianism is not merely a personal preference but a political decision made within the context of a political struggle.

The final contribution in this section is an article by well-known French feminist Monique Wittig. Wittig's conception of human nature is a sharp contrast both with conservative biological determinism and also with the biologically determinist elements in Firestone's work. Going far beyond the relatively familiar feminist claims that "feminine" psychology is socially imposed, Wittig argues that even women's bodies are socially constructed. Nothing about women is "natural": women are made not born.

Some radical feminists have glorified what they perceive as women's special nature. Wittig rejects this tendency in radical feminism. She argues that true women's liberation goes not only beyond the liberal ideal of equal opportunity for women and men but even beyond the ideal of matriarchy that some radical feminists advocate. True liberation, in Wittig's view, requires the abolition of women and men as classes. Within Wittig's new society, there will be only persons: both women and men will have disappeared.

SOCIALIST FEMINISM

Socialist feminists are committed to the historical materialist method of Marx and Engels. Like traditional Marxists, they see human nature as varying according to changes in the mode of production. However, they challenge the traditional Marxist conception of what constitutes the mode of production. In understanding human society and historical change, Marxists traditionally have focussed on the way in which people have organized to produce and distribute the means of satisfying such needs as the need for food, shelter, and clothing. Socialist feminists argue that this approach is useful for understanding conflicts between classes of men but that it obscures certain features of women's oppression that cut across class lines. In order to make visible women's oppression and to understand its root causes, the conceptual framework of traditional Marxism must be enriched. In particular, our conception of the mode of production must be enlarged so that it includes not only the way in which people have organized to produce and distribute the means of satisfying their need for food, shelter, and clothing, but so that it also includes the way in which people have organized to produce and distribute the means of satisfying their needs for sexuality, nurturance, and babies. Thus, socialist feminists accept the radical feminist insight that women's oppression is at least partially rooted in the so-called personal sphere, and they attempt to incorporate this insight within the conceptual framework provided by historical materialism.

Gayle Rubin's notion of the "sex/gender system" is an attempt to reconceptualise what Marxists call the sphere of reproduction. Rubin argues that the term "reproduction" is misleading in this context, in part because it obscures the possibility of reorganizing this area of human life. Rubin uses the notion of sex/gender system in her speculative but powerful account of the roots of women's oppression. She suggests that women's subordination is rooted in the institution of kinship, the most widely prevailing form of sex/gender system. By enforcing exogamy and by using women in interfamilial exchange, the institution of kinship created and consolidated extrafamilial ties. People would consent to these arrangements, however, only if the sexuality of both girls and boys was repressed, if a norm of heterosexuality was imposed and if a passive feminine nature was created. Rubin argued that those features of human psychology were imposed in infancy, within the context of the male-dominated family.

Rubin was one of the first contemporary feminist theorists to utilize Freudian theory rather than to reject it totally. She believes that Freud provides an acute description of the way in which a typically masculine or feminine psychology is created in originally bisexual infants. Unlike Freud, however, Rubin does not see this process as an inevitable response to the differences in male and female anatomy. Instead, Rubin points out that girls and boys discover their anatomy in a social context that is male-dominated and that assigns tremendous significance to the possession of a penis. Anatomy is destiny only in a society that is obsessed with features of anatomy. In a sexually egalitarian or gender-free society, sexual anatomy would become largely irrelevant, new forms of psychosocial development would appear, and much of Freudian theory would become outdated. There would have been a transformation of the reality that Freud once described so acutely.

The last contribution in this section is an extract from Heidi Hartmann's "The Unhappy Marriage of Marxism and Feminism." Co-authored by Hartmann and Amy Bridges, early drafts of this paper were widely circulated in typescript during the 1970s. In the final version of the paper, Hartmann criticizes prevailing versions of both traditional Marxist and radical feminist theory. She argues that the sex-blind categories of traditional Marxism are inadequate to comprehend the subordination of women; similarly, the class-blind and ahistorical categories of radical feminism, especially the category of patriarchy, are inadequate to comprehend the variety of women's experience, which differs according to many variables such as age, class, race, nationality, and marital status.

Hartmann offers a redefinition of patriarchy in terms of male control over women's labor power, control that is exerted both within the home and outside it. She then begins a discussion of the reciprocal relationship between patriarchy and capitalism and an examination of the ways in which women's experience is determined by this relationship.

She perceives capitalism and patriarchy as mutually interdependent and reinforcing systems; women's liberation requires the abolition of both.

Hartmann makes it clear that socialist feminism is not a completed theory. She herself indicates some of the questions that socialist feminism leaves unanswered; other questions emerge in the following selections.

FEMINISM AND WOMEN OF COLOR

Women of color must deal with the realities that they are both female and nonwhite in a society defined by patriarchy and white supremacy. In addition, many face the added burden of poverty. Taken together, these factors have created unique problems for women of color as they seek to articulate and combat the basis of their oppression.

Although women of color do not utilize any single theoretical framework, their writings invariably reflect a concern that the complexities of race and gender (and often class as well) be explored simultaneously. They caution us against hasty over-generalizations about women's situation, generalizations that have often reflected only the experience of white, middle-class women.

By insisting that feminist theory should always be conscious of race, the writings of many women of color have helped to reveal the class bias as well as the racism of the contemporary feminist movement. Women of color have tended to regard this movement with suspicion if not open hostility. They have correctly identified the issues of the early phase of this movement as issues of concern primarily to white, middle-class or professional women. At the beginning of the contemporary feminist movement, for instance, feminists engaged in a much-needed struggle for the right of women to obtain safe and legal abortions, but for a long time the women's movement remained oblivious to the plight of many women of color who were, and are, struggling against compulsory sterilization and for the right to conceive and bear children without the fear of poverty and degradation. By demonstrating the limited nature of the demands that are still most firmly associated in the public mind with feminism, women of color have exposed the exclusion of issues that concern all poor and working-class women, whatever their race.

Our section on feminism and women of color begins with Elizabeth Hood's discussion of the similarities and differences in the oppression experienced by white women and black women. While recognizing that both groups are oppressed by a "patriarchal system established and operated by white males" which results in "similarities in human destruction," Hood goes on to argue that white women continue to retain certain privileges by virtue of their race. She contends that black and white women will remain divided until white women commit themselves to the eradication of racism as well as male dominance.

In this essay Hood articulates the view held by many women of color that while racism and sexism are both vicious forms of oppression, racism is the more devastating of the two. Because women of color must struggle against both these forms of oppression simultaneously, they face problems that are different from those experienced by white women. Other thinkers who share Hood's view that being black is more difficult than being female have argued that the feminist concept of patriarchy, which identifies men as women's oppressors, misrepresents the situation of black men who, in white society, often have less power than white women. Like Hood, they maintain that insofar as racism is in some ways more powerful and pervasive than male dominance, women will often bond with men of their own race rather than with each other. For this reason, black women and white women will remain separated until the struggle against male dominance is combined with an equally fervent struggle against racist oppression.

Since its first publication in 1979, the *Black Feminist Statement* of the Combahee River Collective has become a classic expression of black feminism. The Collective states that the texture of black women's lives is multilayered, often incorporating oppression on the basis not only of race and sex but of class, age, and sexual preference. Existing political frameworks are inadequate to capture the reality of black women's situation. For instance, a traditional Marxist class analysis, which speaks only of "raceless, sexless workers," ignores real conflicts of interest between these workers and so fails to articulate the true situation of black women. Similarly, radical feminist proposals for women to separate from men divide human beings only on the basis of sex and ignore the interests that black women share with black men. The multifaceted nature of black women's oppression makes it impossible for black women to identify with any groups that focus only on one or two aspects of oppression.

The selections we have chosen by women of color do not offer an alternative feminist framework; rather, they present a test for the adequacy of existing frameworks. Black women need a conceptual framework that will illuminate rather than obscure their situation and that will guide their struggle against the various aspects of their oppression. In seeking to construct such a framework, women of color reveal the way in which every woman's experience is shaped by her race as well as by her sex. By exposing the race (and class) bias hidden within abstract generalizations about "women," women of color force feminist theory to reflect more faithfully the social reality and thus to become more objective. The Combahee River Collective suggests that the single most important criterion for the adequacy of a feminist theory is its ability to explain the situation of black women: "If black women were free, it would mean that everyone else would have to be free since our freedom would necessitate the destruction of all systems of oppression."

CONSERVATISM: Women's Oppression as Biologically Determined

Femininity

Sigmund Freud

. . . In conformity with its peculiar nature, psycho-analysis does not try to describe what a woman is—that would be a task it could scarcely perform—but sets about enquiring how she comes into being, how a woman develops out of a child with a bisexual disposition. . . .

. . . A little girl is as a rule less aggressive, defiant and self-sufficient; she seems to have a greater need for being shown affection and on that account to be more dependent and pliant. It is probably only as a result of this pliancy that she can be taught more easily and quicker to control her excretions: urine and faeces are the first gifts that children make to those who look after them, and controlling them is the first concession to which the instinctual life of children can be induced. One gets an impression, too, that little girls are more intelligent and livelier than boys of the same age; they go out more to meet the external world and at the same time form stronger object-cathexes. I cannot say whether this lead in development has been confirmed by exact observations, but in any case there is no question that girls cannot be described as intellectually backward. These sexual differences are not, however, of great consequence: they can be outweighed by individual variations. For our immediate purposes they can be disregarded.

Both sexes seem to pass through the early phases of libidinal development in the same manner. It might have been expected that in girls there would already have been some lag in aggressiveness in the sadistic-anal phase, but such is not the case. Analysis of children's play has shown our women analysts that the aggressive impulses of little girls leave nothing to be desired in the way of abundance and violence. With their entry into the phallic phase the differences between the sexes are completely eclipsed by their agreements. We are now obliged to recognize that the little girl is a little man. In boys, as we know, this phase is marked by the fact that they have learnt how to derive pleasurable sensations from their small penis and connect its excited state with their ideas of sexual intercourse. Little girls do the same thing with their still smaller clitoris. It seems that with them all their masturbatory acts are carried out on this penis-equivalent, and that the truly feminine vagina is still undiscovered by both sexes. It is true that there are a few isolated reports of early vaginal sensations as well, but it could not be easy to distinguish these from sensations in the anus or vestibulum; in any case they cannot play a great part. We are entitled to keep to our view that in the phallic phase of girls the clitoris is the leading erotogenic zone. But it is not, of course, going to remain so. With the change to femininity the clitoris should wholly or in part hand over its sensitivity, and at the same time its importance, to the vagina. This would be one of the two tasks which a woman has to perform in the course of her development, whereas the more fortunate man has only to continue at the time of his sexual maturity the activity that he has previously carried out at the period of the early efflorescence of his sexuality.

We shall return to the part played by the clitoris; let us now turn to the second task with which a girl's development is burdened. A boy's mother is the first object of his love, and she remains so too during the formation of his Oedipus complex and, in essence, all through his life. For a girl too her first object must be her mother (and the figures of wet-nurses and foster-mothers that merge into her). The first object-cathexes occur in attachment to the satisfaction of the major and simple vital needs, and the circumstances of the care of children are the same for both sexes. But in the Oedipus situation the girl's father has become her love-object, and we expect that in the normal course of development she will find her way from this paternal object to her final choice of an object. In the course of time, therefore, a girl has to change her erotogenic zone and her object—both of which a boy retains. The question then arises of how this happens: in particular, how does a girl pass from her mother to an attachment to her father? or, in other words, how does she pass from her masculine phase to the feminine one to which she is biologically destined? . . .

. . . All these factors—the slights, the disappointments in love, the jealousy, the seduction followed by prohibition—are, after all, also in operation in the relation of a *boy* to his mother and are yet unable to alienate him from the maternal object. Unless we can find something that is specific for girls and is not present or not in the same way present in boys, we shall not have explained the termination of the attachment of girls to their mother.

I believe we have found this specific factor, and indeed where we expected to find it, even though in a surprising form. Where we expected to find it, I say, for it lies in the castration complex. After all, the anatomical distinction [between the sexes] must express itself in psychical consequences. It was, however, a surprise to learn from analyses that girls hold their mother responsible for their lack of a penis and do not forgive her for their being thus put at a disadvantage.

As you hear, then, we ascribe a castration complex to women as well. And for good reasons, though its content cannot be the same as with boys. In the latter the castration complex arises after they have learnt from the sight of the female genitals that the organ which they value so highly need not necessarily accompany the body. At this the boy recalls to mind the threats he brought on himself by his doings with that organ, he begins to give credence to them and falls under the influence of fear of castration, which will be the most powerful motive force in his subsequent development. The castration complex of girls is also started by the sight of the genitals of the other sex. They at once notice the difference and, it must be admitted, its significance too. They feel seriously wronged, often declare that they want to "have something like it too," and fall a victim to "envy for the penis," which will leave ineradicable traces on their development and the formation of their character and which will not be surmounted in even the most favourable cases without a severe expenditure of psychical energy. The girl's recognition of the fact of her being without a penis does not by any means imply that she submits to the fact easily. On the contrary, she continues to hold on for a long time to the wish to get something like it herself and she believes in that possibility for improbably long years; and analysis can show that, at a period when knowledge of reality has long since rejected the fulfilment of the wish as unattainable, it persists in the unconscious and retains a considerable cathexis of energy. The wish to get the longed-for penis eventually in spite of everything may contribute to the motives that drive a mature woman to analysis, and what she may reasonably expect from analysis—a capacity, for instance, to carry on an intellectual profession—may often be recognized as a sublimated modification of this repressed wish.

One cannot very well doubt the importance of envy for the penis. You may take it as an instance of male injustice if I assert that envy and jealousy play an even greater part in the mental life of women than of men. It is not that I think these characteristics are absent in men or that I think they have no other roots in women than envy for the penis; but I am inclined to attribute their greater amount in women to this latter influence. . . .

The discovery that she is castrated is a turning-point in a girl's growth. Three possible lines of development start from it: one leads to sexual inhibition or to neurosis, the second to change of character in the sense of a masculinity complex, the third, finally, to normal femininity. We have learnt a fair amount, though not everything, about all three.

The essential content of the first is as follows: the little girl has hitherto lived in a masculine way, has been able to get pleasure by the excitation of her clitoris and has brought this activity into relation with her sexual wishes directed towards her mother, which are often active ones; now, owing to the influence of her penis-envy, she loses her enjoyment in her phallic sexuality. Her self-love is mortified by the comparison with the boy's far superior equipment and in consequence she renounces her masturbatory satisfaction from her clitoris, repudiates her love for her mother and at the same time not infrequently represses a good part of her sexual trends in general. No doubt her turning away from her mother does not occur all at once, for to begin with the girl regards her castration as an individual misfortune, and only gradually extends it to other females and finally to her mother as well. Her love was directed to her *phallic* mother; with the discovery that her mother is castrated it becomes possible to drop her as an object, so that the motives for hostility, which have long been accumulating, gains the upper hand. This means, therefore, that as a result of the discovery of women's lack of a penis they are debased in value for girls just as they are for boys and later perhaps for men.

You all know the immense aetiological importance attributed by our neurotic patients to their masturbation. They make it responsible for all their troubles and we have the greatest difficulty in persuading them that they are mistaken. In fact, however, we ought to admit to them that they are right, for masturbation is the executive agent of infantile sexuality, from the faulty development of which they are indeed suffering. But what neurotics mostly blame is the masturbation of the period of puberty; they have mostly forgotten that of early infancy, which is what is really in question. . . . From the development of girls, which is what my present lecture is concerned with, I can give you the example of a child herself trying to get free from masturbating. She does not always succeed in this. If envy for the penis has provoked a powerful impulse against clitoridal masturbation but this nevertheless refuses to give way, a violent struggle for liberation ensues in which the girl, as it were, herself takes over the role of her deposed mother and gives expression to her entire dissatisfaction with her inferior clitoris in her efforts against obtaining satisfaction from it. Many years later, when her masturbatory activity has long since been suppressed, an interest still persists which we must interpret as a defence against a temptation that is still dreaded. It manifests itself in the emergence of sympathy for those to whom similar difficulties are attributed, it plays a part as a motive in contracting a marriage and, indeed, it may determine the choice of a husband or lover. Disposing of early infantile masturbation is truly no easy or indifferent business.

Along with the abandonment of clitoridal masturbation a certain amount of activity is renounced. Passivity now has the upper hand, and the girl's turning to her father is accomplished principally with the help of passive instinctual impulses. You can see that a wave of development like this, which clears the phallic activity out of the way, smooths the ground for femininity. If too much is not lost in the course of it through repression, this femininity may turn out to be normal. The wish with which the girl turns to her father is no doubt originally the wish for the penis which her mother has refused her and which she now expects from her father. The feminine situation is only established, however, if the wish for a penis is replaced by one for a baby, if, that is, a baby takes the place of a penis in accordance with an ancient symbolic equivalence. It has not escaped us that the girl has wished for a baby earlier, in the undisturbed phallic phase: that, of course, was the meaning of her playing with dolls. But that play was not in fact an expression of her femininity; it served as an identification with her mother with the intention of substituting activity for passivity. *She* was playing the part of her mother and the doll was herself: now she could do with the baby everything that her mother used to do with her. Not until the emergence of the wish for a penis does the doll-baby become a baby from the girl's father, and thereafter the aim of the most powerful feminine wish. Her happiness is great if later on this wish for a baby finds fulfilment in reality, and quite especially so if the baby is a little boy who brings the longed-for penis with him. Often enough in her combined picture of "a baby from her father" the emphasis is laid on the baby and her father left unstressed. In this way the ancient masculine wish for the possession of a penis is still faintly visible through the femininity now achieved. But perhaps we ought rather to recognize this wish for a penis as being *par excellence* a feminine one.

With the transference of the wish for a penis-baby on to her father, the girl has entered the situation of the Oedipus complex. Her hostility to her mother, which did not need to be freshly created, is now greatly intensified, for she becomes the girl's rival, who receives from her father everything that she desires from him. For a long time the girl's Oedipus complex concealed her pre-Oedipus attachment to her mother from our view, though it is nevertheless so important and leaves such lasting fixations behind it. For girls the Oedipus situation is the outcome of a long and difficult development; it is a kind of preliminary solution, a position of rest which is not soon abandoned, especially as the beginning of the latency period is not far distant. And we are now struck by a difference between the two sexes, which is probably momentous, in regard to the relation of the Oedipus complex to the castration complex. In a boy the Oedipus complex, in which he desires his mother and would like to get rid of his father as being a rival, develops naturally from the phase of his phallic sexuality. The threat of castration compels him, however, to give up that attitude. Under the impression of the danger of losing his penis, the Oedipus complex is abandoned, repressed and, in the most normal cases, entirely destroyed, and a severe super-ego is set up as its heir. What happens with a girl is almost the opposite. The castration complex prepares for the Oedipus complex instead of destroying it; the girl is driven out of her attachment to her mother through the influence of her envy for the penis and she enters the Oedipus situation as though into a haven of refuge. In the absence of fear of castration the chief motive is lacking which leads boys to surmount the Oedipus complex. Girls remain in it for an indeterminate length of time; they demolish it late and, even so, incompletely. In these circumstances the formation of the super-ego must suffer; it cannot attain the strength and independence which give it its cultural significance, and feminists are not pleased when we point out to them the effects of this factor upon the average feminine character.

To get back a little. We mentioned as the second possible reaction to the discovery of female castration the development of a powerful masculinity complex. By this we mean that the girl refuses, as it were, to recognize the unwelcome fact and, defiantly rebellious, even exaggerates her previous masculinity, clings to her clitoridal activity and takes refuge in an idenfication with her phallic mother or her father. What can it be that decides in favour of this outcome? We can only suppose that it is a constitutional factor, a greater amount of activity, such as is ordinarily characteristic of a male. However that may be, the essence of this process is that at this point in development the wave of passivity is avoided which opens the way to the turn towards femininity. The extreme achievement of such a masculinity complex would appear to be the influencing of the choice of an object in the sense of manifest homosexuality. Analytic experience teaches us, to be sure, that female homosexuality is seldom or never a direct continuation of infantile masculinity. Even for a girl of this kind it seems necessary that she should take her father as an object for some time and enter the Oedipus situation. But afterwards, as a result of her inevitable disappointments from her father, she is driven to regress into her early masculinity complex. The significance of these disappointments must not be exaggerated; a girl who is destined to become feminine is not spared them, though they do not have the same effect. The predominance of the constitutional factor seems indisputable; but the two phases in the development of female homosexuality are well mirrored in the practices of homosexuals, who play the parts of mother and baby with each other as often and as clearly as those of husband and wife.

What I have been telling you here may be described as the prehistory of women. It is a product of the very last few years and may have been of interest to you as an example of detailed analytic work. . . .

It is not my intention to pursue the further behavior of femininity through puberty to the period of maturity. Our knowledge, moreover, would be insufficient for the purpose. But I will bring a few features together in what follows. Taking its prehistory as a starting-point, I will only emphasize here that the development of femininity remains exposed to disturbance by the residual phenomena of the early masculine period. Regressions to the fixations of the pre-Oedipus phases very frequently occur; in the course of some women's lives there is a repeated alternation between periods in which masculinity or femininity gains the upper hand. Some portions of what we men call "the enigma of women" may perhaps be derived from this expression of bisexuality in women's lives. But another question seems to have become ripe for judgement in the course of these researches. We have called the motive force of sexual life "the libido." Sexual life is dominated by the polarity of masculine-feminine; thus the notion suggests itself of considering the relation of the libido to this antithesis. It would not be surprising if it were to turn out that each sexuality had its own special libido appropriated to it, so that one sort of libido would pursue the aims of a masculine sexual life and another sort those of a feminine one. But nothing of the kind is true. There is only one libido, which serves both the masculine and the feminine sexual functions. To it itself we cannot assign any sex; if, following the conventional equation of activity and masculinity, we are inclined to describe it as masculine, we must not forget that it also covers trends with a passive aim. Nevertheless the juxtaposition "feminine libido" is without any justification. Furthermore, it is our impression that more constraint has been applied to the libido when it is pressed into the service of the feminine function, and that—to speak teleologically—Nature takes less careful account of its [that function's] demands than in the case of masculinity. And the reason for this may lie—thinking once again teleologically—in the fact that the accomplishment of the aim of biology has been entrusted to the aggressiveness of men and has been made to some extent independent of women's consent.

The sexual frigidity of women, the frequency of which appears to confirm this disregard, is a phenomenon that is still insufficiently understood. Sometimes it is psychogenic and in that case accessible to influence; but in other cases it suggests the hypothesis of its being constitutionally determined and even of there being a contributory anatomical factor.

I have promised to tell you of a few more psychical peculiarities of mature femininity, as we come across them in analytic observation. We do not lay claim to more than an average validity for these assertions; nor is it always easy to distinguish what should be ascribed to the influence of the sexual function and what to social breeding. Thus, we attribute a larger amount of narcissism to femininity, which also affects women's choice of object, so that to be loved is a stronger need for them than to love. The effect of penis-envy has a share, further, in the physical vanity of women, since they are bound to value their charms more highly as a late compensation for their original sexual inferiority. Shame, which is considered to be a feminine characteristic *par excellence* but is far more a matter of convention than might be supposed, has as its purpose, we believe, concealment of genital deficiency. We are not forgetting that at a later time shame takes on other functions. It seems that women have made few contributions to the discoveries and inventions in the history of civilization; there is, however, one technique which they may have invented—that of plaiting and weaving. If that is so, we should be tempted to guess the unconscious motive for the achievement. Nature herself would seem to have given the model which this achievement imitates by causing the growth at maturity of the pubic hair that conceals the genitals. The step that remained to be taken lay in making the threads adhere to one another, while on the body they stick into the skin and are only matted together. If you reject this idea as fantastic and regard my belief in the influence of lack of a penis on the configuration of femininity as an *idée fixe,* I am of course defenceless.

The determinants of women's choice of an object are often made unrecogniz-able by social conditions. Where the choice is able to show itself freely, it is often made in accordance with the narcissistic ideal of the man whom the girl had wished to become. If the girl has remained in her attachment to her father—that is, in the Oedipus complex—her choice is made according to the paternal type. Since, when she turned from her mother to her father, the hostility of her ambivalent relation remained with her mother, a choice of this kind should guarantee a happy marriage. But very often the outcome is of a kind that presents a general threat to such a settlement of the conflict due to ambivalence. The hostility that has been left behind follows in the train of the positive attachment and spreads over on to the new object. The woman's husband, who to begin with inherited from her father, becomes after a time her mother's heir as well. So it may easily happen that the second half of a woman's life may be filled by the struggle against her husband, just as the shorter first half was filled by her rebellion against her mother. When this reaction has been lived through, a second marriage may easily turn out very much more satisfying. Another alteration in a woman's nature, for which lovers are unprepared, may occur in a marriage after the first child is born. Under the influence of a woman's becoming a mother herself, an identification with her own mother may be revived, against which she had striven up till the time of her marriage, and this may attract all the available libido to itself, so that the compulsion to repeat reproduces an unhappy marriage between her parents. The difference in a mother's reaction to the birth of a son or a daughter shows that the old factor of lack of a penis has even now not lost its strength. A mother is only brought unlimited satisfaction by her relation to a son; this is altogether the most perfect, the most free from ambivalence of all human relations. A mother can transfer to her son the ambition which she has been obliged to suppress in herself, and she can expect from him the satisfaction of all that has been left over in her of her masculinity complex. Even a marriage is not made secure until the wife has succeeded in making her husband her child as well and in acting as a mother to him.

A woman's identification with her mother allows us to distinguish two strata: the pre-Oedipus one which rests on her affectionate attachment to her mother and takes her as a model, and the later one from the Oedipus complex which seeks to get rid of her mother and take her place with her father. We are no doubt justified in saying that much of both of them is left over for the future and that neither of them is adequately surmounted in the course of development. But the phase of the affectionate pre-Oedipus attachment is the decisive one for a woman's future: during it preparations are made for the acquisition of the characteristics with which she will later fulfil her role in the sexual function and perform her invaluable social tasks. It is in this identification too that she acquires her attractiveness to a man, whose Oedipus attachment to his mother it kindles into passion. How often it happens, however, that it is only his son who obtains what he himself aspired to! One gets an impression that a man's love and a woman's are a phase apart psychologically.

The fact that women must be regarded as having little sense of justice is no doubt related to the predominance of envy in their mental life; for the demand for justice is a modification of envy and lays down the condition subject to which one can put envy aside. We also regard women as weaker in their social interests and as having less capacity for sublimating their instincts than men. The former is no doubt derived from the dissocial quality which unquestionably characterizes all sexual relations. Lovers find sufficiency in each other, and families too resist inclusion in more comprehensive associations. The aptitude for sublimation is subject to the greatest individual variations. On the other hand I cannot help mentioning an impression that we are constantly receiving during analytic practice. A man of about thirty strikes us as a youthful, somewhat unformed individual, whom we expect to make powerful use of the possibilities for development opened up to him by analysis. A woman of the same age, however, often frightens us by her psychical rigidity and unchangeability. Her libido has taken up final positions and seems incapable of exchanging them for others. There are no paths open to further development; it is as though the whole process had already run its course and remains thenceforward insusceptible to influence—as though, indeed, the difficult development to femininity had exhausted the possibilities of the person concerned. . . .

Sex

Edward O. Wilson

Sex is central to human biology and a protean phenomenon that permeates every aspect of our existence and takes new forms through each step in the life cycle. Its complexity and ambiguity are due to the fact that sex is not designed primarily for reproduction. . . .

Why, then, has sex evolved?

The principal answer is that sex creates diversity. And diversity is the way a parent hedges its bets against an unpredictably changing environment. Imagine a case of two animal species, both of which consist entirely of individuals carrying two genes. Let us arbitrarily label one gene *A* and the other *a*. For instance, these genes might be for brown (*A*) versus blue (*a*) eye color, or right-handedness (*A*) versus left-handedness (*a*). Each individual is *Aa* because it possesses both genes. Suppose that one species reproduces without sex. Then all the offspring of every parent will be *Aa*.

The other population uses sex for reproduction; it produces sex cells, each of which contains only one of the genes, *A* or *a*. When two individuals mate they combine their sex cells, and since each adult contributes sex cells bearing either *A* or *a*, three kinds of offspring are possible: *AA, Aa,* and *aa*. So, from a starting population of *Aa* individuals, asexual parents can produce only *Aa* offspring, while sexual parents can produce *AA, Aa,* and *aa* offspring. Now let the environment change—say a hard winter, a flood, or the invasion of a dangerous predator—so that *aa* individuals are favored. In the next generation, the sexually reproducing population will have the advantage and will consist predominantly of *aa* organisms until conditions change to favor, perhaps, *AA* or *Aa* individuals.

Diversity, and thus adaptability, explains why so many kinds of organisms bother with sexual reproduction. They vastly outnumber the species that rely on the direct and simple but, in the long run, less prudent modes of sexless multiplication. . . .

The quintessential female is an individual specialized for making eggs. The large size of the egg enables it to resist drying, to survive adverse periods by consuming stored yolk, to be moved to safety by the parent, and to divide at least a few times after fertilization before needing to ingest nutrients from the outside. The male is defined as the manufacturer of the sperm, the little gamere. A sperm is a minimum cellular unit, stripped down to a head packed with DNA and powered by a tail containing just enough stored energy to carry the vehicle to the egg.

When the two gametes unite in fertilization they create an instant mixture of genes surrounded by the durable housing of the egg. By cooperating to create zygotes, the female and male make it more likely that at least some of their offspring will survive in the event of a changing environment. A fertilized egg differs from an asexually reproducing cell in one fundamental respect: it contains a newly assembled mixture of genes.

The anatomical difference between the two kinds of sex cell is often extreme. In particular, the human egg is eighty-five thousand times larger than the human sperm. The consequences of this gametic dimorphism ramify throughout the biology and psychology of human sex. The most important immediate result is that the female places a greater investment in each of her sex cells. A woman can expect to produce only about four hundred eggs in her lifetime. Of these a maximum of about twenty can be converted into healthy infants. The costs of bringing an infant to term and caring for it afterward are relatively enormous. In contrast, a man releases 100 million sperm with each ejaculation. Once he has achieved fertilization his purely physical commitment has ended. His genes will benefit equally with those of the female, but his investment will be far less than hers unless she can induce him to contribute to the care of the offspring. If a man were given total freedom to act, he could theoretically inseminate thousands of women in his lifetime.

The resulting conflict of interest between the sexes is a property of not only human beings but also the majority of animal species. Males are characteristically aggressive, especially toward one another and most intensely during the breeding season. In most species, assertiveness is the most profitable male strategy. During the full period of time it takes to bring a fetus to term, from the fertilization of the egg to the birth of the infant, one male can fertilize many females but a female can be fertilized by only one male. Thus if males are able to court one female after another, some will be big winners and others will be absolute losers, while virtually all healthy females will succeed in being fertilized. It pays males to be aggressive, hasty, fickle, and undiscriminating. In theory it is more profitable for females to be coy, to hold back until they can identify males with the best genes. In species that rear young, it is also important for the females to select males who are more likely to stay with them after insemination.

Human beings obey this biological principle faithfully. It is true that the thousands of existing socieites are enormously variable in the details of their sexual mores and the division of labor between the sexes. This variation is based on culture. Societies mold their customs to the requirements of the environment and in so doing duplicate in totality a large fraction of the arrangements encountered throughout the remainder of the animal kingdom: from strict monogamy to extreme forms of polygamy, and from a close approach to unisex to extreme differences between men and women in behavior and dress. People change their attitudes consciously and at will; the reigning fashion of a society can shift within a generation. Nevertheless, this flexibility is not endless, and beneath it all lie general features that conform closely to the expectations from evolutionary theory. So let us concentrate initially on the biologically significant generalities and defer, for the moment, consideration of the undeniably important plasticity controlled by culture.

We are, first of all, moderately polygynous, with males initiating most of the changes in sexual partnership. About three-fourths of all human societies permit the taking of multiple wives, and most of them encourage the practice by law and custom. In contrast, marriage to multiple husbands is sanctioned in less than one percent of societies. The remaining monogamous societies usually fit that category in a legal sense only, with concubinage and other extramarital stratagems being added to allow de facto polygyny.

Because women are commonly treated by men as a limiting resource and hence as valued property, they are the beneficiaries of hypergamy, the practice of marrying upward in social position. Polygyny and hypergamy are essentially complementary strategies. In diverse cultures men pursue and acquire, while women are protected and battered. Sons sow wild oats and daughters risk being ruined. When sex is sold, men are usually the buyers. It is to be expected that prostitutes are the despised members of society; they have abandoned their valuable reproductive investment to strangers. . . .

Anatomy bears the imprint of the sexual division of labor. Men are on the average 20 to 30 percent heavier than women. Pound for pound, they are stronger and quicker in most categories of sport. The proportion of their limbs, their skeletal torsion, and the density of their muscles are particularly suited for running and throwing, the archaic specialties of the ancestral hunter-gatherer males. The world track records reflect the disparity. . . .

It is of equal importance that women match or surpass men in a few other sports, and these are among the ones further removed from the primitive techniques of hunting and aggression: long-distance swimming, the more acrobatic events of gymnastics, precision (but not distance) archery, and small-bore rifle shooting. As sports and sport-like activities evolve into more sophisticated channels dependent on skill and agility, the overall achievements of men and women can be expected to converge more closely.

The average temperamental differences between the human sexes are also consistent with the generalities of mammalian biology. Women as a group are less assertive and physically aggressive. The magnitude of the distinction depends on the culture. It ranges from a tenuous, merely statistical difference in egalitarian settings to the virtual enslavement of women in some extreme polygynous societies. But the variation in degree is not nearly so important as the fact that women differ consistently in this qualitative manner regardless of the degree. The fundamental average difference in personality traits is seldom if ever transposed.

The physical and temperamental differences between men and women have been amplified by culture into universal male dominance. History records not a single society in which women have controlled the political and economic lives of men. Even when queens and empresses ruled, their intermediaries remained primarily male. At the present writing not a single country has a woman as head of state, although Golda Meir of Israel and Indira Gandhi of India were, until recently, assertive, characteristic leaders of their countries. In about 75 percent of societies studied by anthropologists, the bride is expected to move from the location of her own family to that of her husband, while only 10 percent require the reverse exchange. Lineage is reckoned exclusively through the male line at least five times more frequently than it is through the female line. Men have traditionally assumed the positions of chieftains, shamans, judges, and warriors. Their modern technocratic counterparts rule the industrial states and head the corporations and churches.

These differences are a simple matter of record—but what is their significance for the future? How easily can they be altered?

It is obviously of vital social importance to try to make a value-free assessment of the relative contributions of heredity and environment to the differentiation of behavioral roles between the sexes. Here is what I believe the evidence shows: modest genetic differences exist between the sexes; the behavioral genes interact with virtually all existing environments to create a noticeable divergence in early psychological development; and the divergence is almost always widened in later psychological development by cultural sanctions and training. Societies can probably cancel the modest genetic differences entirely by careful planning and training, but the convergence will require a conscious decision based on fuller and more exact knowledge than is now available.

The evidence for a genetic difference in behavior is varied and substantial. In general, girls are predisposed to be more intimately sociable and less physically venturesome. From the time of birth, for example, they smile more than boys. This trait may be especially revealing, since as I showed earlier the infant smile, of all human behaviors, is most fully innate in that its form and function are virtually invariant. Several independent studies have shown that newborn females respond more frequently than males with eyes-closed, reflexive smiling. The habit is soon replaced by deliberate, communicative smiling that persists into the second year of life. Frequent smiling then becomes one of the more persistent of female traits and endures through adolescence and maturity. By the age of six months, girls also pay closer attention to sights and sounds used in communication than they do to nonsocial stimuli. Boys of the same age make no such distinction. The ontogeny then proceeds as follows: one-year-old girls react with greater fright and inhibition to clay faces, and they are more reluctant to leave their mothers' sides in novel situations. Older girls remain more affiliative and less physically venturesome than boys of the same age. . . .

In Western cultures boys are also more venturesome than girls and more physically aggressive on the average. Eleanor Maccoby and Carol Jacklin, in their review *The Psychology of Sex Differences,* concluded that this male trait is deeply rooted and could have a genetic origin. From the earliest moments of social play, at age 2 to 2½ years, boys are more aggressive in both words and actions. They have a larger number of hostile fantasies and engage more often in mock fighting, overt threats, and physical attacks, which are directed preferentially at other boys during efforts to acquire dominance status. Other studies, summarized by Ronald P. Rohner, indicate that the differences exist in many cultures. . . .

So at birth the twig is already bent a little bit—what are we to make of that? It suggests that the universal existence of sexual division of labor is not entirely an accident of cultural evolution. But it also supports the conventional view that the enormous variation among societies in the degree of that division is due to cultural evolution. Demonstrating a slight biological component delineates the options that future societies may consciously select. Here the second dilemma of human nature presents itself. In full recognition of the struggle for women's rights that is now spreading throughout the world, each society must make one or the other of the three following choices:

Condition its members so as to exaggerate sexual differences in behavior. This is the pattern in almost all cultures. It results more often than not in domination of women by men and exclusion of women from many professions and activities. But this need not be the case. In theory at least, a carefully designed society with strong sexual divisions could be richer in spirit, more diversified, and even more productive than a unisex society. Such a society might safeguard human rights even while channeling men and women into different occupations. Still, some amount of social injustice would be inevitable, and it could easily expand to disastrous proportions.

Train its members so as to eliminate all sexual differences in behavior. By the use of quotas and sex-biased education it should be possible to create a society in which men and women *as groups* share equally in all professions, cultural activities, and even, to take the absurd extreme, athletic competition. Although the early predispositions that characterize sex would have to be blunted, the biological differences are not so large as to make the undertaking impossible. Such control would offer the great advantage of eliminating even the hint of group prejudice (in addition to individual prejudice) based on sex. It could result in a much more harmonious and productive society. Yet the amount of regulation required would certainly place some personal freedoms in jeopardy, and at least a few individuals would not be allowed to reach their full potential.

Provide equal opportunities and access but take no further action. To make no choice at all is of course open to all cultures. Laissez-faire on first thought might seem to be the course most congenial to personal liberty and development, but this is not necessarily true. Even with identical education for men and women and equal access to all professions, men are likely to maintain disproportionate representation in political life, business, and science. Many would fail to participate fully in the equally important, formative aspects of child rearing. The result might be legitimately viewed as restrictive of the complex emotional development of individuals. Just such a divergence and restriction has occurred in the Israeli kibbutzim, which represents one of the most powerful experiments in egalitarianism conducted in modern times.

From the time of the greatest upsurge of the kibbutz movement, in the 1940s and 1950s, its leaders promoted a policy of complete sexual equality, of encouraging women to enter roles previously reserved for men. In the early years it almost worked. The first generation of women were ideologically committed, and they shifted in large numbers to politics, management, and labor. But they and their daughters have regressed somewhat toward traditional roles, despite being trained from birth in the new culture. Furthermore, the daughters have gone further than the mothers. They now demand and receive a longer period of time each day with their children, time significantly entitled "the hour of love." Some of the most gifted have resisted recruitment into the higher levels of commercial and political leadership, so that the representation in these roles is far below that enjoyed by the same generation of men. It has been argued that this reversion merely represents the influence of the strong patriarchal tradition that persists in the remainder of Israeli society, even though the role division is now greater inside the kibbutzim than outside. The Israeli experience shows how difficult it is to predict the consequences and assess the meaning of changes in behavior based on either heredity or ideology.

From this troubling ambiguity concerning sex roles one firm conclusion can be drawn: the evidences of biological constraint alone cannot prescribe an ideal course of action. However, they can help us to define the options and to assess the price of each. The price is to be measured in the added energy required for education and reinforcement and in the attrition of individual freedom and potential. And let us face the real issue squarely: since every option has a cost, and concrete ethical principles will rarely find universal acceptance, the choice cannot be made easily. In such cases we could do well to consider the wise counsel of Hans Morgenthau: "In the combination of political wisdom, moral courage and moral judgment, man reconciles his political nature and his moral destiny. That this conciliation is nothing more than a *modus vivendi,* uneasy, precarious, and even paradoxical, can disappoint only those who prefer to gloss over and to distort the tragic contradictions of human existence with the soothing logic of a specious concord." I am suggesting that the contradictions are rooted in the surviving relics of our prior genetic history, and that one of the most inconvenient and senseless, but nevertheless unavoidable of these residues is the modest predisposition toward sex role differences. . . .

LIBERALISM: Women's Oppression as Unfair Discrimination

The Subjection of Women

John Stuart Mill

The object of this Essay is to explain as clearly as I am able, the grounds of an opinion which I have held from the very earliest period when I had formed any opinions at all on social or political matters, and which, instead of being weakened or modified, has been constantly growing stronger by the progress of reflection and the experience of life: That the principle which regulates the existing social relations between the two sexes—the legal subordination of one sex to the other—is wrong in itself, and now one of the chief hindrances to human improvement; and that it ought to be replaced by a principle of perfect equality, admitting no power or privilege on the one side, nor disability on the other.

The very words necessary to express the task I have undertaken, show how arduous it is. But it would be a mistake to suppose that the difficulty of the case must lie in the insufficiency or obscurity of the grounds of reason on which my conviction rests. The difficulty is that which exists in all cases in which there is a mass of feeling to be contended against. So long as an opinion is strongly rooted in the feelings, it gains rather than loses in stability by having a preponderating weight of argument against it. For if it were accepted as a result of argument, the refutation of the argument might shake the solidity of the conviction; but when it rests solely on feeling, the worse it flares in argumentative contest, the more persuaded its adherents are that their feeling must have some deeper ground, which the arguments do not reach; and while the feeling remains, it is always throwing up fresh intrenchments of argument to repair any breach made in the old. And there are so many causes tending to make the feelings connected with this subject the most intense and most deeply-rooted of all those which gather round and protect old institutions and customs, that we need not wonder to find them as yet less undermined and loosened than any of the rest by the progress of the great modern spiritual and social transition; nor suppose that the barbarisms to which men cling longest must be less barbarisms than those which they earlier shake off. . . .

In the first place, the opinion in favour of the present system, which entirely subordinates the weaker sex to the stronger, rests upon theory only; for there never has been trial made of any other; so that experience, in the sense in which it is vulgarly opposed to theory, cannot be pretended to have pronounced any verdict. And in the second place, the adoption of this system of inequality never was the result of deliberation, or forethought, or any social ideas, or any notion whatever of what conducted to the benefit of humanity or the good order of society. It arose simply from the fact that from the very earliest twilight of human society, every woman (owing to the value attached to her by men, combined with her inferiority in muscular strength) was found in a state of bondage to some man. Laws and systems of polity always begin by recognising the relations they find already existing between individuals. They convert what was a mere physical fact into a legal right, give it the sanction of society, and principally aim at the substitution of public and organized means of asserting and protecting these rights, instead of the irregular and lawless conflict of physical strength. Those who had already been compelled to obedience became in this manner legally bound to it. Slavery, from being a mere affair of force between the master and the slave, became regularized and a matter of compact among the masters, who, binding themselves to one another for common protection, guaranteed by their collective strength the private possessions of each, including his slaves. In early times, the great majority of the male sex were slaves, as well as the whole of the female. And many ages elapsed, some of them ages of high cultivation, before any thinker was bold enough to question the rightfulness and the absolute social necessity, either of the one slavery or of the other. . . .

If people are mostly so little aware how completely, during the greater part of the duration of our species, the law of force was the avowed rule of general conduct, any other being only a special and exceptional consequence of peculiar ties—and from how very recent a date it is that the affairs of society in general have been even pretended to be regulated according to any moral law; as little do people remember or consider, how institutions and customs which never had any ground but the law of force, last on into ages and states of general opinion which never would have permitted their first establishment. Less than forty years ago, Englishmen might still by law hold human beings in bondage as saleable property; within the present century they might kidnap them and carry them off, and work them literally to death. This absolutely extreme case of the law of force, condemned by those who can tolerate almost every other form of arbitrary power, and which, of all others, presents features the most revolting to the feelings of all who look at it from an impartial position, was the law of civilized and Christian England within the memory of persons now living: and in one half of Anglo-Saxon America three or four years ago, not only did slavery exist, but the slave trade, and the breeding of slaves expressly for it, was a general practice between slave states. Yet not only was there a greater strength of sentiment against it, but, in England at least, a less amount either of feeling or of interest in favour of it, than of any other of the customary abuses of force: for its motive was the love of gain, unmixed and undisguised; and those who profited by it were a very small numerical fraction of the country, while the natural feeling of all who were not personally interested in it, was unmitigated abhorrence. So extreme an instance makes it almost superfluous to refer to any other; but consider the long duration of absolute monarchy. In England at present it is the almost universal conviction that military despotism is a case of the law of force, having no other origin or justification. Yet in all the great nations of Europe except England it either still exists, or has only just ceased to exist, and has even now a strong party favourable to it in all ranks of the people, especially among persons of station and consequence. Such is the power of an established system, even when far from universal, when not only in almost every period of history there have been great and well-known examples of the contrary system, but these have almost invariably been afforded by the most illustrious and most prosperous communities. In this case, too, the possessor of the undue power, the person directly interested in it, is only one person, while those who are subject to it and suffer from it are literally all the rest. The yoke is naturally and necessarily humiliating to all persons, except the one who is on the throne, together with, at most, the one who expects to succeed to it. How different are these cases from that of the power of men over women! I am not now prejudging the question of its justifiableness. I am showing how vastly more permanent it could not but be, even if not justifiable, than these other dominations which have nevertheless lasted down to our own time. Whatever gratification of pride there is in the possession of power, and whatever personal interest in its exercise, is in this case not confined to a limited class, but common to the whole male sex. Instead of being, to most of its supporters, a thing desirable chiefly in the abstract, or, like the political ends usually contended for by factions, of little private importance to any but the leaders; it comes home to the person and hearth of every male head of a family, and of every one who looks forward to being so. The clodhopper exercises, or is to exercise, his share of the power equally with the highest nobleman. And the case is that in which the desire of power is the strongest: for every one who desires power, desires it most over those who are nearest to him, with whom his life is passed, with whom he has most concerns in common, and in whom any independence of his authority is oftenest likely to interfere with his individual preferences. If, in the other cases specified, power manifestly grounded only on force, and having so much less to support them, are so slowly and with so much difficulty got rid of, much more must it be so with this, even if it rests on no better foundation than those. We must consider, too, that the possessors of the power have facilities in this case, greater than in any other, to prevent any uprising against it. Every one of the subjects lives under the very eye, and almost, it may be said, in the hands, of one of the masters—in closer intimacy with him than with any of her fellow-subjects; with no means of combining against him, no power of even locally overmastering him, and, on the other hand, with the strongest motives for seeking his favour and avoiding to give him offence. In struggles for political emancipation, everybody knows how often its champions are bought off by bribes, or daunted by terrors. In the case of women, each individual of the subject-class is in a chronic state of bribery and intimidation combined. In setting up the standard of resistance, a large number of the leaders, and still more of the followers, must make an almost complete sacrifice of the pleasures or the alleviations of their own individual lot. If ever any system of privilege and enforced subjection had its yoke tightly riveted on the necks of those who are kept down by it, this has. . . .

All causes, social and natural, combine to make it unlikely that women should be collectively rebellious to the power of men. They are so far in a position different from all other subject classes, that their masters require something more from them than actual service. Men do not want solely the obedience of women, they want their sentiments. All men, except the most brutish, desire to have, in the woman most nearly connected with them, not a forced slave but a willing one, not a slave merely, but a favourite. They have therefore put everything in practice to enslave their minds. The masters of all other slaves rely, for maintaining obedience, on fear; either fear of themselves, or religious fears. The masters of women wanted more than simple obedience, and they turned the whole force of education to effect their purpose. All women are brought up from the very earliest years in the belief that their ideal of character is the very opposite to that of men; not self-will, and government by self-control, but submission, and yielding to the control of others. All the moralities tell them that it is the duty of women, and all the current sentimentalities that it is their nature, to live for others; to make complete abnegation of themselves, and to have no life but in their affections. And by their affections are meant the only ones they are allowed to have—those to the men with whom they are connected, or to the children who constitute an additional and indefeasible tie between them and a man. When we put together three things—first, the natural attraction between opposite sexes; secondly, the wife's entire dependence on the husband, every privilege or pleasure she has being either his gift, or depending entirely on his will; and lastly, that the principal object of human pursuit, consideration, and all objects of social ambition, can in general be sought or obtained by her only through him, it would be a miracle if the object of being attractive to men had not become the polar star of feminine education and formation of character. And, this great means of influence over the minds of women having been acquired, an instinct of selfishness made men avail themselves of it to the utmost as a means of holding women in subjection, by representing to them meekness, submissiveness, and resignation of all individual will into the hands of a man, as an essential part of sexual attractiveness. Can it be doubted that any of the other yokes which mankind have succeeded in breaking, would have subsisted till now if the same means had existed, and had been as sedulously used, to bow down their minds to it? If it had been made the object of the life of every young plebeian to find personal favour in the eyes of some patrician, of every young serf with some seigneur; if domestication with him, and a share of his personal affections, had been held out as the prize which they all should look out for, the most gifted and aspiring being able to reckon on the most desirable prizes; and if, when this prize had been obtained, they had been shut out by a wall of brass from all interests not centering in him, all feelings and desires but those which he shared or inculcated; would not serfs and seigneurs, plebeians and patricians, have been as broadly distinguished at this day as men and women are? and would not all but a thinker here and there, have believed the distinction to be a fundamental and unalterable fact in human nature?

The preceding considerations are amply sufficient to show that custom, however universal it may be, affords in this case no presumption, and ought not to create any prejudice, in favour of the arrangements which place women in social and political subjection to men. But I may go farther, and maintain that the course of history, and the tendencies of progressive human society, afford not only no presumption in favour of this system of inequality of rights, but a strong one against it; and that, so far as the whole course of human improvement up to this time, the whole stream of modern tendencies, warrants any inference on the subject, it is, that this relic of the past is discordant with the future, and must necessarily disappear.

For, what is the peculiar character of the modern world—the difference which chiefly distinguishes modern institutions, modern social ideas, modern life itself, from those of times long past? It is, that human beings are no longer born to their place in life, and chained down by an inexorable bond to the place they are born to, but are free to employ their faculties, and such favourable chances as offer, to achieve the lot which may appear to them most desirable. Human society of old was constituted on a very different principle. All were born to a fixed social position, and were mostly kept in it by law, or interdicted from any means by which they could emerge from it. As some men are born white and others black, so some were born slaves and others freemen and citizens; some were born patricians, others plebeians; some were born feudal nobles, others commoners and *roturiers*. A slave or serf could never make himself free, nor, except by the will of his master, become so. In most European countries it was not till towards the close of the middle ages, and as a consequence of the growth of regal power, that commoners could be ennobled. Even among nobles, the eldest son was born the exclusive heir to the paternal possessions, and a long time elapsed before it was fully established that the father could disinherit him. Among the industrious classes, only those who were born members of a guild, or were admitted into it by its members, could lawfully practise their calling within its local limits; and nobody could practise any calling deemed important, in any but the legal manner—by processes authoritatively prescribed. Manufacturers have stood in the pilory for presuming to carry on their business by new and improved methods. In modern Europe, and most in those parts of it which have participated most largely in all other modern improvements, diametrically opposite doctrines now prevail. Law and government do not undertake to prescribe by whom any social or industrial operation shall or shall not be conducted, or what modes of conducting them shall be lawful. These things are left to the unfettered choice of individuals. Even the laws which required that workmen should serve an apprenticeship, have in this country been repealed: there being ample assurance that in all cases in which an apprenticeship is necessary, its necessity will suffice to enforce it. The old theory was, that the least possible should be left to the choice of the individual agent; that all he had to do should, as far as practicable, be laid down for him by superior wisdom. Left to himself he was sure to go wrong. The modern conviction, the fruit of a thousand years of experience is, that things in which the individual is the person directly interested, never go right but as they are left to his own discretion; and that any regulation of them by authority, except to protect the rights of others, is sure to be mischievous. This conclusion, slowly arrived at, and not adopted until almost every possible application of the contrary theory had been made with disastrous result, now (in the industrial department) prevails universally in the most advanced countries, almost universally in all that have pretensions to any sort of advancement. It is not that all processes are supposed to be equally good, or all persons to be equally qualified for everything; but that freedom of individual choice is now known to be the only thing which procures the adoption of the best processes, and throws each operation into the hands of those who are best qualified for it. Nobody thinks it necessary to make a law that only a strong-armed man shall be a blacksmith. Freedom and competition suffice to make blacksmiths strong-armed men, because the weak-armed can earn more by engaging in occupations for which they are more fit. In consonance with this doctrine, it is felt to be an overstepping of the proper bounds of authority to fix beforehand, on some general presumption, that certain persons are not fit to do certain things. It is now thoroughly known and admitted that if some such presumptions exist, no such presumption is infallible. Even if it be well grounded in a majority of cases, which it is very likely not to be, there will be a minority of exceptional cases in which it does not hold; and in those it is both an injustice to the individuals, and a detriment to society, to place barriers in the way of their using their faculties for their own benefit and for that of others. In the cases, on the other hand, in which the unfitness is real, the ordinary motives of human conduct will on the whole suffice to prevent the incompetent person from making, or from persisting in, the attempt.

If this general principle of social and economical science is not true; if individuals, with such help as they can derive from the opinion of those who know them, are not better judges than the law and the government, of their own capacities and vocation; the world cannot too soon abandon this principle, and return to the old system of regulations and disabilities. But if the principle is true, we ought to act as if we believed it, and not to ordain that to be born a girl instead of a boy, any more than to be born black instead of white, or a commoner instead of a nobleman, shall decide the person's position through all life—shall interdict people from all the more elevated social positions, and from all, except a few, respectable occupations. Even were we to admit the utmost that is ever pretended as to the superior fitness of men for all the functions now reserved to them, the same argument applies which forbids a legal qualification for members of Parliament. If only once in a dozen years the conditions of eligibility exclude a fit person, there is a real loss, while the exclusion of thousands of unfit persons is no gain; for if the constitution of the electoral body disposes them to choose unfit persons, there are always plenty of such persons to choose from. In all things of any difficulty and importance, those who can do them well are fewer than the need, even with the most unrestricted latitude of choice; and any limitation of the field of selection deprives society of some chances of being served by the competent, without ever saving it from the incompetent.

At present, in the more improved countries, the disabilities of women are the only case, save one, in which laws and institutions take persons at their birth, and ordain that they shall never in all their lives be allowed to compete for certain things. . . .

The social subordination of women thus stands out an isolated fact in modern social institutions; a solitary breach of what has become their fundamental law; a single relic of an old world of thought and practice exploded in everything else, but retained in the one thing of most universal interest. . . .

The least that can be demanded is, that the question should not be considered as prejudged by existing fact and existing opinion, but open to discussion on its merits, as a question of justice and expediency; the decision on this, as on any of the other social arrangements of mankind, depending on what an enlightened estimate of tendencies and consequences may show to be most advantageous to humanity in general, without distinction of sex. And the discussion must be a real discussion, descending to foundations, and not resting satisfied with vague and general assertions. It will not do, for instance, to assert in general terms, that the experience of mankind has pronounced in favour of the existing system. Experience cannot possibly have decided between two courses, so long as there has only been experience of one. If it be said that the doctrine of the equality of the sexes rests only on theory, it must be remembered that the contrary doctrine also has only theory to rest upon. All that is proved in its favour by direct experience, is that mankind have been able to exist under it, and to attain the degree of improvement and prosperity which we now see; but whether that prosperity has been attained sooner, or is now greater, than it would have been under the other system, experience does not say. On the other hand, experience does say, that every step in improvement has been so invariably accompanied by a step made in raising the social position of women, that historians and philosophers have been led to adopt their elevation or debasement as on the whole the surest test and most correct measure of the civilization of a people or an age. Through all the progressive period of human history, the condition of women has been approaching nearer to equality with men. This does not of itself prove that the assimilation must go on to complete equality; but it assuredly affords some presumption that such is the case.

Neither does it avail anything to say that the *nature* of the two sexes adapts them to their present functions and position, and renders these appropriate to them. Standing on the ground of common sense and the constitution of the human mind, I deny that any one knows, or can know, the nature of the two sexes, as long as they have only been seen in their present relation to one another. If men had ever been found in society without women, or women without men, or if there had been a society of men and women in which the women were not under the control of the men, something might have been positively known about the mental and moral differences which may be inherent in the nature of each. What is now called the nature of women is an eminently artificial thing—the result of forced repression in some directions, unnatural stimulation in others. It may be asserted without scruple, that no other class of dependents have had their character so entirely distorted from its natural proportions by their relation with their masters; for, if conquered and slave races have been, in some respects, more forcibly repressed, whatever in them has not been crushed down by an iron heel has generally been let alone, and if left with any liberty of development, it has developed itself according to its own laws; but in the case of women, a hot-house and stove cultivation has always been carried on of some of the capabilities of their nature, for the benefit and pleasure of their masters. . . .

Hence, in regard to that most difficult question, what are the natural differences between the two sexes—a subject on which it is impossible in the present state of society to obtain complete and correct knowledge—while almost everybody dogmatizes upon it, almost all neglect and make light of the only means by which any partial insight can be obtained into it. This is, an analytic study of the most important department of psychology, the laws of the influence of circumstances on character. For, however great and apparently ineradicable the moral and intellectual differences between men and women might be, the evidence of their being natural differences could only be negative. Those only could be inferred to be natural which could not possibly be artificial—the residuum, after deducting every characteristic of either sex which can admit of being explained from education or external circumstances. The profoundest knowledge of the laws of the formation of character is indispensable to entitle any one to affirm even that there is any difference, much more what the difference is, between the two sexes considered as moral and rational beings; and since no one, as yet, has that knowledge, (for there is hardly any subject which, in proportion to its importance, has been so little studied), no one is thus far entitled to any positive opinion on the subject. Conjectures are all that can at present be made; conjectures more or less probable, according as more or less authorized by such knowledge as we yet have of the laws of psychology, as applied to the formation of character.

Even the preliminary knowledge, what the differences between the sexes now are, apart from all questions as to how they are made what they are, is still in the crudest and most incomplete state. . . .

One thing we may be certain of—that what is contrary to women's nature to do, they never will be made to do by simply giving their nature free play. The anxiety of mankind to interfere in behalf of nature, for fear lest nature should not succeed in effecting its purpose, is an altogether unnecessary solicitude. What women by nature cannot do, it is quite superfluous to forbid them from doing. What they can do, but not so well as the men who are their competitors, competition suffices to exclude them from; since nobody asks for protective duties and bounties in favour of women; it is only asked that the present bounties and protective duties in favour of men should be recalled. If women have a greater natural inclination for some things than for others, there is no need of laws or social inculcation to make the majority of them do the former in preference to the latter. Whatever women's services are most wanted for, the free play of competition will hold out the strongest inducements to them to undertake. And, as the words imply, they are most wanted for the things for which they are most fit; by the apportionment of which to them, the collective faculties of the two sexes can be applied on the whole with the greatest sum of valuable result.

The general opinion of men is supposed to be, that the natural vocation of a woman is that of a wife and mother. I say, is supposed to be, because, judging from acts—from the whole of the present constitution of society—one might infer that their opinion was the direct contrary. They might be supposed to think that the alleged natural vocation of women was of all things the most repugnant to their nature; insomuch that if they are free to do anything else—if any other means of living, or occupation of their time and faculties, is open, which has any chance of appearing desirable to them—there will not be enough of them who will be willing to accept the condition said to be natural to them. If this is the real opinion of men in general, it would be well that it should be spoken out. I should like to hear somebody openly enunciating the doctrine (it is already implied in much that is written on the subject)—"It is necessary to society that women should marry and produce children. They will not do so unless they are compelled. Therefore it is necessary to compel them." The merits of the case would then be clearly defined. It would be exactly that of the slaveholders of South Carolina and Louisiana. "It is necessary that cotton and sugar should be grown. White men cannot produce them. Negroes will not, for any wages which we choose to give. *Ergo* they must be compelled." An illustration still closer to the point is that of impressment. Sailors must absolutely be had to defend the country. It often happens that they will not voluntarily enlist. Therefore there must be the power of forcing them. How often has this logic been used! and, but for one flaw in it, without doubt it would have been successful up to this day. But it is open to the retort—First pay the sailors the honest value of their labour. When you have made it as well worth their while to serve you, as to work for other employers, you will have no more difficulty than others have in obtaining their services. To this there is no logical answer except "I will not": and as people are now not only ashamed, but are not desirous, to rob the labourer of his hire, impressment is no longer advocated. Those who attempt to force women into marriage by closing all other doors against them, lay themselves open to a similar retort. If they mean what they say, their opinion must evidently be, that men do not render the married condition so desirable to women, as to induce them to accept it for its own recommendations. It is not a sign of one's thinking the boon one offers very attractive, when one allows only Hobson's choice, "that or none." And here, I believe, is the clue to the feelings of those men, who have a real antipathy to the equal freedom of women. I believe they are afraid, not lest women should be unwilling to marry, for I do not think that any one in reality has that apprehension; but lest they should insist that marriage should be on equal conditions; lest all women of spirit and capacity should prefer doing almost anything else, not in their own eyes degrading, rather than marry, when marrying is giving themselves a master, and a master too of all their earthly possessions. And truly, if this consequence were necessarily incident to marriage, I think that the apprehension would be very well founded. I agree in thinking it probable that few women, capable of anything else, would, unless under an irresistible *entrainement,* rendering them for the time insensible to anything but itself, choose such a lot, when any other means were open to them of filling a conventionally honourable place in life: and if men are determined that the law of marriage shall be a law of despotism, they are quite right, in point of mere policy, in leaving to women only Hobson's choice. But, in that case, all that has been done in the modern world to relax the chain on the minds of women, has been a mistake. They never should have been allowed to receive a literary education. Women who read, much more women who write, are, in the existing constitution of things, a contradiction and a disturbing element: and it was wrong to bring women up with any acquirements but those of an odalisque, or of a domestic servant.

Sex Roles: The Argument from Nature

Joyce Trebilcot[1]

I am concerned here with the normative question of whether, in an ideal society, certain roles should be assigned to females and others to males. In discussions of this issue, a great deal of attention is given to the claim that there are natural psychological differences between the sexes. Those who hold that at least some roles should be sex roles generally base their view primarily on an appeal to such natural differences, while many of those advocating a society without sex roles argue either that the sexes do not differ in innate psychological traits or that there is no evidence that they do.[2] In this paper I argue that whether there are natural psychological differences between females and males has little bearing on the issue of whether society should reserve certain roles for females and others for males.

Let me begin by saying something about the claim that there are natural psychological differences between the sexes. The issue we are dealing with arises, of course, because there are biological differences among human beings which are bases for designating some as females and others as males. Now it is held by some that, in addition to biological differences between the sexes, there are also natural differences in temperament, interests, abilities, and the like. In this paper I am concerned only with arguments which appeal to these psychological differences as bases of sex roles. Thus I exclude, for example, arguments that the role of jockey should be female because women are smaller than men or that boxers should be male because men are more muscular than women. Nor do I discuss arguments which appeal directly to the reproductive functions peculiar to each sex. If the physiological processes of gestation or of depositing sperm in a

---

[1]The first version of this paper was written in 1973 and read at the meeting of the American Philosophical Association, Western Division, April 1974. I have learned and changed a great deal since then; and what I write now would not appear under the rubric "liberal feminism."—J. T., 1983.

[2]For support of sex roles, see, for example, Aristotle, *Politics,* Book I . . . ; and Erik Erikson, "Womanhood and the Inner Space," *Identity: Youth and Crisis* (New York, W. W. Norton & Co., 1968). Arguments against sex roles may be found, for example, in J. S. Mill, *The Subjection of Women* . . . (reprinted in this volume).

vagina are, apart from any psychological correlates they may have, bases for sex roles, these roles are outside the scope of the present discussion.

It should be noted, however, that virtually all those who hold that there are natural psychological differences between the sexes assume that these differences are determined primarily by differences in biology. . . . But here we are concerned not with the etiology of allegedly natural differences between the sexes but rather with the question of whether such differences, if they exist, are grounds for holding that there should be sex roles.

That a certain psychological disposition is natural only to one sex is generally taken to mean in part that members of that sex are more likely to have the disposition, or to have it to a greater degree, than persons of the other sex. The situation is thought to be similar to that of height. In a given population, females are on the average shorter than males, but some females are taller than some males, as suggested by Figure 1. The shortest members of the population are all females, and the tallest are all males, but there is an area of overlap. For psychological traits, it is usually assumed that there is some degree of overlap and that the degree of overlap is different for different characteristics. Because of the difficulty of identifying natural psychological characteristics, we have of course little or no data as to the actual distribution of such traits.

I shall not undertake here to define the concept of role, but examples include voter, librarian, wife, president. A broad concept of role might also comprise, for example, being a joker, a person who walks gracefully, a compassionate person. The genders, femininity and masculinity, may also be conceived as roles. On this view, each of the gender roles includes a number of more specific sex roles, some of which may be essential to it. For example, the concept of femininity may be construed in such a way that it is necessary to raise a child in order to be fully feminine, while other feminine roles—teacher, nurse, charity worker—are not essential to gender. In the arguments discussed below, the focus is on sex roles rather than genders, but, on the assumption that the genders are roles, much of what is said applies, *mutatis mutandis,* to them.

A sex role is a role performed only or primarily by persons of a particular sex. Now if this is all we mean by "sex role," the problem of whether there should be sex roles must be dealt with as two separate issues: "Are sex roles a good thing?" and "Should society enforce sex roles?" One might argue, for example, that sex roles have value but that, even so, the demands of individual autonomy and freedom are such that societal institutions and practices should not enforce

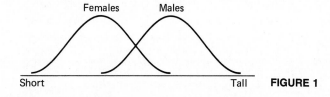

Females   Males

Short   Tall   **FIGURE 1** correlations between roles and sex. But the debate over sex roles is of course mainly a discussion about the second question, whether society should enforce these correlations. The judgment that there should be sex roles is generally taken to mean not just that sex-exclusive roles are a good thing, but that society should promote such exclusivity.

In view of this, I use the term "sex role" in such a way that to ask whether there should be sex roles is to ask whether society should direct women into certain roles and away from others, and similarly for men. A role is a sex role then (or perhaps an "institutionalized sex role") only if it is performed exclusively or primarily by persons of a particular sex *and* societal factors tend to encourage this correlation. These factors may be of various kinds. Parents guide children into what are taken to be sex-appropriate roles. Schools direct students into occupations according to sex. Marriage customs prescribe different roles for females and males. Employers and unions may refuse to consider applications from persons of the "wrong" sex. The media carry tales of the happiness of those who conform and the suffering of the others. The law sometimes penalizes deviators, individuals may ridicule and condemn role crossing and smile on conformity. Societal sanctions such as these are essential to the notion of sex role employed here.

I turn now to a discussion of the three major ways the claim that there are natural psychological differences between the sexes is held to be relevant to the issue of whether there should be sex roles.

1 INEVITABILITY

It is sometimes held that if there are innate psychological differences between females and males, sex roles are inevitable. The point of this argument is not, of course, to urge that there should be sex roles, but rather to show that the normative question is out of place, that there will be sex roles, whatever we decide. The argument assumes first that the alleged natural differences between the sexes are inevitable; but if such differences are inevitable, differences in behavior are inevitable; and if differences in behavior are inevitable, society will inevitably be structured so as to enforce role differences according to sex. Thus, sex roles are inevitable.

For the purpose of this discussion, let us accept the claim that natural psychological differences are inevitable. We assume that there are such differences and ignore the possibility of their being altered, for example, by evolutionary change or direct biological intervention. Let us also accept the second claim, that behavioral differences are inevitable. Behavioral differences could perhaps be eliminated even given the assumption of natural differences in disposition (for example, those with no natural inclination to a certain kind of behavior might nevertheless learn it), but let us waive this point. We assume then that behavioral differences, and hence also role differences, between the sexes are inevitable. Does it follow that there must be sex roles, that is, that the institutions and practices of society must enforce correlations between roles and sex?

Surely not. Indeed, such sanctions would be pointless. Why bother to direct women into some roles and men into others if the pattern occurs regardless of the nature of society? Mill makes the point elegantly in *The Subjection of Women:* "The anxiety of mankind to interfere in behalf of nature, for fear lest nature should not succeed in effecting its purpose, is an altogether unnecessary solicitude."

It may be objected that if correlations between sex and roles are inevitable, societal sanctions enforcing these correlations will develop because people will expect the sexes to perform different roles and these expectations will lead to behavior which encourages their fulfillment. This can happen, of course, but it is surely not inevitable. One need not act so as to bring about what one expects.

Indeed, there could be a society in which it is held that there are inevitable correlations between roles and sex but institutionalization of these correlations is deliberately avoided. What is inevitable is presumably not, for example, that every woman will perform a certain role and no man will perform it, but rather that most women will perform the role and most men will not. For any individual, then, a particular role may not be inevitable. Now suppose it is a value in the society in question that people should be free to choose roles according to their individual needs and interests. But then there should not be sanctions enforcing correlation between roles and sex, for such sanctions tend to force some individuals into roles for which they have no natural inclination and which they might otherwise choose against.

I conclude then that, even granting the assumptions that natural psychological differences, and therefore role differences, between the sexes are inevitable, it does not follow that there must be sanctions enforcing correlations between roles and sex. Indeed, if individual freedom is valued, those who vary from the statistical norm should not be required to conform to it.

2 WELL-BEING

The argument from well-being begins with the claim that, because of natural psychological differences between the sexes, members of each sex are happier in certain roles than in others, and the roles which tend to promote happiness are different for each sex. It is also held that if all roles are equally available to everyone regardless of sex, some individuals will choose against their own well-being. Hence, the argument concludes, for the sake of maximizing well-being there should be sex roles: society should encourage individuals to make "correct" role choices.

Suppose that women, on the average, are more compassionate than men. Suppose also that there are two sets of roles, "female" and "male," and that because of the natural compassion of women, women are happier in female than in male roles. Now if females and males overlap with respect to compassion, some men have as much natural compassion as some women, so they too will be happier in female than in male roles. Thus, the first premise of the argument from well-being should read: Suppose that, because of natural psychological differences between the sexes, *most* women are happier in female roles and *most* men in male roles. The argument continues: If all roles are equally available to everyone, some of the women who would be happier in female roles will choose against their own well-being, and similarly for men.

Now if the conclusion that there should be sex roles is to be based on these premises, another assumption must be added—that the loss of the potential well-being resulting from societally produced adoption of unsuitable roles by individuals in the overlapping areas of the distribution is *less* than the loss that would result from "mistaken" free choices if there were no sex roles. With sex roles, some individuals who would be happier in roles assigned to the other sex perform roles assigned to their own sex, and so there is a loss of potential happiness. Without sex roles, some individuals, we assume, choose against their own well-being. But surely we are not now in a position to compare the two systems with respect to the number of mismatches produced. Hence, the additional premise required for the argument, that overall well-being is greater with sex roles than without them, is entirely unsupported.

Even if we grant, then, that because of innate psychological differences between the sexes members of each sex achieve greater well-being in some roles than in others, the argument from well-being does not support the conclusion that there should be sex roles. In our present state of knowledge, there is no reason to suppose that a sex role system which makes no discriminations within a sex would produce fewer mismatches between individuals and roles than a system in which all roles are open equally to both sexes.

3 EFFICIENCY

If there are natural differences between the sexes in the capacity to perform socially valuable tasks, then, it is sometimes argued, efficiency is served if these tasks are assigned to the sex with the greatest innate ability for them. Suppose, for example, that females are naturally better than males at learning foreign languages. This means that, if everything else is equal and females and males are given the same training in a foreign language, females, on the average, will achieve a higher level of skill than males. Now suppose that society needs interpreters and translators and that in order to have such a job one must complete a special training program whose only purpose is to provide persons for these roles. Clearly, efficiency is served if only individuals with a good deal of natural ability are selected for training, for the time and effort required to bring them to a given level of proficiency is less than that required for the less talented. But suppose that the innate ability in question is normally distributed within each sex and that the sexes overlap (see Figure 2). If we assume that a sufficient number of candidates can be recruited by considering only persons in the shaded

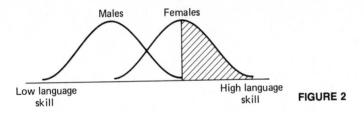

FIGURE 2

area, they are the only ones who should be eligible. There are no men in this group. Hence, although screening is necessary in order to exclude nontalented women, it would be inefficient even to consider men, for it is known that no man is as talented as the talented women. In the interest of efficiency, then, the occupational roles of interpreter and translator should be sex roles; men should be denied access to these roles, but women who are interested in them, especially talented women, should be encouraged to pursue them.

This argument is sound. That is, if we grant the factual assumptions and suppose also that efficiency for the society we are concerned with has some value, the argument from efficiency provides one reason for holding that some roles should be sex roles. This conclusion of course is only *prima facie*. In order to determine whether there should be sex roles, one would have to weigh efficiency, together with other reasons for such roles, against reasons for holding that there should not be sex roles. The reasons against sex roles are very strong. They are couched in terms of individual rights—in terms of liberty, justice, equality of opportunity. Efficiency by itself does not outweigh these moral values. Nevertheless, the appeal to nature, if true, combined with an appeal to the value of efficiency, does provide one reason for the view that there should be sex roles.

The arguments I have discussed here are not the only ones which appeal to natural psychological differences between the sexes in defense of sex roles, but these three arguments—from inevitability, well-being, and efficiency—are, I believe, the most common and the most plausible ones. The argument from efficiency alone, among them, provides a reason—albeit a rather weak reason—for thinking that there should be sex roles. I suggest, therefore, that the issue of natural psychological differences between women and men does not deserve the central place it is given, both traditionally and currently, in the literature on this topic.

It is frequently pointed out that the argument from nature functions as a cover, as a myth to make patriarchy palatable to both women and men. Insofar as this is so, it is surely worthwhile exploring and exposing the myth. But of course most of those who use the argument from nature take it seriously and literally, and this is the spirit in which I have dealt with it. Considering the argument in this way, I conclude that whether there should be sex roles does not depend primarily on whether there are innate psychological differences between the sexes. The question is, after all, not what women and men naturally are, but what kind of society is morally justifiable. In order to answer this question, we must appeal to the notions of justice, equality, and liberty. It is these moral concepts, not the empirical issue of sex differences, which should have pride of place in the philosophical discussion of sex roles.

Bill of Rights

National Organization for Women (NOW)

I   Equal Rights Constitutional Amendment
II   Enforce Law Banning Sex Discrimination in Employment
III   Maternity Leave Rights in Employment and in Social Security Benefts
IV   Tax Deduction for Home and Child Care Expenses for Working Parents
V   Child Care Centers
VI   Equal and Unsegregated Education
VII   Equal Job Training Opportunities and Allowances for Women in Poverty
VIII   The Right of Women to Control Their Reproductive Lives

WE DEMAND

Exception

I That the United States Congress immediately pass the Equal Rights Amendment to the Constitution to provide that "Equality of rights under the law shall not be denied or abridged by the United States or by any State on account of sex," and that such then be immediately ratified by the several States.

II That equal employment opportunity be guaranteed to all women, as well as men, by insisting that the Equal Employment Opportunity Commission enforces the prohibitions against sex discrimination in employment under Title VII of the Civil Rights Act of 1964 with the same vigor as it enforces the prohibitions against racial discrimination.

III That women be protected by law to ensure their rights to return to their jobs within a reasonable time after childbirth without loss of seniority or other accrued benefits, and be paid maternity leave as a form of social security and/or employee benefit.

IV Immediate revision of tax laws to permit the deduction of home and child care expenses for working parents.

V That child care facilities be established by law on the same basis as parks, libraries, and public schools, adequate to the needs of children from the pre-school years through adolescence, as a community resource to be used by all citizens from all income levels.

VI That the right of women to be educated to their full potential equally with men be secured by Federal and State Legislation, eliminating all discrimination and segregation by sex, written and unwritten, at all levels of education, including colleges, graduate and professional schools, loans and fellowships, and Federal and State training programs such as the Job Corps.

VII The right of women in poverty to secure job training, housing, and family allowances on equal terms with men, but without prejudice to a parent's right to remain at home to care for his or her children; revision of welfare legislation and poverty programs which deny women dignity, privacy and self-respect.

VIII The right of women to control their own reproductive lives by removing from penal codes laws limiting access to contraceptive information and devices and laws governing abortion.

TRADITIONAL MARXISM:
Women's Oppression
as a Result of the Class System

The Origin of the Family, Private Property, and the State

Friedrich Engels

. . . According to the materialistic conception, the determining factor in history is, in the final instance, the production and reproduction of immediate life. This, again, is of a twofold character: on the one side, the production of the means of existence, of food, clothing and shelter and the tools necessary for that production; on the other side, the production of human beings themselves, the propagation of the species. The social organization under which the people of a particular historical epoch and a particular country live is determined by both kinds of production: by the stage of development of labor on the one hand and of the family on the other. The lower the development of labor and the more limited the amount of its products, and consequently, the more limited also the wealth of the society, the more the social order is found to be dominated by kinship groups. However, within this structure of society based on kinship groups the productivity of labor increasingly develops, and with it private property and exchange, differences of wealth, the possibility of utilizing the labor power of others, and hence the basis of class antagonisms: new social elements, which in the course of generations strive to adapt the old social order to the new conditions, until at last their incompatibility brings about a complete upheaval. In the collision of the newly developed social classes, the old society founded on kinship groups is broken up. In its place appears a new society, with its control centered in the state, the subordinate units of which are no longer kinship associations, but local associations; a society in which the system of the family is completely dominated by the system of property, and in which there now freely develop those class antagonisms and class struggles that have hitherto formed the content of all *written* history. . . .

Morgan was the first person with expert knowledge to attempt to introduce a definite order into the history of primitive man; so long as no important additional material makes changes necessary, his classification will undoubtedly remain in force.

Of the three main epochs—savagery, barbarism, and civilization—he is concerned, of course, only with the first and the transition to the third. . . .

Reconstructing thus the past history of the family, Morgan, in agreement with most of his colleagues, arrives at a primitive stage when unrestricted sexual freedom prevailed within the tribe, every woman belonging equally to every man and every man to every woman. . . .

According to Morgan, from this primitive state of primiscuous intercourse there developed, probably very early:

1 THE CONSANGUINE FAMILY, THE FIRST STAGE OF THE FAMILY

Here the marriage groups are separated according to generations: all the grandfathers and grandmothers within the limits of the family are all husbands and wives of one another; so are also their children, the fathers and mothers; the latter's children will form a third circle of common husbands and wives; and their children, the great-grandchildren of the first group, will form a fourth. In this form of marriage, therefore, only ancestors and progeny, and parents and children, are excluded from the rights and duties (as we would say) of marriage with one another. Brothers and sisters, male and female cousins of the first, second, and more remote degrees, are all brothers and sisters of one another, and *precisely for that reason* they are all husbands and wives of one another. At this stage the relationship of brother and sister also includes as a matter of course the practice of sexual intercourse with one another. In its typical form, such a family would consist of the descendants of a single pair, the descendants of these descendants in each generation being again brothers and sisters, and therefore husbands and wives, of one another. . . .

2 THE PUNALUAN FAMILY

If the first advance in organization consisted in the exclusion of parents and children from sexual intercourse with one another, the second was the exclusion of sister and brother. On account of the greater nearness of age, this second advance was infinitely more important, but also more difficult, than the first. It was effected gradually, beginning probably with the exclusion from sexual intercourse of one's own brothers and sisters (children of the same mother) first in isolated cases and then by degrees as a general rule (even in this century exceptions were found in Hawaii), and ending with the prohibition of marriage even between collateral brothers and sisters, or, as we should say, between first, second, and third cousins. It affords, says Morgan, "a good illustration of the operation of the principle of natural selection." There can be no question that the tribes among whom inbreeding was restricted by this advance were bound to develop more quickly and more fully than those among whom marriage between brothers and sisters remained the rule and the law. How powerfully the influence of this advance made itself felt is seen in the institution which arose directly out of it and went far beyond it—the gens, which forms the basis of the social order of most, if not all, barbarian peoples of the earth and from which in Greece and Rome we step directly into civilization.

After a few generations at most, every original family was bound to split up. The practice of living together in a primitive communistic household which prevailed without exception till late in the middle stage of barbarism set a limit, varying with the conditions but fairly definite in each locality, to the maximum size of the family community. As soon as the conception arose that sexual intercourse between children of the same mother was wrong, it was bound to exert its influence when the old households split up and new ones were founded (though these did not necessarily coincide with the family group). One or more lines of sisters would form the nucleus of the one household and their own brothers the nucleus of the other. It must have been in some such manner as this that the form which Morgan calls the punaluan family originated out of the consanguine family. According to the Hawaiian custom, a number of sisters, natural or collateral (first, second or more remote cousins) were the common wives of their common husbands, from among whom, however, their own brothers were excluded. These husbands now no longer called themselves brothers, for they were no longer necessarily brothers, but punalua—that is, intimate companion, or partner. Similarly, a line of natural or collateral brothers had a number of women, *not* their sisters, as common wives, and these wives called one another *punalua*. This was the classic form of family structure [*Familienformation*] in which later a number of variations was possible, but whose essential feature was the mutually common possession of husbands and wives within a definite family circle, from which, however, the brothers of the wives—first one's own and later also collateral—and conversely also the sisters of the husbands, were excluded. . . .

In all forms of group family, it is uncertain who is the father of a child; but it is certain who its mother is. Though she calls *all* the children of the whole family her children and has a mother's duties toward them, she nevertheless knows her own children from the others. It is therefore clear that in so far as group marriage prevails, descent can only be proved on the *mother's* side and that therefore only the *female* line is recognized. And this is in fact the case among all peoples in the period of savagery or in the lower stage of barbarism. . . .

3 THE PAIRING FAMILY

A certain amount of pairing, for a longer or shorter period, already occurred in group marriage or even earlier; the man had a chief wife among his many wives (one can hardly yet speak of a favorite wife), and for her he was the most important among her husbands. This fact has contributed considerably to the confusion of the missionaries, who have regarded group marriage sometimes as promiscuous community of wives, sometimes as unbridled adultery. But these customary pairings were bound to grow more stable as the gens developed and the classes of "brothers" and "sisters" between whom marriage was impossible became more numerous. The impulse given by the gens to the prevention of marriage between blood relatives extended still further. Thus among the Iroquois and most of the other Indians at the lower stage of barbarism, we find that marriage is prohibited between *all* relatives enumerated in their system—which includes several hundred degrees of kinship. The increasing complication of these prohibitions made group marriages more and more impossible; they were displaced by the *pairing family*. In this stage, one man lives with one woman, but the relationship is such that polygamy and occasional infidelity remain the right of the men, even though for economic reasons polygamy is rare, while from the woman the strictest fidelity is generally demanded throughout the time she lives with the man and adultery on her part is cruelly punished. The marriage tie can, however, be easily dissolved by either partner; after separation, the children still belong as before to the mother alone. . . .

Thus the history of the family in primitive times consists in the progressive narrowing of the circle, originally embracing the whole tribe, within which the two sexes have a common conjugal relation. The continuous exclusion, first of nearer, then of more and more remote relatives, and at last even of relatives by marriage, ends by making any kind of group marriage practically impossible. Finally, there remains only the single, still loosely linked pair, the molecule with whose dissolution marriage itself ceases. This in itself shows what a small part individual sex love, in the modern sense of the word, played in the rise of monogamy. Yet stronger proof is afforded by the practice of all peoples at this stage of development. Whereas in the earlier forms of the family, men never lacked women but, on the contrary, had too many rather than too few, women had now become scarce and highly sought after. Hence it is with the pairing marriage that there begins the capture and purchase of women—widespread *symptoms*, but no more than symptoms, of the much deeper change that had occurred. . . .

The pairing family, itself too weak and unstable to make an independent household necessary or even desirable, in no wise destroys the communistic household inherited from earlier times. Communistic housekeeping, however, means the supremacy of women in the house; just as the exclusive recognition of the female parent, owing to the impossibility of recognizing the male parent with certainty, means that the women—the mothers—are held in high respect. One of the most absurd notions taken over from 18th century enlightenment is that in the beginning of society woman was the slave of man. Among all savages and all barbarians of the lower and middle stages, and to a certain extent of the upper stage also, the position of women is not only free, but honorable. As to what it still is in the pairing marriage, let us hear the evidence of Ashur Wright, for many years missionary among the Iroquois Senecas:

> As to their family system, when occupying the old long houses [communistic households comprising several families], it is probable that some one clan [gens] predominated, the women taking in husbands, however, from the other clans [gentes]. . . . Usually, the female portion ruled the house. . . . The stores were in common; but woe to the luckless husband or lover who was too shiftless to do his share of the providing. No matter how many children, or whatever goods he might have in the house, he might at any time be ordered to pick up his blanket and budge; and after such orders it would not be healthful for him to attempt to disobey. The house would be too hot for him; and . . . he must retreat to his own clan [gens]; or, as was often done, go and start a new matrimonial alliance in some other. The women were the great power among the clans [gentes], as everywhere else. They did not hesitate, when occasion required, "to knock off the horns," as it was technically called, from the head of a chief, and send him back to the ranks of the warriors [Morgan, 1963: 464 *fn*].

The communistic household, in which most or all of the women belong to one and the same gens, while the men come from various gentes, is the material foundation of that supremacy of the women which was general in primitive times, and which it is Bachofen's third great merit to have discovered. The reports of travelers and missionaries, I may add, to the effect that women among savages and barbarians are overburdened with work in no way contradict what has been said. The division of labor between the two sexes is determined by quite other causes than by the position of women in society. Among peoples where the women have to work far harder than we think suitable, there is often much more real respect for women than among our Europeans. The lady of civilization, surrounded by false homage and estranged from all real work, has an infinitely lower social position than the hard-working woman of barbarism, who was regarded among her people as a real lady (lady, *frowa, Frau*—mistress) and who was also a lady in character. . . .

The first beginnings of the pairing family appear on the dividing line between savagery and barbarism; they are generally to be found already at the upper stage of savagery, but occasionally not until the lower stage of barbarism. The pairing family is the form characteristic of barbarism, as group marriage is characteristic of savagery and monogamy of civilization. To develop it further, to strict monogamy, other causes were required than those we have found active hitherto. In the single pair the group was already reduced to its final unit, its two-atom molecule: one man and one woman. Natural selection, with its progressive exclusions from the marriage community, had accomplished its task;

there was nothing more for it to do in this direction. Unless new, *social* forces came into play, there was no reason why a new form of family should arise from the single pair. But these new forces did come into play.

We now leave America, the classic soil of the pairing family. No sign allows us to conclude that a higher form of family developed here or that there was ever permanent monogamy anywhere in America prior to its discovery and conquest. But not so in the Old World.

Here the domestication of animals and the breeding of herds had developed a hitherto unsuspected source of wealth and created entirely new social relations. Up to the lower stage of barbarism, permanent wealth had consisted almost solely of house, clothing, crude ornaments and the tools for obtaining and preparing food—boat, weapons, and domestic utensils of the simplest kind. Food had to be won afresh day by day. Now, with their herds of horses, camels, asses, cattle, sheep, goats, and pigs, the advancing pastoral peoples—the Semites on the Euphrates and the Tigris, and the Aryans in the Indian country of the Five Streams (Punjab), in the Ganges region, and in the steppes then much more abundantly watered by the Oxus and the Jaxartes—had acquired property which only needed supervision and the rudest care to reproduce itself in steadily increasing quantities and to supply the most abundant food in the form of milk and meat. All former means of procuring food now receded into the background; hunting, formerly a necessity, now became a luxury.

But to whom did this new wealth belong? Originally to the gens, without a doubt. Private property in herds must have already started at an early period, however. Is it difficult to say whether the auther of the so-called first book of Moses regarded the patriarch Abraham as the owner of his herds in his own right as head of a family community or by right of his position as actual hereditary head of a gens. What is certain is that we must not think of him as a property owner in the modern sense of the word. And it is also certain that at the threshold of authentic history we already find the herds everywhere separately owned by heads of families, as are the artistic products of barbarism (metal implements, luxury articles and, finally, the human cattle—the slaves).

For now slavery had also been invented. To the barbarian of the lower stage, a slave was valueless. Hence the treatment of defected enemies by the American Indians was quite different from that at a higher stage. The men were killed or adopted as brothers into the tribe of the victors; the women were taken as wives or otherwise adopted with their surviving children. At this stage human labor power still does not produce any considerable surplus over and above its maintenance costs. That was no longer the case after the introduction of cattle breeding, metalworking, weaving and, lastly, agriculture. Just as the wives whom it had formerly been so easy to obtain had now acquired an exchange value and were bought, so also with labor power, particularly since the herds had definitely become family possessions. The family did not multiply so rapidly as the cattle. More people were needed to look after them; for this purpose use could be made of the enemies captured in war, who could also be bred just as easily as the cattle themselves.

Once it had passed into the private possession of families and there rapidly begun to augment, this wealth dealt a severe blow to the society founded on pairing marriage and the matriarchal gens. Pairing marriage had brought a new element into the family. By the side of the natural mother of the child it placed its natural and attested father with a better warrant of paternity, probably, than that of many a "father" today. According to the division of labor within the family at that time, it was the man's part to obtain food and the instruments of labor necessary for the purpose. He therefore also owned the instruments of labor, and in the event of husband and wife separating, he took them with him, just as she retained her household goods. Therefore, according to the social custom of the time, the man was also the owner of the new source of subsistence, the cattle, and later of the new instruments of labor, the slaves. But according to the custom of the same society, his children could not inherit from him. For as regards inheritance, the position was as follows:

At first, according to mother right—so long, therefore, as descent was reckoned only in the female line—and according to the original custom of inheritance within the gens, the gentile relatives inherited from a deceased fellow member of their gens. His property had to remain within the gens. His effects being insignificant, they probably always passed in practice to his nearest gentile relations—that is, to his blood relations on the mother's side. The children of the dead man, however, did not belong to his gens, but to that of their mother; it was from her that they inherited, at first conjointly with her other blood-relations, later perhaps with rights of priority; they could not inherit from their father because they did not belong to his gens within which his property had to remain. When the owner of the herds died, therefore, his herds would go first to his brothers and sisters and to his sister's children, or to the issue of his mother's sisters. But his own children were disinherited.

Thus on the one hand, in proportion as wealth increased it made the man's position in the family more important than the woman's, and on the other hand created an impulse to exploit this strengthened position in order to overthrow, in favor of his children, the traditional order of inheritance. This, however, was impossible so long as descent was reckoned according to mother right. Mother right, therefore, had to be overthrown, and overthrown it was. This was by no means so difficult as it looks to us today. For this revolution—one of the most decisive ever experienced by humanity—could take place without disturbing a single one of the living members of a gens. All could remain as they were. A simple decree sufficed that in the future the offspring of the male members should remain within the gens, but that of the female should be excluded by being transferred to the gens of their father. The reckoning of descent in the female line and the matriarchal law of inheritance were thereby overthrown, and the male line of descent and the paternal law of inheritance were substituted for them. As to how and when this revolution took place among civilized peoples, we have no knowledge. It falls entirely within prehistoric times. But that it *did* take place is more than sufficiently proved by the abundant traces of mother right which have been collected. . . .

The overthrow of mother right was the *world historical defeat of the female sex.* The man took command in the home also; the woman was degraded and reduced to servitude; she became the slave of his lust and a mere instrument for the production of children. This degraded position of the woman, especially conspicuous among the Greeks of the heroic and still more of the classical age, has gradually been palliated and glossed over, and sometimes clothed in a milder form; in no sense has it been abolished.

The establishment of the exclusive supremacy of the man shows its effects first in the patriarchal family, which now emerges as an intermediate form. Its essential characteristic is not polygyny, of which more later, but "the organization of a number of persons, bond and free, into a family under paternal power for the purpose of holding lands and for the care of flocks and herds. . . . (In the Semitic form) the chiefs, at least, lived in polygamy. . . . Those held to servitude and those employed as servants lived in the marriage relation" [Morgan, 1963: 474].

Its essential features are the incorporation of unfree persons and paternal power; hence the perfect type of this form of family is the Roman. The original meaning of the word "family" (*familia*) is not that compound of sentimentality and domestic strife which forms the ideal of the present-day philistine; among the Romans it did not at first even refer to the married pair and their children but only to the slaves. *Famulus* means domestic slave, and *familia* is the total number of slaves belonging to one man. As late as the time of Gaius, the *familia, id est patrimonium* (family, that is, the patrimony, the inheritance) was bequeathed by will. The term was invented by the Romans to denote a new social organism whose head ruled over wife and children and a number of slaves, and was invested under Roman paternal power with rights of life and death over them all.

> This term, therefore, is no older than the ironclad family system of the Latin tribes, which came in after field agriculture and after legalized servitude, as well as after the separation of the Greeks and Latins [Morgan, 1963: 478].

Marx adds:

> The modern family contains in germ not only slavery (*servitus*) but also serfdom, since from the beginning it is related to agricultural services. It contains *in miniature* all the contradictions which later extend throughout society and its state.

Such a form of family shows the transition of the pairing family to monogamy. In order to make certain of the wife's fidelity and therefore of the paternity of the children, she is delivered over unconditionally into the power of the husband; if he kills her, he is only exercising his rights. . . .

4 THE MONOGAMOUS FAMILY

It develops out of the pairing family, as previously shown, in the transitional period between the upper and middle stages of barbarism; its decisive victory is one of the signs that civilization is beginning. It is based on the supremacy of the man, the express purpose being to produce children of undisputed paternity; such paternity is demanded because these children are later to come into their father's property as his natural heirs. It is distinguished from pairing marriage by the much greater strength of the marriage tie, which can no longer be dissolved at either partner's wish. As a rule, it is now only the man who can dissolve it and put away his wife. The right of conjugal infidelity also remains secured in him, at any rate by custom (the *Code Napoléon* explicitly accords it to the husband as long as he does not bring his concubine into the house), and as social life develops he exercises his right more and more; should the wife recall the old form of sexual life and attempt to revive it, she is punished more severely than ever.

. . . It is the existence of slavery side by side with monogamy, the presence of young, beautiful slaves belonging unreservedly to the *man,* that stamps monogamy from the very beginning with its specific character of monogamy *for the woman only,* but not for the man. And that is the character it still has today. . . .

This is the origin of monogamy as far as we can trace it back among the most civilized and highly developed people of antiquity. It was not in any way the fruit of individual sex love, with which it had nothing whatever to do; marriages remained as before marriages of convenience. It was the first form of the family to be based not on natural but on economic conditions—on the victory of private property over primitive, natural communal property. The Greeks themselves put the matter quite frankly; the sole exclusive aims of monogamous marriage were to make the man supreme in the family and to propagate, as the future heirs to his wealth, children indisputably his own. Otherwise, marriage was a burden, a duty which had to be performed whether one liked it or not to gods, state, and one's ancestors. In Athens the law exacted from the man not only marriage but also the performance of a minimum of so-called conjugal duties.

Thus when monogamous marriage first makes its appearance in history, it is not as the reconciliation of man and woman, still less as the highest form of such a reconciliation. Quite the contrary monogamous marriage comes on the scene as the subjugation of the one sex by the other; it announces a struggle between the sexes unknown throughout the whole previous prehistoric period. In an old unpublished manuscript written by Marx and myself in 1846, I find the words: "The first division of labor is that between man and woman for the propagation of children." And today I can add: The first class opposition that appears in history coincides with the development of the antagonism between man and woman in monogamous marriage, and the first class oppression coincides with that of the female sex by the male. Monogamous marriage was a great historical step forward; nevertheless, together with slavery and private wealth, it opens the period that has lasted until today in which every step forward is also relatively a step backward, in which prosperity and development for some is won through the misery and frustration of others. It is the cellular form of civilized society in which the nature of the oppositions and contradictions fully active in that society can be already studied. . . .

. . . With the rise of the inequality of property—already at the upper stage of barbarism, therefore—wage labor appears sporadically side by side with slave labor, and at the same time, as its necessary correlate, the professional prostitution of free women side by side with the forced surrender of the slave. Thus the heritage which group marriage has bequeathed to civilization is double-edged, just as everything civilization brings forth is double-edged, double-tongued, divided against itself, contradictory: here monogamy, there hetaerism with its most extreme form, prostitution. For hetaerism is as much a social institution as any other; it continues the old sexual freedom—to the advantage of the men. Actually, not merely tolerated but gaily practiced by the ruling classes particularly, it is condemned in words. But in reality this condemnation never falls on the men concerned, but only on the women; they are despised and outcast in order that the unconditional supremacy of men over the female sex may be once more proclaimed as a fundamental law of society. . . .

Thus, wherever the monogamous family remains true to its historical origin and clearly reveals the antagonism between the man and the woman expressed in the man's exclusive supremacy, it exhibits in miniature the same oppositions and contradictions as those in which society has been moving, without power to resolve or overcome them, ever since it split into classes at the beginning of civilization. . . .

Our jurists, of course, find that progress in legislation is leaving women with no further ground of complaint. Modern civilized systems of law increasingly acknowledge first, that for a marriage to be legal it must be a contract freely entered into by both partners and secondly, that also in the married state both partners must stand on a common footing of equal rights and duties. If both these demands are consistently carried out, say the jurists, women have all they can ask.

This typically legalist method of argument is exactly the same as that which the radical republican bourgeois uses to put the proletarian in his place. The labor contract is to be freely entered into by both partners. But it is considered to have been freely entered into as soon as the law makes both parties equal on *paper*. The power conferred on the one party by the difference of class position, the pressure thereby brought to bear on the other party—the real economic position of both—that is not the law's business. Again, for the duration of the labor contract, both parties are to have equal rights in so far as one or the other does not expressly surrender them. That economic relations compel the worker to surrender even the last semblance of equal rights—here again, that is no concern of the law.

In regard to marriage, the law, even the most advanced, is fully satisfied as soon as the partners have formally recorded that they are entering into the marriage of their own free consent. What goes on in real life behind the juridical scenes, how this free consent comes about—that is not the business of the law and the jurist. And yet the most elementary comparative jurisprudence should show the jurist what this free consent really amounts to. In the countries where an obligatory share of the paternal inheritance is secured to the children by law and they cannot therefore be disinherited—in Germany, in the countries with French law and elsewhere—the children are obliged to obtain their parents' consent to their marriage. In the countries with English law, where parental consent to a marriage is not legally required, the parents on their side have full freedom in the testamentary disposal of their property and can disinherit their children at their pleasure. It is obvious that in spite and precisely because of this fact freedom of marriage among the classes with something to inherit is in reality not a whit greater in England and America than it is in France and Germany.

As regards the legal equality of husband and wife in marriage, the position is no better. The legal inequality of the two partners bequeathed to us from earlier social conditions is not the cause but the effect of the economic oppression of the woman. In the old communistic household, which comprised many couples and their children, the task entrusted to the women of managing the household was as much a public, a socially necessary industry as the procuring of food by the men. With the patriarchal family and still more with the single monogamous family, a change came. Household management lost its public character. It no longer concerned society. It became a *private service;* the wife became the head servant, excluded from all participation in social production. Not until the coming of modern large-scale industry was the road to social production opened to her again—and then only to the proletarian wife. But it was opened in such a manner that, if she carries out her duties in the private service of her family, she remains excluded from public production and unable to earn; and if she wants to take part in public production and earn independently, she cannot carry out family duties. And the wife's position in the factory is the position of women in all branches of business, right up to medicine and the law. The modern individual family is founded on the open or concealed domestic slavery of the wife, and modern society is a mass composed of these individual families as its molecules.

In the great majority of cases today, at least in the possessing classes, the husband is obliged to earn a living and support his family, and that in itself gives him a position of supremacy without any need for special legal titles and privileges. Within the family he is the bourgeois, and the wife represents the proletariat. In the industrial world, the specific character of the economic oppression burdening the proletariat is visible in all its sharpness only when all special legal privileges of the capitalist class have been abolished and complete legal equality of both classes established. The democratic republic does not do away with the oppression of the two classes; on the contrary, it provides the clear field on which the fight can be fought out. And in the same way, the peculiar character of the supremacy of the husband over the wife in the modern famliy, the necessity of creating real social equality between them and the way to do it, will only be seen in the clear light of day when both possess legally complete equality of rights. Then it will be plain that the first condition for the liberation of the wife is to bring the whole female sex back into public industry, and that this in turn demands that the characteristic of the monogamous family as the economic unit of society be abolished.

Women:
Caste, Class, or Oppressed Sex?

Evelyn Reed

The new stage in the struggle for women's liberation already stands on a higher ideological level than did the feminist movement of the last century. Many of the participants today respect the Marxist analysis of capitalism and subscribe to Engels's classic explanation of the origins of women's oppression. It came about through the development of class society, founded upon the family, private property, and the state.

But there still remain considerable misunderstandings and misinterpretations of Marxist positions, which have led some women who consider themselves radicals or socialists to go off course and become theoretically disoriented. Influenced by the myth that women have always been handicapped by their childbearing functions, they tend to attribute the roots of women's oppression, at least in part, to biological sexual differences. In actuality its causes are exclusively historical and social in character.

Some of these theorists maintain that women constitute a special class or caste. Such definitions are not only alien to the views of Marxism but lead to the false conclusion that it is not the capitalist system but men who are the prime enemy of women. I propose to challenge this contention.

The findings of the Marxist method, which have laid the groundwork for explaining the genesis of women's degradation, can be summed up in the following propositions:

First, women were not always the oppressed or "second" sex. Anthropology, or the study of prehistory, tells us the contrary. Throughout primitive society, which was the epoch of tribal collectivism, women were the equals of men and recognized by man as such.

Second, the downfall of women coincided with the breakup of the matriarchal clan commune and its replacement by class-divided society with its institutions of the patriarchal family, private property and state power.

The key factors which brought about this reversal in woman's social status came out of the transition from a hunting and food-gathering economy to a far higher mode of production based upon agriculture, stock raising and urban crafts. The primitive division of labor between the sexes was replaced by a more complex social division of labor. The greater efficiency of labor gave rise to a sizable surplus product, which led first to differentiations and then to deepgoing divisions among the various segments of society.

By virtue of the directing roles played by men in large-scale agriculture, irrigation and construction projects, as well as in stock raising, this surplus wealth was gradually appropriated by a hierarchy of men as their private property. This, in turn, required the institution of marriage and the family to fix the legal ownership and inheritance of a man's property. Through monogamous marriage the wife was brought under the complete control of her husband who was thereby assured of legitimate sons to inherit his wealth.

As men took over most of the activities of social production, and with the rise of the family institution, women became relegated to the home to serve their husbands and families. The state apparatus came into existence to fortify and legalize the institutions of private property, male dominion and the father-family, which later were sanctified by religion.

This, briefly, is the Marxist approach to the origins of woman's oppression. Her subordination did not come about through any biological deficiency as a sex. It was the result of the revolutionary social changes which destroyed the equalitarian society of the matriarchal gens or clan and replaced it with a patriarchal class society which, from its birth, was stamped with discriminations and inequalities of many kinds, including the inequality of the sexes. The growth of this inherently oppressive type of socioeconomic organization was responsible for the historic downfall of women.

But the downfall of women cannot be fully understood, nor can a correct social and political solution be worked out for their liberation, without seeing what happened at the same time to men. It is too often overlooked that the patriarchal class system which crushed the matriarchy and its communal social relations also shattered its male counterpart, the fratriarchy—or tribal brotherhood of men. Woman's overthrow went hand in hand with the subjugation of the mass of toiling men to the master class of men. . . .

Speaking in a loose and popular way, it is possible to refer to women as an inferior "caste"—as is sometimes done when they are also called "slaves" or "serfs"—when the intent is merely to indicate that they occupy the subordinate position in male-dominated society. The use of the term "caste" would then only expose the impoverishment of our language, which has no special word to indicate womankind as the oppressed sex. But more than this seems to be involved, if we judge from the paper by Roxanne Dunbar dated February 1970 which supersedes her previous positions on this question.

In that document she says that her characterization of women as an exploited caste is nothing new; that Marx and Engels likewise "analyzed the position of the female sex in just such a way." This is simply not the case. Neither Marx in *Capital,* nor Engels in *The Origin of the Family, Private Property, and the State,* nor in any writings by noted Marxists from Lenin to Luxemburg on this matter, has woman been defined by virtue of her sex as a "caste." Therefore this is not a mere verbal squabble over the misuse of a term. It is a distinct departure from Marxism, although presented in the name of Marxism.

I would like clarification from Roxanne Dunbar on the conclusions she draws from her theory. For, if all women belong to an inferior caste, and all men belong to the superior caste, it would consistently follow that the central axis of a struggle for liberation would be a "caste war" of all women against all men to bring about the liberation of women. This conclusion would seem to be confirmed by her statement that "we live under an international caste system. . . ."

This assertion is equally non-Marxist. What Marxists say is that we live under an international *class* system. And they further state that it will require not a caste war, but a *class struggle*—of all the oppressed, male and female alike—to consummate women's liberation along with the liberation of all the oppressed masses. Does Roxanne Dunbar agree or disagree with this viewpoint on the paramount role of the class struggle?

Her confusion points up the necessity for using precise language in a scientific exposition. However downtrodden women are under capitalism, they are not chattel slaves any more than they are feudal serfs or members of an inferior caste. The social categories of slave, serf and caste refer to stages and features of past history and do not correctly define the position of women in our society.

If we are to be precise and scientific, women should be defined as an "oppressed *sex*."

Turning to the other position, it is even more incorrect to characterize women as a special "class." In Marxist sociology a class is defined in two interrelated ways: by the role it plays in the processes of production and by the stake it has in the ownership of property. Thus the capitalists are the major power in our society because they own the means of production and thereby control the state and direct the economy. The wage workers who create the wealth own nothing but their labor power, which they have to sell to the bosses to stay alive.

Where do women stand in relation to these polar class forces? They belong to all strata of the social pyramid. The few at the top are part of the plutocratic class; more among us belong to the middle class; most of us belong to the proletarian layers of the population. There is an enormous spread from the few wealthy women of the Rockefeller, Morgan and Ford families to the millions of poor women who subsist on welfare dole. *In short, women, like men, are a multiclass sex.*

This is not an attempt to divide women from one another but simply to recognize the actual divisions that exist. The notion that all women as a sex have more in common than do members of the same class with one another is false. Upper-class women are not simply bedmates of their wealthy husbands. As a rule they have more compelling ties which bind them together. They are economic, social and political bedmates, united in defense of private property, profiteering, militarism, racism—and the exploitation of other women.

To be sure, there can be individual exceptions to this rule, especially among young women today. We remember that Mrs. Frank Leslie, for example, left a $2 million bequest to further the cause of women's suffrage, and other upper-class women have devoted their means to secure civil rights for our sex. But it is quite another matter to expect any large number of wealthy women to endorse or support a revolutionary struggle which threatens their capitalist interests and privileges. Most of them scorn the liberation movement, saying openly or implicitly, "What do we need to be liberated from?"

Is it really necessary to stress this point? Tens of thousands of women went to the Washington antiwar demonstrations in November 1969 and again in May 1970. Did they have more in common with the militant men marching beside them on that life-and-death issue—or with Mrs. Nixon, her daughters, and the wife of the attorney general, Mrs. Mitchell, who peered uneasily out of her window and saw the specter of another Russian Revolution in those protesting masses? Will the wives of bankers, generals, corporation lawyers, and big industrialists be firmer allies of women fighting for liberation than working-class men, black and white, who are fighting for theirs? Won't there be both men and women on both sides of the class struggle? If not, is the struggle to be directed against men as a sex rather than against the capitalist system?

It is true that all forms of class society have been male-dominated and that men are trained from the cradle on to be chauvinistic. But it is not true that men as such represent the main enemy of women. This crosses out the multitudes of downtrodden, exploited men who are themselves oppressed by the main enemy of women, which is the capitalist system. These men likewise have a stake in the liberation struggle of the women; they can and will become our allies.

Although the struggle against male chauvinism is an essential part of the tasks that women must carry out through their liberation movement, it is incorrect to make that the central issue. This tends to conceal or overlook the role of the ruling powers who not only breed and benefit from all forms of discrimination and oppression but are also responsible for breeding and sustaining male chauvinism. Let us remember that male supremacy did not exist in the primitive commune, founded upon sisterhood and brotherhood. Sexism, like racism, has its roots in the private property system.

A false theoretical position easily leads to a false strategy in the struggle for women's liberation. Such is the case with a segment of the Redstockings who state in their *Manifesto* that "women are an oppressed *class*." If all women compose a class then all men must form a counterclass—the oppressor class. What conclusion flows from this premise? That there are no men in the oppressed class? Where does this leave the millions of oppressed white working men who, like the oppressed blacks, Chicanos and other minorities, are exploited by the monopolists? Don't they have a central place in the struggle for social revolution? At what point and under what banner do these oppressed peoples of all races and both sexes join together for common action against their common enemy? To oppose women as a class against men as a class can only result in a diversion of the real class struggle.

Isn't there a suggestion of this same line in Roxanne Dunbar's assertion that female liberation is the basis for social revolution? This is far from Marxist strategy since it turns the real situation on its head. Marxists say that social revolution is the basis for full female liberation—just as it is the basis for the liberation of the whole working class. In the last analysis the real allies of women's liberation are all those forces which are impelled for their own reasons to struggle against and throw off the shackles of the imperialist masters.

The underlying source of women's oppression, which is capitalism, cannot be abolished by women alone, nor by a coalition of women drawn from all classes. It will require a worldwide struggle for socialism by the working masses, female and male alike, together with every other section of the oppressed, to overthrow the power of capitalism, which is centered today in the United States. . . .

RADICAL FEMINISM: Women's Oppression as the Fundamental Oppression

The Dialectic of Sex

Shulamith Firestone

Sex class is so deep as to be invisible. Or it may appear as a superficial inequality, one that can be solved by merely a few reforms, or perhaps by the full integration of women into the labor force. But the reaction of the common man, woman, and child—"*That?* Why you can't change *that!* You must be out of your mind!"—is the closest to the truth. We are talking about something every bit as deep as that. This gut reaction—the assumption that, even when they don't know it, feminists are talking about changing a fundamental biological condition —is an honest one. That so profound a change cannot be easily fit into traditional categories of thought, e.g., "political," is not because these categories do not apply but because they are not big enough: radical feminism bursts through them. If there were another word more all-embracing than *revolution* we would use it.

Until a certain level of evolution had been reached and technology had achieved its present sophistication, to question fundamental biological conditions was insanity. Why should a woman give up her precious seat in the cattle car for a bloody struggle she could not hope to win? But, for the first time in some countries, the preconditions for feminist revolution exist—indeed, the situation is beginning to *demand* such a revolution.

The first women are fleeing the massacre, and, shaking and tottering, are beginning to find each other. Their first move is a careful joint observation, to resensitize a fractured consciousness. This is painful: No matter how many levels of consciousness one reaches, the problem always goes deeper. It is everywhere. The division yin and yang pervades all culture, history, economics, nature itself; modern Western versions of sex discrimination are only the most recent layer. To so heighten one's sensitivity to sexism presents problems far worse than the black militant's new awareness of racism: Feminists have to question, not just all of *Western* culture, but the organization of culture itself, and further, even the very organization of nature. Many women give up in despair: if *that's* how deep it goes they don't want to know. Others continue strengthening and enlarging the movement, their painful sensitivity to female oppression existing for a purpose: eventually to eliminate it.

Before we can act to change a situation, however, we must know how it has arisen and evolved, and through what institutions it now operates. Engels' "[We must] examine the historic succession of events from which the antagonism has sprung in order to discover in the conditions thus created the means of ending the conflict." For feminist revolution we shall need an analysis of the dynamics of sex war as comprehensive as the Marx-Engels analysis of class antagonism was for the economic revolution. More comprehensive. For we are dealing with a larger problem, with an oppression that goes back beyond recorded history to the animal kingdom itself.

In creating such an analysis we can learn a lot from Marx and Engels: Not their literal opinions about women—about the condition of women as an oppressed class they know next to nothing, recognizing it only where it overlaps with economics—but rather their analytic *method.*

Marx and Engels outdid their socialist forerunners in that they developed a method of analysis which was both *dialectical* and *materialist.* The first in centuries to view history dialectically, they saw the world as process, a natural flux of action and reaction, of opposites yet inseparable and interpenetrating. Because they were able to perceive history as movie rather than as snapshot, they attempted to avoid falling into the stagnant "metaphysical" view that had trapped so many other great minds. (This sort of analysis itself may be a product of the sex division, as discussed in Chapter 9.) They combined this view of the dynamic interplay of historical forces with a materialist one, that is, they attempted for the first time to put historical and cultural change on a real basis, to trace the development of economic classes to organic causes. By understanding thoroughly the mechanics of history, they hoped to show men how to master it.

Socialist thinkers prior to Marx and Engels, such as Fourier, Owen, and Bebel, had been able to do no more than moralize about existing social inequalities, positing an ideal world where class privilege and exploitation should not exist—in the same way that early feminist thinkers posited a world where male privilege and exploitation ought not exist—by mere virtue of good will. In both cases, because the early thinkers did not really understand how the social injustice had evolved, maintained itself, or could be eliminated, their ideas existed in a cultural vacuum, utopian. Marx and Engels, on the other hand, attempted a scientific approach to history. They traced the class conflict to its real economic origins, projecting an economic solution based on objective economic preconditions already present: the seizure by the proletariat of the means of production would lead to a communism in which government had withered away, no longer needed to repress the lower class for the sake of the higher. In the classless society the interests of every individual would be synonymous with those of the larger society.

But the doctrine of historical materialism, much as it was a brilliant advance over previous historical analysis, was not the complete answer, as later events bore out. For though Marx and Engels grounded their theory in reality, it was only a *partial* reality. Here is Engels' strictly economic definition of historical materialism from *Socialism: Utopian or Scientific:*

> Historical materialism is that view of the course of history which seeks the *ultimate* cause and the great moving power of all historical events in the economic development of society, in the changes of the modes of production and exchange, in the consequent division of society into distinct classes, and in the struggles of these classes against one another. (Italics mine)

Further, he claims:

> . . . that all past history with the exception of the primitive stages was the history of class struggles; that these warring classes of society are always the products of the modes of production and exchange—in a word, of the economic conditions of their time; that the *economic* structure of society always furnishes the real basis, starting from which we can alone work out the *ultimate* explanation of the whole superstructure of juridical and political institutions as well as of the religious, philosophical, and other ideas of a given historical period. (Italics mine)

It would be a mistake to attempt to explain the oppression of women according to this strictly economic interpretation. The class analysis is a beautiful piece of work, but limited: although correct in a linear sense, it does not go deep enough. There is a whole sexual substratum of the historical dialectic that Engels at times dimly perceives, but because he can see sexuality only through an economic filter, reducing everything to that, he is unable to evaluate in its own right.

Engels did observe that the original division of labor was between man and woman for the purposes of childbreeding; that within the family the husband was the owner, the wife the means of production, the children the labor; and that reproduction of the human species was an important economic system distinct from the means of production. . . .

But Engels has been given too much credit for these scattered recognitions of the oppression of women as a class. In fact he acknowledged the sexual class system only where it overlapped and illuminated his economic construct. Engels didn't do so well even in this respect. But Marx was worse: There is a growing recognition of Marx's bias against women (a cultural bias shared by Freud as well as all men of culture), dangerous if one attempts to squeeze feminism into an orthodox Marxist framework—freezing what were only incidental insights of Marx and Engels about sex class into dogma. Instead, we must enlarge historical materialism to *include* the strictly Marxian, in the same way that the physics of relativity did not invalidate Newtonian physics so much as it drew a circle around it, limiting its application—but only through comparison—to a smaller sphere. For an economic diagnosis traced to ownership of the means of production, even of the means of *r*eproduction, does not explain everything. There is a level of reality that does not stem directly from economics.

The assumption that, beneath economics, reality is psychosexual is often rejected as ahistorical by those who accept a dialectical materialist view of history because it seems to land us back where Marx began: groping through a fog of utopian hypotheses, philosophical systems that might be right, that might be wrong (there is no way to tell), systems that explain concrete historical developments by *a priori* categories of thought; historical materialism, however, attempted to explain "knowing" by "being" and not vice versa.

But there is still an untried third alternative: We can attempt to develop a materialist view of history based on sex itself. . . .

Let us try to develop an analysis in which biology itself—procreation—is at the origin of the dualism. The immediate assumption of the layman that the unequal division of the sexes is "natural" may be well-founded. We need not immediately look beyond this. Unlike economic class, sex class sprang directly from a biological reality: men and women were created different, and not equally privileged. Although, as De Beauvoir points out, this difference of itself did not necessitate the development of a class system—the domination of one group by another—the reproductive *functions* of these differences did. The biological family is an inherently unequal power distribution. The need for power leading to the development of classes arises from the psychosexual formation of each individual according to this basic imbalance, rather than, as Freud, Norman O. Brown, and others have, once again overshooting their mark, postulated, some irreducible conflict of Life against Death, Eros vs. Thanatos.

The *biological family*—the basic reproductive unit of male/female/infant, in whatever form of social organization—is characterized by these fundamental—if not immutable—facts:

1 That women throughout history before the advent of birth control were at the continual mercy of their biology—menstruation, menopause, and "female ills," constant painful childbirth, wetnursing and care of infants, all of which made them dependent on males (whether brother, father, husband, lover, or clan, government, community-at-large) for physical survival.

2 That human infants take an even longer time to grow up than animals, and thus are helpless and, for some short period at least, dependent on adults for physical survival.

3 That a basic mother/child interdependency has existed in some form in every society, past or present, and thus has shaped the psychology of every mature female and every infant.

4 That the natural reproductive difference between the sexes led directly to the first division of labor at the origins of class, as well as furnishing the paradigm of caste (discrimination based on biological characteristics).

These biological contingencies of the human family cannot be covered over with anthropological sophistries. Anyone observing animals mating, reproducing, and caring for their young will have a hard time accepting the "cultural relativity" line. For no matter how many tribes in Oceania you can find where the connection of the father to fertility is not known, no matter how many matrilineages, no matter how many cases of sex-role reversal, male housewifery, or even empathic labor pains, these facts prove only one thing: the amazing *flexibility* of human nature. But human nature is adaptable *to* something, it is, yes, determined by its environmental conditions. And the biological family that we have described has existed everywhere throughout time. Even in matriarchies where woman's fertility is worshipped, and the father's role is unknown or unimportant, if perhaps not on the genetic father, there is still some dependence of the female and the infant on the male. And though it is true that the nuclear family is only a recent development, one which, as I shall attempt to show, only intensifies the psychological penalties of the biological family, though it is true that throughout history there have been many variations on this biological family, the contingencies I have described existed in all of them, causing specific psychosexual distortions in the human personality.

But to grant that the sexual imbalance of power is biologically based is not to lose our case. We are no longer just animals. And the Kingdom of Nature does not reign absolute. . . .

The "natural" is not necessarily a "human" value. Humanity has begun to outgrow nature: we can no longer justify the maintenance of a discriminatory sex class system on grounds of its origins in Nature. Indeed, for pragmatic reasons alone it is beginning to look as if we *must* get rid of it (see Chapter 10).

The problem becomes political, demanding more than a comprehensive historical analysis, when one realizes that, though man is increasingly capable of freeing himself from the biological conditions that created his tyranny over women and children, he has little reason to want to give this tyranny up. As Engels said, in the context of economic revolution:

> It is the law of division of labor that lies at the basis of the division into classes [Note that this division itself grew out of a fundamental biological division]. But this does not prevent the ruling class, once having the upper hand, from consolidating its power at the expense of the working class, from turning its social leadership into an intensified exploitation of the masses.

Though the sex class system may have originated in fundamental biological conditions, this does not guarantee once the biological basis of their oppression has been swept away that women and children will be freed. On the contrary, the new technology, especially fertility control, may be used against them to reinforce the entrenched system of exploitation.

So that just as to assure elimination of economic classes requires the revolt of the underclass (the proletariat) and, in a temporary dictatorship, their seizure of the means of *production,* so to assure the elimination of sexual classes requires the revolt of the underclass (women) and the seizure of control of *reproduction:* not only the full restoration to women of ownership of their own bodies, but also their (temporary) seizure of control of human fertility—the new population biology as well as all the social institutions of childbearing and childrearing. And just as the end goal of socialist revolution was not only the elimination of the economic class *privilege* but of the economic class *distinction* itself, so the end goal of feminist revolution must be, unlike that of the first feminist movement, not just the elimination of male *privilege* but of the sex *distinction* itself: genital differences between human beings would no longer matter culturally. (A reversion to an unobstructed *pansexuality*—Freud's "polymorphous perversity" —would probably supersede hetero/homo/bi-sexuality.) The reproduction of the species by one sex for the benefit of both would be replaced by (at least the option of) artificial reproduction: children would be born to both sexes equally, or independently of either, however one chooses to look at it; the dependence of the child on the mother (and vice versa) would give way to a greatly shortened dependence on a small group of others in general, and any remaining inferiority to adults in physical strength would be compensated for culturally. The division of labor would be ended by the elimination of labor altogether (cybernation). The tyranny of the biological family would be broken. . . .

STRUCTURAL IMPERATIVES

Before we talk about revolutionary alternatives, let's summarize—to determine the specifics that must be carefully excluded from any new structures. Then we can go on to "utopian speculation" directed by at least negative guidelines.

We have seen how women, biologically distinguished from men, are culturally distinguished from "human." Nature produced the fundamental inequality— half the human race must bear and rear the children of all of them—which was later consolidated, institutionalized, in the interests of men. Reproduction of the species cost women dearly, not only emotionally, psychologically, culturally but even in strictly material (physical) terms: before recent methods of contraception, continuous childbirth led to constant "female trouble," early aging, and death. Women were the slave class that maintained the species in order to free the other half for the business of the world—admittedly often its drudge aspects, but certainly all its creative aspects as well.

This natural division of labor was continued only at great cultural sacrifice: men and women developed only half of themselves, at the expense of the other half. The division of the psyche into male and female to better reinforce the reproductive division was tragic: the hypertrophy in men of rationalism, aggressive drive, the atrophy of their emotional sensitivity was a physical (war) as well as a cultural disaster. The emotionalism and passivity of women increased their suffering (we cannot speak of them in a symmetrical way, since they were victimized as a class by the division). Sexually men and women were channeled into a highly ordered—time, place, procedure, even dialogue— heterosexuality restricted to the genitals, rather than diffused over the entire physical being.

I submit, then, that the first demand for any alternative system must be:

1 *The freeing of women from the tyranny of their reproductive biology by every means available, and the diffusion of the childbearing and childrearing role to the society as a whole, men as well as women.* There are many degrees of this. Already we have a (hard-won) acceptance of "family planning," if not contraception for its own sake. Proposals are imminent for day-care centers, perhaps even twenty-four-hour child-care centers staffed by men as well as women. But this, in my opinion, is timid if not entirely worthless as a transition. We're talking about *radical* change. And though indeed it cannot come all at once, radical goals must be kept in sight at all times. Day-care centers buy women off. They ease the immediate pressure without asking why that pressure is on *women.*

At the other extreme there are the more distant solutions based on the potentials of modern embryology, that is, artificial reproduction, possibilities still so frightening that they are seldom discussed seriously. We have seen that the fear is to some extent justified: in the hands of our current society and under the direction of current scientists (few of whom are female or even feminist), any attempted use of technology to "free" anybody is suspect. But we are speculating about post-revolutionary systems, and for the purposes of our discussion we shall assume flexibility and good intentions in those working out the change.

To thus free women from their biology would be to threaten the *social* unit that is organized around biological reproduction and the subjection of women to their biological destiny, the family. Our second demand will come also as a basic contradiction to the family, this time the family as an *economic* unit:

2 *The full self-determination, including economic independence, of both women and children.* To achieve this goal would require fundamental changes in our social and economic structure. This is why we must talk about a feminist socialism: in the immediate future, under capitalism, there could be at best a token integration of women into the labor force. For women have been found exceedingly useful and cheap as a transient, often highly skilled labor supply,[1] not to mention the economic value of their traditional function, the reproduction and rearing of the next generation of children, a job for which they are now patronized (literally and thus figuratively) rather than paid. But whether or not officially recognized, these are essential economic functions. Women, in this present capacity, are the very foundation of the economic superstructure, vital to its existence.[2] The paeans to self-sacrificing motherhood have a basis in reality: Mom *is* vital to the American way of life, considerably more than apple pie. She is an institution without which the system really *would* fall apart. In official capitalist terms, the bill for her economic services[3] might run as high as

[1]Most bosses would fail badly had they to take over their secretaries' job, or do without them. I know several secretaries who sign without a thought their bosses' names to their own (often brilliant) solutions. The skills of college women especially would cost a fortune reckoned in material terms of male labor.

[2]Margaret Benston ("The Political Economy of Women's Liberation," *Monthly Review,* September 1969), in attempting to show that women's oppression is indeed economic—though previous economic analysis has been incorrect—distinguishes between the male superstructure economy based on *commodity* production (capitalist ownership of the means of production, and wage labor), and the pre-industrial reduplicative economy of the family, production for immediate *use.* Because the latter is not part of the *official* contemporary economy, its function at the basis of that economy is often overlooked. Talk of drafting women into the superstructure commodity economy fails to deal with the tremendous amount of necessary production of the traditional kind now performed by women without pay: Who will do it?

[3]The Chase Manhattan Bank estimates a woman's over-all domestic work week at 99.6 hours. Margaret Benston gives her minimal estimate for a *childless* married woman at 16 hours, close to half of a regular work week; a *mother* must spend at least six or seven days a week working close to 12 hours.

one-fifth of the gross national product. But payment is not the answer. To pay her, as is often discussed seriously in Sweden, is a reform that does not challenge the basic division of labor and thus could never eradicate the disastrous psychological and cultural consequences of that division of labor.

As for the economic independence of children, that is really a pipe dream, realized as yet nowhere in the world. And, in the case of children too, we are talking about more than a fair integration into the labor force; we are talking about the abolition of the labor force itself under a cybernetic socialism, the radical restructuring of the economy to make "work," i.e., wage labor, no longer necessary. In our post-revolutionary society adults as well as children would be provided for—irrespective of their social contributions—in the first equal distribution of wealth in history.

We have now attacked the family on a double front, challenging that around which it is organized: reproduction of the species by females and its outgrowth, the physical dependence of women and children. To eliminate these would be enough to destroy the family, which breeds the power psychology. However, we will break it down still further.

3 *The total integration of women and children into all aspects of the larger society.* All institutions that segregate the sexes, or bar children from adult society, e.g., the elementary school, must be destroyed. *Down with school!*

These three demands predicate a feminist revolution based on advanced technology. And if the male/female and the adult/child cultural distinctions are destroyed, we will no longer need the sexual repression that maintains these unequal classes, allowing for the first time a "natural" sexual freedom. Thus we arrive at:

4 *The freedom of all women and children to do whatever they wish to do sexually.* There will no longer be any reason *not* to. (Past reasons: Full sexuality threatened the continuous reproduction necessary for human survival, and thus, through religion and other cultural institutions, sexuality had to be restricted to reproductive purposes, all nonreproductive sex pleasure considered deviation or worse; The sexual freedom of women would call into question the fatherhood of the child, thus threatening patrimony; Child sexuality had to be repressed because it was a threat to the precarious internal balance of the family. These sexual repressions increased proportionately to the degree of cultural exaggeration of the biological family.) In our new society, humanity could finally revert to its natural polymorphous sexuality—all forms of sexuality would be allowed and indulged. The fully sexuate mind, realized in the past in only a few individuals (survivors), would become universal. Artificial cultural achievement would no longer be the only avenue to sexuate self-realization: one could now realize oneself fully, simply in the process of being and acting. . . .

Lesbians in Revolt

Charlotte Bunch

The development of Lesbian-Feminist politics as the basis for the liberation of women is our top priority: this article outlines our present ideas. In our society which defines all people and institutions for the benefit of the rich, white male, the Lesbian is in revolt. In revolt because she defines herself in terms of women and rejects the male definitions of how she should feel, act, look, and live. To be a Lesbian is to love oneself, woman, in a culture that denegrates and despises women. The Lesbian rejects male sexual/political domination; she defies his world, his social organization, his ideology, and his definition of her as inferior. Lesbianism puts women first while the society declares the male supreme. Lesbianism threatens male supremacy at its core. When politically conscious and organized, it is central to destroying our sexist, racist, capitalist, imperialist system.

Male society defines Lesbianism as a sexual act, which reflects men's limited view of women: they think of us only in terms of sex. They also say Lesbians are not real women, so a real woman is one who gets fucked by men. We say that a Lesbian is a woman whose sense of self and energies, including sexual energies, center around women—she is woman identified. The woman-identified-woman commits herself to other women for political, emotional, physical, and economic support. Women are important to her. She is important to herself. Our society demands that commitment from women be reserved for men.

The Lesbian, woman-identified-woman, commits herself to women not only as an alternative to oppressive male/female relationships but primarily because she *loves* women. Whether consciously or not, by her actions, the Lesbian has recognized that giving support and love to men over women perpetuates the system that oppresses her. If women do not make a commitment to each other, which includes sexual love, we deny ourselves the love and value traditionally given to men. We accept our second class status. When women do give primary energies to other women, then it is possible to concentrate fully on building a movement for our liberation.

Woman-identified Lesbianism is, then, more than a sexual preference, it is a political choice. It is political because relationships between men and women are essentially political, they involve power and dominance. Since the Lesbian actively rejects that relationship and chooses women, she defies the established political system.

Of course, not all Lesbians are consciously woman-identified, nor are all committed to finding common solutions to the oppression they suffer as women and Lesbians. Being a Lesbian is part of challenging male supremacy, but not the end. For the Lesbian or heterosexual woman, there is no individual solution to oppression.

The Lesbian may think that she is free since she escapes the personal oppression of the individual male/female relationship. But to the society she is still a woman, or worse, a visible Lesbian. On the street, at the job, in the schools, she is treated as an inferior and is at the mercy of men's power and whims. (I've never heard of a rapist who stopped because his victim was a Lesbian.) This society hates women who love women, and so, the Lesbian, who escapes male dominance in her private home, receives it doubly at the hands of male society; she is harassed, outcast, and shuttled to the bottom. Lesbians must become feminists and fight against woman oppression, just as feminists must become Lesbians if they hope to end male supremacy.

U.S. society encourages individual solutions, apolitical attitudes, and reformism to keep us from political revolt and out of power. Men who rule, and male leftists who seek to rule, try to depoliticize sex and the relations between men and women in order to prevent us from acting to end our oppression and challenging their power. As the question of homosexuality has become public, reformists define it as a private question of who you sleep with in order to sidetrack our understanding of the politics of sex. For the Lesbian-Feminist, it is not private; it is a political matter of oppression, domination, and power. Reformists offer solutions which make no basic changes in the system that oppresses us, solutions which keep power in the hands of the oppressor. The only way oppressed people end their oppression is by seizing power: People whose rule depends on the subordination of others do not voluntarily stop oppressing others. Our subordination is the basis of male power.

SEXISM IS THE ROOT OF ALL OPPRESSION

The first division of labor, in pre-history, was based on sex: men hunted, women built the villages, took care of children, and farmed. Women collectively controlled the land, language, culture, and the communities. Men were able to conquer women with the weapons that they developed for hunting when it became clear that women were leading a more stable, peaceful, and desirable existence. We do not know exactly how this conquest took place, but it is clear that the original imperialism was male over female: the male claiming the female body and her service as his territory (or property).

Having secured the domination of women, men continued this pattern of suppressing people, now on the basis of tribe, race, and class. Although there have been numerous battles over class, race, and nation during the past 3000 years, none has brought the liberation of women. While these other forms of oppression must be ended, there is no reason to believe that our liberation will come with the smashing of capitalism, racism, or imperialism today. Women will be free only when we concentrate on fighting male supremacy.

Our war against male supremacy does, however, involve attacking the latter day dominations based on class, race, and nation. As Lesbians who are outcasts from every group, it would be suicidal to perpetuate these man-made divisions among ourselves. We have no heterosexual privileges, and when we publicly assert our Lesbianism, those of us who had them lose many of our class and race privileges. Most of our privileges as women are granted to us by our relationships to men (fathers, husbands, boyfriends) whom we now reject. This does not mean that there is no racism or class chauvinism within us, but we must destroy these divisive remnants of privileged behavior among ourselves as the first step toward their destruction in the society. Race, class, and national oppressions come from men, serve ruling class white men's interests, and have no place in a woman-identified revolution.

LESBIANISM IS THE BASIC THREAT TO MALE SUPREMACY

Lesbianism is a threat to the ideological, political, and economic basis of male supremacy. The Lesbian threatens the ideology of male supremacy by destroying the lie about female inferiority, weakness, passivity, and by denying women's "innate" need for men. Lesbians literally do not need men (even for procreation if the science of cloning is developed).

The Lesbian's independence and refusal to support one man undermines the personal power that men exercise over women. Our rejection of hetereosexual sex challenges male domination in its most individual and common form. We offer all women something better than submission to personal oppression. We offer the beginning of the end of collective and individual male supremacy. Since men of all races and classes depend on female support and submission for practical tasks and feeling superior, our refusal to submit will force some to examine their sexist behavior, to break down their own destructive privileges over other humans, and to fight against those privileges in other men. They will have to build new selves that do not depend on oppressing women and learn to live in social structures that do not give them power over anyone.

Hetereosexuality separates women from each other; it makes women define themselves through men; it forces women to compete against each other for men and the privilege which comes through men and their social standing. Heterosexual society offers women a few privileges as compensation if they give up their freedom: for example, mothers are respected and "honored," wives or lovers are socially accepted and given some economic and emotional security, a woman gets physical protection on the street when she stays with her man, etc. The privileges give hetereosexual women a personal and political stake in maintaining the status quo.

The Lesbian receives none of these heterosexual privileges or compensations since she does not accept the male demands on her. She has little vested interest in maintaining the present political system since all of its institutions—church, state, media, health, schools—work to keep her down. If she understands her oppression, she has nothing to gain by supporting white rich male America and much to gain from fighting to change it. She is less prone to accept reformist solutions to women's oppression.

Economics is a crucial part of woman oppression, but our analysis of the relationship between capitalism and sexism is not complete. We know that

Marxist economic theory does not sufficiently consider the role of women or Lesbians, and we are presently working on this area.

However, as a beginning, some of the ways that Lesbians threaten the economic system are clear: In this country, women work for men in order to survive, on the job and in the home. The Lesbian rejects this division of labor at its roots; she refuses to be a man's property, to submit to the unpaid labor system of housework and childcare. She rejects the nuclear family as the basic unit of production and consumption in capitalist society.

The Lesbian is also a threat on the job because she is not the passive/part-time woman worker that capitalism counts on to do boring work and be part of a surplus labor pool. Her identity and economic support do not come through men, so her job is crucial and she cares about job conditions, wages, promotion, and status. Capitalism cannot absorb large numbers of women demanding stable employment, decent salaries, and refusing to accept their traditional job exploitation. We do not understand yet the total effect that this increased job dissatisfaction will have. It is, however, clear that as women become more intent upon taking control of their lives, they will seek more control over their jobs, thus increasing the strains on capitalism and enhancing the power of women to change the economic system.

LESBIANS MUST FORM OUR OWN MOVEMENT
TO FIGHT MALE SUPREMACY

Feminist-Lesbianism, as the most basic threat to male supremacy, picks up part of the Women's Liberation analysis of sexism and gives it force and direction. Women's Liberation lacks direction now because it has failed to understand the importance of heterosexuality in maintaining male supremacy and because it has failed to face class and race as real differences in women's behavior and political needs. As long as straight women see Lesbianism as a bedroom issue, they hold back the development of politics and strategies which would put an end to male supremacy and they give men an excuse for not dealing with their sexism.

Being a Lesbian means ending identification with, allegiance to, dependence on, and support of heterosexuality. It means ending your personal stake in the male world so that you join women, individually and collectively, in the struggle to end your oppression. Lesbianism is the key to liberation and only women who cut their ties to male privilege can be trusted to remain serious in the struggle against male dominance. Those who remain tied to men, individually or in political theory, cannot always put women first. It is not that heterosexual women are evil or do not care about women. It is because the very essence, definition, and nature of heterosexuality is men first. Every woman has experienced that desolation when her sister puts her man first in the final crunch: heterosexuality demands that she do so. As long as women still benefit from heterosexuality, receive its privileges and security, they will at some point have to betray their sisters, especially Lesbian sisters who do not receive those benefits.

Women in women's liberation have understood the importance of having meetings and other events for women only. It has been clear that dealing with men divides us and saps our energies and that it is not the job of the oppressed to explain our oppression to the oppressor. Women also have seen that collectively, men will not deal with their sexism until they are forced to do so. Yet, many of these same women continue to have primary relationships with men individually and do not understand why Lesbians find this oppressive. Lesbians cannot grow politically or personally in a situation which denies the basis of our politics: that Lesbianism is political, that heterosexuality is crucial to maintaining male supremacy.

Lesbians must form our own political movement in order to grow. Changes which will have more than token effects on our lives will be led by woman-identified Lesbians who understand the nature of our oppression and are therefore in a position to end it.

One Is Not Born a Woman

Monique Wittig

A materialist feminist approach to women's oppression destroys the idea that women are a "natural group": "a social group of a special kind, a group perceived *as natural,* a group of men considered as materially specific in their bodies." A lesbian society destroys the artificial (social) fact constituting women as a "natural group." A lesbian society pragmatically reveals that the division from men of which women have been the object is a political one and shows how we have been ideologically re-built into a "natural group." In our case, ideology goes far since our bodies as well as our minds are the product of this manipulation. We have been compelled in our bodies and in our minds to correspond, feature by feature, with the *idea* of nature that has been established for us. Distorted to such an extent that our deformed body is what they call "natural," is what is supposed to exist as such before oppression. Distorted to such an extent that at the end oppression seems to be a consequence of this "nature" in ourselves (a nature which is only an *idea*). What a materialist analysis does by reasoning, a lesbian society accomplishes in fact: not only is there no natural group "women" (we lesbians are a living proof of it) but as individuals as well we question "woman," which for us, as for Simone de Beauvoir thirty years ago, is only a myth. She said: "One is not born, but becomes a woman. No biological, psychological, or economic fate determines the figure that the human female presents in society; it is civilization as a whole that produces this creature, intermediate between male and eunuch, which is described as feminine."

However, most of the feminists and lesbian-feminists in America and elsewhere still believe that the basis of women's oppression *is biological as well as* historical. Some of them even claim to find their sources in Simone de

Beauvoir. The belief in mother-right and in a "prehistory" when women would have created civilization (because of a biological predisposition), while the coarse and brutal men would have hunted (because of a biological predisposition), does not make the biological approach any better. It is still the same method of finding in women and men a biological explanation of their division, outside of social facts. For me this could never constitute a lesbian approach since it assumes that the basis of society or the beginning of society lies in heterosexuality. Matriarchies are no less heterosexual than patriarchies: it's only the sex of the oppressor that changes. Furthermore, not only is this conception still a prisoner of the categories of sex (woman and man), but it keeps to the idea that the capacity to give birth (biology) is what defines a woman. Although practical facts and ways of living contradict this theory in lesbian society, there are lesbians who affirm that "women and men are different species or races (the words are used interchangeably); men are biologically inferior to women; male violence is a biological inevitability . . ." By doing this, by admitting that there is a "natural" division between women and men, we naturalize history, we assume that men and women have always existed and will always exist. Not only do we naturalize history, but also consequently we naturalize the social phenomena which express our oppression, making change impossible. For example, instead of seeing giving birth as a forced production, we see it as a "natural," "biological" process, forgetting that in our societies births are planned (demography), forgetting that we ourselves are programmed to produce children, while this is the only social activity "short of war" that presents such a great danger of death. Thus, as long as we will be "unable to abandon by will or impulse a lifelong and centuries old commitment to childbearing as *the* female creative act," having control of the production of children will mean much more than the mere control of the material means of this production. Women will have to abstract themselves from the definition "woman" which is imposed upon them.

A materialist feminist approach shows that what we take for the cause or origin of oppression is in fact only the *mark* imposed by the oppressor: the "myth of woman," plus its material effects and manifestations in the appropriated consciousnesses and bodies of women. Thus, the mark does not preexist oppression. Colette Guillaumin, a French sociologist, has shown that before the socio-economical reality of black slavery, the concept of race did not exist (at least not in its modern meaning: it was applied to the lineage of families). However, now, race, exactly like sex, is taken as an "immediate given," a "sensible given," "physical features." They appear as though they existed prior to reasoning, belonging to a natural order. But what we believe to be a physical and direct perception is only a sophisticated and mythic construction, an "imaginary formation" which reinterprets physical features through the network of relationships in which they are perceived. (They are seen *black,* therefore they *are* black; they are seen *women,* therefore they *are* women. But before being *seen* that way, they first had to be *made* that way.) A lesbian consciousness should always remember how "unnatural," compelling, totally oppressive, and destructive being "woman" was for us in the old days before the women's liberation movement. It was a political obligation and those who resisted it were accused of not being "real" women. But then we were proud of it, since in the accusation there was already something like a shadow of victory: the avowal by the oppressor that "woman" is not something that goes without saying, since to be one, one has to be a "real" one (what about the others?). We were also confronted by the accusation of wanting to be men. We still are by certain lesbians and feminists who believe that one has to become more and more of a woman as a political obligation. But to refuse to be a woman does not mean that one has to become a man. And for her who does want to become a man: in what way is her alienation different from wanting to become a woman? At least for a woman, wanting to become a man proves that she escaped her initial programming. But even if she wants to, she cannot become a man. For becoming a man would demand from a woman having not only the outside appearance of a man but his consciousness as well, that is, the consciousness of one who disposes by right of at least two natural "slaves" during his life span. This is impossible since precisely one feature of lesbian oppression consists of making women out of reach for us, since women belong to men. Thus a lesbian *has to* be something else, not-woman, not-man, a product of society not a product of "nature," for there is no "nature" in society.

The refusal to become heterosexual always meant to refuse to become a man or a woman, consciously or not. For a lesbian this goes further than the refusal of the role "woman." It is the refusal of the economic, ideological and political power of a man. This, we lesbians, and non-lesbians as well, have experienced before the beginning of the lesbian and feminist movement. However, as Andrea Dworkin emphasizes, many lesbians recently "have increasingly tried to transform the very ideology that has enslaved us into a dynamic, religious, psychologically compelling celebration of female biological potential." Thus, some avenues of the feminist and lesbian movement lead us back to the myth of woman which was created by men especially for us, and with it we sink back into a natural group. Thirty years ago Simone de Beauvoir destroyed the myth of woman. Ten years ago we stood up to fight for a sexless society. Now we find ourselves entrapped in the familiar deadlock of "woman is wonderful." Thirty years ago Simone de Beauvoir underlined particularly the false consciousness which consists of selecting among the features of the myth (that women are different from men) those which look good and using them as a definition for women. What the concept of "woman is wonderful" accomplishes is that it retains for defining women the best features which oppression has granted us and it does not radically question the categories "man" and "woman." It puts us in a position of fighting within the class "women" not as the other classes do, for the disappearance of our class, but for the defense of "woman" and its reinforcement. It leads us to develop with complacency "new" theories about our specificity: thus, we call our passivity "non-violence." The ambiguity of the term "feminist" sums up the whole situation. What does "feminist" mean? Feminist is formed with the word "femme," "woman," and means "someone who fights for women." For many of us it means "someone who fights for women as a class and for the disappearance of this class." For many others it means "someone who fights for woman and her defense"—for the myth then and its reinforcement. But why was the word "feminist" chosen? We chose to call ourselves "feminists" ten years ago, not in order to identify ourselves with the oppressor's definition of us, but rather to affirm that our movement had a history and to emphasize the political link with the old feminist movement.

It is, then, this movement that we can question for its meaning of "feminism." It so happens that feminism in the last century could never resolve its contradictions on the subject of nature/culture, woman/society. Women started to fight for themselves as a group and rightly considered that they shared common features. But for them these features were natural and biological rather than social. They went so far as to adopt pseudo-Darwinist theories of evolution. They did not believe like Darwin, however, "that women were less evolved than men, but they did believe that male and female natures had diverged in the course of evolutionary development and that society at large reflected this polarization . . . The failure of early feminism was that it only attacked the Darwinist charge of female inferiority, while accepting the foundations of this charge—namely, the view of woman as 'unique'." And finally it was women scholars—and not feminists who scientifically destroyed this theory. But the early feminists had failed to regard history as a dynamic process which develops from conflicts of interests. Furthermore, they still believed that the cause (origin) of their oppression lay within themselves (among black people only the Uncle Toms believed this). And therefore feminists, after some astonishing victories, found themselves at an impasse for lack of reasons for fighting. They upheld the illogical principle of "equality in difference," an idea now being born again. They fell back into the trap which threatens us once again: the myth of woman.

Thus it remains historically for us to define our oppression in materialist terms, to say that women are a class, which is to say that the category "woman," as well as "man," is a political and economic category, not an eternal one. Our fight aims to suppress men as a class, not through a genocidal, but a political struggle. Once the class "men" disappears, women as a class will disappear as well, for there are no slaves without masters. Our first task, it seems, is to always thoroughly disassociate "women" (the class within which we fight) and "woman," the myth. For "woman" does not exist for us: it is only an imaginary formation, while "women" is the product of a social relationship. Furthermore we have to destroy the myth within and outside ourselves. "Woman" is not each one of us, but the political and ideological formation which negates "women" (the product of a relation of exploitation). "Woman" is there to confuse us, to hide the reality "women." In order to become a class and to be aware of it, we have first to kill the myth "woman" even in its most seductive aspects. . . .

To destroy "woman" does not mean to destroy lesbianism, for a lesbian is not a woman and does not love a woman, given that we agree with Christine Delphy that what "makes" woman is a personal dependency on a man (as opposed to an impersonal dependency on a boss). Lesbian is the only concept that I know of which is beyond the categories of sex (woman and man), because lesbian societies are not based upon women's oppression and because the designated subject (lesbian) is *not* a woman either economically or politically or ideologically. Furthermore, what we aim at is not the disappearance of lesbianism, which provides the only social form that we can live in, but the destruction of heterosexuality—the political system based on women's oppression, which produces the body of thought of the difference between the sexes to explain women's oppression.

Beyond or within this class consciousness, this science/experience, while in the separateness of one's ego, do we still have to fight to exist as an autonomous entity? There is no doubt that we have to fight for this entity, since we are left with nothing, once we reject the basic determination "woman" and "man," once we have no more attributes by which to identify ourselves (I am this or that). We are for the first time in history confronted with the necessity of existing as a person.

SOCIALIST FEMINISM:
The Inseparability of Gender and Class Oppression

A View of Socialist Feminism

Charlotte Perkins Gilman Chapter of the New American Movement

We believe that socialist feminism is essential to the struggle for the liberation of all women and the destruction of capitalism. We derive roots, strength, and direction from the feminist movement and from the socialist movement. Yet we believe that neither approach alone can achieve our goals for economic justice and a society where all women and men are equal. Socialist feminism provides a synthesis of both movements, while providing its unique perspective, vision, strategies, and contributions to theory.

AS FEMINISTS

As feminists, we see sexism as a primary focus; we fight against all forms and facets of sexism. We attack the inferior economic and legal status of women. We oppose the sexual division of labor, in which men and women have different responsibilities for home and family and unequal work divisions in the outside work place. We struggle for control of reproduction: for the freedom to choose contraception, abortion, or sterilization when we want them, but never to have any imposed, as they are on many poor and minority women. We challenge societal definitions of "femininity" and "masculinity" and seek freedom to define ourselves as we wish. We see "personal" issues as aspects of ourselves and society that are basic to change—sexuality, life-style, and family.

AS SOCIALISTS

As socialists, we see ourselves involved in the historic struggle of working people against a system which creates poverty in the midst of wealth; alienating work in a technological society; divisions between black and white, male and female, workers in this country and abroad; capitalism. All people who struggle against capitalism and for a socialist society must work together to challenge that system and its institutions.

THE TENSION

There remains a tension between socialism and feminism. Each regards its own particular focus as primary, and the other as secondary. Socialists insist on their unifying analysis, yet feminists can point to past failures of the left to address either the oppression women face, or the sexism within the left itself.

We must insist on a socialist-feminist movement because:

1 Sexism has a life of its own. It has existed throughout human history, under every economic system.

2 Capitalism determines the particular forms of sexism in a capitalist society. The subjugation of women contributes to capitalists' domination of society.

Any movement which fails to deal with *both* of these fundamental realities cannot succeed. Thus, we believe socialist-feminism is the necessary approach for both feminists and socialists.

WHY SOCIALIST FEMINISM?

The demands of feminism cannot be met by capitalist society. In order to achieve such goals as the elimination of sex roles, free 24-hour day care, and women's control over their own bodies, women must not only struggle to build a strong women's movement, but must work along with other oppressed groups. Socialist feminism moves beyond an attempt to create equality of women within the system to a struggle for equality within a new system that is not dependent on male domination or any exploitation of one group by another. This results in seeing feminism within a larger revolutionary context. For example, when we organize for day care, we challenge the power structure and economic system that are responsible for the present inadequacies. We expose the priorities and interests of those people who are determining and carrying out the current policies. We explore the implications of socialized child care, and its effect on working women and men.

WHY FEMINIST SOCIALISM?

Even though women are divided by class society, we are all united by our oppression as women. Just as women cannot achieve their full liberation except under socialism, so socialism cannot truly succeed unless all people are free from exploitation, manipulation, and prejudice.

Feminism provides the key to the cultural dimension of any successful revolutionary movement. Traditional socialist politics has focused on the public realms of "politics," goods production outside the home, and material needs. But feminism has taught us that the personal *is* political; that production in the "private" world of the home, while invisible under capitalism, is economically and socially critical; and that our culture, as well as our economic system, gives some people power over other people's lives. Any movement which ignores these learnings will surely fail, for it warps its vision and cuts itself off from the strength and knowledge of the female half of the working class. The fight against sexism reinforces the essential recognition that what is important is not just redistribution of goods, but a change in authority, control, and ideas.

Sexism's roots are deep; we must struggle not only against the institutions that maintain it, but against our own roles and attitudes. Feminism brings to the movement an attention to relationships *within* the movement, to the nature and functions of leadership, and to the importance of working collectively.

Women's pain and anger are real. When the broad interests of women and the interests of the working class seem to conflict, it is our task to clarify the interrelationships of those movements and seek programs that speak to all women's needs from a class perspective. Socialists committed to working for a society that is against all forms of oppression and exploitation must join in the struggle against sexism and together with other oppressed people fight for a new social and economic order.

The Traffic in Women:
Notes on the "Political Economy" of Sex[1]

Gayle Rubin

The literature on women—both feminist and anti-feminist—is a long rumination on the question of the nature and genesis of women's oppression and social subordination. The question is not a trivial one, since the answers given it determine our visions of the future, and our evaluation of whether or not it is realistic to hope for a sexually egalitarian society. More importantly, the analysis of the causes of women's oppression forms the basis for any assessment of just what would have to be changed in order to achieve a society without gender hierarchy. Thus, if innate male aggression and dominance are at the root of female oppression, then the feminist program would logically require either the extermination of the offending sex, or else a eugenics project to modify its character. If sexism is a by-product of capitalism's relentless appetite for profit, then sexism would wither away in the advent of a successful socialist revolution. If the world historical defeat of women occurred at the hands of an armed patriarchal revolt, then it is time for Amazon guerrillas to start training in the Adirondacks. . . .

Marx once asked: "What is a Negro slave? A man of the black race. The one explanation is as good as the other. A Negro is a Negro. He only becomes a slave in certain relations. A cotton spinning jenny is a machine for spinning cotton. It becomes *capital* only in certain relations. Torn from these relationships it is no more capital than gold in itself is money or sugar is the price of sugar" (Marx, 1971b:28). One might paraphrase: What is a domesticated woman? A female of the species. The one explanation is as good as the other. A woman is a woman. She only becomes a domestic, a wife, a chattel, a playboy bunny, a prostitute, or a human dictaphone in certain relations. Torn from these relationships, she is no more the helpmate of man than gold in itself is money . . . etc. What then are these relationships by which a female becomes an oppressed woman? The place to begin to unravel the system of relationships by which women become the prey of men is in the overlapping works of Claude Lévi-Strauss and Sigmund Freud. The domestication of women, under other names, is discussed at length in both of their *oeuvres*. In reading through these works, one begins to have a sense of a systematic social apparatus which takes up females as raw materials and fashions

[1]Acknowledgments are an inadequate expression of how much this paper, like most, is the product of many minds. They are also necessary to free others of the responsibility for what is ultimately a personal vision of a collective conversation. I want to free and thank the following persons: Tom Anderson and Arlene Gorelick, with whom I co-authored the paper from which this one evolved; Rayna Reiter, Larry Shields, Ray Kelly, Peggy White, Norma Diamond, Randy Reiter, Frederick Wyatt, Anne Locksley, Juliet Mitchell, and Susan Harding, for countless conversations and ideas; Marshall Sahlins, for the revelation of anthropology; Lynn Eden, for sardonic editing; the members of Women's Studies 340/004, for my initiation into teaching; Sally Brenner, for heroic typing; Susan Lowes, for incredible patience; and Emma Goldman, for the title.

domesticated women as products. Neither Freud nor Lévi-Strauss sees his work in this light, and certainly neither turns critical glance upon the processes he describes. Their analyses and descriptions must be read, therefore, in something like the way in which Marx read the classical political economists who preceded him (on this, see Althusser and Balibar, 1970:11–69). Freud and Lévi-Strauss are in some sense analogous to Ricardo and Smith: They see neither the implications of what they are saying, nor the implicit critique which their work can generate when subjected to a feminist eye. Nevertheless, they provide conceptual tools with which one can build descriptions of the part of social life which is the locus of the oppression of women, of sexual minorities, and of certain aspects of human personality within individuals. I call that part of social life the "sex/gender system," for lack of a more elegant term. As a preliminary definition, a "sex/gender system" is the set of arrangements by which a society transforms biological sexuality into products of human activity, and in which these transformed sexual needs are satisfied. . . .

I will return later to a refinement of the definition of a sex/gender system. First, however, I will try to demonstrate the need for such a concept by discussing the failure of classical Marxism to fully express or conceptualize sex oppression. This failure results from the fact that Marxism, as a theory of social life, is relatively unconcerned with sex. In Marx's map of the social world, human beings are workers, peasants, or capitalists; that they are also men and women is not seen as very significant. By contrast, in the maps of social reality drawn by Freud and Lévi-Strauss, there is a deep recognition of the place of sexuality in society, and of the profound differences between the social experience of men and women.

MARX

There is no theory which accounts for the oppression of women—in its endless variety and monotonous similarity, cross-culturally and throughout history—with anything like the explanatory power of the Marxist theory of class oppression. Therefore, it is not surprising that there have been numerous attempts to apply Marxist analysis to the question of women. There are many ways of doing this. It has been argued that women are a reserve labor force for capitalism, that women's generally lower wages provide extra surplus to a capitalist employer, that women serve the ends of capitalist consumerism in their roles as administrators of family consumption, and so forth.

However, a number of articles have tried to do something much more ambitious—to locate the oppression of women in the heart of the capitalist dynamic by pointing to the relationship between housework and the reproduction of labor (see Benston, 1969; Dalla Costa, 1972; Larguia and Dumoulin, 1972; Gerstein, 1973; Vogel, 1973; Secombe, [1973]; Gardiner, 1974; Rowntree, M. & J., 1970). To do this is to place women squarely in the definition of capitalism, the process in which capital is produced by the extraction of surplus value from labor by capital. . . .

But to explain women's usefulness to capitalism is one thing. To argue that this usefulness explains the genesis of the oppression of women is quite another. It is precisely at this point that the analysis of capitalism ceases to explain very much about women and the oppression of women.

Women are oppressed in societies which can by no stretch of the imagination be described as capitalist.. . . Capitalism has taken over, and rewired, notions of male and female which predate it by centuries. No analysis of the reproduction of labor power under capitalism can explain foot-binding, chastity belts, or any of the incredible array of Byzantine, fetishized indignities, let alone the more ordinary ones, which have been inflicted upon women in various times and places. The analysis of the reproduction of labor power does not even explain why it is usually women who do domestic work in the home, rather than men.

In this light it is interesting to return to Marx's discussion of the reproduction of labor. What is necessary to reproduce the worker is determined in part by the biological needs of the human organism, in part by the physical conditions of the place in which it lives, and in part by cultural tradition. Marx observed that beer is necessary for the reproduction of the English working class, and wine necessary for the French.

> . . . . *the number and extent of his* [the worker's] *so-called necessary wants, as also the modes of satisfying them, are themselves the product of historical development,* and depend therefore to a great extent on the degree of civilization of a country, more particularly on the conditions under which, and consequently on the habits and degree of comfort in which, the class of free labourers has been formed. *In contradistinction therefore to the case of other commodities, there enters into the determination of the value of labour-power a historical and moral element.* . . . (Marx, 1972:171, my italics)

It is precisely this "historical and moral element" which determines that a "wife" is among the necessities of a worker, that women rather than men do housework, and that capitalism is heir to a long tradition in which women do not inherit, in which women do not lead, and in which women do not talk to god. It is this "historical and moral element" which presented capitalism with a cultural heritage of forms of masculinity and femininity. It is within this "historical and moral element" that the entire domain of sex, sexuality, and sex oppression is subsumed. And the briefness of Marx's comment only serves to emphasize the vast area of social life which it covers and leaves unexamined. Only by subjecting this "historical and moral element" to analysis can the structure of sex oppression be delineated.

ENGELS

In *The Origin of the Family, Private Property, and the State,* Engels sees sex oppression as part of capitalism's heritage from prior social forms. Moreover, Engels integrates sex and sexuality into his theory of society. . . . The idea that the "relations of sexuality" can and should be distinguished from the "relations of production" is not the least of Engels' intuitions:

According to the materialistic conception, the determining factor in history is, in the final instance, the production and reproduction of immediate life. *This again, is a twofold character: on the one hand, the production of the means of existence, of food, clothing, and shelter and the tools necessary for that production; on the other side, the production of human beings themselves,* the propagation of the species. The social organization under which the people of a particular historical epoch and a particular country live is determined by both kinds of production: by the stage of development of labor on the one hand, and of the family on the other . . . (Engels, 1972:71–72; my italics)

This passage indicates an important recognition—that a human group must do more than apply its activity to reshaping the natural world in order to clothe, feed, and warm itself. We usually call the system by which elements of the natural world are transformed into objects of human consumption the "economy." But the needs which are satisfied by economic activity even in the richest, Marxian sense, do not exhaust fundamental human requirements. A human group must also reproduce itself from generation to generation. The needs of sexuality and procreation must be satisfied as much as the need to eat, and one of the most obvious deductions which can be made from the data of anthropology is that these needs are hardly ever satisfied in any "natural" form, any more than are the needs for food. Hunger is hunger, but what counts as food is culturally determined and obtained. Every society has some form of organized economic activity. Sex is sex, but what counts as sex is equally culturally determined and obtained. Every society also has a sex/gender system—a set of arrangements by which the biological raw material of human sex and procreation is shaped by human, social intervention and satisfied in a conventional manner, no matter how bizarre some of the conventions may be.[2]

The realm of human sex, gender, and procreation has been subjected to, and changed by, relentless social activity for millennia. Sex as we know it—gender

---

[2]That some of them are pretty bizarre, from our point of view, only demonstrates the point that sexuality is expressed through the intervention of culture (see Ford and Beach, 1972). Some examples may be chosen from among the exotica in which anthropologists delight. Among the Banaro, marriage involves several socially sanctioned sexual parternerships. When a woman is married, she is initiated into intercourse by the sib-friend of her groom's father. After bearing a child by this man, she begins to have intercourse with her husband. She also has an institutionalized partnership with the sib-friend of her husband. A man's partners include his wife, the wife of his sib-friend, and the wife of his sib-friend's son (Thurnwald, 1916). Multiple intercourse is a more pronounced custom among the Marind Anim. At the time of marriage, the bride has intercourse with all the members of the groom's clan, the groom coming last. Every major festival is accompanied by a practice known as *otiv-bombari*, in which semen is collected for ritual purposes. A few women have intercourse with many men, and the resulting semen is collected in coconut-shell buckets. A Marind male is subjected to multiple homosexual intercourse during initiation (Van Baal, 1966). Among the Etoro, heterosexual intercourse is taboo for between 205 and 260 days a year (Kelly, 1974). In much of New Guinea, men fear copulation and think that it will kill them if they engage in it without magical precautions (Glasse, 1971; Meggitt, [1964]). Usually, such ideas of feminine pollution express the subordination of women. But symbolic systems contain internal contradictions, whose logical extensions sometimes lead to inversions of the propositions on which a system is based. In New Britain, men's fear of sex is so extreme that rape appears to be feared by men rather than women. Women run after the men, who flee from them, women are the sexual aggressors, and it is bridegrooms who are reluctant (Goodale and Chowning, 1971). Other interesting sexual variations can be found in Yalmon (1963) and K. Gough (1959).

identity, sexual desire and fantasy, concepts of childhood—is itself a social product. We need to understand the relations of its production, and forget, for awhile, about food, clothing, automobiles, and transistor radios. In most Marxist tradition, and even in Engels' book, the concept of the "second aspect of material life" has tended to fade into the background, or to be incorporated into the usual notions of "material life." Engels' suggestion has never been followed up and subjected to the refinement which it needs. But he does indicate the existence and importance of the domain of social life which I want to call the sex/gender system.

Other names have been proposed for the sex/gender system. The most common alternatives are "mode of reproduction" and "patriarchy." It may be foolish to quibble about terms, but both of these can lead to confusion. All three proposals have been made in order to introduce a distinction between "economic" systems and "sexual" systems, and to indicate that sexual systems have a certain autonomy and cannot always be explained in terms of economic forces. "Mode of reproduction," for instance, has been proposed in opposition to the more familiar "mode of production." But this terminology links the "economy" to production, and the sexual system to "reproduction." It reduces the richness of either system, since "productions" and "reproductions" take place in both. Every mode of production involves reproduction—of tools, labor, and social relations. We cannot relegate all of the multi-faceted aspects of social reproduction to the sex system. Replacement of machinery is an example of reproduction in the economy. On the other hand, we cannot limit the sex system to "reproduction" in either the social or biological sense of the term. A sex/gender system is not simply the reproductive moment of a "mode of production." The formation of gender identity is an example of production in the realm of the sexual system. And a sex/gender system involves more than the "relations of procreation," reproduction in the biological sense.

The term "patriarchy" was introduced to distinguish the forces maintaining sexism from other social forces, such as capitalism. But the use of "patriarchy" obscures other distinctions. Its use is analogous to using capitalism to refer to all modes of production, whereas the usefulness of the term "capitalism" lies precisely in that it distinguishes between the different systems by which societies are provisioned and organized. Any society will have some system of "political economy." Such a system may be egalitarian or socialist. It may be class stratified, in which case the oppressed class may consist of serfs, peasants, or slaves. The oppressed class may consist of wage laborers, in which case the system is properly labeled "capitalist." The power of the term lies in its implication that, in fact, there are alternatives to capitalism.

Similarly, any society will have some systematic ways to deal with sex, gender, and babies. Such a system may be sexually egalitarian, at least in theory, or it may be "gender stratified," as seems to be the case for most or all of the known examples. But it is important—even in the face of a depressing history—to maintain a distinction between the human capacity and necessity to create a sexual world, and the empirically oppressive ways in which sexual worlds have been organized. Patriarchy subsumes both meanings into the same term. Sex/gender system, on the other hand, is a neutral term which refers to the domain and indicates that oppression is not inevitable in that domain, but is the product of the specific social relations which organize it.

Finally, there are gender-stratified systems which are not adequately described as patriarchal. Many New Guinea societies (Enga, Maring, Bena Bena, Huli, Melpa, Kuma, Gahuku-Gama, Fore, Marind Anim, ad nauseum; see Berndt, 1962; Langness, 1967; Rappaport, 1975; Read, 1952; Meggitt, [1964]; Glasse, 1971; Strathern, 1972; Reay, 1959; Van Baal, 1966; Lindenbaum, 1973) are viciously oppressive to women. But the power of males in these groups is not founded on their roles as fathers or patriarchs, but on their collective adult maleness, embodied in secret cults, men's houses, warfare, exchange networks, ritual knowledge, and various initiation procedures. Patriarchy is a specific form of male dominance, and the use of the term ought to be confined to the Old Testament-type pastoral nomads from whom the term comes, or groups like them. Abraham was a Patriarch—one old man whose absolute power over wives, children, herds, and dependents was an aspect of the institution of fatherhood, as defined in the social group in which he lived.

Whichever term we use, what is important is to develop concepts to adequately describe the social organization of sexuality and the reproduction of the conventions of sex and gender. We need to pursue the project Engels abandoned when he located the subordination of women in a development within the mode of production.[3] To do this, we can imitate Engels in his method rather than in his results. Engels approached the task of analyzing the "second aspect of material life" by way of an examination of a theory of kinship systems. Kinship systems are and do many things. But they are made up of, and reproduce, concrete forms of socially organized sexuality. Kinship systems are observable and empirical forms of sex/gender systems.

KINSHIP
(ON THE PART PLAYED BY SEXUALITY
IN THE TRANSITION FROM APE TO "MAN")

To an anthropologist, a kinship system is not a list of biological relatives. It is a system of categories and statuses which often contradict actual genetic relationships. There are dozens of examples in which socially defined kinship statuses take precedence over biology. The Nuer custom of "woman marriage" is a case in point. The Nuer define the status of fatherhood as belonging to the person in whose name cattle bridewealth is given for the mother. Thus, a woman can be married to another woman, and be husband to the wife and father of her

---

[3]Engels thought that men acquired wealth in the form of herds and, wanting to pass this wealth to their own children, overthrew "mother right" in favor of patrilineal inheritance. "The overthrow of mother right was the *world historical defeat of the female sex.* The man took command of the home also; the woman was degraded and reduced to servitude; she became the slave of his lust and a mere instrument for the production of children" (Engels, 1972:120–21; italics in original). As has been often pointed out, women do not necessarily have significant social authority in societies practicing matrilineal inheritance (Schneider and Gough, [1961]).

children, despite the fact that she is not the inseminator (Evans-Pritchard, 1951:107–09).

In pre-state societies, kinship is the idiom of social interaction, organizing economic, political, and ceremonial, as well as sexual, activity. One's duties, responsibilities, and privileges vis-à-vis others are defined in terms of mutual kinship or lack thereof. The exchange of goods and services, production and distribution, hostility and solidarity, ritual and ceremony, all take place within the organizational structure of kinship. The ubiquity and adaptive effectiveness of kinship has led many anthropologists to consider its invention, along with the invention of language, to have been the developments which decisively marked the discontinuity between semi-human hominids and human beings (Sahlins, 1960; Livingstone, 1969; Lévi-Strauss, 1969). . . .

In taking up Engels' project of extracting a theory of sex oppression from the study of kinship, we have the advantage of the maturation of ethnology since the nineteenth century. We also have the advantage of a peculiar and particularly appropriate book, Lévi-Strauss' *The Elementary Structures of Kinship*. This is the boldest twentieth-century version of the nineteenth-century project to understand human marriage. It is a book in which kinship is explicitly conceived of as an imposition of cultural organization upon the facts of biological procreation. It is permeated with an awareness of the importance of sexuality in human society. It is a description of society which does not assume an abstract, genderless human subject. On the contrary, the human subject in Lévi-Strauss's work is always either male or female, and the divergent social destinies of the two sexes can therefore be traced. Since Lévi-Strauss sees the essence of kinship systems to lie in an exchange of women between men, he constructs an implicit theory of sex oppression. . . .

"VILE AND PRECIOUS MERCHANDISE" —MONIQUE WITTIG

. . . *The Elementary Structures* is in part a radical gloss on another famous theory of primitive social organization, Mauss' *Essay on the Gift* (See also Sahlins, 1972; Chap. 4). It was Mauss who first theorized as to the significance of one of the most striking features of primitive societies: the extent to which giving, receiving, and reciprocating gifts dominates social intercourse. In such societies, all sorts of things circulate in exchange—food, spells, rituals, words, names, ornaments, tools, and powers.

> Your own mother, your own sister, your own pigs, your own yams that you have piled up, you may not eat. Other people's mothers, other people's sisters, other people's pigs, other people's yams that they have piled up, you may eat. (Arapesh, cited in Lévi-Strauss, 1969:27)

In a typical gift transaction, neither party gains anything. In the Trobriand Islands, each household maintains a garden of yams and each household eats yams. But the yams a household grows and the yams it eats are not the same. At harvest time, a man sends the yams he has cultivated to the household of his sister; the household in which he lives is provisioned by his wife's brother (Malinowski, 1929). Since such a procedure appears to be a useless one from the point of view of accumulation or trade, its logic has been sought elsewhere. Mauss proposed that the significance of gift giving is that it expresses, affirms, or creates a social link between the partners of an exchange. Gift giving confers upon its participants a special relationship of trust, solidarity, and mutual aid. One can solicit a friendly relationship in the offer of a gift; acceptance implies a willingness to return a gift and a confirmation of the relationship. Gift exchange may also be the idiom of competition and rivalry. There are many examples in which one person humiliates another by giving more than can be reciprocated. Some political systems, such as the Big Man systems of highland New Guinea, are based on exchange which is unequal on the material plane. An aspiring Big Man wants to give away more goods than can be reciprocated. He gets his return in political prestige.

Although both Mauss and Lévi-Strauss emphasize the solidary aspects of gift exchange, the other purposes served by gift giving only strengthen the point that it is an ubiquitous means of social commerce. Mauss proposed that gifts were the threads of social discourse, the means by which such societies were held together in the absence of specialized governmental institutions. "The gift is the primitive way of achieving the peace that in civil society is secured by the state. . . . Composing society, the gift was the liberation of culture" (Sahlins, 1972:169, 175).

Lévi-Strauss adds to the theory of primitive reciprocity the idea that marriages are a most basic form of gift exchange, in which it is women who are the most precious of gifts. He argues that the incest taboo should best be understood as a mechanism to insure that such exchanges take place between families and between groups. Since the existence of incest taboos is universal, but the content of their prohibitions variable, they cannot be explained as having the aim of preventing the occurrence of genetically close matings. Rather, the incest taboo imposes the social aim of exogamy and alliance upon the biological events of sex and procreation. The incest taboo divides the universe of sexual choice into categories of permitted and prohibited sexual partners. Specifically, by forbidding unions within a group it enjoins marital exchange between groups.

> The prohibition on the sexual use of a daughter or a sister compels them to be given in marriage to another man, and at the same time it establishes a right to the daughter or sister of this other man. . . . The woman whom one does not take is, for that very reason, offered up. (Lévi-Strauss, 1969:51)

> The prohibition of incest is less a rule prohibiting marriage with the mother, sister, or daughter, than a rule obliging the mother, sister, or daughter to be given to others. It is the supreme rule of the gift. . . . (Ibid:481)

The result of a gift of women is more profound than the result of other gift transactions, because the relationship thus established is not just one of reciprocity, but one of kinship. The exchange partners have become affines, and their descendents will be related by blood: "Two people may meet in friendship and exchange gifts and yet quarrel and fight in later times, but intermarriage connects them in a permanent manner" (Best, cited in Lévi-Strauss, 1969:481). . . .

The exchange of women does not necessarily imply that women are objectified, in the modern sense, since objects in the primitive world are imbued with highly personal qualities. But it does imply a distinction between gift and giver. If women are the gifts, then it is men who are the exchange partners. And it is the partners, not the presents, upon whom reciprocal exchange confers its quasi-mystical power of social linkage. The relations of such a system are such that women are in no position to realize the benefits of their own circulation. As long as the relations specify that men exchange women, it is men who are the beneficiaries of the product of such exchanges—social organization.

> The total relationship of exchange which constitutes marriage is not established between a man and a woman, but between two groups of men, and the woman figures only as one of the objects in the exchange, not as one of the partners. . . . This remains true even when the girl's feelings are taken into consideration, as, moreover, is usually the case. In acquiescing to the proposed union, she precipitates or allows the exchange to take place, she cannot alter its nature. . . . (Lévi-Strauss in ibid.115)[4]

To enter into a gift exchange as a partner, one must have something to give. If women are for men to dispose of, they are in no position to give themselves away.

> "What woman," mused a young Northern Melpa man, "is ever strong enough to get up and say, 'Let us make *moka,* let us find wives and pigs, let us give our daughters to men, let us wage war, let us kill our enemies!' No indeed not! . . . they are little rubbish things who stay at home simply, don't you see?" (Strathern, 1972:161)

What women indeed! The Melpa women of whom the young man spoke can't get wives, they *are* wives, and what they get are husbands, an entirely different matter. The Melpa women can't give their daughters to men, because they do not have the same rights in their daughters that their male kin have, rights of bestowal (although *not* of ownership).

The "exchange of women" is a seductive and powerful concept. It is attractive in that it places the oppression of women within social systems, rather than in biology. Moreover, it suggests that we look for the ultimate locus of women's oppression within the traffic in women, rather than within the traffic in merchandise. It is certainly not difficult to find ethnographic and historical examples of trafficking in women. Women are given in marriage, taken in battle, exchanged for favors, sent as tribute, traded, bought, and sold. Far from being confined to the "primitive" world, these practices seem only to become more pronounced and commercialized in more "civilized" societies. Men are of course also trafficked—but as slaves, hustlers, athletic stars, serfs, or as some other catastrophic social status, rather than as men. Women are transacted as slaves,

---

[4]The analysis of society as based on bonds between men by means of women makes the separatist responses of the women's movement thoroughly intelligible. Separatism can be seen as a mutation in social structure, as an attempt to form social groups based on unmediated bonds between women. It can also be seen as a radical denial of men's "rights" in women, and as a claim by women of rights in themselves.

serfs, and prostitutes, but also simply as women. And if men have been sexual subjects—exchangers—and women sexual semi-objects—gifts—for much of human history, then many customs, clichés, and personality traits seem to make a great deal of sense (among others, the curious custom by which a father gives away the bride). . . .

Kinship systems do not merely exchange women. They exchange sexual access, genealogical statuses, lineage names and ancestors, rights and *people*—men, women, and children—in concrete systems of social relationships. These relationships always include certain rights for men, others for women. "Exchange of women" is a shorthand for expressing that the social relations of a kinship system specify that men have certain rights in their female kin, and that women do not have the same rights either to themselves or to their male kin. In this sense, the exchange of women is a profound perception of a system in which women do not have full rights to themselves. The exchange of women becomes an obfuscation if it is seen as a cultural necessity, and when it is used as the single tool with which an analysis of a particular kinship system is approached.

If Lévi-Strauss is correct in seeing the exchange of women as a fundamental principle of kinship, the subordination of women can be seen as a product of the relationships by which sex and gender are organized and produced. The economic oppression of women is derivative and secondary. But there is an "economics" of sex and gender, and what we need is a political economy of sexual systems. We need to study each society to determine the exact mechanisms by which particular conventions of sexuality are produced and maintained. The "exchange of women" is an initial step toward building an arsenal of concepts with which sexual systems can be described. . . .

Although every society has some sort of division of tasks by sex, the assignment of any particular task to one sex or the other varies enormously. In some groups, agriculture is the work of women, in others, the work of men. Women carry the heavy burdens in some societies, men in others. There are even examples of female hunters and warriors, and of men performing child-care tasks. Lévi-Strauss concludes from a survey of the division of labor by sex that it is not a biological specialization, but must have some other purpose. This purpose, he argues, is to insure the union of men and women by making the smallest viable economic unit contain at least one man and one woman.

> The very fact that it [the sexual division of labor] varies endlessly according to the society selected for consideration shows that . . . it is the mere fact of its existence which is mysteriously required, the form under which it comes to exist being utterly irrelevant, at least from the point of view of any natural necessity . . . the sexual division of labor is nothing else than a device to institute a reciprocal state of dependency between the sexes. (Lévi-Strauss, 1971:347–48)

The division of labor by sex can therefore be seen as a "taboo": a taboo against the sameness of men and women, a taboo dividing the sexes into two mutually exclusive categories, a taboo which exacerbates the biological differences between the sexes and thereby *creates* gender. The division of labor can also be seen as a taboo against sexual arrangements other than those containing at least one man and one woman, thereby enjoining heterosexual marriage. . . .

At the most general level, the social organization of sex rests upon gender, obligatory heterosexuality, and the constraint of female sexuality.

Gender is a socially imposed division of the sexes. It is a product of the social relations of sexuality. Kinship systems rest upon marriage. They therefore transform males and females into "men" and "women," each an incomplete half which can only find wholeness when united with the other. Men and women are, of course, different. But they are not as different as day and night, earth and sky, yin and yang, life and death. In fact, from the standpoint of nature, men and women are closer to each other than either is to anything else—for instance, mountains, kangaroos, or coconut palms. The idea that men and women are more different from one another than either is from anything else must come from somewhere other than nature. Furthermore, although there is an average difference between males and females on a variety of traits, the range of variation of those traits shows considerable overlap. There will always be some women who are taller than some men, for instance, even though men are on the average taller than women. But the idea that men and women are two mutually exclusive categories must arise out of something other than a nonexistent "natural" opposition. Far from being an expression of natural differences, exclusive gender identity is the suppression of natural similarities. It requires repression: in men, of whatever is the local version of "feminine" traits; in women, of the local definition of "masculine" traits. The division of the sexes has the effect of repressing some of the personality characteristics of virtually everyone, men and women. The same social system which oppresses women in its relations of exchange, oppresses everyone in its insistence upon a rigid division of personality.

Furthermore, individuals are engendered in order that marriage be guaranteed. Lévi-Strauss comes dangerously close to saying that heterosexuality is an instituted process. If biological and hormonal imperatives were as overwhelming as popular mythology would have them, it would hardly be necessary to insure hetereosexual unions by means of economic interdependency. Moreover, the incest taboo presupposes a prior, less articulate taboo on homosexuality. A prohibition against *some* heterosexual unions assumes a taboo against *non*-heterosexual unions. Gender is not only an identification with one sex; it also entails that sexual desire be directed toward the other sex. The sexual division of labor is implicated in both aspects of gender—male and female it creates them, and it creates them heterosexual. The suppression of the homosexual component of human sexuality, and by corollary, the oppression of homosexuals, is therefore a product of the same system whose rules and relations oppress women. . . .

In summary, some basic generalities about the organization of human sexuality can be derived from an exegesis of Lévi-Strauss's theories of kinship. These are the incest taboo, obligatory heterosexuality, and an asymmetric division of the sexes. The asymmetry of gender—the difference between exchanger and exchanged—entails the constraint of female sexuality. Concrete kinship systems will have more specific conventions, and these conventions vary a great deal. While particular socio-sexual systems vary, each one is specific, and individuals within it will have to conform to a finite set of possibilities. Each new generation must learn and become its sexual destiny, each person must be encoded with its appropriate status within the system. It would be extraordinary for one of us to calmly assume that we would conventionally marry a mother's brother's daughter, or a father's sister's son. Yet there are groups in which such a marital future is taken for granted.

Anthropology, and descriptions of kinship systems, do not explain the mechanisms by which children are engraved with the conventions of sex and gender. Psychoanalysis, on the other hand, is a theory about the reproduction of kinship. Psychoanalysis describes the residue left within individuals by their confrontation with the rules and regulations of sexuality of the societies to which they are born. . . .

The salvage of psychoanalysis from its own motivated repression is not for the sake of Freud's good name. Psychoanalysis contains a unique set of concepts for understanding men, women, and sexuality. It is a theory of sexuality in human society. Most importantly, psychoanalysis provides a description of the mechanisms by which the sexes are divided and deformed, of how bisexual, androgynous infants are transformed into boys and girls.[5] Psychoanalysis is a feminist theory *manqué*.

THE OEDIPUS HEX

. . . It is in explaining the acquisition of "femininity" that Freud employs the concepts of penis envy and castration which have infuriated feminists since he first introduced them. The girl turns from the mother and represses the "masculine" elements of her libido as a result of her recognition that she is castrated. She compares her tiny clitoris to the larger penis, and in the face of its evident superior ability to satisfy the mother, falls prey to penis envy and a sense of inferiority. She gives up her struggle for the mother and assumes a passive feminine position vis-à-vis the father. Freud's account can be read as claiming that femininity is a consequence of the anatomical differences between the sexes. He has therefore been accused of biological determinism. Nevertheless, even in his most anatomically stated versions of the female castration complex, the "inferiority" of the woman's genitals is a product of the situational context: the girl feels less "equipped" to possess and satisfy the other. If the pre-Oedipal lesbian were not confronted by the heterosexuality of the mother, she might draw different conclusions about the relative status of her genitals.

---

[5]"In studying women we cannot neglect the methods of a science of the mind, a theory that attempts to explain how women become women and men, men. The borderline between the biological and the social which finds expression in the family is the land psychoanalysis sets out to chart, the land where sexual distinction originates." (Mitchell, 1971:167).

OEDIPUS REVISITED

. . . The psychoanalytic theory of femininity is one that sees female development based largely on pain and humiliation, and it takes some fancy footwork to explain why anyone ought to enjoy being a woman. At this point in the classic discussions biology makes a triumphant return. The fancy footwork consists in arguing that finding joy in pain is adaptive to the role of women in reproduction, since childbirth and defloration are "painful." Would it not make more sense to question the entire procedure? If women, in finding their place in a sexual system, are robbed of libido and forced into a masochistic eroticism, why did the analysis not argue for novel arrangements, instead of rationalizing the old ones?

Freud's theory of femininity has been subjected to feminist critique since it was first published. To the extent that it is a rationalization of female subordination, this critique has been justified. To the extent that it is a description of a process which subordinates women, this critique is a mistake. As a description of how phallic culture domesticates women, and the effects in women of their domestication, psychoanalytic theory has no parallel (see also Mitchell, 1971 and 1974; Lasch, 1974). And since psychoanalysis is a theory of gender, dismissing it would be suicidal for a political movement dedicated to eradicating gender hierarchy (or gender itself). We cannot dismantle something that we underestimate or do not understand. The oppression of women is deep; equal pay, equal work, and all of the female politicians in the world will not extirpate the roots of sexism. Lévi-Strauss and Freud elucidate what would otherwise be poorly perceived parts of the deep structures of sex oppression. They serve as reminders of the intractability and magnitude of what we fight, and their analyses provide preliminary charts of the social machinery we must rearrange.

WOMEN UNITE TO OFF THE OEDIPAL RESIDUE OF CULTURE

The precision of the fit between Freud and Lévi-Strauss is striking. Kinship systems require a division of the sexes. The Oedipal phase divides the sexes. Kinship systems include sets of rules governing sexuality. The Oedipal crisis is the assimilation of these rules and taboos. Compulsory heterosexuality is the product of kinship. The Oedipal phase constitutes heterosexual desire. Kinship rests on a radical difference between the rights of men and women. The Oedipal complex confers male rights upon the boy, and forces the girl to accommodate herself to her lesser rights.

This fit between Lévi-Strauss and Freud is by implication an argument that our sex/gender system is still organized by the principles outlined by Lévi-Strauss, despite the entirely nonmodern character of his data base. The more recent data on which Freud bases his theories testifies to the endurance of these sexual structures. If my reading of Freud and Lévi-Strauss is accurate, it suggests that the feminist movement must attempt to resolve the Oedipal crisis of culture by reorganizing the domain of sex and gender in such a way that each individual's Oedipal experience would be less destructive. The dimensions of such a task are difficult to imagine, but at least certain conditions would have to be met.

Several elements of the Oedipal crisis would have to be altered in order that the phase not have such disastrous effects on the young female ego. The Oedipal phase institutes a contradiction in the girl by placing irreconcilable demands upon her. On the one hand, the girl's love for the mother is induced by the mother's job of child care. The girl is then forced to abandon this love because of the female sex role—to belong to a man. If the sexual division of labor were such that adults of both sexes cared for children equally, primary object choice would be bisexual. If heterosexuality were not obligatory, this early love would not have to be suppressed, and the penis would not be overvalued. If the sexual property system were reorganized in such a way that men did not have overriding rights in women (if there was no exchange of women) and if there were no gender, the entire Oedipal drama would be a relic. In short, feminism must call for a revolution in kinship.

The organization of sex and gender once had functions other than itself—it organized society. Now, it only organizes and reproduces itself. The kinds of relationships of sexuality established in the dim human past still dominate our sexual lives, our ideas about men and women, and the ways we raise our children. But they lack the functional load they once carried. One of the most conspicuous features of kinship is that it has been systematically stripped of its functions—political, economic, educational, and organizational. It has been reduced to its barest bones—*sex and gender*.

Human sexual life will always be subject to convention and human intervention. It will never be completely "natural," if only because our species is social, cultural, and articulate. The wild profusion of infantile sexuality will always be tamed. The confrontation between immature and helpless infants and the developed social life of their elders will probably always leave some residue of disturbance. But the mechanisms and aims of this process need not be largely independent of conscious choice. Cultural evolution provides us with the opportunity to seize control of the means of sexuality, reproduction, and socialization, and to make conscious decisions to liberate human sexual life from the archaic relationships which deform it. Ultimately, a thorough-going feminist revolution would liberate more than women. It would liberate forms of sexual expression, and it would liberate human personality from the straightjacket of gender. . . .

The sex/gender system is not immutably oppressive and has lost much of its traditional function. Nevertheless, it will not wither away in the absence of oppression. It still carries the social burden of sex and gender, of socializing the young, and of providing ultimate propositions about the nature of human beings themselves. And it serves economic and political ends other than those it was originally designed to further (cf. Scott, 1965). The sex/gender system must be reorganized through political action.

Finally, the exegesis of Lévi-Strauss and Freud suggests a certain vision of feminist politics and the feminist utopia. It suggests that we should not aim for the elimination of men, but for the elimination of the social system which creates sexism and gender. I personally find a vision of an Amazon matriarchate, in which men are reduced to servitude or oblivion (depending on the possibilities for parthenogenetic reproduction), distasteful and inadequate. Such a vision maintains gender and the division of the sexes. It is a vision which simply inverts the arguments of those who base their case for inevitable male dominance on ineradicable and *significant* biological differences between the sexes. But we are not only oppressed *as* women, we are oppressed by having to *be* women, or men as the case may be. I personally feel that the feminist movement must dream of even more than the elimination of the oppression of women. It must dream of the elimination of obligatory sexualities and sex roles. The dream I find most compelling is one of an androgynous and genderless (though not sexless) society, in which one's sexual anatomy is irrelevant to who one is, what one does, and with whom one makes love.

THE POLITICAL ECONOMY OF SEX

It would be nice to be able to conclude here with the implications for feminism and gay liberation of the overlap between Freud and Lévi-Strauss. But I must suggest, tentatively, a next step on the agenda: a Marxian analysis of sex/gender systems. Sex/gender systems are not ahistorical emanations of the human mind; they are products of historical human activity.

We need, for instance, an analysis of the evolution of sexual exchange along the lines of Marx's discussion in *Capital* of the evolution of money and commodities. There is an economics and a politics to sex/gender systems which is obscured by the concept of "exchange of women.". . . .

In short, there are other questions to ask of a marriage system than whether or not it exchanges women. Is the woman traded for a woman, or is there an equivalent? Is this equivalent only for women, or can it be turned into something else? If it can be turned into something else, is it turned into political power or wealth? On the other hand, can bridewealth be obtained only in marital exchange, or can it be obtained from elsewhere? Can women be accumulated through amassing wealth? Can wealth be accumulated by disposing of women? Is a marriage system part of a system of stratification? . . .

Sexual systems cannot, in the final analysis, be understood in complete isolation. A full-bodied analysis of women in a single society, or throughout history, must take *everything* into account: the evolution of commodity forms in women, systems of land tenure, political arrangements, subsistence technology, etc. Equally important, economic and political analyses are incomplete if they do not consider women, marriage, and sexuality. . . .

This sort of endeavor is, in the final analysis, exactly what Engels tried to do in his effort to weave a coherent analysis of so many of the diverse aspects of social life. He tried to relate men and women, town and country, kinship and state, forms of property, systems of land tenure, convertibility of wealth, forms of exchange, the technology of food production, and forms of trade, to name a few, into a systematic historical account. Eventually, someone will have to write a new version of *The Origin of the Family, Private Property, and the State,* recognizing the mutual interdependence of sexuality, economics, and politics without underestimating the full significance of each in human society.

BIBLIOGRAPHY

Althusser, Louis, and Balibar, Etienne. 1970. *Reading Capital.* London: New Left Books.

Benston, Margaret. 1969. "The Political Economy of Women's Liberation." *Monthly Review* 21, no. 4: 13–27.

Berndt, Ronald. 1962. *Excess and Restraint.* Chicago: University of Chicago Press.

Dalla Costa, Mariarosa, and James, Selma. 1972. *The Power of Women and the Subversion of the Community.* Bristol: Falling Wall Press.

Engels, Frederick. 1972. *The Origin of the Family, Private Property, and the State,* edited by Eleanor Leacock. New York: International Publishers.

Evans-Pritchard, E. E. 1951. *Kinship and Marriage among the Nuer.* London: Oxford University Press.

Ford, Clellan, and Beach, Frank. 1972. *Patterns of Sexual Behavior.* New York: Harper.

Gardiner, Jean. 1974. "Political Economy of Female Labor in Capitalist Society." Unpublished manuscript.

Gerstein, Ira. 1973. "Domestic Work and Capitalism." *Radical America* 7, nos. 4 and 5: 101–28.

Glasse, R. M. 1971. "The Mask of Venery." Paper read at the 70th Annual Meeting of the American Anthropological Association, New York City, December 1971.

Goodale, Jane C., and Chowning, Ann. 1971. "The Contaminating Woman." Paper read at the 70th Annual Meeting of the American Anthropological Association.

Gough, Kathleen. 1959. "The Nayars and the Definition of Marriage." *Journal of the Royal Anthropological Institute* 89: 23–24.

Kelly, Raymond. 1974. "Witchcraft and Sexual Relations: An Exploration of the Social and Semantic Implications of the Structure of Belief." Paper read at the 73rd Annual Meeting of the American Anthropological Association, Mexico City.

Langness, L. L. 1967. "Sexual Antagonism in the New Guinea Highlands: A Bena Bena Example." *Oceania* 37, no. 3: 161–77.

Larguia, Isabel, and Cumoulin, John. 1972. "Towards a Science of Women's Liberation." *NACIA Newsletter* 6, no. 10: 3–20.

Lasch, Christopher. 1974. "Freud and Women." *New York Review of Books* 21, no. 15: 12–17.

Levi-Strauss, Claude. 1969. *The Elementary Structures of Kinship.* Boston: Beacon Press.
———. 1971. "The Family." In *Man, Culture, and Society,* edited by H. Shapiro. London: Oxford University Press.

Lindenbaum, Shirley. 1973. "A Wife Is the Hand of Man." Paper read at the 72nd Annual Meeting of the American Anthropological Association.

Livingstone, Frank. 1969. "Genetics, Ecology, and Origins of Incest and Exogamy." *Current Anthropology* 10, no. 1: 45–49.

Malinowski, Bronislaw. 1929. *The Sexual Life of Savages.* London: Routledge and Kegan Paul.

Marx, Karl. 1971. *Wage-Labor and Capital*. New York: International Publishers.

———. 1972. *Capital*, vol. 1. New York: International Publishers.

Meggit, M. J. 1964. "Male-Female Relationships in the Highlands of Australian New Guinea." *American Anthropologist* 66, no. 4, part 2: 204–24.

Mitchell, Juliet. 1971. *Women's Estate*. New York: Vintage.

———. 1974. *Psychoanalysis and Feminism*. New York: Pantheon.

Rappaport, Roy, and Buchbinder, Georgeda. 1975. "Fertility and Death among the Maring." In *Sex Roles in the New Guinea Highlands,* edited by Paula Brown and G. Buchbinder. Cambridge, Mass.: Harvard University Press.

Read, Kenneth. 1952. "The Nama Cult of the Central Highlands, New Guinea." *Oceania* 23, no. 1: 1–25.

Reay, Marie. 1959. *The Kuma*. London: Cambridge University Press.

Rowntree, M. and J. 1970. "More on the Political Economy of Women's Liberation." *Monthly Review* 21, no. 8:26–32.

Sahlins, Marshall. 1960. "The Origin of Society." *Scientific American* 203, no. 3: 76–86.

———. 1972. *Stone Age Economics*. Chicago: Aldine-Atherton.

Schneider, David, and Gough, Kathleen, eds. 1961. *Matrilineal Kinship*. Berkeley: University of California Press.

Scott, John Finley. 1965. "The Role of Collegiate Sororities in Maintaining Class and Ethnic Endogamy." *American Sociological Review* 30, no. 4: 415–26.

Secombe, Wally. 1973. "Housework Under Capitalism." *New Left Review* 83: 3–24.

Strathern, Marilyn. 1972. *Women in Between*. New York: Seminar.

Thurnwald, Richard. 1916. "Banaro Society." *Memoirs of the American Anthropological Association* 3, no. 4: 251–391.

Van Baal, J. 1966. *Dema*. The Hague: Nijhoff.

Vogel, Lise. 1972. "The Earthly Family." *Radical America* 7, nos. 4 and 5: 9–50.

Yalman, Nur. 1963. "On the Purity of Women in the Castes of Ceylon and Malabar." *Journal of the Royal Anthropological Institute* 93, no. 1: 25–58.

The Unhappy Marriage of Marxism and Feminism: Towards a More Progressive Union[1]

Heidi I. Hartmann

The "marriage" of marxism and feminism has been like the marriage of husband and wife depicted in English common law: marxism and feminism are one, and that one is marxism.[2] Recent attempts to integrate marxism and feminism are unsatisfactory to us as feminists because they subsume the feminist struggle into the "larger" struggle against capital. To continue our simile further, either we need a healthier marriage or we need a divorce.

The inequalities in this marriage, like most social phenomena, are no accident. Many marxists typically argue that feminism is at best less important than class conflict and at worst divisive of the working class. This political stance produces an analysis that absorbs feminism into the class struggle. Moreover, the analytic power of marxism with respect to capital has obscured its limitations with respect to sexism. We will argue here that while marxist analysis provides essential insight into the laws of historical development, and those of capital in particular, the categories of marxism are sex-blind. Only a specifically feminist analysis reveals the systemic character of relations between men and women. Yet feminist analysis by itself is inadequate because it has been blind to history and insufficiently materialist. Both marxist analysis, particularly its historical and materialistic method, and feminist analysis, especially the identification of patriarchy as a social and historical structure, must be drawn upon if we are to understand the development of western capitalist societies and the predicament of women within them. In this essay we suggest a new direction for marxist feminist analysis. . . .

I MARXISM AND THE WOMAN QUESTION

The woman question has never been the "feminist question." The feminist question is directed at the causes of sexual inequality between women and men, of male dominance over women. Most marxist analyses of women's position

---

[1]Earlier drafts of this essay appeared in 1975 and 1977 coauthored with Amy B. Bridges. Unfortunately, because of the press of current commitments, Amy was unable to continue with this project, joint from its inception and throughout most of its long and controversial history. Over the years many individuals and groups offered us comments, debate, and support. . . . This is a substantially abridged version of the essay as it appeared in *Women and Revolution,* edited by Lydia Sargent (Boston: South End Press, 1981). A more complete version was also published in *Capital and Class* in the summer of 1979. . . .

[2]Often paraphrased as "the husband and wife are one and that one is the husband," English law held that "by marriage, the husband and wife are one person in law: that is, the very being or legal existence of the women is suspended during the marriage, or at least is incorporated and consolidated into that of the Husband," I. Blackstone, *Commentaries,* 1965, pp. 442–445, cited in Kenneth M. Davidson, Ruth B. Ginsburg, and Herma H. Kay, *Sex Based Discrimination* (St. Paul, Minn.: West Publishing Co., 1974), p. 117.

take as their question the relationship of women to the economic system, rather than that of women to men, apparently assuming the latter will be explained in their discussion of the former. Marxist analysis of the woman question has taken [several] forms. All see women's oppression in our connection (or lack of it) to production. Defining women as part of the working class, these analyses consistently subsume women's relation to men under workers' relation to capital. . . . All attempt to include women in the category working class and to understand women's oppression as another aspect of class oppression. In doing so all give short shrift to the object of feminist analysis, the relations between women and men. While our "problems" have been elegantly analyzed, they have been misunderstood. The focus of marxist analysis has been class relations; the object of marxist analysis has been understanding the laws of motion of capitalist society. While we believe marxist methodology *can* be used to formulate feminist strategy, these marxist feminist approaches discussed above clearly do not do so; their marxism clearly dominates their feminism.

As we have already suggested, this is due in part to the analytical power of marxism itself. Marxism is a theory of the development of class society, of the accumulation process in capitalist societies, of the reproduction of class dominance, and of the development of contradictions and class struggle. Capitalist societies are driven by the demands of the accumulation process, most succinctly summarized by the fact that production is oriented to exchange, not use. In a capitalist system production is important only insofar as it contributes to the making of profits, and the use value of products is only an incidental consideration. Profits derive from the capitalists' ability to exploit labor power, to pay laborers less than the value of what they produce. The accumulation of profits systematically transforms social structure as it transforms the relations of production. The reserve army of labor, the poverty of great numbers of people and the near-poverty of still more, these human reproaches to capital are by-products of the accumulation process itself. From the capitalist's point of view, the reproduction of the working class may "safely be left to itself."[3] At the same time, capital creates an ideology, which grows up along side it, of individualism, competitiveness, domination, and in our time, consumption of a particular kind. Whatever one's theory of the genesis of ideology one must recognize these as the dominant values of capitalist societies.

Marxism enables us to understand many aspects of capitalist societies: the structure of production, the generation of a particular occupational structure, and the nature of the dominant ideology. Marx's theory of the development of capitalism is a theory of the development of "empty places." Marx predicted, for example, the growth of the proletariat and the demise of the petit bourgeoisie. More precisely and in more detail, Braverman among others has explained the creation of the "places" clerical worker and service worker in

---

[3]This is a paraphrase. Karl Marx wrote: "The maintenance and reproduction of the working class is, and must ever be, a necessary condition to the reproduction of capital. But the capitalist may safely leave its fulfillment to the labourer's instincts of self-preservation and propagation." [*Capital* (New York: International Publishers, 1967), Vol. 1, p. 572.]

advanced capitalist societies.[4] Just as capital creates these places indifferent to the individuals who fill them, the categories of marxist analysis, class, reserve army of labor, wage-laborer, do not explain why particular people fill particular places. They give no clues about why *women* are subordinate to *men* inside and outside the family and why it is not the other way around. *Marxist categories, like capital itself, are sex-blind.* The categories of marxism cannot tell us who will fill the empty places. Marxist analysis of the woman question has suffered from this basic problem.

Towards More Useful Marxist Feminism

Marxism is also a *method* of social analysis, historical dialectical materialism. By putting this method to the service of feminist questions, Juliet Mitchell and Shulamith Firestone suggest new directions for marxist feminism. Mitchell says, we think correctly, that

> It is not "our relationship" to socialism that should *ever* be the question—it is the use of scientific socialism [what we call marxist method] as a method of analyzing the specific nature of our oppression and hence our revolutionary role. Such a method, I believe needs to understand radical feminism, quite as much as previously developed socialist theories.[5]

As Engels wrote:

> According to the materialistic conception, the determining factor in history is, in the final instance, the production and reproduction of immediate life. This, again, is of a twofold character: on the one side, the production of the means of existence, of food, clothing, and shelter and the tools necessary for that production; on the other side, the production of human beings themselves, the propagation of the species. The social organization under which the people of a particular historical epoch live is determined by both kinds of production. . . .[6]

This is the kind of analysis Mitchell has attempted. In her first essay, "Women: The Longest Revolution," Mitchell examines both market work and the work of reproduction, sexuality, and childrearing.[7]

Mitchell does not entirely succeed, perhaps because not all of women's work counts as production for her. Only market work is identified as production; the other spheres (loosely aggregated as the family) in which women work are identified as ideological. Patriarchy, which largely organizes reproduction, sexuality, and childrearing, has no material base for Mitchell. *Women's Estate,* Mitchell's expansion of this essay, focuses much more on developing the analysis

---

[4]Harry Braverman, *Labor and Monopoly Capital* (New York: Monthly Review Press, 1975).

[5]Juliet Mitchell, *Women's Estate* (New York: Vintage Books, 1973), p. 92.

[6]Frederick Engels, *The Origin of the Family, Private Property, and the State,* edited with an introduction by Eleanor Burke Leacock, New York International Publishers, 1972, "Preface to the First Edition," pp. 71–72. The continuation of this quotation reads, ". . . by the stage of development of labor on the one hand and of the family on the other." It is interesting that, by implication, labor is excluded from occurring within the family; this is precisely the blind spot we want to overcome in this essay.

[7]Juliet Mitchell, "Women: The Longest Revolution," *New Left Review,* No. 40 (November–December 1966), pp. 11–37, also reprinted by the New England Free Press.

of women's market work than it does on developing the analysis of women's work within the family. The book is much more concerned with women's relation to, and work for, capital than with women's relation to, and work for, men; more influenced by marxism than by radical feminism. . . .

Shulamith Firestone bridges marxism and feminism by bringing materialist analysis to bear on patriarchy.[8] Her use of materialist analysis is not as ambivalent as Mitchell's. The dialectic of sex, she says, is the fundamental historical dialectic, and the material base of patriarchy is the work women do reproducing the species. The importance of Firestone's work in using marxism to analyze women's position, in asserting the existence of a material base to patriarchy, cannot be overestimated. But it suffers from an overemphasis on biology and reproduction. What we need to understand is how sex (a biological fact) becomes gender (a social phenomenon). It is necessary to place all of women's work in its social and historical context, not to focus only on reproduction. Although Firestone's work offers a new and feminist use of marxist methodology, her insistence on the primacy of men's dominance over women as the cornerstone on which all other oppression (class, age, race) rests, suggests that her book is more properly grouped with the radical feminists than with the marxist feminists. Her work remains the most complete statement of the radical feminist position. . . .

II RADICAL FEMINISM AND PATRIARCHY

The great thrust of radical feminist writing has been directed to the documentation of the slogan "the personal is political." Women's discontent, radical feminists argued, is not the neurotic lament of the maladjusted, but a response to a social structure in which women are systematically dominated, exploited, and oppressed. Women's inferior position in the labor market, the male-centered emotional structure of middle class marriage, the use of women in advertising, the so-called understanding of women's psyche as neurotic—popularized by academic and clinical psychology—aspect after aspect of women's lives in advanced capitalist society was researched and analyzed. The radical feminist literature is enormous and defies easy summary. At the same time, its focus on psychology is consistent. The New York Radical Feminists' organizing document was "The Politics of the Ego." "The personal is political" means for radical feminists, that the original and basic class division is between the sexes, and that the motive force of history is the striving of men for power and domination over women, the dialectic of sex.[9]

---

[8]Shulamith Firestone, *The Dialectic of Sex* (New York: Bantam Books, 1971).

[9]"Politics of Ego: A Manifesto for New York Radical Feminists," can be found in *Rebirth of Feminism*, ed. Judith Hole and Ellen Levine (New York: Quadrangle Books, 1971), pp. 440–443. "Radical feminists" are those feminists who argue that the most fundamental dynamic of history is men's striving to dominate women. 'Radical' in this context does *not* mean anti-capitalist, socialist, counter-cultural, etc., but has the specific meaning of this particular set of feminist beliefs or group of feminists. Additional writings of radical feminists, of whom the New York Radical Feminists are probably the most influential, can be found in *Radical Feminism*, ed. Ann Koedt (New York: Quadrangle Press, 1972).

Accordingly, Firestone rewrote Freud to understand the development of boys and girls into men and women in terms of power.[10] Her characterizations of what are "male" and "female" character traits are typical of radical feminist writing. The male seeks power and domination; he is egocentric and individualistic, competitive and pragmatic; the "technological mode," according to Firestone, is male. The female is nurturant, artistic, and philosophical; the "aesthetic mode" is female.

No doubt, the idea that the aesthetic mode is female would have come as quite a shock to the ancient Greeks. Here lies the error of radical feminist analysis: the dialectic of sex as radical feminists present it projects male and female characteristics as they appear in the present back into all of history. Radical feminist analysis has greatest strength in its insights into the present. Its greatest weakness is a focus on the psychological which blinds it to history.

The reason for this lies not only in radical feminist method, but also in the nature of patriarchy itself, for patriarchy is a strikingly resilient form of social organization. Radical feminists use patriarchy to refer to a social system characterized by male domination over women. Kate Millett's definition is classic:

> our society . . . is a patriarchy. The fact is evident at once if one recalls that the military, industry, technology, universities, science, political offices, finances—in short, every avenue of power within the society, including the coercive force of the police, is entirely in male hands.[11]

This radical feminist definition of patriarchy applies to most societies we know of and cannot distinguish among them. The use of history by radical feminists is typically limited to providing examples of the existence of patriarchy in all times and places.[12] For both marxist and mainstream social scientists before the women's movement, patriarchy referred to a system of relations between men, which formed the political and economic outlines of feudal and some pre-feudal societies, in which hierarchy followed ascribed characteristics. Capitalist societies are understood as meritocratic, bureaucratic, and impersonal by bourgeois

---

[10]Focusing on power was an important step forward in the feminist critique of Freud. Firestone argues, for example, that if little girls "envied" penises it was because they recognized that little boys grew up to be members of a powerful class and little girls grew up to be dominated by them. Powerlessness, not neurosis, was the heart of women's situation. More recently, feminists have criticized Firestone for rejecting the usefulness of the concept of the unconscious. In seeking to explain the strength and continuation of male dominance, recent feminist writing has emphasized the fundamental nature of gender-based personality differences, their origins in the unconscious, and the consequent difficulty of their eradication. See Dorothy Dinnerstein, *The Mermaid and the Minotaur* (New York: Harper Colophon Books, 1977), Nancy Chodorow, *The Reproduction of Mothering* (Berkeley: University of California Press, 1978), and Jane Flax, "The Conflict Between Nurturance and Autonomy in Mother-Daughter Relationships and Within Feminism," *Feminist Studies*, Vol. 4, no. 2 (June 1978), pp. 141–189.

[11]Kate Millett, *Sexual Politics* (New York: Avon Books, 1971), p. 25.

[12]One example of this type of radical feminist history is Susan Brownmiller's *Against Our Will, Men, Women, and Rape* (New York: Simon & Shuster, 1975).

social scientists; marxists see capitalist societies as systems of class domination.[13] For both kinds of social scientists neither the historical patriarchal societies nor today's western capitalist societies are understood as systems of relations between men that enable them to dominate women.

Towards a Definition of Patriarchy

We can usefully define patriarchy as a set of social relations between men, which have a material base, and which, though hierarchical, establish or create interdependence and solidarity among men that enable them to dominate women. Though patriarchy is hierarchical and men of different classes, races, or ethnic groups have different places in the patriarchy, they also are united in their shared relationship of dominance over their women; they are dependent on each other to maintain that domination. Hierarchies "work" at least in part because they create vested interests in the status quo. Those at the higher levels can "buy off" those at the lower levels by offering them power over those still lower. In the hierarchy of patriarchy, all men, whatever their rank in the patriarchy, are bought off by being able to control at least some women. There is some evidence to suggest that when patriarchy was first institutionalized in state societies, the ascending rulers literally made men the heads of their families (enforcing their control over their wives and children) in exchange for the men's ceding some of their tribal resources to the new rulers.[14] Men are dependent on one another (despite their hierarchical ordering) to maintain their control over women.

The material base upon which patriarchy rests lies most fundamentally in men's control over women's labor power. Men maintain this control by excluding women from access to some essential productive resources (in capitalist societies, for example, jobs that pay living wages) and by restricting women's sexuality.[15] Monogamous heterosexual marriage is one relatively recent

[13]For the bourgeois social science view of patriarchy, see, for example, Weber's distinction between traditional and legal authority, *Max Weber: The Theories of Social and Ecoonomic Organization,* ed. Talcott Parson (New York: The Free Press, 1964), pp. 328–357. These views are also discussed in Elizabeth Fee, "The Sexual Politics of Victorian Social Anthropology," *Feminist Studies,* Vol. 1, nos. 3–4 (Winter–Spring 1973), pp. 23–29, and in Robert A. Nisbet, *The Sociological Tradition* (New York: Basic Books, 1966), especially Chapter 3, "Community."

[14]See Viana Muller, "The Formation of the State and Oppression of Women: Some Theoretical Considerations and a Case Study in England and Wales," *Review of Radical Political Economics,* Vol. 9, no. 3 (Fall 1977), pp. 7–21.

[15]The particular ways in which men control women's access to important economic resources and restrict their sexuality vary enormously, both from society to society, from subgroup to subgroup, and across time. The examples we use to illustrate patriarchy in this section, however, are drawn primarily from the experience of whites in western capitalist countries. The diversity is shown in *Toward an Anthropology of Women,* ed. Rayna Rapp Reiter (New York: Monthly Review Press, 1975), *Woman, Culture and Society,* ed. Michelle Rosaldo and Louise Lamphere (Stanford, California: Stanford University Press, 1974), and *Females, Males, Families: A Biosocial Approach,* by Liba Leibowitz (North Scituate, Massachusetts: Duxbury Press, 1978). The control of women's sexuality is tightly linked to the place of children. An understanding of the demand (by men and capitalists) for children is crucial to understanding changes in women's subordination.

Where children are needed for their present or future labor power, women's sexuality will tend to be directed toward reproduction and childrearing. When children are seen as superfluous, women's

and efficient form that seems to allow men to control both these areas. Controlling women's access to resources and their sexuality, in turn, allows men to control women's labor power, both for the purpose of serving men in many personal and sexual ways and for the purpose of rearing children. The services women render men, and which exonerate men from having to perform many unpleasant tasks (like cleaning toilets) occur outside as well as inside the family setting. Examples outside the family include the harrassment of women workers and students by male bosses and professors as well as the common use of secretaries to run personal errands, make coffee, and provide "sexy" surroundings. Rearing children, whether or not the children's labor power is of immediate benefit to their fathers, is nevertheless a crucial task in perpetuating patriarchy as a system. Just as class society must be reproduced by schools, work places, consumption norms, etc., so must patriarchal social relations. In our society children are generally reared by women at home, women socially defined and recognized as inferior to men, while men appear in the domestic picture only rarely. Chidren raised in this way generally learn their places in the gender hierarchy well. Central to this process, however, are the areas outside the home where patriarchal behaviors are taught and the inferior position of women enforced and reinforced: churches, schools, sports, clubs, unions, armies, factories, offices, health centers, the media, etc.

The material base of patriarchy, then, does not rest solely on childrearing in the family, but on all the social structures that enable men to control women's labor. The aspects of social structures that perpetuate patriarchy are theoretically identifiable, hence separable from their other aspects. Gayle Rubin has increased our ability to identify the patriarchal element of these social structures enormously by identifying "sex/gender systems":

> a "sex/gender system" is the set of arrangements by which a society transforms biological sexuality into products of human activity, and in which these transformed sexual needs are satisfied.[16]

We are born female and male, biological sexes, but we are created woman and man, socially recognized genders. *How* we are so created is that second aspect of the *mode* of production of which Engels spoke, "the production of human beings themselves, the propagation of the species."

How people propagate the species is socially determined. If, biologically, people are sexually polymorphous, and society were organized in such a way that all forms of sexual expression were equally permissible, reproduction would result only from some sexual encounters, the heterosexual ones. The strict

---

sexuality for other than reproductive purposes is encouraged, but men will attempt to direct it towards satisfying male needs. The Cosmo girl is a good example of a woman "liberated" from childrearing only to find herself turning all her energies toward attracting and satisfying men. Capitalists can also use female sexuality to their own ends, as the success of Cosmo in advertising consumer products shows.

[16]Gayle Rubin, "The Traffic in Women," in *Anthropology of Women,* ed. Reiter, p. 159.

division of labor by sex, a social invention common to all known societies, creates two very separate genders and a need for men and women to get together for economic reasons. It thus helps to direct their sexual needs toward heterosexual fulfillment, and helps to ensure biological reproduction. In more imaginative societies, biological reproduction might be ensured by other techniques, but the division of labor by sex appears to be the universal solution to date. Although it is theoretically possible that a sexual division of labor not imply inequality between the sexes, in most known societies, the socially acceptable division of labor by sex is one which accords lower status to women's work. The sexual division of labor is also the underpinning of sexual subcultures in which men and women experience life differently; it is the material base of male power which is exercised (in our society) not just in not doing housework and in securing superior employment, but psychologically as well.

How people meet their sexual needs, how they reproduce, how they inculcate social norms in new generations, how they learn gender, how it feels to be a man or a woman—all occur in the realm Rubin labels the sex/gender system. Rubin emphasizes the influence of kinship (which tells you with whom you can satisfy sexual needs) and the development of gender specific personalities via child-rearing and the "oedipal machine." In addition, however, we can use the concept of the sex/gender system to examine all other social institutions for the roles they play in defining and reinforcing gender hierarchies. Rubin notes that theoretically a sex/gender system could be female dominant, male dominant, or egalitarian, but declines to label various known sex/gender systems or to periodize history accordingly. We choose to label our present sex/gender system patriarchy, because it appropriately captures the notion of hierarchy and male dominance which we see as central to the present system.

Economic production (what marxists are used to referring to as *the* mode of production) and the production of people in the sex/gender sphere both determine "the social organization under which the people of a particular historical epoch and a particular country live," according to Engels. The whole of society, then, can be understood by looking at both these types of production and reproduction, people and things.[17] There is no such thing as "pure capitalism," nor does "pure patriarchy" exist, for they must of necessity coexist. What exists is patriarchal capitalism, or patriarchal feudalism, or egalitarian hunting/gathering societies, or matriarchal horticultural societies, or patriarchal horticultural societies, and so on. There appears to be no necessary connection between *changes* in the one aspect of production and changes in the other. A society could undergo transition from capitalism to socialism, for example, and

[17]Himmelweit and Mohun point out that both aspects of production (people and things) are logically necessary to describe a mode of production because by definition a mode of production must be capable of reproducing itself. Either aspect alone is not self-sufficient. To put it simply the production of things requires people, and the production of people requires things. Marx, though recognizing a capitalism's need for people did not concern himself with how they were produced or what the connections between the two aspects of production were. See Himmelweit and Mohun, "Domestic Labour and Capital," *Cambridge Journal of Economics*, Vol. 1, no. 1 (March 1977), pp. 15–31.

remain patriarchal.[18] Common sense, history, and our experience tell us, however, that these two aspects of production are so closely intertwined, that change in one ordinarily creates movement, tension, or contradiction in the other.

Radical hierarchies can also be understood in this context. Further elaboration may be possible along the lines of defining color/race systems, arenas of social life that take biological color and turn it into a social category, race. Racial hierarchies, like gender hierarchies, are aspects of our social organization, of how people are produced and reproduced. They are not fundamentally ideological; they constitute that second aspect of our mode of production, the production and reproduction of people. It might be most accurate then to refer to our societies not as, for example, simply capitalist, but as patriarchal capitalist white supremacist. In Part III below, we illustrate one case of capitalism adapting to and making use of racial orders and several examples of the interrelations between capitalism and patriarchy.

Capitalist development creates the places for a hierarchy of workers, but traditional marxist categories cannot tell us who will fill which places. Gender and racial hierarchies determine who fills the empty places *Patriarchy is not simply hierarchical organization,* but hierarchy in which *particular* people fill *particular* places. It is in studying patriarchy that we learn why it is women who are dominated and how. While we believe that most known societies have been patriarchal, we do not view patriarchy as a universal, unchanging phenomenon. Rather patriarchy, the set of interrelations among men that allow men to dominate women, has changed in form and intensity over time. It is crucial that the hierarchy among men, and their differential access to patriarchal benefits, be examined. Surely, class, race, nationality, and even marital status and sexual orientation, as well as the obvious age, come into play here. And women of different class, race, national, marital status, or sexual orientation groups are subjected to different degrees of patriarchal power. Women may themselves exercise class, race, or national power, or even patriarchal power (through their family connections) over men lower in the patriarchal hierarchy than their own male kin.

To recapitulate, we define patriarchy as a set of social relations which has a material base and in which there are hierarchical relations between men and solidarity among them which enable them in turn to dominate women. The material base of patriarchy is men's control over women's labor power. That control is maintained by excluding women from access to necessary economically productive resources and by restricting women's sexuality. Men exercise their control in receiving personal service work from women, in not having to do housework or rear children, in having access to women's bodies for sex, and in feeling powerful and being powerful. The crucial elements of patriarchy as we

[18]For an excellent discussion of one such transition to socialism, see Batya Weinbaum, "Women in Transition to Socialism: Perspectives on the Chinese Case," *Review of Radical Political Economics,* Vol. 8, no. 1 (Spring 1976), pp. 34–58.

currently experience them are: heterosexual marriage (and consequent homophobia), female childrearing and housework, women's economic dependence on men (enforced by arrangements in the labor market), the state and numerous institutions based on social relations among men—clubs, sports, unions, professions, universities, churches, corporations, and armies. All of these elements need to be examined if we are to understand patriarchal capitalism.

Both hierarchy and interdependence among men and the subordination of women are *integral* to the functioning of our society; that is, these relationships are *systemic*. We leave aside the question of the creation of these relations and ask, can we recognize patriarchal relations in capitalist societies? Within capitalist societies we must discover those same bonds between men which both bourgeois and marxist social scientists claim no longer exist, or are, at the most, unimportant leftovers. Can we understand how these relations among men are perpetuated in capitalist societies? Can we identify ways in which patriarchy has shaped the course of capitalist development?

III THE PARTNERSHIP OF PATRIARCHY AND CAPITAL

How are we to recognize patriarchal social relations in capitalist societies? It appears as if each woman is oppressed by her own man alone; her oppression seems a private affair. Relationships among men and among families seem equally fragmented. It is hard to recognize relationships among men, and between men and women, as *systematically* patriarchal. We argue, however, that patriarchy as a system of relations between men and women exists in capitalism, and that in capitalist societies a healthy and strong partnership exists between patriarchy and capital. Yet if one begins with the concept of patriarchy and an understanding of the capitalist mode of production, one recognizes immediately that the partnership of patriarchy and capital was not inevitable; men and capitalists often have conflicting interests, particularly over the use of women's labor power. Here is one way in which this conflict might manifest itself: the vast majority of men might want their women at home to personally service them. A smaller number of men, who are capitalists, might want most women (not their own) to work in the wage labor market. In examining the tensions of this conflict over women's labor power . . . we will be able to identify the material base of patriarchal relations in capitalist societies, as well as the basis for the partnership between capital and patriarchy.

Industrialization and the Development of Family Wages

. . . Family wages may be understood as a resolution of the conflict over women's labor power which [occurred] between patriarchal and capitalist interests [in the nineteenth century].

Family wages for most adult men imply men's acceptance, and collusion in, lower wages for others, young people, women and socially defined inferior men as well (Irish, blacks, etc., the lowest groups in the patriarchal hierarchy who are denied many of the patriarchal benefits). Lower wages for women and children and inferior men are enforced by job segregation in the labor market, in turn maintained by unions and management as well as by auxiliary institutions like schools, training programs, and even families. Job segregation by sex, by insuring that women have the lower paid jobs, both assures women's economic dependence on men and reinforces notions of appropriate spheres for women and men. For most men, then, the development of family wages secured the material base of male domination in two ways. First, men have the better jobs in the labor market and earn higher wages than women. The lower pay women receive in the labor market both perpetuates men's material advantage over women and encourages women to choose wifery as a career. Second, then, women do housework, childcare, and perform other services at home which benefit men directly.[19] Women's home responsibilities in turn reinforce their inferior labor market position.[20]

The resolution that developed in the early twentieth century can be seen to benefit capitalist interests as well as patriarchal interests. Capitalists, it is often argued, recognized that in the extreme conditions which prevailed in the early nineteenth century industrialization, working class families could not adequately reproduce themselves. They realized that housewives produced and maintained healthier workers than wage-working wives and that educated children became better workers than noneducated ones. The bargain, paying family wages to men and keeping women home, suited the capitalists at the time as well as the male workers. Although the terms of the bargain have altered over time, it is still true that the family and women's work in the family serve capital by providing a labor force and serve men as the space in which they exercise their privilege. Women, working to serve men and their families, also serve capital as consumers.[21] The family is also the place where dominance and submission are learned, as Firestone, the Frankfurt School, and many others have explained.[22] Obedient children become obedient workers, girls and boys each learn their proper roles.

[19]The importance of the fact that women perform labor services for men in the home cannot be overemphasized. As Pat Mainardi said in "The Politics of Housework," "[t]he measure of your oppression is his resistance" (in *Sisterhood is Powerful,* ed. Robin Morgan [New York: Vintage Books, 1970], p. 451). Her article, perhaps as important for us as Firestone on love, is an analysis of power relations between women and men as exemplified by housework.

[20]Libby Zimmerman has explored the relation of membership in the primary and secondary labor markets to family patterns in New England. See her *Women in the Economy: A Case Study of Lynn, Massachusetts, 1760–1974* (Unpublished Ph.D dissertation, Heller School, Brandeis, 1977). Batya Weinbaum is currently exploring the relationship between family roles and places in the labor market. See her "Redefining the Question of Revolution," *Review of Radical Political Economics,* Vol. 9, no. 3 (Fall 1977), pp. 54, 78, and *The Curious Courtship of Women's Liberation and Socialism* (Boston: South End Press, 1978). Additional studies of the interaction of capitalism and patriarchy can be found in Zillah Eisenstein, ed., *Capitalist Patriarchy and the Case for Socialist Feminism* (New York: Monthly Review Press, 1978).

[21]See Batya Weinbaum and Amy Bridges, "The Other Side of the Paycheck: Monopoly Capital and the Structure of Consumption," *Monthly Review,* Vol. 28, no. 3 (July–August 1976), pp. 88–103, for a discussion of women's consumption work.

[22]For the view of the Frankfurt School, see Max Horkheimer, "Authority and the Family," in *Critical Theory* (New York: Herder & Herder, 1972) and Frankfurt Institute of Social Research, "The Family," in *Aspects of Sociology* (Boston: Beacon, 1972).

While the family wage shows that capitalism adjusts to patriarchy, the changing status of children shows that patriarchy adjusts to capital. Children, like women, came to be excluded from wage labor. As children's ability to earn money declined, their legal relationship to their parents changed. At the beginning of the industrial era in the United States, fulfilling children's need for their fathers was thought to be crucial, even primary, to their happy development; fathers had legal priority in cases of contested custody. As children's ability to contribute to the economic well-being of the family declined, mothers came increasingly to be viewed as crucial to the happy development of their children, and gained legal priority in cases of contested custody.[23] Here patriarchy adapted to the changing economic role of children: when children were productive, men claimed them; as children became unproductive, they were given to women. . . .

With respect to capitalism and patriarchy, the adaptation, or mutual accommodation, took the form of the development of the family wage in the early twentieth century. The family wage cemented the partnership between patriarchy and capital. Despite women's increased labor force participation, particularly rapid since World War II, the family wage is still, we argue, the cornerstone of the present sexual division of labor—in which women are primarily responsible for housework and men primarily for wage work. Women's lower wages in the labor market (combined with the need for children to be reared by someone) assure the continued existence of the famliy as a necessary income pooling unit. The family, supported by the family wage, thus allows the control of women's labor by men both within and without the family.

Though women's increased wage work may cause stress for the family (similar to the stress Kautsky and Engels noted in the nineteenth century), it would be wrong to think that as a consequence, the concepts and the realities of the family and of the sexual division of labor will soon disappear. The sexual division of labor reappears in the labor market, where women work at women's jobs, often the very jobs they used to do only at home—food preparation and service, cleaning of all kinds, caring for people, and so on. As these jobs are low-status and low-paying patriarchal relations remain intact, though their material base shifts somewhat from the family to the wage differential, from family-based to industrially-based patriarchy.[24]

The prediction of nineteenth century marxists that patriarchy would wither away in the face of capitalism's need to proletarianize everyone has not come true. Not only did marxists underestimate the strength and flexibility of patriarchy, they also overestimated the strength of capital. They envisioned the new social force of capitalism, which had torn feudal relations apart, as virtually all-powerful. . . .

If the first element of our argument about the course of capitalist develop-

---

[23]Carol Brown, "Patriarchal Capitalism and the Female-Headed Family," *Social Scientist* (India); no. 40–41 (November–December 1975), pp. 28–39.

[24]Carol Brown, in "Patriarchal Capitalism," argues, for example, that we are moving from "family based" to "industrially-based patriarchy within capitalism.

ment is that capital is not all-powerful, the second is that capital is tremendously flexible. Capital accumulation encounters preexisting social forms, and both destroys them and adapts to them. The adaptation of capital can be seen as a reflection of the *strength* of these preexisting forms to persevere in new environments. Yet even as they persevere, they are not unchanged. The ideology with which race and sex are understood today, for example, is strongly shaped by the particular ways racial and sexual divisions are reinforced in the accumulation process. . . .

Industrially based patriarchal relations are enforced in a variety of ways. Union contracts which specify lower wages, lesser benefits, and fewer advancement opportunities for women are not just atavistic hangovers—a case of sexist attitudes or male supremacist ideology—they maintain the material base of the patriarchal system. While some would go so far as to argue that patriarchy is already absent from the family (see, for example, Stewart Ewen, *Captains of Consciousness*),[25] we would not. Although the terms of the compromise between capital and patriarchy are changing as additional tasks formerly located in the family are capitalized, and the location of the deployment of women's labor power shifts,[26] it is nevertheless true, as we have argued above, that the wage differential caused by extreme job segregation in the labor market reinforces the family, and, with it, the domestic division of labor, by encouraging women to marry. The "ideal" of the family wage—that a man can earn enough to support an entire family—may be giving way to a new ideal that both men and women contribute through wage earning to the cash income of the family. The wage differential, then, will become increasingly necessary in perpetuating patriarchy, the male control of women's labor power. The wage differential will aid in *defining* women's work as secondary to men's at the same time it necessitates women's actual continued economic dependence on men. The sexual division of labor in the labor market and elsewhere should be understood as a manifestation of patriarchy which serves to perpetuate it.

Many people have argued that though the partnership between capital and patriarchy exists now, it may *in the long run* prove intolerable to capitalism; capital may eventually destroy both familial relations and patriarchy. The argument proceeds logically that capitalist social relations (of which the family is not an example) tend to become universalized, that women will become increasingly able to earn money and will increasingly refuse to submit to subordination in the family, and that since the family is oppressive particularly

---

[25]Stewart Ewen, *Captains of Consciousness* (New York: Random House, 1976).

[26]Jean Gardiner, in "Women's Domestic Labour," *New Left Review*, no. 89, Jan.–Feb. 1975, pp. 47–58, clarifies the cause for the shift in location of women's labor, from capital's point of view. She examines what capital needs (in terms of the level of real wages, the supply of labor, and the size of markets) at various stages of growth and of the business cycle. She argues that in times of boom or rapid growth it is likely that socializing housework (or more accurately capitalizing it) would be the dominant tendency, and that in times of recession, housework will be maintained in its traditional form. In attempting to assess the likely direction of the British economy, however, Gardiner does not assess the economic needs of patriarchy. We argue in this essay that unless one takes patriarchy as well as capital into account one cannot adequately assess the likely direction of the economic system.

to women and children, it will collapse as soon as people can support themselves outside it.

We do not think that the patriarchal relations embodied in the family can be destroyed so easily by capital, and we see little evidence that the family system is presently disintegrating. Although the increasing labor force participation of women has made divorce more feasible, the incentives to divorce are not overwhelming for women. Women's wages allow very few women to support themselves and their children independently and adequately. The evidence for the decay of the traditional family is weak at best. The divorce rate has not so much increased, as it has evened out among classes; moreover, the remarriage rate is also very high. Up until the 1970 census, the first-marriage age was continuing its historic decline. Since 1970 people seem to have been delaying marriage and childbearing, but most recently, the birth rate has begun to increase again. It is true that larger proportions of the population are now living outside traditional families. Young people, especially, are leaving their parents' homes and establishing their own households before they marry and start traditional families. Older people, especially women, are finding themselves alone in their own households, after their children are grown and they experience separation or death of a spouse. Nevertheless, trends indicate that the new generations of young people will form nuclear families at some time in their adult lives in higher proportions than ever before. The cohorts, or groups of people, born since 1930 have much higher rates of eventual marriage and childrearing than previous cohorts. The duration of marriage and childrearing may be shortening, but its incidence is still spreading.[27]

The argument that capital destroys the family also overlooks the social forces which make family life appealing. Despite critiques of nuclear families as psychologically destructive, in a competitive society the family still meets real needs for many people. This is true not only of long-term monogamy, but even more so for raising children. Single parents bear both financial and psychic burdens. For working class women, in particular, these burdens make the "independence" of labor force participation illusory. Single parent families have recently been seen by policy analysts as transitional family formations which become two-parent families upon remarriage.[28]

It could be that the effects of women's increasing labor force participation are found in a declining sexual division of labor within the family, rather than in more frequent divorce, but evidence for this is also lacking. Statistics on who does housework, even in families with wage-earning wives, show little change in

[27]For the proportion of people in nuclear families, see Peter Uhlenberg, "Cohort Variations in Family Life Cycle Experiences of U.S. Females," *Journal of Marriage and the Family,* Vol. 36, no. 5 (May 1974), pp. 284–92. For remarriage rates see Paul C. Glick and Arthur J. Norton, "Perspectives on the Recent Upturn in Divorce and Remarriage," *Demography,* Vol. 10 (1974), pp. 301–14. For divorce and income levels see Arthur J. Norton and Paul C. Glick, "Marital Instability: Past, Present, and Future," *Journal of Social Issues,* Vol. 32, no. 1 (1976), pp. 5–20. Also see Mary Jo Bane, *Here to Stay: American Families in the Twentieth Century* (New York: Basic Books, 1976).

[28]Heather L. Ross and Isabel B. Sawhill, *Time of Transition: The Growth of Families Headed by Women* (Washington, D.C.: The Urban Institute, 1975).

recent years; women still do most of it.[29] The double day is a reality for wage-working women. This is hardly surprising since the sexual division of labor outside the family, in the labor market, keeps women financially dependent on men—even when they earn a wage themselves. The future of patriarchy does not, however, rest solely on the future of familial relations. For patriarchy, like capital, can be surprisingly flexible and adaptable.

Whether or not the patriarchal division of labor, outside the family and elsewhere, is "ultimately" intolerable to capital, it is shaping capitalism now. As we illustrate below, patriarchy both legitimates capitalist control and delegitimates certain forms of struggle against capital.

Ideology in the Twentieth Century

Patriarchy, by establishing and legitimating hierarchy among men (by allowing men of all groups to control at least some women), reinforces capitalist control, and capitalist values shape the definition of patriarchal good. . . .

If we examine the characteristics of men as radical feminists describe them—competitive, rationalistic, dominating—they are much like our description of the dominant values of capitalist society.

This "coincidence" may be explained in two ways. In the first instance, men, as wage laborers, are absorbed in capitalist social relations at work, driven into the competition these relations prescribe, and absorb the corresponding values.[30] The radical feminist description of men was not altogether out of line for capitalist societies. Secondly, even when men and women do not actually behave in the way sexual norms prescribe, men *claim for themselves* those characteristics which are valued in the dominant ideology. So, for example, the authors of *Crestwood Heights* found that while the men, who were professionals, spent their days manipulating subordinates (often using techniques that appeal to fundamentally irrational motives to elicit the preferred behavior), men and women characterized men as "rational and pragmatic." And while the women devoted great energies to studying scientific methods of child-rearing and child development, men and women in Crestwood Heights characterized women as "irrational and emotional."[31]

[29]See Kathryn E. Walker and Margaret E. Woods *Time Use: A Measure of Household Production of Family Goods and Services* (Washington, D.C.: American Home Economics Association, 1976; and Heidi I. Hartmann, "The Family as the Locus of Gender, Class, and Political Struggle: The Example of Housework," *Signs: Journal of Women in Culture and Society,* Vol. 6, no. 3 (Spring 1981).

[30]This should provide some clues to class differences in sexism, which we cannot explore here.

[31]See John R. Seeley, et al., *Crestwood Heights* (Toronto: University of Toronto Press, 1956), pp. 382–94. While men's place may be characterized as "in production" this does not mean that women's place is simply "not in production"—her tasks, too, are shaped by capital. Her nonwage work is the resolution, on a day-to-day basis, of production for exchange with socially determined need, the provision of use values in a capitalist society (this is the context of consumption). See Weinbaum and Bridges, "The Other Side of the Paycheck," for a more complete discussion of this argument. The fact that women provide "merely" use values in a society dominated by exchange values can be used to denigrate women.

This helps to account not only for "male" and "female" characteristics in capitalist societies, but for the particular form sexist ideology takes in capitalist societies. Just as women's work serves the dual purpose of perpetuating male domination and capitalist production, so sexist ideology serves the dual purpose of glorifying male characteristics/capitalist values, and denigrating female characteristics/social need. If women were degraded or powerless in other societies, the reasons (rationalizations) men had for this were different. Only in a capitalist society does it make sense to look down on women as emotional or irrational. As epithets, they would not have made sense in the renaissance. Only in a capitalist society does it make sense to look down on women as "dependent." "Dependent" as an epithet would not make sense in feudal societies. Since the division of labor ensures that women as wives and mothers in the family are largely concerned with the production of use values, the denigration of these activities obscures capital's inability to meet socially determined needs at the same time that it degrades women in the eyes of men, providing a rationale for male dominance. An example of this may be seen in the peculiar ambivalence of television commercials. On one hand, they address themselves to the real obstacles to providing for socially determined needs: detergents that destroy clothes and irritate skin, shoddily made goods of all sorts. On the other hand, concern with these problems must be denigrated; this is accomplished by mocking women, the workers who must deal with these problems.

A parallel argument demonstrating the partnership of patriarchy and capitalism may be made about the sexual division of labor in the work force. The sexual division of labor places women in low-paying jobs, and in tasks thought to be appropriate to women's role. Women are teachers, welfare workers, and the great majority of workers in the health fields. The nurturant roles that women play in these jobs are of low status because capitalism emphasizes personal independence and the ability of private enterprise to meet social needs, emphases contradicted by the need for collectively provided services. As long as the social importance of nurturant tasks can be denigrated because women perform them, the confrontation of capital's priority on exchange value by a demand for use values can be avoided. In this way, it is not feminism but sexism that divides and debilitates the working class.

IV TOWARDS A MORE PROGRESSIVE UNION

Many problems remain for us to explore. Patriarchy as we have used it here remains more a descriptive term than an analytic one. If we think marxism alone inadequate, and radical feminism itself insufficient, then we need to develop new categories. What makes our task a difficult one is that the same features, such as the division of labor, often reinforce both patriarchy and capitalism, and in a thoroughly patriarchal capitalist society, it is hard to isolate the mechanisms of patriarchy. Nevertheless, this is what we must do. We have pointed to some starting places: looking at who benefits from women's labor power, uncovering the material base of patriarchy, investigating the mechanisms of hierarchy and solidarity among men. The questions we must ask are endless.

Can we speak of the laws of motion of a patriarchal system? How does patriarchy generate feminist struggle? What kinds of sexual politics and struggle between the sexes can we see in societies other than advanced capitalist ones? What are the contradictions of the patriarchal system and what is their relation to the contradictions of capitalism?. . . .

Feminism and the Class Struggle

. . . The struggle against capital and patriarchy cannot be successful if the study and practice of the issues of feminism is abandoned. A struggle aimed only at capitalist relations of oppression will fail, since their underlying supports in patriarchal relations of oppression will be overlooked. And the analysis of patriarchy is essential to a definition of the kind of socialism useful to women. While men and women share a need to overthrow capitalism they retain interests particular to their gender group. It is not clear—from our sketch, from history, or from male socialists—that the socialism being struggled for is the same for both men and women. For a humane socialism would require not only consensus on what the new society should look like and what a healthy person should look like, but more concretely, it would require that men relinquish their privilege.

As women we must not allow ourselves to be talked out of the urgency and importance of our tasks, as we have so many times in the past. We must fight the attempted coercion, both subtle and not so subtle, to abandon feminist objectives.

This suggests two strategic considerations. First, a struggle to establish socialism must be a struggle in which groups with different interests form an alliance. Women should not trust men to liberate them after the revolution, in part, because there is no reason to think they would know how; in part, because there is no necessity for them to do so. In fact their immediate self-interest lies in our continued oppression. Instead we must have our own organizations and our own power base. Second, we think the sexual division of labor within capitalism has given women a practice in which we have learned to understand what human interdependence and needs are. While men have long struggled *against* capital, women know what to struggle *for*.[32] As a general rule, men's position in patriarchy and capitalism prevents them from recognizing both human needs for nurturance, sharing, and growth, and the potential for meeting those needs in a nonhierarchical, nonpatriarchial society. But even if we raise their consciousness, men might assess the potential gains against the potential losses and choose the status quo. Men have more to lose than their chains.

As feminist socialists, we must organize a practice which addresses both the struggle against patriarchy and the struggle against capitalism. We must insist

[32]Lise Vogel, "The Earthly Family," *Radical America,* Vol. 7, no. 4–5 (July–October 1973), pp. 9–50.

that the society we want to create is a society in which recognition of interdependence is liberation rather than shame, nurturance is a universal, not an oppressive practice, and in which women do not continue to support the false as well as the concrete freedoms of men.

FEMINISM AND WOMEN OF COLOR:
The Inseparability of Gender, Class, and Racial Oppression

Black Women, White Women: Separate Paths to Liberation

Elizabeth F. Hood

Many changes have occurred in the roles of blacks and women during the past 40 years with respect to their functions in American society and the awareness of the impact of their collective behavior. World events and technological changes affected the producer-consumer roles of the two groups. The contemporary black civil rights movement and the ensuing woman's liberation movement stimulated changes in the organized behavior of these recognized minorities.

The involvement of the U.S. in World War II was a historical force that changed the destiny of blacks and females. Millions of blacks left the rural South to work in industrial plants. Over 200,000 took federal civil service jobs. For blacks, the new freedom to participate in political activities stimulated interest in organizing around their needs and aspirations. Membership in unions offered job protection and the chance for increased benefits. Awareness of additional opportunities in white-collar, skilled, and semi-skilled jobs heightened the black concern for moving ahead. Emerging people, their expectations rose.

Changes in locales did not eliminate the on-going discrimination against blacks in employment, education, the armed forces, and housing. Prospects of "doing better" intensified the smoldering resentment and frustration which characterized the black experience in America. The stage was set for a vigorous protest against the system—a protest which would take place in the courts, at lunch counters, in the streets, on buses, at the polls, in the schools, and any place where inequality existed.

During the four years of World War II, six and one-half million women left their kitchens for paid jobs. A substantial majority of these females in the labor force were married (75 percent) and over the age of 35 (60 percent). Many returned to their ironing boards at the end of the war, but the reality of the working woman persisted. Some struggled to retain the daycare centers established for mothers participating in the war effort. Popular women's magazines portrayed the average woman contentedly admiring colorful wall paper in her sunny breakfast room; but studies of young girls revealed that they admired the independence and flexibility of their mothers who worked. Woman's image as a member of the labor force gradually became entrenched.

Women, as blacks, increased the awareness of themselves as underpaid, underappreciated workers. They saw differences both in size of paychecks and in institutional attitudes towards their special needs as persons. Only an impetus was necessary for them to take collective action against sex discrimination. The black civil rights movement proved to be their catalyst for change.

Black and white women recognized the commonalities in their oppression and those forces operating to establish the "structured conduciveness" for changing their situations.[1] Yet the two groups did not form a close alliance against their common enemy, the patriarchal system. This paper will focus upon some of the reasons why black and white women relate differently to the contemporary women's rights movement with respect to the following factors: (1) the historical forces which shaped the black protest and the women's liberation movements; (2) differences between black and white women in terms of the impact of sexism and racism; (3) and the special problems of black women as doubly oppressed people.

The protracted black struggle dates back to 1619. Recurring women's liberation movements followed the black demands for equality of opportunity and its logical companion, equality of benefits. Both groups, as victims, fight the same oppressor—the patriarchal system dominated by white males. The ideology of this system creates and maintains controlling structures which keep blacks and women in the states of dependency, deprived of "prestige, power, and advantages in society."[2]

Racism and sexism (both of which include class distinctions) are then the intertwining oppressive structures operating under this paternalistic patriarchalism. Racism defines blacks as inferior beings and assigns them race-coded roles in the economy. Menial jobs, low pay and limited opportunities for advancement are the plagues of black workers. Sexism keeps women in their places— women playing out their sex-coded roles—ornaments, toys, servants, underpaid laborers. Racism and sexism are related evils in the system, affecting their subjects in strikingly similar ways.

As expected, in terms of ultimate goals, sexism and racism achieve the same ends: the adult male culture of an industrial society characterized by advanced technology excludes blacks and women from assimilation into the power structures. Women struggle to express their femaleness through achieving companionship with men and bearing children. At the same time, they resist the sole definition of themselves in terms of marriage and motherhood. Their

---

[1] William H. Chafe, *Women and Equality* (New York: Oxford University Press, 1977), p. 99.
[2] Gunnar Myrdal, Appendix 5, "A Parallel to the Negro Problem," *An American Dilemma* (New York: Harper and Brothers, 1944), p. 1077.

demands for equal access and equal benefits reflect human yearning for the fulfillment of creative potentials and the utilization of acquired skills.

Blacks are highly visible minorities. They cannot escape the yoke of oppression. Racism not only exploits them as an abundant, cheap source of labor, it destroys their culture and prevents the group from maintaining economically and socially stable communities. The dominant culture, through its institutional practices, either attacks or disrespects the essence of the black self-concept—physical appearance, language, traditions, customs and religion. Denied the privilege of defining themselves, black chldren are restricted in their choices of routes to mature personhood.

Radical feminists narrow these black options to three:[3] (1) they may yield to the oppressor and accept his definitions of what is adult male and female (with the crumbs allowed); (2) they may opt out of the "normal" mainstream by committing themselves to crime, homosexuality, or drugs; (3) or they may choose the more healthy path of revolution. The third choice is extremely difficult, given the insidious nature of racism. Racism holds the carrot and sticks of fancy titles, big cars, elegant clothing, and mansion-like houses. A limited number of blacks manage to get the baubles and bangles. Racism labels those who fail: lazy, stupid, welfare-addicted, fun-lovers, and baby factories.

To perpetuate the structure of racism, the patriarchal system engages its "best" minds in activities designated to establish scientific reasons for abusing blacks.[4] From Europe came the Malthusian principles of the "rightness" of "whiteness," especially the Teutonic standard of "whiteness." The legacy of Thomas Malthus, *Essay on the Principle of Population (1826),* is embodied in all the attempts at genocide against the "inferior" races on the bases of their "low" intelligence, tendencies to overbreed, and proclivities to immoral and criminal behavior.

Racism is the linking chain which binds all the master plans designed to destroy black people: psychological tests to establish mental inferiority, the unequal distribution of wealth to ensure poverty, inadequate diets which may cause physical illness and mental retardation, substandard housing in communities lacking clean air, shortages of dental and medical care, unequal educational opportunities, and federally-subsidized involuntary sterilizations.[5]

In spite of their shared oppression, with its resulting similarities in human destruction, blacks and women have not developed a close alliance in the cause of human rights. Historical forces decree the choice between the "allegiance to black skin and the allegiance to sex."[6] A crucial controlling force in the divisions

[3]Shulamith Firestone, *The Dialectic of Sex: The Case for Feminist Revolution* (New York: William Morrow and Co., 1970), p. 111.

[4]Allan Chase, *The Legacy of Malthus: The Social Case of the New Scientific Racism* (New York: Alfred A. Knopf Co., 1977), p. 6.

[5]Ibid., pp. 2–23 (Chapter I, "The Genesis and Functions of Scientific Racism" includes a discussion of the effects of scientific racism).

[6]Catherine Stimpson, "Thy Neighbor's Wife, Thy Neighbor's Servant: Women's Liberation and Black Civil Rights," *Woman in Sexist Society: Studies in Power and Powerlessness,* ed. Vivian Gornick and Barbara K. Maran (New York: Basic Books, 1971), p. 622.

between lines of white and black women is the nature of the relationship of white women to white men. White women belong to the worlds of their fathers, grandfathers, brothers, uncles, cousins and family friends. Life with their husbands and lovers separates them from other women, weakening their collective consciousness of oppression. Varying amounts of privilege and differing levels of wealth affect white women's perceptions of the degrees of their disadvantage. Many white women define liberation as the access to those thrones traditionally occupied by white men—positions in the kingdoms which support racism.[7]

There are substantive differences between the treatment accorded black and white women, regardless of the individual white woman's feelings about her personal life style. White women suffer less violence than black women. They are more acceptable to society at large, and therefore, are in positions to influence, if only indirectly, the decisions of those in power.[8]

Racism, on the other hand, affects the psychological structures of black people without separating them from each other. With limited exceptions, most metropolitan areas have "black bottoms." Local housing restrictions, supported by the courts and federal housing policies, have operated to ensure the continued existence of the "black community," whether it is across the tracks, by the river, in Harlem, or downtown. Black identity emerges, then, from the collective history of a separate group in a place where freedom, autonomy, and distinctive cultural forms existed.[9] Despite the roles which blacks assume in efforts to cope with a racist power structure, most are painfully aware of their actual positions in American society. Uncle Tom, black Sambo and Aunt Jemima never erase the reality of blackness. The black ghetto is a natural breeder of protest.

The relationship between the black protest and the women's protest may be traced back to the anti-slavery crusade. Contemporary white feminists acknowledge the emergence of early female leadership for women's rights from women's efforts on behalf of blacks.[10] Elizabeth Cady Stanton and Angelina Grimke Weld, leaders of the first Women's Rights Conference at Seneca Falls, New York, in 1848, had worked tirelessly for the cause of Abolition.

The reasons why trained, economically secure women identified closely with the plight of the slaves are significant to the understanding of the contemporary woman's rights movement. Many of the female abolitionists had grown up in slavery-hating families with deeply-rooted moral and religious convictions against the institution.[11] Beyond this perceived wrongness in human bondage, however, lay the disquieting fact of the woman as slave. White women, encountering the oppression of blacks, faced the reality of their own lives in

---

[7]Rosemary Radford Reuther, *New Woman: New Earth* (New York: The Seabury Press, 1975), p. 122.

[8]Chafe, op. cit., p. 52.

[9]Ibid., pp. 55–57.

[10]Stimpson, op. cit., p. 624.

[11]Ibid., p. 627.

servitude to their fathers and husbands. Without the ballot, they were politically powerless. Their limited influence derived from whatever status they were able to obtain from their association with the white men in their lives.

Woman's indirect power-by-association was, at best, tenuous. Objectified as chattel property, women depended upon the benevolence of their masters.[12] Social institutions reinforced the rights of men to decide what was "judicious" in those matters concerning women: separation and divorce, child custody, domestic violence, trial by a jury of peers, and commitment to institutions for the insane. Those casting the judgements, in the traditions of their times, usually decided in favor of the acknowledged male right to conduct the affairs of society in accordance with the existing power structures.

In-depth views of the system of slavery not only raised women's consciousness of the facts of their lives, but provided them with some practical skills essential to waging battles in their own behalf.[13] Women developed the organizational expertise necessary to engaging in extended social struggles. They began shattering time-honored stereotypes of themselves as compliant, silent partners to men. Casting out taboos against female participation in public life, women used the pen and the spoken word to express their indignation.

White women often imitated the oratorical style of the black "Pilgrim," Sojourner Truth. Lucretia Mott, Abby Kelly Foster, Maria W. Stewart, and Angelina Grimke boldly and confidently faced their audiences. Risking insults and physical injuries from unsympathetic men and women, the female slavery fighters continued their agitation. Toughness and efficiency were the by-products of their efforts.

Practical women, the female antislavery soldiers, made political use of their identification with slavery. At the close of the Civil War, they directed their attention to getting the vote for women as well as for black men. Sojourner Truth, the black feminist, in true democratic posture, joined the white women in their demands for suffrage:

> There is a great stir about colored men getting their rights, but not a word about the colored women; and if colored men get their rights, and not colored women theirs, you see the colored men will be masters over the women, and it will be just as bad as before. So I am for keeping the thing going while things are stirring; because if we wait till it is still, it will take a great while to get it going again.[14]

White male abolitionists had no great passion for women's suffrage. The logical outcome of their efforts, reasoned the majority, was the enfranchisement of black males.

Black leaders, though sympathetic to the women, sensed the political opposition to woman's suffrage. The Republican Party and most women objected to the enfranchisement of females. Linking the women's suffrage to black suffrage might increase the wrath of white men and, in the confusion,

[12]Ibid., p. 626.

[13]Ibid., p. 630.

[14]Sojourner Truth, quoted in History of Woman's Suffrage (New York: The National American Woman Suffrage Association, 1922), vol. 2, p. 193.

cause black men to miss their cherished goal. Frederick Douglass, a staunch supporter of women's rights, reaffirmed his loyalty to the cause of blacks:

> While the Negro is mobbed, beaten, shot, stabbed, hanged, burnt, and is the target of all that is malignant in the North and all that is murderous in the South, his claims may be preferred by me without exposing in any wise myself to the imputation of narrowness or meanness towards the cause of women.[15]

The truth in Frederick Douglass' words became the truth for most blacks engaged in liberation struggles: blackness was by far more difficult and energy-draining than femaleness; white women tended to value their whiteness above sex; exploitation notwithstanding, every white person in the U.S. had the power to discriminate against blacks.

After the adoption of the Fifteenth Amendment in 1870, white feminists expressed resentment at the idea of illiterate black men possessing power over educated white women. They abandoned attempts to form alliances with blacks and organized women's rights groups of upperclass white females. One popular organization, the National American Women's Suffrage Association, organized chapters in the South during the 1890s. Conservative in their racial attitudes, some members of state chapters openly condoned racism. One of the notoriously racist speeches was given by Miss Belle Kearney, a feminist and orator from Mississippi. In 1903, speaking in New Orleans, Miss Kearney articulated what she understood as the position of the National American Women's Suffrage Association:

> Just as surely as the North will be forced to turn to the South for the nation's salvation, just so surely will the South be compelled to look to its Anglo Saxon women as the medium through which to retain the supremacy of the white race over the African.[16]

A lesson from the disintegration of the coalition of blacks and women's rights workers is the fate of friendship when the self-interest of one party conflicts with that of another. Logically, given the opportunity, black men would not defer their right to the ballot in the interest of white women. The demand for woman's suffrage was fair and just. The wider patriarchal society was unyielding in its position. Membership in the culture of their white male oppressors was, by far, too important to white women for them to stage an open rebellion. They chose to remain in that system as disenfranchised citizens until they won the vote on August 26, 1920.

Blacks have never stopped their press for civil rights; white involvement in this press has been sporadic, some "friendly" whites maintaining working relationships with the less nationalistic black organizations. In the 1960s the

---

[15]Frederick Douglass, *Life and Writings of Frederick Douglass,* Vol. IV, ed. Philip S. Foner (New York: Philip S. Foner, 1950), pp. 212–13.

[16]Belle Kearney, quoted in *The Ideas of the Woman Suffrage Movement 1890–1920,* Aileen Kraditor (New York: Columbia University Press, 1965).

black civil rights movement again stimulated a contemporary woman's liberation movement. Black men, black women, white men and white women joined in the struggle to obtain civil rights for blacks. By 1966, however, blacks had taken the leadership in their own struggle. White women then began to organize in their own interests.

Both black women and white women observed that women had been written out of the leadership functions of the black protest, often being relegated to the routine, fellowship tasks. Pauli Murray, a noted black female attorney, observed that no woman was invited to present a major address at the August 28, 1963, March on Washington.[17] One reason given for the exclusion of women from highly visible participation on the occasion was trite: "They cannot agree upon a delegate."

The black civil rights movement of the '60s brought about a resurgence of the consciousness of women, black and white, to their actual roles and positions in American society. Once again the white woman saw herself as the ornament and servant of the white man; the black woman encountered her double oppression, being black and female.

This consciousness of themselves as victims of a paternalistic structure energized women of different racial groups to self-liberating activity. Being black, however, was still more difficult than being female. Black women could only accept a "limited sisterhood" with white women—equal pay for equal work, federally subsidized day care, the right to choose abortion, legal protection against domestic violence and rape, affirmative action in training programs and employment, more representation in the media, and entry into traditional male structures of the world of work.

The contemporary white women's movement failed in many respects to identify with the problems of black women. The history and life situations of blacks shape their reality—a reality which often varies greatly from that of upper-income white women. Reality for the black woman is the presence of problems peculiar to her group, most of which arise from the triple burdens of racism, sexism, and poverty.

A critical concern to black women is their image in American society. History books, the media and scientific racism send out the stereotyped message: black women as matriarchs emasculate black men and thereby prevent the formation of healthy black family and community structures. From these unhealthy families and pathological communities flow the diseases of poverty, low educational achievement, prostitution, drug abuse, and unemployment. This line of reasoning establishes the black woman as the "evil one," rather than the victim.

The images of the sapphire-like black woman leading the weak black man by a leash and "bossing" her children spilled over into the formulation of government policies towards blacks. Exercising this license to portray black families negatively and without examining the data on black families critically, Daniel Patrick

---

[17]Pauli Murray, "Jim Crow and June Crow," in *Black Women in White America: A Documentary History,* ed. Gerda Lerner (New York: Vintage Books, 1973), p. 596.

Moynihan concluded in his infamous report: "At the heart of the deterioration of the fabric of Negro society is the deterioration of the Negro family. This is the fundamental source of the weakness of the Negro community at the present time."[18]

This "myth of the matriarchy" is in itself racist. Black women who head their families do so in most instances out of necessity, rather than choice. Their heritage of slavery and racial oppression predetermine the possibility of them struggling through the childbearing years (25–44) without economically able husbands. Pauli Murray documented from the statistics of 1960 the factors that force black women into the role of head-of-house: there were 93.3 black males to every 100 black females, making competition for a spouse difficult; black women were widowed earlier than white women; and racism strained black marriages to the point of extremely high rates of separation and divorce.[19]

Fifteen years later, Murray's profile of the disadvantages suffered by black women, particularly those measured by income, had not changed. Between 1950 and 1975 the position of black women remained at the bottom rung of the economic ladder, with them having the lowest median income in comparison with white men, black males and white females. Figures in Table 1 compiled from reports of the U.S. Bureau of the Census validate the contention that black women earn the least money and form the smallest proportion of workers in the $10,000 and above income bracket.[20]

Regardless of occupational title and median earnings, black women in husband-wife families make greater contributions to the total income of their families. Data from the U.S. Bureau of the Census support this conclusion.[21] The amount of spendable money generally available to the black married woman is less than that for her white female counterpart. In 1970, the average white woman in the North and West whose total family income was $14,022, earned $3,537 and contributed 25.2 percent of her wages to the family. During the same year in the North and West, when the average family income was $12,403 and the black woman earned $4,015, her wages accounted for 32.4 percent of the family income. Employed black women whose husbands have white collar jobs still invest larger percentages of their incomes in the operation of their families.

Since black men at all economic levels earn less than white men, black women cannot withdraw from competition in the labor market. They not only assist their husbands in providing necessities for their families, but often make real differences in the standards by which their families will live.

Society, infested with racism, compares black women unfavorably to white

[18]Daniel Patrick Moynihan, "The Negro Family: The Case for National Action," quoted in *Black Families in White America,* Andrew Billingsley (Englewood Cliffs, New Jersey: Prentice-Hall, Inc., 1968), p. 199.

[19]Op. cit., p. 597.

[20]Table 666, U.S. Bureau of the Census, Current Population Reports, Series P-60, No. 105, p. 413.

[21]Table 663, U.S. Bureau of the Census, Current Population Reports, Series P-23, N. 39, and P-60, No. 161, p. 411.

TABLE 1
MONEY INCOME—PERCENT DISTRIBUTION OF RECEIPTS

Sex, race	Median income, 1975	Percent earning above $10,000 in 1975
White male	$9,300	46.9
Black male	5,560	24.9
White female	3,420	10.4
Black female	3,107	7.8

Compiled from Table 666, U.S. Bureau of the Census, Current Population Reports, Series P-60, No. 105, p. 413.

women. Ethnic studies usually portray the immigrant woman in ethnic groups as a helpmate. She becomes a doer when circumstances force her into the role of head-of-the-household. Literature on European born women refers to their courage and strength when faced with rearing their families alone. The dominant Jewish mother is prized for the manner in which she molds her children in the traditions of her group.[22] Black women who, because of racial discrimination, require many times more strength to cope with family life alone, are often the recipients of harsh criticism and negative labels. Unmotivated, lazy and immoral are adjectives frequently applied to the black woman forced to accept public assistance. Yet, these women are merely adapting to the conditions forced upon them by a racist society.[23]

Studies of black family life do reveal a positive "unnatural superiority" identified in many black women—a superiority which functions to ensure the survival of the race and the transmission of black culture.[24] Often deprived of supportive males, black women must teach their children both how to survive and how to cope with the tensions related to their blackness in a racist society.

Regardless of family income level, black females are socialized differently from white females. Joyce Ladner's study of the life-orientations of poor females in a public housing development in St. Louis provides insightful information about the manner in which poor black females are introduced early to the harsh fact: you must be able to care for yourself economically and emotionally.[25]

The fantasy of prince charming whisking them off to a happy-ever-after life is absent from the lives of young black females who grow up in economically stable homes. Epstein found that young black females learn early, even when they are bound for such careers as law, medicine, college teaching and engineering, the

[22]Stephen Birmingham, *Our Crowd: The Great Jewish Families of New York* (New York: Harper and Row, 1967).

[23]Jessie Bernard. *Marriage and Family Among Negroes* (Englewood Cliffs, New Jersey: Prentice-Hall Book Co., 1966), p. 39.

[24]Ibid., pp. 68–70.

[25]Joyce A. Ladner, *Tomorrow's Tomorrow* (New York: Doubleday Book Co., 1971).

possibility that they will be the single female head of the household.[26] The black woman at the top professional level is far less likely than her white counterpart to meet, marry, and spend her life with a man whose skills and income compare favorably with her own.

Racism causes black male-female relationships to differ from those between white males and white females. Radical white feminists often view the patriarchal system as the eternal triangle—the white male as father-controller, the white female as the powerless, but respected mother figure, and the black woman as the sex object, a degraded figure.[27] In this structure, the black male, deprived of his manhood, becomes the pimp. If he attempts to obtain power equal to that of the white man, he is figuratively (and sometimes, literally) castrated. According to this model, then, the black male and black female, both powerless beings, are pitted against each other in their efforts to obtain favors from the white father figure.

From centuries of humiliation, the black male often emerged as the "psychological casualty" because the white ideology gave him a marginal status as husband and father. Because she was sex object and useful in many servant roles, the black female ruled the cabin and provided the continuity for the black family. It was she, not her mate, to whom the black child was forced to look as a source of identity. The white master, grand patriarch of the plantation, heaped frustration upon the black male in his roles as husband, father and head-of-the-household.[28]

This humiliation of the black man continued after physical slavery ended. He was not permitted to integrate into the mainstream of socioeconomic life. Lacking the means of making a stable livelihood to support his family, many black men fled, drifted, rotted in prisons, or died early and violently.[29] In spite of this severe oppression, most black men and women fought tenaciously to preserve their family units.

Black men and women, aware of themselves as powerless persons, and conscious of the real power of the white man, and the power-by-association of the white female, often experience difficulties in establishing long-term relationships characterized by respect and trust. The quotation from Gail Stokes is one black woman's summation of a real tension recurring in relationships between black men and women:

> The oppressor has determined to keep you running, and you, in turn, have been determined to keep me barefoot and pregnant. For each blow that the man rains on your head, you come home and rain triple blows upon my already weary and battered skull.[30]

---

[26]Cynthia Fuchs Epstein, "Positive Effects of the Multiple Negative: Explaining the Success of Black Professional Women," in *Changing Women in a Changing Society,* ed. Joan Huber (Chicago: University of Chicago Press, 1973), pp. 163–64.

[27]Firestone, op. cit., pp. 109–10.

[28]Reuther, op. cit., p. 118.

[29]Ibid., p. 119.

[30]Gail A. Stokes, "Black Woman to Black Man," in *The Black Family: Essays and Studies,* ed. Robert Staples (Belmont, California: Wadsworth Publishing Co., 1971), p. 159.

. . . In bygone times you have cursed me and labeled me a wretched bitch because of my blasphemies against your name, your condition, your attitude. Yet, these blasphemies were justified, because when I looked at you, I saw a free man, forgetting me and lusting after the white man, the white woman, the white status symbol.[31]

The socialization process differs between blacks and whites in other measurable ways, creating distance and suspicion. Chafe allows that courts of judicial and public opinion tend to favor white women with respect to: concern for and action against violence levelled at white women; the acceptability of the physical appearance of white women; the provisions of benefits which will ensure white women to being reared in genteel, refined circumstances; and the toleration of white illogical hate often hurled at blacks.[32]

Black women, in spite of their oftenkept silence are painfully aware of a "Miss Anne" complex that society creates in white women: the knowledge and use of their power to ignore and disrespect black women. Fannie Lou Hamer, the late civil rights activist from Mississippi, did not keep silent about the way in which she sensed that white women treated black women as "dirt."

But you know, sometimes I really feel more sorrier for the white woman than I feel for ourselves because she has been caught up in this thing, caught up feeling very special, and folks, I'm going to put it on the line, because my job is not to make people feel comfortable—(drowned out by applause). You've been caught up in this thing because, you know, you worked my grandmother, and after that you worked my mother, and then finally you got hold of me. And you really thought, people—you might try and cool it now, but I been watching you, baby. You thought that you was more a white woman, you had this kind of angel feeling that you were untouchable. You know that? There's nothing under the sun that made you believe that you was just like me, that under this white pigment of skin is red blood, just like under this black skin of mine. So we was used as black women over and over and over.

. . . In the past, I don't care how poor this white woman was in the South she felt like she was more than us. In the North, I don't care how poor or how rich this white woman has been, she still felt like she was more than us. But coming to the realization of the thing, her freedom is shackled in chains to mine, and she realizes for the first time that she is not free until I am free. The point about it, the male influence in this country—you know the white male, didn't go and brainwash the black man and the black woman, he brainwashed his wife too . . . He made her think that she was an angel.[33]

Black women feel even more bitterness, and at times, outrage, over what they view as the white woman's pragmatic use of both her sex and color to realize personal gains from the system. The public schools provided many battle fronts for white females. Newspapers and television screens flashed pictures of white women hurling invectives at blacks as they attempted to enroll their children in desegregated public schools. North and South, from Boston to New Orleans, white women acted in their self-interest: preserving the "cleanliness" and

[31]Ibid., p. 161.
[32]Chafe, op. cit., pp. 52–53.
[33]Fannie Lou Hamer, "It's In Your Hands," in *Black Women in White America: A Documentary History,* ed. Gerda Lerner (New York: Vintage Books, 1973), pp. 610–11.

quality of their neighborhood schools. To many white women who support equality among the sexes, the concept of either desegregated or integrated neighborhoods and schools is synonymous with the destruction of their sacred rights to "ethnic purity." Their actions confirm the stability of their marriage to the system.

In terms of choice of weapons to oppress blacks, white women have shown a striking similarity to white men. Charging "reverse discrimination," they have challenged in the courts affirmative action programs designed to attract, recruit and train members of minority groups. For example: Frances Henson, a white female brought an action against the University of Arkansas on June 12, 1975, charging the University with depriving her of the equal protection of the law by accepting minority students into its law school with lesser qualifications. Ms. Henson's case was dismissed by the Court of Appeals on the basis that she had not been injured by the law school's minority preference admission system and that she would not have been admitted in its absence.[34] The cases of Janet Lynn Timmerman v. the University of Toledo[35] and Doris Stewart v. New York University[36] also charge the defendants with racial discrimination, alleging that less "qualified" minority applicants had been selected over them. Timmerman and Stewart were not upheld. In the case of Stewart, the judge ruled: "Indeed, the Law School's minority admissions policy is a good faith effort by the school to correct past discrimination."[37]

The cases of Henson, Timmerman, and Stewart are examples of the manner in which white women use their "whiteness" when it serves their interests. Affirmative action policies and programs designed to attract, recruit and provide supportive services for members of minority groups in training programs and professional schools have not lessened the opportunities for whites as a group. On the contrary, white enrollment in professional schools increased dramatically between 1968 and 1976: in law schools it rose 64 percent; in medical schools, 49 percent; and in undergraduate programs, 45 percent. Competition for the limited number of slots in professional schools prompted white women to imitate white men by charging "reverse discrimination."

Black people, as other poor minority groups, live with the specter of genocide—the ultimate threat to their continued existence. There is evidence to support the conclusion that white women *do* participate in some of the actions designed to control population growth among the poor and members of the "inferior" races. Each year, conservative figures estimate, 200,000 plus poor people in the U.S. are subjected to irreversible sterilization procedures.[38] Medical personnel, male and female, subsidized by federal policies and funds, support a sterilization program in the U.S. estimated to exceed Nazi Germany's

---

[34]Henson v. University of Arkansas, 519 F. 2d 576 (8th Cir. 1975).
[35]Timmerman v. University of Toledo, 421 F. Supp. 464 (N.D. Ohio, 1976).
[36]Stewart v. New York University, 430 F. Supp. 1305 (S.D. New York, 1976).
[37]Ibid., p. 1317.
[38]Chase, op. cit., p. 23.

sterilization program between 1933 and 1945. Medicare, Medicaid and other health plans for the poor and the affluent will reimburse a surgeon up to 90 percent of the costs of any sterilization procedure.[39] Yet, only 50 percent of matching federal funds are provided for the costs of abortion.

The black and poor are urged to choose "voluntary" sterilization as their method of family planning. The "package deal" is a regular service in many North American hospitals. This plan requires that a woman desiring abortion undergo a simultaneous sterilization procedure as a condition for the approval of the abortion.[40] Of the teaching hospitals surveyed on the issue, 53.6 agreed that they made this requirement for some of their patients.

Black women in particular have been victimized by the "Mississippi Appendectomies," procedures by which women undergo tubal ligations and hysterectomies at the same time.[41] Since 12,000 women die per year from hysterectomies, the "Mississippi Appendectomy" poses a greater risk to the life of the patient.[42]

Members of the medical profession receive both support and approval for their punitive actions towards poor and minority women. Chase reports the results of a 1965 Gallup Poll of American opinion from coast to coast on the following question: "Sometimes unwed mothers on relief continue to have illegitimate children and get relief money for each new child born. What do you think should be done in the case of these women? How about the children?" Out of every five Americans replying to this poll, one said, "Sterilize the woman."[43]

Quantifiable differences between black and white women exist in all spheres of life—family income, education, employment opportunities, housing, access to leisure-time activities, the arts, etc. Racism, in its virulence, places black women at the bottom of the heap economically and socially. Since white women do not struggle against racism with a fervor equal to that of their antisexist campaigns, there is no exact parallel between them and black women. Simply stated, white women as a group continue to value their whiteness above their sex.

In summary, black people and white women are oppressed groups under the patriarchal system established and operated by white males through racist and sexist structures. These two groups share many of the same disabilities resulting from their inferior status in society. The destinies of both have been shaped by technological changes and world events. Black women and white women act out the sex-coded rules defined for them by the dominant society. The problems of the two groups of women differ, however. Black women also labor under the cross of racism—a cross which is more oppressive than sexism.

The unwillingness of white women to identify with the special problems of black women and the white female's refusal to take the offensive against racism set up barriers between the two groups. Black-white coalitions for civil rights have not been effective instruments in the struggle to eliminate racism. The

---

[39]Ibid., p. 18.
[40]Ibid., p. 18.
[41]Ibid., p. 18.
[42]Chase, op. cit., p. 21.
[43]Ibid., p. 21.

problem of sexism, therefore, cannot command the undivided attention of blacks.

The manner in which the patriarchal system awards benefits and secures allegiance from its constituents prevails against a viable coalition of black and white women in the immediate future. Each group is socialized to view the other as the enemy, rather than focusing upon the common enemy. This socialization process includes the structured sexist and racist policies and practices operating in all institutions controlled by the dominant society. Policies and practices enslave the minds of white women, but permit them to retain many of the advantages available to white men. Both racism and sexism exploit black women. Racism, however, destroys black women, black men, and their off-spring.

White women and black women cannot unite in their struggle against sexism until both groups recognize the functions of sexism and racism as controlling structures in a system that presupposes inequality between the sexes and the races. White women cannot be free until they reject all the forms of racism that separate them from black people. In the struggle for human rights, black and white women will follow separate paths so long as either group harbors illusions about the possibility of freedom becoming a reality before the existing structures of racism and sexism crumble.

A Black Feminist Statement

Combahee River Collective

We are a collective of black feminists who have been meeting together since 1974.[1] During that time we have been involved in the process of defining and clarifying our politics, while at the same time doing political work within our own group and in coalition with other progressive organizations and movements. The most general statement of our politics at the present time would be that we are actively committed to struggling against racial, sexual, heterosexual, and class oppression and see as our particular task the development of integrated analysis and practice based upon the fact that the major systems of oppression are interlocking. The synthesis of these oppressions creates the conditions of our lives. As black women we see black feminism as the logical political movement to combat the manifold and simultaneous oppressions that all women of color face.

[1]This statement is dated April 1977.

We will discuss four major topics in the paper that follows: (1) The genesis of contemporary black feminism; (2) what we believe, i.e., the specific province of our politics; (3) the problems in organizing black feminists, including a brief herstory of our collective; and (4) black feminist issues and practice.

1   THE GENESIS OF CONTEMPORARY BLACK FEMINISM

Before looking at the recent development of black feminism, we would like to affirm that we find our origins in the historical reality of Afro-American women's continuous life-and-death struggle for survival and liberation. Black women's extremely negative relationship to the American political system (a system of white male rule) has always been determined by our membership in two oppressed racial and sexual castes. As Angela Davis points out in "Reflections on the Black Woman's Role in the Community of Slaves," black women have always embodied, if only in their physical manifestation, an adversary stance to white male rule and have actively resisted its inroads upon them and their communities in both dramatic and subtle ways. There have always been black women activists—some known, like Sojourner Truth, Harriet Tubman, Frances E. W. Harper, Ida B. Wells Barnett, and Mary Church Terrell, and thousands upon thousands unknown—who had a shared awareness of how their sexual identity combined with their racial identity to make their whole life situation and the focus of their political struggles unique. Contemporary black feminism is the outgrowth of countless generations of personal sacrifice, militancy, and work by our mothers and sisters.

A black feminist presence has evolved most obviously in connection with the second wave of the American women's movement beginning in the late 1960s. Black, other Third World, and working women have been involved in the feminist movement from its start, but both outside reactionary forces and racism and elitism within the movement itself have served to obscure our participation. In 1973 black feminists, primarily located in New York, felt the necessity of forming a separate black feminist group. This became the National Black Feminist Organization (NBFO).

Black feminist politics also have an obvious connection to movements for black liberation, particularly those of the 1960s and 1970s. Many of us were active in those movements (civil rights, black nationalism, the Black Panthers), and all of our lives were greatly affected and changed by their ideology, their goals, and the tactics used to achieve their goals. It was our experience and disillusionment within these liberation movements, as well as experience on the periphery of the white male left, that led to the need to develop a politics that was antiracist, unlike those of white women, and antisexist, unlike those of black and white men.

There is also undeniably a personal genesis for black feminism, that is, the political realization that comes from the seemingly personal experiences of individual black women's lives. Black feminists and many more black women who do not define themselves as feminists have all experienced sexual oppression as a constant factor in our day-to-day existence.

Black feminists often talk about their feelings of craziness before becoming conscious of the concepts of sexual politics, patriarchal rule, and, most importantly, feminism, the political analysis and practice that we women use to struggle against our oppression. The fact that racial politics and indeed racism are pervasive factors in our lives did not allow us, and still does not allow most black women, to look more deeply into our own experiences and define those things that make our lives what they are and our oppression specific to us. In the process of consciousness-raising, actually life-sharing, we began to recognize the commonality of our experiences and, from that sharing and growing consciousness, to build a politics that will change our lives and inevitably end our oppression.

Our development also must be tied to the contemporary economic and political position of black people. The post-World War II generation of black youth was the first to be able to minimally partake of certain educational and employment options, previously closed completely to black people. Although our economic position is still at the very bottom of the American capitalist economy, a handful of us have been able to gain certain tools as a result of tokenism in education and employment which potentially enable us to more effectively fight our oppression.

A combined antiracist and antisexist position drew us together initially, and as we developed politically we addressed ourselves to heterosexism and economic oppression under capitalism.

2 WHAT WE BELIEVE

Above all else, our politics initially sprang from the shared belief that black women are inherently valuable, that our liberation is a necessity not as an adjunct to somebody else's but because of our need as human persons for autonomy. This may seem so obvious as to sound simplistic, but it is apparent that no other ostensibly progressive movement has ever considered our specific oppression a priority or worked seriously for the ending of that oppression. Merely naming the pejorative stereotypes attributed to black women (e.g., mammy, matriarch, Sapphire, whore, bulldagger), let alone cataloguing the cruel, often murderous, treatment we receive, indicates how little value has been placed upon our lives during four centuries of bondage in the Western hemisphere. We realize that the only people who care enough about us to work consistently for our liberation is us. Our politics evolve from a healthy love for ourselves, our sisters, and our community which allows us to continue our struggle and work.

This focusing upon our own oppression is embodied in the concept of identity politics. We believe that the most profound and potentially the most radical politics come directly out of our own identity, as opposed to working to end somebody else's oppression. In the case of black women this is a particularly repugnant, dangerous, threatening, and therefore revolutionary concept because it is obvious from looking at all the political movements that have preceded us that anyone is more worthy of liberation than ourselves. We reject pedestals, queenhood, and walking ten paces behind. To be recognized as human, levelly human, is enough.

We believe that sexual politics under patriarchy is as pervasive in black women's lives as are the politics of class and race. We also often find it difficult to separate race from class from sex oppression because in our lives they are most often experienced simultaneously. We know that there is such a thing as racial-sexual oppression which is neither solely racial nor solely sexual, e.g., the history of rape of black women by white men as a weapon of political repression.

Although we are feminists and lesbians, we feel solidarity with progressive black men and do not advocate the fractionalization that white women who are separatists demand. Our situation as black people necessitates that we have solidarity around the fact of race, which white women of course do not need to have with white men, unless it is their negative solidarity as racial oppressors. We struggle together with black men against racism, while we also struggle with black men about sexism.

We realize that the liberation of all oppressed peoples necessitates the destruction of the political-economic systems of capitalism and imperialism as well as patriarchy. We are socialists because we believe the work must be organized for the collective benefit of those who do the work and create the products and not for the profit of the bosses. Material resources must be equally distributed among those who create these resources. We are not convinced, however, that a socialist revolution that is not also a feminist and antiracist revolution will guarantee our liberation. We have arrived at the necessity for developing an understanding of class relationships that takes into account the specific class position of black women who are generally marginal in the labor force, while at this particular time some of us are temporarily viewed as doubly desirable tokens at white-collar and professional levels. We need to articulate the real class situation of persons who are not merely raceless, sexless workers, but for whom racial and sexual oppression are significant determinants in their working/economic lives. Although we are in essential agreement with Marx's theory as it applied to the very specific economic relationships he analyzed, we know that this analysis must be extended further in order for us to understand our specific economic situation as black women.

A political contribution which we feel we have already made is the expansion of the feminist principle that the personal is political. In our consciousness-raising sessions, for example, we have in many ways gone beyond white women's revelations because we are dealing with the implications of race and class as well as sex. Even our black women's style of talking/testifying in black language about what we have experienced has a resonance that is both cultural and political. We have spent a great deal of energy delving into the cultural and experimental nature of our oppression out of necessity because none of these matters have ever been looked at before. No one before has ever examined the multilayered texture of black women's lives.

As we have already stated, we reject the stance of lesbian separation because it is not a viable political analysis or strategy for us. It leaves out far too much and far too many people, particularly black men, women, and children. We have a great deal of criticism and loathing for what men have been socialized to be in this society: what they support, how they act, and how they oppress. But we do not have the misguided notion that it is their maleness, per se—i.e., their biological maleness—that makes them what they are. As black women we find any type of biological determinism a particularly dangerous and reactionary basis upon which to build a politic. We must also question whether lesbian separatism is an adequate and progressive political analysis and strategy, even for those who practice it, since it so completely denies any but the sexual sources of women's oppression, negating the facts of class and race.

3 PROBLEMS IN ORGANIZING BLACK FEMINISTS

During our years together as a black feminist collective we have experienced success and defeat, joy and pain, victory and failure. We have found that it is very difficult to organize around black feminist issues, difficult even to announce in certain contexts that we *are* black feminists. We have tried to think about the reasons for our difficulties, particularly since the white women's movement continues to be strong and to grow in many directions. In this section we will discuss some of the general reasons for the organizing problems we face and also talk specifically about the stages in organizing our own collective.

The major source of difficulty in our political work is that we are not just trying to fight oppression on one front or even two, but instead to address a whole range of oppressions. We do not have racial, sexual, heterosexual, or class privilege to rely upon, nor do we have even the minimal access to resources and power that groups who possess any one of these types of privilege have.

The psychological toll of being a black woman and the difficulties this presents in reaching political consciousness and doing political work can never be underestimated. There is a very low value placed upon black women's psyches in this society, which is both racist and sexist. As an early group member once said: "We are all damaged people merely by virtue of being black women." We are dispossessed psychologically and on every other level, and yet we feel the necessity to struggle to change our condition and the condition of all black women. In "A Black Feminist's Search for Sisterhood," Michele Wallace arrives at this conclusion:

> We exist as women who are black who are feminists, each stranded for the moment, working independently because there is not yet an environment in this society remotely congenial to our struggle—because, being on the bottom, we would have to do what no one else has done: we would have to fight the world.[2]

Wallace is not pessimistic but realistic in her assessment of black feminists'

[2]Michele Wallace, "A Black Feminist's Search for Sisterhood," *The Village Voice,* 28 July 1975, pp. 6–7.

position, particularly in her allusion to the nearly classic isolation most of us face. We might use our position at the bottom, however, to make a clear leap into revolutionary action. If black women were free, it would mean that everyone else would have to be free since our freedom would necessitate the destruction of all the systems of oppression.

Feminism is, nevertheless, very threatening to the majority of black people because it calls into question some of the most basic assumptions about our existence, i.e., that gender should be a determinant of power relationships. Here is the way male and female roles were defined in a black nationalist pamphlet from the early 1970s.

> We understand that it is and has been traditional that the man is the head of the house. He is the leader of the house/nation because his knowledge of the world is broader, his awareness is greater, his understanding is fuller and his application of this information is wiser. . . . After all, it is only reasonable that the man be the head of the house because he is able to defend and protect the development of his home. . . . Women cannot do the same things as men—they are made by nature to function differently. Equality of men and women is something that cannot happen even in the abstract world. Men are not equal to other men, i.e., ability, experience, or even understanding. The value of men and women can be seen as in the value of gold and silver—they are not equal but both have great value. We must realize that men and women are a complement to each other because there is no house/family without a man and his wife. Both are essential to the development of any life.[3]

The material conditions of most black women would hardly lead them to upset both economic and sexual arrangements that seem to represent some stability in their lives. Many black women have a good understanding of both sexism and racism, but because of the everyday constrictions of their lives cannot risk struggling against them both.

The reaction of black men to feminism has been notoriously negative. They are, of course, even more threatened than black women by the possibility that black feminists might organize around our own needs. They realize that they might not only lose valuable and hard-working allies in their struggles but that they might also be forced to change their habitually sexist ways of interacting with and oppressing black women. Accusations that black feminism divides the black struggle are powerful deterrents to the growth of an autonomous black women's movement.

Still, hundreds of women have been active at different times during the three-year existence of our group. And every black woman who came, came out of a strongly felt need for some level of possibility that did not previously exist in her life.

When we first started meeting early in 1974 after the NBFO first eastern regional conference, we did not have a strategy for organizing, or even a focus.

---

[3]Mumininas of Committee for Unified Newark, *Mwanamke Mwananchi (The Nationalist Woman)*, Newark, N.J., c. 1971, pp. 4–5.

We just wanted to see what we had. After a peroid of months of not meeting, we began to meet again late in the year and started doing an intense variety of consciousness-raising. The overwhelming feeling that we have is that after years and years we had finally found each other. Although we were not doing political work as a group, individuals continued their involvement in lesbian politics, sterilization abuse and abortion rights work. Third World Women's International Women's Day activities, and support activity for the trials of Dr. Kenneth Edelin, Joan Little, and Inez Garcia. During our first summer, when membership had dropped off considerably, those of us remaining devoted serious discussion to the possibility of opening a refuge for battered women in a black community. (There was no refuge in Boston at that time.) We also decided around that time to become an independent collective since we had serious disagreements with NBFOs bourgeois-feminist stance and their lack of a clear political focus.

We also were contacted at that time by socialist feminists, with whom we had worked on abortion rights activities, who wanted to encourage us to attend the National Socialist Feminist Conference in Yellow Springs. One of our members did attend and despite the narrowness of the ideology that was promoted at that particular conference, we became more aware of the need for us to understand our own economic situation and to make our own economic analysis.

In the fall, when some members returned, we experienced several months of comparative inactivity and internal disagreements which were first conceptualized as a lesbian-straight split but which were also the result of class and political differences. During the summer those of us who were still meeting had determined the need to do political work and to move beyond consciousness-raising and serving exclusively as an emotional support group. At the beginning of 1976, when some of the women who had not wanted to do political work and who also had voiced disagreements stopped attending of their own accord, we again looked for a focus. We decided at that time, with the addition of new members, to become a study group. We had always shared our reading with each other, and some of us had written papers on black feminism for group discussion a few months before this decision was made. We began functioning as a study group and also began discussing the possibility of starting a black feminist publication. We had a retreat in the late spring which provided a time for both political discussion and working out interpersonal issues. Currently we are planning to gather together a collection of black feminist writing. We feel that it is absolutely essential to demonstrate the reality of our politics to other black women and believe that we can do this through writing and distributing our work. The fact that individual black feminists are living in isolation all over the country, that our own numbers are small, and that we have some skills in writing, printing, and publishing makes us want to carry out these kinds of projects as a means of organizing black feminists as we continue to do political work in coalition with other groups.

4 BLACK FEMINIST ISSUES AND PRACTICE

During our time together we have identified and worked on many issues of particular relevance to black women. The inclusiveness of our politics makes us concerned with any situation that impinges upon the lives of women, Third World, and working people. We are of course particularly committed to working on those struggles in which race, sex, and class are simultaneous factors in oppression. We might, for example, become involved in workplace organizing at a factory that employs Third World women or picket a hospital that is cutting back on already inadequate health care to a Third World community, or set up a rape crisis center in a black neighborhood. Organizing around welfare or daycare concerns might also be a focus. The work to be done and the countless issues that this work represents merely reflect the pervasiveness of our oppression.

Issues and projects that collective members have actually worked on are sterilization abuse, abortion rights, battered women, rape, and health care. We have also done many workshops and educationals on black feminism on college campuses, at women's conferences, and most recently for high school women.

One issue that is of major concern to us and that we have begun to publicly address is racism in the white women's movement. As black feminists we are made constantly and painfully aware of how little effort white women have made to understand and combat their racism, which requires among other things that they have a more than superficial comprehension of race, color, and black history and culture. Eliminating racism in the white women's movement is by definition work for white women to do, but we will continue to speak to and demand accountability on this issue.

In the practice of our politics we do not believe that the end always justifies the means. Many reactionary and destructive acts have been done in the name of achieving "correct" political goals. As feminists we do not want to mess over people in the name of politics. We believe in collective process and a nonhierarchical distribution of power within our own group and in our vision of a revolutionary society. We are committed to a continual examination of our politics as they develop through criticism and self-criticism as an essential aspect of our practice. As black feminists and lesbians we know that we have a very definite revolutionary task to perform and we are ready for the lifetime of work and struggle before us.

SUGGESTIONS FOR FURTHER READING:
Part Two

This selected bibliography includes works on feminist anthropology, feminist psychology, and feminist political theory. It excludes those important works from which excerpts appear already in this book. The reader is reminded that in Part Three of this book the feminist theories are applied to specific social issues. Hence, the suggestions for further reading on work, the family, and sexuality given at the end of Part Three also constitute further readings in feminist theory.

Barrett, Michele: *Women's Oppression Today: Problems in Marxist Feminist Analysis,* Verso, London, 1980.

Building Feminist Theory: Essays from Quest, Longman, New York, 1981.

Bunch, Charlotte, and Nancy Myron (eds.): *Class and Feminism,* Diana Press, Baltimore, 1974.

Clark, Lorenne M. G., and Lynda Lange: *The Sexism of Social and Political Theory: Women and Reproduction from Plato to Nietzsche,* University of Toronto Press, Toronto, 1979.

De Beauvoir, Simone: *The Second Sex,* Knopf, New York, 1953.

Daly, Mary: *Gyn/Ecology: The Metaethics of Radical Feminism,* Beacon, Boston, 1978.

Dinnerstein, Dorothy: *The Mermaid and the Minotaur: Sexual Arrangements and Human Malaise,* Harper Colophon, New York, 1977.

Eisenstein, Zillah: *Capitalist Patriarchy and the Case for Socialist Feminism,* Monthly Review Press, New York, 1979.

————: *The Radical Future of Liberal Feminism,* Longman, New York, 1981.

Elshtain, Jean Bethke: *Public Man, Private Woman: Women in Social and Political Thought,* Princeton University Press, Princeton, N.J., 1981.

English, Jane: *Sex Equality,* Prentice-Hall, Englewood Cliffs, N.J., 1977.

Fisher, Elizabeth: *Women's Creation: Sexual Evolution and the Shaping of Society,* Doubleday, New York, 1979.

Foreman, Ann: *Femininity as Alienation: Women and the Family in Marxism and Psychoanalysis.* Pluto, London, 1977.

Gilligan, Carol: *In a Different Voice: Psychological Theory and Women's Development,* Harvard, Cambridge, Mass., 1982.

Griffin, Susan: *Women and Nature: The Roaring Inside Her,* Harper Colophon, New York, 1978.

Hooks, Bell: *Ain't I a Woman: Black Women and Feminism,* South End Press, Boston, 1981.

Hull, Gloria T., Patricia Bell Scott, and Barbara Smith: *All the Women Are White, All the Blacks are Men, But Some of Us Are Brave: Black Women's Studies,* Feminist Press, Old Westbury, N.Y., 1982.

Jaggar, Alison M.: *Feminist Politics and Human Nature,* Littlefield Adams, Totowa, N.J., 1983.

Koedt, Anne, Ellen Levine, and Anita Rapone: *Radical Feminism,* Quadrangle, New York, 1973.

Kuhn, Annette, and AnnMarie Wolpe: *Feminism and Materialism: Women and Modes of Production,* Routledge & Kegan Paul, London and Boston, 1978.

Lenin, V. I. *The Emancipation of Women,* International, New York, 1934.

MacCormack, Carol P., and Marilyn Strathern (eds.): *Nature, Culture and Gender,* Cambridge, Cambridge, 1980.

Mitchell, Juliet: *Woman's Estate,* Pantheon, New York, 1971.

———: *Psycho-Analysis and Feminism: Freud, Reich, Laing and Women,* Vintage, New York, 1974.

Moraga, Cherrie, and Gloria Anzaldua: *This Bridge Called my Back: Writings by Radical Women of Color,* Persephone, Mass., 1981.

Okin, Susan Moller: *Women in Western Political Thought,* Princeton, Princeton, N.J., 1979.

Reiter, Rayna R. (ed.): *Toward an Anthropology of Women,* Monthly Review, New York, 1975.

Rosaldo, Michelle Zimbalist, and Louise Lamphere (eds.): *Women, Culture and Society,* Stanford University Press, Stanford, Calif., 1974.

Sargent, Lydia (ed.): *Women and Revolution: A Discussion of the Unhappy Marriage of Marxism and Feminism:* South End Press, Boston, 1981.

Schechter, Susan: *Women and Male Violence,* South End Press, Boston, 1982.

Spretnak, Charlene (ed.): *The Politics of Women's Spirituality: Essays on the Rise of Spiritual Power Within the Feminist Movement,* Anchor, New York, 1982.

Warren, Mary Anne: *The Nature of Woman: An Encyclopedia and Guide to the Literature,* Edgepress, Inverness, Calif., 1980.

Wittig, Monique: *Les Guerilleres,* Avon, New York, 1973.

Wollstonecraft, Mary: *A Vindication of the Rights of Woman,* 1792.

Vetterling-Braggin, Mary: *"Femininity," "Masculinity," and "Androgyny": A Modern Philosophical Discussion,* Littlefield Adams, Totowa, N.J., 1982.

THREE

APPLYING THE FRAMEWORKS: PAID LABOR

There is no career more exciting or exacting for a woman than marriage to a great man.

Mrs. Georgina Battiscombe
In her biography of Mrs. Gladstone

We must start with the realization that, as much as women want to be good scientists or engineers, they want first and foremost to be womanly companions for men.

Bruno Bettelheim

But no one can evade the fact, that in taking up a masculine calling, studying, and working in a man's way, woman is doing something not wholly in agreement with, if not directly injurious to, her feminine nature.

Carl Jung

True women's liberation does not lie in a formalistic or material equality with the other sex, but in the recognition of that specific in the feminine personality—the ability of a woman to be a mother.

Pope Paul VI

More than twenty years after the signing of the federal equal pay act and the establishment of the Equal Employment Opportunity Commission, women wage earners continue to be paid between 57 and 59 cents for each dollar paid to male wage earners and black women continue to earn less than all other workers, black or white, male or female. Although some assume that these figures reflect the fact that women tend to be employed in secretarial or clerical jobs while men obtain employment in high paying fields like construction or the professions, further study shows that this explanation is not adequate. Women tend to receive lower pay than men simply because they are women. For example, a recent study shows that women who earn a Harvard Ph.D. average $23,000 a year, $7,000 a year less than the $30,000 average salary for men with these credentials. The discrepancy between male and female graduates of the Harvard School of Public Health is even greater: the salary of male graduates is $37,800, whereas that of female graduates is $21,300. In other words, even women who manage to graduate from one of the United States' most prestigious graduate schools find themselves subject to dramatic economic discrimination once they enter the job market. In fact, statistics indicate that women workers who have graduated from college still earn less during their lifetime than those males who have completed eighth grade.

Further, in spite of full-color photos in glossy magazines showing "the first woman locomotive engineer" or "the first female jockey," 70 percent of women currently employed are concentrated in just twenty different job categories, only five more than in 1905. Women are highly represented in the service areas, social work, nursing, primary school teaching, etc., and systematically excluded from other kinds of work.

These facts of economic life in the 1980s illustrate a continued division of labor by sex within the paid labor force, a division by which women are allocated the lower paying and lower status jobs. The ways we explain and evaluate this sexual division of labor will differ dramatically depending upon the particular theoretical framework we use to organize and evaluate social reality. Indeed, while the existence of a sexual division of labor will be seen as problematic according to most frameworks, at least one, the conservative, will fail to identify the division as a problem at all.

CONSERVATISM

As we have seen, the conservative tends to view many capacities of human beings as biologically determined and therefore unchangeable. It is not surprising, then, to find that conservatism regards the sexual division within paid labor as the natural expression of biological differences between women and men. Conservatives point to differences in physiology, hormonal balance, and genetic composition as suiting women and men for different tasks. Some crude versions of conservative theory actually claim that women (unlike men) are biologically suited to perform repetitive detailed labor for long periods of time. Others argue that women alone are suited to caring for young children because they are naturally patient and nurturing and thus can cope with the constant demands of infants and small children. In the selection included here Tiger and Fox emphasize different "emotional, intellectual and social skills and enthusiasm" as the basis for what they maintain is a virtually universal division of labor according to gender.

What is characteristic of conservative theory is that it treats the sexual division of labor as essentially natural and usually goes on to equate the perpetuation of this "natural" division with a just and good state of affairs. It gives little if any consideration to the role of socialization in maintaining the sexual division of labor and tends to ignore anthropological evidence citing societies in which heavy manual labor is routinely the responsibility of women rather than of men. In fact, it ignores our own recent experience in the United States during World War II, when thousands of women were mobilized to take over the jobs in heavy industry vacated by men who went off to fight.

LIBERALISM

The liberal theorist is less concerned with the origins of the sexual division of labor in the past than with bringing about the equitable treatment of all members of society in the present. This is understandable when we remind ourselves that liberalism grew up as a theory to press for the legal and social rights of the rising bourgeoisie against a feudal order that apportioned rights on the basis of birth and inherited position. Liberalism argues for the equal opportunity of all human beings to acquire education and training commensurate with their ability and the opportunity to use that training to achieve whatever place in the society the individual is able. Thus liberalism maintains, not that all individuals can attain the same achievements but rather that gender in itself is no more a proper criterion for determining what opportunities an individual should have than was nobility of birth. Given equal opportunities, different individuals will prove themselves suited to different jobs and careers, and the removal of discrimination in the area of employment will permit all individuals to fulfill themselves to the greatest extent possible.

Appeals to individual self-fulfillment and distributive justice are not the only arguments that the liberal uses in defending the distribution of jobs through a competition in which each individual has an equal opportunity. This method of job distribution is also claimed to maximize each individual's contribution to society as a whole. Hence we find in liberal feminist writings, from Mary Wollstonecraft and J. S. Mill right up to the present time, constant references to the general advantages that are supposed to accrue to society through the fuller utilization of women's talents. It is interesting to note that these liberal feminist arguments are modern applications of Adam Smith's classic belief that, when each individual pursues her or his own economic self-interest, the "invisible hand" of Providence, working through a market economy, will coordinate these selfish strivings so that the net consequences are to the benefit of all.

In the contemporary period, liberal feminists, especially the National Organization for Women (NOW), have been the moving force behind the campaign to pass the Equal Rights Amendment (the ERA) to the United States Constitution. Focusing on discrimination in employment as perhaps the biggest problem facing women today, the liberal feminist views the ERA as a way of ensuring women's legal equality in the areas of employment and business. Many liberal feminists have sought to speed up the process of equalization by developing programs designed to prevent informal discrimination and to counteract its past effects. Thus special efforts are made to recruit qualified women candidates for job training programs from which traditionally they have been excluded. One recommendation that has been made in a variety of forms involves what its opponents call "reverse discrimination." According to this recommendation, qualified female candidates for available positions should be preferred over male candidates for a limited period of time. In our first selection, Hardy Jones offers a liberal justification for such a policy, arguing that the alternative to giving women and minorities temporary preference is not an absence of discrimination but rather the perpetuation of discrimination based on race and gender.

Another area of feminist concern is the issue of sexual harassment. Liberal feminists argue that this pervasive but secret form of harassment in fact constitutes a type of sex discrimination. Federal studies show that the vast majority of women who work for pay experience some form of sexual harassment on their jobs. Like incidents of rape, the majority of such cases have gone unreported in the past, partly out of fear of reprisals, partly because the victims have often blamed themselves. The situation is changing now as feminists reconceptualize sexual harassment as another abuse of male power, similar in many ways to rape. Lin Farley discusses sexual harassment and outlines some of the tactics that liberal feminists have developed for dealing with it.

TRADITIONAL MARXISM

Traditional Marxism opposes the sexual division of labor that keeps some women out of the paid labor force entirely and relegates others to its lowest ranks. However, Marxists do not believe that this division can be eliminated entirely as long as capitalism persists. They argue that the existence of a group of poorly paid workers who can be marshalled in and out of the work force at will is necessary for the capitalist to maintain and increase profits. Profits depend on having workers produce considerably more value than is returned to them in the form of their wages. Marxists call this difference "surplus value." The capitalist maximizes profits by extracting as much labor as possible from workers while keeping their wages as low as possible. Because of competition between workers for jobs, low wages paid to women and third-world workers keep the average wage of all workers down. In addition, the existence of a pool of nonemployed but potential workers means that all employed workers know that others are available to take their jobs if their productivity falls, and bosses are quick to point this out. For these reasons, the traditional Marxist argues that the sexual division of labor is not accidental but a necessary aspect of capitalism. The way to struggle against this division, according to traditional Marxists, is to struggle against capitalism. The Marxist urges that women become part of the paid labor force so that, as full members of the working class, they can struggle with men to overthrow the system of private property and class domination. The reader is urged to review the concluding pages of Engels's discussion in Part Two of this volume for the classic statement of this position.

In this section Margaret Benston provides a contemporary version of Engels's analysis of the relation between woman's work and her status in society. In particular, Benston asks whether women's labor occupies a unique position within the economy at large. She observes that, for the most part, even those women who work outside the home are given exclusive responsibility for housework, an activity which, under the capitalist system of commodity production, is not considered "real" work. Benston concludes that housework must be industrialized in order to be recognized as significant, and women must be integrated into public labor if the basis for their oppression is to be removed. Because the roots of women's oppression ultimately are ecocomic, the traditional Marxist argues that legal equality will not liberate women but that it is a preliminary step to exposing the underlying differences in power and wealth that predominate in class society and that rob all working people of dignity and freedom.

Many Marxists support the ERA because they agree with Engels that it is important to expose the inadequacy of establishing mere legal equality. Passage of the ERA will help people to realize that women will not have genuine equality as long as they are economically dependent on men. Other Marxists oppose the ERA on the grounds that it will bring little if any relief to working-class women. They see it as a threat to the gains made in protective legislation by all workers and fear that bosses will use it as an excuse to remove rules mandating rest periods, prohibiting mandatory night work, etc., many of which were instituted originally in order to permit women equal access to jobs. In addition, they fear that emphasis on the ERA will delude women into defining equality in legalistic terms so that feminists will mistakenly hail the passage of the ERA as a kind of ultimate victory and fail to recognize that a formal end to discrimination will leave untouched the inequalities in wealth and power that have the fundamental determining effect on people's lives.

RADICAL FEMINISM

The most significant contribution of radical feminism may have been its insight that the personal is political. In an attempt to counter what they perceive as undue liberal and Marxist emphasis on the so-called public world, radical feminists have tended to focus more sharply on male dominance in so-called private life. For radical feminism, women's subordinate position in paid labor is merely a symptom of the deeper sexual divisions that have their roots in men's control of women's sexual and childbearing capacities.

As we saw in Part Two, many radical feminists advocate separation from men as a strategy for social change. For most women, it is presently impossible to withdraw from the male-dominated world of paid labor, but some women have been able to create ways of supporting themselves that also support the feminist movement. The 1970s saw a proliferation of small feminist businesses, including feminist banks, credit unions, health care facilities, restaurants, and bookshops. These businesses were not run primarily as profit-making ventures; they were designed to fill a genuine need for women and simultaneously to create models for alternatives to the prevailing capitalist or male mode of operation. Jennifer Woodul identifies some of the alternatives with which feminists experimented.

On the surface there would appear to be considerable similarity in the response that liberal feminists and radical feminists make to the discrimination experienced by women in the world of paid labor. Both liberal and radical feminists wish to organize aspects of economic life so that women may hold positions of power. The significant difference in their reactions is that liberals see power for women in society as it exists as being an end in itself. Radical feminists, on the other hand, view the achievement of power for women in the existing system as being merely the way to enable women to force significant changes in that system.

Writing in the 1980s, Maida Tilchen discusses the difficulties that feminist businesses have encountered, particularly the economic pressures imposed by the larger economic system. Tilchen's discussion suggests that it may be impossible to establish feminism within one business. A number of feminist businesses still survive, however, and all the evidence is not yet in regarding their contribution to large-scale social change.

SOCIALIST FEMINISM

The socialist feminist is concerned as much with women's work in the home as with women's work in the paid labor force. Socialist feminists argue that an adequate understanding of women's position in either sphere requires an understanding of women's position in the other. Because women are taught to consider themselves primarily as wives and mothers, they accept lower-rank jobs at disproportionately low wages and can be marshalled in and out of the paid labor force according to the needs of the capitalist class. The lower wages available to women make it appear rational for wives rather than husbands to stay at home and to take primary responsibility for housework. Thus women's subordination in each sphere of work reinforces their subordination in the other. Women's liberation requires a transformation of how work is organized both inside and outside the home.

Socialist feminist theory rejects the traditional dichotomy between home and so-called workplace. It insists that domestic work is indeed work. Traditional Marxist theorists have offered varying analysis of the nature of women's work in the home, focussing sometimes on women's role in reproducing labor power, sometimes on women's role in facilitating the consumption of commodities (cooking macaroni so that it becomes edible) and sometimes on women's responsibility for providing emotional support to men. Thus they have shown how women's domestic labor provides an essential contribution to the maintenance of the capitalist system. Socialist feminist theorists have supplemented traditional Marxist analyses by pointing out how sex segregation in the labor market tends to force women into a subordinate position at home and thus reinforces male dominance as well as capitalism. For socialist feminism, the distinction between home and so-called workplace is an ideological division that gives undue emphasis to men's "public" work and devalues the social and historical importance of women's "private" work in the home.

While liberal feminists were among the first to campaign actively for equal pay for equal work, socialist feminists argue that it is necessary to reevaluate the worth of the work that women do and have redefined the equal pay issue as equal pay for comparable work. They argue that differentials in pay between a truck driver and a clerical worker do not reflect real differences in skills, training, social utility, or other relevant factors. Instead, they reflect the fact that one job is traditionally defined as a male occupation while the other is traditionally reserved for females. For this reason, socialist feminists contend that the demand for equal pay for equal work cannot strike at the heart of women's economic inferiority.

Socialist feminists argue that differentials in pay fulfill a political as well as an economic purpose. Apart from the obvious economic advantages to employers of undervaluing women's work, pay differentials between the sexes serve to divide and subdue those women and men who might challenge the existing distribution of wealth and income. Socialist feminists argue that an adequate analysis of the sexual division of labor and the severe economic discrimination practiced against women, minorities, and minority women must recognize the role that racism and sexism play in dividing workers and thus maintaining the capitalist class in its position of power. In this respect, socialist feminists tend to be in agreement with the traditional Marxist analysis, which they regard as correct, though incomplete.

Natalie Sokoloff argues that our understanding of women's position and exploitation in the paid labor force can be further refined once we recognize that all women who work for pay (whether or not they are married or have children) are seen (and often see themselves) as working mothers. In this way, women's position in the home and their position in the labor force reinforce each other. In both cases that position is defined by the needs of patriarchy and capitalism.

Socialist feminists agree with Nancy Hartsock that we must rethink our definition of work. Because most of the work presently available to us is so unsatisfying, it is easy to mistakenly assume that work is intrinsically unpleasant. Socialist feminists reject this assumption and hold instead the fundamental Marxist belief that work is the essential human activity. According to this view, participation in creative forms of production is necessary not only for human progress but also for individuals' development as complete and satisfied human beings. Only the capitalist and male-dominated organization of work turns it into drudgery. Socialist feminists are concerned with developing new ways of defining and organizing work so as to maximize its creative and life-affirming character.

WOMEN OF COLOR

While black men earn less than white men and white women earn less than all men, black women earn less than all other workers. This statistic reflects a reality experienced by all women of color—the fact that they suffer a two-fold exploitation—on the basis of both their race and their sex. Although all women are victims of sex segregation in the labor force, women of color find the jobs available to them even more restricted than those offered to white women. About the only area of the economy where women of color outnumber white workers is in the percentage unemployed.

Among the worst-off of all wage workers are those women of color who come as immigrants to the industrially developed nations or who remain in their homelands (Korea, Mexico, Thailand, the Philippines, the West Indies) to work in factories owned by foreign corporations. Both our selections in this section deal with women who were not born in the industrially developed nations.

In response to labor militancy during the 1970s and out of the desire to continue to maximize profits while undermining the strength of a unionized workforce, many large American firms have closed existing industrial facilities in the United States and have moved part or even all of their industrial operations into third-world nations where labor is cheap and plentiful. They are aided by the policies of corrupt governments in these nations who are more than willing to work with American corporations to maximize their profits at the expense of the health and safety of their workforce. Between 80 and 90 percent of the workers exploited in this way are female, and most of these women earn between $3 and $5 *a day* for long hours of tedious and precise labor. Barbara Ehrenreich and Annette Fuentes document the situation faced by such women throughout the third world. The picture they present is of women of color victimized both by prevailing racist and sexist stereotypes and by large American or multinational corporations whose racist and sexist practices produce large stock dividends for wealthy American or European stockholders at incredible human cost.

It is important for feminists to see that the fate of women born abroad is connected directly with the fate of native-born British or American women. Not only are women of color exploited by the same system of male-dominated capitalism that also exploits native-born women, but the superexploitation of women of color also exerts a downward pressure on the wages of all women—and, indeed, on the wages of male workers as well. White women cannot be liberated at the expense of women of color. By looking at the situation of all women wage workers, we can understand more clearly how the liberation of women of color is necessary for the liberation of all women.

CONSERVATISM

Give and Take

Lionel Tiger
Robin Fox

One thing that every system has to take into account is the sexual division of labor. We have maintained elsewhere in this book that the degree and nature of the participation of men and women in the economy is very different. We suggested that this goes back to the evolution of the hunting animal, where male and female were assigned radically different tasks, each essential to the success and survival of the group, and that therefore they were subjected to very different kinds of selection pressure. We can come to the same conclusions about economic as political division of labor, but the details differ insofar as women are of necessity deeply involved in the economy at the same time that they are shut out completely from any political activity. But it can be predicted that in each case men will want to keep them from controlling the system, and women will be unlikely to make effective inroads on any scale into the centers of economic power. The roots of this dilemma are deep in our history. Women did not hunt.

Some of the physical differences between males and females, which are related to different roles during our formative evolution, have already been discussed, but it is necessary here to note some of them briefly in order to root behavior directly in its biological context. These differences are first of all based on clear reproductive distinctions. Female reproductive physiology places simple structural limits on what women can do. They must have wider pelvises than men, because the birth canal must accommodate the infant's large head; therefore they use more energy in locomotion, because their hips swing wider from side to side. In addition, the fat deposits on their buttocks are heavy and use up precious energy. Accordingly, women cannot run as quickly or for as long as men. Of course, there is a normal curve of variation here as elsewhere, and some women will run faster than some men; the curve of variations of the male and female will overlap, but the curves are nonetheless real and significant. This is true also of the ability to throw objects such as balls and spears—a matter obviously relevant to a hunting animal. Furthermore, females adapt less readily than males to changes in temperature—a considerable hazard in hot environments. We now know that there are predictable and disruptive effects on female performance that depend on their menstrual cycles; and it remains an abiding index of male callousness to female realities that rarely are these normal and foreseeable stimuli considered in arranging work and even domestic schedules. (This can become positively inequitable when females are engaged in crucial tests of various kinds. For example, some reports indicate that females achieve some fourteen-percent-lower grades on examination during the premenstrual days, when they are at a considerable disadvantage. Depending on the nature of the examination in question, a woman may be affected for her entire career because she could not demonstrate the ability she normally has. Conversely, if she were to confront this examination at mid-cycle, her performance might be better than usual. In another milieu, the first female Russian astronaut has argued that while women could do the tasks men do, it was still necessary to take the menstrual cycle into account in managing the routines of space flight.)

There is a series of other differences of this kind that could be described, but it is clearly more relevant today to focus less upon explicitly physical features of work performance than upon those involving emotional, intellectual, and social skills and enthusiasm. There are, after all, relatively few jobs in industrial societies that demand strength of arm and speed of foot so greedily that females could not meet the needs. Women can and do drive huge trucks and airplanes, operate elaborate machines, and physically cope with the air-conditioned cabins and power-assisted controls of huge cranes and earth movers. There is very little justification for assuming that any job that men now do women could not do too. And vice versa: aside from bearing and suckling children, there is no characteristically women's work that some husky baritone copilot could not do. Our ideas about equality and the right to widespread social participation of men and women all urge us overwhelmingly in the direction of a society in which male and female roles are more or less interchangeable and in which no particular cachet or stigma attaches to men doing what was once women's work, or the other way around.

But the reality falls far short of the ideal. The potentialities are felt only weakly in what actually still goes on. One of the few general rules about human cultures that anthropologists can safely affirm is that in all known societies a distinction is made between "women's work" and "men's work." The inconsistencies in attitudes are plentiful and comical from one society to another; in one place, men will carry water and women will plant yams, while ten villages away the inhabitants will defend with high intensity the obviously correct proposition that women must carry water and men plant yams. So the first point is that even where the distinctions are not especially reasonable or defensible, they are inevitably made. The next general feature of this division of labor by sex is that some jobs are widely thought to be the rightful provinces of males, and others of females. Hunting, the manufacture of weapons, and the construction of boats are almost universally thought to be male, while such tasks as grinding seeds and gathering nuts are reckoned females' work nearly everywhere. This follows understandably from the hunting past.

But what is not easily understandable is the extraordinary persistence of the division of labor by sex in societies with different forms and levels of industrialization, different climates, different histories, and varying notions about the good man, the good woman, and the good life. This must be explained.

We have already indicated how persistent male-female differences both baffled ideologists and violated the laws of chance. There is no particular reason why females must be part of formal politics. But women must work, and they must be part of the economy, any economy. Of course, in broad terms, they always are, to the extent that they do housework, prepare food, mind and socialize children, and attend to the clothing of their family. That this is not regarded as work in the sense that factory labor is, is a conceit of economic analysis, and part, besides, of a general devaluation of intimate (as opposed to public) activity—a devaluation that applies to the do-it-yourself man who contributes nothing to the Gross National Product when he builds himself a bookshelf but pushes it up two hundred dollars when he buys one from a shop. Women have to be in on the economy. But a basic element of the biogrammar here seems to be that they have to be in on only specially defined terms; there appears to be a tendency to define some work as female and some as male, and to maintain the distinction whatever the content and whatever the cost. This is the same principle of male-bond-female-exclusion that, in politics, so rudely circumscribed the female role. In economic matters, since females cannot be excluded totally, at least they can be segregated into some set specific activities.

But does it go deeper even than this? We argued that the central arena of politics was male because of differences in male and female potentials for successful large-scale competitive bonding. Insofar as the central arena of economic life demands similar organization, we would expect males to dominate it. Where business and industry, or the organization of production consumption and exchange, generally demand cohort activity, it will be male cohorts who will be in evidence. Where control is involved, men will work together and women will be excluded or allowed in only if they agree to play male roles in a male fashion. Women usually lend themselves to this strategy by agreeing that it is not specific female skills that they bring to their roles as executives, and that in simply filling male positions they are substitute males. This attitude strictly delimits female behavior in business.

It also accounts for the pressures against overt sexuality on the job. Seductive arts are disruptive of male cohesion. The outlaw band or the board of directors assumes that they are not part of its normal routines, and women who want seriously to play the power game must leave their false eyelashes at home.

This may seem a facetious point, but it is a point that underlies a very serious truth. False eyelashes are supplements to female courtship-display behavior. They enhance the "recognition flutter" and coy covering of the dilating pupils in courtship exchanges. As such they are part of the apparatus that aids in promoting and cementing the courtship bond. This is a male-female bond and operates in the arena of sexual competition and eventual mating. It is outside of and inimical to the male-made bond that operates in the politicoeconomic arena for purpose of cohort formation and maintenance in the pursuit of effective defense and predation. This is a point difficult, of course, to prove, yet it seems clear enough: that one serious if tragicomic reason for the difficulty females experience in male work groups is not that males dislike females but rather that the force of their enthusiasm for females can disrupt the work and endanger the integrity of groups of men.

We needn't waste sympathy on men harassed by such enthusiasm for women that they reject them as colleagues and force them into occupational ghettos so the precious male mystique will remain undisturbed. Our suggestion is that it is not malice alone, and not prejudice only, and not just cultural lag and individual fear that stimulate an obvious antifemale inequity. The same pattern emerges both in countries that devalue women and in countries that eagerly support them. The opportunities for women in the economy of the United States have declined over the past sixty years, though the number of women with advanced and technical education has increased enormously. The Israeli experience, both in and out of the kibbutz, is even more discouraging to those who looked to their ideology about sexual equality to produce radical social change. And in Russia itself, the first and most important revolutionary society, the position of women has not been improved in any sense commensurate with either the expressed idealism of the community or its willingness to try relatively egalitarian socioeconomic forms and approaches to the ownership and control of wealth.

So it cannot be a conspiracy of men against women that once swept the world that now—so apparently securely—sets limits to the range of female options to enter the powerful macrostructures of economic life. The evidence against conspiracy comes from too heterogeneous a set of places: females are obviously able to do the tasks men can—that is, when they are given the opportunity; males are unlikely to have deliberately thought up ways of maintaining women in their homes for domestic and sexual convenience and then brainwashed them to accept such an exploitative situation—if exploitative it is. Perhaps, as with some of the other bonds, we are dealing here with a regularity of the biogrammar that has to do with ancient forms of survival that mark us still today. That the thrilling and elaborate innovations of our technology seem to have relatively little effect on the work relationships of men and women attests either to the unimportance of technology—which is foolish—or to the importance of the biogrammar. Though puritans and Calvinists will shrink at the thought, it may be true that social relationships are more important than work encounters, and the apparent rigidity of the sexual division of labor represents both men and women "voting with their feet" for the notion that difference does not necessarily connote inferiority or superiority, and that the division of labor is not necessarily the squalid display of human invidiousness that, for example, racism undoubtedly is. The sexual division of labor has no racial home. The analogy is faulty because sex differences are important biologically and tangible behaviorally, whereas racial ones are unimportant biologically and meaningless behaviorally. The bad analogy confuses policy even more than it confuses people: to avoid the consequences of racism, it is imperative that all people be treated equally, but to avoid the features of the sexual division of labor that many men and women find undesirable, it may be necessary to treat men and women differently and not deny their real biologies in the name of theoretical equities. . . .

LIBERALISM

On the Justifiability of Reverse Discrimination

Hardy E. Jones

The topic of reverse discrimination in hiring excites strong passions on all sides. It is a complex issue, the difficulty of which is reflected in divisive, often volatile debates. In the following discussion I shall consider whether and why preferential treatment for members of certain groups is permissible. I assume that discrimination against females and blacks is wrong and unjust. The issue is whether employment discrimination against white males in favor of less-qualified persons of another sex or color is morally justifiable. Another crucial assumption is that employers are able and willing to use objective standards for determining relevant qualifications—that they have access to, and can follow, nonsexist and nonracist criteria.

I shall adumbrate four aims in view of which a comprehensive social program of reverse discrimination may be justified. These are worthy goals which, were there no serious countervailing considerations, should surely be sufficient to justify preferential treatment.

1 *To ensure that past discrimination against females and blacks does not continue.* It takes some societies a long time to cease, finally and completely, patterns of injustice that have prevailed for generations. Legislative acts and constitutional amendments often simply do not do the job. A comprehensive, tightly administered social program involving reverse discrimination in hiring would help bring past and continuing injustice to a halt. Blacks and females may feel, quite understandably, that in order for them not to be discriminated *against* they must be discriminatingly *favored.*

2 *To offer, officially and explicitly, a symbolic denunciation of our racist and sexist past.* A program of reverse discrimination, suitably touted and carefully advertised, might serve well as such a symbol. Among other benefits, such a program could have the salutary effect of encouraging victims to work hard to offset the often sadly debilitating consequences of injustice. Further, this gesture might represent a confession of past wrong and a resolution to be more just. Employers might be encouraged voluntarily to stop discriminating against blacks and females.

3 *To provide role models for victimized blacks and females.* One good way for persons to shake off the shackles of past injustice is to become aware of others, relevantly similar to them, who have good jobs. By noting quite directly that these others are succeeding in respectable positions, persons may be encouraged to proceed vigorously in pursuit of satisfying careers for themselves.

4 *To compensate victims of discrimination by preferring them over beneficiar-*

ies of injustice. It seems only just to give those who have been treated unjustly extra benefits and, in this way, to make some effort toward "evening the score." Those to benefit directly from the preferential treatment may not have been discriminated against, but they may have suffered from previous unjust acts toward their ancestors. The effects of past discriminatory acts may have deprived them of the wealth, education, health, and employment essential to equal-opportunity competition. The white males to be discriminated against may not have perpetrated the injustices, but many have greatly benefited from them. So it seems proper that they now be deprived of still further fruits, in the form of jobs, of past acts of unjust discrimination. This position may be buttressed by reflection on how people have come to have the qualifications they possess. The better-qualified white males might have been far less qualified had they not reaped the benefits of an unjust system which favored them at every turn. And the now lesser-qualified blacks and females might have been much better qualified if they and their ancestors had received equal, fair treatment from the start. The meritocratic views holds that persons deserve jobs on the basis of merit or ability—whatever their qualifications now happen to be. The position set out here rejects this "meritocracy of present qualifications." What is also relevant is how people have gotten qualifications and what their qualifications would have been if certain crucial aspects of their histories had been different.

The notion employed here may be thought of as "counterfactual meritocracy." On this view, people are deserving, at least within certain limits, of jobs on the basis of what their qualifications would have been if they had been neither victims nor beneficiaries of past injustice. In principle there is nothing wrong with a fair meritocracy. What makes the usual meritocracy pernicious is its allowance of past injustice to penetrate, or spill over into, the present by refusing to factor out the unjust causes of present qualifications. The fair counterfactual meritocracy, whatever its defects, is not subject to this criticism. There is also a forward-looking feature of the basic position. The future qualifications of job applicants, as well as present and "what would have been" qualifications, are relevant. If a presently lesser-qualified person, a victim of past injustice, can increase his level of competence by being offered the position, then there is some reason for preferring him to a beneficiary of past injustice whose future qualifications will become no higher.

All of these appear to be eminently good reasons for instituting a compensatory program of reverse discrimination. But there are serious objections that must be conscientiously confronted. I shall state the difficulties with reverse discrimination, assess their relative strengths, and suggest how they might be resolved.

1

Perhaps the most nearly devastating objection to a scheme based on the notion of "counterfactual meritocracy" is that it requires vastly more knowledge about individual cases than we have any reasonable prospect of obtaining. If we do not know that the particular white male to be passed over (in favor of the lesser-qualified black or female) has benefited from past injustice in obtaining his qualifications, then we run the risk of unfairly discriminating against him. And there is surely a very strong, widely shared intuition that "two wrongs do not make a right"—that we cannot rightly rectify past injustice by committing further injustices. It is very difficult to know the truth of counterfactual claims about what a white male's qualification would have been without the benefits of injustice, of what a black person's qualifications would have been without the liabilities of injustice. We might be tempted just to throw up our hands in frustration and say "Who knows?" Recognizing the lack of special favors and facing more severe competition, the white male might have worked harder to obtain high qualifications. Being confronted with less formidable obstacles to overcome, the black might have felt less of a challenge and might never have worked as hard to obtain his qualifications. And without injustice many other factors could have worked differently in the lives of both. So how could one ever know where either would have ended up when it came time to apply for a job? The perfect working of the counter-factual meritocracy would seem to require the existence of an ideal social observer, in possession of all knowledge as to how individuals have benefited and suffered from injustice—and how things would have been in a just world. Not having this sort of God's-eyeview, we seem destined to lack enough knowledge to implement a fair program of reverse discrimination. Furthermore, even if human means of obtaining the requisite knowledge were developed, their use might be very costly—so costly that everyone in the society would suffer.

The objection is a serious one, and I do not have a fully satisfactory answer. Three points, however, seem noteworthy. First, the risk of unfair treatment of white males can be greatly reduced by establishing small minimal differentials between the better and lesser qualifications. A black female could get the job if she were slightly less qualified. If the difference between the two is very small at present, then it would seem likely that without past injustice the black female would have acquired much better qualifications. Only a cursory knowledge of racist and sexist injustice in American history is necessary to know that discrimination has been widespread, touching the lives of virtually everyone to some degree.

This point suggests a second reply. Lacking the knowledge of a godlike social observer, we are not totally ignorant either. We know a lot about how injustice has affected many individuals. And we can learn more through extensive interviews with individuals and inquiries into the social conditions of their childhood environments. The program could involve setting up hearings for this purpose. In cases in which only a small fraction of the needed knowledge is obtainable, the job could standardly go to the presently more qualified. The program need not be entirely scrapped for lack of complete knowledge of all the cases that may arise.

The third reply is based on an analogy with the administration of criminal justice. In many cases it is very difficult to get enough evidence to know whether an accused person is guilty or innocent. There are great risks involved in a trial system with an attached schedule of punishments. Some innocent people will be found guilty and punished for crimes they did not commit, some guilty persons will be found not guilty and escape the punishment they deserve. We are aware of these uncertainties: yet we are not thereby deterred from implementing a system of indictments, trials, and punishments. Apparently it is thought that the risks of committing injustice are worth taking. If we are reasonable in proceeding with this sort of system, then we would not be obviously unreasonable to institute a program of reverse discrimimition with its attendant risks of unfair treatment of white male applicants. Indeed, the injustice of not hiring a deserving white male seems far less serious than the injustice of punishing an innocent person. The latter may happen less often, but when it does occur we countenance something akin to tragedy. With the generally better opportunities most white males have, it does not seem tragic to prefer unfairly some black female for a particular job. Furthermore, more injustice may result from not having a program of reverse discrimination than from having one. For if we hire solely on the basis of present qualifications, then it is likely that many "counterfactually deserving" but actually less-qualified females and blacks will lose out in favor of white males. Not having a program of reverse discrimination runs the risk of more extensively victimizing persons already unfairly treated. Such a risk seems far more serious than that of unfairly preferring blacks or females to white males who have thus far not been victimized.

The three replies go a way toward meeting the first objection to my scheme to counterfactual meritocracy. In the absence of perfectly adequate knowledge of the individual cases, we must rely on certain roughly reliable indices of past injustice. For purposes of implementing the program initially, rather crude indicators would probably have to be used. "Being black" would be taken as an index of being a victim of past discrimination, and "being a white male" an index of being a beneficiary of past injustice. As knowledge progresses and as we gain experience with the workings of the system, more complex and refined indices could be introduced.

2

Another cluster of objections relates to the administration of the program on a class or group basis. There are serious problems in offering preferential treatment to persons because they are members of a group most of whose members are victims of injustice, and in discriminating against persons because they are members of a group in which most of the members are beneficiaries of injustice.

One of these difficulties is simply that not everyone who deserves compensation will get it. Only a segment of the group of black persons (or female persons) can be given jobs within a preferential-hiring scheme. The appropriate reply here is that reverse discrimination is only *one* way of compensating *some* victimized persons for some of the wrongs done to them. It cannot rectify all past injustice to members of unfairly treated minority groups. There are many other ways to provide compensation, and the operation of a program of reverse discrimination in hiring does not preclude their being tried. Perhaps some more broadly based program could compensate all victims more fairly and efficiently than the more limited program of preferential hiring. However, without such a program, it is surely unobjectionable to compensate as many as possible within our unfortunate limitations. The fact that we cannot compensate everyone does not justify us in compensating no one. The civil-law system of compensating negligently injured persons does not work perfectly so as to insure that every victim receives his due. Still, in the absence of a fairer and more efficient system, the present one is worth keeping. A well-designed system of preferential hiring would seem to be analogous.

But there is a still more serious problem. The programs based on the notion of a counterfactual meritocracy would presumably allow market criteria to determine which members of the groups get jobs (and thus receive compensation). The members must still compete for positions, and the best qualified will obtain them. One result will be that those who have suffered most lose out to those who have suffered least. The better qualified are those most likely to have suffered less from past injustice, and those who are most victimized will be the lesser qualified. So those who are less deserving of compensation will receive it at the expense of those who are more deserving. The compensation will not be distributed in proportion to the degree of liabilities resulting from injustice. . . .

A partial answer to this objection has already been suggested. The proposed system is very imperfect, but in the absence of a better one it seems worth pursuing. If the amount of injustice rectified is greater than that incidentally committed, the program would seem to be worthwhile. Furthermore, other types of compensation could be provided to those victimized persons who lose out in the competition for jobs. As our knowledge of degrees of victimization grows, such information can be incorporated so as to dispense positions proportionately to past injustice. Though extremely important, the objection does not appear to be devastating.

3

The next major difficulty may be labelled the "efficiency objection." It is arguable that, even with knowledge that would allow perfect correlations between being a certain sort of person and being deserving of a certain degree of compensation, the program would be a social disaster. The counterfactual meritocracy, administered comprehensively and assiduously, would drastically reduce efficiency and productivity. To maintain these at acceptable levels, jobs must be allocated on the basis of *actual* qualifications rather than hypothetical "what would have been" qualifications. Everyone in the society will suffer if too many of the lesser qualified are given job preference over better-qualified applicants. Those who are already victims probably will suffer even more than the rest. Poorer, more disadvantaged students, for example, have the greatest need of the very best instructors in their schools. Again, some of what has already been said is applicable here. Other compensatory programs may be useful in making up for the losses suffered by some members of minority groups as a result of the effort to aid the others. Reverse discrimination in hiring is not the only viable method of providing compensation.

Unless the losses in efficiency and productivity are so great that they produce injustice, a trade-off between efficiency and fairness seems justified. Surely the society can afford to tolerate some reduction in efficiency for the sake of rectifying past injustice. It would also be possible to build into the program methods of minimizing inefficiency. One way to do this would be to establish a "threshold of minimal qualifications" variable from job to job. No applicant could fall below this standard and still be hired, and no one would be hired if he were clearly unqualified. But the very best qualified might be passed over without unacceptable losses of efficiency. Another efficiency-conserving device is a "maximum differential of qualification," again varying perhaps from job to job. This would insure that a lesser qualified black or female applicant would not be hired if that person were far less qualified than someone else, The differential would have to be small enough so as to minimize inefficiency, yet large enough so that at least some victimized, lesser-qualified persons are given preference. These suggestions are rather vague, even amorphous; but they at least indicate how the efficiency issue could be handled.

4

At least as serious is the "white male objection." The program of preferential hiring works so that white male applicants, new candidates for new or newly available positions, bear the major burden of providing compensation. They are the ones who primarily suffer from this rectification of past injustice. Though most white males have probably benefited from discrimination against others, they are by no means the only ones who have done so. Though some have actually perpetrated injustices against blacks and females, different individuals are more largely responsible for the unfair treatment. And though many white males have tolerated injustices, virtually everyone else has also. Such facts make a commonly asked question especially pressing. Why must young white males be the ones to make the heavy sacrifices imposed by a program of compensatory justice? The costs of rectification would seem to be unfairly shared among members of a large group of beneficiaries of past injustice.

The ultimate force of the objection hinges on just how much injustice would be committed by the program as compared with how much can be rectified by its implementation. Not having a program of reverse discrimination and running the society on the model of an actual meritocracy brooks injustice by allowing the effects of past unfairness to penetrate into the future. The failure to have compensatory treatment is a failure to rectify injustice; but it also allows former injustices partially to prevail and to remain infused in our present society. So, all things considered, the amount of injustice tolerated without reverse discrimination may exceed that involved in making white males bear the burden. Such a conclusion is admittedly distasteful and unsatisfying.

There is a more utopian, vastly less realistic way of viewing the matter. Those white males who already have jobs have probably benefited more from past injustice than have the new applicants for newly available positions. Some evidence for this consists in the fact that the former have (and in many cases have had for a long time) secure, satisfying, often lucrative positions. Many of these positions were acquired during the days when there was not ever the pretense of fair treatment and equal opportunity for blacks and females. Also, many of these well-entrenched individuals are actual perpetrators, not mere beneficiaries, of injustice to members of minority groups. As a group they are probably much more "guilty" than the young white males who confront the dismal job market for the first time. It seems only fair that those who presently have jobs share the burdens of rectification. One way to do this might be to legislate a heavy tax, a "beneficiary of injustice" tax. The money could be spent to create new jobs and to provide needed social services to victims of unfair discrimination. These points are also suggestive of a more tantalizing, potentially very alarming vision. All jobs in the society could simply be subject to being vacated and then refilled. Everyone (well-entrenched, formerly secure veterans as well as hopeful new candidates) would have to apply for the jobs. The positions would then be filled—of necessity on a gradual, piecemeal basis—in accordance with criteria of justice and merit. A general redistribution of jobs could be accomplished. This would provide the proper rectification of past injustice in such a way that no particular group is unfairly treated.

This scheme is subject to the objections already discussed. The "knowledge objection" and the "efficiency objection" would become especially acute. Very complicated procedures and criteria would have to be devised so as to provide much knowledge about degrees of benefit and victimization. And it would become difficult to determine the appropriate balances between justice and efficiency. As difficult as they are, such problems are not clearly insurmountable. I should emphasize that this proposal is highly speculative. There is virtually no chance of its being very seriously considered and tried. Members of our society will not be willing to institute it. But this program ideally could become the most practically feasible, the most fair, and the most intellectually fascinating means of rectifying the gross injustices of the past.

5

I conclude with the "self-respect objection." If blacks and females know that they have been given jobs because of their group membership and that they have been chosen over better-qualified individuals, they may suffer severe losses of self-respect. Whereas if a person knows he deserves his job in virtue of his merit, ability, and prospects for success, then he will have a strong feeling of dignity and self-worth. Reverse discrimination would be counterproductive with regard to the purposes of having a job. At least one main motivation in seeking a position is the enhancement of one's self-esteem. Such an aim is defeated if persons are not hired solely because of their possession of the very best qualifications.

It is too easy to exaggerate the importance of this difficulty and thus to deemphasize the benefits of a program of compensatory hiring. The problem could possibly be avoided by deceiving job-seekers and making them believe that only the best qualified are hired. This is not likely to be a very workable solution. It would be difficult to carry out the deception on a massive scale, and those who discover the truth may suffer even greater losses of self-respect from having been lied to. Another way of dealing with the problem would be both more sincere and more effective. One could emphasize to persons given the preferential treatment that they would have been best qualified if they had not been victims of injustice. If this is correct and if the central claims of this paper are sound, then people selected for jobs can have the appropriate and secure feeling that, whatever detractors may say, they are getting what they deserve.

Dealing with Sexual Harassment

Lin Farley

The sexual harassment of women at work arose out of man's need to maintain his control of female labor. This tactic of nonreciprocal aggression is a major element in the maintenance of job segregation by sex. It ensures that female wages stay low, weakens women's employment position by undermining female seniority, and keeps women divided so they are incapable of organizing to change their situation.

Working women, by and large, have succumbed to this male extortion by escaping sexual aggression at the expense of their jobs or by keeping their jobs at the expense of their self-respect. They have forfeited their independence and equality at work either way. Meanwhile, the pervasiveness of the aggression has taken a toll of women's drive and desire to work that is beyond calculation. Work itself is a precondition of women's liberation. However, instead of liberation, women find the promise of equality inherent in modern work canceled out by sexual harassment. The abuse maintains the age-old requirement of the Patriarchy: that woman shall serve man with her labor and pay for the right to do so with her body.

The obvious solution is a totally integrated work force with both sexes sharing equally in all jobs and all authority throughout the hierarchies of business power. This kind of change, however, will require nothing less than an alteration in the balance of power at work. This will have to be effected by women. There is only one way women can accomplish it: by unifying and organizing themselves into a cohesive force that will protect their rights at work as vigorously as men will fight to preserve the status quo. Organization is the key to ending sexual harassment. This necessity, however, is often obscured by concern at helping the victims. Assistance of this kind is an immediate necessity, but altering the balance of power at work is the only long-term solution. Working women deserve not just aid for their mistreatment but an end of the victimization altogether.

Significantly, present legal recourse can go part of the way toward accomplishing both tasks. Currently, perpetrators of harassment can be prosecuted under present criminal laws that pertain to sexual assault—rape, extortion, and solicitation for prostitution. These laws have been invoked rarely in cases involving sexual harassment primarily because work is viewed as a world unto itself—also because of social attitudes that have denied the serious nature of the behavior while simultaneously assuming both parties to be equally culpable (if, in fact, the woman wouldn't be viewed as more culpable). In view of our increased understanding of this type of aggression, however, there should be more pressure on law-enforcement officials to make arrests.

This effort can take advantage of the lobbying about rape that has already been done with police departments so that male attitudes, once an initial unfamiliarity with sexual harassment is overcome, may be expected to be more cooperative than ever before. Of course, widespread prosecution will continue to remain problematic. Male attitudes, despite improvement, still constitute a strong obstacle. Women's reluctance to seek redress from the police in the face of this hostility will also continue. Even so, the advantages of criminal prosecution (and this cannot be stressed enough) are well worth the trouble. Any significant increase in enforcement of these laws will act as a deterrent; the abuse has only flourished in part because it has been spared the stigma of criminal activity.

Civil legal remedies are frequently less immediate than criminal prosecution, and their usefulness as a real deterrent is questionable. But they often prove more beneficial to the female victim by redressing some of the financial harm that has attended her victimization. Of all the civil remedies available, Title VII of the 1964 Civil Rights Act offers the best chance for potential redress by providing remuneration for lost pay, legal fees, and the possibility of reinstatement on the job. As the chapter on legal recourse makes clear, however, male attitudes are serious obstacles to enforcement and future prosecution of this issue under Title VII remains in serious jeopardy. In addition, the present three-year backlog in EEOC cases presents another deterrent. Society's condoning of this lengthy time lag between injury and adjudication casts grave doubt as to the more-than-symbolic intent of the legislation.

Aside from legal redress, there is a third widely-advocated remedy—women simply must become more active. Assertiveness training programs for women at work have sprung up all around the country, generally for the best of motives—to counter women's socialization to submissiveness and to reinforce assertiveness. It is believed this will enhance women's success at work by better enabling them to handle their discrimination. This kind of training is effective only up to a point, however, and it would be a grave mistake to rely on this training to combat sexual harassment. In the first place, the problem is not women's behavior, and in the second place, the aggression succeeds largely because women have no recourse at work, not because they can't stand up to it.

About the best that can be said for this kind of "solution," then, is that in some situations, for some women, it may help them deal with it a little better. Sandra Driggs of Communications Perspectives in San Francisco says:

> Be smart. If you find yourself in job difficulties because of sexual pressures, take time to analyze the situation. Build your own case, get documentation. Put it in writing. Get memos. Try and develop a case of the way it is affecting your job evaluations and performance. Don't just behave as if he automatically has the upper hand. This comes under the general heading of "Cover Your Ass"

All of the preceding indicates that, while some things can be done once the aggression has begun, this frequently will not prevent the end result of job loss. Law enforcement is punitive rather than preventive except in the sense that punishment is believed or hoped to be a deterrent. In the meantime, however, the extortion has succeeded. Only a completely inclusive solution to sexual harassment will ensure a future for women at work that is free of this abuse. Grievance procedures are at present completely inadequate. Women do not trust in-house avenues of employee redress, and for the most part this is grounded in accurate assessments of the range of male power that will be arrayed against them.

The hope of working women for a substantial change in the work environment has been evidenced in recent years by their efforts in demanding better working conditions. Grass-roots working women's organizations have sprung up all across the country and include: Women Office Workers in New York City, 9–5 in Boston, Women Employed in Chicago, Women Organized for Employment in San Francisco, and Union W.A.G.E. in Oakland. They draw their members from among the mass of unorganized working women who have no other way to articulate their needs, voice their complaints, or channel their demands for change. They are hybrid groups, neither pure women's rights nor pure labor rights, but an amalgam of both evidencing women's great need for organizations that will advance their cause as *women at work*.

These groups represent significant progress; nevertheless they cannot supply the full solution. Women on the job, inside the workplace, must gather their collective strength.

Sexual harassment will be stopped when women finally take control of their own labor power via collective bargaining and striking to regain their rights.

This will be a long fight, but it is the inevitable future. The sexual harassment of women at work is an intolerable working condition that negatively affects everyone. It is as onerous to women as rape, and as important as abortion because it involves the right to control their own bodies. It is this *sine qua non* which is at the core of all three issues. Women's stamina, energy, and courage in the battles on rape and abortion have made recent history; because of sexual harassment they will change the face of modern work as well. It is only a question of time. Women are 40 percent of the work force now. This percentage is expected to grow, and these numbers alone bespeak a power base which only lacks organization to make itself felt. Humor has always played a large part in the cover-up of sexual harassment, but women will have the last laugh. The sexual harassment men have used to keep women subordinate will ultimately prove the issue by which working women will unite.

ELEVEN WAYS TO FIGHT SEXUAL HARASSMENT

1 Sexual harassment is Criminal Activity. Rape because it occurs in an office or factory is no less a crime than elsewhere in our society. The same holds true for sexual assault, abuse, misuse and physical violation. No less importantly, when a manager, boss, supervisor or foreman tells a woman she can't get a job or keep one without "putting out" sexually, he is soliciting for prostitution. All of these forms of sexual harassment are *already* outlawed by criminal statutes. Take your complaint to your local police department. Don't be timid. Demand your protection under the law. Prosecute your assailant.

2 Sexual Harassment on-the-job is Sex Discrimination. Because this abuse deprives women of the right to equal employment opportunity, you can seek justice and/or compensation under a variety of government enforcement agencies:

• The Equal Employment Opportunity Commission (EEOC) is the federal remedy. Within 180 days of filing a complaint with the EEOC you can obtain a lawyer (often on a contingency basis which means you pay nothing until the successful conclusion of your suit) and you can, if fired, sue for re-instatement to your job plus up to three years back-pay dating from the time of termination.

• Closer to home, your local city or state human rights agency is empowered to intervene in your behalf at any point you experience sexual harassment. This can be before or after you are either forced to quit your job and/or are fired. All it takes is a phone call to determine if you have a complaint. Don't wait! Act immediately. You have nothing to lose and it could save your job.

• Private suits are a third legal option. You can sue for damages as a result of the trauma of being coerced sexually on your job. Consult a lawyer.

3 You deserve Unemployment Compensation. A bill now pending in the New York State Legislature will make sexual harassment good cause for leaving a job; Wisconsin has already passed a similar statute. File your claim immediately. Fair and just economic compensation for sexual harassment that results in loss of employment is your right.

4 File a Grievance/Go to your Union. Internal grievance procedures and unions are your on-the-job remedies. Use them. Even if you feel they will not take your claim seriously or are prejudiced against your complaint, these channels must be pursued if you are serious about stopping sexual harassment. No court, for example, can rule in favor of a female complainant if she has not first exhausted all internal remedies.

5 Document Your Case. Your job is in jeopardy from the second the sexual harassment begins. Prepare yourself accordingly. Keep memos that detail the attacks. For example, "On such and such day and time, so and so came into my office, met me in the hall, cornered me in the elevator and he either/and-or said or did thus." You don't have to post these memos on the company bulletin board, but you should send them privately to someone else at work, preferably a superior. Now you have a record of the harassment. Combined with your good employment record this documentation can eventually save your job.

6 Take Direct Action. This is particularly successful with co-workers. State your discomfort, say "NO" immediately. If necessary, pinch back. Many men will stop when faced by a determined woman who forcefully communicates that this behavior is intolerable.

7 Get Help from Women's Groups. The experience of sexual harassment at work is a serious trauma. Women's organizations including N.O.W. and a variety of local working women's organizations such as the Alliance Against Sexual Coercion in Boston, the Interfaith Project on Working Women in Philadelphia and Work Options for Women in Wichita, Kansas are on your side. You need their emotional/legal resources. Don't hesitate. If your town doesn't have a women's organization to deal with women's job problems—start one.

8 Use the Power of the Press. Never underestimate the value of adverse publicity. Go public. Expose the situation. Sexual harassment can only succeed in secrecy and public exposure is a great asset.

9 Female Solidarity on-the-job is a Powerful Weapon. Ask for help from your female co-workers. Give help without being asked. Become friends of the women with whom you work. The company and the harasser can always pick us off one-by-one. When we stand up together we have power—the power of unity in numbers. Just think, he can fire you, but he can't fire all ten of you in the office at the same time.

10 Organize. This is the *whole* solution. When women have organized to protect their rights on-the-job as vigorously as men have organized to protect theirs, the world of work for women will be transformed. This is the future. It won't be long before a national women's union or federation of unions of women will negotiate decent working conditions for all women who work for pay, but you can begin now. Form a women's committee, a women's caucus, a female rap group. You have nothing to lose and your job may depend on it.

11 In school. While it is not strictly on-the-job, female students in University and College graduate schools frequently are blocked by sexual harassment from obtaining the degrees necessary to get skilled jobs. Because the abuse in this setting deprives women of the right to an equal education, students should file grievances against the offending professor as well as sue the institution under all the government statutes and agencies which prohibit sex discrimination in education.

TRADITIONAL MARXISM

Women and Society

V. I. Lenin

Capitalism combines formal equality with economic and, consequently, social inequality. This is one of the principal distinguishing features of capitalism, one that is mendaciously screened by the supporters of the bourgeoisie, the liberals, and that is not understood by the petty-bourgeois democrats. Out of this distinguishing feature of capitalism, by the way, the necessity arises, while fighting resolutely for economic equality, openly to recognize capitalist inequality and, under certain conditions, even to include this open recognition of inequality as a basis for the proletarian state organization (the Soviet constitution).

But capitalism *cannot* be consistent even with regard to formal equality (equality before the law, "equality" between the well-fed and the hungry, between the property-owner and the propertyless). And one of the most flagrant manifestations of this inconsistency is the *inferior position* of woman compared with man. Not a single bourgeois state, not even the most progressive, republican democratic state, has brought about complete equality of rights.

But the Soviet Republic of Russia promptly wiped out, *without any exception,* every trace of inequality in the legal status of woman, and secured her complete equality in its laws.

It is said that the level of culture is best characterized by the legal status of woman. There is a grain of profound truth in this saying. From this point of view, only the dictatorship of the proletariat, only the socialist state, could achieve and did achieve a higher level of culture.

Therefore, the foundation (and consolidation) of the first Soviet Republic— and alongside and in connection with this, the Communist International— inevitably lends a new, unparalleled, powerful impetus to the working women's movement.

For, when we speak of those who, under capitalism, were directly or indirectly, wholly or partially oppressed, it is precisely the Soviet system, and the Soviet system only, that secures democracy. This is clearly demonstrated by the position of the working class and the poor peasants. It is clearly demonstrated by the position of women.

But the Soviet system represents the final decisive conflict for the *abolition of classes,* for economic and social equality. *For us,* democracy, even democracy for those who were oppressed under capitalism, including democracy for the oppressed sex, *is inadequate.*

The working women's movement has for its object the fight for the economic and social, and not merely formal, equality of woman. The main task is to draw the women into socially productive labor, extricate them from "domestic slavery," free them of their stultifying and humiliating resignation to the perpetual and exclusive atmosphere of the kitchen and nursery.

It is a long struggle, requiring a radical remaking both of social technique and of customs. But this struggle will end with the complete triumph of communism.

The Political Economy of Women's Liberation

Margaret Benston

The position of women rests, as everything in our complex society, on an economic base.

Eleanor Marx and Edward Aveling

The "woman question" is generally ignored in analyses of the class structure of society. This is so because, on the one hand, classes are generally defined by their relation to the means of production and, on the other hand, women are not supposed to have any unique relation to the means of production. The category seems instead to cut across all classes; one speaks of working-class women, middle-class women, etc. The status of women is clearly inferior to that of men,[1] but analysis of this condition usually falls into discussing socialization, psychology, interpersonal relations, or the role of marriage as a social institution.[2] Are these, however, the primary factors? In arguing that the roots of the secondary status of women are in fact economic, it can be shown that women as a group do indeed have a definite relation to the means of production and that this is different from that of men. The personal and psychological factors then follow from this special relation to production, and a change in the latter will be a necessary (but not sufficient) condition for changing the former.[3] If this special relation of women to production is accepted, the analysis of the situation of women fits naturally into a class analysis of society.

The starting point for discussion of classes in a capitalist society is the

[1]Marlene Dixon, "Secondary Social Status of Women." (Available from US. Voice of Women's Liberation Movement, 1940 Bissell, Chicago, Illinois 60614.)

[2]The biological argument is, of course, the first one used, but it is not usually taken seriously by socialist writers. Margaret Mead's *Sex and Temperament* is an early statement of the importance of culture instead of biology.

[3]This applies to the group or category as a whole. Women as individuals can and do free themselves from their socialization to a great degree (and they can even come to terms with the economic situation in favorable cases), but the majority of women have no chance to do so.

distinction between those who own the means of production and those who sell their labor power for a wage. As Ernest Mandel says:

> The proletarian condition is, in a nutshell, the lack of access to the means of production or means of subsistence which, in a society of generalized commodity production, forces the proletarian to sell his labor power. In exchange for this labor power he receives a wage which then enables him to acquire the means of consumption necessary for satisfying his own needs and those of his family.
>
> This is the structural definition of wage earner, the proletarian. From it necessarily flows a certain relationship to his work, to the products of his work, and to his overall situation in society, which can be summarized by the catchword alienation. But there does not follow from this structural definition any necessary conclusions as to the level of his consumption . . . the extent of his needs, or the degree to which he can satisfy them.[4]

We lack a corresponding structural definition of women. What is needed first is not a complete examination of the symptoms of the secondary status of women, but instead a statement of the material conditions in capitalist (and other) societies which define the group "women." Upon these conditions are built the specific superstructures which we know. An interesting passage from Mandel points the way to such a definition:

> The commodity . . . is a product created to be exchanged on the market, as opposed to one which has been made for direct consumption. *Every commodity must have both a use-value and an exchange-value.*
>
> It must have a use-value or else nobody would buy it. . . . A commodity without a use-value to anyone would consequently be unsalable, would constitute useless production, would have no exchange-value precisely because it had no use-value.
>
> On the other hand, every product which has use-value does not necessarily have exchange-value. It has an exchange-value only to the extent that the society itself, in which the commodity is produced, is founded on exchange, is a society where exchange is a common practice. . . .
>
> In capitalist society, commodity production, the production of exchange-values, has reached its greatest development. It is the first society in human history where the major part of production consists of commodities. It is not true, however, that all production under capitalism is commodity production. Two classes of products still remain simple use-value.
>
> The first group consists of all things produced by the peasantry for its own consumption, everything directly consumed on the farms where it is produced. . . .
>
> The second group of products in capitalist society which are not commodities but remain simple use-value consists of all things produced in the home. Despite the fact that considerable human labor goes into this type of household production, it still remains a production of use-values and not of commodities. Every time a soup is made or a button sewn on a garment, it constitutes production, but it is not production for the market.

---

[4]Ernest Mandel, "Workers Under Neocapitalism," paper delivered at Simon Fraser University. (Available through the Department of Political Science, Sociology and Anthropology, Simon Fraser University, Burnaby, B.C., Canada.)

The appearance of commodity production and its subsequent regularization and generalization have radically transformed the way men labor and how they organize society.[5]

What Mandel may not have noticed is that his last paragraph is precisely correct. The appearance of commodity production has indeed transformed the way that *men* labor. As he points out, most household labor in capitalist society (and in the existing socialist societies, for that matter) remains in the premarket stage. This is the work which is reserved for women and it is in this fact that we can find the basis for a definition of women.

In sheer quantity, household labor, including child care, constitutes a huge amount of socially necessary production. Nevertheless, in a society based on commodity production, it is not usually considered "real work" since it is outside of trade and the market place. It is pre-capitalist in a very real sense. This assignment of household work as the function of a special category "women" means that this group *does* stand in a different relation to production than the group "men." We will tentatively define women, then, as that group of people who are responsible for the production of simple use-values in those activities associated with the home and family.

Since men carry no responsibility for such production, the difference between the two groups lies here. Notice that women are not excluded from commodity production. Their participation in wage labor occurs but, as a group, they have no structural responsibility in this area and such participation is ordinarily regarded as transient. Men, on the other hand, are responsible for commodity production; they are not, in principle, given any role in household labor. For example, when they do participate in household production, it is regarded as more than simply exceptional; it is demoralizing, emasculating, even harmful to health. (A story on the front page of the *Vancouver Sun* in January 1969 reported that men in Britain were having their health endangered because they had to do too much housework!)

The material basis for the inferior status of women is to be found in just this definition of women. In a society in which money determines value, women are a group who work outside the money economy. Their work is not worth money, is therefore valueless, is therefore not even real work. And women themselves, who do this valueless work, can hardly be expected to be worth as much as men, who work for money. In structural terms, the closest thing to the condition of women is the condition of others who are or were also outside of commodity production, i.e., serfs and peasants.

In her recent paper on women, Juliet Mitchell introduces the subject as follows: "In advanced industrial society, women's work is only marginal to the total economy. Yet it is through work that man changes natural conditions and thereby produces society. Until there is a revolution in production, the labor

---

[5]Ernest Mandel, *An Introduction to Marxist Economic Theory* (New York: Merit Publishers, 1967), pp. 10–11.

situation will prescribe women's situation within the world of men."[6] The statement of the marginality of women's work is an unanalyzed recognition that the work women do is *different* from the work that men do. Such work is not marginal, however; it is just not wage labor and so is not counted. She even says later in the same article, "Domestic labor, even today, is enormous if quantified in terms of productive labor." She gives some figures to illustrate: In Sweden, 2,340 million hours a year are spent by women in housework compared with 1,290 million hours spent by women in industry. And the Chase Manhattan Bank estimates a woman's overall work week at 99.6 hours.

However, Mitchell gives little emphasis to the basic economic factors (in fact she condemns most Marxists for being "overly economist") and moves on hastily to superstructural factors, because she notices that "the advent of industrialization has not so far freed women." What she fails to see is that no society has thus far industrialized housework. Engels points out that the "first premise for the emancipation of women is the reintroduction of the entire female sex into public industry. . . . And this has become possible not only as a result of modern large-scale industry, which not only permits the participation of women in production in large numbers, but actually calls for it and, moreover, strives to convert private domestic work also into a public industry."[7] And later in the same passage: "Here we see already that the emancipation of women and their equality with men are impossible and must remain so as long as women are excluded from socially productive work and restricted to housework, which is private." What Mitchell has not taken into account is that the problem is not simply one of getting women into *existing* industrial production but the more complex one of converting private production of household work into public production.

For most North Americans, domestic work as "public production" brings immediate images of Brave New World or of a vast institution—a cross between a home for orphans and an army barracks—where we would all be forced to live. For this reason, it is probably just as well to outline here, schematically and simplistically, the nature of industrialization.

A pre-industrial production unit is one in which production is small-scale and reduplicative; i.e., there are a great number of little units, each complete and just like all the others. Ordinarily such production units are in some way kinbased and they are multi-purpose, fulfilling religious, recreational, educational, and sexual functions along with the economic function. In such a situation, desirable attributes of an individual, those which give prestige, are judged by more than purely economic criteria: for example, among approved character traits are proper behavior to kin or readiness to fulfill obligations.

Such production is originally not for exchange. But if exchange of commodi-

---

[6]Juliet Mitchell, "Women: The Longest Revolution," *New Left Review*, December 1966.

[7]Frederick Engels, *Origin of the Family, Private Property and the State* (Moscow: Progress Publishers, 1968), Chapter IX, p. 158. The anthropological evidence known to Engels indicated primitive woman's dominance over man. Modern anthropology disputes this dominance but provides evidence for a more nearly equal position of women in the matrilineal societies used by Engles as examples. The arguments in this work of Engels do not require the former dominance of women but merely their former equality, and so the conclusions remain unchanged.

ties becomes important enough, then increased efficiency of production becomes necessary. Such efficiency is provided by the transition to industrialized production which involves the elimination of the kin-based production unit. A large-scale, non-reduplicative production unit is substituted which has only one function, the economic one, and where prestige or status is attained by economic skills. Production is rationalized, made vastly more efficient, and becomes more and more public—part of an integrated social network. An enormous expansion of man's productive potential takes place. Under capitalism such social productive forces are utilized almost exclusively for private profit. These can be thought of as *capitalized* forms of production.

If we apply the above to housework and child rearing, it is evident that each family, each household, constitutes an individual production unit, a pre-industrial entity, in the same way that peasant farmers or cottage weavers constitute pre-industrial production units. The main features are clear, with the reduplicative, kin-based, private nature of the work being the most important. (It is interesting to notice the other features: the multipurpose functions of the family, the fact that desirable attributes for women do not center on economic prowess, etc.) The rationalization of production effected by a transition to large-scale production has not taken place in this area.

Industrialization is, in itself, a great force for human good; exploitation and dehumanization go with capitalism and not necessarily with industrialization. To advocate the conversion of private domestic labor into a public industry under capitalism is quite a different thing from advocating such conversion in a socialist society. In the latter case the forces of production would operate for human welfare, not private profit, and the result should be liberation, not dehumanization. In this case we can speak of *socialized* forms of production.

These definitions are not meant to be technical but rather to differentiate between two important aspects of industrialization. Thus the fear of the barracks-like result of introducing housekeeping into the public economy is most realistic under capitalism. With socialized production and the removal of the profit motive and its attendant alienated labor, there is no reason why, *in an industrialized society,* industrialization of housework should not result in better production, i.e., better food, more comfortable surroundings, more intelligent and loving child-care, etc., than in the present nuclear family.

The argument is often advanced that, under neocapitalism, the work in the home has been much reduced. Even if this is true, it is not structurally relevant. Except for the very rich, who can hire someone to do it, there is for most women, an irreducible minimum of necessary labor involved in caring for home, husband, and children. For a married woman without children this irreducible minimum of work probably takes fifteen to twenty hours a week; for a woman with small children the minimum is probably seventy or eighty hours a week.[8]

[8]Such figures can easily be estimated. For example, a married woman without children is expected each week to cook and wash up (10 hours), clean house (4 hours), do laundry (1 hour), and shop for food (1 hour). The figures are *minimum* times required each week for such work. The total, 16 hours, is probably unrealistically low; even so, it is close to half of a regular work week. A mother with young children must spend at least six or seven days a week working close to 12 hours.

(There is some resistance to regarding child-rearing as a job. That labor is involved, i.e., the production of use-value, can be clearly seen when exchange-value is also involved—when the work is done by baby sitters, nurses, child-care centers, or teachers. An economist has already pointed out the paradox that if a man marries his housekeeper, he reduces the national income, since the money he gives her is no longer counted as wages.) The reduction of housework to the minimums given is also expensive; for low-income families more labor is required. In any case, household work remains structurally the same—a matter of private production.

One function of the family, the one taught to us in school and the one which is popularly accepted, is the satisfaction of emotional needs: the needs for closeness, community, and warm secure relationships. This society provides few other ways of satisfying such needs; for example, work relationships or friend-ships are not expected to be nearly as important as a man-woman-with-children relationship. Even other ties of kinship are increasingly secondary. This function of the family is important in stabilizing it so that it can fulfill the second, purely economic, function discussed above. The wage-earner, the husband-father, whose earnings support himself, also "pays for" the labor done by the mother-wife and supports the children. The wages of a man buy the labor of two people. The crucial importance of this second function of the family can be seen when the family unit breaks down in divorce. The continuation of the economic function is the major concern where children are involved; the man must continue to pay for the labor of the woman. His wage is very often insufficient to enable him to support a second family. In this case his emotional needs are sacrificed to the necessity to support his ex-wife and children. That is, when there is a conflict the economic function of the family very often takes precedence over the emotional one. And this is a society which teaches that the major function of the family is the satisfaction of emotional needs.[9]

As an economic unit, the nuclear family is a valuable stabilizing force in capitalist society. Since the production which is done in the home is paid for by the husband-father's earnings, his ability to withhold his labor from the market is much reduced. Even his flexibility in changing jobs is limited. The woman, denied an active place in the market, has little control over the conditions that govern her life. Her economic dependence is reflected in emotional dependence, passivity, and other "typical" female personality traits. She is conservative, fearful, supportive of the status quo.

Furthermore, the structure of this family is such that it is an ideal consump-tion unit. But this fact, which is widely noted in Women's Liberation literature, should not be taken to mean that this is its primary function. If the above analysis is correct, the family should be seen primarily as a production unit for housework and child-rearing. *Everyone* in capitalist society is a consumer; the structure of the family simply means that it is particularly well suited to encourage consumption. Women in particular *are* good consumers; this follows

[9]For evidence of such teaching, see any high school text on the family.

naturally from their responsibility for matters in the home. Also, the inferior status of women, their general lack of a strong sense of worth and identity, make them more exploitable than men and hence better consumers.

The history of women in the industrialized sector of the economy has depended simply on the labor needs of that sector. Women function as a massive reserve army of labor. When labor is scarce (early industrialization, the two world wars, etc.) then women form an important part of the labor force. When there is less demand for labor (as now under neocapitalism) women become a surplus labor force—but one for which their husbands and not society are economically responsible. The "cult of the home" makes its reappearance during times of labor surplus and is used to channel women out of the market economy. This is relatively easy since the pervading ideology ensures that no one, man or woman, takes women's participation in the labor force very seriously. Women's real work, we are taught, is in the home; this holds whether or not they are married, single, or the heads of households.

At all times household work is the responsibility of women. When they are working outside the home they must somehow manage to get both outside job and housework done (or they supervise a substitute for the housework). Women, particularly married women with children, who work outside the home simply do two jobs; their participation in the labor force is only allowed if they continue to fulfill their first responsibility in the home. This is particularly evident in countries like Russia and those in Eastern Europe where expanded opportunities for women in the labor force have not brought about a corresponding expansion in their liberty. Equal access to jobs outside the home, while one of the preconditions for women's liberation, will not in itself be sufficient to give equality for women; as long as work in the home remains a matter of private production and is the responsibility of women, they will simply carry a double work-load.

A second prerequisite for women's liberation which follows from the above analysis is the conversion of the work now done in the home as private production into work to be done in the public economy.[10] To be more specific, this means that child-rearing should no longer be the responsibility solely of the parents. Society must begin to take responsibility for children; the economic dependence of women and children on the husband-father must be ended. The other work that goes on in the home must also be changed—communal eating places and laundries for example. When such work is moved into the public sector, then the material basis for discrimination against women will be gone.

These are only preconditions. The idea of the inferior status of women is deeply rooted in the society and will take a great deal of effort to eradicate. But once the structures which produce and support that idea are changed then, and only then, can we hope to make progress. It is possible, for example, that a change to communal eating places would simply mean that women are moved

---

[10]This is stated clearly by early Marxist writers besides Engels. Relevant quotes from Engels have been given in the text. . . .

from a home kitchen to a communal one. This *would* be an advance, to be sure, particularly in a socialist society where work would not have the inherently exploitative nature it does now. Once women are freed from private production in the home, it will probably be very difficult to maintain for any long period of time a rigid definition of jobs by sex. This illustrates the interrelation between the two preconditions given above: true equality in job opportunity is probably impossible without freedom from housework, and the industrialization of housework is unlikely unless women are leaving the home for jobs.

The changes in production necessary to get women out of the home might seem to be, in theory, possible under capitalism. One of the sources of women's liberation movements may be the fact that alternative capitalized forms of home production now exist. Day care is available, even if inadequate and perhaps expensive; convenience foods, home delivery of meals, and take-out meals are widespread; laundries and cleaners offer bulk rates. However, cost usually prohibits a complete dependence on such facilities, and they are not available everywhere, even in North America. These should probably then be regarded as embryonic forms rather than completed structures. However, they clearly stand as alternatives to the present system of getting such work done. Particularly in North America, where the growth of "service industries" is important in maintaining the growth of the economy, the contradictions between these alternatives and the need to keep women in the home will grow.

The need to keep women in the home arises from two major aspects of the present system. First, the amount of unpaid labor performed by women is very large and very profitable to those who own the means of production. To pay women for their work, even at minimum wage scales, would imply a massive redistribution of wealth. At present, the support of a family is a hidden tax on the wage earner—his wage buys the labor power of two people. And second, there is the problem of whether the economy can expand enough to put all women to work as a part of the normally employed labor force. The war economy has been adequate to draw women partially into the economy but not adequate to establish a need for all or most of them. If it is argued that the jobs created by the industrialization of housework will create this need, then one can counter by pointing to (1) the strong economic forces operating for the status quo and against capitalization discussed above, and (2) the fact that the present service industries, which somewhat counter these forces, have not been able to keep up with the growth of the labor force as presently constituted. The present trends in the service industries simply create "underemployment" in the home; they do not create new jobs for women. So long as this situation exists, women remain a very convenient and elastic part of the industrial reserve army. Their incorporation into the labor force on terms of equality—which would create pressure for capitalization of housework—is possible only with an economic expansion so far achieved by neocapitalism only under conditions of full-scale war mobilization.

In addition, such structural changes imply the complete breakdown of the present nuclear family. The stabilizing consuming functions of the family, plus the ability of the cult of the home to keep women out of the labor market, serve neocapitalism too well to be easily dispensed with. And, on a less fundamental level, even if these necessary changes in the nature of household production were achieved under capitalism it would have the unpleasant consequence of including *all* human relations in the cash nexus. The atomization and isolation of people in Western society is already sufficiently advanced to make it doubtful if such complete psychic isolation could be tolerated. It is likely in fact that one of the major negative emotional responses to women's liberation movements may be exactly such a fear. If this is the case, then possible alternatives—cooperatives, the kibbutz, etc.—can be cited to show that psychic needs for community and warmth can in fact be better satisfied if other structures are substituted for the nuclear family.

At best the change to capitalization of housework would only give women the same limited freedom given most men in capitalist society. This does not mean, however, that women should wait to demand freedom from discrimination. There *is* a material basis for women's status; we are not merely discriminated against, we are exploited. At present, our unpaid labor in the home is necessary if the entire system is to function. Pressure created by women who challenge their role will reduce the effectiveness of this exploitation. In addition, such challenges will impede the functioning of the family and may make the channeling of women out of the labor force less effective. All of these will hopefully make quicker the transition to a society in which the necessary structural changes in production can actually be made. That such a transition will require a revolution I have no doubt; our task is to make sure that revolutionary changes in the society do in fact end women's oppression.

RADICAL FEMINISM

What's This about Feminist Businesses?

Jennifer Woodul

It is time for feminist businesses to deal with questions and criticisms which are popping up within the women's movement. I've recently read several articles and participated in a well-attended community rap group on the subject of feminist businesses and the general economics of the women's community. The same issues come up over and over—vital ones for all of us to deal with more effectively than we've done in the past. As a member of the Olivia Records Collective, I'd like to respond here to the article which appeared in *off our backs*, Jan./Feb. 1976, by Hannah Darby and Brooke Williams: "God, Mom and Apple Pie: 'Feminist' Business as an Extension of the American Dream."

INVENTION, NOT SOLUTION

The gist of the problem as seen by Hannah and Brooke is that feminism and capitalism are antithetical; therefore, that *feminist business* is a *contradiction.* While it seems clear to me that the two above ideologies are indeed incompatible, I conclude that *feminist business* is an *invention.* Feminist business is an attempt to get power for women right now. It is not, and I don't think feminist businesswomen have ever claimed it was, a *solution* to the problem of women-oppression, nor the final means of *taking* power.

One of my assumptions in writing this article is that capitalism is a patriarchal development. As such, it's been characterized by two elements which make it especially repugnant to feminists. They are: 1. exploitation of the labor workers that goes to the accumulation of profit that goes to an elite, providing them with living standards unavailable to workers, and 2. exploitation of the consumer by selling overpriced, low quality, useless, and unnecessary products. The basic process which supports this system of domination is the selling of goods or services at a price which affords a surplus of money, leading to accumulation of money. That's where we get interested as feminists: we do need money. Since it's not yet within our scope to do away with an oppressive system, is it possible to use the basics of that system to our own advantage, while avoiding 1 and 2 above? And, going even further, can we actually prepare ourselves for a feminist world at the same time?

Another assumption is that feminism presupposes a socialist economy of some kind. Communism was not invented by Marx, as we know. It has been an integral part of matriarchal society, and, in one form or another, is a continual guiding principle as feminists today decide what things we want to keep in our world. It is my firm contention that feminist businesses are not to be accused of revisionism with regard to long term goals and strategies.

PRIORITIES

As political workers, there are a number of things that we should hold as priorities in any sort of plan that we put forth. Can this plan help women to change, to think politically, to identify themselves with the oppression of women globally? And can this plan concretely improve the lives of women at the same time—materially and psychologically? (For further development, see "Reform Tool Kit," Charlotte Bunch, in *Quest,* Volume I, number 1.) A major premise here is that the material improvement of the lives of women, the psychological improvement as well, represent CONTROL and that control means POWER. Over the past few years, we've discovered different ways to make our minds and bodies stronger—to take our personal power. Olivia and other feminist businesses believe that we now need to take our economic power. State power is a ways down the road, but just because we don't start with it, that doesn't mean we're not on the way to getting it.

First of all, I think it's important to point out that feminist businesses are not just "selling products which promote the idea of equality," as "God, Mom and Apple Pie" defines them, and they are not just "alternatives." Feminist businesses are the mainstream, the wave of the future. They are woman-designed to meet our own needs and to become what *we* want. They are superb inventions which test out our feminist principles in crises of the everyday decisions which are momentous because they have everything to do with our survival—politically and economically. Feminist businesses and feminist businesswomen are putting their lives and their livelihoods on the line in order to invent a way to gain actual power for women.

What makes a business feminist then? It should offer women something that they need, something relevant to their lives. However, as Brooke and Hannah point out, "products do not affect the nature of business as such." We agree. The nature of business will be changed by feminist operation of it. There should be structures for worker input, working toward meaningful worker control. Salaries should be set within a narrow range, with consideration of each woman's particular needs as well as her role in the company. Structures should be clear to all and determined on concrete bases. Decision-making methods should be set out, with the understanding that decision-making must presume responsibility. There must be a consciousness of accountability to the women's community. There must be a commitment to channel money back into the community or the movement. Finally, there must be a commitment to radical change—to the goals of economic and political power for women. . . .

BETTER CREATIONS THAN ASHES

Of course it's ironic that women who claim to be anti-capitalist are using capitalist strategies as a road to liberation. We are the first to agree with that. But it's also terribly creative. If we thought there were other ways to accumulate economic clout AT THIS TIME we might never feel the need to use capitalist strategies. We feel that until this movement doesn't have to depend on the good will of a few women with money any more, until the workers in the movement are freed from having to work for the Man, the movement will remain middle-class oriented and steered by middle-class women. Feminist businesses, by creating jobs with worker control and offering them to women with less class or race privilege are taking positive steps to change that balance of power. We feel that it's useless to advocate more and more "political action" if some of it doesn't result in the permanent material improvement of the lives of women.

Recently I read an article about a group of sewing machine operators in Thailand who tired of their oppressive work conditions and locked out the management. These women then proceeded to reorganize the company according to their own principles of worker/woman control. The result of their labor was that within a short time they tripled their individual wages and were able to sell the product at a lower price. They did *not* burn down the factory because it was capitalistic. That's the kind of thing Olivia wants to do—that many feminist businesses have in mind—not just following a capitalistic map and forming a carbon copy of the society that oppresses us. We want to take concrete steps toward creating *feminist structures that work*. We are part of a process of revolutionary change. . . .

Women's Music: Politics for Sale?

Maida Tilchen

. . . ECONOMICS: REVERSE EXPLOITATION?

The most often heard complaint about women's music is that "The prices are too high!!" With albums costing $7.50, and concert tickets reaching $7.50 in many cities, audience members are sometimes unable to, or refuse to, purchase women's music products.

Anyone within the industry will tell you that the prices are high because costs are high. The women of Galaxia Records once sided with the audience. They told me, "The first time we went to a concert, before we got involved in this, we thought, 'oh wow, you get 800 women and you charge $5 each, all that money. We should do that.' And then it happened to us. We produced a concert in Boston and lost $1200 on it. Why? Because the expenses are incredible."

During its first years, women's music concerts were often held in church basements or university meeting rooms. The sound systems were non-existent or borrowed. Advertising was by simple flyers and word-of-mouth. The local producers who brought in a touring musician made no money, and often paid losses out of their own pockets. All work was done by volunteers, and the musician was happy if her expenses were covered.

Today's audiences expect more, and today's industry feels they should get it. Says producer Polly Laurelchild, "I feel that women deserve the best. I'm not going to spend a hundred dollars less and have crummy sound. Another thing is location. The concert should be accessible to many communities. We chose to present Mary Watkins and Linda Tillery at a theatre near the black community.

"There has to be respect for the artist and the audience, and one thing that shows that respect is the quality of performance. You can enhance it by having a good hall and good tech, or make it sound much worse with a poor hall and poor teching. So it is a choice that's political, and artistic, and a matter of pride.

"I want people to know that money isn't being spent frivolously. For example, the Berklee Performance Center [in Boston] costs more than Sanders Theatre [at Harvard University], but at Sanders you have to bring in the lights and sound and you end up paying more for everything."

Polly is concerned that producers burn out quickly. Not only are few paid, but they also take the financial risks. Performers are sympathetic when concerts lose money, but none have offered to take reduced pay. Allegra Productions has a seed fund which is built up by successful concerts and donations, but which can be quickly dissipated by concerts which lose money. Says Polly, "It's not so much losing money on one concert. But if there's a whole trend of people not coming out in enough quantity to support the cost of an event, over and over again, and you know that the only concerts you can count on to make money are the same four women—Holly, Cris, Margie, and Meg—there's not much appeal to being a four-artist production company. But you can't afford to just lose money, either."

Record companies also must recover their high costs. It takes $15,000 to make an LP on a very tight budget, not including promotion, salaries, or additional pressings. The recording studio may cost $100 an hour, and some albums require 100 hours of studio time. There is also the cost of pressing the record, which has risen with the price of vinyl's main ingredient, petroleum. Sometimes an even higher expense than the record itself is the jacket. Most printers insist on a minimum order of 5000, although the record company may only press an initial run of 1000 records.

Consumers of women's records often expect the prices to be lower than those of the straight music industry. In fact, the small record producer is at a distinct disadvantage. Just as 20 pounds of sunflower seeds will cost less per pound than the one-pound package, pressing the 7000 or so copies that the average women's music record sells costs much more per unit than the seven million copies of Billy Joel's latest hit album cost CBS.

Another problem for small record companies is cash flow. When a record comes out, it may sell extremely well. But distributors don't pay the record company their share of the money for 60 days or more. As a result, the record company may not be able to pay the bills for making the record. And the cost of the record never stops—if it is selling well, more copies wlll have to be pressed and jackets printed. Advertising costs are ongoing. One of the Galaxia women told me, "See all these white hairs I have? They never used to be there." The women of Galaxia estimate that they have put $50,000 of their own and borrowed money into their company in three years, and they have to reinvest all returns.

Another area of cost is distribution. The straight industry keeps its costs down by using huge central warehouses. In women's music, the network of independent distributors gets the record from the company to the store, but the cost of shipping and packaging is added on, plus the distributor's share. The retail store actually takes a bigger cut than the distributor.

One new twist in album prices involves the discounting of women's music records. Last January, the Harvard Coop, a huge straight record store, advertised several new albums for $4.99. Suspecting a plot to undercut the local women's store, I investigated and discovered that this was an advertising promotion that Galaxia had done with the Coop. Galaxia had plenty of records, but little cash, so they gave the Coop free records, and the Coop paid for the expensive newspaper ads for the sale. According to distributor Trish Karlinski, the sale did not take business away from the women's store, but probably did attract new buyers to women's music, buyers who might never go into the women's store.

Another factor in costs is wages. Women today are much less willing to do unpaid volunteer work. Says Polly Laurelchild, "I certainly respect somebody who doesn't have the money to put out for something that is in some cases a luxury. On the other hand, I have a certain reaction to those who think that everything that is women's or alternative has to be cheap-cheap-cheap to the point where it's a kind of "reverse exploitation." It comes down to exploitation of labor. In a food co-op, people give their time to get something back for less. But here it's a case of only a few people giving their time. At Allegra, we've gotten from 25¢ an hour to the best we ever got, $2.50 an hour. It's not something you do for money, but you always hope to get paid for your work because it's an important validation and it's also economically impractical to put out a lot of energy and get nothing back financially. People still have to live." Or, as Holly Near says, "It's hard when I see the people that I work with working for 15 hours a day and not paying themselves and somebody complains about a $6.50 ticket price. That puts me on edge."

Often musicians' salaries are suspected as the cause of high prices. Polly Laurelchild told me, "People have expectations that they make a lot of money. They say, 'they have all these pretty clothes, and what happy lives they must lead, and how stuck up they all are.' But these ideas are largely untrue."

The artists claim they are not paid well, and few are working full time as musicians. Record royalties usually amount to only a few cents per record. Concert fees, even for nationally known artists, run as low as $250 and rarely run over $1000. Kay Gardner says that *ten years* ago a beginning classical artist for Columbia records would have been paid more for a concert.

Says Maxine Feldman, "I don't know what some of the other performers get paid. Some I know, and if I was getting paid that, it would be more than I've made in a year. But they've earned it, I don't resent them for making money. I think it's terrific. I think we should all make money. We're all kind of scraping by. They've earned it, you just go out there and figure out how you can make it."

BUSINESS: "*I AM THE COLLECTIVE*"

Most women I spoke to were quick to point out that the real economic problem lies not within the women's community, but within the unequal role of women in our society. As the Galaxia women said, "If women had attained equality, we'd all be a lot bigger. Women are paid so little that there is no money to recycle."

How have economic realities affected women's music? The trend seems to be toward sounder business practices and a refusal to be "reversely exploited." It is not clear yet what affect such strategies will have on women's music. Combining good business practices and feminist ideals is a prime example of what Alix Dobkin calls "living with contradictions." Kay Gardner told me, "You cannot have high political ideals and run a business. Let's put it this way: most of the political ideals are anti-capitalism, whether they are Marxist or whatever you want to name them. It's very hard to have a high anti-capitalist ideal and be running a business in a capitalist manner.

"What one has to do is to think about her ideas very carefully, about what is pragmatic and what isn't, what can be done right away and what can't. We have these ideals that we can change 10,000 years of slavery in ten years of feminism! It's impossible. It's a long slow process. There has been incredible growth in the last ten years, but it's going to take time and we have to look at the overall view. We can't just be looking at the Now and the political import of the very moment. We have to look at it from years and years and where we're going to go in those years. If we're going to go that way in a capitalistic manner, what we do is earn money. Businesses want to earn money. What you do with it is what's important. How do you run your business? Do you run it by cutting off people's heads? Or do you run it with some heart, too? Is business totally a mental thing, or can it also be an emotional thing?

"A lot of that we've had to learn. I certainly have. I didn't know a damn thing about money when I went into business. I had no concept of what it was, because that was the boys' game. Well, it's our game too. If we want to succeed and get our music out, we have to learn how to do it in a business-like way, without compromising our political ideals. But we cannot be totally ideological and run a capitalist business. We have to be practical. And to think, how can we combine the two without selling out one way or the other? I don't want to sell out my beliefs, yet I might want to run a good business and make a profit so I can live instead of scrounging around. Women in women's music do not make money."

Part of the trend towards good business practice has apparently been the abandonment of the collective structure. The Berkeley Women's Music Collective, a band organized as a collective, disbanded in 1979 after six years. According to June Millington, Olivia Records no longer is structured collectively.

The women of Galaxia Records gave me an example of why they have not attempted a collective decision-making structure, although they do try to involve everyone concerned in the decision-making process:

"Somebody has to make decisions. For instance, we have had situations in which people with equal say in a group had a conflict and they were deadlocked. We were being charged by the studio while they argued. If it had been a collective, because they all had the same power, the record might have stopped production. We finally tried to talk the people out of the deadlock, and when nothing worked, we had to decide. At a certain point somebody had to say 'stop.' Of course, later on people laughed about it, but at that moment it was a dead serious decision. But, basically, we always try to have people work it out first, and as a last resort use a stronger approach."

June Millington feels that collective decision-making is too slow. She has never worked in a band where all the members had equal power, and pointed out that even the Beatles had a leader, John Lennon. For Cris Williamson's national tour last year, June was hired specifically as bandleader, which freed Cris from some tasks. June believes that there has to be a hierarchy, although not an imposed one. "I think if people realize what's going on, then they can, for their own benefit, give someone else power or exchange power, and have different responsibilities. Hopefully this will be out of respect for what other people can do, and what your piece will be in the whole puzzle."

I asked Maxine Feldman if her coffeehouse will be run by a collective. "I am the collective," replied Maxine. . . .

OUTREACH: ROCK AND ROLL SUICIDE?

"Outreach" and "cross-over" are two terms heard a lot in women's music these days. "Outreach" means to go after new individual buyers. "Cross-over" means to acquire another specifically defined audience in addition to the women's audience, such as the jazz or classical audience. Both are strategies that virtually all the record companies are exploring currently.

First of all, it is important to examine at whom outreach is being aimed. Somehow, the concept awakens fears in many lesbians' minds that they will have to share their women's music favorites with Top 40 rock and roll audiences. The women I spoke with had a very specific cross-over audience in mind.

Kay Gardner hopes to sell her meditation-inducing flute music to the New Age market. "It's not really a cross-over, because there's an awful lot of parallelism between the women's movement and the New Age movement. There is an awful lot of sexism in the New Age movement, but we have our problems, too—a lot of racism in our movement. We all have things to work out. But there are basic things that we agree on, like nuclear energy, self-sufficient living, natural fibres and natural foods. I'm very interested in holistic healing, and in healing with my music, and some of the New Age people are too, so I have to go to the people who I think my music will reach."

Galaxia Records hopes that its products will each find another cross-over market. Their *Womens Symphonic Works* album is already doing extremely well in the classical market. *Side By Side,* an historical album about the suffrage movement, has been selling steadily to schools and libraries. Robin Flower's album sells to bluegrass and country audiences.

Mary Watkins and Alive! reach a jazz audience. Artists who are women of color also hope to reach audiences of color. In Boston this effort has been aided by having their concerts in locations convenient to the black communities, and by encouraging radio stations aimed at black listeners to play their records. Holly Near hopes that we will see women's music in styles such as musical comedy or opera. "I'd like to see these ideas move out into a lot of different musical forms rather than people thinking that if you're going to do conscious lyrics you therefore have to perform in a certain style. If we make very rigid limits on what's OK and what isn't, then people will look at those rigid limits and say 'I can't fit in there.' And then we'll end up all being the same, which is rather boring. Let's celebrate our differences instead.''

Cross-over also works in another direction. Some artists have brought their original audiences over to women's music. Betsy Rose and Cathy Winter have played in straight folk clubs for years. They hope to create a two-way bridge between folk and women's music. Holly Near was a successful performer in the anti-war music scene. When she started singing more feminist and lesbian music, many of her straight anti-war followers felt that she was abandoning them. By associating her current music with the anti-nuke movement, Holly hopes to satisfy both of her groups of fans. . . .

OUTREACH:
CREEPING UP VERSUS WINNING 'EM OVER

The fear that lesbian audiences seem to have is that in its effort to reach larger and different audiences, the political message of women's music will be diluted, disguised, or discarded. There seem to be two strategies that are being considered for use by lesbian performers in playing before straight audiences.

Holly Near has the "creep up and surprise 'em" theory. "For example, when I go on these TV shows, I won't walk right out and say, 'Hi, I'm a lesbian feminist who believes in da-da-da.' I walk out and smile and talk about growing up on a farm, sing a country love song, and say 'see you next year.' Hopefully, they'll think that the music is real pretty and next time they go to a record store they'll buy it. Then they'll get an earful!! I don't have to discourage them right off the bat. I know that there's people who might say that that was manipulative, but art is. It's very manipulative. I think that when it is used conscientiously and caringly then it's a good thing.

"When I started doing feminist things, people in the anti-war movement got scared that I had lost my global politics. Now that I'm doing more outreach concerts, a lot of lesbian feminists are afraid I'm losing my lesbian politics. There's always a fear that somebody is going to cop out or blow it or betray. It matters so much to people that there's just terror that something is going to be lost. I feel that there are women who can do radical lesbian concerts, and do them very well. And there are women doing different kinds of work from different places. I feel that I do real good work in an outreach situation. I feel like I'm real apple pie. I can take very complex situations and present them to a group of people who fear those subjects and help people get over that. Maybe some people would like to see me do a more strict, hard-line kind of work. I think I'm using my skills better in another environment. I wish there were hundreds of people doing concerts, then we wouldn't have to worry what everybody is doing."

Producer Polly Laurelchild says, "Of course there's always some danger in the sense of somebody not choosing to make the message more subtly, but choosing to disguise that she's a lesbian. It's important for us not to pretend we're something we aren't. However, people who want to do heavy outreach to new groups must respect the sensibilities of that group. I don't mean you have to disguise that you're a lesbian, but you definitely don't walk into a working-class neighborhood, advertise all over the place to get people to your show, and then the first song is 'I'm a lesbian.' You would turn a lot of people off that way. You can sing songs that don't deny and cancel out who you are, and establish a rapport and then kind of slide the message in subtly. The next time you go back, you can maybe make it more strongly."

The other tactic is the "win 'em over" theory. Maxine Feldman feels this way. "I work very hard when I'm performing to win an audience over. It really hasn't mattered who is there—straight, gay, or whatever. By the end of the evening, straight people are thinking about what I've said, because I always remind them that there's at least one in their family. Hopefully I've educated them to a positive place. I can laugh at myself, and I make them laugh at themselves, by poking fun at stereotypes, and poking fun at who they think that I am. And then I blow that up in their face and get them totally confused and that gets rid of that. I've destroyed the myths.

"I look at it as that's who I am, a lesbian feminist, and I'm going to talk and sing about it, and be prideful about it. I'm not going to be in a moderate fence-straddling position." . . .

CONCLUSIONS?

Where will women's music be heading? How will lesbian audiences respond? It seems to me there are two directions that seem likely. One is to increase outreach. This might meet more financial needs, and serve political purposes. It may also mean larger concerts, higher prices, and, possibly, alienation of lesbians. The other direction is towards smallness: a coffeehouse circuit, smaller concerts, cassette tapes. The drawbacks: lack of money, and possibly a "private party" atmosphere.

Most likely, because it already is happening, women's music will go in both these directions simultaneously. I hope it is obvious from this article that audiences have a lot of responsibility in keeping their music flowing. Although I hate to see it as an either/or situation, the fact is that within women's communities, money is limited. There is probably going to be a very clear connection between the choices of lesbians and the future of women's music.

SOCIALIST FEMINISM

Women's Work

The Progressive

In 1903, socialist Kate Richards O'Hare recalled the hostility she faced when she wanted to work in a machine shop. "If one girl learned the machinist trade," the men argued, "others would, and soon the shops would be overrun by women, and *wages would go down as they have in every trade women have entered.*"

The recent Supreme Court ruling that women may sue to obtain comparable pay for comparable work is chilling news to corporate executives; they know very well why women's pay averages only 59 per cent of men's: The jobs women hold have been systematically devalued because women hold them.

For a long time, women bought the idea that they are paid less because they do work that is worth less. And so, particularly over the last decade, some of them fought their way into higher-paid male ranks—into coal mines and executive suites. But most remained where they were: 80 per cent of all women who work are stuck in the low-paid clerical and service slots traditionally reserved for them.

The notion that women who want higher pay for their labor must leave those jobs and move into male-dominated categories is both impractical and sexist, implying that secretaries are paid less than plumbers because they are worth less. Advocates of comparable pay, who know that secretaries are paid less because they are women, want to get rid of gender as a determinant of wages. And there's the rub:

If we do not assign wages by gender (or by race or national origin), how *shall* we assign them? By skill? But what of the people whose jobs require little skill but great tolerances for stress? And if we add stress to the pay formula, what about those whose jobs require little skill and stress tolerance—but because of that very fact are boring and bland and, in some cases, demeaning?

As we recognize the difficulty of finding "fair" criteria for determining income, we come up against the possibility that fairness has nothing to do with it. Indeed, wage scales have other functions than fair allocation of income—other functions, too, than providing incentives for hard work or accumulation of skills. One principal function of wage scales is to keep people in their places: to legitimize the power of those at the top and encourage humility in those at the bottom.

High salaries, after all, confer status; they confirm the importance of those who command General Motors and the Bell System. Low wages confirm the lack of status, the unimportance and low worth of those who occupy the bottom rungs of the ladder. Unable to accumulate either the capital or confidence to escape from their low-paying ranks or to demand a more equitable sharing of disagreeable work, those at the bottom keep on performing tedious or dirty tasks for those at the top.

And those in the middle have high incentive to behave themselves and do what they're told, lest they sink to the ranks below them.

If the notion of "comparable worth" were truly to take hold in this country, we would soon see that the assignment of worth by sex, race, or national origin is merely the most blatant of arbitrary assignments—that the custom of paying a corporate president fifty or a hundred times the wage of a file clerk is an arbitrary social decision.

Arbitrary—but not without purpose, for the wage scale, whoever fills the various slots, has significant reasons for being: It keeps the work force divided and unable to take control of the workplace, and it prevents an entire class of people from acquiring skills, so they can be more easily controlled.

Thus, efforts to reform the wage scale are inherently radical; they could knock the foundations out from under our stratified economy. It is important that women engaged in the fight for comparable pay recognize the radical nature of their cause, and the potential consequences if it succeeds. Otherwise, they may find themselves entangled in absurd and sophistic debates over pay formulas—arguments that are absurd because their very assumptions are absurd.

It is tactically important, too, to recognize that the appeal to "fairness," however easy or difficult it may be to determine what is fair, has never gotten any group very far in the United States. Blacks know. Hispanics know, women *should* know that if they get what they want it will not be because it is "fair" but because they have confronted the system with a credible threat of disruption. Affirmative action programs of the last decade gave some women more than they would otherwise have had—but only because push came to shove and the institutions in question were afraid they would lose Federal funds or licenses or contracts. Clout is what counts, and clout comes ultimately not from judges in courtrooms but from organizing, striking, demonstrating—practicing politics in streets and workplaces as well as at the polls.

The importance of the Supreme Court's recent ruling is basically political: It is a wedge, however slender (the Court did not establish women's right to comparable pay—only their right to sue for it). It may be the impetus needed to create a strong labor movement among women workers. Only a month after the Supreme Court ruling 2,000 city employees in San Jose, California, went on strike over the issue of comparable pay. "The issue is not equal pay for women; it is equal pay for work of comparable value," said a local official of the American Federation of State, County, and Municipal Employes.

Formidable obstacles to organizing women workers have been raised. With every paycheck, women have been told their work is worth little. And so they have said to themselves, "Why strike, when anyone could type this letter, when there will always be someone to replace me?"

But coal miners and trash collectors and steel workers have felt the same way, only to come to grips at last with the Big Lie of low pay—the lie that they were worth little. If women join them, in large numbers, the lords of the economy have good reason to fear, as they already know. Last November, months before the Supreme Court ruling, *Business Week* predicted that "comparable worth may be the civil rights issue of the 1980s," and added, with a shudder, that "it would cost employers billions in payroll dollars." Ultimately, it could cost them something even more important: the power they derive from keeping a large part of the work force in its place.

Motherwork and Working Mothers

Natalie J. Sokoloff

The material and ideological oppression of women is supported by the structure of the work women do with and through their bodies and their labor—bearing and rearing children in society. Motherhood can be understood as an institutionally organized experience.[1] It is neither the bearing nor the rearing of children that is oppressive; rather, it is the institution of motherhood as organized by and for patriarchy in U.S. capitalism that makes women into mothers as we know them. It is therefore understandable when many women say they want to be or like being mothers, but vehemently dislike the institution of motherhood as it is organized in our society.

THE HISTORICAL DEVELOPMENT OF MOTHERHOOD AS AN INSTITUTION

The responsibility of women as full-time wives/mothers/homemakers is a uniquely twentieth century idea for the masses of women in the U.S. The effort by male owners of industry, male workers, and male-dominated unions in the 19th and 20th centuries to make market work "men's work" and the unwaged sphere of home work "women's work" was manifest in the development of protective legislation, child labor laws, intensified segregation of the labor force, and the creation of the family wage.[2] Prior to the institutionalization of the family wage for men engaged in wage labor, "public opinion expected women and children to earn at least sufficiently for their own maintenance, and men's wages were based

[1]See, e.g., Adrienne Rich, *Of Woman Born: Motherhood as Experience and Institution* (New York: W. W. Norton, 1976).
[2]Jessie Bernard, *The Future of Motherhood* (New York: Penguin Books, 1974).

on the assumption that they did so."[3] The family wage was supposed to change this by providing a man with a "wage sufficient to allow the women to stay home, raise children and maintain the family, rather than having all members of the family out at work."[4]

The historically evolved definition of the personal world of the home as women's arena and of the social, powerful world outside as men's, allowed for the construction of the institution of motherhood as we understand it today. The ideological underpinning for this belief is the identity of women with their "natural" role in the family. Most of all, it was a woman's role as *childrearer* that put her, and kept her, in the home. This new ideology emphasized her biological features—womb and breast—and allegedly innate maternal instincts for the social role of mothering.

Changes in the role of women as full-time mothers occurred "under the guise of a policy toward children."[5] Culminating in the progressive era (1900–1917) and the "doctrine of the tender years" (in the 1920s), the full-time work of motherhood and homemaking was assigned to women.

Children, no longer productive members of their families, as in agricultural times or the very early industrial labor market, had become an economic burden to their parents. Someone had to take care of them. The capitalist mode of production needed a healthy, well-disciplined and well-trained current and future labor force. In addition, in the 19th century, men did not want to compete with the masses of women and children working in the market. At the same time, women at home provided men with someone to take care of their household needs to make sure they were able to return to their jobs the next day. The family wage helped ensure it would be women who continued to perform these tasks.

Making motherhood, domesticity, and subservience to men acceptable to women is a major development that took place in the 19th century. Women did not simply give up their function of producing domestic goods. They had to be convinced of the importance of their new role as producers of use-values, rather than exchange values (the mark of worth in capitalism). The elements of this new ideology that had to be asserted as "natural" were (1) children require full-time, undivided adult attention, (2) women are specially endowed to provide this care, and care for the homes their husbands need to ensure the reproduction of their labor power; and (3) domesticity not only shields women from the evils of the outside world, but also brings them certain rewards of status which are mediated through their families.

This all depended on a new conception of human nature: where Puritan parents were previously told that their children were fundamentally sinful, 19th

---

[3]Ivy Pinchbeck, *Women Workers and the Industrial Revolution* (London: Frank Cass, 1969). As quoted in Laura Oren, "The Welfare of Women in Laboring Families: England, 1860–1950." *Feminist Studies* 1 (Winter–Spring, 1973), p. 108.

[4]Eli Zaretsky, "The Effects of the Economic Crisis on the Family" in *U.S. Capitalism in Crisis.* Edited by Crisis Reader Editorial Collective. (New York: Union for Radical Political Economics, 1978), p. 211.

[5]Ibid.

century philosophy told mothers that their babies were innocent and pure.[6] They had to be shielded from the corrupting influences of the outside world. As a palliative, women were told that without ever leaving home, they could exert a powerful influence over society through their sons. Through this new role, which nature allegedly equipped only them to handle, women could reform the whole of society. Thus, the idea that children were innocent and malleable helped to explain and justify women's confinement to the home.

In addition, women's relegation to the home in industrial capitalism also was supposed to lead to an elevation of maternal qualities since they served as nurturant supporters and moral models for both children and husbands.

The ideal of full-time motherhood was clearly class and strata based. In the late 19th and early 20th centuries, the ideal woman's role became exemplified by the wives and daughters of entrepreneurs and merchant capitalists of the northeastern U.S. In fact, the cult of true womanhood—idleness, leisure, frailty, conspicuous and preferably wasteful consumption—depended on the hard labor of many immigrant and slave women who staffed households, acted as wet nurses and nannies for children of the rich, and were personal maids of these ladies of leisure. Moreover, this cult of true womanhood not only depended on the bye work and factory work of those miserably poor women who helped produce the goods bought for these fashionable homes, but also was totally contradicted by the way poor working women were treated by the factory owners; *their* female biology—menstruation, childbirth, and nursing—were completely ignored by the factory owners.[7]

Over the course of the 20th century, however, the mark of class superiority for men of all levels of the working class became the wife who did not work for wages. (This ideology should be separated from the fact that poor women always have had to work for wages.) The books that began to appear espousing these new values of "scientific motherhood" and "domestic science" were geared especially for the emerging "middling classes" of mass production monopoly capitalism.

At the same time that this 20th century ideology of individual and isolated "motherhood" was spreading, bolstered by the "science" of mothering developing in schools and literature, there was the contradictory reality of an ever-increasing employment of women in the labor market. The mass production of the monopoly capitalist era has necessitated continually increasing consumption by the working class. By the 1920s, with the introduction of mass advertising, mass consumption was essential to the development of capitalism, and it was necessary for women to do this consuming.

The demand for full-time mothering responsibility for women in our society, resulted in a series of further contradictions. As women were becoming

[6]Barbara Easton, "Industrialization and Femininity: A Case Study of Nineteenth Century New England" in *Social Problems* 23 (April, 1976).

[7]Barbara Ehrenreich and Diedre English, "The Manufacture of House Work" in *Socialist Revolution* 26 (October–December, 1975). *Complaints and Disorders* (New York: Faculty Press, 1975).

increasingly employed in the labor market, full time motherhood became the ideal. Second, women were being relegated to the home as their primary responsibility just as technology made possible modern birth control and bottle feeding. Third, while women have been increasingly convinced of their "maternal instincts" and the "naturalness" of their roles as mothers, they were told by a whole movement of male experts how to be good mothers. Fourth, as middle class women were more effectively able to control their family size with modern contraception, they were spending more and more time with children. The expansion of children's individual needs took over and controlled more of women's time and energy. They became specialists par excellence in mothering.[8]

During the 1930s and after World War II, the intensification of specialization and the sexual division of labor reinforced attempts to keep women out of the labor force. In the late 1940s, the ideology of the "isolated nuclear family" served to mask the social reality of the rapidly increasing participation of women, especially married women, in the labor force. Despite the fact that women were working in increasing numbers, they were supposed to believe that their real identity lay in family duties. Even during the war, with the massive influx of women into factories and war work, women's wage work was projected as an extension of their family duties, to be revoked when the war was over. This ideology was supported with contracts and agreements for the women to give up their jobs—to their husbands and to their male neighbors—when the men returned from overseas.[9]

Although more and more women have entered the labor force in the 1960s and 1970s, and it is no longer desirable to deny their presence, women are still employed as *women,* and particularly as *mothers.* In fact, the extensive research in mainstream family sociology as early as 1960 about working women in terms of "role conflict" or "working mothers," alerts us to the crucial importance of women being treated as "mothers" in the labor force.

THE RELATIONSHIP OF MOTHERHOOD TO WAGED LABOR

Thus, not only is the definition of women's work in the home as mother determined by and for patriarchal capitalism, but it is crucial in determining what happens to women in the labor market today. When women go into waged labor, they do so as *mothers.* This may be understood in at least the following ways:

1 Most importantly, women enter the labor market in order to fulfill their duty as mothers in the home—to secure money to buy goods and services for their families that previous generations of mothers used to produce in the home.

---

[8]Nancy Chodorow, "Mothering, Male Dominance, and Capitalism" in *Capitalist Patriarchy and the Case for Socialist Feminism.* Edited by Zillah Eisenstein. (New York: Monthly Review Press, 1979).

[9]Joan Ellen Trey, "Women in the War Economy" in *Review of Radical Political Economy* 4 July, 1972, pp. 40–57.

2 Once in the labor market, women—all women—are treated as mothers—former, actual, or potential.

3 As paid market workers, women continue to do "mothering" on the job.

Before we explore each of these in more detail, however, we need a clearer understanding of the work that is mothering.

The physical and emotional work of women in the home has been termed "motherwork" by Jessie Bernard.[10] "Motherwork" consists of several different and interconnected features. Specifically, these are: (1) *mothering* which consists of the emotional and physical care of infants and children: touching, rocking, smiling, feeding, teaching, diaper-changing, playing, disciplining, etc.; and (2) *added housework* caused by infants and children. This includes the extra cooking, cleaning, laundering, shopping, sewing, driving, waiting, etc. necessitated by caring for children.[11]

Neither the "mothering" nor the "added housework" components are simple phenomena. The "mothering" component of motherwork is not limited to infants and small children. As Bernard suggests, "the stroking, support, loving care and healing which women supplied to all family members in the home according to the Victorian model remains; it is still written into the role script of all women workers no less than mothers."[12] With regard to the "added housework" component, Bernard suggests that with small children the physical work involved in motherwork requires an enormous amount of housework. When the children are older, however, it may involve part-time, outside jobs.

Now, let us return to each of our three explanations of how this "motherwork" extends into the job market: i.e., when women go into waged labor, they go as *mothers*.

First, women enter the labor market to buy the goods and services they need in their jobs as mothers. Just as industrial capitalism pushed goods that had been produced by women out of the home, monopoly capitalism also has increasingly pushed out services. In post World War II U.S., women needed jobs to pay both for services as well as goods for their children, previously provided at home: education, health care, nursing, psychotherapy, birthing of babies, food preparation, clothing, shoes, washing machines. In monopoly capitalism, goods and services increasingly are found only in the market. It has become cheaper to produce such things as clothing by mass production rather than in the home. It follows, then, that under capitalism, it is necessary that the women who work in the home be able to work in the market as well. Women are both "finely tuned customers," and also "workers in home, ready for integration outside the

[10]Jessie Bernard, p. 116.

[11]It has been estimated that housework with no children at home consists of 1000 hours per year. With a child over the age of six, this figure increases to 1500 per year. But with a child under six, 2000 hours are required. There are only 8760 hours in an entire year. (See Jessie Bernard.) Thus, 5½ hours a day are spent in housework in a household with a child under 6. This does not include bathing, diapering, disciplining, playing, feeding, soothing the child, etc.

[12]Jessie Bernard, p. 116.

home."[13] Hence, keeping women in the role of mother *and* employing them as such in the market is a profitable solution to capitalism's needs. On the one hand, women are employed to provide goods and services from which the economy can profit directly. On the other hand, many other tasks remain for women to do in the home at no cost to the economy. This results in lower wages for women in the market and segregates them so they do not compete there with men.

Contradictions abound between women's position as mothers and their position as wage earners. First, having children increases costs to the family and increases the likelihood of women having to work outside the home, even though they are supposed to be staying at home and doing full-time child care. Second, while men are affirmed in their double relation of wage earner and breadwinner, women often see their roles as good mothers in conflict with their roles in the labor force, especially in relation to the emotional and physical well-being of their children. Further, while women's "femininity" is supposedly enhanced as mothers in the service of husbands and children, once in waged labor, women's desirability as sexual objects comes into conflict with their femininity as mothers and wives at home. Not only is patriarchy affected by this but so, too, is capital. One important mechanism for dealing with this contradiction has been the expansion of the sex segregation of the labor force through the threat of sexual harassment. For example, women are segregated off from men in lower paid and less powerful jobs. On the one hand, this tends to protect them from being sexually harassed by male co-workers (although not necessarily from male supervisors). On the other hand, it reminds women of their dependence on men for protection outside this supposedly safe sex-segregated work space. More recently, however, all forms of violence against women including sexual harassment on the job and rape in marriage are being fought against by women as they move between motherwork at home and motherwork in the market.

A second major consequence of the extension of motherwork from the home to the market is that when women enter the labor market they are treated as mothers—past, actual or potential. This phenomenon is attested to by the increasing literature treating employed women as "working mothers" rather than as "employees". Further, the old rationalization for not advancing women is often still used. If the woman is single or newly married and without children, she will not be given a responsible job with high wages since, it is said, she will probably leave when she has a chance to marry and have children. If she has children, the rationalization given is that she will be unreliable because of the need to be absent if her children are sick. This apologia persists despite the fact that male turnover and absenteeism rates are similar to women's, the crucial difference being that women have traditionally left the market for lack of child care and other family services, while men have left a particular job for personal

---

[13]Roslyn Baxandall, Elizabeth Ewen and Linda Gordon, "The Working Class Has Two Sexes" in *Monthly Review* 28 (July–August, 1976), pp. 1–9.

advancement.[14] Men's reasons for leaving are always more acceptable, for men are perceived as workers, women are perceived as mothers.

More recently, during the economic crises of the mid 1970s, the charge of women's "instability and unreliability" as workers abated since it became economically worthwhile for a company to exploit women as part-time workers.[15] Mothers of school age children are now said to be stable, conscientious, and appreciative of companies' tailoring work hours to their family schedules. Furthermore, because women are "mothers first" and because only men are paid a family wage, women are always classified as "secondary workers" in the family. This assumption holds true whether the woman is single, a grandmother, married, or divorced. Being viewed as a mother in a nuclear family rationalizes the low wages of all women throughout their lives as waged laborers.

This tendency to use women's status as mothers and therefore only "secondary workers" as a rationalization for lower wages is being increasingly challenged by women. The current women's movement, which has recognized the oppressive contradiction of women's "double day," encourages women to fight against labor market inequalities. By filing complaints with the Equal Employment Opportunity Commission—in accordance with Title VII of the Civil Rights Act of 1964—women are refusing to accept their lower status in the job market. However, because of the interrelatedness of women's work in the labor force and their roles in the home, the fight against lower status also requires an understanding of their total reproductive position. Therefore, women are struggling against the control of their bodies for male benefit and profit—both by husbands in the home and male bosses on the job. A major focus of the women's liberation movement since its rebirth in the 1960s has been on reproductive rights. Political action has been organized to demand the regaining of women's control of their bodies. The fight against involuntary sterilization of third world and poor white women and, more recently, against chemical and other companies which require women to be sterilized before they are hired or kept in hazardous jobs, reflects this focus.

Finally, as we all know, "motherwork" does not end at home. Women perform such mothering tasks on the job as nurturing, soothing, healing, teaching, and giving sexual comfort and ego support. Even unmarried women with no children of their own must mother men at work. These mothering tasks are sometimes paid for—as nurses, teachers, social workers, etc.—and sometimes simply appropriated—boosting the boss's ego, making coffee, getting his reports into final shape before typing them, doing housecleaning tasks to help present the boss to the public, etc.

[14]See R. D. Barron and G. M. Norris, "Sexual Divisions and the Dual Labor Market" in *Dependence and Exploitation in Work and Marriage*. Edited by Diana Leonard Barker and Shelia Allen. (London: Longmans, 1976).

[15]See Jerry Flint "Growing Part-Time Work Force Has Major Impact on Economy" in *New York Times,* (April 12, 1977), pp. 1, 56.

Here, too, the contradictory patriarchal aspects of "motherwork," hitherto private in the family, become publicly visible in waged labor. Women, both individually and collectively, have begun to challenge non job-related demands. Moreover, they are increasingly becoming aware of the unwaged work done at home in their mothering tasks, for which they are now being paid in the market. Not only does this put pressure on capitalism, as women learn that the unpaid work they do benefits the ruling class's profits, but it intensifies the contradictions within patriarchy: on the one hand, women and men have similar interest at home in providing for their families, on the other hand, in the market, men's and women's interests are very different. This in turn is threatening to men, as their wives must continuously increase their labor force participation to keep up with rising inflation.

Thus it is that women's role as mother in the patriarchal capitalist home reinforces their treatment as mothers in a labor market organized to benefit men and capital, which in turn reinforces their work as mothers in the home. These relations of reciprocal reinforcement should not obscure the fact that a multitude of conflicts emerge in this situation. Women's role as mothers is in the interest of capital and affects the outcome of class struggle; likewise, women's role as mothers in the home is in the interest of men, but simultaneously, is the historical outcome of struggles between men and women. Thus, although the relations between patriarchy and capitalism appear to mesh, their linkages can and will be broken. Motherwork at home and motherwork in the market are intimately linked. They need not be. It is out of the contradictory nature of this relationship that new possibilities for women and mothers will emerge.

Staying Alive

Nancy Hartsock

Gray is the color of work without purpose or end, and the cancer of hopelessness creeping through the gut.

Marge Piercy
To Be of Use

You're there just to filter people and filter telephone calls . . . . You're treated like a piece of equipment, like the telephone. You come in at nine, you open the door, you look at the piece of machinery, you plug in the headpiece. That's how my day begins. You tremble when you hear the first ring. After that, it's sort of downhill. . . .

I don't have much contact with people. You can't see them. You don't know if they're laughing, if they're being satirical or being kind. So your conversations become very abrupt. I notice that in talking to people. My conversations would be very short and clipped, in short sentences, the way I talk to people all day on the telephone. . . . When I'm talking to someone at work, the telephone rings and the conversation is interrupted. So I never bother finishing sentences or finishing thoughts. I always have this feeling of interruption. . . . There isn't a ten minute break in the whole day that's quiet. . . . You can't think, you can't even finish a letter. So you do quickie things, like read a chapter in a short story. It has to be short term stuff. . . . I always dream I'm alone and things are quiet. I call it the land of no-phone, where there isn't any machine telling me where I have to be every minute. The machine dictates. This crummy little machine with buttons on it—you've got to be there to hear it, but it pulls you. You know you're not doing anything, not doing a hell of a lot for anyone. Your job doesn't mean anything. Because you're just a little machine. A monkey could do what I do. It's really why I can't quit the job. I really don't know what talents I may have. And I don't know where to go to find out. I've been fostered so long at school and I didn't have time to think about it.

Studs Terkel
Working

Whether we work for wages or not, most of us have come to accept that we work because we must. We know that the time we spend on things important to us must somehow be found outside the time we work to stay alive. We have forgotten that work is in fact fundamental to our development as human beings, that it is a source of our sense of accomplishment, and an important aspect of our sense of self.

Work is an especially important question for feminists since in our capitalist and patriarchal society the work that women do goes unrecognized, whether it is done for wages or not. Housework is not defined as work at all, but rather as a "natural" activity, or an expression of love. Only in the last few years have women as a group demanded that housework be recognized as important work. Women who work for wages simply have two jobs—the one, though unimportant and temporary, recognized as work, and the other, completely unrecognized.

The liberation of women—and all human beings—depends on understanding that work is essential to our development as individuals and on creating new places in our lives for our work. We must develop a new conception of work itself. To begin this process, we must clarify what is wrong with the capitalist and patriarchal organization of work and define the requirements of *human* work. We must critically evaluate the ways we are structuring work in feminist organizations, where we can experiment, and invent ways to use our work for our development as human beings.

ESTRANGED LABOR

The receptionist has described the way most of us feel about our work—that it is not important and that the pace is often set by machines or by people who are not involved in the work itself. Work is something we must do, however painful.

In our society, work is, almost by definition, something we cannot enjoy. Time at work is time we do not have for ourselves—time when creativity is cut off, time when our activity is structured by rules set down by others. The increasing use of unskilled labor (or more precisely, the skills everyone is taught in public schools), and the increasing application of scientific management techniques in manufacturing, the office, and even the home (as home economics) all contribute to the feeling that many jobs could be done by machines and that people should not have to do them. In these respects, housework does not differ fundamentally from women's wage work. Housewives too experience the isolation described by the receptionist, while the phrase "just a housewife" expresses the cultural devaluation of housework.

The work most of us do has been described by Marx as estranged labor—time and activity taken from us and used against us. Work that should be used for our growth as well-rounded human beings is used instead to diminish us, to make us feel like machines. Estranged labor distorts our lives in a number of ways, most of them illustrated by the receptionist's description of her work.[1] She expresses what Marx described as our separation from our own activity at work when she says, "the machine dictates. This crummy little machine with buttons on it," so that "you can't think."[2] We are not in control of our actions during the time we work; our time belongs to those who have the money to buy our time. Women's time in particular is not our own but is almost always controlled by men. Our time is not our own even away from work. The rhythms of estranged labor infect our leisure time as well; our work exhausts us, and we need time to recover from it. As a result we spend much of our leisure time in passive activities—watching television, listening to the radio, or sleeping.

In addition, Marx pointed out that our work separates us from others, preventing real communication with our fellow workers. Often our work separates us physically from others. Some manufacturers deliberately put working stations too far apart for conversation among employees. But just as often, we are kept from real contact with others not by actual physical barriers but by roles, status differences, and hierarchies. The receptionist points out that although she is surrounded by people, she has little contact with them. Competition on the job also separates us from others. We are forced into situations in which our own promotion or raise means that someone else cannot advance, situations where we can benefit only by another's loss.

Patriarchy, too, in giving men more power over women, separates us from real contact with other human beings. And here, too, the patterns of our lives at work invade our leisure as well. The receptionist says, "I never answer the phone at home. It carries over. The way I talk to people has changed. Even when my mother calls, I don't talk to her very long. I want to *see* people to talk

---

[1]All this is more true for working- and lower-class women than for middle-class professional women. Women who are lawyers, for example, have much more control over their work, but the patterns that are so clear for most women (whether we work for wages or not) also structure and limit the ability of any woman to control her own work.

[2]Studs Terkel, *Working* (New York: Pantheon, 1972), p. 30.

to them. But now, when I see them, I talk to them like I was talking on the telephone. . . . I don't know what's happened."[3]

Finally, estranged labor prevents us from developing as well-rounded people and keeps us from participating in the life of the community as a whole. Marx argued that rather than participating in community work for joint purposes, our survival as individuals becomes primary for us, and prevents us from recognizing our common interests.[4] Our own activity, especially our actions in our work, separates us from other people and from the people we ourselves could become. We work only because we must earn enough money to satisfy our physical needs. Yet by working only to survive, we are participating in our own destruction as real, social individuals. Worst of all, even though we recognize the dehumanization our work forces on us, we are powerless as individuals to do anything about it. Patriarchy and capitalism work together to define "women's work" as suited only to creatures of limited talent and ambition; the sex segregation of the labor market ensures that women's work will be especially dehumanizing. The receptionist speaks for most of us when she says she doesn't know what she wants to do. We all have talents we are not developing but we don't really know what they are. As she says, we haven't really had the chance to find out.

WORK: THE CENTRAL HUMAN ACTIVITY

Because of the perverted shape of work in a patriarchal, capitalist society, we have forgotten that work is a central human activity, the activity through which the self-creation of human beings is accomplished.[5] Work is a definition of what it is to be human—a striving first to meet physical needs and later to realize all our human potentialities. Marx argues that our practical activity, or work in the largest sense, is so fundamental that social reality itself is made up of human activity (work).[6]

Our work produces both our material existence and our consciousness. Both consciousness and material life grow out of our efforts to satisfy physical needs, a process that leads to the production of new needs. These efforts, however, are more than the simple production of physical existence. They made up a "definite mode of life." "As individuals express their life, so they are. What they are, therefore, coincides with their production, both with *what* they produce and with *how* they produce. The nature of individuals thus depends on the material conditions determining their production."[7] Here individuality must be understood as a social phenomenon, that human existence in all its forms must be seen

---

[3]Ibid.

[4]Karl Marx, *Economic and Philosophic Manuscripts of 1844,* ed. Dirk Struik (New York: International Publishers, 1964), pp. 112–13. The account of alienation is taken from pp. 106–19.

[5]Herbert Marcuse, *Studies in Critical Philosophy,* tr. Joris De Bres (Boston: Beacon Press, 1973), p. 14; Karl Marx, *1844 Manuscripts,* pp. 113, 188.

[6]Karl Marx, *Capital* (New York: International Publishers, 1967), 1:183–84.

[7]Karl Marx and Frederick Engels, *The German Ideology,* ed. C. J. Arthur (New York: International Publishers, 1970), pp. 42, 59.

as the product of human activity—that is, activity and consciousness "both in their content and in their *mode of existence,* are *social: social* activity and *social* mind."[8]

Finally, Marx argued that the realization of all human potential is possible only as and when human beings as a group develop their powers and that these powers can be realized only through the cooperative action of all people over time.[9] Thus, although it is human work that structures the social world, the structure is imposed not by individuals but by generations, each building on the work of those who came before. Fully developed individuals, then, are products of human work over the course of history.[10]

As we saw, however, capitalism perverted human work, has distorted the self-creation of real individuals. The fact that a few use the time of a majority for their own profit or their own pleasure makes work into a means to life rather than life itself. The work we do has become estranged labor; and as a result, our humanity itself is diminished. Our work has become a barrier to our self-creation, to the expansion and realization of our potential as human beings. Work in a capitalist and patriarchal society means that in our work and in our leisure we do not affirm but deny ourselves; we are not content but unhappy; we do not develop our own capacities, but destroy our bodies and ruin our minds.[11]

By contrast, creative work could be understood as play, and as an expression of ourselves. "In creative work as well as genuine play, exhaustion is not deadening. . . . When one selects the object of work, determines its method, and creates its configuration, the consciousness of time tends to disappear. While clock-watching is a characteristic disease of those burdened with alienated labor, [when we work creatively], we lose ourselves, and cease to measure our activities in so many units of minutes and hours. . . .[12]

ALTERNATIVES TO ESTRANGED LABOR

The perversion of our work, then, is the perversion of our lives as a whole. Thus our liberation requires that we recapture our work. Ultimately we can do this only by reordering society as a whole and directing it away from domination, competition, and the isolation of women from each other. What would work be like in such a society? What models can we look to for guidance about ways to reorganize work?

We know that a feminist restructuring of work must avoid the monotonous jobs with little possibility of becoming more creative and the fragmentation of people through the organization of work into repetitive and unskilled tasks. Although we have some ideas about what such a reorganization of work would

---

[8]Karl Marx, *1844 Manuscripts,* p. 137.
[9]Ibid., p. 17.
[10]Karl Marx, *The Grundrisse,* tr. Martin Nicolaus (Middlesex, England: Penguin, 1973), p. 162.
[11]Marx, *1844 Manuscripts,* p. 110.
[12]Stanley Aronowitz, *False Promises* (New York: McGraw-Hill, 1973), p. 62.

look like, the real redefinition of work can occur only in practice. While our alternative institutions cannot fully succeed so long as we live in a society based on private profit rather than public good—a society in which work and human development are polar opposites—feminist organizations provide a framework within which to experiment. The organizations we build are an integral part of the process of creating political change and, in the long run, can perhaps serve as proving grounds for new institutions.

Some examples of alternatives to estranged labor occur in science fiction. There are worlds, for example, in which high status relieves one from the necessity to consume and provides a chance to work. To move up in that world means to move from a life of high consumption to a life of low consumption and work. In *The Female Man,* Joanna Russ describes a world where no one works more than three hours at a time on any one job except in emergencies, and the workweek is only sixteen hours. Yet, she says, Whilewayans work all the time. Marge Piercy, in *Woman on the Edge of Time,* shows us a future in which all the work is done by machines, and women no longer bear children. The high level of technology makes it possible for people to work at things that satisfy them, and spend only a small part of their time on supervising and overseeing the production.[13]

There are, however, contemporary alternatives. The Chinese restructuring of work does not depend on changes in technology but rather operates on two assumptions: first, creativity is an aspect of all kinds of labor, and ordinary women and men on ordinary jobs can make innovations and contributions to society that deserve honor and reward; second, all work that helps build a new society should be treated with the new significance previously accorded only to mental labor. The Chinese, too, have been concerned with avoiding the star mentality, and have argued instead that those who are capable of helping others should make that, rather than their own advancement, a priority. Thus, in China, to lead means to be at the *center* of a group rather than in front of others.[14]

These examples of alternatives to estranged labor draw our attention to the organization of the labor process itself. Feminists, in developing new organizational forms, have been concerned with two related factors that structure the estranged labor process in our society—the use of power as domination, both in the workplace and elsewhere, and the separation of mental from manual work. By understanding the ways these two aspects of estranged labor mold the labor process as a whole, we can correct some of the mistakes we have made as a movement and avoid making others in the future.

[13]Respectively, Frederick Pohl, "The Midas Plague," in *The Science Fiction Hall of Fame,* ed. Ben Bova (New York: Avon, 1973); Joanna Russ, *The Female Man* (New York: Bantam, 1975), pp. 53–56; and Marge Piercy, *Woman on the Edge of Time* (New York: Knopf, 1976).

[14]See Marilyn Young, "Introduction," *Signs* 2, no. 1 (Autumn 1976): 2, and Mary Sheridan, "Young Women Leaders," *Signs* 2, no. 1 (Autumn 1976): 66.

POWER AND POLITICAL CHANGE

In an article on power, I argued that social theorists have generally conceptualized power as "the ability to compel obedience, or as control and domination."[15] Power must be power over someone—something possessed, a property of an actor such that he[16] can alter the will or actions of others in a way which produces results in conformity with his own will.[17] Social theorists have argued that power, like money, is something possessed by an actor that has value in itself as well as being useful for obtaining other valued things.

That power can be compared with money in capitalist society supports Marx's claim that the importance of the market leads to the transformation of all human activity into patterns modeled on monetary transactions.[18] In this society, where human interdependence is fundamentally structured by markets and the exchange of money, power as domination of others (or the use of power to "purchase" certain behavior, which diminishes rather than develops us), is what most of us confront in our work.

There are other definitions of power. Berenice Carroll points out that in *Webster's International Dictionary* (1933), power is first defined as "ability, whether physical, mental, or moral, to act; the faculty of doing or performing something," and is synonymous with "strength, vigor, energy, force, and ability." The words "control" and "domination" do not appear as synonyms.[19] In this definition of power, energy and accomplishment are understood to be satisfying in themselves. This understanding of power is much closer to what the women's movement has sought, and this aspect of power is denied to all but a few women; the experience described by the receptionist can scarcely be characterized as effective interaction with the environment.

Feminists have rightly rejected the use of power as domination and as a property analogous to money, but in practice our lack of clarity about the differences between the two concepts of power has led to difficulties about leadership, strength, and achievement. In general, feminists have not recognized that power understood as energy, strength, and effectiveness need not be the same as power that requires the domination of others.

We must, however, recognize and confront the world of traditional politics in which money and power function in similar ways. For those of us who work in "straight" jobs (whether paid or not) and work part-time in feminist organizations, the confrontation occurs daily. Those of us who work full-time for feminist organizations confront power as domination most often when our organizations

[15]"Political Change: Two Perspectives on Power," *Quest* 1, no. 1 (Summer 1974): 10–25.

[16]"He" and "men" here refer specifically to men and not women.

[17]See Bertrand Russell, *Power, A New Social Analysis* (N. P., 1936), p. 35, cited by Anthony de Crespigny and Alan Wertheimer, *Contemporary Political Theory* (New York: Atherton Press, 1970), p. 22; Harold Lasswell and Abrahan Kaplan, *Power and Society* (New Haven: Yale University Press, 1950), p. 76; Talcott Parsons, "On the Concept of Political Power," in *Political Power,* ed. Roderick Bell, David V. Edwards, and R. Harrison Wagner (New York: Free Press, 1969), p. 256.

[18]Marx, *Grundrisse,* p. 65.

[19]Berenice Carroll, "Peace Research: The Cult of Power" (paper presented to the American Sociological Association, Denver, Colorado (September 1971), pp. 6–7.

try to make changes in the world. Creating political change requires that we set up organizations based on power defined as energy and strength, groups that are structured, not tied to the personality of a single individual, and whose structures do not permit the use of power to dominate others in the group. At the same time, our organizations must be effective in a society in which power is a means of making others do what they do not wish to do.

MENTAL AND MANUAL LABOR

One of the characteristics of advanced capitalist society is the separation of the conception of work from its execution.[20] This division between mental and manual labor—which also shapes the process of estranged labor—is an expression of the power relations between the rulers and the ruled, and is closely related to the concept of power as domination. Having power and dominating others is commonly associated with conceptual or mental work; subordination, with execution, or with manual (routine) work. Women form a disproportionate number of those who do routine work and rarely are insiders in capitalist rituals and symbols of know-how.

As the Chinese have recognized, subordination and lack of creativity are not features of routine work itself but rather are aspects of the socialist relations within which the work takes place. A feminist restructuring of work requires creating a situation in which thinking and doing, planning and routine work, are parts of the work each of us does; it requires creating a work situation in which we can both develop ourselves and transform the external world. Our work itself would provide us with satisfaction and with the knowledge that we were learning and growing. It would be an expression of our own individuality and power in the world.

THE DEVELOPMENT OF A FEMINIST WORKPLACE

Specific questions about how to restructure the labor process can be grouped under the two general headings of problems of power and problems about the division between mental and manual labor. Attention to these two factors can provide several specific guidelines. First, overcoming the domination of a few over the majority of workers in an organization requires that we have control over our own time and activity. Second, we need to develop possibilities for cooperative rather than competitive and isolated work; we need to develop ways for people to work together on problems rather than for one (perhaps more experienced) person to give orders to another.

We need to recognize the importance of enabling people to become fully developed rather than one-sided. We need to make sure that women can learn new skills well enough to innovate and improve on what they have been taught.

---

[20]Harry Braverman, *Labor and Monopoly Capital* (New York: Monthly Review Press), especially pp. 70–121.

We need to make space for changes in interests and skills over time. We need to include elements of both mental and manual work, both planning and routine execution, in every job we create. Finally, we must recognize the importance of responsibility as a source of power (energy) for individual members of feminist organizations. To have responsibility for a project means to have the respect of others in the group, and usually means as well that we must develop our capacities to fulfill that responsibility. The lines of responsibility must be clear, and unless the organization is large, they will often end with a single individual. Having responsibility for some parts of the work done by a group allows us not only to see our own accomplishments but also to expand ourselves by sharing in the accomplishments of others.[21] We are not superwomen, able to do everything. Only by sharing in the different accomplishments of others can we participate in the activities of all women.

COLLECTIVES AND COOPERATIVES WORK

Given these general guidelines, how should we evaluate one of the most common forms of the organization of work—the collective? Here I am concerned about one type of collective—a group that insists that the work done by each member should be fundamentally the same. This kind of organization is widespread in the women's movement, although not all groups that call themselves collectives function in this way. For example, the Olivia Records collective maintains all lines of individual responsibility for different areas of work.[22]

Just as the women's movement erred in its almost universal condemnation of leaders—and its mistaken identification of women who achieved with those who wanted to dominate—we have, through working in collectives, many times simply reacted against the separation of conception from execution. Collective work is our answer to the isolation, competitiveness, and the monotony of the routine work forced on us in capitalist workplaces. But collectives can at the same time reproduce some of the worst features of estranged labor—the separation of the worker from her own activity, the loss of control over her work, and the separation from real cooperative work—that is, work *with* rather than simply beside others. It can cut us off from real growth as individuals. This happens when collectives reproduce power as domination of others and at the same time reintroduce the division between conception and execution.

Informal rather than formal domination of some members of the collective by others often results from the attempt to avoid hierarchical domination by

---

[21]As Marx put it, "I would have been for you the mediator between you and the species and thus been acknowledged and felt by you as a completion of your own essence and a necessary part of yourself and have thus realized that I am confirmed both in your thought and in your love. In my expression of my life I would have fashioned your expression of your life, and thus in my own activity have realized my own essence, my human, communal essence." In David McLellan, *The Thought of Karl Marx* (New York: Viking, 1969), p. 32.

[22]Ginny Berson, "Olivia: We Don't Just Process Records," *Sister* 7, no. 2 (December–January 1976): 8–9.

avoiding formal structure altogether. What is in theory the control of the entire group over its work becomes in fact the domination of some members of the group by others. Some members of the group lose control over their work to those who are more aggressive, although perhaps not more skilled. Also, informal decision making, which assumes that every collective member has the same amount to contribute in every area, can result in reducing opportunities for cooperative work, work that recognizes, combines and uses the differing skills and interests of members of the group to create something none could do alone.

In the attempt to make sure that every task is done by every member of the group, those who were less involved in setting up particular tasks are deprived of a sense of accomplishment—a sense that their activity is an individual and unique expression of why they are, a contribution to the group from which the group as a whole can benefit. By rotating all members through the various tasks of the group, and by insisting that every member of a collective do every activity that the group as a whole is engaged in, the collective, in practice, treats its members as interchangeable and equivalent parts. It reproduces the assembly line of the modern factory, but instead of running the work past the people, people are run past the work.

We are not all equally capable of planning and doing every task of the groups in which we are involved, although we may have some special skills in a particular area. For example, while I am incapable of doing layout or pasteup for *Quest,* I am a competent editor. If much of the work done by one member of the collective has been designed and planned by someone else, the accomplishment and creativity involved in designing a system for doing routine work is not possible. Instead, the tasks are already planned and one learns new operations, planned by someone else. The separation between conception and execution has not been overcome.

One reply to this criticism is that learning skills is important and that collectives provide a place to learn new skills. While we can agree that women very much need to learn new skills, it takes time to reach the point where we can be creative with a new skill. We need to *learn* skills rather than simply try out new things. One of the best ways to learn a skill completely is to be entrusted with full responsibility for one or more aspects of the operation.

In sum, my criticism of this form of collective work is that it is simply a reaction against being forced by the capitalist, patriarchal organization of work to do a single task over and over again. Requiring each of us to do everything is not a creative response and cannot provide a real alternative to estranged labor. A creative response allowing us to move toward unalienated labor requires that we examine the root causes rather than the surface appearances of estranged labor in our society. We should recognize, for example, that learning skills by working for long periods of time on one aspect of the activities of a group does not necessarily produce the estranged labor of capitalist society. If we recognize that the problem is not simply doing one kind of work for a long period of time but rather results from the social relations that surround the work process— power as domination of others, and the separation of conception from execution in our work—we can respond to the real problems of work in feminist organizations. Thus, learning skills means not only learning the physical operations involved in a particular kind of work but learning how to organize and set up that work in the best way—from the perspectives both of efficiency and of self-development.

CONCLUSIONS: THE FRAGILITY OF ALTERNATIVES

Even if we correctly identify the factors that structure the labor process in our society, the alternatives we construct can be only very tenuous. Work in feminist organizations will exist in the tension between reformism and conformity on the one hand and simple reaction to work in our society on the other. Our strategies for change and the internal organization of work must grow out of the tension between using our organizations as instruments for both taking and transforming power in a society structured by power understood only as domination and using our organizations to build models for a society based on power understood as energy and initiative. Work in feminist organizations must be a way of expressing and sharing with others who we are and what we can do, a means of developing ourselves, as well as a place to contribute to the struggle for liberation. There are real pressures to reproduce the patterns of estranged labor in the interests of efficiency and taking power. At the same time, there are pressures to oppose estranged labor by insisting that each of us do every job. We can develop correct strategies only by critically examining the practical work we have done as we attempt to maintain organizations in which power is recognized as energy and in which we work to overcome the divisions between mental and manual labor.

FEMINISM AND WOMEN OF COLOR

We're in Britain for the Money

Norma Steele

I came to England from Jamaica in 1962, a year after my parents. Why did my parents send for me? So I could escape the drudgery and the kind of housework mapped out for West Indian women, escape the poverty mapped out for Black women. That is, to be brought up in a house and a society where we thought there would be less physical work, to be able to get the kind of education which gives access to a better job—a job with more pay and less work.

I can tell you, and any other Jamaican woman can tell you, that housework in Jamaica is really tough, whether you live in the town or in the country. I have lived in both the town (with my parents) and in the country (with my grandparents). In the country, there are very few rented houses and plenty of work—hard unpaid work. People have to build their own homes from the cheapest material available, cheap timber. Cheap in the short run that is, because it's expensive to keep up. There are not many homes with electricity and running water, so cooking is done on kerosene stoves or over open fires in an outhouse. (The smoke from the fire would be too much in the house.) Water has to be carried from a spring and could be some miles away. Firewood has to be gathered. Inside the house, all work has to be done without the aid of machines. Shopping has to be done every day as nothing stays fresh for long in the summer months—not even in an icebox, and of course ice is expensive, and there is little chance of getting any if you live far from the main roads. But at least there's plenty of space for the kids to play and you don't have to watch them all the time.

In the town, there's a desperate shortage of houses, and rents are very high. You have four or five separate one-storey houses with a courtyard in the middle. We just call it a yard as although all kinds of activities go on there—from raising chickens to washing clothes at the communal standpipe—certainly it's no place for courting. Each house usually contains four rooms, each occupied by separate families who share a communal kitchen and shower rooms. All the children share playing in the dusty yard. Can you imagine, the noise from the children, the fighting, the stench from the chicken coops and goat droppings? All the emotional housework of trying to keep sane and keep the children safe, and worrying about them while working on a second job. Because you take on a paid job to maintain yourself and the children as there are hardly any State benefits.

Paid jobs are mainly limited to domestic work—going to clean other people's houses, washing their clothes, cooking for them, waiting on them—and all you get in return is a pittance. All that housework and then home again, to start all over again doing physical and emotional housework. And the mothers ask, "Is there no end to this struggle, this vicious circle of housework, housework? Life must be easier abroad."

So you work harder to save up the fare, taking on a third and even fourth job, and the children work harder to get good grades in school and to learn to speak English or French "correctly"—and also take on paid jobs to help themselves and their mothers. Because they all feel and know that things will be better soon—as soon as they get to England. Everybody thinks so because all the white people they know not only say England is better but they all have big houses, big cars, fine clothes and lots of money. Your mother is even working for a white family that pays more than the Black families, and they have a washing machine and a vacuum cleaner. As part of the upheaval, as children we accept we will have to stay with Grannie or an aunt in the country for a while until our mother saves up and sends for us. In the meantime at least we will get parcels of clothes with money for school fees and food.

But when I arrived in the great metropolis, my school grades weren't good enough—although the exams had been based on the British exams. My mother was still forced to go out to work, but even worse, she wound up doing night shift work—working as a nurse in a hospital. We had to share a house with other people. Other Black and white people. The women, including the white women (some of whom were also from different countries), were working as cleaners, nurses—doing low paid dirty jobs in the service industries. Having to do housework in the mornings and the rest in the evenings. And this was really hard as the house was damp and cold and no matter how much cleaning and polishing you did, it still looked grubby and smelt dank. The women also had to cook and clean for their men and for the single men too, as this was easier than having to clean up after them as they weren't used to housework. My mother, though, would tell me not to do anything for the men. They assumed that because I was a girl I should be doing housework. But my mother told me she didn't bring me here for that. She had to put up with cleaning up after the patients and with cleaning the house and she was determined I shouldn't have to do the same. She had to do all this for us, and also she had to help the rest of the family here and in Jamaica. So I was to make sure I worked hard at school and got on.

My mother had to really struggle on that one wage to look after us here and send money home. My parents were divorced shortly after coming here and at first she fought hard to get some money from my father. But then she decided she wouldn't bother, as each time he came round he wanted something in return and she wasn't going to have that. She wanted the money but she didn't want any more work, which is what it would mean each time my father came round. Scenes of quarrelling, big trauma and temper tantrums were not unusual.

She already had enough coping with me, as while I was the good girl at school, at home it was another matter. I would cuss my mother, tell her she didn't speak well, how I hated Jamaican food, and complain she never turned up at parent-teacher meetings. Whenever I look back I remember how I treated her all those years, and the pain and grief I must have caused her. And I see all the housework she still has to do, that my grandmother does, that my great-grandmother had done, my aunts and cousins—and all that work for free. All that slave labour without a wage, without being paid. And here I see all the wealth in England and in Paris and in New York that was created and continues to be created by our labour and we are still so poor.

White women are also poor, and this is what Black women have seen by immigrating to England. White women are also forced to do unpaid housework and are also forced to take on low-paid second jobs. And when you look at the wealth in London and look at the ordinary women (which are the great majority) you can see they are not getting the wealth of these countries. Women's lack of money is international. As women we produce workers for the wars, we produce workers for the factories, the mines—for all the dangerous but profit-making industries of the world. For without our well cared for, able-bodied children—the past and future workers of society—there wouldn't be a British Empire or French Empire or Dutch Empire or whatever Empire, and there wouldn't be these multi-corporations.

So when Black women come to Britain, the U.S. or any other metropolitan countries—the countries where the money is—we are here, there, for the money, not the weather. And when our children refuse to take on low-paid dirty jobs, when mothers refuse to work at home without being paid, when women refuse to take second jobs with long hours, poor equipment, dirty work—it is out of struggles that have gone on for hundreds of years that we are refusing to continue working for free or for a pittance.

Life on the Global Assembly Line

Barbara Ehrenreich
Annette Fuentes

In Ciudad Juarez, Mexico, Anna M. rises at 5 A.M. to feed her son before starting on the two-hour bus trip to the maquiladora (factory). He will spend the day along with four other children in a neighbor's one-room home. Anna's husband, frustrated by being unable to find work for himself, left for the United States six months ago. She wonders, as she carefully applies her new lip gloss, whether she ought to consider herself still married. It might be good to take a night course, become a secretary. But she seldom gets home before eight at night, and the factory, where she stitches brassieres that will be sold in the United States through J. C. Penney, pays only $48 a week.

In Penang, Malaysia, Julie K. is up before the three other young women with whom she shares a room, and starts heating the leftover rice from last night's supper. She looks good in the company's green-trimmed uniform, and she's proud to work in a modern, American-owned factory. Only not quite so proud as when she started working three years ago—she thinks as she squints out the door at a passing group of women. Her job involves peering all day through a microscope, bonding hair-thin gold wires to a silicon chip destined to end up inside a pocket calculator, and at 21, she is afraid she can no longer see very clearly.

Every morning between four and seven, thousands of women like Anna and Julie head out for the day shift. In Ciudad Juárez, they crowd into *ruteras* (run-down vans) for the trip from the slum neighborhoods to the industrial parks on the outskirts of the city. In Penang they squeeze, 60 or more at a time, into buses for the trip from the village to the low, modern factory buildings of the Bayan Lepas free trade zone. In Taiwan, they walk from the dormitories—where the night shift is already asleep in the still-warm beds—through the checkpoints in the high fence surrounding the factory zone.

This is the world's new industrial proletariat: young, female. Third World. Viewed from the "first world," they are still faceless, genderless "cheap labor," signaling their existence only through a label or tiny imprint—"made in Hong Kong," or Taiwan, Korea, the Dominican Republic, Mexico, the Philippines. But they may be one of the most strategic blocks of womenpower in the world of the 1980s. Conservatively, there are 2 million Third World female industrial workers employed now, millions more looking for work, and their numbers are rising every year. Anyone whose image of Third World women features picturesque peasants with babies slung on their backs should be prepared to update it. Just in the last decade, Third World women have become a critical element in the global economy and a key "resource" for expanding multinational corporations.

It doesn't take more than second-grade arithmetic to understand what's happening. In the United States, an assembly-line worker is likely to earn, depending on her length of employment, between $3.10 and $5 an hour. In many Third World countries, a woman doing the same work will earn $3 to $5 a *day*. According to the magazine "Business Asia," in 1976 the average hourly wage for unskilled work (male or female) was 55 cents in Hong Kong, 52 cents in South Korea, 32 cents in the Philippines, and 17 cents in Indonesia. The logic of the situation is compelling: why pay someone in Massachusetts $5 an hour to do what someone in Manila will do for $2.50 a day? Or, as a corollary, why pay a male worker anywhere to do what a female worker will do for 40 to 60 percent less?

And so, almost everything that can be packed up is being moved out to the Third World; not heavy industry, but just about anything light enough to travel—garment manufacture, textiles, toys, footwear, pharmaceuticals, wigs, appliance parts, tape decks, computer components, plastic goods. In some industries, like garment and textile, American jobs are lost in the process, and the biggest losers are women, often black and Hispanic. But what's going on is much more than a matter of runaway shops. Economists are talking about a "new international division of labor," in which the process of production is broken down and the fragments are dispersed to different parts of the world. In general, the low-skilled jobs are farmed out to the Third World, where labor costs are minuscule, while control over the overall process and technology remains safely at company headquarters in "first world" countries like the United States and Japan.

The American electronics industry provides a classic example: circuits are printed on silicon wafers and tested in California; then the wafers are shipped to Asia for the labor-intensive process by which they are cut into tiny chips and bonded to circuit boards; final assembly into products such as calculators or military equipment usually takes place in the United States. Garment manufacture too is often broken into geographically separated steps, with the most repetitive, labor-intensive jobs going to the poor countries of the southern hemisphere. Most Third World countries welcome whatever jobs come their way in the new division of labor, and the major international development agencies —like the World Bank and the United States Agency for International Development (AID)—encourage them to take what they can get.

So much any economist could tell you. What is less often noted is the *gender* breakdown of the emerging international division of labor. Eighty to 90 percent of the low-skilled assembly jobs that go to the Third World are performed by women—in a remarkable switch from earlier patterns of foreign-dominated industrialization. Until now, "development" under the aegis of foreign corporations has usually meant more jobs for men and—compared to traditional agricultural society—a diminished economic status for women. But multinational corporations and Third World governments alike consider assembly-line work—whether the product is Barbie dolls or missile parts—to be "women's work."

One reason is that women can, in many countries, still be legally paid less than men. But the sheer tedium of the jobs adds to the multinationals' preference for women workers—a preference made clear, for example, by this ad from a Mexican newspaper: *We need female workers; older than 17, younger than 30; single and without children; minimum education primary school, maximum education one year of preparatory school* [high school]; *available for all shifts.*

It's an article of faith with management that only women can do, or will do, the monotonous, painstaking work that American business is exporting to the Third World. Bill Mitchell, whose job is to attract United States businesses to the Bermudez Industrial Park in Ciudad, Ciudad Juárez told us with a certain macho pride: "A man just won't stay in this tedious kind of work. He'd walk out in a couple of hours." The personnel manager of a light assembly plant in Taiwan told anthropologist Linda Gail Arrigo: "Young male workers are too restless and impatient to do monotonous work with no career value. If displeased, they sabotage the machines and even threaten the foreman. But girls? At most, they cry a little."

In fact, the American businessmen we talked to claimed that Third World women genuinely enjoy doing the very things that would drive a man to assault and sabotage. "You should watch these kids going into work," Bill Mitchell told us. "You don't have any sullenness here. They smile." A top-level management consultant who specializes in advising American companies on where to relocate their factories gave us this global generalization: "The [factory] girls genuinely enjoy themselves. They're away from their families. They have spending money. They can buy motorbikes, whatever. Of course it's a regulated experience too—with dormitories to live in—so it's a healthful experience."

What is the real experience of the women in the emerging Third World industrial work force? The conventional Western stereotypes leap to mind: You can't really compare, the standards are so different. . . . Everything's easier in warm countries. . . . They really don't have any alternatives. . . . Commenting on the low wages his company pays its women workers in Singapore, a Hewlett-Packard vice-president said, "They live much differently here than we do. . . ." But the differences are ultimately very simple. To start with, they have less money.

The great majority of the women in the new Third World work force live at or near the subsistence level for one person, whether they work for a multinational corporation or a locally owned factory. In the Philippines, for example, starting wages in U.S.-owned electronics plants are between $34 to $46 a month, compared to a cost of living of $37 a month; in Indonesia the starting wages are actually about $7 a month less than the cost of living. "Living," in these cases, should be interpreted minimally: a diet of rice, dried fish, and water—a Coke might cost a half-day's wages—lodging in a room occupied by four or more other people. Rachael Grossman, a researcher with the Southeast Asia Resource Center, found women employees of U.S. multinational firms in Malaysia and the Philippines living four to eight in a room in boardinghouses, or squeezing into tiny extensions built onto squatter huts near the factory. Where companies do provide dormitories for their employees, they are not of the "healthful," collegiate variety implied by our corporate informant. Staff from the American Friends Service Committee report that dormitory space is "likely to be crowded with bed rotation paralleling shift rotation—while one shift works, another sleeps, as many as twenty to a room." In one case in Thailand, they found the dormitory "filthy," with workers forced to find their own place to sleep among "splintered floorboards, rusting sheets of metal, and scraps of dirty cloth."

Wages do increase with seniority, but the money does not go to pay for studio apartments or, very likely, motorbikes. A 1970 study of young women factory workers in Hong Kong found that 88 percent of them were turning more than half their earnings over to their parents. In areas that are still largely agricultural (such as parts of the Philippines and Malaysia), or places where male unemployment runs high (such as northern Mexico), a woman factory worker may be the sole source of cash income for an entire extended family.

But wages on a par with what an 11-year-old American could earn on a paper route, and living conditions resembling what Engels found in 19th-century Manchester are only part of the story. The rest begins at the factory gate. The work that multinational corporations export to the Third World is not only the most tedious, but often the most hazardous part of the production process. The countries they go to are, for the most part, those that will guarantee no interference from health and safety inspectors, trade unions, or even free-lance reformers. As a result, most Third World factory women work under conditions that already have broken or will break their health—or their nerves—within a few years, and often before they've worked long enough to earn any more than a subsistence wage.

Consider first the electronics industry, which is generally thought to be the safest and cleanest of the exported industries. The factory buildings are low and modern, like those one might find in a suburban American industrial park. Inside, rows of young women, neatly dressed in the company uniform or T-shirt, work quietly at their stations. There is air conditioning (not for the women's comfort, but to protect the delicate semiconductor parts they work with), and high-volume piped-in Bee Gees hits (not so much for entertainment, as to prevent talking).

For many Third World women, electronics is a prestige occupation, at least compared to other kinds of factory work. They are unlikely to know that in the United States the National Institute on Occupational Safety and Health (NIOSH) has placed electronics on its select list of "high health-risk industries using the greatest number of toxic substances." If electronics assembly work is risky here, it is doubly so in countries where there is no equivalent of NIOSH to even issue warnings. In many plants toxic chemicals and solvents sit in open containers, filling the work area with fumes that can literally knock you out. "We have been told of cases where ten to twelve women passed out at once," an AFSC field worker in northern Mexico told us, "and the newspapers report this as 'mass hysteria.' "

In one stage of the electronics assembly process, the workers have to dip the circuits into open vats of acid. According to Irene Johnson and Carol Bragg, who toured the National Semiconductor plant in Penang, Malaysia, the women who do the dipping "wear rubber gloves and boots, but these sometimes leak, and burns are common." Occasionally, whole fingers are lost. More commonly, what electronics workers lose is the 20/20 vision they are required to have when they are hired. Most electronics workers spend seven to nine hours a day peering through microscopes, straining to meet their quotas.

One study in South Korea found that most electronics assembly workers developed severe eye problems after only one year of employment: 88 percent had chronic conjunctivitis; 44 percent became near-sighted; and 19 percent developed astigmatism. A manager for Hewlett-Packard's Malaysia plant, in an interview with Rachael Grossman, denied that there were any eye problems. "These girls are used to working with 'scopes.' We've found no eye problems. But it sures makes me dizzy to look through those things."

Electronics, recall, is the "cleanest" of the exported industries. Conditions in the garment and textile industry rival those of any 19th-century (or 20th—see below) sweatshop. The firms, generally local subcontractors to large American chains such as J. C. Penney and Sears, as well as smaller manufacturers, are usually even more indifferent to the health of their employees than the multinationals. Some of the worst conditions have been documented in South Korea, where the garment and textile industries have helped spark that country's "economic miracle." Workers are packed into poorly lit rooms, where summer temperatures rise above 100 degrees. Textile dust, which can cause permanent lung damage, fills the air. When there are rush orders, management may require forced overtime of as much as 48 hours at a stretch, and if that seems to go beyond the limits of human endurance, pep pills and amphetamine injections are thoughtfully provided. In her diary (originally published in a magazine now banned by the South Korean government) Min Chong Suk, 30, a sewing-machine operator, wrote of working from 7 A.M. to 11:30 P.M. in a garment factory: "When [the apprentices] shake the waste threads from the clothes, the whole room fills with dust, and it is hard to breathe. Since we've been working in such dusty air, there have been increasing numbers of people getting tuberculosis, bronchitis, and eye diseases. Since we are women, it makes us so sad when we have pale, unhealthy, wrinkled faces like dried-up spinach. . . . It seems to me that no one knows our blood dissolves into the threads and seams, with sighs and sorrow."

In all the exported industries, the most invidious, inescapable health hazard is stress. On their home ground United States corporations are not likely to sacrifice productivity for human comfort. On someone else's home ground, however, anything goes. Lunch breaks may be barely long enough for a woman to stand in line at the canteen or hawkers' stalls. Visits to the bathroom are treated as privilege; in some cases, workers must raise their hands for permission to use the toilet, and waits up to a half hour are common. Rotating shifts—the day shift one week, the night shift the next—wreak havoc with sleep patterns. Because inaccuracies or failure to meet production quotas can mean substantial pay losses, the pressures are quickly internalized; stomach ailments and nervous problems are not unusual in the multinationals' Third World female work force. In some situations, good work is as likely to be punished as slow or shoddy work. Correspondent Michael Flannery, writing for the AFL-CIO's *American Federationist,* tells the story of 23-year-old Basilia Altagracia, a seamstress who stitched collars onto ladies' blouses in the La Romana (Dominican Republic) free trade zone (a heavily guarded industrial zone owned by Gulf & Western Industries, Inc.):

"A nimble veteran seamstress, Miss Altagracia eventually began to earn as much as $5.75 a day. . . . 'I was exceeding my piecework quota by a lot.' . . . But then, Altagracia said, her plant supervisor, a Cuban emigré, called her into his office. 'He said I was doing a fine job, but that I and some other of the women were making too much money, and he was being forced to lower what we earned for each piece we sewed.' On the best days, she now can clear barely $3, she said, 'I was earning less, so I started working six and seven days a week. But I was tired and I could not work as fast as before.'" Within a few months, she was too ill to work at all.

As if poor health and the stress of factory life weren't enough to drive women into early retirement, management actually encourages a high turnover in many industries. "As you know, when seniority rises, wages rise," the management consultant to U. S. multinationals told us. He explained that it's cheaper to train a fresh supply of teenagers than to pay experienced women higher wages. "Older" women, aged 23 or 24, are likely to be laid off and not rehired.

We estimate, based on fragmentary data from several sources, that the multinational corporations may already have used up (cast off) as many as 6 million Third World workers—women who are too ill, too old (30 is over the hill in most industries), or too exhausted to be useful any more. Few "retire" with any transferable skills or savings. The lucky ones find husbands.

The unlucky ones find themselves at the margins of society—as bar girls, "hostesses," or prostitutes.

At 21, Julie's greatest fear is that she will never be able to find a husband. She knows that just being a "factory girl" is enough to give anyone a bad reputation. When she first started working at the electronics company, her father refused to speak to her for three months. Now, every time she leaves Penang to go back to visit her home village she has to put up with a lecture on morality from her older brother—not to mention a barrage of lewd remarks from men outside her family. If they knew that she had actually gone out on a few dates, that she had been to a discotheque, that she had once kissed a young man who said he was a student . . . Julie's stomach tightens as she imagines her family's reaction. She tries to concentrate on the kind of man she would like to marry: an engineer or technician of some sort, someone who had been to California, where the company headquarters are located and where even the grandmothers wear tight pants, and lipstick—someone who had a good attitude about women. But if she ends up having to wear glasses, like her cousin who worked three years at the "scopes," she might as well forget about finding anyone to marry her.

One of the most serious occupational hazards that Julie and millions of women like her may face is the lifelong stigma of having been a "factory girl." Most of the cultures favored by multinational corporations in their search for cheap labor are patriarchal in the grand old style: any young woman who is not under the wing of a father, husband, or older brother must be "loose." High levels of unemployment among men, as in Mexico, contribute to male resentment of working women. (Ironically, in some places the multinationals have increased male unemployment—for example, by paving over fishing and farming villages to make way for industrial parks.) Add to all this the fact that certain companies—American electronics firms are in the lead—actively promote Western-style sexual objectification as a means of insuring employee loyalty: there are company-sponsored cosmetics classes, "guess whose legs these are" contests, and swimsuit-style beauty contests where the prize might be a free night for two in a fancy hotel. Corporate-promoted Westernization only heightens the hostility many men feel toward any independent working women —having a job is bad enough, wearing jeans and mascara to work is going too far.

Anthropologist Patricia Fernandez, who has worked in a *maquiladora* herself, believes that the stigmatization of working women serves, indirectly, to keep them in line. "You have to think of the kind of socialization that girls experience in a very Catholic—or, for that matter, Muslim—society. The fear of having a 'reputation' is enough to make a lot of women bend over backward to be 'respectable' and ladylike, which is just what management wants." She points out that in northern Mexico, the tabloids delight in playing up stories of alleged vice in the *maquiladoras*—indiscriminate sex on the job, epidemics of venereal disease, fetuses found in factory rest rooms. "I worry about this because there are those who treat you differently as soon as they know you have a job at a *maquiladora*," one woman told Fernandez. "Maybe they think that if you have to work, there is a chance you're a whore."

And there is always a chance you'll wind up as one. Probably only a small minority of Third World factory workers turn to prostitution when their working days come to an end. But it is, as for women everywhere, the employment of last resort, the only thing to do when the factories don't need you and traditional society won't—or, for economic reasons, can't—take you back. In the Philippines, the brothel business is expanding as fast as the factory system. If they can't use you one way, they can use you another.

There has been no international protest about the exploitation of Third World women by multinational corporations—no thundering denunciations from the floor of the United Nations' general assembly, no angry resolutions from the Conference of the Non-Aligned Countries. Sociologist Robert Snow, who has been tracing the multinationals on their way south and eastward for years, explained why: "The Third World governments *want* the multinationals to move in. There's cutthroat competition to attract the corporations."

The governments themselves gain little revenue from this kind of investment, though—especially since most offer tax holidays and freedom from export duties in order to attract the multinationals in the first place. Nor do the people as a whole benefit, according to a highly placed Third World woman within the UN. "The multinationals like to say they're contributing to development," she told us, "but they come into our countries for one thing—cheap labor. If the labor stops being so cheap, they can move on. So how can you call that development? It depends on the people being poor and staying poor." But there are important groups that do stand to gain when the multinationals set up shop in their countries: local entrepreneurs who subcontract to the multinationals: Harvard- or Berkeley-educated "technocrats" who become local management; and government officials who specialize in cutting red tape for an "agent's fee" or an outright bribe.

In the competition for multinational investment, local governments advertise their women shamelessly, and an investment brochure issued by the Malaysian government informs multinational executives that: "The manual dexterity of the Oriental female is famous the world over. Her hands are small, and she works fast with extreme care. . . . Who, therefore, could be better qualified by nature and inheritance, to contribute to the efficiency of a bench-assembly production line than the Oriental girl?"

The Royal Thai Embassy sends American businesses a brochure guaranteeing that in Thailand, "the relationship between the employer and employee is like that of a guardian and ward. It is easy to win and maintain the loyalty of workers as long as they are treated with kindness and courtesy." The facing page offers a highly selective photo-study of Thai womanhood: giggling shyly, bowing submissively, and working cheerfully on an assembly line.

Many "host" governments are willing to back up their advertising with whatever amount of brutality it takes to keep "their girls" just as docile as they look in the brochures. Even the most polite and orderly attempts to organize are likely to bring down overkill doses of police repression:

• In Guatemala in 1975 women workers in a North American-owned factory producing jeans and jackets drew up a list of complaints that included insults by management, piecework wages that turned out to be less than the legal minimum, no overtime pay, and "threats of death." In response, the American boss made a quick call to the local authorities to report that he was being harassed by "Communists." When the women reported for work the next day they found the factory surrounded by two fully armed contingents of military police. The "Communist" ringleaders were picked out and fired.

• In the Dominican Republic, in 1978, workers who attempted to organize at the La Romana industrial zone were first fired, then obligingly arrested by the local police. Officials from the AFL-CIO have described the zone as a "modern slave-labor camp," where workers who do not meet their production quotas during their regular shift must stay and put in unpaid overtime until they do meet them, and many women workers are routinely strip-searched at the end of the day. During the 1978 organizing attempt, the government sent in national police in full combat gear and armed with automatic weapons. Gulf & Western supplements the local law with its own company-sponsored motorcycle club, which specializes in terrorizing suspected union sympathizers.

• In Inchon, South Korea, women at the Dong-II Textile Company (which produces fabrics and yarn for export to the United States), had succeeded in gaining leadership in their union in 1972. But in 1978 the government-controlled, male-dominated Federation of Korean Trade Unions sent special "action squads" to destroy the women's union. Armed with steel bars and buckets of human excrement, the goons broke into the union office, smashed the office equipment, and smeared the excrement over the women's bodies and in their hair, eyes, and mouths.

Crudely put (and incidents like this do not inspire verbal delicacy), the relationship between many Third World governments and the multinational corporations is not very different from the relationship between a pimp and his customers. The governments advertise their women, sell them and keep them in line for the multinational "johns." But there are other parties to the growing international traffic in women—such as the United Nations' Industrial Development Organization (UNIDO), the World Bank, and the United States government itself.

UNIDO, for example, has been a major promotor of "free trade zones." These are enclaves within nations that offer multinational corporations a range of creature comforts, including: freedom from paying taxes and export duties; low-cost water power, and buildings; exemption from whatever labor laws may apply in the country as a whole; and, in some cases, such security features as barbed-wire, guarded checkpoints, and government-paid police.

Then there is the World Bank, which over the past decade has lent several billion dollars to finance the roads, airports, power plants, and even the first-class hotels that multinational corporations need in order to set up business in Third World countries. The Sri Lankan garment industry, which like other Third World garment industries survives by subcontracting to major Western firms, was set up on the advice of the World Bank and with a $20 million World Bank loan. This particular experiment in "development" offers young women jobs at a global low of $5 for a six-day week. Gloria Scott, the head of the World Bank's Women and Development Program, sounded distinctly uncomfortable when we asked her about the bank's role in promoting the exploitation of Third World women. "Our job is to help eliminate poverty. It is not our responsibility if the multinationals come in and offer such low wages. It's the responsibility of the governments." However, the Bank's 1979 World Development Report speaks strongly of the need for "wage restraint" in poor countries.

But the most powerful promoter of exploitative conditions for Third World women workers is the United States government itself. For example, the notoriously repressive Korean textile industry was developed with the help of $400 million in aid from the U.S. State Department. Malaysia became a low-wage haven for the electronics industry, thanks to technical assistance financed by AID and to U.S. money (funneled through the Asian Development Bank) to set up free trade zones. Taiwan's status as a "showcase for the free world" and a comfortable berth for multinationals is the result of three decades of financial transfusions from the United States. On a less savory note, the U.S. funds an outfit called the Asian-American Free Labor Institute, whose ostensible purpose is to encourage "free" (*i.e.*, non-Communist) trade unions in Asia, but whose actual mission is to discourage any truly militant union activity. AAFLI works closely with the Federation of Korean Trade Unions, which was responsible for the excrement-smearing incident described above.

But the most obvious form of United States involvement, according to Lenny Siegel, the director of the Pacific Studies Center, is through "our consistent record of military aid to Third World governments that are capitalist, politically repressive, and are not striving for economic independence." Ironically, says Siegel, there are "cases where the United States made a big investment—through groups like AAFLI or other kinds of political pressure—to make sure that any unions that formed would be pretty tame. Then we put in even more money to support some dictator who doesn't allow unions at all." And if that doesn't seem like a sufficient case of duplicate spending, the U.S. government also insures (through the Overseas Private Investment Corporation) outward-bound multinationals against any lingering possibility of insurrection or expropriation.

What does our government have to say for itself? It's hard to get a straight answer—the few parts of the bureaucracy that deal with women and development seem to have little connection with those that are concerned with larger foreign policy issues. A spokesman for the Department of State told us that if multinationals offer poor working conditions (which he questioned), this was not their fault: "There are just different standards in different countries." Offering further evidence of a sheltered life, he told us that "corporations today are generally more socially responsible than even ten years ago. . . . We can expect them to treat their employees in the best way they can." But he conceded in response to a barrage of unpleasant examples, "Of course, you're going to have problems wherever you have human beings doing things." Our next stop was the Women's Division within AID. Staffer Emmy Simmons was aware of the criticisms of the quality of employment multinationals offer, but cautioned that "we can get hung up in the idea that it's exploitation without really looking at the alternatives for women." AID's concern, she said, was with the fact that population is outgrowing the agricultural capacity of many Third World countries, dislocating millions of people. From her point of view, multinationals at least provide some sort of alternative: "These people have to go somewhere."

Anna, for one, has nowhere to go but the maquiladora. Her family left the farm when she was only six, and the land has long since been bought up by a large commercial agribusiness company. After her father left to find work north of the border, money was scarce in the household for years. So when the factory where she now works opened in the early 1970s, Anna felt it was "the best thing that had ever happened" to her. As a wage-earner, her status rose compared to her brothers with their on-again, off-again jobs. Partly out of her new sense of confidence, she agreed to meet with a few other women one day after work to talk about wages and health conditions. That was the way she became what management called a "labor agitator" when, six months later, 90 percent of the day shift walked out in the company's first south-of-the-border strike.

Women like Anna—or Julie K. in Malaysia—need their jobs desperately. They know the risks of organizing. Beyond that, there's the larger risk that—if they do succeed in organizing—the company can always move on in search of a still-docile, job-hungry work force. Yet thousands of women in the Third World's industrial work force have chosen to fight for better wages and working conditions. Few of these struggles reach the North American media. We know of them from reports, often fragmentary, from church and support groups.

• Nuevo Laredo, Mexico, 1973: 2,000 workers at Transitron Electronics walked out in solidarity with a small number of workers who had been unjustly fired. Two days later, 8,000 striking workers met and elected a more militant union leadership.

• Mexicali, Mexico, 1974: 3,000 workers, locked out by Mextel (a Mattel subsidiary), set up a 24-hour guard to prevent the company from moving in search of cheaper labor. After two months of confrontations, the company moved away.

• Bangkok, Thailand, 1976: 70 young women locked their Japanese bosses out and took control of the factory. They continued to make and sell jeans and floppy hats for export, paying themselves 150 percent more than their bosses had.

• South Korea, 1977: 3,000 women at the American-owned Signetics plant went on a hunger strike for a 46.8 percent wage hike above the 39 cents an hour they were receiving. Since an actual walkout would have been illegal, they remained in the plant and held a sit-in in the cafeteria. They won a 23 percent increase.

• South Korea, 1978: 1,000 workers at the Mattel toy company in Seoul, which makes Barbie dolls and Marie Osmond dolls, staged a work slowdown to protest their 25 cents-an-hour wages and 12-hour shifts.

• South Korea, 1979: 200 young women employees of the YH textile-and-wig factory staged a peaceful vigil and fast to protest the company's threatened closing of the plant. On August 11, the fifth day of the vigil, more than 1,000 riot police, armed with clubs and steel shields, broke into the building where the women were staying and forcibly dragged the women out. Twenty-one-year-old Kim Kyong-suk was killed during the melee. It was her death that touched off widespread rioting throughout Korea that many thought led to the overthrow of President Park Chung Hee.

• Ciudad Juárez, Mexico; September, 1980: 1,000 women workers occupied an American Hospital Supply Corporation factory. They demanded better working conditions, paid vacations, and recognition of the union of their choice. The women, who are mostly in their teens and early twenties, began the occupation when 180 thugs, which the company claims were paid by a rival union, entered the factory and beat up the women's leaders. The occupation is over, but the struggle goes on.

Regarding the 1979 vigil in South Korea, Robert Snow points out: "Very few people realize that an action which began with 200 very young women factory workers led to the downfall of a government. In the 1980s, Third World factory women like this are going to be a political force to reckon with." So far, feminism, first-world style, has barely begun to acknowledge the Third World's new industrial womanpower. Jeb Mays and Kathleen Connell, cofounders of the San Francisco-based Women's Network on Global Corporations (see listing at right) are two women who would like to change that. "There's still this idea of the Third World woman as 'the other'—someone exotic and totally unlike us," Mays and Connell told us. "But now we're talking about women who wear the same styles in clothes, listen to the same music, and may even work for the same corporation. That's an irony the multinationals have created. In a way, they're drawing us together as women."

Saralee Hamilton, an AFSC staff organizer of a 1978 conference on "Women and Global Corporations" (held in Des Moines, Iowa) says: "The multinational corporations have deliberately targeted women for exploitation. If feminism is going to mean anything to women all over the world, it's going to have to find new ways to resist corporate power internationally." She envisions a global network of grass-roots women capable of sharing experiences, transmitting information, and —eventually—providing direct support for each other's struggles. It's a long way off; few women anywhere have the money for intercontinental plane flights or even long-distance calls, but at least we are beginning to see the way. "We all have the same hard life," wrote Korean garment worker Min Chong Suk. "We are bound together with one string."

APPLYING THE FRAMEWORKS: FAMILY

It goes far to reconcile me to being a woman, that I reflect that I am thus in no danger of marrying one.

Lady Wortley Montagu

The point remains, however, that movement toward sex equality is restructured by the fact that our most intimate human relation is the heterosexual one of marriage. This places a major brake on the development of sex solidarity among women. . . .

Allice Rossi

The primary role of women is in the home and family . . . men still need a good mother to come to with their little troubles. Women should provide a place of refuge where the husband and children can return from a busy, confused and complex world.

Belle Spafford, President, Women's Auxiliary, Church of
Jesus Christ of Latter-day Saints

Nowhere is woman treated according to the merit of her work, but rather as a sex. It is therefore almost inevitable that she should pay for her right to exist, to keep a position in whatever line, with sex favors. Thus it is merely a question of degree whether she sells herself to one man, in or out of marriage, or to many men.

Emma Goldman

The women's liberation movement that erupted in the late 1960s differed from earlier feminist movements both in focus and in strategy. A particularly striking innovation of contemporary feminism has been its increased emphasis on the family. As we shall see shortly, contemporary feminists of all persuasions have discovered a variety of grounds for criticizing the traditional definition of women's place as in the home. To replace the prevailing model of the nuclear family, in which the husband was primarily responsible for breadwinning and the wife for homemaking, the new feminists argued for the viability and even superiority of a number of alternatives.

Because of their challenges to the prevailing family ideal, feminists have often been blamed for the so-called breakdown of the family. Spiralling divorce rates, extramarital sexuality, teenage drug abuse, pregnancy, and runaways, even the recently revealed prevalence of incest, have all been attributed to the pernicious influence of feminism. Feminists have been accused of encouraging women to eschew marriage or to neglect their family duties by seeking selfish fulfilment outside the home. In consequence of the sinister influence of feminism, women are supposed to have been defeminized and men emasculated.

Contrary to these accusations, and contrary perhaps to what some feminists would like to believe, it seems more likely that feminism is a response to changing circumstances than that it has ignited fundamental social change. The massive influx of women into wage labor, for instance, dates from World War II rather than from the rise of contemporary feminism in the late 1960s. Women's retreat into the home during the 1950s was only a temporary interruption in a much longer-term twentieth century drift into paid labor. Similarly, women's readiness to seize and develop feminist critiques of the family seems more likely to have resulted from a deep dissatisfaction with existing family arrangements rather than from an unthinking submission to feminist demagoguery.

The late 1960s and early 1970s saw widespread experimentation with new forms of the family, experiments ranging from single parenthood to spouse-swapping to communal living. In the late 1970s and early 1980s, many of these experiments were abandoned. Nevertheless, the preeminence of the traditional nuclear family has not been restored: large numbers of children now live in single-parent homes or in homes where both parents work for wages—when they are not unemployed. These new forms of the family bring their own problems and a corresponding nostalgia for the traditional family. In the late 1970s, the so-called New Right in the United States achieved considerable power on the basis of an avowedly conservative program whose core was the reinstatement of what it defined as traditional family values.

Regardless of New Right propaganda, changing economic circumstances make it impossible for most people to return to the traditional nuclear family, even if they want to do so. What should replace the traditional family, however, is less clear, and so the debate continues. Within this debate, feminists are an increasingly vocal minority, and in the following section we present a range of feminist views on the issue of the family.

CONSERVATISM

Given the biological determinist presuppositions of conservative theory, the conservative view of the family is easy to predict, at least in outline. Conservatives take the traditional nuclear family as biologically given and attempt to defend, on biological grounds, the traditional division of labor between the sexes, according to which the woman is responsible for domestic work and child care while the man's task is "to protect against the outside world and to show how to meet this world successfully." Note that conservatives take for granted that the outside world is hostile and competitive.

Tiger and Fox argue that the healthy psychic development of a human individual requires that a strong mother-child bond should be established right at the start of a human infant's life and that this bond should be maintained for a substantial part of childhood.Tiger and Fox's argument is biological in at least two respects. On the one hand, they believe that the necessity for a strong mother-child bond is "the ground rule of human biogrammar." To support this claim, they cite many examples of the abnormal behavior of animals which have been deprived of their mothers, and they also mention the unfortunate situation of children in orphanages. Leaving aside the questionability of arguments from analogy with animals, an obvious objection to Tiger and Fox's argument is that children in orphanages have been deprived of more than their mother: they have been deprived of a whole family context, including father, siblings, grandparents, etc. What justifies Tiger and Fox in claiming that the undoubted misery of many orphans is due specifically to maternal deprivation? To answer this question, Tiger and Fox have another biological argument: they claim that the mother's place as one term in this primary bond with the infant is determined by her ability to suckle and by the fact that she is "emotionally programmed to be responsive to the growing child." They imply that a man is not biologically equipped to enter into a primary bond with an infant. Hence, the kinds of social relations into which men and women may enter are determined in an important way by our biology.

Bruno Bettelheim also believes that men and women, respectively, should engage in very different sorts of relations with their children. For Bettelheim, the proper role of the mother is to provide emotional intimacy for the child and to take her or his side "no matter what"; the proper role for the father, on the other hand, is to set an example of "dedication to higher issues" which give "a meaning to life above and beyond the everyday experiences." In arguing for this division of psychic as well as physical labor, Bettelheim is wise enough to avoid arguments from analogies with animals, but he does, nevertheless, appeal to a biological argument very similar to that used by Tiger and Fox. That is to say, he claims that women are equipped for the physical and emotional work of child care as a result of the biological processes of pregnancy, birth, and breastfeeding. Unable to undergo these processes, men are not suited to child care: a man's function in society is "moral, economic, political." Despite the fact that his article purports to discuss the role of men, Bettelheim does not explain what specific biological capacities fit men for moral, economic, and political functions and what specific biological deficiencies make women ill-equipped to perform them. An informed guess, however, suggests that Bettelheim would use a Freudian justification for his claim.

LIBERAL FEMINISM

We know that liberals are skeptical of alleged biological determinations of human society, and hence we can predict a rejection of the sorts of arguments used by conservatives. In fact, one of the main sparks of the contemporary feminist movement was Betty Friedan's publication in 1964 of *The Feminine Mystique,* a slashing attack on the conservative view that women could and should find their supreme happiness and fulfillment in domesticity. Since that time, a dominant strand in the women's movement has been a critique of the assumption that women are uniquely suited for housework and child care.

Liberal feminists confront a dilemma when they criticize the contemporary definition of women as housewives. On the one hand, classical liberalism traditionally has made a sharp distinction between the public and the private spheres of an individual's life: the public sphere affects other persons and is therefore a proper subject for legal regulation; the private sphere is considered to affect no one but oneself and hence should be outside the realm of legal intervention. For classical nineteenth-century liberals, one's home and living arrangements fell within the private sphere. On the other hand, however, one of the important insights of the contemporary feminist movement has been that the personal is political, a claim that, if accepted, obliterates the traditional public/private distinction.

Twentieth century liberal feminists attempt an uneasy compromise between the view that family life is private and the view that it is political. In line with the traditional liberal account of social relations as contractual, liberal feminists propose to define domestic arrangements in terms of a contract, imposing responsibilities on each party which should be enforced, perhaps legally; at the same time, however, liberals believe that individuals should be able to design whatever type of contract suits them best. Thus, liberals have no theoretical grounds for objecting to any particular type of living arrangement so long as it is chosen freely by the partners concerned. Living together, homosexual marriage, group marriage, open marriage, communal living, even traditional marriage are all acceptable to the liberal feminist, because different individuals will find fulfillment in different living arrangements and because, for the liberal, an individual's domestic arrangements are ultimately her private concern.

This extreme tolerance may appear to conflict with the liberal feminist's condemnation of the traditional housewife role. To resolve the contradiction, we have to view the liberal as objecting, not to the role of housewife as such, but merely to the fact that women are channeled into it by the lack of equal opportunity in other fields. Once women have equal opportunity for paid jobs, liberals believe that we can be sure that any woman who elects to be a housewife is doing so out of free choice. Of course, we should recognize as equally valid the choice of a man to be a househusband.

Ann Crittenden Scott suggests that the viability of the occupation "houseworker" should be guaranteed by the payment of a wage to the houseworker. In evaluation of her arguments, it is important to notice that she does not suggest that the wage be paid by the state as some other feminists have proposed; instead, she recommends payment by the spouse. This would, of course, perpetuate the notion that a family's internal structure and, indeed, its survival are a matter only for the individuals concerned and not for society as a whole. It is interesting to speculate how far Scott's proposal is compatible with the liberal ideal of equality between the partners in marriage, as it makes one partner into the employee of the other.

Alix Kates Shulman's example of a "marriage agreement" may seem to be a paradigm of the contractual liberal approach. We should note, however, one feature of her proposed contract that is nonliberal and that conflicts with Scott's proposal. According to Shulman's contract, the allocation of tasks is not determined completely by the bargaining power of each of the contractees in the marriage market. In other words, the man is not allowed to use his greater earning power as a way of giving his job more importance and buying out of an equal share of the domestic work. To justify this restriction by liberal principles, we must assume that is it merely a temporary restriction on contracts necessary to compensate for past sexism. Past sexist practices have put men in a better position to compete in the labor market and have relegated women to domestic work. The liberal must argue that this pattern will be self-perpetuating if a limitation is not made on permissible contracts: men will continue to buy out of housework and women will never get a chance to compete in the labor market. But once a situation of equality of opportunity for the sexes has been established, the liberal would consistently have to drop this restriction on domestic contracts. To prohibit individuals from being houseworkers would go right against the fundamental liberal principles of individual choice and noninterventionism.

In our selections on liberalism, we have included only discussions of heterosexual marriage, but it is easy to see how the same approach can also be used to set up many other types of domestic arrangements which would be equally justified on liberal principles.

TRADITIONAL MARXISM

We have seen in Part Two of this book that traditional Marxism locates the roots of women's oppression within the monogamous family. From this analysis, it would seem to follow that the traditional Marxist would recommend women's exit from the monogamous family as a precondition for our liberation. But this is true only in a rather special sense.

In ordinary usage, "monogamy" tends to have the meaning of emotional and sexual exclusivity. For Marx and Engels, however, it was a more technical term denoting the marriage of a man and woman *in which the man controls the family's wealth.* Hence, marriages between individuals who own no property, for example, between members of the working class, are not monogamous in this sense. This is what Marx and Engels mean when, in the piece we have excerpted from *The Communist Manifesto,* they talk about the "practical absence of the family among the proletarians." For Marx and Engels, then, so-called monogamous marriage is primarily an economic institution rather than an emotional or sexual one. From the very beginning, Engels says "the sole exclusive aims of monogamous marriage were to make the man supreme in the family, and to propagate as the future heirs to his wealth, children indisputably his own."

From this account of monogamous marriage, we can see that when traditional Marxists propose to liberate women from monogamy, they are recommending the abolition of a certain kind of economic institution rather than of a certain kind of emotional or sexual arrangement. Hence, their criticism of the bourgeois family is not that this family is emotionally or sexually restrictive, but rather that it is founded on what Engels calls "the open or concealed domestic slavery of the wife." As Marx and Engels put it in *The Communist Manifesto,* "The bourgeois sees in his wife a mere instrument of production." In order to free women from this slavery, traditional Marxists believe that "the first condition for the liberation of the wife is to bring the whole female sex back into public industry." Lenin says:

> Notwithstanding all the laws emancipating women, she continues to be a *domestic slave,* because *petty housework* crushes, strangles, stullifies, and degrades her, chains her to the kitchen and the nursery, and she wastes her labour on barbarously unproductive, petty, nerve-racking, stullifying and crushing drudgery. The real *emancipation of women,* real communism, will begin only where and when an all-out struggle begins (led by the proletariat wielding state power) against this petty housekeeping, or rather when its *wholesale transformation* into a large-scale socialist economy begins. (V. I. Lenin, *On the Emancipation of Women,* Progress Publishers, Moscow, p. 61.)

Therefore, traditional Marxists have always argued for the industrialization and socialization of housework as a precondition of women's liberation. One example of such an argument is Margaret Benston's article in this book.

Because capitalist society cannot accommodate the demand for the socialization of housework, the demand to bring women full time into public production is often hailed as a revolutionary demand. But it is, of course, an economic demand, namely, the demand for "the abolition of the monogamous family as the economic unit of society." Traditional Marxists have no objection to heterosexual marriage as a *social* unit and usually take it for granted that people will continue to live in heterosexual couples during and after the revolution. Hence, they see no need to liberate women or men from monogamy in its ordinary, nontechnical sense of emotional or sexual exclusiveness.

Turning to the traditional Marxist authors represented in this section, we see that, in the excerpt from *The Communist Manifesto,* Marx and Engels occupy themselves exclusively with an attack on the bourgeois family. Many years later, in *The Origin of the Family, Private Property and the State,* Engels claimed that working-class marriages are already egalitarian, since the wife as well as the husband has to work for a wage and so is not dependent on him for support. Under capitalism, Marx and Engels argue, the ties between family members are really economic rather than emotional in nature: because the male controls the family wealth, the wives of the bourgeoisie are, in reality, prostitutes. For women to be equal with men in the family, Marx and Engels imply that the institution of private property, which gives males the real power, must be eliminated. They do not discuss in any detail the form of future living arrangements after class society has been abolished.

Our other piece in this section is some extracts from the Cuban Family Code. Since 1959 Cubans have been striving to build their unique form of socialist society, and they view the equality of women in marriage as an integral part of this task. Within the Cuban Family Code, some asymmetries in the rights and obligations of men and women remain, and, later in this anthology, we reprint some feminist criticisms of the Code. Whether or not these criticisms are justified, it is important to acknowledge how far the Cuban Family Code progresses beyond the traditional nuclear family ideal. Cuba is still the only country in the world, for instance, that has written into law the obligation of both partners to perform necessary housework.

In conclusion, it should be noted that traditional Marxism, unlike other contemporary versions of feminism, does not question the heterosexual family as a sexual and emotional unit. Its main challenge is to the economic supremacy of the husband within the family.

RADICAL FEMINISM

Radical feminists reject the premises of each of the views we have discussed so far: they reject the biological determinism of the conservatives; they reject the liberal belief that one's living arrangements are a matter of personal preference; and they reject the traditional Marxist belief that all that is wrong with heterosexual marriage is its economic context in capitalism. Unlike all the other theorists so far, many radical feminists see heterosexual marriage as the primary institution for the oppression of women: hence, they believe that women's liberation is not possible so long as marriage survives in its present form.

This conclusion follows from Firestone's analysis of the roots of women's oppression as being embedded in the prehistoric biological family. (See Part Two.) But radical feminists urge the abolition of marriage whether or not they accept Firestone's analysis. Sheila Cronan, for instance, describes the contemporary institution of marriage as a form of slavery. All radical feminists agree that heterosexual marriage is bound to oppress women as long as it is situated in the context of a society that is overwhelmingly male-dominated. Only if male dominance were eliminated could the possibility of reinstituting heterosexual marriage be considered, and even then the partners should not be given special privileges over and above the participants in other types of relationships.

Janice Raymond's article "Female Friendship" does not focus directly on the family, at least as families traditionally have been conceived. Like all radical feminists, Raymond rejects traditional, patriarchal ways of conceptualising social reality and seeks to develop new concepts that will foreshadow the complete social transformation that radical feminists envision. Elaborating on the radical feminist claim that the personal is political, Raymond seeks deliberately to blur the lines that ordinarily are drawn between family members and political associates, between lovers, friends and comrades. She replaces these distinctions with the concept of "Gyn/affection," which she defines as a continuum of female friendship. Raymond's "Gyn/affection" is similar to Rich's concept of the lesbian continuum (outlined in our section on sexuality), but Raymond refuses to equate "Gyn/affection" with lesbianism, even though she sees a close relation between them. She views "Gyn/affection" as both a cause and a result of women's power, as both a means and an end in itself, as both personal fulfillment and religious and political inspiration.

SOCIALIST FEMINISM

Socialist feminism's chief contribution to feminist theory may have been in the area of the family. Socialist feminists too have sought to develop the radical feminist insight that the personal is political. Our socialist feminist selections on the family are all different from those that we printed in the first edition of *Feminist Frameworks,* a tribute to the continuing development of socialist feminist theorizing in this area.

Our first selection in this section raises some questions about the Cuban Family Code. Jane Flax is critical of the exclusive state support of heterosexual coupling over other forms of sexual relationships and she wonders whether the development of children's potentialities is assisted or hindered when they are raised within nuclear families. A context for Flax's questions and perhaps some ideas for answering them may be found in the socialist feminist reflections that follow immediately.

A number of socialist feminist theorists have challenged the tendency, prevalent in academic sociology, in Marxist scholarship, and even within the community at large, to assume that "the family" is a single unit with a single set of interests and functions. Hartmann's paper is an example of such a socialist feminist challenge. Hartmann recognizes that, for certain purposes, it is useful to view the family as a unit: family members do share certain interests that may coincide or conflict with the interests of families from the same or different races or classes. To view the family invariably as a single unit, however, obscures the fact that the interests of some family members may conflict with those of others: most evidently, the interests of wives may conflict with the interests of husbands. Hartmann shows that, regardless of class, nationality, or even whether they work outside the home, women are still primarily responsible for housework and average many more hours total work per week than do their husbands. The domestic labor of wives creates increased leisure time for husbands and Hartmann takes this to be evidence that nuclear families, even those in which the wives work outside the home, function to perpetuate patriarchy or male dominance as well as capitalism.

Nancy Chodorow uses a different argument to come to a similar conclusion. Chodorow begins by pointing to certain general characteristics of contemporary masculinity and femininity. On her view, adult femininity is characterized by close intrafamilial relationships with particular individuals, by concern with affectional interests and by empathy and identification with others. By contrast, adult masculinity is defined by impersonal and abstract occupational categories, by instrumental ties, and by separation from others. Especially it is defined by a rejection of the empathetic world of women.

Chodorow argues that the prevailing sexual division of labor in parenting produces male and female individuals whose personality characteristics prepare and predispose them to assume their sex-defined roles. In her explanation, Chodorow follows a number of other socialist feminist theorists by utilizing a version of Freudian theory, in her case, the version known as object-relations theory. Chodorow shares Freud's basic assumption that children's gender, including their sexual orientation, is learned rather than innate; however, her account focuses on children's relationships with their early love objects rather than with their own anatomy. Chodorow points out that the traditional division of labor in parenting assigns primary responsibility for infant care to the mother, while the father is usually absent for most of a child's infancy. As a result, it is relatively easy for girls to learn femininity from their mothers, since they are in close proximity with them from birth. By contrast, their fathers' absence makes it more difficult for boys to acquire masculine gender identification; consequently masculinity often is more precarious and fragile than feminine gender identification.

In Chodorow's view, the sexually differentiated personality types that result from exclusive female parenting are well adapted for the perpetuation both of capitalism and of male dominance. Thus the prevailing organization of parenting produces boys who feel a strong need to prove their masculinity by success in the external world and who respect external authority rather than internal standards. It produces girls who derive their primary fulfilment from relationships, who have difficulty separating from others, and who are eager to mother.

Marxist scholars have long argued that the traditional nuclear family is a cornerstone of the capitalist economic system. They have shown that the bourgeois family is a conduit for the accumulation of capital through inheritance, and they have argued that the working-class family fulfils other vital economic functions, such as providing a reserve army of labor, maintaining a high level of aggregate demand for consumer goods, and performing cheaply the socially necessary work of child rearing, care of the sick, and personal maintenance. From the 1930s on, theorists such as Wilhelm Reich, Herbert Marcuse, and members of the Frankfort School have even utilized Freudian theory to argue that the nuclear family produces an authoritarian personality type that is well suited to the hierarchical capitalist economic system. Hartmann, Chodorow, and other socialist feminist theorists do not deny these traditional Marxist analyses, but they argue that such analyses do not tell the whole story about the nuclear family. In particular, traditional Marxist analyses obscure the fact that the nuclear family is also a bulwark of male dominance. Women's liberation will not follow automatically from socialism, or from any transformation of the "public" economy. Socialist feminists argue that women's subordination within the so-called public realm is inseparable from their subordination in the so-called private realm. The liberation of women will require fundamental changes in the family.

FEMINISM AND WOMEN OF COLOR

Although mainstream sociology has often tended to overgeneralize about "the family," its treatment of black families has been an exception to this rule. Even liberal sociology has defined black families as deviant, and a primary aspect of their deviance supposedly consists in black families being matriarchal. On the basis of this definition, academic sociologists have blamed innumerable problems in the black community, from drug addiction to male unemployment, on to the allegedly dominating and "castrating" black women. Even some members of the black community have accepted this interpretation of black families, and their acceptance has resulted in a backlash against any version of black feminism.

Bell Hooks exposes contemporary allegations of black matriarchy as racist and sexist myths. Within modern society, black women have never been matriarchs; instead, they have constituted perhaps the most systematically oppressed and socially powerless group. What white sociologists perceive as matriarchy is in fact a heroic struggle by black women to hold their families together in the face of immense racist and sexist pressures to disintegrate. Prevailing conceptions of black women's position in their families must be completely revised.

Where Bell Hooks challenges mainstream sociology, Mina Davis Caulfield challenges mainstream feminism. She argues that feminist critiques of "the family" have failed to recognize that families function differently in different classes and ethnic groups. The nuclear family may indeed have been a major institution in subordinating white women by enforcing their economic dependence on their husbands. Women of color, however, have often experienced their families very differently, as networks of survival and support, with a sexual division of labor that is much less rigid than it is in white families. Instead of perceiving their husbands as dominant overlords from whom they need to escape, women of color are more likely to want to draw their husbands into their survival networks.

Just as closer attention to women's experience made evident the incompleteness and consequent male bias of traditional Marxist analyses of the family, so closer attention to the actual experience of women of color makes evident the incompleteness and consequent ethnocentrism of prevailing feminist theories of the family.

CONSERVATISM

Mother-Child Bonding

Lionel Tiger
Robin Fox

. . . Our first example of the bonding process was the mating, or "pair" bond. But there is an even more fundamental bond that all mammals at least have to respect—the bond between mother and child. Even in those mammalian species without pair bonds, where mating is brief and where the sexes part immediately after the mating season, the association of the young with the mother remains important. This is particularly true in all those species where the young are relatively dependent. Whether or not the pair bond will figure significantly in the social system seems to depend on factors associated with territoriality on the one hand, and the nature of the protection needed for the mother and young on the other. In some cases the mother and children can fend for themselves. The breeding season of the hamster, for example, lasts only about a week. During this time the males invade female burrows and then retire to their own. The mother and babies stay in the maternal burrow during the brief maturation period, after which the young disperse and the process starts all over again. With slower-maturing young this is not so easily arranged. Sometimes, as with wolves, pairs form and rear the young together. But with many ungulates, like the red deer, a group of females with their offspring, led by an older hind, form the ongoing social unit. Males associate with these "harems" only at the rutting period.

The reason behind the invariability of the mother-child bond in mammals—as compared with the extreme variability of the male-female bond—is very simple: suckling. Mammals after all are by definition the animals that suckle their young. With this evolutionary innovation the basis is laid for a greater development of sociality than can be found elsewhere in nature. This in turn follows from the longer period of dependency and immaturity in mammalian young. The young of an animal that mature quickly are fully formed both physically and socially at an early stage. Those that mature slowly have plenty of time to *learn* their sociality and incorporate greater variety into their behavior. As we go up the phylogenetic scale of mammals, we find several trends: life span increases; the gestation period becomes longer; the period of immaturity lengthens; the suckling period is extended; the size of the litter decreases until single births are most common. All these factors conspire to delay the maturity of the young animal as long as possible, to prevent his becoming fully formed too quickly.

In all these matters man is the supermammal. He does not achieve this by somehow overcoming or denying or surpassing his mammalian nature, but by exaggerating it. Of all mammals it is man who capitalizes most on the biological particularities of his order. This means that he exaggerates the *behavioral* characteristics—an increase in learning ability dependent on the greater size and complexity of the brain, an even more pronounced period of mother-child dependency, a greater emotional lability, a more elaborate sexuality, more complex play, more spectacular aggressivity, a greater propensity for bonding, a more extended system of communications, and so on. But all this rests on the bedrock of the mother-child bond, itself a product of the live-birth-and-suckling syndrome that is the defining characteristic of the zoological order to which we belong.

The mammalian mother has to suckle the child so that it can live, flourish, and eventually breed. But again, the higher we mount the scale of mammalian complexity, the more it becomes true that something other than simple feeding is involved in the mother-child relationship—particularly when, as with bottle-feeding, actual suckling is unnecessary. The further we move from the governance of primary instincts into the arena of learned abilities, the more it becomes essential for the slowly growing young animal to get its learning *right*. A great deal of its most important learning occurs early and involves those experiences that will provide the foundations for further learning. Since this is the time when the young will be intensively suckling, nature has no option but to make the mother-child bond the matrix for the basic learning processes of the maturing animal.

Simply on the basis of what we know about the social mammals in general, we can predict that if the mother-child bond does not go right, the unfortunate youngster may never get any of his *other* bonds right. The first instruction in the programs says: "Form a close and emotionally satisfying bond with the mother; when completed, move on to form x number of bonds, in the following order." Ultimately the "nonbreeding" bond with the mother has to be transformed into a "breeding" bond with a member of the opposite sex. If the initial instructions are not properly followed, the rest of the program may be jeopardized and emerge in an attenuated or skewed form. At worst the wrongly programmed animal may not be able to breed at all and thus be lost to the gene pool; at best it may breed but put the programming of its own offspring in danger.

Sometimes nature tries to make sure of the bond by relatively mechanical means. These, like all instinctive mechanisms, have the advantage of sureness—but they can also go disastrously awry because of their otherwise advantageous rigidity. The idea of "imprinting" is now firmly established in both the ethological literature and the popular imagination. In some animals (*e.g.,* most species of duck) the young learn quickly and dramatically to associate with the first moving object of a given size and color that they see—or even more generally with any larger object that they encounter at a specific period in their development. They will follow and respond to this object in predictable and specified ways. The "object," of course, is almost always their mother, but if for some reason it is something else, the program is totally and irreversibly confused, and a duckling may become attached to a dog or an ethologist or a scientist's boot. The unfortunate creature accepts this object as of its own "species"; once the animal matures, the inexorably confused program instructs it to mate with the only other member of its "species," with comic and yet pathetic results. Zoo animals, to the distress of zoological societies and breeders, thus fixate on their keepers and fail to breed with their own kind. But this is rare. Usually the creature makes the appropriate fixation, and often this is ensured by such devices as having mother and child isolated for a period immediately after the birth. This is common in mammals and gives time for the bond to be formed exclusively with the mother animal, who will then be followed incessantly, turned to in danger, and generally used as a base providing security for forays into the outside world.

Ethologists, with some accuracy, have established "critical periods" during which various types of imprinting take place in various species. But even if the "learning" involved is not of this rather dramatic and rigid character—as is the case with higher mammals—it is nevertheless like it in that it must take place at certain times and in certain ways, and that its outcome determines to a large extent the future performance of the creature. For example, some infants for some reason may not take easily to food, and some mothers may be unwilling or temperamentally incapable of suckling or otherwise feeding them. As we have noted, these characteristics will simply not reproduce themselves in the gene pool if the infant dies or later cannot breed. And, again, the infant may be permanently damaged in a behavioral sense because it has not learned the first rule of the behavioral biogrammar that allows him or her to go on.

This sounds drastic, and it is. There is a striking similarity between behavioral "malnutrition" and food malnutrition. It is now absolutely clear that children deprived of good food—chiefly the substances contained in milk—when they are very young can never wholly recover. For one thing, their growth rates are adversely affected. This has evident consequences for other features of their development. Also, it has been shown recently that the lack of protein in the newborn's diet inhibits the little body's development of myelin, which is necessary if brain cells are to form in the appropriate sequence. Brain damage results as surely from deprivation in the first weeks and months of life as it does from a concussion later.

Development is also closely tied to social patterns, and there is a close connection between behavior and food—one without the other will not do. There is no point in going into an attractive restaurant staffed with capable and friendly waiters who do not serve food; it is just as unpleasant to eat good food in an environment in which one is harassed and abused. For the infant it is a far more desperate matter. Children in orphanages get the food but not the behavior; infants of loving but poor parents may get the behavior, but they will not get the food. In both cases, if the children live to become adults they will be less effective and more frail than their counterparts who were raised by competent mothers and given suitable food.

Our proposal is that the mother-infant bond precedes all others in time— which is obvious—and is the basis for the development of the other bonds that humans are "programmed" to be likely to have. What is the evidence for a statement both so simple and so portentous of complexities to come?

The maladjusted adult has frequently been traced back to the disturbed child, and the disturbed child to the unloved infant. Psychoanalysts argue among themselves about the most vulnerable period of the mother-child relationship. Some favor a late date, some argue for the first few months, some stress the moment of birth itself with its attendant traumas, while still others look into the darkness of the womb—which does in fact contain a living child capable of psychic upset. In any event, the child *is* born in a very "fetal" state—one of the means of extending its dependency and hence its maturation period. But all agree that basic disturbances in the early stages will adversely affect proper passage through the later ones. Many of these explanations and arguments seem overelaborate. A convergence of work in child psychiatry and the study of animal behavior suggests that something rather simple is behind all this, even if the simplicity is disguised by the jargon term "separation trauma." Nature intended mother and child to be together. It is at once as simple and as profound as that. If they are separated when the bond should be forming, it forms imperfectly, if at all. The child suffers a deep sense of loss and even physical distress. And though the mother may not be clear about what has happened to her, she too may suffer—from feelings of depression and inadequacy.

The mother is totally essential to the well-being of the child. Remove her, and its world collapses. This dependence is based on the suckling tendency of mammals, but it does not wholly hinge on food. It is largely a matter of emotional security, of which food is but a part. The human mother is a splendid mammal—the epitome of her order. Her physiology is more highly developed for suckling behavior—with permanent breasts, for example—than any of her cousins, except domesticated ungulates bred specially for milk-giving. But more than this, she is, like any other mammal, emotionally programmed to be responsive to the growing child. Her whole physiology from the moment she conceives is changed not only to accommodate the sheer business of parturition but also to cope with this physical extension of her body for years after the event. Animal experiments have shown that the softness and texture of the mother—and even her smell—are more important to the child than simply her milk supply, although without the latter, in most "wild" conditions, it would not live. Primate infants deprived of real mothers will adapt best to mechanical substitutes that are alike in *texture* to their real parent, in preference to those that simply provide milk but no warmth.

Whatever the value of the substitute, the young animal, psychically, is permanently damaged by the separation. The male may never learn to relate to females, with the consequence that his sexual identity will be confused. The female will almost certainly fail in her task as a mother by ignoring her own offspring, as she was ignored herself. Anyone who has seen the grief, the listlessness, the obvious and heartrending despair of infant monkeys deprived, in an experiment, of maternal care, will echo the sentiments of the man who performed the experiment. He declared: "Thank God we only have to do it once to prove the point."

The point is proved time and time again in human society. Brief separations of mother and child are bad enough, but excessive separations are devastating. Nature is ruthless about this. In the case of some animals, if the mother is not able to find the child immediately at birth, respond to its cries, and above all, lick it from head to foot, she will treat it as a stranger and refuse to suckle it when it is later presented to her. Yet in the name of sanitation we risk tampering with this delicate system by taking babies away from their mothers on the maternity wards moments after they are born. Monkey infants that lose their mothers develop all the characteristics of autistic children, even to the endless rocking and crouching—with little chance of becoming fully functioning adults. Our orphanages and nurseries are full of children wholly or partly so deprived who also rock and grieve and make only painfully insecure adjustments to the adult world.

The practice of taking infants from their mothers during the first five days of life is an example of the acceptance of hygiene and comfort as of greater importance than the possibility of behavioral disruption—if this is even considered. In some of the most sophisticated and admirable places on earth—the wards of excellent hospitals—newborn organisms emerge from their mothers' wombs in a demanding and exciting process to face a suddenly novel environment containing unmuted sounds, swirls of unfamiliar air, and the impressive movements of hands and bodies. Often the mother of such a confused and needy creature is drugged and will sleep for many hours after this first potential social encounter with her child. The neonate itself may be somewhat under the influence of her drugs and in any event will be quickly removed in a plastic basket from her presence to a ward of a dozen or two similar creatures, many crying, all under high light, and all handled by skilled nurses—part of whose professional skill must be that denial of the special treatment which seems to mark how women treat their own children as opposed to the children of others. The child will be labeled by a card on its container, and some mothers will confuse their own child with another, and the more naive among them will question their competence as mothers; if they cannot even recognize their child, how can they possibly cope with it?

This plight has to be seen in the context of the improved health of mothers and infants. It is probably true that there are important advantages to having the mother rest after the single most trying of all predictable human actions. The question here is about the effects of systems—which are perhaps useful for mothers and certainly efficient for hospitals—on the essential bond between mother and infant. On theoretical and empirical grounds there is a real and disturbing possibility that—with effects difficult to measure—some human babies and their mothers encounter in the act of birth a fact of technology and custom that may make more uncertain the elaboration of a bond begun *in utero*, a bond severely interrupted at just that point when presumably some forceful recreation of the certainty and strength of uterine environment is most necessary.

The mother-child bond is the basic instruction in the human bonding program, and the ground rule of the human biogrammar. If this rule is not learned, the human may not learn to "speak" behaviorally, just as, if he does not learn the difference between subject and predicate, he will never be able to handle the verbal grammar. What he "learns," essentially, is the ability to make successful bonds in general. Bonds depend on feelings, and the mother-deprived child is most commonly described as "affectless"—lacking the motive power to love or care. It is here that the groundwork for "emotional maturity" is laid: that the child will eventually become an adult capable of the full sexual experience and of complete parental behavior. In general, he learns to be confident in his own ability to explore; he develops self-confidence and security. Young monkeys with mothers will move off to enjoy the pleasures of curiosity, whereas maternally deprived monkeys will be afraid to. Successful bonding in later life depends to a great extent on this tendency to explore. This program of security/exploration is so easily interfered with—especially in "advanced" societies—that a large number of people end up by making only partial adjustments in all these areas, to the detriment of their social relationships.

It is just as important to note that the instructions are also quite precise about the termination of the bond—which begins with the gross physiological act of weaning and ends with the transference of emotional ties onto peers and mates. If the mother ignores the instructions to terminate the bond, the results can be just as disastrous as if the child continues to talk baby talk into adulthood: its chances of communicating effectively with other adults are severely curtailed. "Maternal overprotection"—the continuation into adolescence of the relationship appropriate to childhood—extends the mother-child program to a time when the "child-child" and "child-other-adult" programs should be coming into play. . . .

Fathers Shouldn't Try to Be Mothers

Bruno Bettelheim

What is Father's job? What should he stand for in his children's eyes?

Once the answers were quite clear. Today they're not so simple.

A very popular German verse goes: "It's as easy to become a father as it is difficult to be one." And this is said of the German father, who was at all times master of the house, whose word was law for wife and children. If being a father was difficult for him, how much more tenuous is the modern American father's position!

Being one myself and having had intimate experience with the inner feelings of many other fathers, I know of the confusion and utter bafflement which the modern father often feels. He does more for his children and with them, than his father did. Nevertheless, instead of feeling more of a father he feels less so. Nor are matters helped much by the many comic strips, radio and TV programs that either frankly ridicule fathers or depict them as silly boys. These things are not only damaging to the way his wife and children see the father, but also to the way he sees himself.

In the old-fashioned family the father, through his work, provided for the family's physical existence and, he hoped, its emotional well-being. He set an example for standards of behavior and enforced them. He was the protector and the breadwinner—in a time when the bread was harder to win and the family knew it.

Nowadays, with earning and living conditions improved, most children know no fear of want. This security, desirable as it is in itself, tends to obscure the importance of a father's contribution both in his own eyes and in those of his children. Though well aware himself of how hard he works, he no longer finds the recognition at home that used to be the reward for his efforts.

This is not all. When the father comes home and is tacitly expected (or openly asked) to take over the care of the children; when he is received with an account of what went wrong during the day, as if nothing could possibly have gone wrong during his day at work; or with the request to do things around the house—the impression is conveyed to the child that he has been more or less loafing all day and Mother now expects him to start on the serious tasks. That the father accepts this as the right order of things supports other notions the child gets from his storybooks and primers where the father's work, if depicted at all, is with rare and laudable exceptions shown as easy pleasure. The text sometimes says he is hard-working but the pictures which make a much deeper impression on the child, don't show it. The storybook farmers or mail carriers hardly ever work in sleet or rain, nor does sweat run down their foreheads or soak their shirts though the sun burns down strongly. There are never work accidents or any layoffs.

Furthermore, whether or not the father was a good provider used not to be questioned in the child's mind. If he did not provide as much as he might, the child probably did not know it. Nowadays all this is changed. The mass media see to that. They harass the child with how desirable it is to have a new car or dishwasher and how easy these are to get.

In many other ways, too, and in many families, the father's importance as a breadwinner is undermined. The general panacea that modern psychology seems to offer is that we now have better parent-child relationships. But how is a father to relate to his children?

Today's father is often advised to participate in infant care as much as the mother does, so that he, too, will be as emotionally enriched as she. Unfortunately, this is somewhat empty advice because the male physiology and that part of his psychology based on it are not geared to infant care.

Not that there is anything wrong in a father's giving the baby a bottle. Far from it. He should certainly do so whenever the situation requires it or he enjoys it. What is wrong is to think that this adds to his parenthood. What is wrong is a thinking based on what I can best term division of labor rather than on inherent function; a thinking that disregards physiology, denies that our emotions have their deepest roots in it; a thinking that separates activities from the emotions we bring to them.

Nowadays women assume, or have had thrust upon them by technological and social change, many roles in society which until recently were masculine prerogatives. Perhaps that is why they now expect men to assume some of the tasks once reserved for women, and men have become ready to accept such demands. But infant care and chld-rearing, unlike choice of work, are not activities in which who should do what can be decided independently of physiology.

For example, just reviewing the mother's function reveals some of the reasons why fathers have a much harder time with their fatherhood than mothers do with motherhood. I believe it is due to the essential difference in their biological roles.

Nine months of growth and profound physiological changes in the mother precede the arrival of a baby, permitting her to prepare not only *physiologically, but emotionally* for the coming child. The birth act itself, *the dramatic changes in her body, all impress upon her what a momentous event has taken place.* Great as a father's desire for a child may be, there are certainly no physiological changes within him to accompany the arrival of the new family member. And afterwards, he has no close relationship with a child that can compare with that of a nursing mother. For her, nursing creates a cycle of tension and relief, of need and fulfillment that is directly connected with her bodily functions and gives her a wonderful feeling of importance and well-being. The father, on the other hand, simply continues to pursue his normal occupation, may even feel a need to do better at it. But he undergoes no physiological and emotional changes comparable to the mother's, has no comparable feelings of contributing intimately and directly to the baby's welfare. Probably he is dimly aware that the physiological underpinning for getting his own satisfaction by administering intimately to the needs of the infant is lacking. When he tries to find greater fulfillment of his fatherhood by doing more for the child along the lines only mothers used to follow, the result is that he finds less rather than more fulfillment, not only for his fatherhood, but also for his manhood.

The completion of womanhood is largely through motherhood, but fulfillment of manhood is not achieved largely through fatherhood. The fulfillment of manhood is achieved by making a contribution to society as a whole, an impulse which is quickened when a responsible man becomes a father. Without a child, there seems little reason why a man should wish to perpetuate society, to plan beyond the reaches of his life; why he should plant trees, the fruits of which will not ripen while he can still enjoy them. But the relationship between father and child never was and cannot now be built principally around chld-caring experiences. It is built around a man's function in society: moral, economic, political.

The father who read the Scriptures to his family, impressed on his child that his interest was concentrated on matters transcending daily toil, matters that gave a meaning to life above and beyond the everyday experiences. Though the child did not understand the content of the Scriptures, his father's concern with them, and what the child dimly felt they stood for, made a lasting impression on him. This example of a deep concern for matters beyond the day-to-day struggle made the head of the family a father just as much as his providing the wherewithal for the family. Thus the old-fashioned father influenced the personality of his child not so much through what he did with the child as through the importance of what he, the father, was concerned with. It was the depth of his dedication to higher issues which gave a broader scope to the child's life. This the modern father can still contribute. How? Today much of a father's positive relationship to his child is built up around playing games, working around the house, fixing the car or other leisure-time activities—and not around the father's function in society. When these activities remain mere enjoyment, many modern fathers become play companions rather than parents. A meaningful parent is that father who manages to use such activities for conveying to the child what a man should be like in meeting life, in mastering it and its responsibilities.

When a father plays games and gets carried away by a childish desire to win, gets angry, upset or argumentative about rules, the child's confidence in him can be undermined. Also, in working together with their children, there are fathers who are more intent on getting done with the job than on using it to teach the child what it means to be a man.

For example, when a child watches his father slowly sawing through wood and even helps with his own little saw, the child may be daydreaming of how someday he will clear a large forest and build a city. The act of "doing together" shows the child the validity of his daydreams of future greatness because, while he dreamed them, something real was observed by his father. That the father's achievement required hard work, thinking, planning, is another important lesson that the child must learn, provided the work he has to do himself is not too hard.

So often it has been those men who have long and arduously daydreamed about a better world they would build who later become those best able to do it in reality. While those who were too soon made familiar with hardship as often as not learned to avoid it in later life, and to escape from it.

Contrary to such psychological facts, the opinion is widespread that hard work in childhood is the best training for meeting future hardships. The wish to get real work out of the child is often camouflaged behind high-sounding statements about its enhancing his self-respect. The child will recognize and resent our selfish motives.

These are some of the bad consequences of confused roles for the modern father who at one time is pal, at another the strict supervisor. The child can never be sure what attitude to expect. One of the most important factors contributing to the security of the child is the father's inner consistency. The father's attitude ought to be both strong and understanding, so that the child can afford to become angry and still feel secure nothing untoward will happen.

Provided such inner attitudes obtain, it is true that carefully planned and shared leisure-time activities—games, hikes, picnics, making things—can cement and add new enjoyment to a father and child relationship. They can be as satisfying for the father as the child. Although it has become fashionable for fathers to say they do not care what work their children choose to do when they grow up, many men hope that their sons will follow in their footsteps, take over the business, enter the same occupation, profession or company. Understandably, a father looks forward to the time when his child is grown enough so that he can teach him his craft. Unfortunately, a good many years are required by modern education, and by the time a child reaches the age at which he can learn a craft from his father, the child has also reached the developmental stage of late adolescence or early maturity, when his desire for independence from his parents stands in the way of such an undertaking. More often than not the father's dream that he will truly become a father by making a man out of his son through the handing down of a craft ends in deep disappointment for both of them. Actually no important teaching can take place once the child has reached maturity.

Most fathers realize this, at least to some degree. That is why we see efforts to build up a child's relation to his father at a much earlier age, and around paternal activities in which the child is better able to share. So intense has been the emphasis on "doing things together" that many fathers worry about the relatively short time they can spend with their children. This need not be a serious handicap. If a child sees his father for a few hours a day, he assumes that what his father is and how he acts during the time, is what he is and how he acts when he is away. When a father feels deeply for his child during the few hours he is with him the child is convinced he feels that way all the time. If the father is able to answer the child's questions about life, the child assumes he can answer all important questions. If the father remains calm and in command of himself in the small emergencies around the house the child will feel that, come hell or high water, his father can always control an emergency. And this gives the child the security he needs to meet life—a security far more important than just the act of playing ball or checkers or soldiers with his father.

The issue, as I see it, in this question of the modern father's role, is that in our society fathers have assumed too much the role of an "also ran." No longer is there one central figure in the home—the mother—whose sole or at least major function is to provide physical, physiological, emotionally intimate satisfaction to the members of the family and another equally important person—the father—whose role is clearly to protect against the outside world and to teach how to meet this world successfully. Since both parents try to do both, neither parent is experienced by the child as a secure haven for either. We all need both: someone who always takes our side and sees things our way, no matter what; and also someone who, though definitely on our side, can be relied on to give us sound advice even if it goes against our wishes, who responds to our needs by seeing them in a broader perspective.

Fathers will have to accept and be satisfied with the fact that their contribution will be less immediately obvious to the young child than the mother's. But how important to the child to have a father whose greater objectivity can be trusted in all emergencies just because he is not so immediately involved in the picayune squabbles; to be able to rely on the judgment of a father who is known to think beyond the problems of the moment to their far-reaching implications and consequences.

The child's view of the world and himself will be deeply influenced by the father's quiet confidence; the inner security which permits him freely and graciously to admit an error, which gives him the freedom not to think poorly of himself if a colleague earns more money, which permits him not to blame his difficulties on others or to become defensive about them. In this matter of being a father, as in everything, it is not the externals that count, but the inner convictions and the ability to put them into practice.

LIBERALISM

A Marriage Agreement

Alix Kates Shulman

When my husband and I were first married a decade ago, "keeping house" was less of a burden than a game. We both worked full-time jobs and we each pretty much took care of ourselves. We had a small apartment which stayed empty most of each day so that taking care of it was very little trouble. Every couple of weeks we'd spend a Saturday morning cleaning and taking our laundry to the laundromat. Though I usually did the cooking, our meals were casual and simple. We shopped for food together after work; sometimes we ate out; we had our breakfast at a diner near work; sometimes my husband cooked; there were few dishes. In the evenings we went for long walks and weekends we spent in Central Park. Our domestic life was beautifully uncomplicated.

Then our first child was born. I quit my job to stay home with him. Our domestic life was suddenly very complicated. When our second child was born, domestic life, the only life I had any longer, became a tremendous burden.

Once we had children, we totally accepted the sex-roles society assigns. My husband worked all day in an office and I was at home, so the domestic burden fell almost entirely on me. We had to move to a larger apartment to accommodate the children. Keeping it minimally livable was no longer a matter of an hour or two a week but took hours of every day: children make unbelievable messes. Our one meal a day for two people turned into a half a dozen meals a day for anywhere from one to four people at a time, and everyone ate different food. To shop for this brood—or even just to run out for a quart of milk—became a major project. It meant putting on snowsuits, boots, and mittens, getting strollers or carriages up and down stairs, and scheduling the trip so it did not interfere with someone's feeding or nap or illness or some other domestic job. Laundry turned from a weekly to a daily chore. And all this tumult started for me at six in the morning and didn't let up until nine at night, and *still* there wasn't time enough to do everything.

But even more burdensome than the physical work of child-rearing was the relentless responsibility I had for the children. There was literally nothing I could do or even contemplate without having to consider first how the children would be affected. Answering their questions alone ruled out for me such a minimum of privacy as a private *mental* life. They were always *there*. I couldn't read or think. If there ever was a moment to read, I read to them.

My husband's job began keeping him at work later and later, and sometimes took him out of town. If I suffered from too much domesticity, he suffered from too little. The children were usually asleep when he got home and I was too exhausted to talk. He became a stranger. Though he had sometimes, when we were first married, cooked for the two of us, that was no longer possible. A meal had become a major complicated production, in which timing counted heavily and someone might be crying in the background. No longer could we decide at the last moment what we felt like having for supper. And there were always dishes in the sink.

As the children grew up, our domestic arrangement seemed increasingly odious to me. I took free-lance work to do at home in order to keep some contact with the world, but I had to squeeze it into my "free" time. My husband, I felt, could always change his job if the pressure was too great, but I could never change mine. When I finally began to see my situation from a woman's liberation point of view, I realized that the only way we could possibly survive as a family (which we wanted to do) was to throw out the old sex roles we had been living by and start again. Wishing to be once more equal and independent as we had been when we had met, we decided to make an agreement in which we could define our roles our own way. We wanted to share completely the responsibility for caring for our household and for raising our children, by then five and seven. We recognized that after a decade of following the traditional sex roles we would have to be extremely vigilant and wary of backsliding into our old domestic habits. If it was my husband's night to take care of the children, I would have to be careful not to check up on how he was managing; if the baby sitter didn't show up for him, it would have to be *his* problem.

When our agreement was merely verbal, it didn't work; our old habits were too firmly established. So we made a formal agreement instead, based on a detailed schedule of family duties and assignments. Eventually, as the old roles and habits are replaced, we may be able to abandon the formality of our arrangement, but now the formality is imperative. Good intentions are simply not enough.

Our agreement is designed for our particular situation only in which my husband works all day at a job of his choice, and I work at home on a free-lance basis during the hours the children are in school (from 8:30 till 3:00). If my husband or I should change jobs, income, or working hours, we would probably have to adjust our agreement to the altered circumstances. Now, as my husband makes much more money than I do, he pays for most of our expenses.

MARRIAGE AGREEMENT

I Principles

We reject the notion that the work which brings in more money is the more valuable. The ability to earn more money is already a privilege which must not be compounded by enabling the larger earner to buy out of his/her duties and put the burden on the one who earns less, or on someone hired from outside.

We believe that each member of the family has an equal right to his/her own time, work, value, choices. As long as all duties are performed, each person may use his/her extra time any way he/she chooses. If he/she wants to use it making money, fine. If he/she wants to spend it with spouse, fine. If not, fine.

As parents we believe we must share all responsibility for taking care of our children and home—not only the work, but the responsibility. At least during the first year of this agreement, *sharing responsibility* shall mean:

1 Dividing the *jobs* (see "Job Breakdown" below); and
2 Dividing the *time* (see "Schedule" below) for which each parent is responsible

In principle, jobs should be shared equally, 50-50, but deals may be made by mutual agreement. If jobs and schedule are divided on any other than a 50-50 basis, then either party may call for a re-examination and redistribution of jobs or a revision of the schedule at any time. Any deviation from 50-50 must be for the convenience of both parties. If one party works overtime in any domestic job, she/he must be compensated by equal extra work by the other. For convenience, the schedule may be flexible, but changes must be formally agreed upon. The terms of this agreement are rights and duties, not privileges and favors.

II Job Breakdown

A Children

1 Mornings: Waking children; getting their clothes out, making their lunches; seeing that they have notes, homework, money, passes, books, etc.; brushing their hair; giving them breakfast; making coffee for us.
2 Transportation: Getting children to and from lessons, doctors, dentists, friends' houses, park, parties, movies, library, etc. Making appointments.
3 Help: Helping with homework, personal problems, projects like cooking,

making gifts, experiments, planting, etc.; answering questions, explaining things.

4 Nighttime: Getting children to take baths, brush their teeth, go to bed, put away their toys and clothes; reading with them; tucking them in and having night-talks, handling if they wake and call in the night.

5 Babysitters: Getting babysitters, which sometimes takes an hour of phoning.

6 Sickcare: Calling doctors, checking out symptoms, getting prescriptions filled, remembering to give medicine, taking days off to stay home with sick child; providing special activities.

7 Weekends: All above, plus special activities (beach, park, zoo, etc.).

B Housework

8 Cooking: Breakfasts; dinners; (children, parents, guests).

9 Shopping: Food for all meals; housewares; clothing and supplies for children.

10 Cleaning: Dishes daily; apartment weekly, bi-weekly, or monthly.

11 Laundry: Home laundry; making beds; drycleaning (take and pick up).

III Schedule

(The numbers on the following schedule refer to Job Breakdown list.)

1 Mornings: Every other week each parent does all.

2 and 3 Transportation and Help: Parts occurring between 3:00 and 6:30 pm, fall to wife. She must be compensated (see 10 below). Husband does all weekend transportation and pickups after 6:00. The rest is split.

4 Nighttime (and all Help after 6:30): Husband does Tuesday, Thursday, and Sunday. Wife does Monday, Wednesday, and Saturday. Friday is split according to who has done extra work during the week.

5 Babysitters must be called by whoever the sitter is to replace. If no sitter turns up, the parent whose night it is to take responsibility must stay home.

6 Sickcare: This must still be worked out equally, since now wife seems to do it all. (The same goes for the now frequently declared school closings for so-called political protest, whereby the mayor gets credit at the expense of the mothers of young children. The mayor only closes the schools, not the places of business or the government offices.)

7 Weekends: Split equally. Husband is free all of Saturday, wife is free all of Sunday, except that the husband does all weekend transportation, breakfasts, and special shopping.

8 Cooking: Wife does all dinners except Sunday nights; husband does all weekend breakfasts (including shopping for them and dishes). Sunday dinner, and any other dinners on his nights of responsibility if wife isn't home. Breakfasts are divided week by week. Whoever invites the guests does shopping, cooking, and dishes; if both invite them, split work.

9 Shopping: Divide by convenience. Generally, wife does local daily food shopping, husband does special shopping for supplies and children's things.

10 Cleaning: Husband does all the house-cleaning, in exchange for wife's extra childcare (3:00 to 6:30 daily) and sick care. Dishes: same as 4.

11 Laundry: Wife does most home laundry. Husband does all dry cleaning delivery and pick up. Wife strips beds, husband remakes them.

After only four months of strictly following our agreement, our daughter said one day to my husband, "You know, Daddy, I used to love Mommy more than you, but now I love you both the same."

The Value of Housework

Ann Crittenden Scott

. . . According to economists at the Chase Manhattan Bank, housewives are doing gratis work worth at least $257.53 a week on the current labor market, and they are performing a dozen or so tasks, any one of which, outside the home, would be an independent profession with its own salary. [See the table "Women's Work."]

Chase's calculations don't even include some of the most important tasks performed by women who work at home. Aside from their daily "jobs," they act as teachers for their children and as hostesses and frequently secretaries for their husbands. And tying all these roles together, balancing time and allocating energies, is a managerial skill that, according to one economist, is equivalent to the functions performed by an independent entrepreneur of a small fairly complex business.

WOMAN'S WORK

Job	Hours per week	Rate per hour	Value per week	Job	Hours per week	Rate per hour	Value per week
Nursemaid	44.5	$2.00	$89.00	Laundress	5.9	$2.50	$14.75
Dietitian	1.2	4.50	5.40	Seamstress	1.3	3.25	4.22
Food buyer	3.3	3.50	11.55	Practical nurse	.6	3.75	2.25
Cook	13.1	3.25	42.58	Maintenance man	1.7	3.00	5.10
Dishwasher	6.2	2.00	12.40	Gardener	2.3	3.00	6.90
Housekeeper	17.5	3.25	56.88	Chauffeur	2.0	3.25	6.50
			Total	$257.53 or $13,391.56 a year*			

*[Note omitted.]
Source: Chase Manhattan Bank, 1972.

In fact, if the job weren't considered "woman's work," there is little doubt that its challenges, its variety, and its flexibility would appeal to many men. For many individuals, these rewards more than outweigh the long hours—sometimes 13 to 14 hours per day—and the hard, often routine work. But what man would want a position that guarantees no independent income, no Social Security, not even a living wage? And worse, which has, in this male-dominated culture, in spite of all propaganda to the contrary, almost no status at all?

For the truth is, although the housewife may take justifiable pride in the home she works so hard to maintain, housework is not viewed as dignified or respected employment. The housewife is the subject of endless jokes and social put-downs; she is patronized, condescended to, and considered unemployed. All too often, the woman who has chosen to be a housewife and stays home with her children is looked upon as lazy, untalented, or someone who "doesn't really work." . . .

Some economists maintain that housewives' services are excluded from the GNP because it is impossible to impute a value to them, but a number of other nonmarket items are figured into the accounts—the value of agricultural commodities produced and consumed by a family, for instance, or the value of owner-occupied dwellings. Although it might not be easy to set a price for unpaid housework, it would surely be within the capability of interested economists. And it might help correct the impression that those 30 million Americans are living off the fat of the land.

According to Gardner Ackley, Chairman of the President's Council of Economic Advisers under President Johnson, the "failure to recognize the value of these productive services is a source of serious bias in the national product." Under the existing method of accounting, for example, every time a woman leaves home to take a job, the move is counted as an addition to the GNP, instead of simply a shift in the type of work being done. Since more women have been entering the job market in recent years, this makes the GNP look as though it is growing faster than it really is. Conversely, by leaving housework out of the GNP, economists have vastly underestimated the total amount of productive work being done. By one calculation, housewives' services probably amount to about one-fourth of the current level of GNP, or $250 billion—and that's not even counting all the unpaid volunteer work that women perform for hospitals, charities, political candidates, and other worthy causes. . . .

One of the main reasons the housewife's bearing and caring for children, her cooking, cleaning, chauffeuring, and shopping are scoffed at, ignored, or taken for granted, is because it is work being done by a woman. Men who cook are chefs; women are just cooks. Men who handle finances are accountants; women are simply bookkeepers. Men who plan and order supplies are purchasing agents; women who do the same are only consumers. Not so long ago when men were secretaries and bank tellers, the jobs were the training grounds for executive positions. When performed by women, those tasks are likely to be dead-end jobs.

An explicit downgrading of the work done by women is found in the

Dictionary of Occupational Titles, a Labor Department publication that defines some 22,000 occupations and serves as a standard reference for government and industry. Each occupation is rated on a skill scale from a high of 1 to a low of 887. Listed at the 878 level are homemakers, foster mothers, child-care attendants, home health aides, nursery school teachers, and practical nurses. A marine mammal handler, on the other hand, has a ranking of 328, a hotel clerk 368, and a barber 371. Obviously, "woman's work" doesn't measure up. Ultimately, the only way to achieve any real equality between the sexes is to abolish sex roles altogether; to put an end to woman's work and man's work, and to develop the concept and value of human work.

One way to achieve this might come from making marriage a true partnership, legally and financially, as well as personally. Both partners, for example, should have equal rights to all income and property, acquired during marriage, as well as to its management and control. If one partner works outside the home, then half of his or her salary should by law belong to the other party, and the partners could decide between themselves how the household expenses should be handled. . . .

Another proposal giving credence to the idea of equality between the sexes would have the law assure the wife a salary for the housework she performs. This salary would reflect the value of her individual services, what she could be earning in the labor market, or the official minimum wage. She could receive a percentage of her husband's salary to be paid by him or paid directly by his employer in the same way as the military sends allotment checks to the wives of servicemen who are stationed overseas. If she is paid by her husband, her salary would not be subject to tax, since it was already taxed once when the husband received it. Since the husband would in fact be the "employer," he would be expected to pay the basic household expenses of food, clothing, and shelter, allowing his wife to spend her salary as she chose, on her own personal needs, on her family, savings, or investment. If she worked outside the home and did all the housework, too, she would get paid for both jobs. If a husband and wife each did half of the housework, they would receive no household salary, or they could split a salary. A husband who refused to pay his wife for housework could be taken to domestic court for a determination of her proper salary. . . .

Still, the idea of a salary for housewives arouses strong opposition—and sometimes among housewives themselves. Many feel that they receive payment enough in the love and affection from their families. "No amount of money could make you do some of the things you have to do," says one Dallas suburbanite. "You only do it for love." Others resent the notion of trying to place a crass, monetary value on that labor of love. "How could you place a value on some of the functions of mothering, of being there when people need you, of making sure that everything in the household happens smoothly and on time?" asks New York economist Alfred Eichner. "It wouldn't be a realistic exercise. What makes a household a home is people sacrificing themselves. No money could buy a comparable commitment, just as money can't buy a good soldier."

That may be, but because a service is invaluable seems a poor reason to turn it into servitude, and it's a little late to be romanticizing a housewife's martyrdom on the altar of love. Elizabeth Janeway, in her book, *Man's World, Woman's Place,* has some astute things to say about the dangers of being paid in emotional capital alone. As she sees it, women who work at home have no objective means of judging their own value or skills. They must become "managers of emotions," in Kenneth Keniston's phrase, who keep their successes on a private and personal level, and live vicariously on the praise and success of others. The situation can all too often turn normal family encounters into opportunities for emotional manipulation and blackmail.

A more practical argument against salaries for housework is simply this: in most families, after all the basic bills are paid, there is no money left over for a salary for anybody. A household wage might therefore benefit only the more affluent wives. And many feminists worry that the idea would only reinforce the association of housework with "woman's work," and make the eventual goal of abolishing sex roles more difficult than ever to achieve. "The husband would just be employing his wife as a servant," complains one activist, "and who wants that?"

Some advocates overcome this objection by suggesting that the salary need not be actually paid unless the marriage is dissolved. At that time the wife's "back wages" could be awarded to her as a sort of "severance pay." Others have suggested that the portion of the family income allotted to the wife as salary be used to buy an annuity or pension, payable if the marriage went aground—a sort of forced savings against the possibility of divorce. And in that event, instead of receiving alimony, with all its connotations of charity, the wife would receive accrued income, or reparations, for the labor she had put into the job of marriage. The New York Chapter of NOW is extending that idea by pushing for family insurance. In cases of divorce, such an insurance policy would guarantee the homeworking wife an income, determined by number of children and length of marriage.

Today, housewives still don't enjoy basic rights and safeguards that workers in factories and offices have long taken for granted. "The rights to support of women and children are much more limited than is generally known," stated a recent report by the Labor Department. "A married woman living with her husband can, in practice, only get what he chooses to give her." In all but eight states, for example, a husband's earnings are his separate personal property and his wife has no legal claim on them, or on any property accumulated in his name. Nor does she have any right to compensation for the labor she may have put into the marriage. He can make and spend his own money, build up his own estate, without her participation or knowledge of what is happening.

Another way for a housewife to collect her well-earned salary might be to place housework in the category of jobs covered by the Social Security system. A similar proposal was recently made by the West German government, after a poll revealed that 86 percent of the population was in favor of housewives receiving their own pension. Under the proposed law, all houseworkers would register for Social Security as individuals, so that they could take their own pensions into marriage, and out of it again if divorce occurred. Whatever their work pattern, they could collect a full pension. During marriage, if the houseworker had no other income, the other spouse would contribute to the plan for both. In justifying the proposed change, the West German government declared that "to be a housewife is a full job . . . as much a career as any other. . . . Economists agree that the work done at home contributes to the family income, for if it were done professionally, unmanageable costs would be added to the household's budget."

The inequalities of the current Social Security system in the United States are a result of the fact that housewives are considered "nonworking" women. Because the system is based on contributions from employer and employee, and she has neither employer nor salary, she gets no benefits from the system except Medicare. Everything is dependent on her husband's pension. If she is widowed and at least 62, she receives only 82½ percent of the benefits he had earned. If she is divorced, she receives nothing unless she was married at least 20 years and can show that he is contributing or was ordered to contribute to her support. And if she has worked outside the home for a time, as most women do, she must choose, upon retirement, either her own benefit or half of her husband's, whichever is larger. She can't receive both, even though both have been earned. That means the government benefits from their marriage by retaining more cash than it would have done had this man and woman remained single.

There has been some agitation in Congress to correct these inequities in the Social Security system, but virtually no initiatives have been taken to grant women full pensions, or any kind of salaries for housework.

But, in an unorganized way, things are changing. At least 50 percent of American women 18 years and over (and almost 40 percent of women with children under 18) are in the labor force, and who-knows-how-many men are in the kitchen. The growth of child-care centers and businesses supplying household services also suggests a new fate for housework in the future. But these trends are not change enough.

Nothing will be enough until the working woman—wherever she works—is free to earn a living in any way that she chooses. "Occupation: Houseworker" is a viable and respectable choice for anyone, male or female, provided it is treated as such, socially and economically. If it were, the houseworker could at last be recognized as a professional member of the American labor force, paid for her or his labor, time, and skills.

TRADITIONAL MARXISM

The Family

Karl Marx
Friedrich Engels

. . . Abolition of the family! Even the most radical flare up at this infamous proposal of the Communists.

On what foundation is the present family, the bourgeois family, based? On capital, on private gain. In its completely developed form this family exists only among the bourgeoisie. But this state of things finds its complement in the practical absence of the family among the proletarians, and in public prostitution.

The bourgeois family will vanish as a matter of course when its complement vanishes, and both will vanish with the vanishing of capital.

Do you charge us with wanting to stop the exploitation of children by their parents? To this crime we plead guilty.

But, you will say, we destroy the most hallowed of relations, when we replace home education by social.

And your education! Is not that also social, and determined by the social conditions under which you educate, by the intervention, direct or indirect, of society, by means of schools, etc.? The Communists have not invented the intervention of society in education; they do but seek to alter the character of that intervention, and to rescue education from the influence of the ruling class.

The bourgeois clap-trap about the family and education, about the hallowed co-relation of parent and child, becomes all the more disgusting, the more, by the action of Modern Industry, all family ties among the proletarians are torn asunder, and their children transformed into simple articles of commerce and instruments of labour.

But you Communists would introduce community of women, screams the whole bourgeoisie in chorus.

The bourgeois sees in his wife a mere instrument of production. He hears that the instruments of production are to be exploited in common, and, naturally, can come to no other conclusion than that the lot of being common to all will likewise fall to the women.

He has not even a suspicion that the real point aimed at is to do away with the status of women as mere instruments of production.

For the rest, nothing is more ridiculous than the virtuous indignation of our bourgeois at the community of women which, they pretend, is to be openly and officially established by the Communists. The Communists have no need to introduce community of women; it has existed almost from time immemorial.

Our bourgeois, not content with having the wives and daughters of their proletarians at their disposal, not to speak of common prostitutes, take the greatest pleasure in seducing each others' wives.

Bourgeois marriage is in reality a system of wives in common and thus, at the most, what the Communists might possibly be reproached with, is that they desire to introduce, in substitution for a hypocritically concealed, an openly legalised community of women. For the rest, it is self-evident that the abolition of the present system of production must bring with it the abolition of the community of women springing from that system, *i.e.,* of prostitution both public and private. . . .

Excerpts from the Cuban Family Code

Executive Branch, Council of Ministers

I, OSVALDO DORTICOS TORRADO, President of the Republic of Cuba, HEREBY PROCLAIM: That the Council of Ministers has approved and I have signed the following:

WHEREAS: The equality of citizens resulting from the elimination of private property over the means of production and the extinction of classes and all forms of exploitation of human beings by others is a basic principle of socialist society being constructed by our people, a principle which must be explicitly and fully reflected in the provisions of our legislation.

WHEREAS: Obsolete judicial norms from the bourgeois past which are contrary to equality and discriminatory with regard to women and children born out of wedlock still exist in our country, these norms must be replaced by others fully in keeping with the principles of equality and the realities of our socialist society, which is constantly and dynamically advancing.

WHEREAS: The socialist concept of the family is based on the fundamental consideration that it constitutes an entity in which social and personal interests are present and closely linked in view of the fact that it is the elementary cell of society and, as such, contributes to its development and plays an important role in the upbringing of the new generations. Moreover, as the center for relations of common existence between men and women and between them and their children and between all of them with their relatives, it meets deep-rooted human needs in the social field and in the field of affection for the individual.

WHEREAS: The concept expressed above and the importance which, with this in mind, our socialist society assigns to the family, make it advisable that the judicial norms on this subject be separated from other legislation and constitute the Family Code.

WHEREAS: Adoption and tutelage are institutions which normally and general-ly correspond to the family, it is convenient that the judicial norms which cover them be included in the Family Code, especially when the relationship between adoptive parent and adopted child are similar to those between parents and their children.

WHEREAS: The draft version of the Family Code was drawn up on the basis of the ideas and assumptions contained in the preceding Whereases, by the Law Study Commission and its Secretariat and presented to the Deputy Prime Ministers, Ministers, heads of central agencies and other officials for their individual examination. Their comments and suggestions were taken into account for the improvement of the draft which had been prepared.

WHEREAS: The draft version of the Family Code was submitted for broad and far-reaching discussion by all the people through the Committees for the Defense of the Revolution, Central Organization of Cuban Trade Unions, Federation of Cuban Women, National Association of Small Farmers, Federa-tion of University Students of Cuba, Federation of Students of Intermediate Education and a number of state and social agencies and was approved in full and section by section by a majority of more than 98 per cent of those who participated in the meetings and assemblies held for this purpose.

WHEREAS: In spite of the general approval, the Secretariat of the Law Study Commission carefully studied each and every one of the more than 4000 observations which were made regarding 121 of the 166 articles and, regardless of the number of those who voted for them, accepted and included in the final version all suggestions which it felt were rational and useful for the goals of the proposed legislation.

THEREFORE: By virtue of the powers vested in it the Council of Ministers has resolved to enact the following

LAW NO. 1289

FAMILY CODE
PRELIMINARY TITLE:
ON THE OBJECTIVES OF THIS CODE

ARTICLE   This Code regulates judicially the institutions of the family—marriage, divorce, parent-child relations, obligation to provide alimony, adop-tion and tutelage—with the main objectives of contributing to:

—the strengthening of the family and of the ties of affection and reciprocal respect between its members;

—the strengthening of legally formalized or judicially recognized marriage, based on absolute equality of rights between men and women;

—the most effective fulfillment by parents of their obligations regarding the protection, moral upbringing and education of their children so they can develop fully in every field as worthy citizens of a socialist society;

—the absolute fulfillment of the principle of equality of all children.

CHAPTER II:
RELATIONS BETWEEN HUSBAND AND WIFE

Section One:
Rights and Duties between Husband and Wife

ARTICLE 24 Marriage is established with equal rights and duties for both partners.

ARTICLE 25 Partners must live together, be loyal, considerate, respectful and mutually helpful to each other.

The rights and duties that this Code establishes for partners will remain in effect as long as the marriage is not legally terminated, even if the partners do not live together for any well-founded reason.

ARTICLE 26 Both partners must care for the family they have created and each must cooperate with the other in the education, upbringing and guidance of the children according to the principles of socialist morality. They must participate, to the extent of their capacity or possibilities, in the running of the home, and cooperate so that it will develop in the best possible way.

ARTICLE 27 The partners must help meet the needs of the family they have created with their marriage, each according to his or her ability and financial status. However, if one of them only contributes by working at home and caring for the children, the other partner must contribute to this support alone, without prejudice to his duty of cooperating in the above-mentioned work and care.

ARTICLE 28 Both partners have the right to practice their profession or skill and they have the duty of helping each other and cooperating in order to make this possible and to study or improve their knowledge. However, they must always see to it that home life is organized in such a way that these activities are coordinated with their fulfillment of the obligations posed by this Code.

Section Two:
The Economic Basis of Matrimony

ARTICLE 29 The economic basis of matrimony will be joint property of goods as contemplated in this Code.

This will prevail from the moment a marriage is formalized or from the date a union is initiated in the cases covered by Article 19 and it will cease when the marriage is terminated for any reason.

ARTICLE 30 In line with the bases mentioned in the above article, the following will be considered joint property:

1 the salaries or wages, retirement pensions, benefits and other pensions or other income obtained by one or both partners during the marriage as a result of work done or from the social security fund;

2 The goods and the rights acquired by virtue of a purchase made during the marriage with common funds, regardless of whether the purchased item is for joint use or for one of the partners;

3 the benefits, rents or interests received or acquired during the marriage

from goods or items which are considered joint property or those which are the individual property of either partner. . . .

Section Three:
Responsibilities and Obligations
Involved in Joint Property of Goods

ARTICLE 33   The joint property of goods will involve the following responsibilities:

1 support of the family and meeting of the expenses resulting from the education and upbringing of children of both or one of the partners;
2 all debts and obligations arising during the marriage which were taken on and assumed by either partner, except in the cases when the consent of both was required to assume them;
3 the rent or interests derived during the marriage from the obligations to which the goods which were the property of the individual partners and those which are joint property are subject;
4 minor repair work or upkeep of individual property during the marriage. . . .

CHAPTER III:
TERMINATION OF MARRIAGE

. . . Section Four: Divorce

ARTICLE 49   Divorce will result in the dissolution of the matrimonial ties and all the other effects mentioned in this section.

ARTICLE 50   Divorce can only be obtained by means of a judicial decree.

ARTICLE 51   Divorce will take effect by common agreement or when the court determines that there are factors which have led the marriage to lose its meaning for the partners and for the children and, thus, for society as a whole.

ARTICLE 52   For the purposes of this law it is understood that marriage loses its meaning for the partners and for the children and, thus, for society as a whole when there are causes which create an objective situation in which the marriage is no longer, or cannot be in the future, the union of a man and a woman in a manner adequate to exercise the rights, fulfill the obligations and obtain the objectives mentioned in Articles 24–28 inclusive.

ARTICLE 53   Either one of the partners can take action to obtain a divorce. . . .

ARTICLE 56   If the partners have lived together for more than a year or if children have been born during their marriage, the court, when handing down the decree of divorce, will grant an alimony for one of them in the following cases:

1 the partner who does not have a paying job and lacks other means of support. This will be temporary and it will be paid by the other partner for six months if there are no minor children in his or her care and guardianship, or for a year if there are, so the beneficiary can obtain a paying job;

2 the partner who because of age, disability, illness or other insurmountable obstacle is unable to work and lacks other means of support. In this case the alimony will continue as long as the obstacle exists.

ARTICLE 57   In the decree of divorce the court will grant *patria potestas*, establishing as a rule that both parents shall retain it over their minors.

However, the court may grant it to the parent whom it feels should have it, when this is required by the interests of the minors, outlining the reasons why one or the other is deprived of it.

Likewise, the court may determine, outlining its basis for doing so, the negation of *patria potestas* to both parents when this is necessary for the interests of the children, in which case the children will be placed under tutelage.

ARTICLE 58   In the decree of divorce the court must determine which of the parents will have guardianship and care over the children born during the marriage and will take the necessary measures so the children can maintain adequate communication with the parent that is not entrusted with their guardianship and care.

For the purpose of the provisions in the previous paragraphs, the court will be guided by the rules established in Articles 88, 89, and 90.

ARTICLE 59   Support of minors is a duty of both parents even if they do not have *patria potestas* over them or even if the children are not under their guardianship and care or even if they are enrolled in an educational institution. In accordance with this norm, the court, in its decree of divorce, will set the amount of alimony to be paid by the parent who does not have the minors under his or her guardianship and care.

ARTICLE 60   The amount of alimony for minors will be determined by their normal expenses and the income of the parents, in order to determine the responsibility of the latter in a proportionate manner. . . .

TITLE I: MARRIAGE
CHAPTER I: MARRIAGE IN GENERAL

Section One:
Marriage and Its Establishment

ARTICLE 2   Marriage is the voluntarily established union between a man and a woman who are legally fit to do so, in order to live together. Marriage will have a legal effect only when it is formalized or recognized in keeping with the rules established in this Code.

ARTICLE 3   Women and men who are more than 18 years old are authorized to marry. Those who are less than 18 years old are not.

In spite of the contents of the above paragraph, under exceptional circumstances and for justified reasons the parents or other relatives in lieu of them, or in other cases, the court, can grant permission to those who are under 18 to formalize their marriage, as long as the girl is at least 14 and the boy at least 16 years old. . . .

ARTICLE 6   Once their marriage is ended for any reason, either of the partners has the right to formalize a new marriage anytime afterward.

However, in order to facilitate a determination of paternity, the woman whose marriage has ended and is going to formalize a new one within the next 300 days, must prove by means of a medical certificate, provided by a state medical institution, whether or not she is pregnant.

If the certificate indicates she is pregnant, the paternity of the partner in the previous marriage will be assumed. All types of legally admissible evidence can be presented to counter this assumption. If the woman has given birth before the aforementioned 300 days no certificate will be required for the formalization of a new marriage. . . .

TITLE II:
RELATIONS BETWEEN PARENTS AND CHILDREN

CHAPTER I:
RECOGNITION OF PATERNITY

Section One:
Recognition and Registration

ARTICLE 65   All children are equal and they have equal rights and duties with regard to their parents, regardless of the latter's civil status.

ARTICLE 66   In the case of a formalized or judicially recognized marriage, the registration of the birth of a child in the Civil Register by one of the parents will have legal standing with respect to both.

ARTICLE 67   The registration of the birth of a child and the recognition of paternity by parents who are not married must be done by both, either together or separately.

ARTICLE 68   In the case of the previous article, when only the mother seeks to have the birth of a child registered and she states the name of the father, he will be summoned to appear before the head of the Civil Register and notified that if he does not appear within 30 days to accept or deny paternity the child will be registered as his. Following this period and if there is no challenge to the paternity, the registration will become binding and once this has been done the challenge can only be carried out by means of the corresponding procedure, within a year.

If there is a denial of paternity the child will be registered without mentioning the name of the father, the latter may recognize paternity at a later date, provided the mother agrees. If not, they must proceed in the manner outlined in the final paragraph of the previous article.

ARTICLE 69   When the mother appears to have the child registered without mentioning the name of the father, the latter may recognize paternity at a later date, provided the mother agrees. If not, they must proceed in the manner outlined in the final paragraph of the previous article. . . .

ARTICLE 73   The first last name of the children will be that of the father and the second last name the first last name of the mother.

If the name of only one parent appears on the birth certificate of a child born outside of the framework of the situation described in Article 66, he will have the last names of that parent or repeat the last name in case of one last name only. . . .

CHAPTER II:
RELATIONSHIP BETWEEN PARENTS AND CHILDREN

Section One:
Patria Potestas and Its Exercise

ARTICLE 82   Minors are under the *patria potestas* of their parents.

ARTICLE 83   The exercise of *patria potestas* corresponds jointly to both parents.

It will correspond solely to one of them as a result of the death of the other or as a result of suspension or deprivation of its exercise.

ARTICLE 84   The children are obliged to respect, show consideration for and help their parents and to obey them while under their *patria potestas*.

ARTICLE 85   *Patria potestas* entails the following rights· and duties of the parents:

1 Keeping the children under their guardianship and care; making every possible effort to provide them with a stable home and adequate nourishment; caring for their health and personal hygiene; providing them with the means of recreation fitting their age which are within their possibilities; giving them the proper protection; seeing to their good behavior and cooperating with the authorities in order to overcome any situation or environmental factor that may have an unfavorable effect on their training and development;

2 Seeing to the education of their children; inculcating them with the love for learning; seeing to it that they attend school; seeing to their adequate technical, scientific and cultural improvement in keeping with their aptitude and vocation and the demands posed by the country's development; and collaborating with the educational authorities in school programs and activities;

3 Training their children to be useful citizens; inculcating them with the love for their country, respect for the country's symbols and their country's values, the spirit of internationalism, the standards of coexistence, and socialist morality; respect for social property and the property and personal rights of others;

arousing the respect of their children by their attitude toward them; and teaching them to respect the authorities, their teachers and every other person;

4 Administering and caring for their children's property; seeing to it that their children use and enjoy in a proper manner whatever property they have; and not to sell, exchange or give any such property except in the interest of the children and pursuant to the requisites of this Code;

5 Representing their children in every judicial action or arrangement in which they are involved; giving their authorization in those cases where full capacity for taking action is required; and taking action opportunely and in due fashion to defend the children's interests and property.

ARTICLE 86   The parents are invested with the authority to reprimand and set straight adequately and moderately those children under their *patria potestas*.. . . .

Section Two:
Guardianship and Care and Communication
between Parents and Children

. . . ARTICLE 89.—In case there is no arrangement or the arrangement is detrimental to the material or moral interests of the children, the question will be settled by the competent court, which will decide on the basis of what is more beneficial to the minors. Under equal conditions, the court will generally decide that the children be left under the care of the parent in whose company they have been until the disagreement arose. Preference is given to the mother in the case that the children lived with both father and mother, unless special reasons make another solution advisable. . . .

RADICAL FEMINISM

Marriage

Sheila Cronan

Marriage has been a subject which has generated considerable controversy in the Women's Movement. So far as I know, no group other than The Feminists has publicly taken a stand against marriage, although I'm sure it has been a topic of discussion in most. . . .

The Feminists decided to examine the institution of marriage as it is set up by law in order to find out whether or not it did operate in women's favor. It became increasingly clear to us that the institution of marriage "protects" women in the same way that the institution of slavery was said to "protect" blacks—that is, that the word "protection" in this case is simply a euphemism for oppression.

We discovered that women are not aware of what marriage is really about. We are given the impression that love is the purpose of marriage—after all, in the ceremony, the wife promises to "love, honor, and cherish" her husband and the husband promises to "love, honor, and protect" his wife. This promise, which women believe to be central to the marriage contract, is viewed as irrelevant by the courts. For example, in a well-known case here in New York State, a woman attempted to obtain an annulment on the grounds that her husband had told her that he loved her prior to the marriage and then afterward admitted that he did not and never would. This was held *not* to give grounds for annulment,[1] despite the fact that the man committed fraud, which is normally grounds for nullifying any contract.

There is nothing in most marriage ceremonies specifically referring to sex, yet the courts have held that "the fact that a party agrees to and does enter into the marriage implies a promise to consummate the marriage by cohabitation, so that failure to do so gives grounds for annulment on the basis of fraud in the inducement."[2] An annulment was granted to a New York man on the grounds that his wife was unable to have sex with him due to an incurable nervous condition.[3]

But then, one might ask, how is this particularly oppressive to women? After all, men also enter into marriage with the understanding that love is central. Many of us, in examining our personal histories, however, have suspected that "love" has a different meaning for men than it does for women. This has been substantiated by a study done by a man, Clifford R. Adams of Penn State

---

[1]*Schaeffer v. Schaeffer,* 160 AppDiv 48, 144 NYS 774.
[2]Eugene R. Canudo, *Law of Marriage, Divorce and Adoption* (Gould Publications, 1966), p. 20.
[3]*Hiebink v. Hiebink,* 56 NYS(2) 394, aff'd 269 AppDiv 786, 56 NYS(2) 397.

University, who spent thirty years researching the subconscious factors involved in mate selection, studying 4000 couples. His conclusion was:

> When a man and a woman gaze into each other's eyes with what they think are love and devotion, they are not seeing the same thing. . . . For the woman, the first things she seeks are love, affection, sentiment. She has to feel loved and wanted. The second is security, then companionship, home and family, community acceptance, and sixth, sex. But for the man sex is at the top of the list, not at the bottom. It's second only to companionship. The single category of love-affection-sentiment is *below* sex.[4]

Sex is compulsory in marriage. A husband can legally force his wife to have sexual relations with him against her will, an act which if committed against any other woman would constitute the crime of rape. Under law, "a husband cannot be guilty of raping his own wife by forcing her to have sexual intercourse with him. By definition, the crime [of rape] is ordinarily that of forcing intercourse on someone other than the wife of the person accused."[5] Thus the threat of force is always present even if it is not necessary for the man to exert it—after all, most women are aware of the " 'right' of the husband to insist on and the 'duty' of the wife to 'submit' "[6] to sexual intercourse.

It is clear that the compulsory nature of sex in marriage operates to the advantage of the male. The husband theoretically has the duty to have intercourse with his wife also, but this normally cannot occur against his will. Furthermore, as far as the enjoyment of the sex act is concerned, figures show that men (with the exception of impotent men who generally cannot have sex at all) nearly always experience orgasm when they have sex. Women, however, are not so fortunate. Surveys have shown that:

> fifteen to twenty percent of all [American] married women have never had an orgasm. About fifty percent reach orgasm on a "now and then" basis, meaning that they experience full culmination about one sex act out of three. Thirty to thirty-five percent of American wives say that they "usually" reach orgasm, meaning that they get there two out of three times or thereabouts. Only a very few women can claim that they have an orgasm every time they take part in sexual activities.[7]

Thus sex as practiced in American marriages clearly benefits the male far more than the female. Despite the emphasis that has recently been put on the husband's duty to give pleasure to his wife, this is not happening most of the time, and we all know that intercourse without orgasm is at best a waste of time. From the above figures we see that 70 percent of American wives have this boring and often painful experience over two-thirds of the time.

---

[4]Reported in *Glamour Magazine,* November, 1969, p. 214.

[5]Harriet F. Pilpel and Theodora Zavin, *Your Marriage and the Law* (New York: Collier Books, 1964), p. 215.

[6]*Ibid.,* p. 64.

[7]L. T. Woodward, M. D., *Sophisticated Sex Techniques in Marriage* (New York: Lancer Books, 1967), p. 18.

In Alabama's legal code of 1852 two clauses, standing in significant juxtaposition, recognized the dual character of the slave.

The first clause confirmed his status as property—the right of the owner to his "time, labor and services" and to his obedient compliance with all lawful commands. . . .

The second clause acknowledged the slave's status as a person. The law required that masters be humane to their slaves, furnish them adequate food and clothing, and provide care for them during sickness and in old age. In short, the state endowed masters with obligations as well as rights and assumed some responsibility for the welfare of the bondsmen.[8]

The following is a description of marital responsibilities:

The legal responsibilities of a wife are to live in the home established by her husband; to perform the domestic chores (cleaning, cooking, washing, etc.) necessary to help maintain that home; to care for her husband and children.

The legal responsibilities of a husband are to provide a home for his wife and children; to support, protect and maintain his wife and children.[9]

The word "slave" is usually defined as a person owned by another and forced to work without pay for, and obey, the owner. Although wives are not bought and sold openly, I intend to show that marriage is a form of slavery. We are told that marriage is an equitable arrangement entered into freely by both husband and wife. We have seen above that this is not true with regard to the sexual aspect of marriage—that in this respect marriage is clearly set up to benefit the male. It also is not true with regard to the rest of the marital responsibilities.

Women believe that they are voluntarily giving their household services, whereas the courts hold that the husband is legally entitled to his wife's domestic services and, further, that she *cannot be paid* for her work.

As part of the rights of consortium, the husband is entitled to the services of his wife. If the wife works outside the home for strangers she is usually entitled to her own earnings. But domestic services or assistances which she gives the husband are generally considered part of her wifely duties. The wife's services and society are so essential a part of what the law considers the husband is entitled to as part of the marriage that it will not recognize any agreement between the spouses which provides that the husband is to pay for such services or society. In a Texas case David promised his wife, Fannie, that he would give her $5000 if she would stay with him while he lived and continue taking care of his house and farm accounts, selling his butter and doing all the other tasks which she had done since their marriage. After David's death, Fannie sued his estate for the money which had been promised her. The court held that the contract was unenforceable since Fannie had agreed to do nothing which she was not already legally and morally bound to do as David's wife.[10]

---

[8]Kenneth M. Stampp, *The Peculiar Institution* (New York: Vintage Books, 1956), p. 192.

[9]Richard T. Gallen, *Wives' Legal Rights* (New York: Dell Publishing Co., 1967), pp. 4–5.

[10]Pilpel and Zavin, *op. cit.,* p. 65. For a New York case similar to the Texas one cited, see *Garlock v. Garlock,* 279 NY 337.

Whereas the legal responsibilities of the wife include providing all necessary domestic services—that is, maintaining the home (cleaning, cooking, washing, purchasing food and other necessities, etc.), providing for her husband's personal needs and taking care of the children—the husband in return is obligated only to provide her with basic maintenance—that is, bed and board. Were he to employ a live-in servant in place of a wife, he would have to pay the servant a salary, provide her with her own room (as opposed to "bed"), food, and the necessary equipment for doing her job. She would get at least one day a week off and probably would be required to do considerably less work than a wife and would normally not be required to provide sexual services.

Thus, being a wife is a full-time job for which one is not entitled to pay. Does this not constitute slavery? Furthermore, slavery implies a lack of freedom of movement, a condition which also exists in marriage. The husband has the right to decide where the couple will live. If he decides to move, his wife is obligated to go with him. If she refuses, he can charge her with desertion. This has been held up by the courts even in certain cases where the wife would be required to change her citizenship.[11] In states where desertion is grounds for divorce (forty-seven states plus the District of Columbia), the wife would be the "guilty party" and would therefore be entitled to no monetary settlement.

The enslavement of women in marriage is all the more cruel and inhumane by virtue of the fact that it appears to exist with the consent of the enslaved group. Part of the explanation for this phenomenon lies in the fact that marriage has existed for so many thousands of years—the female role has been internalized in so many successive generations. If people are forced into line long enough, they will begin to believe in their own inferiority and to accept as natural the role created for them by their oppressor. Furthermore, the society has been so structured that there is no real alternative to marriage for women. Employment discrimination, social stigma, fear of attack, sexual exploitation are only a few of the factors that make it nearly impossible for women to live as single people. Furthermore, women are deceived as to what the nature of marriage really is. We have already seen how we are made to believe that it is in our interest. Also, marriage is so effectively disguised in glowing, romantic terms that young girls rush into it excitedly, only to discover too late what the real terms of the marriage contract are.

The marriage contract is the only important legal contract in which the terms are not listed. It is in fact a farce created to give women the illusion that they are consenting to a mutually beneficial relationship when in fact they are signing themselves into slavery. . . .

While wives are "owned" by their husbands in the same sense that slaves are owned by their masters—that is, that the master is entitled to free use of the slave's labor, to deny the slave his human right to freedom of movement and control over his own body—the scarcity of slaves resulted in their monetary value. Any man can take a wife and although he is legally required to support

[11]Gallen, *op. cit.*, p. 6.

her, there is very little anyone can do if he is unable to fulfill this responsibility. Thus many women are forced to work outside the home because their husbands are unemployed or are not making enough money to support the family. This in no way absolves us from our domestic and child care duties, however.[12]

Since marriage constitutes slavery for women, it is clear that the Women's Movement must concentrate on attacking this institution. Freedom for women cannot be won without the abolition of marriage. Attack on such issues as employment discrimination is superfluous; as long as women are working for nothing in the home we cannot expect our demands for equal pay outside the home to be taken seriously.

Furthermore, marriage is the model for all other forms of discrimination against women. The relationships between men and women outside of marriage follow this basic pattern. Although the law does not officially sanction the right of a man to force his sweetheart to have sex with him, she would find it very difficult to prove rape in the courts, especially if they have had a regular sexual relationship. Also, it is not unusual for a man to expect his girl friend to type his term papers, iron his shirts, cook dinner for him, and even clean his apartment. This oppressive relationship carries over into employment and is especially evident in the role of the secretary, also known as the "office wife."

One of the arguments in the Movement against our attacking marriage has been that most women are married. This has always seemed strange to me as it is like saying we should not come out against oppression since all women are oppressed. Clearly, of all the oppressive institutions, marriage is the one that affects the most women. It is logical, then, that if we are interested in building a mass movement of women, this is where we should begin.

Another argument against attacking marriage has been that it is dying out anyway. The evidence cited for this is usually the growing rate of divorce. But the high rate of remarriage among divorced persons shows that divorce is not evidence for the decline of marriage. We have seen that divorce is in fact a further abuse so far as women's interests are concerned. And the fact is that marriage rates have been on the increase. From 1900 to 1940 approximately one half of all American women over twenty years of age were married at any given time. After 1940 the figure began to rise noticeably; by 1960 it had reached the rate of two-thirds of all women over twenty.[13]

The Women's Movement must address itself to the marriage issue from still another point of view. The marriage relationship is so physically and emotionally draining for women that we must extricate ourselves if for no other reason than to have the time and energy to devote ourselves to building a feminist revolution.

The Feminists have begun to work on the issue of marriage. It is only a beginning, however; all women must join us in this fight.

[12]Gallen, *op. cit.*, p. 7.
[13]*American Women: Report of the President's Commission on the Status of Women*, 1963, p. 6.

Female Friendship[1]

Janice Raymond

Virginia Woolf tells us how she searched for a tradition of female friendship in literature—". . . those unsaid or half-said words, which form themselves, no more palpably than the shadows of moths on the ceiling, when women are alone, unlit by the capricious and coloured light of the other sex."[2] In the midst of this search, Woolf found meagre evidence that "Chloe liked Olivia," i.e., that women are drawn to women. However, the evidence is deceiving.

Women have been friends for millennia. Women have been each other's best friends, relatives, stable companions, emotional and economic supporters, and faithful lovers. But this tradition of female friendship, like much else in women's lives, has been distorted, dismantled, destroyed—in summary, to use Mary Daly's term, *dismembered*.[3] The dismembering of female friendship is initially the dismembering of the woman-identified Self.[4] The lack of Self-love is grafted onto the female self under patriarchy. Women who do not love their Selves cannot love others like their Selves. . . .

I do not wish to romanticize the subject of female friendship. In a woman-hating society, female friendship has been tabooed to the extent that there are women who hate their Selves and other women, or who, at best, are indifferent to women. The obstacles to female friendship have taken solid root in their lives, and it is they who believe and act out the fiction that women never have been nor ever can be friends. This book does not pretend that all women can be friends. . . .

All kinds of women have been/are friends in spite of this primordial patriarchal taboo against female friendship and the enormous pressures put on women to exist for men. There are women who have been/are *for* women. Women must learn to identify such women. Women must also learn to identify their friends. This is a process that is not realized by anything as simple as the wearing of an identification card. . . .

A central premise of my book is that buried deep in the past, present, and future of female Be-ing, there is an original and primary attraction of women for women, manifested by many different women in many different ways. Women who have manifested, and who do manifest this affection for women, initially care about their Selves and thus do not denigrate others like their Selves. . . .

---

[1]This article is excerpted from the introduction to the forthcoming book *Geneology of Female Friendship*. A longer version was published in the first issue of *Trivia*, pp. 5–26.

[2]Virgina Woolf, *A Room of One's Own* (New York: Harcourt, Brace & World, 1929), p. 88.

[3]Daly uses this term in *Gyn/Ecology: The Metaethics of Radical Feminism* (Boston: Beacon Press, 1978) to indicate the way in which women have been deprived of our history and traditions, and encouraged to forget by "patriarchal erasure of our tradition." As the female body has been dismembered, so too has women's memory of our heritage.

[4]Again I use Mary Daly's device of capitalizing *Self* to distinguish between the man-made feminine self, "the imposed/internalized false 'self'" of women, and the authentic Self which women are re-creating.

GYN/AFFECTION, HETERO-RELATIONS, AND LESBIANISM

There are certain words that will recur throughout my work. The most frequent one is *Gyn/affection*. Generally, Gyn/affection can be defined as woman-to-woman attraction, influence, and movement. In many ways, Gyn/affection is a synonym for female friendship. The word Gyn/affection, however, has a meaning context of its own which helps to elucidate how I am using the term *female friendship* throughout this book. Dictionary definitions of *affection* and *affect* shed further light on the meaning of Gyn/affection.

The more commonly understood meaning of affection is a feeling, emotion, fondness, attachment, and love for another. In this sense, Gyn/affection connotes the passion that women feel for women, i.e., the experience of profound attraction for, and movement toward, the original female Self and toward other women. There is another meaning to affection, however, which conveys more than the personal movement of one woman towards another. Affection in this sense means the state of influencing, acting upon, moving, and impressing; and of being influenced, acted upon, moved, and impressed by other women. Virginia Woolf expressed this in saying, "Only women stir my imagination." She might have added, "Only women stir me to action and power."

Women who *affect* women stimulate response and action; bring about a change in living; stir and arouse emotion, ideas, and activities that defy dichotomies between the personal and political aspects of affection. Thus Gyn/affection means personal and political movement of women toward each other. . . .

While it is true that certain kinds of political activity are and have to be possible between persons who are not friends, both politics and friendship are restored to a deeper meaning when they are brought together; i.e., when political activity proceeds from a shared affection, vision, and spirit, and when friendship has a more expansive political effect. I maintain that we need to create a feminist politics based on friendship. And we need an ideal of friendship that is realized in investing women with personal and socio-economic power. A genuine friendship goes beyond the world of the Self's *relations* with other Selves to the society in which the female is allowed to grow. . . .

Many Lesbian feminists have pointed to heterosexism as the paradigmatic model for the oppression of women in a patriarchal society. While I agree that we are living in a heterosexist society, I think the wider problem is that we live in a hetero-relational society where all of women's personal, social, political, professional, and economic relations are defined by the ideology that woman is for man. Hetero-relations names more accurately, in my opinion, the ways in which Gyn/affection gets obscured and eclipsed, even for women who are lesbians. For example, there are lesbians who perceive the world and live in it according to hetero-relations; i.e., they are in constant intercourse with men, identifying with male-defined ideologies and with individual men, in order to succeed professionally, to move ahead politically, or simply to feel that they are normal. Some women restrict their Gyn/affection to sexual relationships with women, or they rigidly separate their private existence from their public or professional lives in ways that lack integrity. In a society where women are governed by hetero-relations, Gyn/affection can be and has been confined to the bedroom, or to other private worlds that do not impinge upon the dominant hetero-relational ethos. . . .

The imperative of female friendship is that women be equal to their Selves, equal to the women who have gone before them, and equal to the task of creating a woman-centered existence. This is one of the more important distinctions between radical feminism and liberal and Marxist feminisms: their starting points. The former starts "among the women." The latter begins among and with the men, i.e., in tangential relation to men as a group, whether they be men as oppressors or men as oppressed "brothers." Both brands of feminism investigate and locate women mainly in relation to male persons, history and culture.

The question might be asked, at this point, whether the term Gyn/affection is equated with Lesbianism, the Lesbianism that Mary Daly has purposefully spelled with a capital "L"?[5] If Gyn/affection embraces the totality of a woman's existence with and for her Self and other women, if Gyn/affection means putting one's original Self and other women first, and if Gyn/affection is movement toward other women, then one would expect that women who are Gyn/affectionate and Gyn/affective would be Lesbians. Yet there are different ways in which women acknowledge and live out female friendship. I do not wish to simplify these differences nor to restrict the reality of Gyn/affection to Lesbian Be-ing. While respecting these differences, however, I do not pretend to understand all of them. In particular, I do not understand why Gyn/affection does not translate into Lesbian love for many women. However, my use of the term *Gyn/affection* is expressive of a *continuum of female friendship*. The distinction between Lesbian friendship and Gyn/affection is often not easy to make, but obviously it has been made in the lives of some women. . . .

While my Lesbian feminist sensibility wants to affirm any woman's woman-identified existence and affection for other women as Lesbian, my philosophical and ethical faculties say otherwise.[6] Philosophically, I have the gnawing intuition that this affirmation is logically incorrect, morally shortchanging to women who are Lesbians, and unintentionally patronizing to women who are not Lesbians. . . .

While many Lesbian feminists may wish to include women who live a Gyn/affective and Gyn/affectionate existence as Lesbian, many of these women would not wish to be described as such. I do not think that, in all cases, Lesbian feminists can regard this as Lesbophobia. We must assume that some female friends know and live their own truth and have consciously chosen their own

[5]Daly capitalizes *Lesbian* when the word is used in a woman-identified sense and leaves it in the lower case when it describes women who, although they relate genitally to women, are governed by what I would call hereto-relational standards.

[6]Only a short while ago, I devised the phrase *Lesbian continuun* to describe the woman-identified relationships that Rich, Smith, and Cook describe. In my view, at that time, friendship that was on a Lesbian continuum was imbued with Lesbian meaning, as characterized by the above writers. Now, however, I would prefer to use Gyn/affection and think it more adequately describes all of the complexities involved.

paths. To do otherwise is both patronizing and pretentious—patronizing to women who have consciously chosen men in some ways, no matter how much some of us may disagree with that choice; pretentious in the sense of claiming to know these women better than they know themselves. Some women have viewed with honesty the layers of hetero-relational coercion in their own lives. Nonetheless, they still choose to relate sexually with men. Those choices must be credited with some integrity.

Yet, of course, the question becomes how many women who remain in certain central hetero-relational contexts, most notably heterosexual relationships, do so with clarity of mind, moral integrity, honest scrutiny of hetero-relational coercion, and with Gyn/affection. Marilyn Frye has spoken most pointedly to these questions.

> Millions of heterosexual women give no thought to what heterosexuality is or why they are heterosexual . . . they do not perceive heterosexuality as an option. . . . But well-educated, worldly, politically astute, thoughtful, analytical, feminist women do know perfectly well that there are options, and that Lesbian life is an option that coheres very well with feminist politics. They do choose to be heterosexual.[7]

For Frye, "Respect for that choice (on my part, and on their part) demands that they make that choice intelligible."[8] Just as Lesbian feminists have struggled long and hard to make the choice of Lesbian feminism lucid, heterosexual feminists must show "that their choice can be understood as a *reasonable choice*."[9]

Thus the word Lesbian, in this work, connotes a knowledge of and will to affirm Lesbian living. Many women do not have this Self-clarity and/or active will to live Lesbian lives (including some lesbians). However, they may move in the world of female friendship, and their affinity and struggles for women may be often characterized by intense Gyn/affection. To use the word *Lesbian*, in these cases, is false inclusion. Women who are Lesbian must have a history of perceiving them Selves as such, and the will to assume responsibility for Lesbian acts, erotic and political.

The use of the term *Gyn/affection* throughout this work is an attempt to be logical, honest, and truly inclusive of all women who put each other first in some or in all ways. It is meant to include Lesbians as well as women who, while they are intensely Gyn/affectionate, would not define themselves as Lesbians. Gyn/affection is intended to make honest and honorable distinctions, while at the same time avoiding a simplistic and sentimental inclusiveness. At the same time, my use of the words *Gyn/Affection* and *female friendship* is intended to affirm the vast range, the degrees, and the manifestations of Gyn/affection. In a woman-hating society, the whole range of female friendships and Gyn/affective acts is taboo. More is encoded in this taboo than the male fear of Lesbian

---

[7]Marilyn Frye, "Assignment—Bloomington—1980: Speak on 'Lesbian Perspectives on Women's Studies,'" *Sinister Wisdom* 14 (1980): 6.

[8]Idem.

[9]Ibid., p. 7.

sexuality and eroticism. The ultimate fear that men have, in my opinion, is the threat posed by all dimensions, degrees, and manifestations of women's personal and political movement toward and for each other. . . .

THE "STATE OF ATROCITY" AND THE STATE OF FEMALE FRIENDSHIP

. . . There is pressure in some feminist and particularly in supposedly "liberated" circles to talk cautiously about an independent sphere of female friendship. Some see it as escapist, or as romanticizing a separatism in which women are encouraged to forget the "real world" and go off by themselves, thereby creating a ghetto that is marginal to the "real world." The assertion that men and women do not necessarily belong together strikes many as unenlightened, reactionary, and not furthering "the cause of women"—the "cause of women" being defined as the equality of women with men and the bringing together of women and men. By my standards of female friendship, the "cause of women" is defined first as the bringing together of women by and for our Selves. Self-centering is a necessary political act.

Unless Gyn/affection becomes an intrinsic part of the feminist "political platform," feminism will not fulfill its most basic goals of obliterating the mechanics, institutions, and effects of female colonization in all its forms. The destruction of these systems of oppression and the evolution of female friendship go together. *The political is personal.* Emphasis on the political aspects of feminism expressed in the early adage "The personal is political," has kept many from recognizing that a complete feminist vision must also turn these words around. A purely political definition of the word feminist accenting oppression, struggle, conflict, and resistance is circumscribed and limited. It is as absurd as the Marxist interpretation of the person primarily as worker.

Complete or sustained emphasis on female oppression, or the "State of Atrocity," can have the unintended effect of making the female experience or situation synonymous with the colonization experience. *Feminist* must mean something different—not only women in struggle and conflict with men and male supremacy, but women in concert with our Selves and each other. Feminists must also be defined by the reality of female friendship in our lives. As feminists, women must be for each other. Female friendship gives depth and spirit to a political vision of feminism and is itself a profoundly political act. Without Gyn/affection, our politics and political struggles remain superficial for a limited period of time and only on levels which do not really shake the foundations of patriarchy. When women assert their power of absence to all forms of hetero-relations, we assert a power of presence to our Selves. This is indeed power and powerful.

VISION

Women also need a *vision* of female friendship that conjures up the possibilities of realization in women's lives. "Without vision the people perish." . . .

Vision . . . constitutes a form of "seeing." Perception, of course, depends in large measure on where the viewer stands, in what currents she moves, and with whom she stands and moves. Vision is both descriptive, in terms of recognizing what is, and imaginative, in the sense of perceiving what might be. The two senses of vision must go together. A woman's grasp of "reality," on the boundary of a woman-hating culture, can become tenuous if she does not have some vision of how things can be different, and if there is not, ultimately, some realization of visionary possiblities in her own life. On the other hand, one's vision of the future can become escapist if one does not move and act in the "real" world, which the feminist searcher soon learns is the "unreal" world that men have fabricated. She can only move and act in this world by focusing her anger in the right direction and creatively raging against all states of female atrocities. But it is imperative that she move and act in this world. Vision seeks to illuminate and make us wiser about political reality, change, and action. And vision is also an important means of effecting change and transcending our man-made history. . . .

My vision of female friendship is spiritual and religious, in spite of the debasement of these realities by patriarchal religions and spiritual movements. For men, Gyn/affection raises questions of "ultimate concern" or meaning for women. It is therefore, in part, a religious quest which goes beyond religion's identification with God, gods, or religious organizations. A vision of female friendship is religious in the most basic sense of being derived from its accepted Latin root, *religare,* meaning "to tie" or "to link." As one author has commented: "Its [religion's] role in human life is not to *add* something but to *unify* and to *direct* what is already there. The religious drive is . . . the contextual drive, as it were, manifested in all the others, the comprehensive drive through which they are related."[10]

It is in this sense that I am calling a vision of female friendship religious or spiritual. For I maintain that Gyn/affection has the power to help tie women's lives together, to make connections that have not been made, and to provide a unifying and directing influence in all other areas of female existence in this world. Female friendship should create a network of meaning that transcends women's past, our ordinary lives, and our present. The reality of Gyn/affection begins a journey into an "Otherworld" that, as Mary Daly has described it, is "both discovery and creation of a world other than patriarchy."[11]

It is the perception of female friendship as "Otherworld Journey," as "more than," which also imbues it with religious meaning. The transcendent possibilities of female friendship may be viewed as illusion or as "really real" depending upon whether one transforms question into answer, absence into presence. This vision of Gyn/affection sees female friendship as having revelatory power and as a realization of transcendence which creates for women ever-new possibilities of infinite Be-ing. For many women, what female friendship bestows is the promise and presence of ultimate Be-ing.. . . .

[10]Michael Novak, *Ascent of the Mountain, Flight of the Dove* (New York: Harper & Row, 1971), p. 5.

[11]Daly, *Gyn/Ecology,* p. 1.

SOCIALIST FEMINISM

A Look at the Cuban Family Code

Jane Flax

The Cuban family code was drafted in July 1974. Following extensive discussion throughout the country, the Code was adopted March 8, 1975. The Cubans view the Code as the beginning of a prolonged attack on both sexist attitudes and women's "second shift," i.e., complete responsibility for domestic labor as well as work outside the home. The Code is historically important as one strategy for ending sexism under socialism. It has been praised by many outside Cuba as an exemplary piece of socialist legislation.

As feminists who operate in a different historical context and situation, we must be careful to evaluate the Code in terms of our own needs and principles. The Code raises rather than resolves one of the most difficult issues for feminist theory: the role of the heterosexual family and its place in a liberated society. The Cuban Code explicitly identifies the heterosexual family as the "elementary cell" of society and as the "center for relations of common existence between men and women and between them and their children and between all of them with their relatives."

The Code involves the state, especially the judiciary, in the regulation of marriage, divorce, alimony and child custody and institutionalizes a preference for "judicially recognized" marriages. The family will be supported and strengthened by the state and is recognized as *the* social unit for the satisfaction of "deep rooted human needs in the social field and in the field of affection for the individual." Within the family the absolute equality of the partners is stressed as is their equal responsibility for the satisfaction of all the needs of the family. Family responsibilities should not hinder either partner in the pursuit of her/his skill or profession, but neither should family life suffer as a result of these pursuits.

While these principles are important to the development of equal relations between men and women, many important questions of concern to feminists outside Cuba remain unresolved. The state supported bias towards heterosexuality is extremely troubling. Can patriarchy be completely eliminated without an attack on the channeling of sexuality in exclusively heterosexual directions? What happens to persons whose deeply rooted social needs can only be met by relations with someone of the same sex? Feminists have traced strong connections between the suppression and control of sexuality and the existence of authoritarian social patterns. These connections need to be considered as we conceptualize our ideal social organization.

We must also evaluate the bias towards the family as the center of child development and "domestic" labor and the involvement of the state in legitimating and regulating relations between men and women, parents and children. The nuclear family structure may result in certain forms of psychological development, forms which may preclude full development of individual capacities and true sociability—or it may be essential to such development. Without experimentation with a wide range of forms this central question can never be resolved. Furthermore, we must consider what types of socially necessary labor now performed in the family (cooking, childcare, etc.) should remain there.

While we need means of insuring responsibility between adults and between adults and children, it is not clear that granting the state a monopoly on regulating and legitimating these relations is the solution. Perhaps the feminist ideal will look more like the combination of responsibility and fluidity suggested by Marge Piercy in *Woman on the Edge of Time*.

These issues, while central to feminism, are far from settled. We should learn from the examples of others, but the hard work still lies before us: to develop a feminist theory and practice adequate to our own historical situation, needs and visions. The Cuban family code is an important document for feminists to study, but it should be analyzed with these questions and concerns in mind. . . .

The Family as the Locus of Gender, Class, and Political Struggle: The Example of Housework[1]

Heidi I. Hartmann

Although the last decade of research on families has contributed enormously to our understanding of diversity in family structures and the relationship of family units to various other aspects of social life, it has, it seems to me, generally failed to identify and address sources of conflict within family life. Thus, the usefulness of this research for understanding women's situation has been particularly limited. The persistence and resilience of family forms in the midst of general social change, often forcefully documented in this research, have certainly helped to goad us, as feminists, to consider what women's interests may be in the maintenance of a type of family life that we have often viewed as a primary source of women's oppression. Historical, anthropological, and sociological studies of families have pointed to the many ways in which women and men have

[1]The first draft of this paper was presented at the Rockefeller Foundation Conference on Women, Work, and the Family (New York, September 21–22, 1978), organized by Catherine Stimpson and Tamara Hareven. Many people besides myself have labored over this paper. Among them are Rayna Rapp, Elsa Dixter, and Joan Burstyn. Jack Wells, Judy Stacey, Shelly Rosaldo, Evelyn Glenn, and my study group provided particularly careful reading. . . . This is an abridged version of the article as it appeared in *Signs: Journal of Women in Culture and Society*, 6 (Spring 1981): 366–394.

acted in defense of the family unit, despite the uneven responsibilities and rewards of the two sexes in family life. In failing to focus sufficiently clearly on the differences between women's and men's experiences and interests within families, however, these studies overlook important aspects of social reality and potentially decisive sources of change in families and society as people struggle both within and outside families to advance their own interests. This oversight stems, I think, from a basic commitment shared by many conducting these studies to a view of the family as a unified interest group and as an agent of change in its own right. . . .

In this essay I suggest that the underlying concept of the family as an active agent with unified interests is erroneous, and I offer an alternative concept of the family as a locus of *struggle*. In my view, the family cannot be understood solely, or even primarily, as a unit shaped by affect or kinship, but must be seen as a *location* where production and redistribution take place. As such, it is a location where people with different activities and interests in these processes often come into conflict with one another. I do not wish to deny that families also encompass strong emotional ties, are extremely important in our psychic life, and establish ideological norms, but in developing a Marxist-feminist analysis of the family, I wish to identify and explore the material aspects of gender relations within family units.[2] Therefore, I concentrate on the nature of the work people do in the family and their control over the products of their labor.

In a Marxist feminist view, the organization of production both within and outside the family is shaped by patriarchy and capitalism. Our present social structure rests upon unequal division of labor by class and by gender which generates tension, conflict, and change. These underlying patriarchal and capitalist relations among people, rather than familial relations themselves, are the sources of dynamism in our society. The particular forms familial relations take largely reflect these underlying social forces. For example, the redistribution that occurs within the family between wage earners and non-wage earners is necessitated by the division of labor inherent in the patriarchal and capitalist organization of production. In order to provide a schema for understanding the underlying economic structure of the family form prevalent in modern Western society—the heterosexual nuclear family living together in one household—I do not address in this essay the many real differences in the ways people of different periods, regions, races, or ethnic groups structure and experience family life. I limit my focus in order to emphasize the potential for differing rather than harmonious interrelationships among family members, especially between women and men.

---

[2]In distinguishing between the household—the unit in which people actually live—and the family—the concept of the unit in which they think they should live—Rayna Rapp points to the contradictions that develop because of the juxtaposition of economic and ideological norms in the family/household ("Family and Class in Contemporary America: Notes towards an Understanding of Ideology," *Science and Society* 42 [Fall 1978]: 257–77). In addition, see Lila Leibowitz, *Females, Males, Families, a Biosocial Approach* (North Scituate, Mass.: Duxbury Press, 1978), esp. pp. 6–11, for a discussion of how the family defines ties among its members and to kin beyond it.

The first part of this essay explains the family's role as a location for production and redistribution and speculates about the interaction between the family and the state and about changes in family-state relations. The second part uses the example of housework to illustrate the differences in material interests among family members that are caused by their differing relations to patriarchy and capitalism. Since, as I argue, members of families frequently have different interests, it may be misleading to hold, as family historians often do, that "the family" as a unit resists or embraces capitalism, industrialization, or the state. Rather, people—men and/or women, adults and/or children—use familial forms in various ways. While they may use their "familial" connections or kin groups and their locations in families in any number of projects—to find jobs, to build labor unions, to wage community struggles, to buy houses, to borrow cars, or to share child care—they are not acting only as family members but also as members of gender categories with particular relations to the division of labor organized by capitalism and patriarchy.

Yet tensions between households and the world outside them have been documented by family historians and others, and these suggest that households do act as entities with unified interests, set in opposition to other entities. This seeming paradox comes about because, although family members have distinct interests arising out of their relations to production and redistribution, those same relations also ensure their mutual dependence. Both the wife who does not work for wages and the husband who does, for example, have a joint interest in the size of his paycheck, the efficiency of her cooking facilities, or the quality of their children's education. However, the same historical processes that created households in opposition to (but also in partnership with) the state also augmented the power of men in households, as they became their household heads, and exacerbated tensions within households.

Examples of tensions and conflicts that involve the family in struggle are presented in [the table "Conflicts Involving the Family"]. The family can be a locus of internal struggle over matters related to production or redistribution

CONFLICTS INVOLVING THE FAMILY

Sources of conflict	Conflicts within the household	Conflicts between households and larger institutions
Production issues	*Housework:* Who does it? How? According to which standards? Should women work for wages outside the home or for men inside the home?	*Household production versus production organized by capital and the state:* Fast-food or home-cooked meals? Parent co-operative child care or state regulated child-care centers?
Redistribution issues	*Paycheck(s):* How should the money be spent? Who decides? Should the husband's paycheck be spent on luxuries for him or on household needs?	*Taxes:* Who will make the decisions about how to use the family's resources? Family members or representatives of the state apparatus?

(housework and paychecks, respectively). It can also provide a basis for struggle by its members against larger institutions such as corporations or the state. Will cooking continue to be done at home or be taken over largely by fast-food chains? Will child care continue to be the responsibility of parents or will it be provided by the state outside the home? Such questions signal tensions over the location of production. Tax protest, revolving as it does around the issue of who will make decisions for the family about the redistribution of its resources, can be viewed as an example of struggle between families and the state over redistribution. In this essay I intend to discuss only one source of conflict in any depth—housework—and merely touch upon some of the issues raised by tensions in other arenas. As with most typologies, the categories offered here are in reality not rigidly bounded or easily separable. Rather they represent different aspects of the same phenomena; production and redistribution are interrelated just as are struggles within and beyond households.[3]

PRODUCTION, REDISTRIBUTION, AND THE HOUSEHOLD

. . . In a capitalist system the production of material needs takes place largely outside households, in large-scale enterprises where the productive resources are owned by capitalists. Most people, having no productive resources of their own, have no alternative but to offer their labor power in exchange for wages. Capitalists appropriate the surplus value the workers create above and beyond the value of their wages. One of the fundamental dynamics in our society is that which flows from this production process: wage earners seek to retain as much control as possible over both the conditions and products of their labor, and capitalists, driven by competition and the needs of the accumulation process, seek to wrest control away from the workers in order to increase the amount of surplus value.[4] With the wages they receive, people buy the commodities that they need for their survival. Once in the home these commodities are then transformed to become usable in producing and reproducing people. In our society, which is organized by patriarchy as well as by capitalism, the sexual division of labor by gender makes men primarily responsible for wage labor and women primarily responsible for household production. That portion of household production called housework consists largely in purchasing commodities and transforming them into usable forms. Sheets, for example, must be bought, put on beds, rearranged after every sleep, and washed, just as food must be bought, cleaned, cooked, and served to become a meal. Household production also encompasses the biological reproduction of people and the shaping of their

---

[3]For another typology of struggle, see Gosta Esping-Anderson, Roger Friedland, and Erik Olin Wright, "Modes of Class Struggle and the Capitalist State," *Kapitalistate*, no. 4/5 (Summer 1976), pp. 186–220; and for a critique, see Capitol Kapitalistate Collective, "Typology and Class Struggle: Critical Notes on 'Modes of Class Struggle and the Capitalist State,' " *Kapitalistate*, no. 6 (Fall 1977), pp. 209–15.

[4]See Harry Braverman, *Labor and Monopoly Capital: The Degradation of Work in the Twentieth Century* (New York: Monthly Reivew Press, 1974), as well as Karl Marx, *Capital* (New York: International Publishers, 1967), vol. 1.

gender, as well as their maintenance through housework. In the labor process of producing and reproducing people, household production gives rise to another of the fundamental dynamics of our society. The system of production in which we live cannot be understood without reference to the production and reproduction both of commodities—whether in factories, service centers, or offices—and of people, in households. Although neither type of production can be self-reproducing, together they create and recreate our existence.[5]

The patriarchal and capitalist arrangement of production necessitates a means of redistribution. Because of the class and gender division of labor not everyone has direct access to the economic means of survival. A schematic view of the development of capitalism in Western societies suggests that capitalism generally took root in societies where production and redistribution had taken place largely in households and villages; even though capitalism shifted much production beyond the household, it did not destroy all the traditional ways in which production and redistribution were organized. In preindustrial households, people not only carried on production but also shared their output among themselves (after external obligations such as feudal dues were met), according to established patriarchal relations of authority. In the period of capitalist primitive accumulation, capitalists had to alienate the productive resources that people previously attached to the land had controlled in order to establish the capitalist mode of production based on "free" wage labor. Laborers became "free" to work for capitalists because they had no other means of subsistence and therefore required wages to buy from the capitalists what they had formerly produced in households and villages and exchanged with each other.

With the development of the capitalist mode of production, the old, the young, and women of childbearing age participated less in economic production and became dependent on the wage earners, increasingly adult men. People continued to live in households, however, to reproduce the species and to redistribute resources. Households became primarily income-pooling units rather than income-producing units.[6] The previously established patriarchal division of labor, in which men benefited from women's labor, was perpetuated in a capitalist setting where men became primarily wage laborers but retained the personal services of their wives, as women became primarily "housewives."[7] The interdependence of men and women that arises out of the division of labor by gender was also maintained. The need for the household in capitalism to be an income-pooling unit, a place where redistribution occurs between men and women, arises fundamentally from the patriarchal division of labor. Yet it is

[5]See Susan Himmelweit and Simon Mohun, "Domestic Labour and Capital," *Cambridge Journal of Economics* 1, no. 1 (March 1977): 15–31.

[6]See Heidi Hartmann and Ellen Ross, "The Origins of Modern Marriage" (paper delivered at the Scholar and the Feminist Conference, III, Barnard College, April 10, 1976). Batya Weinbaum, "Women in Transition to Socialism: Perspectives on the Chinese Case," *Review of Radical Political Economics* 8, no. 1 (Spring 1976): 34–58, shows that the family is also an income-pooling unit in China under socialism.

[7]See Heidi Hartmann, "Capitalism, Patriarchy, and Job Segregation by Sex," *Signs: Journal of Women in Culture and Society* 1, no. 3, pt. 2 (Spring 1976): 137–69, for how this came about.

income pooling that enables the household to be perceived as a unit with unitary interests, despite the very different relationships to production of its separate members. Because of the division of labor among family members, disunity is thus inherent in the "unity" of the family. . . .

HOUSEWORK

Some observers have argued that the family is no longer a place where men exericse their power. If patriarchy exists at all for them, it does so only on impersonal, institutional levels. For some analysts working in the Marxist traditions, the inexorable progress of capitalism has eliminated patriarchy within the family and has even given rise to the women's movement, because it weakened patriarchal power just enough to enable women to confront it directly.[8] I wish to argue, however, that, although capitalism has somewhat shifted the locus of control, the family nevertheless remains a primary arena where men exercise their patriarchal power over women's labor. In this section, I review some of the empirical findings on time spent on housework by husbands and wives to support this proposition. I believe that time spent on housework, as well as other indicators of household labor, can be fruitfully used as a measure of power relations in the home.

WHO DOES HOW MUCH HOUSEWORK?

In recent years a number of time-budget studies have measured time spent on housework, as well as other activities such as paid work and leisure. Such studies generally involve having respondents record their activities for specified time intervals (for example, fifteen minutes) for one or two days. The most comprehensively analyzed data on time spent doing housework in the United States are those collected in 1967 and 1968 by Kathryn Walker and Margaret Woods for 1,296 husband-and-wife families in Syracuse, New York.[9] Time diaries were also collected for a representative sample of families in five U.S. cities in 1965 and 1966 as part of the Multinational Comparative Time-Budget Research Project.[10] The University of Michigan Survey Research Center has

[8]Stewart Ewen, *Captains of Consciousness* (New York: McGraw-Hill Book Co., 1976), and Barbara Ehrenreich and Dierdre English, *For Her Own Good: 150 Years of the Experts' Advice to Women* (New York: Anchor Press, 1978), argue that patriarchal control is now exercised by the corporation or the experts, rather than the small guy out there, one to a household. The trenchant review of the weakness of family history by Wini Breines, Margaret Cerullo, and Judith Stacey, "Social Biology, Family Studies and Anti-feminist Backlash," *Feminist Studies* 4, no. 1 (February 1978): 43–67, also suggests that within the family male power over women is declining. Barbara Easton, "Feminism and the Contemporary Family," *Socialist Revolution,* no. 39 (May–June 1978), pp. 11–36, makes a similar argument, as do Linda Gordon and Allen Hunter, "Sex, Family and the New Right: Anti Feminism as a Political Force," *Radical America* 11, no. 6 and 12, no. 1 (November 1977–February 1978): 9–25.

[9]Kathryn E. Walker and Margaret E. Woods, *Time Use: A Measure of Household Production of Family Goods and Services* (Washington, D.C.: American Home Economics Association, 1976).

[10]Alexander Szalai, ed., *The Use of Time* (The Hague: Mouton, 1972).

collected data for representative national samples of families and individuals for 1965–66 and for 1975.[11] Subsequently, a number of smaller studies have been conducted.[12] While the studies all differ in such data collection procedures as sampling (national vs. local, husband-and-wife families vs. individuals) and reporting (interview vs. self-report, contemporaneous vs. retrospective reporting), their findings are remarkably consistent and support rather firm conclusions about who does how much housework.[13] Because Walker and Woods have analyzed their data so extensively, their findings are relied upon here.

Women who have no paid employment outside the home work over fifty hours per week on household chores: preparing and cleaning up after meals, doing laundry, cleaning the house, taking care of children and other family members, and shopping and keeping records. Walker and Woods found that 859 full-time houseworkers (usually labeled "homemakers" or "housewives") worked an average of fitty-seven hours per week. Their husbands, as reported by their wives, spent about eleven hours a week on housework, and children were reported to do about the same amount on average.[14] A study of a national sample of 700 women in 1965 and 1966 found that 357 full-time houseworkers worked an average of 55.4 hours per week.[15] Household production is clearly more than a full-time job according to these time-budget studies.

The way that time spent on housework changes as demands on members' time

[11]James N. Morgan, "A Potpourri of New Data Gathered from Interviews with Husbands and Wives," in *Five Thousand American Families: Patterns of Economic Progress*, vol. 6, *Accounting for Race and Sex Differences in Earnings and Other Analyses of the First Nine Years of the Panel Study of Income Dynamics*, ed. Greg J. Duncan and James N. Morgan (Ann Arbor: University of Michigan, Institute for Social Research [hereafter ISR], 1978), pp. 367–401; Frank Stafford and Greg Duncan, "The Use of Time and Technology by Households in the United States," working paper (Ann Arbor: University of Michigan, ISR, 1977); John P. Robinson, "Changes in American's Use of Time: 1965–1975: A Progress Report," working paper (Cleveland: Cleveland State University, August 1977).

[12]Among the smaller studies are Martin Meissner et al., "No Exit for Wives: Sexual Division of Labour and the Cumulation of Household Demands," *Canadian Review of Sociology and Anthropology* 12 (November 1975): 424–39; Richard A. Berk and Sarah Fenstermaker Berk, *Labor and Leisure at Home: Content and Organization of the Household Day* (Beverly Hills, Calif.: Sage Publications, 1979); and Joseph H. Pleck, "Men's Family Work: Three Perspectives and Some New Data," working paper (Wellesley, Mass.: Wellesley College Center for Research on Women, 1979). New data collection efforts on a larger scale are already under way in several states, coordinated by Kathryn Walker at Cornell University, and planned by the Survey Research Center at the University of Michigan under the coordination of Frank Stafford, Greg Duncan, and John Robinson.

[13]For a discussion of the reliability of time diaries and their compatibility, see John Robinson, "Methodological Studies into the Reliability and Validity of the Time Diary," in *Studies in the Measurement of Time Allocation*, ed. Thomas Juster (Ann Arbor: University of Michigan, ISR, in press); and Joann Vanek, "Keeping Busy: Time Spent in Housework, United States, 1920–1970" (Ph.D. diss., University of Michigan, 1973). Research on the distribution of families at the extremes (e.g., where men and women may be sharing housework equally) would also be very useful.

[14]Kathryn E. Walker, "Time-Use Patterns for Household Work Related to Homemakers' Employment" (paper presented at the 1970 National Agriculture Outlook Conference, Washington, D.C., February 18, 1970), p. 5.

[15]John Robinson and Philip Converse, "United States Time Use Survey" (Ann Arbor, Mich.: Survey Research Center, 1965–66), as reported by Joann Vanek, "Household Technology and Social Status: Rising Living Standards and Status and Residence Differences in Housework," *Technology and Culture* 19 (July 1978): 374.

increase is a good indicator of how patriarchy operates in the home, at least with respect to housework. Much has been made of the potentially equalizing effects of women's increased labor-force participation: as women earn wages they may come to exercise more power both within and outside the family. Time-budget studies [e.g., Figure 1, below] show, however, that husbands of wives who work

FIGURE 1
Time spent on housework and total work by wives and husbands in 1,296 Syracuse, New York, families (1967–68), by wives' hours of employment. Based on data from Kathryn E. Walker and Margaret E. Woods, *Time Use: A Measure of Household Production of Family Goods and Services* (Washington: D.C.: American Home Economics Association, 1976), p. 45; and Kathryn E. Walker, "Time-Use Patterns for Household Work Related to Homemakers' Employment" (paper presented at the 1970 National Agricultural Outlook Conference, Washington, D.C., February 18, 1970), p. 5.

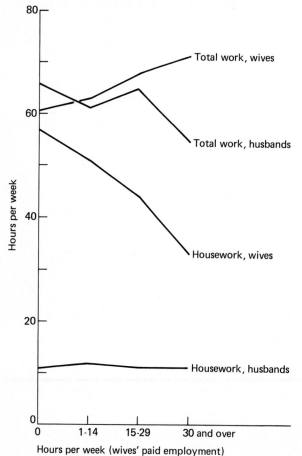

for wages do not spend more time on housework than those husbands whose wives do not work for wages. The Walker and Woods data for Syracuse families show that the more wage work women do, the fewer hours they spend on housework but the longer are their total work weeks. Women who worked for wages thirty or more hours per week had total work weeks of seventy-six hours on average, including an average of thirty-three hours per week spent on housework. Yet men whose wives had the longest work weeks had the shortest work weeks themselves [see Figure 1]. The lack of responsiveness of men's housework time to women's increased wage work is also shown in time-budget data from cities in twelve industrialized countries collected by the Multinational Comparative Time-Budget Research Project in 1965 and 1966. In all countries wage-working wives worked substantially more hours every day than husbands or full-time houseworkers. Employed wives also spent substantially more time on housework on their days off (about double their weekday time), whereas husbands and even full-time houseworkers had the weekends for increased leisure.[16] These findings are corroborated by two later studies, one of 300 couples in Greater Vancouver in 1971, and one of 3,500 couples in the United States in 1976.[17]

A look at the tasks performed by husbands and wives, as well as the time spent, adds to our understanding of the relative burden of housework. Meissner and his associates, examining participation rates of husbands and wives in various tasks for 340 couples, finds that only 26 percent of the husbands reported spending some time cleaning the house (on either of two days reported, one weekday and one weekend day) while 86 percent of their wives did, and that 27 percent of the husbands contributed 2.5 hours per week to cooking, while 93 percent of the wives contributed 8.5 hours. Only seven of the 340 husbands reported doing any laundry, but nearly half their wives did.[18] Meissner and his associates conclude: "These data indicate that most married women do the regular, necessary, and most time consuming work in the household every day. In view of the small and selective contribution of their husbands, they can anticipate doing it for the rest of their lives."[19]

Walker and Woods, examining the percentage of record days that wives and husbands, as well as other household members, participated in various house-

---

[16]John P. Robinson, Philip E. Converse, and Alexander Szalai, "Everyday Life in Twelve Countries," in Szalai, ed., pp. 119, 121.

[17]Meissner et al.; Morgan. One recent survey, the national 1977 Quality of Employment Survey, does, however, indicate that husbands of employed wives do more housework than husbands of full-time houseworkers: about 1.8 hours more per week in household tasks and 2.7 more in child care (quoted in Pleck, pp. 15, 16). These findings are based on data gathered by the retrospective self-reports of 757 married men in interviews rather than by time diaries kept throughout the day. Respondents were asked to "estimate" how much time they spent on "home chores—things like working, cleaning, repairs, shopping, yardwork, and keeping track of money and bills," and on "taking care of or doing things with your child(ren)." The child-care estimates are probably high relative to those from time-budget studies because the latter count only active care; "doing things with your children" would often be classified as leisure.

[18]Meissner et al., p. 430.

[19]Ibid., p. 431.

hold tasks, conclude that while husbands of employed wives participated more often than husbands of nonemployed wives in almost all household tasks, their contributions to the time spent on the tasks were small.[20] One is forced to conclude that the husbands of wage-working wives appear to do more housework by participating more often, but the substance of their contributions remains insignificant.[21] Women are apparently not, for the most part, able to translate their wages into reduced work weeks, either by buying sufficient substitute products or labor or by getting their husbands to do appreciably more housework. In the absence of patriarchy, we would expect to find an equal sharing of wage work and housework; we find no such thing.

The burden of housework increases substantially when there are very young children or many children in the household. The household time-budget data from Walker and Woods's study indicate that in both cases the wife's work week expands to meet the needs of the family while the husband's does not. In families with a child under one year old, the typical full-time houseworker spent nearly seventy hours per week in housework, nearly thirty of it in family (primarily child) care. The typical husband spent five hours per week on family care but reduced his time spent on other housework, so that his total housework did not increase. When the wife was employed for fifteen or more hours per week, the average husband did spend two hours more per week on child care, and his time spent on housework increased to twenty hours (compared to twelve for the husband whose wife did less wage work). Meanwhile, however, his employed wife spent over fifty hours on housework, nearly twenty of them on child care. As Figure 2 indicates, the employed wife's total housework time expands substantially with the presence of young children, while the husband's increases only moderately. Data from a national sample of about 3,500 U.S. husband-and-wife families in the 1976 Panel Study of Income Dynamics also show a pattern of longer housework time for wives with greater family responsibility (indicated by

[20]Husbands of employed wives reported participating in meal preparation on 42 percent of the record-keeping days, while the employed wives participated on 96 percent of the days. Yet the husbands contributed only 10 percent of the time spent on that task, while the wives contributed 75 percent. Similarly, 17 percent of the husbands of employed wives participated in after-meal cleanup, contributing 7 percent of the time. In only two of the seven tasks constituting regular housework, marketing and nonphysical care of the family, did husbands contribute as much as 25 percent of the total time spent on the tasks (tasks defined as nonphysical care of the family are activities that relate to the social and educational development of other family members, such as reading to children or helping them with lessons; pet care is also included in this task). For these two tasks, neither the participation rates nor the proportions of time contributed differed substantially between those husbands whose wives worked for wages and those whose wives did not. It should be noted that the percentage of record days husbands were reported as participating in a particular task is not the same as a straightforward participation rate. For example, a report that husbands participated on half the days could indicate either that all husbands participated every other day or that half the husbands participated both days (Walker and Woods [n. 9 above], pp. 58–59).

[21]The unusual finding reported by Pleck, that husbands of employed wives estimate they spend more time on housework, could be explained by this phenomenon: men *participate* more often, and *think* they are doing more housework. The new time-budget studies will be useful in confirming or denying this change.

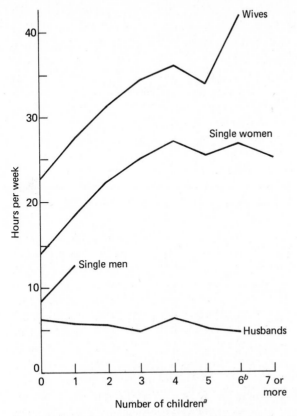

ᵃNumber of other people in household besides husband and wife or single head of household.
ᵇSix or more for husbands and wives.

FIGURE 2
Time spent on housework and family care by husbands and
employed wives in 1,296 Syracuse, New York, families
(1967–68), by age of youngest child. Based on data from
Walker and Woods (see legend to Figure 1), pp. 50, 126.

numbers of children) and nearly total lack of variability in the husbands'
housework time [see Figure 3].[22]

Meissner and his associates developed a ranked set of four combinations of
demands on household time and analyzed the data on changes in the housework
time of husbands and wives in response to these increased levels of demands.
The first level of demand is represented by households with one job and no
children under ten, the second is one job and children under ten, the third is two

[22]Morgan. These data indicate far fewer hours spent on housework than the Walker and Woods
data because they exclude child-care hours and, perhaps as well, because they are based on recall
rather than actual time diaries.

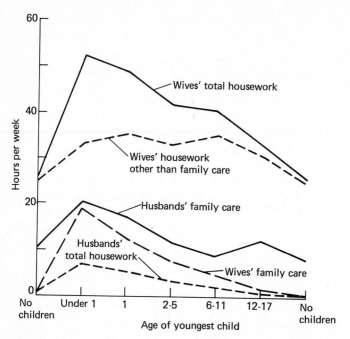

FIGURE 3

Time spent on housework, not including child care, by a national sample
of 5,863 families (1976), by number of children. Based on data in James N.
Morgan, "A Potpourri of New Data Gathered from Interviews with
Husbands and Wives," in *Five Thousand American Families: Patterns of
Economic Progress,* vol. 6, *Accounting for Race and Sex Differences in
Earnings and Other Analyses of the First Nine Years of the Panel Study
of Income Dynamics,* ed. Greg J. Duncan and James N. Morgan (Ann
Arbor: University of Michigan, Institute for Social Research), 1978, p. 370.

jobs and no children under ten, and the fourth is two jobs and children under
ten. The invariance of time husbands spent on housework is corroborated by
their procedure. For the five activities of meals, sleep, gardening, visiting, and
watching television, women lose fourteen hours a week from the least to most
demanding situation, while men gain 14 hours a week.[23] The United States cities
survey of 1965–66 found that among working couples with children, fathers
averaged 1.3 hours more free time each weekday and 1.4 hours more on Sunday
than mothers.[24]

The rather small, selective, and unresponsive contribution of the husband to
housework raises the suspicion that the husband may be a net drain on the
family's resources of housework time—that is, husbands may require more

[23]Meissner et al., p. 433.
[24]John Robinson and Philip Converse, "United States Time Use Survey" (Ann Arbor, Mich.:
Survey Research Center, 1965–66), as reported in Janice N. Hedges and Jeanne K. Barnett,
"Working Women and the Division of Household Tasks," *Monthly Labor Review* (April 1971),
p. 11.

housework than they contribute. Indeed, this hypothesis is suggested by my materialist definition of patriarchy, in which men benefit directly from women's labor power. No direct estimates of housework required by the presence of husbands have, to my knowledge, been made. The Michigan survey data, however, in providing information on the housework time of single parents shed some light on this question. Single women spend considerably less time on housework than wives, for the same size families [sée Figure 3]. They spend less time even when they are compared only to wives who work for wages. It seems plausible that the difference in time spent on housework (approximately eight hours per week) could be interpreted as the amount of increased housework caused by the husband's presence. Unfortunately, because very few time-budget studies solicit information from single women, this estimate of "husband care" cannot be confirmed. Additional estimates can be made, however, from Walker and Woods's data of the minimum time necessary for taking care of a house. For wives who worked in the labor market less than fourteen hours per week, time spent on "regular" housework (all housework minus family care) ranged between forty and forty-five hours for all life-cycle phases (varying ages and numbers of children), while for wives who worked for wages fifteen hours per week or more, time spent on regular housework ranged between twenty-five and thirty-five hours per week [see Figure 2].

These studies demonstrate the patriarchal benefits reaped in housework. First, the vast majority of time spent on housework is spent by the wife, about 70 percent on the average, with both the husband and the children providing about 15 percent on average.[25] Second, the wife is largely responsible for child care. The wife takes on the excess burden of housework in those families where there are very young or very many children; the husband's contribution to housework remains about the same whatever the family size or the age of the youngest child. It is the wife who, with respect to housework at least, does all of the adjusting to the family life cycle. Third, the woman who also works for wages (and she does so usually, we know, out of economic necessity) finds that her husband spends very little more time on housework on average than the husband whose wife is not a wage worker. Fourth, the wife spends perhaps eight hours per week in additional housework on account of the husband. And fifth, the wife spends, on average, a minimum of forty hours a week maintaining the house and husband if she does not work for wages and a minimum of thirty hours per week if she does.

Moreover, while we might expect the receipt of patriarchal benefits to vary according to class, race, and ethnicity, the limited time data we have relating to socioeconomic status or race indicate that time spent on housework by wives is not very sensitive to such differences.[26] The national panel study data, for example, showed no variation in housework time between racial groups.[27] With

[25]Walker and Woods, p. 64.
[26][See the article by Heidi Hartmann on page 172 of this text.]
[27]Morgan, p. 369.

respect to class differences, I have argued elsewhere that the widespread use of household conveniences (especially the less expensive ones) and the decline in the use of servants in the early twentieth century probably increased the similarity of housework across class. In addition, no evidence was found that showed that the larger appliances effectively reduced housework time.[28] Income probably has its most important effect on housework through its effect on women's labor-force participation rates. Wives of husbands with lower incomes are more likely to be in the labor force and therefore experiencing the "double day" of wage work and housework.[29] Wage work, while it shortens the number of hours spent on housework (compared to those of the full-time houseworker), almost certainly increases the burden of the hours that remain. Even for full-time houseworkers, the number and ages of children appear to be more important than income in effect upon housework time.[30]

The relation of the household's wage workers to the capitalist organization of production places households in class relations with each other and determines the household's access to commodities; yet in viewing and understanding women's work in the home—the rearing of children, the maintenance of the home, the serving of men—patriarchy appears to be a more salient feature than class.[31] . . .

WHAT ARE THE PROSPECTS FOR CHANGE?

What is the likelihood that patriarchal power in the home, as measured by who does housework, will decline? What is the likelihood that housework will become equally shared by men and women? Might the amount of time required for housework be reduced? The prospects for change in housework time, while

---

[28]Heidi I. Hartmann, "Capitalism and Women's Work in the Home, 1900–1930" (Ph.D. diss., Yale University, 1974). The Robinson-Converse study found that wives' housework time hovered around forty-two hours per week at all household incomes above $4,000 per year (1965–66 dollars) but was somewhat less, thirty-three hours, when household income was below $4,000 (reported in Vanek, "Household Technology and Social Status," p. 371).

[29]In the Meissner study, fully 36 percent of the wives whose husbands earned under $10,000 (1971 dollars) were in the labor force, whereas no more than 10 percent of those whose husbands earned over $14,000 were in the labor force (Meissner et al., p. 429).

[30]Much additional research, both of the already available data and the forthcoming data, is needed to increase our knowledge of potential variations in housework time.

[31]The salience of patriarchy over class for women's work could probably be shown for many societies; Bangladesh provides one example. In 1977 Mead Cain and his associates collected data on time use from all members of 114 households in a rural Bangladesh village, where control of arable land is the key to economic survival and position. Dichotomizing people's class position by the amount of arable land owned by their households, Cain found that the work days of men with more than one-half acre of land were substantially shorter than those of men with less than one-half acre of land, whereas women in households with more land worked longer hours. The better-off men probably worked about eleven hours *less* per week than the poorer. The better-off women worked about three hours *more* per week than the poorer. In this rural village, Bangladesh women, unlike the men, did not benefit—at least in terms of lighter work loads—from the higher class position of their households (Mead Cain, Syeda Rokeya Khanam, and Shamsun Naher, "Class, Patriarchy, and Women's Work in Bangladesh," *Population and Development Review* 5, no. 3 [September 1979]: 405–38).

dependent on economic and political changes at the societal level, probably hinge most directly on the strength of the women's movement, for the amount and quality of housework services rendered, like the amount of and pay for wage work, result from historical processes of struggle. Such struggle establishes norms that become embodied in an expected standard of living. Time spent on housework by both full-time houseworkers and employed houseworkers has remained remarkably stable in the twentieth century. Kathryn Walker and Joann Vanek for the United States and Michael Paul Sacks for the Soviet Union report that total time spent on housework has not declined significantly from the 1920s to the 1960s.[32] Although time spent on some tasks, such as preparing and cleaning up after meals, has declined, that spent on others—such as shopping, record keeping, and child care—has increased. Even time spent on laundry has increased, despite new easy care fabrics and the common use of automatic home washing machines. A completely satisfactory explanation for the failure of housework time to decline, despite rapid technological change, has not yet been developed, but part of the answer lies in rising standards of cleanliness, child care, and emotional support, as well as in the inherent limitation of technology applied to small decentralized units, that is, typical homes.[33]

Gender struggle around housework may be bearing fruit. Standards may in fact be changing, allowing for a reduction in overall time spent on housework. A recent time-budget study indicates that between 1965 and 1975 housework time may have fallen by as much as six hours per week for full-time houseworkers and four hours for those also employed outside the house.[34] Such a decrease may also be the result of changing boundaries between home and market production; production formerly done by women at home may be increasingly shifted to capitalist production sites. In such cases, the products change as well; home-cooked meals are replaced by fast food.[35] Over time, the boundary between

---

[32]Kathryn E. Walker, "Homemaking Still Takes Time," *Journal of Home Economics* 61, no. 8 (October 1969): 621–24; Joann Vanek, "Time Spent in Housework," *Scientific American* 231 (November 1974): 116–20; Michael Paul Sacks, "Unchanging Times: A Comparison of the Everyday Life of Soviet Working Men and Women between 1923 and 1966," *Journal of Marriage and the Family* 30 (November 1977): 793–805.

[33]Technological innovations within the household—the washing machine, the vacuum cleaner, the dishwasher—have not been effective in reducing household time. Sophisticated robots, microwave ovens, or computer-controlled equipment may yet be able to reduce the time required for maintaining household services at established levels. Yet what technology is developed and made available is also the result of historical processes and the relative strength of particular classes and genders. See Hartmann, *Capitalism and Women's Work.*

[34]Robinson, table 4 (see n. 11 above); Clair Vickry, "Women's Economic Contribution to the Family," in *The Subtle Revolution,* ed. Ralph E. Smith (Washington, D.C.: Urban Institute, 1979), p. 194.

[35]One in four meals is now eaten outside the home (Charles Vaugh, "Growth and Future of the Fast Food Industry," *Cornell Motel and Restaurant Administration Quarterly* [November 1976]), cited in Christine Bose, "Technology and Changes in the Division of Labor in the American Home" (paper delivered at the annual meeting of the American Sociological Association, San Francisco, September 1978). I suspect that the most effective means of reducing housework time involves changing the location of production from the household to the larger economy, but men, acting in their patriarchal interests, may well resist this removal of production from the home, with its attendant loss of personalized services.

home and market production has been flexible rather than fixed, determined by the requirements of patriarchy and capitalism in reproducing themselves and by the gender and class struggles that arise from these processes.

While women's struggles, and perhaps as well capital's interests, may be successfully altering standards for housework and shifting some production beyond the home, prospects within the home for shifting some of the household tasks onto men do not appear to be as good. We have already seen, in our review of the current time-budget studies, that men whose wives work for wages do not spend more time than other married men on housework. This suggests that, even as more women increase their participation in wage labor and share with men the financial burden of supporting families, men are not likely to share the burden of housework with women. The increase in women's labor-force participation has occurred over the entire course of the twentieth century. Walker's comparison of the 1967–68 Syracuse study with studies from the 1920s shows that husbands' work time may have increased at most about a half hour per week, while the work time of women, whether employed outside the home or full-time houseworkers, may have increased by as much as five hours per week.[36] Interestingly, a similar conclusion was reached by Sacks in his comparison of time-budget studies conducted in several cities in the Soviet Union in 1923 and 1966. He found that women's housework time has decreased somewhat, that men's time has not increased, that women still spend more than twice as much time on housework than do men, and that women have a total work week that is still seventeen hours longer than men's. In 1970, fully 90 percent of all Soviet women between the ages of twenty and forty-nine were in the labor force.[37] We are forced to conclude that the increase in women's wage labor will not *alone* bring about any sharing of housework with men. Continued struggle will be necessary. . . .

CONCLUSION

The decentralized home system, which I see as a fundamental result of patriarchy, also meets crucial requirements for the reproduction of the capitalist system.[38] Families can provide crucial services less expensively than does the cash nexus of either the state or capital, especially when economic growth has come to a halt. From capital's point of view, however, the relationship is an uneasy one; capital and the state use the household but do not entirely control it. Despite the spread of capitalism and centralized, bureaucratic states, and their penetration into more and more areas of social life, people in households still manage to retain control over crucial resources and particular areas of decision. Family historians have helped us understand the strength and endurance of

---

[36]Walker, "Homemaking Still Takes Time."

[37]Sacks, "Unchanging Times," p. 801.

[38]Ann R. Markusen has extended the notion of decentralized households as characteristic of patriarchy to explain the development of segregated residential areas in cities. See her "City Spatial Structure. Women's Household Work, and National Urban Policy," *Signs: Journal of Women in Culture and Society* 5, no. 3, suppl. (Spring 1980): S23–S44.

family units and their retention of power in many areas. The family historians may not have been sensitive to power relations within the family, but they have focused on another aspect of the same phenomenon—the interdependence of people within households and their common stance as a household against the incursion of forces that would alienate their resources or their control over decision making. Although I have focused on the potential for conflict among family members, particularly between men and women over housework, I want to point out that the same division of labor that creates the basis for that conflict also creates interdependence as a basis for famliy unity. It is this dual nature of the family that makes the behavior of families so unpredictable and problematic for both capital and the state. In the United States, for example, no one predicted the enormity of the post-World War II baby boom, the size of the subsequent increase in women's labor force participation, the rapid decrease in the birthrate in the late 1960s and early 1970s, or, most recently, the increase in divorce and single parenthood.

With the perspective developed here, these changes in people's household behavior can be understood as responses to conflicts both within and outside households. As Wendy Lutrell, who has also been working on reconceptualizing the family as a locus of tension and conflict, writes: "People can be seen as historical agents acting both independently as individuals *and* dependently as family members. This dual process fuels tensions and conflicts within the family arena and creates one potential for social change. . . . When the state, workplace, community, religion, or family are seen as arenas of struggle, we are forced to abandon a static, functional framework which can only see capitalist institutions as maintaining the status quo."[39]

In some cases, family members face capital or state actions together. In the Brookside strike, miners' wives united with their husbands, supporting their demands and even extending them to community concerns. Struggles around community issues are often initiated by women because of their ties to their neighbors and extended kin, and they are sometimes joined by men disaffected with their lot in patriarchy and capitalism. In New York City, both men and women protested government cuts for preschools and hospitals. In other cases, men and women who are in conflict within the family may seek solutions in the capitalist or state sectors. The recent rapid growth of fast-food eateries can be seen in this light, as can English women's fight for milk allowances from the state to redress income inequality within the family.

In our society both class and gender shape people's consciousness of their situation and their struggles to change those situations. At times it may be appropriate to speak of the family or the household as a unit with common interests, but the conditions which make this possible should be clearly spelled out. The conflicts inherent in class and patriarchal society tear people apart, but the dependencies inherent in them can hold people together.

[39]Wendy Lutrell, "The Family as an Arena of Struggle: New Directions and Strategies for Studying Contemporary Family Life" (paper delivered at a Sociology Colloquium, University of California, Santa Cruz, May 30, 1979), pp. 19, 18.

Gender Personality and the Sexual Sociology of Adult Life

Nancy Chodorow

Hence, there is a typically asymmetrical relation of the marriage pair to the occupational structure.

This asymmetrical relation apparently both has exceedingly important positive functional significance and is at the same time an important source of strain in relation to the patterning of sex roles.

Talcott Parsons
"The Kinship System of the Contemporary United States"

Girls and boys develop different relational capacities and senses of self as a result of growing up in a family in which women mother. These gender personalities are reinforced by differences in the identification processes of boys and girls that also result from women's mothering. Differing relational capacities and forms of identification prepare women and men to assume the adult gender roles which situate women primarily within the sphere of reproduction in a sexually-unequal society.

GENDER IDENTIFICATION AND GENDER ROLE LEARNING

All social scientists who have examined processes of gender role learning and the development of a sense of identification in boys and girls have argued that the asymmetrical organization of parenting in which women mother is the basic cause of significant contrasts between feminine and masculine identification processes.[1] Their discussions range from concern with the learning of appropriate gender role behavior—through imitation, explicit training and admonitions, and cognitive learning processes—to concern with the development of basic gender identity. The processes these people discuss seem to be universal, to the extent that all societies are constituted around a structural split, growing out of women's mothering, between the private, domestic world of women and the public, social world of men.[2] Because the first identification for children of both genders has always been with their mother, they argue, and because children are

[1] For a review of the literature which argues this, see Biller, 1971, *Father, Child.* See also Stoller, 1965, "The Sense of Maleness." For a useful recent formulation, see Johnson, 1975, "Fathers, Mothers."

[2] See Mead, 1949, *Male and Female;* Michelle Z. Rosaldo, 1974, "Women, Culture, and Society"; Nancy Chodorow, 1971, "Being and Doing," and 1974, "Family Structure and Feminine Personality," in Rosaldo and Lamphere, eds., *Women, Culture and Society*, pp. 43–66; Beatrice B. Whiting and John W. M. Whiting, 1975, *Children of Six Cultures;* John Whiting, 1959, "Sorcery, Sin"; Burton and Whiting, 1961, "The Absent Father."

first around women, women's family roles and being feminine are more available and often more intelligible to growing children than masculine roles and being masculine. Hence, male development is more complicated than female because of the difficult shifts of identification which a boy must make to attain his expected gender identification and gender role assumption. Their view contrasts sharply to the psychoanalytic stress on the difficulties inherent in feminine development as girls make their convoluted way to heterosexual object choice.[3]

Because all children identify first with their mother, a girl's gender and gender role identification processes are continuous with her earliest identifications and a boy's are not. A girl's oedipal identification with her mother, for instance, is continuous with her earliest primary identification (and also in the context of her early dependence and attachment). The boy's oedipal crisis, however, is supposed to enable him to shift in favor of an identification with his father. He gives up, in addition to his oedipal and preoedipal attachment to his mother, his primary identification with her.

What is true specifically for oedipal identification is equally true for more general gender identification and gender role learning. A boy, in order to feel himself adequately masculine, must distinguish and differentiate himself from others in a way that a girl need not—must categorize himself as someone apart. Moreover, he defines masculinity negatively as that which is not feminine and/or connected to women, rather than positively.[4] This is another way boys come to deny and repress relation and connection in the process of growing up.

These distinctions remain even where much of a girl's and boy's socialization is the same, and where both go to school and can participate in adulthood in the labor force and other nonfamilial institutions. Because girls at the same time grow up in a family where mothers are the salient parent and caretaker, they also can begin to identify more directly and immediately with their mothers and their mothers' familial roles than can boys with their fathers and men. Insofar as a woman's identity remains primarily as a wife/mother, moreover, there is greater generational continuity in role and life-activity from mother to daughter than there can be from father to son. This identity may be less than totally appropriate, as girls must realistically expect to spend much of their life in the labor force, whereas their mothers were less likely to do so. Nevertheless, family organization and ideology still produce these gender differences, and generate expectations that women much more than men will find a primary identity in the family.

[3]The extent of masculine difficulty varies, as does the extent to which identification processes for boys and girls differ. This variance depends on the extent of the public-domestic split in a subculture of society—the extent to which men, men's work, and masculine activities are removed from the home, and therefore masculinity and personal relations with adult men are hard to come by for a child.

[4]See Richard T. Roessler, 1971, "Masculine Differentiation and Feminine Constancy," *Adolescence,* 6, #22, pp. 187–196; E. M. Bennett and L. R. Cohen, 1959, "Men and Women, Personality Patterns and Contrasts," *Genetic Psychology Monographs,* 59, pp. 101–155; Johnson, 1963, "Sex Role Learning," and 1975, "Fathers, Mothers"; Stoller, 1964, "A Contribution to the Study," 1965, "The Sense of Maleness," and 1968, "The Sense of Femaleness," *Psychoanalytic Quarterly,* 37, #1, pp. 42–55.

Permanent father-absence, and the "father absence" that is normal in our society, do not mean that boys do not learn masculine roles or proper masculine behavior, just as there is no evidence that homosexuality in women correlates with father absence.[5] What matters is the extent to which a child of either gender can form a personal relationship with their object of identification, and the differences in modes of identification that result from this. Mitscherlich, Slater, Winch, and Lynn all speak to these differences.[6] They suggest that girls in contemporary society develop a personal identification with their mother, and that a tie between affective processes and role learning—between libidinal and ego development—characterizes feminine development. By contrast, boys develop a positional identification with aspects of the masculine role. For them, the tie between affective processes and role learning is broken.

Personal identification, according to Slater and Winch, consists in diffuse identification with someone else's general personality, behavioral traits, values, and attitudes. Positional identification consists, by contrast, in identification with specific aspects of another's role and does not necessarily lead to the internalization of the values or attitudes of the person identified with. According to Slater, children preferentially choose personal identification because this grows out of a positive affective relationship to a person who is there. They resort to positional identification residually and reactively, and identify with the perceived role or situation of another when possibilities for personal identification are not available.

In our society, a girl's mother is present in a way that a boy's father, and other adult men, are not. A girl, then, can develop a personal identification with her mother, because she has a real relationship with her that grows out of their early primary tie. She learns what it is to be womanlike in the context of this personal identification with her mother and often with other female models (kin, teachers, mother's friends, mothers of friends). Feminine identification, then, can be based on the gradual learning of a way of being familiar in everyday life, exemplified by the relationship with the person with whom a girl has been most involved.

A boy must attempt to develop a masculine gender identification and learn the masculine role in the absence of a continuous and ongoing personal relationship to his father (and in the absence of a continuously available masculine role model). This positional identification occurs both psychologically and sociologically. Psychologically, as is clear from descriptions of the masculine oedipus complex, boys appropriate those specific components of the masculinity of their father that they fear will be otherwise used against them, but do not as much identify diffusely with him as a person. Sociologically, boys in father-absent and normally father-remote families develop a sense of what it is to be

---

[5]See Biller, 1971, *Father, Child.*

[6]Mitscherlich, 1963, *Society Without the Father,* Philip E. Slater, 1961, "Toward a Dualistic Theory of Identification," *Merrill-Palmer Quarterly of Behavior and Development,* 7, #2, pp. 113–126; Robert F. Winch, 1962, *Identification and Its Familial Determinants;* David B. Lynn, 1959, "A Note on Sex Differences," and 1962, "Sex Role and Parent."

masculine through identification with cultural images of masculinity and men chosen as masculine models.

Boys are taught to be masculine more consciously than girls are taught to be feminine. When fathers or men are not present much, girls are taught the heterosexual components of their role, whereas boys are assumed to learn their heterosexual role without teaching, through interaction with their mother.[7] By contrast, other components of masculinity must be more consciously imposed. Masculine identification, then, is predominantly a gender role identification. By contrast, feminine identification is predominantly *parental:* "Males tend to identify with a cultural stereotype of the masculine role; whereas females tend to identify with aspects of their own mother's role specifically."[8]

Girls' identification processes, then, are more continuously embedded in and mediated by their ongoing relationship with their mother. They develop through and stress particularistic and affective relationships to others. A boy's identification processes are not likely to be so embedded in or mediated by a real affective relation to his father. At the same time, he tends to deny identification with and relationship to his mother and reject what he takes to be the feminine world; masculinity is defined as much negatively as positively. Masculine identification processes stress differentiation from others, the denial of affective relation, and categorical universalistic components of the masculine role. Feminine identification processes are relational, whereas masculine identification processes tend to deny relationship.

These distinctions do not mean that the development of femininity is all sugar and spice for a girl, but that it poses different *kinds* of problems for her than the development of masculinity does for a boy. The feminine identification that a girl attains and the masculine identification about which a boy remains uncertain are valued differently. In their unattainability, masculinity and the masculine role are fantasized and idealized by boys (and often by girls), whereas femininity and the feminine role remain for a girl all too real and concrete. . . .

FAMILY AND ECONOMY

Women's relatedness and men's denial of relation and categorical self-definition are appropriate to women's and men's differential participation in nonfamilial production and familial reproduction. Women's roles are basically familial, and concerned with personal, affective ties. Ideology about women and treatment of them in this society, particularly in the labor force, tend to derive from this familial location and the assumptions that it is or should be both exclusive and primary for women, and that this exclusivity and primacy come from biological sex differences. By contrast, men's roles as they are defined in our society are basically not familial. Though men are interested in being husbands and fathers,

---

[7]Johnson, 1975, "Fathers, Mothers," and Maccoby and Jacklin, 1974, *The Psychology of Sex Differences,* point this out.

[8]D. B. Lynn, 1959, "A Note on Sex Differences," p. 130.

and most men do occupy these roles during their lifetime, ideology about men and definitions of what is masculine come predominantly from men's nonfamilial roles. Women are located first in the sex-gender system, men first in the organization of production.

We can reformulate these insights to emphasize that women's lives, and beliefs about women, define them as embedded in social interaction and personal relationships in a way that men are not. Though men and women participate in both the family and the nonfamilial world, the sexual division of labor is such that women's first association is within the family, a relational institution, and men's is not. Women in our society are primarily defined as wives and mothers, thus in particularistic relation to someone else, whereas men are defined primarily in universalistic occupational terms. These feminine roles and women's family functions, moreover, stress especially affective relationship and the affective aspects of family life. As I discuss in Chapter I, being a mother and wife are increasingly centered on emotional and psychological functions— women's work is "emotional work."[9] By contrast, men's occupational roles, and the occupational world in general, are increasingly without room for affect and particularistic commitments. Women's two interconnected roles, their dual relatedness to men and children, replicate women's internalized relational triangle of childhood—preoccupied alternately with male-female and mother-child issues.

The definitional relatedness of being a wife and mother, and women's intrafamilial responsibility for affectively defined functions, receive further support from the way the family is related socially to the extrafamilial world. Parsons and many feminist theorists point out that it is the husband/father whose occupational role is mainly determinant of the class position and status of the whole family, and sociologists who measure socioeconomic status by *paternal* occupation and education seem to concur. The husband/father thus formally articulates the family in the larger society and gives it its place. And although families increasingly depend on income from both spouses, class position derives ideologically from what the male spouse does. The wife, accordingly, is viewed as deriving her status and class position mainly from her husband, even if she also is in the labor force and contributes to the maintenance of the family's life style. She is seen as a representative of her family, whereas her husband is seen as an independent individual.

The wife/mother role draws on women's personality in another way, as a result of the fundamentally different modes of organization of the contemporary sex-gender system and contemporary capitalism. The activities of a wife/mother have a nonbounded quality. They consist, as countless housewives can attest and as women poets, novelists, and feminist theorists have described, of diffuse

---

[9]This phrase is Arlie Hochschild's. (See Arlie Russell Hochschild, 1975, "The Sociology of Feeling and Emotion: Selected Possibilities," in Marica Millman and Rosabeth Moss Kanter, eds., *Another Voice,* pp. 280–307.) She uses it to refer to the internal work women do to make their feelings accord with how they think they ought to feel. My usage here extends also to work for and upon other people's emotions.

obligations. Women's activities in the home involve continuous connection to and concern about children and attunement to adult masculine needs, both of which require connection to, rather than separateness from, others. The work of maintenance and reproduction is characterized by its repetitive and routine continuity, and does not involve specified sequence or progression. By contrast, work in the labor force—"men's work"—is likely to be contractual, to be more specifically delimited, and to contain a notion of defined progression and product.

Even when men and women cross into the other's sphere, their roles remain different. Within the family, being a husband and father is different from being a wife and mother; as women have become more involved in the family, men have become less so. Parsons's characterization of men's instrumental role in the family may be too extreme, but points us in the right direction. A father's first responsibility is to "provide" for his family monetarily. His emotional contribution is rarely seen as of equal importance. Men's work in the home, in all but a few households, is defined in gender-stereotyped ways. When men do "women's" chores—the dishes, shopping, putting children to bed—this activity is often organized and delegated by the wife/mother, who retains residual responsibility (men "babysit" their own children; women do not). Fathers, though they relate to their children, do so in order to create "independence."[10] This is facilitated by a father's own previous socialization for repression and denial of relation, and his current participation in the public nonrelational world. Just as children know their fathers "under the sway of the reality principle,"[11,12] so also do fathers know their children more as separate people than mothers do.

Outside the family, women's roles and ideology about women are more relational than nonfamilial male roles and ideology about men. Women's work in the labor force tends to extend their housewife, wife, or mother roles and their concern with personal, affective ties (as secretaries, service workers, private household workers, nurses, teachers). Men's work is less likely to have affective overtones—men are craft workers, operatives, and professional and technical workers. . . .

Women's role in the home and primary definition in social reproductive, sex-gender terms are characterized by particularism, concern with affective goals and ties, and a diffuse, unbounded quality. Masculine occupational roles and men's primary definition in the sphere of production are universalistically defined and recruited, and are less likely to involve affective considerations. This nonrelational, economic and political definition informs the rest of their lives. The production of feminine personalities oriented toward relational issues and masculine personalities defined in terms of categorical ties and the repression of relation fits these roles and contributes to their reproduction.

---

[10]See, for example, Johnson, 1975, "Fathers, Mothers"; Parsons and Bales, 1955, *Family, Socialization*; Deutsch, 1944, *Psychology of Women*.

[11]Conscious of him as a separate person, verbally rather than preverbally.

[12]Alice Balint, 1939, "Love for the Mother."

MOTHERING, MASCULINITY, AND CAPITALISM

Women's mothering in the isolated nuclear family of contemporary capitalist society creates specific personality characteristics in men that reproduce both an ideology and psychodynamic of male superiority and submission to the requirements of production. It prepares men for participation in a male-dominant family and society, for their lesser emotional participation in family life, and for their participation in the capitalist world of work.

Masculine development takes place in a family in which women mother and fathers are relatively uninvolved in child care and family life, and in a society characterized by sexual inequality and an ideology of masculine superiority. This duality expresses itself in the family. In family ideology, fathers are usually important and consdered the head of the household. Wives focus energy and concern on their husbands, or at least think and say that they do. They usually consider, or at least claim, that they love these husbands. Mothers may present fathers to children as someone important, someone whom the mother loves, and may even build up their husbands to their children to make up for the fact that these children cannot get to know their father as well as their mother. They may at the same time undercut their husband in response to the position he assumes of social superiority or authority in the family.

Masculinity is presented to a boy as less available and accessible than femininity, as represented by his mother. A boy's mother is his primary caretaker. At the same time, masculinity is idealized or accorded superiority, and thereby becomes even more desirable. Although fathers are not as salient as mothers in daily interaction, mothers and children often idealize them and give them ideological primacy, precisely because of their absence and seeming inaccessibility, and because of the organization and ideology of male dominance in the larger society.

Masculinity becomes an issue in a way that femininity does not. Masculinity does not become an issue because of some intrinsic male biology, nor because masculine roles are inherently more difficult than feminine roles, however. Masculinity becomes an issue as a direct result of a boy's experience of himself in his family—as a result of his being parented by a woman. For children of both genders, mothers represent regression and lack of autonomy. A boy associates these issues with his gender identification as well. Dependence on his mother, attachment to her, and identification with her represent that which is not masculine: a boy must reject dependence and deny attachment and identification. Masculine gender role training becomes much more rigid than feminine. A boy represses those qualities he takes to be feminine inside himself, and rejects and devalues women and whatever he considers to be feminine in the social world.

Thus, boys define and attempt to construct their sense of masculinity largely in negative terms. Given that masculinity is so elusive, it becomes important for masculine identity that certain social activities are defined as masculine and superior, and that women are believed unable to do many of the things defined as socially important. It becomes important to think that women's economic and social contribution cannot equal men's. The secure possession of certain realms, and the insistence that these realms are superior to the maternal world of youth, become crucial both to the definition of masculinity and to a particular boy's own masculine gender identification.[13] . . .

Women's mothering produces a psychological and ideological complex in men concerning women's secondary valuation and sexual inequality. Because women are responsible for early child care and for most later socialization as well, because fathers are more absent from the home, and because men's activities generally have been removed from the home while women's have remained within it, boys have difficulty in attaining a stable masculine gender role identification. Boys fantasize about and idealize the masculine role and their fathers, and society defines it as desirable.

Given that men control not only major social institutions but the very definition and constitution of society and culture, they have the power and ideological means to enforce these perceptions as more general norms, and to hold each other accountable for their enforcement. (This is not solely a matter of force. Since these norms define men as superior, men gain something by maintaining them.)[14] The structure of parenting creates ideological and psychological modes which reproduce orientations to and structures of male dominance in individual men, and builds an assertion of male superiority into the definition of masculinity itself.

The same repressions, denials of affect and attachment, rejection of the world of women and things feminine, appropriation of the world of men and identification with the father that create a psychology of masculine superiority also condition men for participation in the capitalist work world. Both capitalist accumulation and proper work habits in workers have never been purely a matter of economics. Particular personality characteristics and behavioral codes facilitated the transition to capitalism. Capitalists developed inner direction, rational planning, and organization, and workers developed a willingness to come to work at certain hours and work steadily, whether or not they needed money that day.

Psychological qualities become perhaps even more important with the expansion of bureaucracy and hierarchy: In modern capitalism different personality traits are required at different levels of the bureaucratic hierarchy.[15,16] Lower level jobs are often directly and continuously supervised, and are best performed by someone willing to obey rules and conform to external authority. Moving up the hierarchy, jobs require greater dependability and predictability,

---

[13]On these issues, see Lynn 1959, "A Note on Sex Differences," and 1962, "Sex Role and Parent"; Parsons, 1942, "Age and Sex"; Mitscherlich, 1963, *Society Without the Father;* Slater, 1968, *The Glory of Hera;* Mead, 1949, *Male and Female.*

[14]But for discussions of ways that this accountability is actively maintained, see Joseph H. Pleck and Jack Sawyer, *Men and Masculinity,* and Marc F. Fasteau, 1974, *The Male Machine.*

[15]It is certainly possible that these same characteristics apply in all extensively bureaucratic and hierarchical settings (in the U.S.S.R., and Eastern Europe, for instance); however, the work I am drawing on has investigated only the capitalist West, and especially the United States.

[16]My formulation of the personality requirements of the hierarchical firm follows Edwards, 1975, "The Social Relations of Production."

the ability to act without direct and continuous supervision. In technical, professional, and managerial positions, workers must on their own initiative carry out the goals and values of the organization for which they work, making those goals and values their own. Often they must be able to draw on their interpersonal capacities as a skill. Parental child-rearing values and practices (insofar as these latter reflect parental values) reflect these differences. Working class parents are more likely to value obedience, conformity to external authority, neatness, and other "behavioral" characteristics in their children; middle-class parents emphasize more "internal" and interpersonal characteristics like responsibility, curiosity, self-motivation, self-control, and considera-tion.[17]

These behavioral and personality qualities differentiate appropriately accord-ing to the requirements of work in the different strata. But they share an important commonality. Conformity to behavioral rules and external authority, predictability and dependability, the ability to take on others' values and goals as one's own, all reflect an orientation external to oneself and one's own standards, a lack of autonomous and creative self-direction. The nuclear, isolated, neolocal family in which women mother is suited to the production in children of these cross-class personality commitments and capacities. . . .

Contemporary family structure produces not only malleability and lack of internalized standards, but often a search for manipulation. These character traits lend themselves to the manipulations of modern capitalism—to media and product consumerism, to the attempt to legitimate a polity that serves people unequally, and finally to work performance. The decline of the oedipal father creates an orientation to external authority and behavioral obedience. Exclusive maternal involvement and the extension of dependence create a generalized need to please and to "succeed," and a seeming independence. This need to succeed can help to make someone dependable and reliable. Because it is divorced from specific goals and real inner standards but has involved the maintenance of an internal dependent relationship, it can also facilitate the taking of others' goals as one's own, producing the pseudo-independent organization man.

An increasingly father-absent, mother-involved family produces in men a personality that both corresponds to masculinity and male dominance as these are currently constituted in the sex-gender system, and fits appropriately with participation in capitalist relations of production. Men continue to enforce the sexual division of spheres as a defense against powerlessness in the labor market. Male denial of dependence and of attachment to women helps to guarantee both masculinity and performance in the world of work. The relative unavailability of the father and overavailability of the mother create negative definitions of masculinity and men's fear and resentment of women, as well as the lack of inner autonomy in men that enables, depending on particular family constellation and

[17]See Melvin L. Kohn, 1969, *Class and Conformity*.

class origin, either rule-following or the easy internalization of the values of the organization.

Thus, women's and men's personality traits and orientations mesh with the sexual and familial division of labor and unequal ideology of gender and shape their asymmetric location in a structure of production and reproduction in which women are in the first instance mothers and wives and men are workers. This structure of production and reproduction requires and presupposes those specific relational modes, between husband and wife, and mother and children, which form the center of the family in contemporary society. An examination of the way that gender personality is expressed in adulthood reveals how women and men create, and are often committed to creating, the interpersonal relationships which underlie and reproduce the family structure that produced them.

BIBLIOGRAPHY

Balint, Alice, 1939, "Love for the Mother and Mother-Love," pp. 91–108 in Michael Balint, ed., *Primary Love and Psycho-Analytic Technique.* New York, Liveright Publishing, 1965.

Bennett, E. M., and L. R. Cohen, 1959, "Men and Women, Personality Patterns and Contrasts," *Genetic Psychology Monographs,* 59, pp. 101–155.

Biller, Henry B., 1971, *Father, Child, and Sex Role.* Lexington, Mass., D. C. Heath.

Burton, Roger V., and John W. M. Whiting, 1961, "The Absent Father and Cross-Sex Identity," *Merrill-Palmer Quarterly of Behavior and Development,* 7, #2, 1961, pp. 85–95.

Chodorow, Nancy, 1971, "Being and Doing: A Cross-Cultural Examination of the Socialization of Males and Females," pp. 173–197 in Vivian Gornick and Barbara K. Moran, eds., *Woman in Sexist Society: Studies in Power and Powerlessness.* New York, Basic Books.

———, 1974, "Family Structure and Feminine Personality," pp. 43–66 in Michelle Z. Rosaldo and Louise Lamphere, eds., *Woman, Culture and Society.* Stanford, Stanford University Press.

Deutsch, Helene, 1944 and 1945, *Psychology of Women,* vols. 1 and 2. New York, Grune & Stratton.

Edwards, Richard C., 1975, "The Social Relations of Production in the Firm and Labor Market Structure," in Richard C. Edwards, Michael Reich, and David M. Gordon, eds., *Labor Market Segmentation.* Lexington, Mass., D. C. Heath.

Fasteau, Marc.F., 1974, *The Male Machine.* New York, McGraw-Hill.

Hochschild, Arlie Russell, 1975, "The Sociology of Feeling and Emotion: Selected Possibilities," pp. 280–307 in Marcia Millman and Rosabeth Moss Kanter, eds., *Another Voice.* New York, Anchor Books.

Johnson, Miriam, 1963, "Sex Role Learning in the Nuclear Family," *Child Development,* 34, pp. 319–334.

———, 1975, "Fathers, Mothers and Sex-Typing," *Sociological Inquiry,* 45, #1, pp. 15–26.

Kohn, Melvin L., 1969, "A Note on Sex Differences in the Development of Masculine and Feminine Identification," *Psychological Review,* 66, pp. 126–135.

Lynn, David B., 1959, "A Note on Sex Differences in the Development of Masculine and Feminine Identification," *Psychological Review,* 66, pp. 126–135.

———, 1962, "Sex Role and Parent Identification," *Child Development,* 33, pp. 555–564.

Maccoby, Eleanor, and Carol Jacklin, 1974, *The Psychology of Sex Differences.* Stanford, Stanford University Press.

Mead, Margaret, 1949, *Male and Female.* New York, Dell Publishing, 1968.

Mitscherlich, Alexander, 1963, *Society Without the Father: A Contribution to Social Psychology.* New York, Schocken Books, 1970.

Parsons, Talcott, 1942, "Age and Sex in the Social Structure of the United States," in 1964, *Essays in Sociological Theory.* New York, Free Press.

Parsons, Talcott, and Robert F. Bales, 1955, *Family, Socialization and Interaction Process.* New York, Free Press.

Pleck, Joseph H., and Jack Sawyer, 1974, *Men and Masculinity.* New Jersey, Prentice-Hall.

Roessler, Richard T., 1971, "Masculine Differentiation and Feminine Constancy," *Adolescence,* 6, #22, pp. 187–196.

Rosaldo, Michelle Z., 1974, "Woman, Culture, and Society: A Theoretical Overview," in M. Z. Rosaldo and Louise Lamphere, eds., 1974, *Woman, Culture and Society.*

Slater, Philip E., 1961, "Toward a Dualistic Theory of Identification," *Merrill-Palmer Quarterly of Behavior and Development,* 7, #2, pp. 113–126.

———, 1968, *The Glory of Hera: Greek Mythology and the Greek Family.* Boston, Beacon Press.

Stoller, Robert J., 1964, "A Contribution to the Study of Gender Identity," *International Journal of Psycho-Analysis,* 45, pp. 220–226.

———, 1965, "The Sense of Maleness," *Psychoanalytic Quarterly,* 34, pp. 207–218.

———, 1968, "The Sense of Femaleness," *Psychoanalytic Quarterly,* 37, #1, pp. 42–55.

Whiting, Beatrice B., and John W. M. Whiting, 1975, *Children of Six Cultures.* Cambridge, Harvard University Press.

Whiting, John W. M., 1959, "Sorcery, Sin and the Superego: A Cross-Cultural Study of Some Mechanisms of Social Control," pp. 147–168 in Clellan S. Ford, ed., 1967, *Cross-Cultural Approaches: Readings in Comparative Research.* New Haven, Human Relations Area Files.

Winch, Robert F., 1962, *Identification and Its Familial Determinants.* New York, Bobbs-Merrill.

FEMINISM AND WOMEN OF COLOR

The Myth of Black Matriarchy

Bell Hooks

Many of the anti-black-woman stereotypes originated during slavery. Long before sociologists perpetuated theories about the existence of a black matriarchy, white male slaveowners created a body of myths to discredit the contributions of black females; one such myth was the notion that they were all masculinized sub-human creatures. Black female slaves had shown that they were capable of performing so-called "manly" labor, that they were able to endure hardship, pain, and privation but could also perform those so-called "womanly" tasks of housekeeping, cooking, and child rearing. Their ability to cope effectively in a sexist-defined "male" role threatened patriarchal myths about the nature of woman's inherent physiological difference and inferiority. By forcing black female slaves to perform the same work tasks as black male slaves, white male patriarchs were contradicting their own sexist order that claimed woman to be inferior because she lacked physical prowess. An explanation had to be provided to explain why black women were able to perform tasks that were cited by patriarchs as jobs women were incapable of performing. To explain the black female's ability to survive without the direct aid of a male and her ability to perform tasks that were culturally defined as "male" work, white males argued that black slave women were not "real" women but were masculinized sub-human creatures. It is not unlikely that white men feared that white women, witnessing the black female slave's ability to cope as effectively in the work force as men, might develop ideas about social equality between the sexes and encourage political solidarity between black and white women. Whatever the reason, black women posed so great a threat to the existing patriarchy that white men perpetuated the notion that black women possessed unusual masculine-like characteristics not common to the female species. To prove their point, they often forced black women to labor at difficult jobs while black male slaves stood idle.

The unwillingness of present-day scholars to accept as a positive step social equality between the sexes in any sphere led to the formation of the theory that a black matriarchy existed in the black family structure. Male social scientists formulated theories about the matriarchal power of black females to provide an out-of-the-ordinary explanation for the independent and decisive role black women played within the black family structure. Like their slaveowning ancestors, racist scholars acted as if black women fulfilling their role as mothers and economic providers were performing a unique action that needed a new definition even though it was not uncommon for many poor and widowed white women to perform this dual role. Yet they labeled black women matriarchs—a title that in no way accurately described the social status of black women in America. No matriarchy has ever existed in the United States.

At the very time sociologists proclaimed the existence of a matriarchal order in the black family structure, black women represented one of the largest socially and economically deprived groups in America whose status in no way resembled that of a matriarch. Political activist Angela Davis writes of the label matriarch:

> The designation of the black woman as a matriarch is a cruel misnomer because it ignores the profound traumas the black woman must have experienced when she had to surrender her child-bearing to alien and predatory economic interest.

The term matriarch implies the existence of a social order in which women exercise social and political power, a state which in no way resembles the condition of black women or all women in American society. The decisions that determine the way in which black women must live their lives are made by others, usually white men. If sociologists are to casually label black women matriarchs, they should also label female children playing house and acting out the role of mother matriarchs. For in both instances, no real effective power exists that allows the females in question to control their own destiny.

In their article "Is the Black Male Castrated," Jean Bond and Pauline Perry write of the matriarchy myth:

> The casting of this image of the black female in sociological bold relief is both consistent and logical in racist terms, for the so-called Black matriarch is a kind of folk character largely fashioned by whites out of half truths and lies about the involuntary conditions of black women.

The misuse of the term matriarch has led many people to identify any woman present in a household where no male resides a matriarch. Although anthropologists disagree about whether or not matriarchal societies ever really existed, an examination of available information about the supposed social structure of matriarchies proves without any doubt that the social status of the matriarch was in no way similar to that of black women in the United States. Within the matriarchal society woman was almost always economically secure. The economic situation of black women in United States has never been secure. While the average median income of employed black men has in recent years often surpassed the average median income of white females, the wages black women receive on the average remain considerably lower than that of both white females and black males. The matriarch was most often the owner of property. Since black women receive on the average low or middle incomes, only a few individuals are able to secure and hold property. Within the woman-centered society, the matriarch assumes the authoritative role in government and home life. Anthropologist Helen Diner found in her research on matriarchs that the position of the woman was like that of the man in patriarchal society. Commenting on the matriarchal role, Diner states, "If one sees her perform heavy labor while the male lounges or putters about the house, it is because he is not permitted to perform or decide important things."

Although white sociologists would have all Americans believe that the black female is often the "man of the house," this is rarely the case. Even in single-parent homes, black mothers may go so far as to delegate the responsibility of being the "man" to male children. In some single-parent homes where no male is present, it is acceptable for a visiting male friend or lover to assume a decision-making role. Few black women, even in homes where no men are present, see themselves as adopting a "male" role. Concurrently in American political life few black women exercise decision-making power. While it is true that in contemporary times more black women can be seen in the political arena than ever before in history, in proportion to the population of black women this number is relatively small. The Joint Center for Political Studies located in Washington D.C. reported on the extent to which sexism and racism have led to under-representation of black women in government, and their study revealed:

> Black females in America have more than doubled their presence among elected officials in the four years since 1969. Yet, even today, they account for only about 12% of black elected officials and are an "infinitesimally" small percentage of the elected office holders in the nation the survey revealed. The report continues by saying there are about seven million black women of voting age in the country, but they hold only 336 of the more than 520,000 elective offices in the country. Yet the total number of black women office holders today represent about 160% increase over their number four years ago.

Many features that anthropologists claim characterize matriarchal social structure resemble privileges and rights feminists are fighting to obtain. One such feature of matriarchal society was the complete control women had over their bodies. Diner asserts, "Above all the woman possessed free disposition over her body and may interrupt pregnancy whenever she wishes or prevent it all together." The inability of women in modern society to gain control over their bodies in regards to childbirth has been a primary impetus behind the women's liberation movement. Lower class women and consequently many black women have the least control over their bodies. In most states, women with enough money (particularly upper and middle class white women), have always been able to rid themselves of unwanted pregnancies. It has been poor women, black and white, who have had the fewest opportunities to exercise control over their reproductive activities. Diner cites many other characteristics common to matriarchal societies which in no way parallel patterns of behavior common to black women. Studying the preferred sex of children in the matriarchal culture, Diner found, "Female children are preferred because they continue the family which boys cannot." Black women, like most women in patriarchal societies prefer the birth of sons, as our society esteems the male child and often ignores or berates the female child. In the female-dominated state, domestic work was considered degrading to the woman just as it is considered beneath the male's dignity in a male-dominated society. Black women perform most of the domestic work in their own homes and in the homes of others. Marriage in the matriarchal state offered women the same privileges rewarded to men in the patriarchal state. Diner contends:

> In marriage obedience is demanded of the male as was specified in the marriage contracts of ancient Egypt. He also must remain faithful, while the wife remains unencumbered. She also retains the right of divorce and repudiation.

Black women have been restricted in these areas as have most women in patriarchal societies.

As is obvious, this cursory comparison of the status of matriarchs with that of black women reveals few similarities. Although various people have written essays and articles that discredit the theory that a black matriarchy exists, the term continues to be widely used to describe the status of black women. It is readily evoked by those white people who wish to perpetuate negative images of black womanhood. At the onset of the emergence of the matriarchy myth it was used to discredit black women and men. Black women were told that they had overstepped the bonds of femininity because they worked outside the home to provide economic support for their families and that by so doing they had de-masculinized black men. Black men were told that they were weak, effeminate, and castrated because "their" women were laboring at menial jobs.

White male scholars who examined the black family by attempting to see in what ways it resembled the white family structure were confident that their data was not biased by their own personal prejudices against women assuming an active role in family decision-making. But it must be remembered that these white males were educated in an elite institutional world that excluded both black people and many white women, institutions that were both racist and sexist. Consequently, when they observed black families, they chose to see the independence, will power, and initiative of black women as an attack on the masculinity of black men. Their sexism blinded them to the obvious positive benefits to both black men and women that occurred when black females assumed an active role in parenting. They argued that the black woman's performance of an active role in family life both as mothers and providers had deprived black men of their patriarchal status in the home. And this argument was used to explain the large numbers of female-headed households, the assumption being that black men had vacated their parenting roles because of domineering black women, whose dominance was attributed to their being economic providers while black men were unemployed.

The belief that men naturally want to provide for the economic well-being of their families and therefore feel de-masculinized if unemployment or low wages prevent them from so doing seems an out-of-place and totally false assumption in a society where men are taught to expect rewards for their provision. The structure of marriage in patriarchal society is based on a system of exchange, one in which men are traditionally taught to provide economically for women and children in exchange for sexual, housekeeping, and nurturing services. The argument that black men have been emasculated because they were not always able to assume the patriarchal role of provider is based on the assumption that black men feel that they should provide for their families and therefore feel unmanned or guilty if they cannot do so. Yet such an assumption does not appear to be based on actual fact. In many homes, black men who are employed are not eager to give money to wives and children and are even resentful that they are expected to share hard-earned low wages with others. Concurrently, despite the fact that the American capitalist economic structure forces many black men to be unemployed, there are some black men who would rather not work "shit" jobs with endless hassles and little monetary reward if they can survive without them; these men do not have doubts about their masculinity. To many of them a low paying menial job is more an attack on their masculinity than no job at all. While I do not mean to imply that there have not been large numbers of black men concerned with being providers, it is important that we remember that the desire to provide is not an innate male instinct. Surveys of groups of women from all races and classes who attempt to get child care payments from ex-husbands would provide ample evidence of the reluctance of men to assume provider roles. It is more likely that lower-middle and middle class black men who have absorbed standard definitions of masculinity would feel that it is important to provide economically for families and consequently feel ashamed, even de-masculinized if unable to assume the provider role. But at the time of the emergence of the matriarchy myth as popular social theory, the great majority of black men were working class. And among working class men, who are by definition the recipients of low wages and who almost always have difficulty providing for families, achievement of manhood or masculine status is not determined solely on the basis of economics.

An ignorant person hearing an analysis of the black matriarchy theory might easily assume that the jobs black women were able to acquire which enabled them to be providers elevated their status above that of black men, but that was never the case. In actuality many of the service jobs black women were employed to perform forced them into daily contact with racist whites who abused and humiliated them. They may have suffered much more intensely a feeling of being de-humanized and degraded than unemployed black men who stood on street corners all day long. Being employed at a low paying job does not necessarily lead to a positive self-concept. It may very well be that unemployed black men were able to maintain a personal dignity that black women employed in service jobs were forced to surrender in their work arena. I can certainly remember lower class black men in our neighborhood commenting on the fact that some jobs were not worth doing because of the loss of one's personal dignity, whereas black women were made to feel that when survival was the crucial issue, personal dignity should be sacrificed. The black female who thought herself "too good" to do domestic work or other service jobs was often ridiculed for being uppity. Yet everyone sympathized when unemployed black men talked about their inability to accept "the man" bossing them. Sexist thinking made it acceptable for black men to refuse menial work even if they were unable to provide for family and children. Many black men who deserted family and children were not regarded contemptuously even though such behavior on the part of black women should have been condemned.

The argument that black women were matriarchs was readily accepted by black people even though it was an image created by white males. Of all the negative stereotypes and myths that have been used to characterize black womanhood, the matriarchy label has had the greatest impact on the consciousness of many black people. . . .

Imperialism, the Family, and Cultures of Resistance
Mina Davis Caulfield

The contemporary women's movement has insisted on describing women's oppression in terms of women's concrete experience, and on discarding abstract ideologies that prevent honest description. In order to assert the crucial importance of the family and personal life and to develop a critique of women's oppression in the family, we have had to go beyond the idea that only commodity production and public political relations are significant. Unfortunately, we have not used the same honesty in examining the experiences of women in other cultures, especially women in colonial situations. Our emphasis on "sisterhood," on the common oppression of all women by male domination, has contributed to ethnocentrism in our movement. The strength and excitement generated by the concept and practice of sisterhood have caused us to look first or exclusively at those aspects of daily life shared by all females (sex stereotyped roles, devaluation of domestic labor, etc.), without considering the contrasts between our situation as women, and the situation of women in colonial or neocolonial societies.

The family must be examined in relation to imperialism as a system, or we are likely to continue the ethnocentrism that has been important in keeping the movement largely white and culturally Anglo middle class. We have made the small, isolated nuclear household and the non-collective nature of domestic labor—both characteristic of American capitalism—central to our analysis of women's oppression; we cannot assume that our conclusions apply to other societies.

Imperialism does not simply reproduce the capitalist mode of production, either industrial or domestic. Rosa Luxemburg has argued that capitalism "depends in all respects on noncapitalist strata and social organizations existing side by side with it," not only as markets but also as sources of labor power and resources.[1] At the same time, capitalist imperialism seeks to stamp out other modes of economy. Without necessarily accepting her argument as to the necessity of these noncapitalist systems for the continued existence of capitalism, it seems clear that she is pointing out an important contradiction. This tendency of imperialist systems to eradicate other economic and social systems, but at the same time to preserve and exploit them in distorted forms that remain outside the sphere of commodity production, is crucial to an understanding of the relation between imperialism and family structures. In colonial societies family-based economic and social systems are thus simultaneously assaulted and exploited. At the same time such systems are central to the physical survival, cultural identity, and anti-imperialist struggles of the people.

Imperialism assaults the total culture: it does not simply impose foreign domination, introduce new productive forces, or make available new market commodities to a "backward" area. Imperial intrusion deeply affects social structures, economic relations, and cultural traditions; it imposes powerful alien institutions and represents them as inherently—racially and culturally—superior. In response, many colonized peoples have developed resistance strategies centering around new forms of cultural affirmation directly or subtly opposed to the massive imperial affirmation of Western European cultural superiority. . . .

Imperialist assaults on families take many forms. In the first place, families as sources of power frequently constitute real threats to the authority of the invader. Just as imperialists are concerned to dominate and exploit the pre-existing state apparatus, economic system, and religious institutions, so also they seek to eliminate the corporate power of kin groups, especially in those societies which are organized around lineages. Various colonial strategies, such as the forcible introduction of private property in land to replace communal ownership and control, are mechanisms for breaking down the organizational strength of families, as well as for facilitating the appropriation of land for the commercial uses of the "export sector." The Western preference for small, father-headed families does not simply reflect an ethnocentric bias toward the "Christian" norm, but is part of a larger strategy of "divide and rule."

Within the family, the power of men is increased. Insofar as colonial authority is extended to portions of the dominated population, these portions will tend to be male, not female. The Western practice of educating boys rather than girls, the introduction of private property rights to men even in areas of traditional female inheritance, and the religious ideology of male dominance in the Holy Family all reinforce whatever elements of male chauvinism may exist in the traditional culture, and threaten traditions of female independence or equality. At the same time men as well as women are coming under the overall

[1]Rosa Luxemborg, *The Accumulation of Capital* (London, 1963), p. 365.

domination of the colonizers: traditional socializing roles are taken out of the family into mission schools, land is expropriated, customs are outlawed, etc. The family as a whole, whatever its structure, loses power in society, and the increased power of men in relation to women is not accompanied by a net increase in men's power.

The assault on the power of the family and the intensification of male dominance are not the only effects of imperialism on families. Imperialism introduces economic enterprises—plantation agriculture, mining, industry—that typically use colonial labor on an individual basis, regardless of the preexisting productive units (extended families, kin-based cooperative groups, etc.). Slave labor systems are perhaps the ultimate in this individuating pattern, where each worker is bought and sold separately, regardless of family ties; only the very young, below the age of any possible productive output, are recognized as belonging to a collectivity that the master need take into account.

In the slave societies of the West Indies and the Southern United States, despite the planters' indifference or hostility to family bonds, slaves *in their own productive relations* resisted the pressures toward individuation. Through minimal and extended family networks slave women and men devised organizational forms for the survival of the young, and maintained cultural patterns of resistance to and rebellion against the colonizer. In these societies slaves could not depend for survival on the handouts of the masters; autonomous productive systems were clearly present.[2]

Survival strategies included cultivating "provision grounds" after hours in many Caribbean societies, and sharing stolen or illegally hunted and cultivated food in the quarters of North American slaves. In all such strategies, kin or pseudo-kin networks organized primarily by women but including fathers, brothers, and sons provided the organizational framework.[3]

In the Caribbean, such minimal productive systems based on family labor were in many cases extended into society-wide marketing systems. Surpluses were actually generated by these groups, working at night after their long hours in the sugar fields, and women traveled about with them, often illegally, cementing social bonds of many kinds in the process and facilitating the creation of new cultural patterns and organizational communications, leading in many cases to active revolts. In this example, it is clear that we must look not only at the ways in which the colonizer acts to *break down* family solidarity, but also the ways in which the colonized—women, men, and children—act to *maintain, consolidate, and build anew* the basic units in which children can grow and be encultured in the values and relationships that are independent of and in opposition to the imperial culture. There may be many institutions involved in a culture of resistance—religions, educational systems, or the marketing organization described above; but the family is basic, with its forms of economic

---

[2]See my discussion on the data on slavery in Mina Caulfield, "Slavery and the Origins of Black Culture: Elkins Revisited," in Peter Rose, ed., *Slavery and Its Aftermath* (New York, 1970).

[3]See Angela Davis on the central role of women in slave communities.

organization and socializing functions. And it is in the family networks that we see most clearly the rejection of imperialist attempts to isolate each individual worker in his or her productive relations.

This process of isolation is not limited to systems of slave labor. The introduction by imperialism of wage labor cuts workers off from kin groups, and drives a further wedge between men and women. In most colonial situations men are the preferred target for recruitment into wage labor, while women must take on various kinds of double work loads. Generally, women remain responsible for traditional subsistence and nurturing activities, and in addition they take on one or both of two new jobs: wage work at lower rates of pay than men, and the former subsistence jobs of men who are absent from the domestic labor force. In both cases, survival of the family as a group and the biological survival of children become the primary tasks of women. These activities constitute forms of production and reproduction which are *alternative* to complete dependence on the economic systems introduced by the colonizers; by the same token, women and families become the focal points for the perpetuation of alternative systems of values, customs, and culture which are so important in building resistance movements. . . .

Carol Stack, Joyce Ladner, and Nancy Tanner, in their writings on the black family in the United States, have stressed the importance of kin-based networks with women as the key figures in maintaining survival strategies. Carol Stack says of these networks:

> The basis of familial structure and cooperation is not the nuclear family of the middle class, but an extended cluster of kinsmen related chiefly through children but also through marriage and friendship, who align to provide domestic functions. This cluster, or domestic network, is diffused over several kin-based households, and fluctuations in individual household composition do not significantly affect cooperative arrangements.[4]

Putting the point in a more historical framework, Nancy Tanner says:

> The Black American kinship system, as it developed in the United States, has put a premium on flexibility. This has meant maintaining a wide range of bilateral kin ties that can be activated as need arises. Kin often reside together or care for one another's children. Extended kin networks may reach from the rural South to northern cities. These flexible kin ties are an important and historically persistent part of the Black American kinship system.[5]

The migration to urban centers has not destroyed the basic family structure that American blacks have developed to deal with the pressures of colonial existence.

[4]"Sex Roles and Survival Strategies in an Urban Black Community," in Michelle Zimbalist Rosaldo and Louise Lamphere, eds., *Woman, Culture, and Society* (California: Stanford University Press), 1974, p. 114. See also Carol Stack, *All Our Kin: Strategies for Survival in a Black Community* (New York: Harper & Row), 1974.

[5]"Matrifocality in Indonesia and Africa and among Black Americans," in Rosaldo and Lamphere, p. 154.

Black women have been central to the perpetuation of autonomous value systems of the group. These women are far from the "domestic wards" Karen Sacks poses as the fate of women in class societies. As Joyce Ladner says, "One of the chief characteristics defining the Black woman is her realistic approach to her own resources. Instead of becoming resigned to her fate, she has always sought creative solutions to her problems. The ability to utilize her existing resources and yet maintain a forthright determination to struggle against the racist society in whatever overt and subtle ways necessary is one of her major attributes."[6]

The emphasis on resourcefulness, flexibility, and creativity rather than fatalism, passivity, and dependence (qualities usually attributed to women—and to peasants) is crucial: the family forms developed to deal with imperialism cannot be interpreted as foot-dragging, conservative attempts to return to a pre-imperialist "golden age." As Fanon has pointed out,[7] elements of traditional culture are transformed in the process of struggle against oppression; the transformation of families is an example of this process. In looking to future transformations of colonial and neocolonial societies, this long history of the struggles of women and families points to the possible development of new family forms, building on the past but surely not returning to it. I have not meant to imply that precolonial family structures were models of non-oppressive relations; imperialism has tended to reinforce pre-existing forms of male dominance and ideologies of male supremacy. The oppressive aspects of colonized families must be recognized, not minimized; but future transformations of the family will need analysis which goes beyond the assumption that families can only be agents of patriarchal oppression.

Ending imperialism will not necessarily end all forms of oppression of women in these societies, just as building socialism does not guarantee liberation from male domination. To the extent, however, that the struggle against imperialism takes place with the active participation of women and men who are consciously striving for an end to the special forms of exploitation relating to families, that struggle can make use of the creative forces so apparent in the history of colonial peoples. Cultures of resistance are not simply adaptive mechanisms; they embody important alternative ways of organizing production and reproduction and value systems critical of those of the oppressor. Recognition of the special position of families in these cultures and social structures can lead to new forms of struggle, new goals.

The resourcefulness and creativity of women in their domestic strategies of survival have made the family forms characteristic of colonized groups a source of strength for anti-colonial resistance which has been far too little recognized. Furthermore, the importance of these family systems suggests a reason for the relative lack of success of feminist appeals to third-world women. Colonized women are not interested so much in combating the domestic dominance of their

---

[6]*Tomorrow's Tommorrow: the Black Woman* (Garden City, N.Y., 1971), pp. 276–77.
[7]Frantz Fanon, *The Wretched of the Earth* (New York, 1963), pp. 223–25.

husbands (though this may indeed be a problem for them) as in insuring the *inclusion* of men in domestic networks of mutual support. Female solidarity or "sisterhood" does not have the same meaning for women engaged in creating and maintaining extensive female-centered networks for gaining strength in the domestic subsistence and child-rearing areas of production as it has for the isolated housewife in advanced capitalist societies. The idea of social and economic resourcefulness and self-reliance is not new for women in colonial situations. The primary form of oppression experienced by these women is not the intimate dependency that feminists are combating. On the contrary, the direction of female strategies under colonial exploitation has been toward strengthening kin bonds with both women *and* men, and toward resisting the dichotomization of role and responsibility which colonialism fosters.

We know very little about female and family-oriented survival strategies under the wide variety of colonial systems of domination; male bias in anthropology has obscured both the exploitation and the sources of power of women, as many of my sisters in the field are now pointing out. What I have presented here is not a general theory of working and peasant families in the entire colonial and neocolonial world. At the least, there are important contrasts in the degree of intensity of the trends I have noted between societies with highly articulated precolonial class and caste systems such as India, China, and the Islamic countries on the one hand, and the plantation societies I have discussed. More information is needed before a general theory can be advanced; what I am suggesting here is a partial theoretical framework.[8]

We need to listen more to women who are living under neocolonialism and colonialism. Much of American feminism does not speak to their needs or experience. If we are interested in discovering the kinds of social and economic changes necessary for doing away with sexist *and* imperialist domination, we cannot assume that our own experience will tell us how much women everywhere suffer under the oppression of their husbands and fathers, or that our role is to explain to all women who their exploiters really are. Further, we must avoid seeing people who exist under conditions of severe oppression simply as *victims.* Sufferers everywhere don't simply suffer; they fight back, and that very definitely includes the women who live with the types of super-exploitation that I have discussed. To recognize the active resistance of the victims of imperialism is crucial to a consciousness of the common sources of oppression, as well as its diverse forms, a consciousness free of guilt, which will help us fight back against our own suffering.

---

[8]I do not want to leave the impression, however, that what we need is a multitude of North American bourgeois anthropologists descending on colonized populations to seek out and write up such strategies for scholarly journals. The usefulness of such studies to the populations in question is at the very least doubtful. I am reminded of the aftermath of the 1929 revolt of Ibo women, when the British sent two women anthropologists to "study the causes of the riot and to uncover the organizational base that permitted such spontaneity and solidarity among the women" (Nancy Leis, "Women in Groups: Ijaw Women's Associations," in Rosaldo and Lamphere, p. 223). More counterinsurgency research we don't need.

APPLYING THE FRAMEWORKS: SEXUALITY

Pin up on your bed, your mirror, your wall, a sign, lady, until you know it in every part of your being: We were designed to delight, excite, and satisfy the male of the species.
    Real *women know this.*

"J"
The Sensuous Woman

The bride should be advised to allow her husband's sex drive to set their pace and she should attempt to gear her satisfaction to his. If she finds after several months or years that this is not possible, she is advised to consult her physician as soon as she realizes there is a real problem.

Novak's *Textbook of Gynecology,* 1970

I am your best fantasy and your worst fear.

Sign at a gay rights demonstration

The liberated orgasm is any orgasm you like, under any circumstances you find comfortable.

Barbara Seaman
Free and Female, Coward, McCann & Geoghegan, New York, 1972, p. 67.

When I speak of the erotic, then, I speak of it as an assertion of the life-force of women; of that creative energy empowered, the knowledge and use of which we are now reclaiming in our language, our history, our dancing, our loving, our work, our lives.

Audre Lorde

Sexuality, like the family, has been an area of human life that has received little sustained attention from modern political theory. The natural law tradition defined intercourse between married couples as the only natural or normal sexual activity and regarded other sexual practices as sinful or abnormal. Most political theorists, even those who rejected the natural law approach in other areas, were content until the contemporary period to accept this position.

In the twentieth century, sexuality became an issue. The emergence of this issue is correlated with a reduced demand for labor power on farms and factories as a result of new mechanical labor-saving devices, with improvements in health care and sanitary hygiene that resulted in reduced infant mortality rates in the industrial world, and with technological developments that made possible new forms of contraception. Taken together these developments led people to challenge the link between sexuality and reproduction and to raise questions about new modes of sexual expression that were not linked to reproduction. Since it had been women whose sexuality had been most sharply constrained by fear of pregnancy, and whose life options had been most limited by repeated pregnancies, it is not surprising that women were in the forefront of those who challenged traditional views of sexuality.

The rise of the contemporary women's movement gave a new context to women's questions about sexuality. The new feminists showed that women's sexuality had frequently been exploited and degraded and used to sell commodities, even to turn women themselves into commodities. In seeking to reappropriate their sexuality, women have no existing models, for most if not all previous societies have been male-dominated and all have tied sexuality to reproduction. Women therefore have to start from scratch in redefining their sexuality, and the questions that confront them are many: What kinds of relationships and practices enhance our personhood? Who, if anyone, shall we choose as our sexual partner(s)? How can we distinguish between those aspects of our culture that are erotic and reflect a positive attitude toward our bodies and our sexuality and those that are simply exploitative and degrading? How safe are most female contraceptives, and whose sexual freedom have they promoted? What is the best way of integrating sexuality into our lives? The alternative theoretical frameworks we have been examining in this volume offer very different analyses of prevailing sexuality and different criteria for changing it.

CONSERVATISM

Conservative views on sexuality make numerous references to biology. They appeal to behavior among lower animals and insects and to human physiology. According to conservatives' reading of it, biology dictates a sexually active and aggressive role for the man and defines the woman as sexually passive. Anthony Storr cites as evidence for this view the "fact" that the "spermatozoon swims actively, whilst the ovum passively awaits its penetration." Further, we are told that the structure of the female and male sex organs dictates this relation. Man must conquer and woman must submit. Her sexuality has fulfillment through pregnancy as its goal, while his aims and needs focus on pleasure and sexual release. Aggression is portrayed as a necessary part of male sexuality, and its frustration is considered dangerous. Taken to its logical conclusion, the conservative view of male sexuality offered by Storr seems to justify male sexual behavior bordering on rape.

Earlier in this book we saw the conservative fear of any alteration in traditional relations between the sexes. Conservatives are equally fearful of any alternatives to male-dominated heterosexual intercourse. The structure of the vagina and the penis are interpreted as evidence that heterosexual intercourse is the only natural and therefore normal form of sexual activity. Alternative modes of heterosexual activity, as well as lesbianism and male homosexuality, are rejected as unnatural and perverse.

LIBERALISM

Liberals totally reject the conservative insistence that heterosexual intercourse is the only normal and therefore moral permissible form of sexual expression. On the liberal view, there is no reason to suppose that any mode of sexual activity is biologically determined or more natural than any other. Thus, liberals reject the conservative notion that different standards should be used to judge the sexual behavior of women and men—or, indeed, that there should be any specifically sexual rules of conduct. Sexual activity is only one of many forms of human action and interaction. It has no special moral status and should be governed by the same sorts of considerations as any other behavior. Primary among these considerations are the typically liberal values of individual freedom, equal opportunity, and avoidance of harm to others. Some of these values, particularly the emphasis on individual freedom, are expressed in Shere Hite's advice to her readers that they are "to make physical relations with other people, of either sex, anything you like."

At the heart of the liberal position is the view that one's private life should not be subject to social regulation. Sexuality is a private concern, and individuals should be free to pursue fulfillment in any way they choose as long as they do not harm anyone else. Regarded in this way, the choice to earn one's living through prostitution might be defended by the liberal theorist on the grounds that as long as the choice is made freely, society has no right to interfere. It is interesting to recognize, by way of comparison, that what the liberal would regard as a free choice in this case the Marxist would criticize as resulting from economic coercion. The difference in their analyses results from the liberal's acceptance of the public/private distinction and the failure to recognize that people's so-called private lives in fact are shaped by power differentials based on wealth. The Marxist view, on the other hand, situates individual choices within the context of class society where vast inequalities in wealth, power, and opportunities create tremendous variations in real freedom of choice.

Letty Cottin Pogrebin offers advice to parents who wish to raise their children in a nonsexist way. Like all liberal feminists, she rejects the sexual double standard which says that "girls should be good and boys should be careful." The consistent liberal will raise both daughters and sons to assume responsibility for their sexuality by making conscious decisions about the quality of their relationships and by practicing contraception. In rejecting the sexual double standard, liberals also reject the imposition of contrasting and limiting sexual stereotypes. Traditional feminine passivity, for instance, does not prevent young women from engaging in sexual activity; it simply renders them unprepared to deal with the emotional and physical consequences of that activity in a realistic and responsible manner.

In general, the liberal, unlike the conservative, tends to adopt an attitude of tolerance toward lesbianism and male homosexuality as long as these practices are carried out by consenting adults in private. Liberalism rejects the view that homosexuality is an "illness" and places its emphasis on individual fulfillment through varied experimentation and on equal opportunity to pursue pleasure without the structures of highly defined sex roles.

TRADITIONAL MARXISM

In principle, traditional Marxists are far from indifferent to issues of sexuality, especially to issues regarding women's sexuality. Unlike liberal theorists, they do not accept that there should be any area of private life that is exempted from state regulation. Moreover, they acknowledge and condemn the fact that women's sexuality has been controlled and exploited for thousands of years by men.

Although traditional Marxists recognize in principle that sexuality is a political issue, in practice sexuality has been an issue that they have largely ignored. The reason for this lies in the traditional Marxist conception of how historical change occurs. The conceptual framework of traditional Marxism is distinguished by its economic focus: the shape of existing society is seen as determined ultimately by the prevailing economic system. On the traditional Marxist view, therefore, only a transformation of that economic system will bring about fundamental social change.

Because of their emphasis on the primacy of the economy, traditional Marxist theorists have devoted little theoretical attention to the issue of sexuality. What they have produced often has been more a reflection of prevailing prejudices than a consistent extension of Marxist theory. For instance, even though Engels mocks the ethnocentrism of nineteenth-century anthropologists, who only saw "primitive society . . . as a brothel," he himself is quite uncritical in his acceptance of the prevailing condemnation of homosexuality, and the interview with Lenin reprinted here indicates a similar acceptance of popular prejudices.

The position on sexual fulfilment most consistent with traditional Marxist theory is the one taken by Engels when he maintains that a definition of nonexploitative, mutually fulfilling sexual relationships must await the time when differences in power and wealth no longer separate women and men.

RADICAL FEMINISM

Rather than a private or a secondary matter, radical feminism views sexuality as an issue of central political concern. Although male dominance is manifested in all prevailing social institutions, many radical feminists argue that the roots of male dominance lie in the male control of women's sexuality. Men traditionally have defined women as primarily sexual beings and have identified heterosexual intercourse as the norm for sexual activity. If these male views are accepted, it follows that emotional and sexual relationships with men provide the most important opportunities for fulfilment in women's lives.

Ti-Grace Atkinson argues that women who accept this picture are deceived by male ideology. Determined to achieve self-fulfilment as males define it, women "fall in love," a state of hysterical self-deception that allows them to ignore their real situation of humiliating subordination and dependence.

In arguing that heterosexual intercourse should not be the norm of sexual activity, radical feminists draw support from the now popular acceptance of the fact that, for most women, orgasm requires direct clitoral stimulation of the kind that is not ordinarily provided during heterosexual intercourse. Recognition of this fact naturally raises the question why women continue to participate in heterosexual intercourse. Earlier radical feminists suggested that it was because women were deceived by the male ideology of love and romance; more recently, radical feminists have suggested that it is because women have no real choice. Kathleen Barry claims that many women literally are sexual slaves. She demonstrates this by examining a variety of practices from prostitution to marriage. The women on whom she focusses are subjected to physical, sexual, and psychological violence and have no realistic prospect of escape.

Within a context of male dominance, radical feminists argue that heterosexuality not only fails to satisfy women's needs but also, because women are always in a position of relative powerlessness, is necessarily masochistic and perverse for women. Many radical feminists argue that women's sexual needs can be fulfilled only within a lesbian relationship. This is true both because a genuinely loving relationship is possible only between equals and because the unique quality of female sexuality can be best understood by another woman.

In a recent essay that has already become a classic, Adrienne Rich argues against narrow and exclusive definitions of lesbianism. She posits the existence of what she calls a lesbian continuum, a continuum that stretches from overt sexual acts between women at one end to deep emotional or political bonds between women at the other. Her concern is to celebrate lesbianism as the paradigm case of resistance to male dominance and to show that all feminists, and even many women who did not view themselves as feminists, have been lesbian in this sense. Like many radical feminists, Rich takes women's subordination as rooted in male control of women's sexuality; only this analysis justifies Rich's assumption that lesbianism is fundamentally involved in all forms of feminist resistance, even those that on the surface are nonsexual. This analysis also justifies the radical feminist claim that how one expresses one's sexuality is always a political issue, whether or not one is conscious of its political implications.

SOCIALIST FEMINISM

Socialist feminism insists that an adequate understanding of contemporary sexuality must examine how it has been shaped both by capitalism and by male dominance. In contrast with traditional Marxism, which views sexuality as being of secondary importance, both theoretically and politically, Gordon and Hunter argue that contemporary Marxists must pay serious attention to the issues that revolve around family life and sexuality and must recognize those issues as political in a fundamental sense. It is particularly important for radicals, including feminists, to focus on these issues at a time when conservative groups have made so-called personal "life-style" questions central to contemporary political debate.

Many socialist feminists accept the radical feminist claim that male privilege is so pervasive in contemporary society that loving sexual relationships with men are difficult if not impossible. However, socialist feminists reject the radical feminist emphasis on sexual domination as the primary form of women's oppression. For socialist feminists, the antagonism between women and men is structured into the economic as well as the sexual foundation of society and can be eliminated only through a revolutionary transformation of every aspect of contemporary society and of all social relations, not only those between women and men. Ann Ferguson argues that many kinds of feminist activity are required to bring about such fundamental social change. To conceptualize all feminist activity as a form of lesbianism is a distortion of history and an oversimplification of the complexity of the political tasks that confront us.

In opposition to liberalism, socialist feminism claims that the options open to us in our efforts to reconstruct our sexuality are so rigidly molded and limited by society as to provide little genuine freedom of choice. Many socialist feminists argue that the supposed new sexual freedom and the seeming sexual permissiveness of contemporary

American society are in fact illusions. They grow out of the needs of a society organized around the profit motive and the preservation of male privilege. Under such conditions the liberal's emphasis on equal freedom and opportunity to explore our sexuality is deceptive. Male dominance provides stereotypically distorted models of masculinity and femininity as sexually desirable. Capitalism teaches that sexual attractiveness is dependent on a whole range of commodities, from expensive perfume to expensive automobiles. Genuine sexual liberation is possible only when our sexuality is no longer shaped by the need to make profits and to perpetuate male supremacy. Only in such a social context can we discover modes of sexual fulfilment that transcend stereotyping and commodification.

WOMEN OF COLOR

White women attempting to define their sexuality have been offered two images by patriarchal culture. They could choose between goddess or bitch, virgin or whore. They could identify as women with sexual needs and seek to fulfill them or they could choose to be the kind of women men marry—but not both. Women of color have found their options even more limited. Neither the role of goddess nor virgin has been available to them and thus they have been left with "bitch" and "whore." Traditionally white patriarchal society has found it useful to portray both black women and black men as more overtly sexual and less capable of controlling their "animal" instincts than white people. This has led to what Angela Davis refers to as "the myth of the black rapist" as well as its counterpart, "the myth of the bad (or sexually promiscuous) black women." These stereotypical portrayals facilitate the continued exploitation of black women and men. In her essay, Davis explores the way in which the historical persecution of black men through charges of rape motivated by racism further complicates the issue of rape for black women. She also reminds us that black women have had even more difficulty than white women in bringing charges of rape against their attackers.

In addition, while white women coming to terms with their sexuality have found themselves evaluated according to a male-defined, artificial conception of female beauty that most women could never approximate, the reality faced by women of color has been further compounded by racial differences. Thus while all women are subjected to an ideal of feminine beauty that is artificial, degrading and virtually unattainable, women of color find themselves discounted at the outset by a standard that excludes them from the ideal by definition. This creates unique problems for women of color in grappling with their own sexuality as well as creating special problems in the relations between black women and black men.

CONSERVATISM

Aggression in the Relations between the Sexes

Anthony Storr

. . . In the relation between the sexes, the spermatozoon swims actively, whilst the ovum passively awaits its penetration. The anatomy of the sexual organs itself attests the differentiation of the sexual role; and although culture and ontogenetic development may obscure the psychological dichotomy, anatomy and physiology form the inescapable substratum upon which the emotional difference between the sexes stands firm. In simpler creatures than ourselves, it is possible to stimulate the various drives concurrently or separately. Thus, in cichlids, aggression, fear and sexual behaviour can be elicited by appropriate stimuli, or more than one drive set in motion at once. In female cichlids, aggression and sexuality can march together, but fear prevents the male from exercising his sexual function.

It is dangerous to press the analogy too far; but, in ourselves, the parallel is close. Male sexuality, because of the primitive necessity of pursuit and penetration, does contain an important element of aggressiveness; an element which is both recognized and responded to by the female who yields and submits. Moreover, it is impossible for the male human who is frightened of women either himself to become fully aroused or to awake a corresponding response in the female. Impotence in men, whether partial or complete, is invariably the result of fears which may be, and often are, unconscious.

In women, however, the reverse is more generally true. Although women who suffer from excessive fear of the sexual act may also be frigid, it is the aggressive woman who resents the male and who is unconsciously competing with him who constitutes the commoner problem in our culture. A complete and fully satisfying sexual relationship implies emotional commitment on either side. There are many people who, because of the vicissitudes of their childhood development, are unable to achieve this; who cannot trust themselves to love without reserve, and who cannot trust another to love them unequivocally. The emotional insecurity which underlies this lack of faith in other human beings tends to cause different forms of behaviour in the two sexes. Insecure men are frequently less dominant and aggressive than their more confident counterparts. Insecure women commonly display a greater degree of aggressiveness and competitiveness than their more secure sisters.

Moreover, Christianity has for so long taught us to conceive of love in terms of self-sacrifice and gentleness that there are many couples who have never experienced the full splendour of sexuality. Innumerable manuals have instructed husbands to be so restrained, or so careful in their love-making that they have inhibited the aggressive component in sexual congress with the result that their wives' cannot fully respond to them, and they themselves fail to gain complete satisfaction.

The role of aggression in the relation between the sexes may be further underlined by a glance at the so-called sexual deviations. Insecure people who have been unable to achieve complete sexual happiness commonly have sexual phantasies of which they are often deeply ashamed, but which contain, albeit in exaggerated form, the elements of erotic passion which are missing from their actual sexual lives. These phantasies are generally, though not invariably, sadomasochistic in content; that is, concerned with male dominance and female submission in extreme degree. It is significant that there is a difference between the sexes in the type of phantasy which appeals to each. The idea of being seized and borne off by a ruthless male who will wreak his sexual will upon his helpless victim has a universal appeal to the female sex. It is the existence of this phantasy which accounts for the wide popularity of such figures as *The Sheik,* Rhett Butler, or even King Kong. A *frisson* of fear of the more dominant male reinforces rather than inhibits erotic arousal in females; and the phobias of men under the bed or hidden in dark corners which are so common in adolescent girls, invariably contain an element of concealed sexual excitement as well as fear. On the other hand, women, however forceful they may actually be, seldom have phantasies of dominating or humiliating men, although they may take part in erotic activities which involve this in order to please the men who demand it of them.

In contrast to women, men very frequently have sexual phantasies in which they behave sadistically; and a vast erotic literature exists in which women are bound, restricted, rendered helpless or beaten. There is generally a wide gap between phantasy and reality, in that men who find themselves the prey of sadistic imaginations seldom actually hurt their partners, whom they wish to enjoy the role of helpless victim. Psychopathic or psychotic persons may act out sadistic phantasies without regard to the feelings of their partners; but most men who are possessed by such thoughts are actually over-considerate, less demanding and less aggressive than is generally expected of the male.

For those unfamiliar with this area of human experience it is less easy to understand why men also may have masochistic phantasies in which they are at the mercy of dominant females. The explanation is that the regressive wish to be cared for by a powerful figure is common to both sexes. For we all start life as helpless infants, and so both retain the memory, and may pursue the illusion, of an erotic relationship in which we are helpless in the hands of a powerful parent. The female is more prone to regress in this way because of her greater need for a protective figure. It is well recognized that women have a greater need for security than men; that is, for a home in which they can bring up their children, safe in the knowledge that a man will provide and care for them. Men tend to feel restricted by the same situation; caught, and used by the female for her own purposes, and it is of course this difference which accounts for a large part of the battle between the sexes. . . .

LIBERALISM

Redefining Sex

Shere Hite

Our definition of sex belongs to a world view that is past—or passing. Sexuality, and sexual relations, no longer define the important property right they once did; children are no longer central to the power either of the state or the individual. Although all of our social institutions are still totally based on hierarchical and patriarchal forms, patriarchy as a form is really dead, as is the sexuality that defined it. We are currently in a period of transition, although it is unclear as yet to what. The challenge for us now is to devise a more humane society, one that will implement the best of the old values, like kindness and understanding, cooperation, equality, and justice throughout *every* layer of public and private life—a metamorphosis to a more personal and humanized society.

Specifically, in sexual relations—which we should perhaps begin calling simply physical relations—we can again reopen many options. All the kinds of physical intimacy that were channeled into our one mechanical definition of sex can now be reallowed, and rediffused throughout our lives, including simple forms of touching and warm body contact. There need not be a sharp distinction between sexual touching and friendship. Just as women described "arousal" as one of the best parts of sex, and just as they described closeness as the most pleasurable aspect of intercourse, so intense physical intimacy can be one of the most satisfying activities possible—in and of itself.

Although we tend to think of "sex" as one set pattern, one group of activities (in essence, reproductive activity), there is no need to limit ourselves in this way. There is no reason why physical intimacy with men, for example, should always consist of "foreplay" followed by intercourse and male orgasm;[1] and there is no reason why intercourse must always be a part of heterosexual sex. Sex is intimate physical contact for pleasure, to share pleasure with another person (or just alone). You can have sex to orgasm, or not to orgasm, genital sex, or just physical intimacy—whatever seems right to you. There is never any reason to think the "goal" must be intercourse, and to try to make what you feel fit into that context. There is no standard of sexual performance "out there," against which you must measure yourself; you aren't ruled by "hormones" or "biology."

---

[1]This will be discussed from men's point of view in the analysis of the replies received to the questionnaire for men, to be published in the future. [*Editors' note:* The *Hite Report on Male Sexuality* was published in 1981 by Knopf, New York.]

You are free to explore and discover your own sexuality, to learn or unlearn anything you want, and to make physical relations with other people, of either sex, anything you like.

Sex Education for Growing Up Free

Letty Cottin Pogrebin

The usual answer to "How do you make a baby?" goes something like this: "When a man and woman love each other, they get married and the Daddy puts his penis inside the Mommy's vagina and plants a seed and it grows inside the Mommy's tummy and nine months later, a baby comes out."

Sounds right, but this tale is rife with misinformation.

Regardless of how young the child, no basic sex education conversation should give the impression that the anatomical sex difference is solely for making babies. This is not just a half-truth, it's a lie. People have sex without love, marriage, or procreational intent as kids soon enough learn from news about rapes in the neighborhood, or from witnessing a friend's mother share a bedroom with a man who is not her husband.

People make few babies in a lifetime, but they make a lot of love. Let your children think of their parents as lovers. Let them know that male-female sex is primarily for fun. You can add your own morality to that, but don't misrepresent the physical truth.

And ask yourself whether, in hiding your sexual intercourse from your children (which I happen to believe wise), you may also be hiding inadvertently, gestures of affection, a stroke of a wife's or lover's cheek, or a hug that communicates the warmth of adult physical love without its clinical detail. When was the last time your children saw their parents kiss?

A few more suggestions: Don't call the uterus a "tummy," or give Daddy all the moves and let his "seed" upstage her egg. Instead of father "puts," it could be that mother "takes" the penis into her vagina. A verb can change the whole dynamic of the act.

What happens when your children ask for sexual rather than reproductive information? Do your moral standards have double standards?

Most parents say they want their children to know about erotic activity by the time they're teenagers. Yet only 12 parents in 100 have ever talked about sexual intercourse to their children, and fewer than 4 in 100 have ever discussed contraception.[1]

---

[1] E. J. Roberts, et al., *Family Life and Sexual Learning: A Study of the Role of Parents in the Sexual Learning of Children*, Project on Human Development, Population Education, Inc. (New York: 1978) 50. Also *Human Behavior*, February 1979, 32.

What have they discussed? They've "cautioned their sons about not acting like a sissy and their daughters about not acting like a tomboy, or warned their child about sex play and child molestors. On most other aspects of sexual learning . . . parents are remarkably silent."[2] Not because they're prudish, I think, but because they're confused, uncertain, and limited by their own upbringing. They want to have heart-to-heart talks but they're not sure what they believe, and what they fear.[3] They want their children to know more but not to *do* more.[4]

> They believe their daughters should have sexual and emotional fulfillment, but are afraid they'll become promiscuous and unmarriageable. They want their sons to be gentle, open and emotionally expressive but are afraid the boys will become sissies or homosexuals.[5]

You can't have it both ways. You must give up sex role stereotypes if you want to help your children prepare for happy, healthy, and responsible sex lives. You can't hope your daughters will find emotional fulfillment if other parents are not raising sons who can give it. You can't tell your daughter to be good and your son to be careful. . . .

"That male adolescents may 'sow their wild oats' premaritally while females save themselves for marriage is one of the most durable aspects of sexual polarization."[6] That double standard is also laced with hypocrisy: whether or not mothers themselves had sex before marriage, they still disapprove of it for girls up to three times more often than for boys.[7] One mother was barely joking when she quipped that her son could have sex at eighteen, but her daughter should "wait until she's forty-three!"[8]

Another mother defended having never told her twelve-year-old daughter about intercourse and birth control because "she's not into that yet."[9] Of course, when she is "into" sex, it may be too late for a parent to help her out of it without scars. . . .

Let me be blunt. Parents who fail to provide contraceptive information to both girls and boys are guilty of child abuse. Having a child while still a child abuses a girl's body and ruins her life. "Teenage pregnancy is not only a health risk for the mother and child, it is a major cause of high school drop-outs, unemployment and poverty."[10]

Why are Americans willing to tolerate an epidemic of teen pregnancies rather than provide their children with simple contraceptive information? Why are

[2]*Ibid.,* 67, 79.

[3]*Ibid.,* 51, 60.

[4]*Ibid.,* 63.

[5]L. White, "A Sexual Revolution? It's Just a Myth, Harvard Report Says," *Boston Herald-American,* December 17, 1978.

[6]J. Gallatin, *Adolescence and Individuality,* Harper and Row (New York: 1975) 260.

[7]R. Long, "Premarital Sexual Behavior in the Sixties," *Journal of Marriage and the Family,* February 1971, 44.

[8]E. J. Roberts, *op. cit.* 59.

[9]*Ibid.,* 57.

[10]F. S. Jaffe, "Teenage Pregnancies: A Need for Education." Reported to Girls' Clubs of America National Seminar, Racine, Wis., June 1978, 23.

parents unable to face the truth of a daughter's sexual activism even at the risk of destroying her future?

Because virginity, chastity as an institution, helps men assure their paternity, which is basic to the patriarchal transfer of power. But making contraception openly available to girls removes the threat of pregnancy that policed female chastity and instead accepts nonreproductive sex as a female prerogative. And that clear a crack in the links between virginity and "femininity," and between female sexuality and maternity, effectively destroys the sex role imperative: Girls Are Meant to Be Mothers.

Rather than break the back of the patriarchy, we allow one million girl children to become mothers each and every year.[11]

Suppose you agree with Dr. Calderone that "Babies should not be used as a 'punishment' for sexually active girls."[12] But you also disapprove of sex before marriage, or sex without love, or sex before a certain age, or whatever. What then? Then, I think, there are several points for you to ponder:

- If most young people subscribe to a single standard and disregard female virginity, why do you care about it? Might you be using your daughter's chastity as a mark of your own virtue?
- Have you taught your children technical virginity, but neglected sexual ethics? A respected sex educator writes: "Instead of worrying about the distinctions between necking, petting, heavy petting . . . and real intercourse, young people would be better advised to examine their motives. After all, a boy can do wrong even by simply kissing a girl, if he knows that she is not ready for it and that it upsets her. In other words, it is not the type of sexual activity that counts, but the intentions behind it."[13]
- Are you unconsciously programming your daughter for the kind of "feminine" passivity that leads to just the "promiscuous" behavior you fear most? Raise a girl on romantic notions of being "swept off her feet," and she may be prey to any sweet-talking seducer. If premeditated sex (using contraception) strikes her as incompatible with the female role, but being "taken" excuses her sexual activity, she's the perfect potential "victim" of early pregnancy. It is the "good girl" who doesn't ask her parents for birth control advice, and who believes only boys should be "ready for sex."
- Do you know that sexual sophistication reduces rather than increases teen sex activity? "Young people who talk with their parents about sex and contraception tend to delay sexual intercourse and to use contraception. When they do enter into relationships, they tend to be more mature and less exploitive."[14]

[11]I. Fosburgh, "The Make-Believe World of Teenage Maternity," *The New York Times Magazine,* August 7, 1977.

[12]M. S. Calderone, "Nothing Less Than the Truth Will Do . . ." Girls Clubs of America National Seminar, Racine, Wis., June 1978, 30.

[13]F. J. Haeberle, *The Sex Atlas,* Seabury Press (New York: 1978) 172.

[14]S. Gordon and C. Synder, "Tomorrow's Family," *Journal of Current Social Issues,* April 1978, 32.

• Have you objectified your daughter's body? Warnings such as "No boy will buy the cow if he can get the milk free" imply that a girl is a piece of property with finite and depleting value. Parents cannot constantly monitor boys' access to a daughter's body. We can only make her strong enough to define her own boundaries and self-respecting enough to think herself more valuable than a cow.

Eventually you will find the truth unavoidable—as well as nonsexist: The sex drive is comparable for both sexes and their levels of heterosexual activity (kissing, necking, petting) show "remarkable similarity."[15] Although girls, as well as boys, are "doing it," they needn't do themselves damage to pay for their sexuality. They can know about sex—and be prepared for sex—and still decide not to *have* sex. . . .

Let's be honest. I may have persuaded you that sex stereotypes are bad, role-free family life is good, and nonsexist sexuality makes sense. But for many parents, apprehension about nonsexist childrearing boils down to one question: *Will it make my child a homosexual?* . . .

Because penis and vagina *fit,* and the combination reproduces the species, heterosexuality must be normal, natural, and good for us, and homosexuality must be wrong and unnatural, as well as queer, perverted, sick, and bad for us. This sort of biological determinism explains why 62 percent of the American public wants homosexuality "cured," nearly half feel "homosexuality is a social corruption which can cause the downfall of a civilization,"[16] and most parents believe homosexuality is one of the worst things that can happen to anyone. Yet, the facts—when this volatile subject can be viewed factually—prove that homosexuality is neither uncommon, abnormal, nor harmful to its practitioners or anyone else.

When the "naturalness" of heterosexuality is claimed via examples in the animal kingdom, one can point to recorded observations of homosexuality among seagulls, cows, mares, sows, primates, and "most if not all mammals."[17] But more important, among humans, "there is probably no culture from which homosexuality has not been reported,"[18] and no matter what moral or legal prohibitions have been devised through the ages, none have ever eliminated

---

[15]A. M. Vener and C. W. Stewart, "The Sexual Behavior of Adolescents in Middle America," *Journal of Marriage and the Family,* November 1972, 699; "Teen Sex Ed Advisors," *Human Behavior,* August 1977, 62; J. Klemesrud, "Parents Encounter Teen Age Sex," *The New York Times,* June 6, 1978, Cl; P. Y. Miller and W. Simon, "Adolescent Sexual Behavior: Content and Change," *Social Problems,* October 1974, 58–76; R. L. Currier, "Debunking the Doublethink on Juvenile Sexuality," *Human Behavior,* September 1977, 16; C. Tavris, "Good News About Sex," *New York* magazine, December 6, 1976.

[16]E. Levitt and A. Klassen, "Public Attitudes Toward Sexual Behavior," paper presented to the American Ortho-Psychiatric Association, 1973.

[17]M. S. Teitelbaum, ed., *Sex Differences: Social and Biological Perspectives,* Anchor Press (New York, 1976); "Extensive Homosexuality Is Found Among Seagulls Off Coast of California," *The New York Times,* November 23, 1977; "Newsline," *Psychology Today,* March 1977, 30; C. S. Ford and F. A. Beach, *Patterns of Sexual Behavior,* Harper (New York: 1951) 143.

[18]C. S. Ford and F. A. Beach, *Patterns of Sexual Behavior,* Harper (New York: 1951) 22–23; J. Marmor and R. Green, "Homosexual Behavior," in J. Money and H. Musaph, *Handbook of Sexology,* Elsevier/North Holland Biomedical Press, 1977, 1051; J. Money and P. Tucker, *Sexual*

homosexuality.[19] In fact, homosexuality is a greater problem in countries that forbid it than in those that don't.[20] With all the fluctuations of public morality, about 10 percent of the entire population consider themselves exclusively homosexual at any given place and time.[21]

Physically, almost all homosexuals have normal chromosomes, sex hormones, genitals, secondary sex characteristics, bodily proportions, and age of puberty.[22] Psychologically, they are quite unremarkable too.

Even Sigmund Freud (who wasn't always wrongheaded) wrote in a 1935 letter to the mother of a homosexual, "Homosexuality is assuredly no advantage but it is nothing to be ashamed of, no vice, no degradation, it cannot be classified as an illness."[23]

Nearly forty years later, the American Psychiatric Association caught up with Freud and declared that homosexuality "by itself does not necessarily constitute a psychiatric disorder."[24]

Aside from choosing to love members of their own sex, lesbians and homosexual males are, on the average, no different from heterosexuals in gender identity or self-esteem,[25] in "drinking, drug use, thoughts of or attempts at suicide, number and sex of friends, relationships with parents, satisfaction with world and many lifestyle issues."[26] One study actually found lower rates of depression among lesbians;[27] another study measured higher competence and intellectual efficiency;[28] still another found more lesbians (87 percent) than heterosexual women (18 percent) experienced orgasm "almost always";[29] and two important recent reports revealed that homosexuals seem to have more and closer friendships than do heterosexuals, more communication and consideration in lovemaking, are less preoccupied with orgasm and are far *less* likely than heterosexuals to commit child abuse or other sexual crimes. In short, many homosexuals "could well serve as models of social comportment and psychological maturity."[30] . . .

Signatures, Little, Brown (Boston: 1975) 22–23; L. J. Hatterer, M.D., *Changing Homosexuality in the Male,* Delta (New York: 1970) 121–154.

[19]J. Marmor and R. Green, *Ibid.* 1051.

[20]M. Brenton, *The American Male,* Fawcett Publications (Greenwich, Conn.: 1970) 32.

[21]E. M. Almquist, et al., *Sociology: Men, Women and Society,* West Publishing Co. (St. Paul, Minn.: 1978) 452.

[22]M. S. Teitelbaum, *op. cit.* 95.

[23]S. Freud, "Letter to An American Mother," *American Journal of Psychiatry,* 1951, 107, 786–787.

[24]R. D. Lyons, "Psychiatrists, in a Shift, Declare Homosexuality No Mental Illness," *The New York Times,* December 16, 1973, 1.

[25]R. E. Hooberman, *Dissertation Abstracts International,* April 1976, 36, 10A, 6554-A.

[26]A. K. Obserstone and H. Sukoneck, "Homosexuality: Lesbians Life Adjustment—The Same as Straights," paper presented to the American Psychological Association, Chicago, 1975.

[27]B. F. Riess et al. "Psychological Test Data on Female Homosexuality: A Review of the Literature," *Journal of Homosexuality* 1974, 1, 1, 71–85.

[28]*Ibid.*

[29]M. G. Fleener, "The Lesbian Lifestyle," paper presented to the Western Social Sciences Association, Denver, April 1977.

[30]A. P. Bell and M. S. Weinberg, *Homosexualities: A Study of Diversity Among Men & Women,* Simon & Schuster (New York: 1978); W. Masters and V. Johnson, *Homosexuality in Perspective,* Little, Brown (Boston: 1979).

TRADITIONAL MARXISM

Sexual Love

Friedrich Engels

We thus have three principal forms of marriage which correspond broadly to the three principal stages of human development: for the period of savagery, group marriage; for barbarism, pairing marriage; for civilization, monogamy supplemented by adultery and prostitution. Between pairing marriage and monogamy intervenes a period in the upper stage of barbarism when men have female slaves at their command and polygamy is practiced.

As our whole presentation has shown, the progress which manifests itself in these successive forms is connected with the peculiarity that women, but not men, are increasingly deprived of the sexual freedom of group marriage. In fact, for men group marriage actually still exists even to this day. What for the woman is a crime entailing grave legal and social consequences is considered honorable in a man or, at the worst, a slight moral blemish which he cheerfully bears. But the more the hetaerism of the past is changed in our time by capitalist commodity production and brought into conformity with it, the more, that is to say, it is transformed into undisguised prostitution, the more demoralizing are its effects. And it demoralizes men far more than women. Among women, prostitution degrades only the unfortunate ones who become its victims, and even these by no means to the extent commonly believed. But it degrades the character of the whole male world. A long engagement particularly is in nine cases out of ten a regular preparatory school for conjugal infidelity.

We are now approaching a social revolution in which the economic foundations of monogamy as they have existed hitherto will disappear just as surely as those of its complement—prostitution. Monogamy arose from the concentration of considerable wealth in the hands of a single individual—a man—and from the need to bequeath this wealth to the children of that man and of no other. For this purpose, the monogamy of the woman was required, not that of the man, so this monogamy of the woman did not in any way interfere with open or concealed polygamy on the part of the man. But by transforming by far the greater portion, at any rate, of permanent, heritable wealth—the means of production—into social property, the coming social revolution will reduce to a minimum all this anxiety about bequeathing and inheriting. Having arisen from economic causes, will monogamy then disappear when these causes disappear?

One might answer, not without reason: far from disappearing, it will on the contrary begin to be realized completely. For with the transformation of the means of production into social property there will disappear also wage labor, the proletariat, and therefore the necessity for a certain—statistically calculable

—number of women to surrender themselves for money. Prostitution disappears; monogamy, instead of collapsing, at last becomes a reality—also for men.

In any case, therefore, the position of men will be very much altered. But the position of women, of *all* women, also undergoes significant change. With the transfer of the means of production into common ownership, the single family ceases to be the economic unit of society. Private housekeeping is transformed into a social industry. The care and education of the children becomes a public affair; society looks after all children alike, whether they are legitimate or not. This removes all the anxiety about the "consequences," which today is the most essential social—moral as well as economic—factor that prevents a girl from giving herself completely to the man she loves. Will not that suffice to bring about the gradual growth of unconstrained sexual intercourse and with it a more tolerant public opinion in regard to a maiden's honor and a woman's shame? And finally, have we not seen that in the modern world monogamy and prostitution are indeed contradictions, but inseparable contradictions, poles of the same state of society? Can prostitution disappear without dragging monogamy with it into the abyss?

Here a new element comes into play, an element which at the time when monogamy was developing existed at most in embryo—individual sex love.

Before the Middle Ages we cannot speak of individual sex love. That personal beauty, close intimacy, similarity of tastes and so forth awakened in people of opposite sex the desire for **sexual** intercourse, that men and women were not totally indifferent regarding **the** partner with whom they entered into this most intimate relationship—that goes without saying. But it is still a very long way to our sexual love. Throughout the whole of antiquity, marriages were arranged by the parents, and the partners calmly accepted their choice. What little love there was between husband and wife in antiquity is not so much subjective inclination as objective duty, not the cause of the marriage but its corollary. Love relationships in the modern sense only occur in antiquity outside official society. The shepherds of whose joys and sorrows in love Theocritus and Moschus sing, the Daphnis and Chloe of Longus, are all slaves who have no part in the state, the free citizen's sphere of life. Except among slaves, we find love affairs only as products of the disintegration of the old world and carried on with women who also stand outside official society, with *hetaerae*—that is, with foreigners or freed slaves: in Athens from the eve of its decline, in Rome under the Caesars. If there were any real love affairs between free men and free women, these occurred only in the course of adultery. And to the classical love poet of antiquity, old Anacreon, sexual love in our sense mattered so little that it did not even matter to him which sex his beloved was.

Our sex love differs essentially from the simple sexual desire, the Eros, of the ancients. In the first place, it assumes that the person loved returns the love; to this extent the woman is on an equal footing with the man, whereas in the Eros of antiquity she was often not even asked. Secondly, our sex love has a degree of intensity and duration which makes both lovers feel that non-possession and separation are a great, if not the greatest, calamity; to possess one another, they risk high stakes, even life itself. In the ancient world this happened only, if at all, in adultery. And finally, there arises a new moral standard in the judgment of a sexual relationship. We do not only ask, was it within or outside marriage, but also, did it spring from love and reciprocated love or not? Of course, this new standard has fared no better in feudal or bourgeois practice than all the other standards of morality—it is ignored. But neither does it fare any worse. It is recognized, like all the rest, in theory, on paper. And for the present more than this cannot be expected.

At the point where antiquity broke off its advance to sexual love, the Middle Ages took it up again—in adultery. We have already described the knightly love which gave rise to the songs of dawn. From the love which strives to break up marriage to the love which is to be its foundation there is still a long road, which chivalry never fully traversed. Even when we pass from the frivolous Latins to the virtuous Germans we find in the *Nibelungenlied* that although in her heart Kriemhild is as much in love with Siegfried as he is with her, yet when Gunther announces that he has promised her to a knight he does not name, she simply replies: "You have no need to ask me; as you bid me, so will I ever be; whom you, lord, give me as husband, him will I gladly take in troth." It never enters her head that her love can be even considered. Gunther asks for Brünhild in marriage and Etzel for Kriemhild, though they have never seen them. Similarly, in *Gutrun,* Sigebant of Ireland asks for the Norwegian Ute, whom he has never seen, Hetel of Hegelingen for Hilde of Ireland, and finally Siegfried of Morland, Hartmut of Ormany and Herwig of Seeland for Gutrun—and here Gutrun's acceptance of Herwig is for the first time voluntary. As a rule, the young prince's bride is selected by his parents if they are still living or, if not, by the prince himself with the advice of the great feudal lords, who have a weighty word to say in all these cases. Nor can it be otherwise. For the knight or baron, as for the prince of the land himself, marriage is a political act, an opportunity to increase power by new alliances; the interest of the *house* must be decisive, not the wishes of an individual. What chance then is there for love to have the final word in the making of a marriage?

The same thing holds for the guild member in the medieval towns. The very privileges protecting him, the guild charters with all their clauses and rubrics, the intricate distinctions legally separating him from other guilds, from the members of his own guild or from his journeymen and apprentices, already made the circle narrow enough within which he could look for a suitable wife. And who in the circle was the most suitable was decided under this complicated system most certainly not by his individual preference but by the family interests.

In the vast majority of cases, therefore, marriage remained up to the close of the middle ages what it had been from the start—a matter which was not decided by the partners. In the beginning, people were already born married—married to an entire group of the opposite sex. In the later forms of group marriage similar relations probably existed, but with the group continually contracting. In the pairing marriage it was customary for the mothers to settle the marriages of their children; here, too, the decisive considerations are the new ties of kinship which are to give the young pair a stronger position in the gens and tribe. And when, with the preponderance of private over communal property and the interest in its bequeathal father right and monogamy gained supremacy, the dependence of marriages on economic considerations became complete. The *form* of marriage by purchase disappears; the actual practice is steadily extended until not only the woman but also the man acquires a price—not according to his personal qualities but according to his property. That the mutual affection of the people concerned should be the one paramount reason for marriage, outweighing everything else, was and always had been absolutely unheard of in the practice of the ruling classes; that sort of thing only happened in romance—or among the oppressed classes, who did not count.

Such was the state of things encountered by capitalist production when it began to prepare itself, after the epoch of geographical discoveries, to win world power by world trade and manufacture. One would suppose that this manner of marriage exactly suited it, and so it did. And yet—there are no limits to the irony of history—capitalist production itself was to make the decisive breach in it. By changing all things into commodities, it dissolved all inherited and traditional relationships, and in place of time-honored custom and historic right, it set up purchase and sale, "free" contract. And the English jurist H. S. Maine thought he had made a tremendous discovery when he said that our whole progress in comparison with former epochs consisted in the fact that we had passed "from status to contract," from inherited to freely contracted conditions—which, in so far as it is correct was already in *The Communist Manifesto* [Chapter II].

But a contract requires people who can dispose freely of their persons, actions, and possessions and meet each other on the footing of equal rights. To create these "free" and "equal" people was one of the main tasks of capitalist production. Even though at the start it was carried out only half-consciously, and under a religious disguise at that, from the time of the Lutheran and Calvinist Reformation the principle was established that man is only fully responsible for his actions when he acts with complete freedom of will, and that it is a moral duty to resist all coercion to an immoral act. But how did this fit in with the hitherto existing practice in the arrangement of marriages? Marriage according to the bourgeois conception was a contract, a legal transaction, and the most important one of all because it disposed of two human beings, body and mind, for life. Formally, it is true, the contract at that time was entered into voluntarily; without the assent of the persons concerned, nothing could be done. But everyone knew only too well how this assent was obtained and who were the real contracting parties in the marriage. But if real freedom of decision was required for all other contracts, then why not for this? Had not the two young people to be coupled also the right to dispose freely of themselves, of their bodies and organs? Had not chivalry brought sex love into fashion, and was not its proper bourgeois form, in contrast to chivalry's adulterous love, the love of husband and wife? And if it was the duty of married people to love each other, was it not equally the duty of lovers to marry each other and nobody else? Did not this right of the lovers stand higher than the right of parents, relations, and other traditional marriage brokers and matchmakers? If the right of free, personal discrimination broke boldly into the Church and religion, how should it halt before the intolerable claim of the older generation to dispose of the body, soul, property, happiness, and unhappiness of the younger generation?

These questions inevitably arose at a time which was loosening all the old ties of society and undermining all traditional conceptions. The world had suddenly grown almost ten times bigger; instead of one quadrant of a hemisphere, the whole globe lay before the gaze of the West Europeans who hastened to take the other seven quadrants into their possession. And with the old narrow barriers of their homeland fell also the thousand-year-old barriers of the prescribed medieval way of thought. To the outward and the inward eye of man opened an infinitely wider horizon. What did a young man care about the approval of respectability or honorable guild privileges handed down for generations when the wealth of India beckoned to him, the gold and the silver mines of Mexico and Potosi? For the bourgeoisie it was the time of knight-errantry; they, too, had their romance and their raptures of love, but on a bourgeois footing and, in the last analysis, with bourgeois aims.

So it came about that the rising bourgeoisie, especially in Protestant countries where existing conditions had been most severely shaken, increasingly recognized freedom of contract also in marriage, and carried it into effect in the manner described. Marriage remained class marriage, but within the class the partners were conceded a certain degree of freedom of choice. And on paper, in ethical theory and in poetic description, nothing was more immutably established than that every marriage is immoral which does not rest on mutual sexual love and really free agreement of husband and wife. In short, the love marriage was proclaimed as a human right, and indeed not only as a *droit de l'homme,* one of the rights of man, but also, for once in a way, as *droit de la femme,* one of the rights of woman.

This human right, however, differed in one respect from all other so-called human rights. While the latter in practice remain restricted to the ruling class (the bourgeoisie) and are directly or indirectly curtailed for the oppressed class (the proletariat), in the case of the former the irony of history plays another of its tricks. The ruling class remains dominated by the familiar economic influences and therefore only in exceptional cases does it provide instances of really freely contracted marriages, while among the oppressed class, as we have seen, these marriages are the rule.

Full freedom of marriage can therefore only be generally established when the abolition of capitalist production and of the property relations created by it has removed all the accompanying economic considerations which still exert such a powerful influence on the choice of a marriage partner. For then there is no other motive left except mutual inclination.

And as sexual love is by its nature exclusive—although at present this exclusiveness is fully realized only in the woman—the marriage based on sexual love is by its nature individual marriage. We have seen how right Bachofen was in regarding the advance from group marriage to individual marriage as primarily due to the women. Only the step from pairing marriage to monogamy can be put down to the credit of the men, and historically the essence of this was to make the position of the women worse and the infidelities of the men easier. If now the economic considerations also disappear which made women put up with the habitual infidelity of their husbands—concern for their own means of existence and still more for their children's future—then, according to all previous experience, the equality of woman thereby achieved will tend infinitely more to make men really monogamous than to make women polyandrous.

But what will quite certainly disappear from monogamy are all the features stamped upon it through its origin in property relations; these are, in the first place, supremacy of the man and secondly, the indissolubility of marriage. The supremacy of the man in marriage is the simple consequence of his economic supremacy, and with the abolition of the latter will disappear of itself. The indissolubility of marriage is partly a consequence of the economic situation in which monogamy arose, partly tradition from the period when the connection between this economic situation and monogamy was not yet fully understood and was carried to extremes under a religious form. Today it is already broken through at a thousand points. If only the marriage based on love is moral, then also only the marriage is moral in which love continues. But the intense emotion of individual sex love varies very much in duration from one individual to another, especially among men, and if affection definitely comes to an end or is supplanted by a new passionate love, separation is a benefit for both partners as well as for society—only people will then be spared having to wade through the useless mire of a divorce case.

What we can now conjecture about the way in which sexual relations will be ordered after the impending overthrow of capitalist production is mainly of a negative character, limited for the most part to what will disappear. But what will there be new? That will be answered when a new generation has grown up: a generation of men who never in their lives have known what it is to buy a woman's surrender with money or any other social instrument of power; a generation of women who have never known what it is to give themselves to a man from any other considerations than real love or to refuse to give themselves to their lover from fear of the economic consequences. When these people are in the world, they will care precious little what anybody today thinks they ought to do; they will make their own practice and their corresponding public opinion about the practice of each individual—and that will be the end of it.

Lenin on Sexual Love

Clara Zetkin

. . . "I was also told that sex problems are a favourite subject in your youth organisations too, and that there are hardly enough lecturers on this subject. This nonsense is especially dangerous and damaging to the youth movement. It can easily lead to sexual excesses, to overstimulation of sex life and to wasted health and strength of young people. You must fight that too. There is no lack of contact between the youth movement and the women's movement. Our Communist women everywhere should cooperate methodically with young people. This will be a continuation of motherhood, will elevate it and extend it from the individual to the social sphere. Women's incipient social life and activities must be promoted, so that they can outgrow the narrowness of their philistine, individualistic psychology centered on home and family. But this is incidental.

"In our country, too, considerable numbers of young people are busy 'revising bourgeois conceptions and morals' in the sex question. And let me add that this involves a considerable section of our best boys and girls, of our truly promising youth. It is as you have just said. In the atmosphere created by the aftermath of war and by the revolution which has begun, old ideological values, finding themselves in a society whose economic foundations are undergoing a radical change, perish, and lose their restraining force. New values crystallise slowly, in the struggle. With regard to relations between people, and between man and woman, feelings and thoughts are also becoming revolutionised. New boundaries are being drawn between the rights of the individual and those of the community, and hence also the duties of the individual. Things are still in complete, chaotic ferment. The direction and potentiality of the various contradictory tendencies can still not be seen clearly enough. It is a slow and often very painful process of passing away and coming into being. All this applies also to the field of sexual relations, marriage, and the family. The decay, putrescence, and filth of bourgeois marriage with its difficult dissolution, its licence for the husband and bondage for the wife, and its disgustingly false sex morality and relations fill the best and most spiritually active of people with the utmost loathing.

"The coercion of bourgeois marriage and bourgeois legislation on the family enhance the evil and aggravate the conflicts. It is the coercion of 'sacrosanct' property. It sanctifies venality, baseness, and dirt. The conventional hypocrisy of 'respectable' bourgeois society takes care of the rest. People revolt against the prevailing abominations and perversions. And at a time when mighty nations are being destroyed, when the former power relations are being disrupted, when a whole social world is beginning to decline, the sensations of the individual undergo a rapid change. A stimulating thirst for different forms of enjoyment easily acquires an irresistible force. Sexual and marriage reforms in the bourgeois sense will not do. In the sphere of sexual relations and marriage, a revolution is approaching—in keeping with the proletarian revolution. Of course, women and young people are taking a deep interest in the complex tangle of problems which have arisen as a result of this. Both the former and the latter suffer greatly from the present messy state of sex relations. Young people rebel against them with the vehemence of their years. This is only natural. Nothing could be falser than to preach monastic self-denial and the sanctity of the filthy bourgeois morals to young people. However, it is hardly a good thing that sex, already strongly felt in the physical sense, should at such a time assume so much prominence in the psychology of young people. The consequences are nothing short of fatal. Ask Comrade Lilina about it. She ought to have had many experiences in her extensive work at educational institutions of various kinds and you know that she is a Communist through and through, and has no prejudices.

"Youth's altered attitude to questions of sex is of course 'fundamental,' and based on theory. Many people call it 'revolutionary' and 'communist.' They sincerely believe that this is so. I am an old man, and I do not like it: I may be a morose ascetic, but quite often this so-called 'new sex life' of young people—and frequently of the adults too—seems to me purely bourgeois and simply an extension of the good old bourgeois brothel. All this has nothing in common with free love as we Communists understand it. No doubt you have heard about the famous theory that in communist society satisfying sexual desire and the craving for love is as simple and trivial as 'drinking a glass of water.' A section of our youth has gone mad, absolutely mad, over this 'glass-of-water theory.' It has been fatal to many a young boy and girl. Its devotees assert that it is a Marxist theory. I want no part of the kind of Marxism which infers all phenomena and all changes in the ideological superstructure of society directly and blandly from its economic basis, for things are not as simple as all that. A certain Frederick Engels has established this a long time ago with regard to historical materialism.

"I consider the famous 'glass-of-water' theory as completely un-Marxist and, moreover, as anti-social. It is not only what nature has given but also what has become culture, whether of a high or low level, that comes into play in sexual life. Engels pointed out in his *Origin of the Family* how significant it was that the common sexual relations had developed into individual sex love and thus became purer. The relations between the sexes are not simply the expression of a mutual influence between economics and a physical want deliberately singled out for physiological examination. It would be rationalism and not Marxism to attempt to refer the change in these relations directly to the economic basis of society in isolation from its connection with the ideology as a whole. To be sure, thirst has to be quenched. But would a normal person normally lie down in the gutter and drink from a puddle? Or even from a glass whose edge has been greased by many lips? But the social aspect is more important than anything else. The drinking of water is really an individual matter. But it takes two people to make love, and a third person, a new life, is likely to come into being. This deed has a social complexion and constitutes a duty to the community.

"As a Communist I have no liking at all for the 'glass-of-water' theory, despite its attractive label: 'emancipation of love.' Besides, emancipation of love is neither a novel nor a communistic idea. You will recall that it was advanced in fine literature around the middle of the past century as 'emancipation of the heart.' In bourgeois practice it materialised into emancipation of the flesh. It was preached with greater talent than now, though I cannot judge how it was practised. Not that I want my criticism to breed asceticism. That is farthest from my thoughts. Communism should not bring asceticism, but joy and strength, stemming, among other things, from a consummate love life. Whereas today, in my opinion, the obtaining plethora of sex life yields neither joy nor strength. On the contrary, it impairs them. This is bad, very bad, indeed, in the epoch of revolution.

"Young people are particularly in need of joy and strength. Healthy sports, such as gymnastics, swimming, hiking, physical exercises of every description and a wide range of intellectual interests is what they need, as well as learning, study and research, and as far as possible collectively. This will be far more useful to young people than endless lectures and discussions on sex problems and the so-called living by one's nature. *Mens sana in corpore sano.* Be neither monk nor Don Juan, but not anything in between either, like a German philistine. You know the young comrade X. He is a splendid lad, and highly gifted. For all that, I am afraid that he will never amount to anything. He has one love affair after another. This is not good for the political struggle and for the revolution. I will not vouch for the reliability or the endurance of women whose love affair is intertwined with politics, or for the men who run after every petticoat and let themselves in with every young female. No, no, that does not go well with revolution."

Lenin sprang to his feet, slapped the table with his hand and paced up and down the room.

"The revolution calls for concentration and rallying of every nerve by the masses and by the individual. It does not tolerate orgiastic conditions so common among d'Annunzio's decadent heroes and heroines. Promiscuity in sexual matters is bourgeois. It is a sign of degeneration. The proletariat is a rising class. It does not need an intoxicant to stupefy or stimulate it, neither the intoxicant of sexual laxity or of alcohol. It should and will not forget the vileness, the filth and the barbarity of capitalism. It derives its strongest inspiration to fight from its class position, from the communist ideal. What it needs is clarity, clarity, and more clarity. Therefore, I repeat, there must be no weakening, no waste and no dissipation of energy. Self-control and self-discipline are not slavery; not in matters of love either. . . ."

RADICAL FEMINISM

Radical Feminism and Love

Ti-Grace Atkinson

Radical feminism is a new political concept. It evolved in response to the concern of many feminists that there has never been even the beginnings of a feminist analysis of the persecution of women. Until there is such an analysis, no coherent, effective program can be designed to solve the problem. The OCTOBER 17TH MOVEMENT was the first radical feminist group begun and has spent a great deal of its first five months working out the structure and details of a causal class analysis.

The analysis begins with the feminist *raison d'être* that women are a class, that this class is political in nature, and that this political class is oppressed. From this point on, radical feminism separates from traditional feminism. . . .

Since it is clear that men oppress women, and since this oppression is an ongoing process, it was clear to radical feminists that women must understand the *dynamics* of their oppression. Men are the *agents* of the oppression of individual women, and these agents use various means to achieve the subordination of their counter-class. But over thousands of years, men have created and maintained an inclosure of institutionalized oppression to fortify their domination of women by using many institutions and values as vehicles of oppression, e.g., marriage, family, sexual intercourse, love, religion, prostitution. Women are the victims of this oppression. . . .

I propose that the phenomenon of love is the psychological pivot in the persecution of women. Because the internalization of coercion must play such a key functional part in the oppression of women due to their numbers alone, and because of the striking grotesqueness of the one-to-one political units "pairing" the oppressor and the oppressed, the hostile and powerless, and thereby severing the oppressed from any kind of political aide, it is not difficult to conclude that women by definition must exist in a special psycho-pathological state of fantasy both in reference to themselves and to their manner of relating to their counterclass. This pathological condition, considered the most desirable state for any woman to find herself in, is what we know as the phenomenon of love.

Because radical feminists consider the dynamics of their oppression the focal point of their analysis, it is obvious that some theory of "attraction" would be needed. Why do women, even feminists, consort with the enemy? For sex? Very few women ever say that; that's the male-role reason. What nearly all women mutter in response to this is: for love.

There has been very little analytic work done on the notion of "love."[1] This is remarkable, considering the importance of it in ethics and political philosophy. Philosophers usually skirt it or brush it aside by claiming it's irreducible, or irrational. Or they smile and claim it's the sine qua non. All these things may be true and are clues to the political significance of "love": it's basic; it's against individual human interest; a great deal rests upon it.

Any theory of attraction could begin with the definition of the verb to attract: the exertion of a force such as magnetism to draw a person or thing, and susceptibility in the thing drawn. Magnetism is caused by friction or conflict, and the primary relationship between men and women of class confrontation or conflict certainly suffices for the cause of magnetism. Usually the magnetized moves towards the magnet in response to the magnet's power, otherwise the magnetized is immobile.

The woman is drawn to→ attracted by→ desirous of→ *in* love *with*→ the man. She is power*less,* he is power*ful.* The woman is instinctively trying to recoup her definitional and political losses by fusing with the enemy. "Love" is the woman's pitiful deluded attempt to attain the human: by fusing, she hopes to blur the male/female role dichotomy, and that a new division of the human class might prove more equitable: she counts on the illusion she has spun out of herself in order to be able to accept the fusion, to be transferred to the whole and, thus, that the new man will be garbed now equally in her original illusion. Unfortunately, magnetism depends upon inequity: as long as the inequity stands, the fusion may hold (everything else relevant remaining the same); if the inequity changes, the fusion and the magnetism fall with the inequity. A woman can unite with a man as long as she is a woman, i.e., subordinate, and no longer. There's no such thing as a "loving" way out of the feminist dilemma: that it is as a *woman* that women are oppressed, and that in order to be free she must shed what keeps her secure.

The OCTOBER 17TH MOVEMENT recently devoted one of its meetings to a discussion of "love" and tried to analyze together how this phenomenon operated. The main difficulty was, and was left at, understanding the shift from the woman desiring an alliance with the power*ful* to the woman being *in love with* the man. It's clear that love has to do with some transitional or relational factor. But why, exactly? She is going from the political, the power*less* identification, to the individual, one-to-one unit. She is disarming herself to go into the enemy camp. Is love a kind of hysterical state, a *mind*less state therefore a *pain*less state, into which women retreat when the contradiction between the last shreds of their human survival and the everyday contingencies of being a woman becomes most acute?

---

[1] I distinguish between friendship and love. Friendship is a rational relationship which requires the participation of two parties to the mutual satisfaction of both parties. Love can be felt by one party; it is unilateral by nature, and, combined with its relational character, it is thus rendered contradictory and irrational.

Is love a kind of frenzy, or something like a Buddhist immolation, to unite with the One? The love women feel for men is most akin to religious love.

But hysteria might be a more useful paradigm for us since it's limited almost exclusively to women (the word "hysterical" derives from the Greek word for "uterus") and the condition is marked by certain characteristics strikingly similar to those of "love": anxiety converted into functional symptoms of illness, amnesia, fugue, multiple personality.

Female Sexual Slavery

Kathleen Barry

ON STUDYING SEXUAL SLAVERY

There are small prostitution hotels in one part of the North African *quartier* of Paris known as *maisons d'abattage*. I was warned to stay out of this section of the 18th *arrondissement* of Paris because it is dangerous for women, at any time of day or night. But I did walk through the area. I needed to see the *maisons d'abattage*. It was early evening when another woman and I emerged from the Barbes-Rochecauart Metro station. We were jostled and pushed as we made our way through the crowded shopping section. Once we were on the quiet side streets no other women were to be seen. As we walked through the neighborhood streets of this North African section of Paris, we were suddenly struck by the sight of a crowd of about 300 men in a narrow street ahead. We stopped and gazed, assuming there must have been an automobile accident or a fight. The frantic, jostling crowd of men spanned the full width and half the length of the small street. As we approached the rue de la Charbonniere, just above the crowd of pushing and shoving men we saw a small "Hotel" sign.

We continued down the street and around the corner. We stopped again, stunned to see a small neighborhood police station with a smiling policeman standing in the doorway, while about 20 yards away from him, next door but in the same building, was another "Hotel" sign and another group of men, about 100 North Africans pushing, body-to-body, against the gates of the hotel. It was only 6:00 P.M. on Saturday of Easter weekend. The crowds of men were to grow larger as the evening progressed. Although closed prostitution houses are illegal in France, these hotels are not only tolerated but obviously supported by the police.

In each of these *maisons d'abattage* (literal translation: houses of slaughter), six or seven girls each serve 80 to 120 customers a night. On holidays their quota might go up to 150. After each man pays his 30 francs (approximately $6.00) at the door, he is given a towel and ushered into a room. A buzzer sounds after six minutes, and he must leave immediately as another man comes in. The girl never even gets out of bed.

The girls are told that they will get a certain percentage of the money if they meet their quota. From their earnings is deducted the cost of room and meals; after these deductions—with the hotel doing the bookkeeping—the girls always find they are indebted to the house. Giving a false sense of earning money, and subsequent indebtedness, are traditional strategies for keeping enslaved prostitutes from rebelling.

In May 1975 a French doctor submitted a confidential report to UNESCO documenting the torture of prostitutes. The report, which was to become the basis of testimony at the International Women's Year Conference in Mexico City, was based on testimony of patients she had treated who had been held in the *maisons d'abattage*. It indicated that the women were "detained indoors without ever having the right to move outside unaccompanied, were subjected to cruel, inhuman, and degrading treatment. Torture was also used if it was needed to obtain their complete submission. This form of terrorism was aimed at making them totally subject to the wishes of those who benefited from it, either by financial profit or sexual satisfaction." The women were described as being of normal intelligence and in a state of depression and considerable anxiety. "They were passive and apathetic, unable to readjust to freedom."

This is not the kind of work a woman looks for when she considers becoming a prostitute. How do women get to places like Paris's *maison d'abattage?*

From my research, I found the women may be purchased, kidnapped, drawn in through syndicates or organized crime, or fraudulently recruited by fronting agencies which offer jobs, positions with dance companies, or marriage contracts that don't exist. Or they may be procured through seduction by being promised friendship and love. Conning a girl or young woman by feigning friendship or love is undoubtedly the easiest and most frequently employed tactic of slave procurers (and one that is also used for procuring young boys) and it is the most effective. Young women readily respond to male attention and affection and easily become dependent on it. Once a procurer has drawn a young woman in by his attention to her and she commits her affection to him it is relatively easy for him to transport her to a brothel. Sometimes she can quickly be turned out on the streets by simply being asked to; he tells her that if she really loves him she will do it for him. If that fails, if she resists his request, traditional seasoning tactics are employed—beating, rape, torture. Either way she gets hooked. . . .

To study female sexual slavery, . . . traditional methods employed by those who study social life were of little use. One cannot, for example, find a sample population of sexual slaves, survey them, and then generalize from the results. Nor is participant observation a possibility. And interviewing those held in slavery is impossible. I began to look for the women who have escaped. My approach was to find any evidence of sexual slavery wherever I could, and to try to fill out fragmentary facts from interviewing people associated with a particular case. . . .

Once I was convinced of the pervasiveness of the problem, the immediate question facing me was why and how female sexual slavery has remained invisible. First, there is direct suppression of the evidence by authorities. In addition, it is invisible as a problem to those who handle practices of female sexual slavery every day. When I would illustrate to an authority how a particular situation fit the most rudimentary definition of slavery, generally I found that they saw the abuse but accepted sexual exploitation and violence as normal for particular groups of women under specific conditions. I noted how, *after* women are enslaved in their homes or in prostitution, they are accepted as part of the group of women destined for that life. When I challenged authorities, I ran up against the "don't confuse me with the facts" attitude. Despite evidence of force and dehumanizing violence in many cases, they were incredulous that anyone would question prostitution or see it as other than a necessary service for a particular group of women to perform.

Yet other, more subtle effects have contributed to the invisibility of the slave trade. For example, most research on prostitution looks at female motivation rather than the objective conditions which bring many women into prostitution, shifting the causal assumptions from those who traffic women to the psychological states of the women themselves. To those who study the victims of the practice I have called female sexual slavery, these women are the exceptions for whom exceptional behavior is normal; to sociologists they are deviants, to psychologists they are sadomasochists. Their life and experiences are construed as normal for them while they are supposedly different from the rest of us. It is in this kind of contradiction that feminists have learned to look for larger truths about female experience. It is in female sexual slavery that I have found conditions which affect all women. Because of these problems it was necessary for me to develop a perspective for analyzing both the documentation of female sexual slavery and the attitudes that define it as normal, which would reveal self-interest on the part of those who label it. That self-interest may range from the actual profit from the traffic in women to a general participation in the sexual power that accrues to men from female sexual slavery. As I studied the attitudes that accept female enslavement, I realized that a powerful ideology stems from it and permeates the social order. I have named that ideology cultural sadism. . . .

Not all thinking on prostitution accepts violence as normal for prostitutes. Prostitution is both an indication of an unjust social order and an institution that economically exploits women. But when economic power is defined as the causal variable, the sex dimensions of power usually remain unidentified and unchallenged. Consequently, economic analysis has often functioned to undermine the feminist critique of sexual domination that has gone on since the beginning of the women's movement. Feminist analysis of sexual power is often modified to make it fit into an economic analysis which defines economic exploitation as the primary instrument of female oppression. Under that system of thought, institutionalized sexual slavery, such as is found in prostitution, is understood in terms of economic exploitation which results in the lack of economic opportunities for women, the result of an unjust economic order. Undoubtedly economic exploitation is an important factor in the oppression of women, but here we must be concerned with whether or not economic analysis reveals the more fundamental sexual domination of women. As unjust as the economic order may be, this analysis spins off a set of beliefs which again contradict fact. Those beliefs assume:

1 That prostitution is an economic alternative for women who are the objects of discrimination in the larger inequitable job market—despite the fact that pimps are known to take all or almost all of the money earned by their prostitutes.

2 That only lower-class or poor women and girls turn to prostitution—despite the knowledge that most pimps recruit girls who are runaways, many of whom are from middle-class homes.

3 That only ethnic minority women are trapped in prostitution—despite the fact that many white women and girls are visible hooking on the streets, and despite the fact that pimps recruit women based on customer demand and easy availability.

4 That black men from the ghetto have no economic alternatives to pimping —despite the fact that a) most black men from the ghetto do not become pimps; b) that not all pimps are black or from the ghetto; and c) that exploitation, abuse, and enslavement cannot be justified by someone's economic conditions.

By appearing to critique the conditions which lead to prostitution these assumptions actually obscure recognition of sexual domination which is the first cause of sexual power. . . .

Finally, sensationalism has made the traffic invisible. The tendency of writers on this subject to render already horrible events in the format of a lurid novel leaves the impression that the material is less than believable, that it is fiction. Not all slave markets are lustful events where whips crack over writhing, naked bodies. Often they are subdued business transactions. Sensationalism was the method that many turn-of-the-century workers used to bring attention to the traffic in women. The net result of their paternalistic, highly dramatized concern was to characterize the victims as such poor, sweet young things as to make the stories about them unbelievable. The very effort to dramatize and create attention casts suspicion on the veracity of the stories. The issue is not whether a child, teenager, or adult woman is a poor, innocent, sweet young thing. It is, rather, that no one should have the right to force anyone into slavery. . . .

SEXUAL SLAVERY EXISTS WORLDWIDE

A young girl, now a prostitute, was sexually molested and raped by her stepfather regularly for four years. He threatened that if she told her mother he would leave them homeless and penniless . . .

Two runaway girls from Pennsylvania get off a bus in Sacramento. They are kidnapped, raped, and forced into prostitution . . .

A prostitute decides to leave her pimp, and when he hunts her down at her aunt's house, he takes her away with him. As a warning against future escapes, he beats her with the base of a car jack until he fractures her skull . . .

A wife gathers up her 5-year-old twin daughters and leaves home. She is hunted down by her husband, and when he finds her he beats her and fires his shotgun within an inch of her head as a warning in case she tries to run away again . . .

Several thousand teenage girls disappear from Paris every year. The police know but cannot prove that many are destined for Arab harems. An eyewitness reports that auctions have been held in Zanzibar, where European women were sold to Arab customers . . .

In one year, 2,000 girls were reported missing from a rural area of India where procurers had been posing as labor contractors . . .

These women and girls are victims of female sexual slavery. Some have escaped; others have not. When it is organized, female sexual slavery is a highly profitable business that merchandises women's bodies to brothels and harems around the world. Practiced individually, without an organizational network, it is carried out by pimps whose lifestyle and expensive habits are supported by one or two women whom they brutally force to sell their bodies for his profit. The private practice of female sexual slavery is carried out by husbands and fathers who use battery and sexual abuse as a personal measure of their power over their wives and/or daughters. *Female sexual slavery is present in ALL situations where women or girls cannot change the immediate conditions of their existence; where regardless of how they got into those conditions they cannot get out; and where they are subject to sexual violence and exploitation.* Sexual slavery, whether it is carried out by international gangs, or individual pimps, is a highly criminal and clandestine activity, and the slavery carried out by fathers and husbands is kept secret and is socially tolerated as well. Its setting may be an Arab harem, a German eros center, an American pimp pad, or a suburban home. Wherever it is located, it brings both monetary gain and personal satisfaction to its perpetrators.

Female sexual slavery is not an illusive condition; the word "slavery" is not merely rhetorical. This is not some condition in which a woman's or child's need for love allows her to fall into psychological patterns that make it possible for her to accept abuse with love or to feel joy in pain. Slavery is an objective social condition of sexual exploitation and violence. The experiences of sexual slavery documented in this book reveal that it is not a practice that is limited to international traffic but it is pervasive throughout patriarchal societies. . . .

PIMPING: THE OLDEST PROFESSION

The arbitrary and false distinctions made in the nineteenth-century purity crusades between the international traffic in women and local prostitution still dominate thought today. Those distinctions, with the accompanying assumption that women are driven to prostitution (by economics, sadomasochism, or mental deficiency), screen the procurers, hiding their strategies and making pimping appear to be other than what it is.

Together, pimping and procuring are perhaps the most ruthless displays of male power and sexual dominance. As practices they go far beyond the merchandising of women's bodies for the market that demands them. Pimping and procuring are the crystallization of misogyny; they rank among the most complete expressions of male hatred for femaleness. Procuring is a strategy, a tactic for acquiring women and turning them into prostitution; pimping keeps them there. Procuring today involves "convincing" a woman to be a prostitute through cunning, fraud, and/or physical force, taking her against her will or knowledge and putting her into prostitution. . . .

All kinds of women are vulnerable to slave procurers. The assumption that only women of a particular class, race, or age group are potential victims of female sexual slavery has followed from the inability to recognize sexual domination as it underpins all other forms of oppression. It is true that some procuring methods are adapted to particular groups of women and the strategy that works in rural poverty may not work in an urban bus station. But it is primarily procurers and their interests and only secondarily women's age, race or economic class that determine who will end up forced into prostitution.

The other major cause of sex slavery is the social-sexual objectification of women that permeates every patriarchal society in the world. Identifying women first as sexual beings who are responsible for the sexual services of men is the social base for gender-specific sexual slavery. As most women know, being sexually harassed while walking alone down a street, or sitting in a bar or restaurant without a man, is a poignant reminder of our definition as sexual objects. Spurning those advances and reacting against them are likely to draw indignant wrath from the perpetrator, suggesting the extent to which many men assume the sexual objectification of *any* woman as their right. Under such conditions, sexual slavery lurks at the corners of every woman's life. . . .

SEXUAL SLAVERY IN THE FAMILY

Many women and girls directly experience female sexual slavery without ever going out of their homes. For them home replaces brothel; they are wives or daughters who are the victims of husbands or fathers instead of pimps. I am speaking, of course, of wife battery and incest, practices which make the private family instead of the public street or "house" the location of female sexual slavery. In certain cultures these practices take the form of forced marriage, polygyny, veiling, and seclusion of women.

In most nations it is evident that family loyalty supersedes loyalty to one's country. Across cultures the family is the basic unit of individual male power. Whether in the tribal hut, rural cottage, city apartment, or government mansion—each man's home is his castle. And each man's home is private. It is in that privacy that female sexual slavery flourishes.

I am defining female sexual slavery in the family in the same way I defined it in prostitution in Chapter 3: "Female sexual slavery is present in *all* situations where women or girls cannot change the immediate conditions of their existence; where regardless of how they got into those conditions they cannot get out; and where they are subject to sexual violence and exploitation." In addition to being cautioned against the invasion of man's privacy, arguments of cultural relativism are used to discourage examination of the similarities in female sexual slavery as it is practiced through the family across cultures. Cultural relativism asserts that the practices within any specific culture are unique to the values, systems, and practices *within* that culture. For the cultural relativist there are no universal standards and the morality and values of one national culture cannot be compared to that of any other. Cultural relativism dominates social, political and academic thought today and it serves as a justification of many inhuman social practices. If one questions the principles of cultural relativism, one is charged with ethnocentrism. Ethnocentrism assumes that the judgments made about another culture stem from the assumption of the superiority of one's own culture.

These attempts to respect the cultural integrity of different societies, well intentioned though they may be, serve to separate and isolate women in their common experience of sexual domination.

There is nothing unique across cultures in the practices of the enslavement of women except perhaps the diversity in the strategies men employ to carry them out. Female sexual slavery is a global phenomenon. As a form of oppression, it cannot be subject to either the respect or protection given to those cultural practices which mark a culture as distinct from any other, or those that insure privacy to the family unit. Applying the same standard or value to human life across all national cultures lifts considerations of female sexual slavery above arguments of ethnocentrism. Wherever female sexual slavery is practiced and condoned, particularly when it spans across many cultures, no culture can be deemed superior to another. . . .

Wife battery and incest are forms of female sexual slavery that have hitherto been lost under the general rubric of "domestic violence." Sexual violence in the home, resulting in conditions of slavery, is consistently underplayed in research, in police reports, and by social service agencies.

Although female sexual slavery in the family is directly linked to forced prostitution, the interdependency of these two forms of slavery is hidden by the traditional argument that domestic violence breeds domestic violence. This thinking dominates research, police response to calls, and the way social service agencies handle cases. Thus it amounts to justification and self-perpetuation of the practices.

The theory assumes a circular pattern to domestic violence participated in by all members of the family without distinguishing between aggressor and victim. Many wife beaters and beaten wives, according to the circular theory, come from homes where they suffered child abuse or witnessed one parent's abuse of the other and they in turn react to their own children with physical abuse. . . .

As battered women are escaping to shelters and are beginning to speak of their experiences, we are learning the true dimensions of "domestic violence." For example, the directly causal links made by social scientists between spouse battery and child abuse ignore the fact that many wife beaters are not from violent homes. In the Gelles sample, 40 percent of his respondents were *not* abused as children and over 30 percent *never* witnessed abuse of their parents.[1] Wives *don't* seek out abusive husbands because they themselves were abused: according to Roy's survey, 66 percent of the wives had not experienced parental violence as children. And in Gayford's study of 100 battered wives, only 23 percent of the women had been exposed to violence as children, while 51 percent of their husbands had.[2]

It is not necessarily violence that breeds violence. It is the fact that sexually abusive men—pimps, husbands, or fathers—many of whom learn violence at an early age as a means of problem solving, still received sanction for their behavior. Hopelessness doesn't stem from an inescapable pattern of violence into which all members of the family are locked, but from social sanction that results from not punishing the offenders but blaming the female victim.

Family Slavery Is Sexual

Until women began describing their experiences of battery in marriage and feminists made rape an issue of sexual politics, wife battery was viewed as physical aggression but not as *sexual* violence. Likewise, through indepth interviews with victims, incest is now known to be another form of family sexual violence carried out by the father or other male in authority in the family. As such, both wife battery and incest are forms of female sexual slavery. . . .

Family Slavery Is Enforced and Sanctioned

Of the women in Roy's study who had left their violent husbands, one third never tried to get help from the police. They feared reprisals from their husbands or social disgrace and they reported they lacked faith in the police system's ability to respond. That lack of faith was substantiated by the two thirds who did call the police: 90 percent of them reported that the police made no arrests, 70 percent reported the police were not helpful at all.[3] Other research on battered women shows that fewer than 10 percent reported being battered to the police.[4] This pattern is similar to that of rape. However, after seeking support from

---

[1] Richard Gelles, *The Violent Home* [Beverly Hills: Sage Publications, 1972], pages 173–174.

[2] J. J. Gayford, "Wife Battery: A Preliminary Survey of 100 Cases," *British Medical Journal*, 1 [1975], page 196.

[3] Maria Roy, "A Current Survey of 150 Cases," in *Battered Women*, ed. Maria Roy [New York: Van Nostrand Reinhold, 1977], page 33.

[4] Lenore E. Walker, "Who Are the Battered Women?" *Frontiers: A Journal of Women's Studies*, II, no. 1 [Spring 1977], page 52.

other women through rape crisis centers or a battered wives shelter, women are able not only to report the incident to the police but to demand the action to which they are entitled. Yet little is forthcoming from this system in their behalf.

Inaction or noninterference is justified by the police on the same grounds that police don't interfere with pimps beating their prostitutes—often wives, like prostitutes, are initially ambivalent about seeing the man they love taken to jail. Instead of recognizing and dealing directly with the extent of the terror behind their ambivalences, the police withdraw, leaving the violence to the privacy of the couple.

The problem in reporting incest begins with the age of the victim: a child cannot easily go to authorities on her own. If she is not significantly estranged from her mother, the little girl may try to turn to her. But mothers, whether through jealousy or personal guilt over the situation, react with disbelief or denial. Or the mother, caught between loyalty to her husband and to her daughter, may take the husband's side and refuse to believe he could do such a thing. More often than not, girls sense on some level the precarious situation they are in and don't say anything. . . .

Wife battery and incest practices illustrate how the family institutionalizes male power and authority. Exploitative and violent use of that power in the family is sanctioned and justified through inadequate laws to protect women, through poor law enforcement of existing laws, and by keeping the abuse of women and girls in the home, private, and therefore inaccessible to scrutiny. Considering the number of women subjected to wife battery, the numbers of daughters incestually assaulted, the socialization in the family that encourages these practices, and the physical and sexual abuse of children which are preconditions to forced prostitution, the family can no longer be accepted as a neutral social institution but instead is seen as an institution which frequently promotes and protects female sexual slavery. . . .

SEX COLONIZATION

Sex is power is the foundation of patriarchy, and patriarchy is *rule by male right.* Across all national boundaries, male gender (and the power that accrues to it) is first and foremost the basis for power and authority in society. It defines who controls the social and political order. From male authority flows male rights. Those rights, established through the sex-is-power ethic, are exercised first in one-to-one relationships. It is in the private relationship between men and women that fundamental inequality is established. From individual domination, inequality is incorporated into the larger social, political, and economic order. Institutionalized sexism and misogyny—from discrimination in employment, to exploitation through the welfare system, to dehumanization in pornography— stem from the primary sexual domination of women in one-to-one situations.

Female sexual slavery, in all of its forms, is the mechanism for controlling women through the sex-is-power ethic, either directly through enslavement or indirectly using enslavement as a threat that is held over all other women. This is the generalized condition of sex colonization. Enslavement or potential slavery is rarely seen as such either by its aggressors/potential aggressors or by its victims/potential victims. That is the subtlety of long-term sex colonization. . . .

Each male national culture has its own set of beliefs that are contained within an ideology which supports sex colonization. That ideology is perpetuated in the social order through various institutions. Religion often serves as a conduit for ideology. Notions of female promiscuity as illustrated by the rape paradigm stem directly from the Christian ethic in the West. In the Arab world seclusion of women is validated by Islamic law.

But in pluralistic societies, religion is insufficient for the ideology that shores up female sexual slavery. In the West where there is a broad range of beliefs and lifestyles among a vast population, ideology must be conveyed through other forms as well. Pornography will be discussed in the next chapter as a primary institution promoting an ideology of sexual violence. It is the masculinist concept of sexual liberation. It actually can be seen as a kind of "danger belief" in a similar sense as those which view women as uncontrollably promiscuous and therefore a threat to honor.

In pornography women are portrayed as supersexed beings who will devour or destroy men. They are the fantasy of men's fear and loathing of women and as such must be subdued; sexual aggression and violence are the means to bring them under control. In the final analysis, genital mutilation practiced in Africa, crimes of honor practiced in the Mediterranean world, and pornography in the West are equivalent forms, each attempting to control or, if necessary, destroy women through masculinist ideology. Where in the Arab world a woman may be murdered in the most extreme acts of honor, in the West murder of women in snuff films (where women are actually murdered in the climax of sexual pleasure) represents the most extreme condition of the act of male sexual freedom. . . .

WHAT IS PORNOGRAPHY?

Pornography is a practice of cultural sadism as well as a means of diffusing it into the mainstream of accepted behavior and therefore into private lives of individuals. It is the principal medium through which cultural sadism becomes part of the sexual practices of individuals.

The most prevalent theme in pornography is one of utter contempt for women. In movie after movie women are raped, ejaculated on, urinated on, anally penetrated, beaten, and, with the advent of snuff films, murdered in an orgy of sexual pleasure. Women are the objects of pornography, men its largest consumers, and sexual degradation its theme. There are variations on this basic format which are made to appeal to tastes that become eroded or saturated from repetition. Variations include an escalation of violence and the use of children and animals as "exotic" objects. Homosexual pornography, which acts out the same dominant and subordinate roles of heterosexual pornography, appeals not only to gay but also to straight men. Lesbian pornography is made specifically for the titillation of the male consumer. It is what heterosexual men get off on thinking women do together; generally that pornography holds no interest or appeal to those lesbians who might otherwise be interested.

The use of blacks and other ethnic minorities in pornography is less of an appeal to the minority audience than it is a racist representation of blacks for kinky sex. Pornography, in serving its consumer, relies on some of the most pronounced sexual myths and biases of reactionary thought in American society. Pornography presents the stereotype of supersexed blacks and kinky homosexuality and feeds it to the predominately male heterosexual consumer for his private pleasure. Racism and sexism blend with the other characteristics of pornography to provide entertainment based on sexual objectification, violence, and contempt for women. It is the media of misogyny. . . .

ENDING SEXUAL SLAVERY

Because it is invisible to social perception and because of the clandestine nature of its practices, it is presently impossible to statistically measure the incidence of female sexual slavery. But considering the arrested sexual development that is understood to be normal in the male population and considering the numbers of men who are pimps, procurers, members of syndicate and free-lance slavery gangs, operators of brothels and massage parlors, connected with sexual exploitation entertainment, pornography purveyors, wife beaters, child molesters, incest perpetrators, johns (tricks) and rapists, one cannot help but be momentarily stunned by the enormous male population participating in female sexual slavery. The huge number of men engaged in these practices should be cause for declaration of a national and international emergency, a crisis in sexual violence. But what should be cause for alarm is instead accepted as normal social intercourse! . . .

Individual liberty is the other side of female sexual slavery; it is the goal of feminism. For us now the *means* to liberation is as important as the goal. The means, how we get there, will be the basis for the new society we are trying to create. We can effectively challenge sex colonization only by guaranteeing individual liberty to the colonized. Not to safeguard individual liberty would be to substitute one set of colonizers for another as male revolutions have done to women. Therefore, while we condemn and punish those who carry out female sexual slavery, and while we condemn the institutions which perpetuate it, we must take care not to condemn in law or practice the women who work and live in those institutions. Our respect and caring must extend to not just those who are identifiable victims but to all women under the yoke of colonization.

For that reason, and in espousing individual liberty, we must not interfere with women who freely enter marriage and can leave it just as freely. Neither should we interfere with women who enter prostitution freely, be they self-employed professional call girls or high-status African prostitutes, as long as they can freely leave their work any time they choose. I assume that this liberty will take place in the context of increasing participation in new values. As new values are actively disseminated through the population, institutions of sex colonization will become less and less attractive. And I assume that we must determine a woman's ability to freely enter or leave institutions of sex colonization based on her actual conditions and not simply on her perception of them or her desire to participate regardless of the conditions.

The liberty that feminists are demanding for women must be granted to all, whether or not we agree with them. But liberty loses its meaning when women are not in fact free to change their situation or when they participate in limiting others' freedom, as when prostitutes acquire women for their pimps, or when wives cooperate with their husbands' incestuous assaults on their daughters.

These changes are only the beginning of a revolution that has never happened before. It is one that will grow out of united strength of women, a strength derived from new values. What is exciting is that instead of adopting a plan handed over to us, as male revolutionaries unsuccessfully attempted by trying to intimidate us, we are charting our own course to liberation. It must ultimately address all levels of exploitation, particularly the economic and the political; but for women colonized both the economic and political are based in the sexual. The challenge is before us, if we dare. . . .

Compulsory Heterosexuality
and Lesbian Existence

Adrienne Rich

. . . Whatever its origins, when we look hard and clearly at the extent and elaboration of measures designed to keep women within a male sexual purlieu, it becomes an inescapable question whether the issue we have to address as feminists is, not simple "gender inequality," nor the domination of culture by males, nor mere "taboos against homosexuality," but the enforcement of heterosexuality for women as a means of assuring male right of physical, economical, and emotional access.[1] One of many means of enforcement is, of course, the rendering invisible of the lesbian possibility, an engulfed continent which rises fragmentedly to view from time to time only to become submerged again. Feminist research and theory that contributes to lesbian invisibility or

---

[1]For my perception of heterosexuality as an economic institution I am indebted to Lisa Leghorn and Katherine Parker, who allowed me to read their unpublished manuscript, "Redefining Economics" (1980). See their article: "Towards a Feminist Economics: A Global View," *Second Wave* 5, no. 3 (1979): 23–30.

marginality is actually working against the liberation and empowerment of woman as a group.[2]

The assumption that "most women are innately heterosexual" stands as a theoretical and political stumbling block for many women. It remains a tenable assumption, partly because lesbian existence has been written out of history or catalogued under disease; partly because it has been treated as exceptional rather than intrinsic; partly because to acknowledge that for women heterosexuality may not be a "preference" at all but something that has had to be imposed, managed, organized, propagandized, and maintained by force, is an immense step to take if you consider yourself freely and "innately" heterosexual. Yet the failure to examine heterosexuality as an institution is like failing to admit that the economic system called capitalism or the caste system of racism is maintained by a variety of forces, including both physical violence and false consciousness. To take the step of questioning heterosexuality as a "preference" or "choice" for women—and to do the intellectual and emotional work that follows—will call for a special quality of courage in heterosexually identified feminists but I think the rewards will be great: a freeing-up of thinking, the exploring of new paths, the shattering of another great silence, new clarity in personal relationships. . . .

I have chosen to use the terms *lesbian existence* and *lesbian continuum* because the word *lesbianism* has a clinical and limiting ring. *Lesbian existence* suggests both the fact of the historical presence of lesbians and our continuing creation of the meaning of that existence. I mean the term *lesbian continuum* to include a range—through each woman's life and throughout history—of woman-identified experience; not simply the fact that a woman has had or consciously desired genital sexual experience with another woman. If we expand it to embrace many more forms of primary intensity between and among women, including the sharing of a rich inner life, the bonding against male tyranny, the giving and receiving of practical and political support; if we can also hear in it such associations as *marriage resistance* and the "haggard" behavior identified by Mary Daly (obsolete meanings: "intractable," "willful," "wanton," and "unchaste" . . . "a woman reluctant to yield to wooing")[3]—we begin to grasp breadths of female history and psychology which have lain out of reach as a consequence of limited, mostly clinical, definitions of "lesbianism."

---

[2]I would suggest that lesbian existence has been most recognized and tolerated where it has resembled a "deviant" version of heterosexuality; e.g., where lesbians have, like Stein and Toklas, played heterosexual roles (or seemed to in public) and have been chiefly identified with male culture. See also Claude E. Schaeffer, "The Kuterai Female Berdache: Courier, Guide, Prophetess and Warrior," *Ethnohistory* 12, no. 3 (Summer 1965): 193–236. (Berdache: "an individual of a definite physiological sex [m. or f.] who assumes the role and status of the opposite sex and who is viewed by the community as being of one sex physiologically but as having assumed the role and status of the opposite sex" [Schaeffer, p. 231].) Lesbian existence has also been relegated to an upper-class phenomenon, an elite decadence (as in the facination with Paris salon lesbians such as Renée Vivien and Natalie Clifford Barney), to the obscuring of such "common women" as Judy Grahn depicts in her *The Work of a Common Woman* (Oakland, Calif.: Diana Press, 1978) and *True to Life Stories* (Oakland, Calif.: Diana Press, 1978).

[3]Mary Daly, *Gyn/Ecology,* Boston: Beacon Press, 1978.

Lesbian existence comprises both the breaking of a taboo and the rejection of a compulsory way of life. It is also a direct or indirect attack on male right of access to women. But it is more than these, although we may first begin to perceive it as a form of nay-saying to patriarchy, an act of resistance. It has of course included role playing, self-hatred, breakdown, alcoholism, suicide, and intrawoman violence; we romanticize at our peril what it means to love and act against the grain, and under heavy penalties; and lesbian existence has been lived (unlike, say, Jewish or Catholic existence) without access to any knowledge of a tradition, a continuity, a social underpinning. The destruction of records and memorabilia and letters documenting the realities of lesbian existence must be taken very seriously as a means of keeping heterosexuality compulsory for women, since what has been kept from our knowledge is joy, sensuality, courage, and community, as well as guilt, self-betrayal, and pain.[4]

Lesbians have historically been deprived of a political existence through "inclusion" as female versions of male homosexuality. To equate lesbian existence with male homosexuality because each is stigmatized is to deny and erase female reality once again. To separate those women stigmatized as "homosexual" or "gay" from the complex continuum of female resistance to enslavement, and attach them to a male pattern, is to falsify our history. Part of the history of lesbian existence is, obviously, to be found where lesbians, lacking a coherent female community, have shared a kind of social life and common cause with homosexual men. But this has to be seen against the differences: women's lack of economic and cultural privilege relative to men; qualitative differences in female and male relationships, for example, the prevalence of anonymous sex and the justification of pederasty among male homosexuals, the pronounced ageism in male homosexual standards of sexual attractiveness, etc. In defining and describing lesbian existence I would hope to move toward a dissociation of lesbian from male homosexual values and allegiances. I perceive the lesbian experience as being, like motherhood, a profoundly *female* experience, with particular oppressions, meanings, and potentialities we cannot comprehend as long as we simply bracket it with other sexually stigmatized existences. Just as the term "parenting" serves to conceal the particular and significant reality of being a parent who is actually a mother, the term "gay" serves the purpose of blurring the very outlines we need to discern, which are of crucial value for feminism and for the freedom of women as a group.

As the term "lesbian" has been held to limiting, clinical associations in its patriarchal definition, female friendship and comradeship have been set apart

---

[4]"In a hostile world in which women are not supposed to survive except in relation with and in service to men, entire communities of women were simply erased. History tends to bury what it seeks to reject" (Blanche W. Cook, " 'Women Alone Stir My Imagination': Lesbianism and the Cultural Tradition," *Signs: Journal of Women in Culture and Society* 4, no. 4 [Summer 1979]: 719–20). The Lesbian Herstory Archives in New York City is one attempt to preserve contemporary documents on lesbian existence—a project of enormous value and meaning, still pitted against the continuing censorship and obliteration of relationships, networks, communities, in other archives and elsewhere in the culture.

from the erotic, thus limiting the erotic itself. But as we deepen and broaden the range of what we define as lesbian existence, as we delineate a lesbian continuum, we begin to discover the erotic in female terms: as that which is unconfined to any single part of the body or solely to the body itself, as an energy not only diffuse but, as Audre Lorde has described it, omnipresent in "the sharing of joy, whether physical, emotional, psychic," and in the sharing of work; as the empowering joy which "makes us less willing to accept powerlessness, or those other supplied states of being which are not native to me, such as resignation, despair, self-effacement, depression, self-denial."[5] . . .

SOCIALIST FEMINISM

Socialism against Patriarchy

Linda Gordon
Allen Hunter

Socialists of various tendencies, both reformist and revolutionary, have been burdened with a tradition of economism. By economism we mean encouraging working-class struggles for *more* of the same, focusing on the redistribution of what is already delivered by the capitalist system without questioning *what* is produced nor *how* it is produced. The economistic conception of socialism demands redivision of the pie and neglects the basic recipe. Socialists have too often neglected the social relations of production and they also have been resistant to radical perspectives on sex and family issues on the grounds they were not "basic." We are here concerned with the latter which we reject as a mechanistic two-stage model—first people struggle for higher wages and then they think about better sexual relationships—because it is so evidently not true.

Socialists have also neglected sex and family issues on the grounds that working class people *as a class* have conservative views on these issues. We do not accept this evaluation for two reasons. First, it is time socialists stopped imagining a working class composed of white patriarchs. Second, we see no reason why socialists should be more willing to compromise on, say, women's rights than on any number of other currently unpopular socialist principles. Finally, socialists have neglected sex and family issues because radical views on these subjects often came from the middle classes. But so did most socialist theory. The question is not whether or not there will be class alliances; the question is toward what end and with what outlook.

---

[5]Audre Lorde, *Uses of the Erotic: The Erotic as Power,* Out & Out Books Pamphlet no. 3 (New York: Out & Out Books [476 2d Street, Brooklyn, New York 11215], 1979).

The issues currently being raised so successfully by the right justify as strong a socialist response as possible. We think socialists ought to develop programs and organizations that address the dissolution of patriarchy, and the left will also have to make sex, family and women's liberation among our primary issues.

It is not easy to be pro-sex in our culture. The prevailing cultural and commercial manipulation is saturated with sexuality to a degree that simultaneously tantalizes and repels. Not only pornography, but also advertising, slick sex books, fashion, sado-masochistic rock—all these cash in on repressed sexuality. At times people try to hold on to a sense of morality and propriety by arguing that sex should be less important, by prefering to focus on work, friends, or "higher" endeavors. Some socialists and feminists, especially because of their anger about the sexual exploitation of women, adopt anti-sexual or anti-heterosexual attitudes. For many women all heterosexual relations are distorted by male dominance; the view that heterosexual relations are too trying, too full of inequality to be worth attempting, is surely a reasonable one for many women; some substitute homosexual relations, some masturbation, some celibacy. The last—celibacy—is a traditional response, for in the nineteenth century feminism was associated with prudery. As a personal choice the rejection of sexual activity may be appropriate for some, but as a political line it is a loser. Similarly, the substitution of masturbation for relationships seems unlikely to satisfy complex human sexual needs, mixed as they are with desires for love and intimacy.

It is important, if at times difficult, to project a view that endorses, even celebrates, the pleasures of sex; and emphasizes the affinity of sexual delight with free, mutual, sensitive and responsible relationships. The capacity for sexual pleasure and sexual relationships is a universal and creative human capacity. Furthermore, the instinct for sex is related to the capacity for play, in turn closely connected to the imagination of a good life which spurs people to struggle for socialism. Sexual restraint was and still is in some respects, necessary for survival. It is a part of the development of human self-control which maximizes the possibility of human freedom and creativity. But sexual prudery today is a tool of domination of men over women, of old over young, and of class over class. In political practice these questions will be matters for judgment and it would be futile to search for clean and simple sexual morals. Such a search would lead to either moralistic repression or irresponsible individualism. But to deny the importance of the widespread search for sexual pleasure will only blind the Left to a tremendous amount of energy, anti-authoritarian sentiments, and capacity for greater honesty and cooperation already existing in society.

If a socialist politics of sex must be complex, a politics of the family must be even more so. We can be in principle unequivocally pro-sex because sex itself is a human activity that has its own worth and which can be separated from those oppressive power relations that invade it. We do not know whether the family can be separated from its oppressive aspects and remain a stable institution. The family is a remarkably universal social creation. It is so weaved into the systems of domination that it has been extremely difficult for socialists to distinguish its oppressive from its supportive possibilities. We think that a socialist politics should clearly oppose the systematically oppressive relations that the family helps to maintain: age, male, and heterosexual domination. But we also think that socialists should support the search for the satisfactions that families can sometimes provide: emotional and sexual intimacy, child-rearing by caring people, cooperation and sharing. Some people are now searching for and finding these outside of families. Others are living in families in which they are struggling—often with good results—against inequality; many others have no choice but to remain in oppressive families. To denounce the family in our circumstances is at best an abstraction; at worst it may seem contemptuous. But without condemning many people's love and need for their families we can fight against the romantic, reactionary, reassertion of family as an ideal model of authority and community.

Women's liberation is a threat that must run through capitalist politics of sex and the family, but it also needs an independent focus. To view feminism as only a politics of sexual and family change would be to vastly underestimate the breadth of the feminist critique. Commitment to women's liberation also requires changing conditions for women in economic and social structures beyond the family. Opposing discrimination against women in jobs and in the law is part of the struggle against women's oppression in the home and vice versa. The relationship between oppression in family and other institutions is a mutually determining dynamic.

Patriarchy, Sexual Identity, and the Sexual Revolution: Heterosexual Ideology as a Coercive Force

Ann Ferguson

. . . Rich makes two basic assumptions in her defense of the lesbian continuum as a construct for understanding female resistance to patriarchy. First, she assumes that the institution of compulsory heterosexuality is the key mechanism underlying and perpetuating male dominance. Second, she implies that all heterosexual relations are coercive or compulsory relations. No arguments are given to support these crucial assumptions, an omission which I take as a fundamental flaw. While I agree that lesbian and male-male attractions are indeed suppressed cross-culturally and that the resulting institution of heterosexuality is coercive, I do not think it plausible to assume such suppression is sufficient by itself to perpetuate male dominance. It may be one of the mechanisms, but it surely is not the single or sufficient one. Others, such as the control of female biological reproduction, male control of state and political power, and economic systems involving discrimination based on class and race, seem analytically distinct from coercive heterosexuality, yet are causes which support and perpetuate male dominance.

Targeting heterosexuality as the key mechanism of male dominance romanticizes lesbianism and ignores the actual quality of individual lesbian or heterosexual women's lives. Calling women who resist patriarchy the lesbian continuum assumes, not only that all lesbians have resisted patriarchy, but that all true patriarchal resisters are lesbians or approach lesbianism. This ignores, on the one hand, the "old lesbian" subculture that contains many nonpolitical, co-opted, and economically comfortable lesbians. It also ignores the existence of some heterosexual couples in which women who are feminists maintain an equal relationship with men. Such women would deny that their involvements are coercive, or even that they are forced to put second their own needs, their self-respect, or their relationships with women.

Part of the problem is the concept of "compulsory heterosexuality." Sometimes Rich seems to imply that women who are essentially or naturally lesbians are coerced by the social mechanisms of the patriarchal family to "turn to the father," hence to men. But if a girl's original love for her mother is itself due to the social fact that women, and not men, mother, then neither lesbianism nor heterosexuality can be said to be women's natural (uncoerced) sexual preference. If humans are basically bisexual or transsexual at birth, it will not do to suggest that lesbiansm is the more authentic sexual preference for feminists, and that heterosexual feminists who do not change their sexual preference are simply lying to themselves about their true sexuality.

The notion that heterosexuality is central to women's oppression is plausible only if one assumes that it is women's emotional dependence on men as lovers in conjunction with other mechanisms of male dominance (e.g., marriage, motherhood, women's economic dependence on men) which allow men to control women's bodies as instruments for their own purposes. But single mothers, black women, and economically independent women, for example, may in ther heterosexual relations with men escape or avoid these other mechanisms.

Rich's emphasis on compulsory heterosexuality as the key mechanism of male domination implies that the quality of straight women's resistance must be questioned. But this ignores other equally important practices of resistance to male domination, for example, women's work networks and trade unions, and welfare mothers organizing against social service cutbacks. The (perhaps unintended) lesbian-separatist implications of her analysis are disturbing. If compulsory heterosexuality is the problem, why bother to make alliances with straight women from minority and working-class communities around issues relating to sex and race discrimination at the workplace, cutbacks in Medicaid abortions, the lack of day-care centers, cutbacks in food stamps, and questions about nuclear power and the arms race? Just stop sleeping with men, withdraw from heterosexual practices, and the whole system of male dominance will collapse on its own!

A socialist-feminist analysis of male dominance sees the systems that oppress women as more complex and difficult to dislodge than does the utopian and idealist simplicity of lesbian separatism. They are at least *dual* systems,[1] and more likely multiple systems, of dominance which at times support and at times contradict each other: capitalism, patriarchy, heterosexism, racism, imperialism. We need autonomous groups of resisters opposing each of these forms of dominance; but we also need alliances among ourselves. If feminism as a movement is truly revolutionary, it cannot give priority to one form of male domination (heterosexism) to the exclusion of others. One's sexual preference may indeed be a political act, but it is not necessarily the best, nor the paradigmatic, feminist political act. Naming the continuum of resistance to patriarchy the lesbian continuum has the political implication that it is.

To conclude, let me agree with Rich that some transhistorical concepts may be needed to stress the continuity of women's resistance to patriarchy. Nonetheless, the concepts we pick should not ignore either the political complexity of our present tasks as feminists nor our historically specific political consciousness as lesbians. Rich's argument, on the one hand that compulsory heterosexuality is the key mechanism of patriarchy, and on the other hand that the lesbian continuum is the key resistance to it, has both of these unfortunate consequences.

Imperialism and Sexuality

Sheila Rowbotham

. . . A similar imperial onslaught on sexuality, particularly female sexuality, has further eroded the traditional notions women had of their value. The cosmetics industry has mushroomed and created needs as well as products. The female who is the cosmetic ideal is more or less unattainable, no sooner captured she appears in another form. Playing on insecurity and anxiety the advertisers market goods which actually create new fears. Vaginal deodorants make people anxious about sexual odour. Acting on the assumption that women regard themselves through men's eyes as objects of pleasure, advertising and the media project a haunting and unreal image of womanhood. The persistent sense of dislocation between the unrealized female self and the projected female stereotypes has contributed to a feeling of failure. Women are not brought up to cope with the male world of production, work, ideas, power. They find their own preserved world threatened, their value reduced and depreciated, and are given an ideal of femininity which is foisted onto them by ever more powerful forms of the mass media.

[1]Iris Young, "Socialist Feminism and the Limits of Dual Systems Theory," *Socialist Review* 10, no. 50/51 (March-June 1980): 169–88.

The media have considerable power to throw back to us a version of ourselves which is presented as the "norm." This "norm" is not unaffected by changes in society. Women's liberation has brought a sprinkling of adverts which attempt to appeal to dissatisfaction. However, the images of freedom are still completely male-defined. Either girls step out in freedom bras towards a man, or they simply become male fantasies of freedom. Girls replace men behind the wheels of fast sports cars. Advertising has a vested interest in presenting the sexual roles between men and women as clearly defined. But it has also to respond, however bizarrely, to changes in the consciousness of women. It reflects very clearly the production relations general in society. In order to sell commodities women are themselves reduced to commodities. However, if a section of middle-class women manage to alter their position in society through agitation there is no reason why adverts should not present these women with a spurious sense of liberation by inverting male-female roles in certain cases, and presenting men as commodities.

The visual impact of advertisements played a large part in awakening women to their own reflection in advanced capitalism. Immediate images on film and television make explicit areas of experience which have previously existed only in our subterranean selves. The very act of communication makes these sensations and experiences assume a shape, whereas before they were only implicit. New forms of consciousness are offered up by the marketing of new commodities and the mass communication of news and events. As a result, many aspects of life which were considered private and personal before become part of what is normally seen.

Sexual relations between men and women, or between men and men, and between women and women, are very clearly no longer exempt from the penetration of the market and the exposure of the sexual sell. This means that sexuality as the symbol of the natural assumes an importance beyond itself. It also means that political resistance to capitalism has to take on new forms, because the tendency for capitalism to distort all areas of human experience is no longer merely an abstract idea, it is an everyday happening.

Within advanced capitalism the maintenance of the separation of male and female conditioning has also assumed a new acuteness. This is partly because the existing sexual division of labour is still necessary to capitalist production. But also because of the deep and long-established nature of female subordination, and the hold it has over both men's and women's notions of their very identities, any challenge touches on deep and intensely personal areas of consciousness. The idea of romantic love, itself a creation of the bourgeoisie, has undergone innumerable transformations and permutations since it originated. Sexual love has assumed immense significance in containing many aspects of social relations incompatible with the work-discipline of commodity production. Here lurk affection, tenderness, passion, violence, satisfaction, fulfilment, excitement, imagination, religion, madness, fantasy, beauty, sensation, cruelty, transcendence, communion, escape. Weighed down with such unrealizable expectations, and surrounded by such an intolerable state of affairs elsewhere, sexuality has been as incapable as the family of providing a genuine alternative to the wasteland.

Sexual pleasure has an elusive and often exhausted quality. It is unable to compensate for everything denied to human beings in normal life. Not surprisingly it has assumed bizarre and distorted forms under the prevailing production for private profit. Belief in property, possession, domination does not stop at the factory gates. But like the family, sex represents the hope of an alternative. It has become the new "sigh of the oppressed creature, the sentiment of a heartless world, and the soul of soulless conditions." Like religion, which it rivals and replaces, sexuality now "is the fantastic realisation of the human being in as much as the human being possesses no true reality."[1] Love and orgasmic explosion have no proper place in a society in which the end of life is the production of goods, in which work discipline as a thing in itself becomes the guardian of morality. Consequently sexual sensation is packaged, and delivered confined and synthesized in prevailing notions of sexuality—sugar sweet or black leather and net. Sex roles of dominator and dominated are part of the sexual sell. Such notions determine the structure of human fantasy—they are the symbol of everything which is not possible in everyday life.

Sexuality is communicated in the media in a series of images. A hand stroking hair, legs walking into summer, clean-washing-crisp housewives, children with cereal spoons and oral brand satisfactions, the power of money and class selling cigars, motor cars, pale ale—these become the visible shell for accumulated unrealizable desire. The loving emotion and physical excitement in sex become loaded with the great weight of this accumulation. Sexual relations between people start to sag, drop into odd places, assume fantastic shapes, in pornographic fetish, the rituals of desire, or the complacency of hypocritical virtue. Any challenge to the prevailing order of fantasy is a political struggle, just as the criticism of religion in the nineteenth century was political.

It would be foolish not to recognize the resilience of the subterranean imagination. The desecration of capitalism's sanctuaries, where pain and domination, grotesque imagination, masochism and guilt, emotional blackmail, and the thwarted ego have a hothouse life of their own, needs, as Wilhelm Reich understood, a conscious commitment to sexual alternatives in the revolutionary movement. Women's liberation attacked from the start the way in which women were presented in the media. By doing this the whole image of the family, of children, of manliness, became very obvious as well as the distortion of sexuality. The distortions appeared clearly because the old moral taboos were being eroded. Instead of the ethic of thrift, abstinence, and sacrifice which came out of the early stages of capital accumulation, capitalism needs now people who can regulate themselves precisely and on their own initiative at work and spend and consume without repression during their leisure. Though these long-term

---

[1]Marx and Engles, *Gesamtausgabe*, I, i, i, quoted in Karl Marx, *Selected Writings in Sociology and Social Philosophy*, ed. T. B. Bottomore and M. Rubel, Watts, 1956, pp. 26–7. See also Christopher Caudwell, "A Study of Changing Values: Love," in *The Concept of Freedom*, Lawrence & Wishart, 1965.

needs are temporarily contradicted by the creation of new forms of labour-intensive work which need the old kind of openly authoritarian supervision, and by short-term economic problems which involve cutting back on demand, they have already had a considerable social influence.

Much of the talk of permissive society and sexual liberation means merely permission to consume. However, this changing climate has a very important effect on the position of women. For the first time in human society it is possible for women to choose when they become pregnant. This with the panic about population explosion means that the persistent connection between sex and procreation, and the fear in male-dominated society of female sexual pleasure, and often of any sexual act which is not likely to produce children, lose their force to contain women—and men. The implications of these for both women's liberation and gay liberation are apparent.

Contraception, like other technological advances in capitalism, has a dual nature. By immeasurably increasing the possibilities of sexual relationship without fear of pregnancy, contraceptives contribute to a loosening of moral coercion to the "permissive" society. Within such a society the carrot replaces the stick as the prime inducement to cooperation, though the stick is kept for the last resort. As long as sexuality, thus liberated, is confined to a small elite group, who are not within the discipline of commodity production, or as long as the kind of sexuality which is permitted retains, in however bizarre a form, the structure of dominance and abnegation, self-disgust and self-destruction, which within capitalism hold down and limit the human consciousness, it can be accommodated. But whenever the notion of pleasure takes off into a questioning of the need to produce people only to produce things it becomes subversive. Nasty, dirty hippy sex exults in its opposition to commodity production. It parades itself dancing in the streets, becomes gleefully transvestite, many coloured, confuses sexual roles, makes love every day. Then capitalism thinks "how nice," not like those old-fashioned revolutionaries, and sells them a few clothes. The market flourishes and the fashion spreads. Nudity proliferates in the underground papers first, and then in the popular press. But despite its ambiguities, and particularly its ambiguities towards women, the emphasis in the underground on sexual pleasure still contains a threat to commodity production. When it seems to spread to the young working classes capitalism suddenly remembers morality, and in its zealous puritan disguise flays out against the sexuality it had formerly encouraged.

That the cult of free sex contains many distortions and much mystique and illusion is not surprising; what is surprising is the tendency for conservative supporters of capitalism to blame these on contraception, and look back longingly to the romantic nonsense of a mythical former unity, when pregnancy followed pregnancy, when childbirth frequently brought the mother's death, and infant mortality was high. The source of mystique and illusion comes from the mess outside, not from the technology of diaphragm, pill and safe abortion. Contraception, like any other kind of knowledge, is not accumulated in a social vacuum. The course of research by private firms, experiments with poor Third

World women, the lack of concern about the effects on women psychologically and physically, reflect a bias which is profit-oriented, imperialist and male-biased. Women's liberation has consistently demanded abortion and contraception as means of control for women, not as part of a social engineering plan to keep population down to avoid the discontent of the poor. None the less, contraceptives lay the basis for a great explosion in the possibility of female pleasure. The release of the female orgasm from the fatalism, fear and shame of millennia is one of the triumphs of bourgeois technology. The social expression of this release and the shape it assumes in consciousness will depend on the activity of revolutionary human beings in history. Its integration is not impossible within capitalism. The glossy women's magazines are already pushing their own version of sexual liberation. How to undress in front of your husband, how to package yourself for all his sexual fantasies. In a popular book on sex technique published recently women are urged to work like the devil to accent their good features and hide the bad. They are shown how to package themselves for the market and check their tone and volume, to remember they are training their body to become a superb instrument of love. Passivity is rebuked, enthusiastic participation and a close check on "Maintenance, Reclamation and Salvage" recommended.[2] But while increasing female participation in the sexual act is convenient as a compensatory feature of advanced capitalism, the notion of female power to control equally in bed upsets the conditioning of men to dominate and females to acquiesce. This is rather like the unresolved contradiction of how to educate people to work with initiative, and get them to continue to obey orders. Hysteria so long contained in the womb leaps exulting up from under. The female orgasm explodes and scrawls itself generously over the women's lavatory at Willesden railway station, "We are all the same, good or bad, slag or vergin."

---

[2] "J," *Sensuous Woman,* London, 1971, pp. 37–9. I owe this reference to Jenny Moss.

FEMINISM AND WOMEN OF COLOR

Rape, Racism, and the Myth of the Black Rapist

Angela Davis

Some of the most flagrant symptoms of social deterioration are acknowledged as serious problems only when they have assumed such epidemic proportions that they appear to defy solution. Rape is a case in point. In the United States today, it is one of the fastest-growing violent crimes.[1] After ages of silence, suffering and misplaced guilt, sexual assault is explosively emerging as one of the telling dysfunctions of present-day capitalist society. The rising public concern about rape in the United States has inspired countless numbers of women to divulge their past encounters with actual or would-be assailants. As a result, an awesome fact has come to light: appallingly few women can claim that they have not been victims, at one time in their lives, of either attempted or accomplished sexual attacks.

In the United States and other capitalist countries, rape laws as a rule were framed originally for the protection of men of the upper classes, whose daughters and wives might be assaulted. What happens to working-class women has usually been of little concern to the courts; as a result, remarkably few white men have been prosecuted for the sexual violence they have inflicted on these women. While the rapists have seldom been brought to justice, the rape charge has been indiscriminately aimed at Black men, the guilty and innocent alike. Thus, of the 455 men executed between 1930 and 1967 on the basis of rape convictions, 405 of them were Black.[2]

In the history of the United States, the fraudulent rape charge stands out as one of the most formidable artifices invented by racism. The myth of the Black rapist has been methodically conjured up whenever recurrent waves of violence and terror against the Black community have required convincing justifications. If Black women have been conspicuously absent from the ranks of the contemporary anti-rape movement, it may be due, in part, to that movement's indifferent posture toward the frame-up rape charge as an incitement to racist aggression. Too many innocents have been offered sacrificially to gas chambers and lifer's cells for Black women to join those who often seek relief from policemen and judges. Moreover, as rape victims themselves, they have found little if any sympathy from these men in uniforms and robes. And stories about

---

[1]Nancy Gager and Cathleen Schurr, *Sexual Assault: Confronting Rape in America* (New York: Grosset & Dunlap, 1976), p. 1.

[2]Michael Meltsner, *Cruel and Unusual: The Supreme Court and Capital Punishment* (New York: Random House, 1973), p. 75.

police assaults on Black women—rape victims sometimes suffering a second rape—are heard too frequently to be dismissed as aberrations. "Even at the strongest time of the civil rights movement in Birmingham," for example,

> young activists often stated that nothing could protect Black women from being raped by Birmingham police. As recently as December, 1974, in Chicago, a 17-year old Black woman reported that she was gang-raped by 10 policemen. Some of the men were suspended, but ultimately the whole thing was swept under the rug.[3]

During the early stages of the contemporary anti-rape movement, few feminist theorists seriously analyzed the special circumstances surrounding the Black woman as rape victim. The historical knot binding Black women—systematically abused and violated by white men—to Black men—maimed and murdered because of the racist manipulation of the rape charge—has just begun to be acknowledged to any significant extent. Whenever Black women have challenged rape, they usually and simultaneously expose the use of the frame-up rape charge as a deadly racist weapon against their men. As one extremely perceptive writer put it:

> The myth of the black rapist of white women is the twin of the myth of the bad black woman—both designed to apologize for and facilitate the continued exploitation of black men and women. Black women perceived this connection very clearly and were early in the forefront of the fight against lynching.[4]

. . . Racism has always drawn strength from its ability to encourage sexual coercion. While Black women and their sisters of color have been the main targets of these racist-inspired attacks, white women have suffered as well. For once white men were persuaded that they could commit sexual assaults against Black women with impunity, their conduct toward women of their own race could not have remained unmarred. Racism has always served as a provocation to rape, and white women in the United States have necessarily suffered the ricochet fire of these attacks. This is one of the many ways in which racism nourishes sexism, causing white women to be indirectly victimized by the special oppression aimed at their sisters of color.

The experience of the Vietnam War furnished a further example of the extent to which racism could function as a provocation to rape. Because it was drummed into the heads of U.S. soldiers that they were fighting an inferior race, they could be taught that raping Vietnamese women was a necessary military duty. They could even be instructed to "search" the women with their penises.[5] It was the unwritten policy of the U.S. Military Command to systematically encourage rape, since it was an extremely effective weapon of mass terrorism. Where are the thousands upon thousands of Vietnam veterans who witnessed

---

[3]"The Racist Use of Rape and the Rape Charge." A Statement to the Women's Movement From a Group of Socialist Women (Louisville, Ky.: Socialist Women's Caucus, 1974), pp. 5–6.

[4]Gerda Lerner, editor, *Black Women in White America: A Documentary History,* New York, Pantheon Books, 1972, p. 193.

[5]Arlene Eisen-Bergman, *Women in Vietnam,* San Francisco, People's Press, 1975, Part I, Chapter 5.

and participated in these horrors? To what extent did those brutal experiences affect their attitudes toward women in general? While it would be quite erroneous to single out Vietnam veterans as the main perpetrators of sexual crimes, there can be little doubt that the horrendous repercussions of the Vietnam experience are still being felt by all women in the United States today.

It is a painful irony that some anti-rape theorists, who ignore the part played by racism in instigating rape, do not hesitate to argue that men of color are especially prone to commit sexual violence against women. . . .

The myth of the Black rapist continues to carry out the insidious work of racist ideology. It must bear a good portion of the responsibility for the failure of most anti-rape theorists to seek the identity of the enormous numbers of anonymous rapists who remain unreported, untried and unconvicted. As long as their analyses focus on accused rapists who are reported and arrested, thus on only a fraction of the rapes actually committed, Black men—and other men of color—will inevitably be viewed as the villains responsible for the current epidemic of sexual violence. The anonymity surrounding the vast majority of rapes is consequently treated as a statistical detail—or else as a mystery whose meaning is inaccessible.

But why are there so many anonymous rapists in the first place? Might not this anonymity be a privilege enjoyed by men whose status protects them from prosecution? Although white men who are employers, executives, politicians, doctors, professors, etc., have been known to "take advantage" of women they consider their social inferiors, their sexual misdeeds seldom come to light in court. Is it not therefore quite probable that these men of the capitalist and middle classes account for a significant proportion of the unreported rapes? Many of these unreported rapes undoubtedly involve Black women as victims: their historical experience proves that racist ideology implies an open invitation to rape. As the basis of the license to rape Black women during slavery was the slaveholders' economic power, so the class structure of capitalist society also harbors an incentive to rape. It seems, in fact, that men of the capitalist class and their middle-class partners are immune to prosecution because they commit their sexual assaults with the same unchallenged authority that legitimizes their daily assaults on the labor and dignity of working people.

The existence of widespread sexual harassment on the job has never been much of a secret. It is precisely on the job, indeed, that women—especially when they are not unionized—are most vulnerable. Having already established their economic domination over their female subordinates, employers, managers and foremen may attempt to assert this authority in sexual terms. That working-class women are more intensely exploited than their men adds to their vulnerability to sexual abuse, while sexual coercion simultaneously reinforces their vulnerability to economic exploitation.

Working-class men, whatever their color, can be motivated to rape by the belief that their maleness accords them the privilege to dominate women. Yet since they do not possess the social or economic authority—unless it is a white man raping a woman of color—guaranteeing them immunity from prosecution, the incentive is not nearly as powerful as it is for the men of the capitalist class. When working-class men accept the invitation to rape extended by the ideology of male supremacy, they are accepting a bribe, an illusory compensation for their powerlessness.

The class structure of capitalism encourages men who wield power in the economic and political realm to become routine agents of sexual exploitation. The present rape epidemic occurs at a time when the capitalist class is furiously reasserting its authority in face of global and internal challenges. Both racism and sexism, central to its domestic strategy of increased economic exploitation, are receiving unprecedented encouragement. It is not a mere coincidence that as the incidence of rape has arisen, the position of women workers has visibly worsened. So severe are women's economic losses that their wages in relationship to men are lower than they were a decade ago. The proliferation of sexual violence is the brutal face of a generalized intensification of the sexism which necessarily accompanies this economic assault.

Following a pattern established by racism, the attack on women mirrors the deteriorating situation of workers of color and the rising influence of racism in the judicial system, the educational institutions and in the government's posture of studied neglect toward Black people and other people of color. The most dramatic sign of the dangerous resurgence of racism is the new visibility of the Ku Klux Klan and the related epidemic of violent assaults on Blacks, Chicanos, Puerto Ricans and Native Americans. The present rape epidemic bears an extraordinary likeness to this violence kindled by racism.

Given the complexity of the social context of rape today, any attempt to treat it as an isolated phenomenon is bound to founder. An effective strategy against rape must aim for more than the eradication of rape—or even of sexism—alone. The struggle against racism must be an ongoing theme of the anti-rape movement, which must not only defend women of color, but the many victims of the racist manipulation of the rape charge as well. The crisis dimensions of sexual violence constitute one of the facets of a deep and ongoing crisis of capitalism. As the violent face of sexism, the threat of rape will continue to exist as long as the overall oppression of women remains an essential crutch for capitalism. The anti-rape movement and its important current activities— ranging from emotional and legal aid to self-defense and educational campaigns —must be situated in a strategic context which envisages the ultimate defeat of monopoly capitalism.

Scratching the Surface:
Some Notes on Barriers to Women and Loving

Audre Lorde

Racism: *The belief in the inherent superiority of one race over all others and thereby the right to dominance.*

Sexism: *The belief in the inherent superiority of one sex and thereby the right to dominance.*

Heterosexism: *The belief in the inherent superiority of one pattern of loving and thereby its right to dominance.*

Homophobia: *The fear of feelings of love for members of one's own sex and therefore the hatred of those feelings in others.*

The above forms of human blindness stem from the same root—the inability to recognize or tolerate the notion of difference as a beneficial and dynamic human force, and one which is enriching rather than threatening to the defined self.

To a large degree, at least verbally, the black community has moved beyond the "two steps behind her man" mode of sexual relations sometimes mouthed as desirable during the sixties. This was a time when the myth of the black matriarchy as a social disease was being presented by racist forces for an excuse or diversion, to redirect our attentions away from the real sources of black oppression.

For black women as well as black men, it is axiomatic that if we do not define ourselves for ourselves, we will be defined by others—for their use and to our detriment. The development of self-defined black women, ready to explore and pursue our power and interests within our communities, is a vital component in the war for black liberation. The image of the Angolan woman with a baby on one arm and a gun in the other is neither romantic nor fanciful. Black women in this country coming together to examine our sources of strength and support, and to recognize our common social, cultural, emotional, and political interests, is a development which can only contribute to the power of the black community as a whole. For it is only through the coming together of self-actualized individuals, female and male, that any real advances can be made. The old sexual power-relationships based on a dominant/subordinate model between unequals have not served us as a people, nor as individuals.

Black women who define ourselves and our goals beyond the sphere of a sexual relationship can bring to any endeavor the realized focus of a completed and therefore empowered individual. Black women and black men who recognize that the development of their particular strengths and interests does not diminish the other, do not diffuse their energies fighting for control over each other. We focus our attentions against the real economic, political and social forces at the heart of this society which are ripping ourselves and our children and our worlds apart.

Increasingly, despite opposition, black women are coming together to explore and to alter those manifestations of our society which oppress us in ways different from the oppression of black men. This is no threat to black men, and is only seen as one by those black men who choose to embody within themselves those same manifestations of female oppression. For instance, enforced sterilization and unavailable abortions are tools of oppression against black women, as is rape. Only to those black men who are unclear as to the paths of their own self-definition can the self-actualization and self-protective bonding of black women be seen as a threatening development.

Today, the red herring of homophobia and lesbian-baiting is being used in the black community to obscure the true double face of racism/sexism. Black women sharing close ties with each other, politically or emotionally, are not the enemies of black men. Too frequently, however, an attempt to rule by fear tactics is practiced by some black men against those black women who are more ally than enemy. These tactics are sometimes expressed as threats of emotional rejection: "Their poetry wasn't too bad but I couldn't take all those lezzies (lesbians)." The man who says this is warning every black woman present who is interested in a relationship with men—and most black women are—that (1) if she wishes to have her work considered she must eschew any other allegiance except to him and (2) any woman who wishes his friendship and/or support had better not be "tainted" by woman-identified interests.

If such threats of labelling, vilification and/or emotional isolation are not enough to bring black women docilely into camp as followers, or persuade them to avoid each other as political or emotional support for each other, then the rule by terror can be expressed physically, as on the campus of a New York college recently, where black women sought to come together around feminist concerns. Violently threatening phone calls were made to those black women who dared to explore the possibilities of a feminist connection with non-black women. Some of these women, intimidated by these threats and the withdrawal of male approval, did turn against their sisters. When threats did not prevent the attempted coalition of black feminists, the resulting hysteria left some black women beaten and raped. Whether the threats by black men actually led to these assaults, or merely encouraged the climate of hostility within which they could occur, the results upon the women attacked were the same.

Wars and jails have decimated the ranks of black males of marriageable age. The fury of many black heterosexual women against white women who date black men is rooted in this unequal sexual equation, since whatever threatens to widen that equation is deeply and articulately resented. But this is essentially unconstructive resentment because it extends sideways, and can never result in true progress on the issue, because it does not question the vertical lines of power or authority, nor the sexist assumptions which dictate the terms of the competition. And the racism of white women can be better addressed where it is less complicated by their own sexual oppression. In this situation it is not the non-black woman who calls the tune, but rather the black man who turns away from himself in his sisters, or who, through a fear borrowed from white men, reads her strength not as a resource but as challenge.

All too often the message comes loud and clear to black women from black men: "I am the prize and there are not too many of me and remember I can always go elsewhere. So if you want me you'd better stay in your place which is away from each other, or I will call you lesbian and wipe you away." Black women are programmed to define themselves within this male attention and to compete with each other for it, rather than to recognize their common interests.

The tactic of encouraging horizontal or lateral hostility to becloud the real and more pressing issues of oppression is by no means new, nor limited to relations between women. The same tactic is used to continue or exacerbate the separation between black women and black men. In discussions around the hiring and firing of black faculty at universities, the charge is frequently heard that black women are more easily hired than are black men. For this reason, black women's problems of promotion and tenure are not to be considered as important, since they are only "taking jobs away from black men." Here again, energy is being wasted on battles which extend horizontally, over the pitifully few crumbs allowed us, rather than being used in a joining of forces to fight for a more realistic representation of black faculty. This would be a vertical battle against the racist policies of the academic structure itself, one which could result in real power and change. And of course, it is the structure at the top which desires changelessness, and so profits from these apparently endless kitchen wars.

Instead of keeping our attentions focused upon the real enemies, enormous energy is being wasted in the black community today by both black men and heterosexual black women, in anti-lesbian hysteria. Yet women-identified women—those who sought their own destinies and attempted to execute them in the absence of male support—have been around in all of our communities for a long time. As Yvonne Flowers of York College pointed out in a recent discussion, the unmarried aunt, childless or otherwise, whose home and resources were often a welcome haven for different members of the family, was a familiar figure in many of our childhoods. And within the homes of our black communities today, it is not the black lesbian who is battering and raping our under-age girl-children, out of displaced and sickening frustration.

The black lesbian has come under increasing attack from both black men and heterosexual black women. In the same way that the existence of the self-defined black woman is no threat to the self-defined black man, the black lesbian is an emotional threat only to those black women who are unsure of, or unable to, express their feelings of kinship and love for other black women, in any meaningful way. For so long, we have been encouraged to view each other with suspicion, as eternal competitors, or as the visible face of our own self-rejection.

But traditionally, black women have always bonded together in support of each other, however uneasily and in the face of whatever other allegiances which militated against that bonding. We have banded together with each other for wisdom and strength and support, even when it was only in relationship to one man. We need only look at the close—although highly complex and involved—relationship between African co-wives; or at the Amazon warriors of ancient Dahomey, who fought together as the Kings' main and most ferocious body-guard. We need only look at the more promising power wielded by the West African Market Women Associations of today, and those governments which have risen and fallen at their pleasure.

In a verbatim retelling of her life, a 92-year-old Efik-Ibibio woman of Nigeria recalls her love for another woman:

> I had a woman friend to whom I revealed my secrets. She was very fond of keeping secrets to herself. We acted as husband and wife. We always moved hand in glove and my husband and hers knew about our relationship. The villagers nicknamed us twin sisters. When I was out of gear with my husband, she would be the one to restore peace. I often sent my children to go and work for her in return for her kindnesses to me. My husband being more fortunate to get more pieces of land than her husband, allowed some to her, even though she was not my co-wife.[1]

The Fon of Dahomey still have 12 different kinds of marriage, one of which is known as "giving the goat to the buck," where a woman of independent means marries another woman who then may or may not bear children, all of whom will belong to the blood line of the other woman.[2] Some marriages of this kind are arranged to provide heirs for women of means who wish to remain "free," and some are homosexual relationships. Marriages of this kind occur throughout Africa, in several different places among different peoples.[3]

In all of these cases, the women involved are recognized parts of their communities, evaluated not by their sexuality but by their respective places within the community.

While a piece of each black woman remembers the old ways of another place and time, when we enjoyed each other in a sisterhood of work and play and power, other pieces of us, less functional, eye each other with suspicion as we have been programmed to do. In the interests of separation, and to keep us out of touch with our own power, black women have been taught to view each other as always suspect, heartless competitors for the scarce male, the all-important prize that will legitimize our existence. This becomes an ultimate and dehuma-nizing denial of self, no less lethal than that dehumanization of racism which is so closely allied to it.

If the recent hysterical rejection of lesbians in the black community is based solely upon an aversion to the idea of sexual contact between members of the same sex (a contact existing for ages in most of the female compounds across the African continent, from reports) why then is the idea of sexual contact between

---

[1]Andreski, Iris. *Old Wives Tales: Life-Stories of African Women*. Schocken Books. New York. 1970. p. 131.
[2]Herskovits, Melville. *Dahomey*. Northwestern Univ. Press. Evanston. 1967. 2 volumes. i, pp. 320–321.
[3]Ibid., i, p. 322.

black men so much more easily accepted, or unremarked? Is the reality of the imagined threat the existence of a self-motivated, self-defined black woman who will not fear nor suffer some terrible retribution from the gods because she does not necessarily seek her face in a man's eyes, even if he has fathered her children? Female-headed households in the black community are not always situations by default.

The distortion of relationship which says "I disagree with you, or I do not share your lifestyle, so I must destroy you" leaves black people with basically uncreative victories, defeated in any common struggle. That is jugular vein psychology, based on a fallacy which holds that your assertion or affirmation of your self must mean an attack upon my self—or that my defining myself will somehow prevent or retard your self-definition. The supposition that one sex needs the other's acquiescence in order to exist prevents both from moving together as self-defined persons toward a common goal.

This is a prevalent mistake among oppressed peoples, and is based upon the false notion that there is only a limited and particular amount of freedom that must be divided up between us, with the largest and juiciest pieces going as spoils to the victor or the stronger. So instead of joining together to fight for more, we quarrel between ourselves for a larger slice of the one pie. Black women fight between ourselves over men instead of pursuing and using who we are and our strengths; black women and men fight between ourselves over who has more of a right to freedom, instead of seeing each other's struggles as part of our own; black and white women fight between ourselves over who is the more oppressed, instead of seeing those areas in which our causes are the same. (Of course, this last separation is worsened by the intransigent racism that white women too often fail to, or cannot, address in themselves.)

As black women we have the right and responsibility to define ourselves, and to seek our allies in common cause with black men against racism, and with white women against sexism. But most of all as black women we have a right to recognize each other without fear and to love where we choose, for both homosexual and heterosexual black women today share a history of bonding and strength that our particular sexual preferences should not blind us too.

SUGGESTIONS FOR FURTHER READING:
Part Three

PAID LABOR

Amsden, Alice H. (ed.): *The Economics of Women and Work,* Penguin, New York, 1980.

Baxandall, Rosalyn, Linda Gordon, and Susan Reverby (eds.): *America's Working Women: A Documentary History—1600 to the Present,* Vintage, New York, 1976.

Blaxall, Martha, and Barbara Reagan: *Women and the Workplace: The Implications of Occupational Segregation,* The University of Chicago Press, Chicago and London, 1976.

Braverman, Harry: *Labor and Monopoly Capital: The Degradation of Work in the 20th Century,* Monthly Review Press, New York, 1976.

Dalla Costa, Mariarosa: *The Power of Women and the Subversion of the Community,* Falling Wall Press, Bristol, 1975.

Farley, Lin: *Sexual Shakedown: The Sexual Harassment of Women on the Job,* Warner, New York, 1980.

Gilman, Charlotte Perkins: *Women and Economics: The Economic Factor Between Men and Women as a Factor in Social Evolution,* Harper & Row, New York, 1966. Originally published in 1898.

Howe, Louise Kapp: *Pink Collar Workers,* Avon, New York, 1977.

Leghorn, Lisa, and Katherine Parker: *Woman's Worth: Sexual Economics and the World of Women,* Routledge & Kegan Paul, Boston, London, and Henley, 1981.

MacKinnon, Catherine A.: *Sexual Harassment of Working Women: A Case of Sex Discrimination,* Yale, New Haven, Conn., 1979.

Stellman, Jeanne Mager: *Women's Work, Women's Health: Myths and Realities,* Pantheon, New York, 1977.

Tepperman, Jean: *Not Servants, Not Machines: Office Workers Speak Out,* Beacon, Boston, 1976.

FAMILY

Chodorow, Nancy: *The Reproduction of Mothering: Psychoanalysis and the Sociology of Gender,* University of California Press, Berkeley, Los Angeles, London, 1978.

Edmond, Wendy, and Suzie Fleming (eds.): *All Work and No Pay,* Falling Wall Press, Bristol, 1975.

Elshtain, Jean Bethke: *The Family in Political Thought,* University of Massachusetts Press, Amherst, 1982.

Friedan, Betty: *The Feminine Mystique,* Dell, New York, 1970.

Luxton, Meg: *More Than a Labour of Love: Three Generations of Women's Work in the Home,* Women's Educational Press, Toronto, 1980.

Malos, Ellen (ed.): *The Politics of Housework,* Schocken, New York, 1980.

Martin, Del: *Battered Wives,* Pocket Books, New York, 1976.

O'Brien, Mary: *The Politics of Reproduction,* Routledge & Kegan Paul, Boston, London, and Henley, 1981.

Rich, Adrienne: *Of Woman Born: Motherhood as Experience and Institution,* Norton, New York, 1976.

Rubin, Lillian Breslow: *Worlds of Pain: Life in the Working-Class Family,* Basic, New York, 1976.

Stack, Carol B.: *All Our Kin: Strategies for Survivial in a Black Community,* Harper & Row, New York, 1974.

Swerdlow, Amy, Renate Bridenthal, Joan Kelly, and Phyllis Vine: *Household and Kin: Families in Flux,* Feminist Press, Old Westbury, N.Y., 1981.

Strasser, Susan: *Never Done: A History of American Housework,* Pantheon, New York, 1982.

SEXUALITY

Barbach, Lonnie Garfield: *For Yourself: The Fulfilment of Female Sexuality,* Doubleday Anchor, New York, 1976.

Barry, Kathleen: *Female Sexual Slavery,* Prentice-Hall, Enclewood Cliffs, N.J., 1979.

The Boston Women's Health Book Collective, *Our Bodies, Ourselves,* Simon & Schuster, New York, 1973.

Brownmiller, Susan, *Against Our Will: Men, Women and Rape,* Simon & Schuster, New York, 1975.

Clark, Lorenne, and Debra Lewis: *Rape: The Price of Coercive Sexuality,* Women's Educational Press, Toronto, 1977.

Ehrenreich, Barbara, and Deirdre English: *Complaints and Disorders: The Politics of Sickness,* Feminist Press, Old Westbury, N.Y., 1973.

Frankfort, Ellen: *Vaginal Politics,* Bantam, New York, 1973.

Gordon, Linda: *Woman's Body, Woman's Right: A Social History of Birth Control in America,* Penguin, New York, 1977.

Griffin, Susan: *Rape: The Power of Consciousness,* Harper & Row, New York, 1979.

Hite, Shere: *The Hite Report: A Nationwide Study of Female Sexuality,* Dell, New York, 1976.

Lederer, Laura: *Take Back the Night: Women on Pornography,* Morrow, New York, 1980.

Linden, Robin Ruth, Darlene R. Pagano, Diana E. H. Russell, Susan Leigh Star (eds.): *Against Sadomasochism: A Radical Feminist Analysis,* Frog in the Well, East Palo Alto, Calif., 1982.

Myron, Nancy, and Charlotte Bunch: *Lesbianism and the Women's Movement,* Diana Press, Baltimore, 1975.

The Red Collective, *The Politics of Sexuality in Capitalism,* Red Collective and Publications Distribution Cooperative, London, 1978.

Seaman, Barbara: *Free and Female,* Coward, McCann and Geoghegan, New York, 1972.

Smart, Carol, and Barry Smart (eds.): *Women, Sexuality and Social Control,* Routledge & Kegan Paul, Boston, London, and Henley, 1978.

Stimpson, Catharine R., and Ethel Spector Person: *Women, Sex and Sexuality,* The University of Chicago Press, Chicago and London, 1980.

ACKNOWLEDGMENTS

Atkinson, Ti-Grace: "Radical Feminism and Love" from *Amazon Odyssey,* Links Books, New York, 1984.

Barry, Kathleen: *Female Sexual Slavery,* Prentice-Hall, Inc. Englewood Cliffs, N. J. 07632. Copyright © by Kathleen Barry.

Bem, Sandra L., and Daryl J. Bem: "Homogenizing the American Woman," adapted from S. L. Bem and D. J. Bem, "Case Study of a Nonconscious Ideology: Training the Woman to Know Her Place," from *Beliefs, Attitudes and Human Affairs,* by D. J. Bem, Brooks/Cole Publishing Company, 1970, pp. 89–99. Copyright © by S. L. Bem and D. J. Bem, 1973.

Benard, Cheryl, and Edit Schlaffer: "The Man in the Street: Why He Harasses" from *Der Mann auf der Strasse.* Copyright © 1980 by Rowohlt Taschenbuch Verlag GmbH, Reinbek bei Hamburg. Reprinted by permission of Rowholt Taschenbuch Verlag GmbH.

Benston, Margaret: "The Political Economy of Women's Liberation" from *Monthly Review,* September 1969, pp. 13–25. Copyright © 1969 by Monthly Review, Inc. Reprinted by permission of Monthly Review Press.

Bettelheim, Bruno: "Fathers Shouldn't Try to Be Mothers," *Parents Magazine,* October 1956, pp. 40 and 126–129. Copyright © 1956, Parents Magazine Enterprises. Reprinted from *Parents* by permission.

Bunch, Charlotte: "Lesbians in Revolt" from *Lesbianism and the Women's Movement,* Diana Press, Oakland, Calif., 1975, pp. 29–37.

Caulfield, Mina Davis: "Imperialism, the Family, and Cultures of Resistance," from *Socialist Revolution* (now called *Socialist Review*), 20, vol. 4, no. 2, pp. 67–85.

Chase Manhattan Bank: Figure of the worth of a woman's work.

Chodorow, Nancy: "Gender, Personality and the Sexual Sociology of Adult Life," from "The Sexual Sociology of Adult Life" in *The Reproduction of Mothering: Psychoanalysis and the Sociology of Gender.* Berkeley, Los Angeles, London: The University of California Press, 1978, pp. 173–190.

Combahee River Collective: "A Black Feminist Statement," from *Capitalist Patriarchy and the Case for Socialist Feminism,* edited by Zillah R. Eisenstein, pp. 362–372. Copyright © 1979 by Zillah R. Eisenstein. Reprinted by permission of Monthly Review Press.

Cronan, Shelia: "Marriage," *Notes from the Third Year: Women's Liberation,* pp. 62–66. Copyright © 1971 by Notes from the Second Year, Inc., P.O. Box AA, Old Chelsea Station, New York, N.Y. 10011.

Davis, Angela: "Rape, Racism, and the Myth of the Black Rapist" from *Women, Race and Class,* by Angela Davis. Pp. 172–201. Copyright © 1981 by Angela Davis. Reprinted by permission of Random House, Inc.

Dreifus, Claudia: "Sterilizing the Poor" from *Seizing Our Bodies,* edited by Claudia Dreifus. New York: Vintage, 1978, pp. 105–120. First appeared in *The Progressive,* 409 East Main Street, Madison, Wisconsin 53703. Copyright © 1975, The Progressive, Inc.

Ehrenreich, Barbara: "The Politics of Talking in Couples: Conversus Interruptus and Other Disorders," May 1981, *Ms. Magazine,* pp. 46–48.

Ehrenreich, Barbara, and Annette Fuentes: "Life on the Global Assembly Line," January 1981, *Ms. Magazine,* pp. 53–59 and 71.

Engels, Friedrich: *The Origin of the Family, Private Property and the State,* International Publishers Company, Inc., New York, 1942, 1970, pp. 87–138, 138–145.

Farley, Lin: "Dealing with Sexual Harrassment," from *Sexual Shakedown: The Sexual Harrassment of Women on the Job,* by Lin Farley. New York: McGraw-Hill, 1978. Reprinted by permission of McGraw-Hill.

Farley, Lin: "Eleven Ways to Fight Sexual Harrassment" from *Sexual Shakedown: The Sexual Harrassment of Women on the Job,* by Lin Farley. New York: Warner Books. Copyright © 1978 by Lin Farley. Reprinted by permission of the author (James Seligmann, agent).

Ferguson, Ann: "Patriarchy, Sexual Identity, and the Sexual Revolution" *Signs: Journal of Woman in Culture and Society,* 1981, vol. 7, no. 1, pp. 158–172.

Firestone, Shulamith: "The Dialectic of Sex" from pp. 1–5, 8–11, 205–209 in *The Dialectic of Sex* by Shulamith Firestone. Copyright © by Shulamith Firestone. Abridged by permission of William Morrow & Company.

Flax, Jane: "A Look at the Cuban Family Code," from *Quest Magazine.* Copyright © Jane Flax, 1978. Pp. 87–88.

Freud, Sigmund: "Femininity," from *New Introductory Lectures on Psychoanalysis* by Sigmund Freud, translated from the German and edited by James Strachey. Copyright © 1965, 1964 by James Strachey. Copyright © 1933 by Sigmund Freud. Copyright renewed 1961 by W. J. H. Sprott. Reprinted by permission of W. W. Norton & Company, Inc. Pp. 158–184.

Gillespie, Marcia Ann: "The Myth of the Strong Black Woman," from *Essence Magazine,* August 1982, pp. 58–60. Copyright © 1982 by Marcia Ann Gillespie.

Charlotte Perkins Gilman Chapter: *A View of Socialist Feminism,* Charlotte Perkins Gilman Chapter, New American Movement, 110 N. Estes Drive, Chapel Hill, N.C. 27514.

Gordon, Linda, and Allen Hunter: "Socialism against Patriarchy," from *Sex, Family and the New Right* by Linda Gordon and Allen Hunter, Radical America, November 1977–February 1978.

Gould, Robert E.: "Measuring Masculinity by the Size of a Paycheck," *Ms. Magazine* June 1973, pp. 18–21. Copyright © 1973 by Ms. Magazine Corp. Reprinted with permission.

Hartmann, Heidi I.: "The Family as the Locus of Gender, Class, and Political Struggle: The Example of Housework," *Signs: Journal of Women in Culture and Society,* 1981, vol. 6, no. 3, pp. 366–394.

Hartmann, Heidi I.: "The Unhappy Marriage of Marxism and Feminism: Towards a More Progressive Union," from *Women and Revolution,* edited by Linda Sargent. Boston: South End Press. Copyright © by Heidi I. Hartman. Reprinted by permission of South End Press and the author. Pp. 1–41.

Hartsock, Nancy: "Staying Alive." First appeared in *Quest: A Feminist Quarterly,* vol. III, no. 3, Winter 1976–1877, pp. 111–122. Copyright © 1976–1977 by Nancy Hartsock.

Herman, Alexis M.: "Still . . . Small Change for Black Women," from *Ms. Magazine* February 1979, pp. 96 and 98.

Hite, Shere: "Redefining Sex," from *The Hite Report* by Shere Hite. Copyright © 1976 by Shere Hite. Reprinted with permission of Macmillan Publishing Company.

Hood, Elizabeth: "Black Women, White Women: Separate Paths to Liberation," *Black Scholar,* April 1978. Reprinted by permission of *Black Scholar.*

Hooks, Bell: "The Myth of the Black Matriarchy" from *Ain't I a Woman: Black Women and Feminism,* pp. 71–78. Copyright © 1981 by Gloria Watkins. Reprinted by permission of South End Press and the author.

Jones, Hardy: "On the Justifiability of Reverse Discrimination," from *Reverse Discrimination,* edited by Barry R. Gross. Buffalo, New York: Prometheus Books, 1977, pp. 348–357. Copyright © 1977 by Prometheus Books. Reprinted by permission of Prometheus Books.

Lenin, V. I.: "Women and Society," from *The Woman: Selections from the Writings of Marx, Engels, Lenin and Stalin,* International Publishers Company, Inc., New York, 1938, pp. 62–63.

London, Linda: "Women Bear the Brunt of Economic Crises," previously unpublished paper, reprinted by permission of the author, who is Community Education Coordinator at Women Helping Women, Cincinnati.

Lorde, Audre: "Scratching the Surface: Some Notes on Barriers to Women and Loving," from *The Black Scholar,* April 1978, pp. 31–35.

Mainardi, Pat: "The Politics of Housework" from *Sisterhood Is Powerful,* Vintage Books, New York, 1970, pp. 447–454.

Maupin, Joyce: "Older Working Women," from WOMEN: *A Journal of Liberation,* vol. 4, no. 2, 1975, p. 14. Copyright © 1975 by WOMEN: A Journal of Liberation, 3028 Greenmount Ave., Baltimore, Md. 21218.

McNamara, Colleen: "I Just Don't Know If I Can Make It," *Up From Under,* vol. 1, no. 4, Winter 1971–1972, p. 34.

Mill, J. S.: "The Subjection of Women," from *Essays on Sex Equality* by John Stuart Mill and Harriet Taylor Mill, edited and with an introductory essay by Alice S. Rossi. Chicago and London: University of Chicago Press, 1970, pp. 125–156.

Moss, Zoe: "It Hurts to Be Alive and Obsolete," from *Sisterhood Is Powerful,* Random House, Inc., New York, 1970, pp. 170–175. Copyright © 1970 by Robin Morgan (ed.). Reprinted by permission of Random House, Inc.

National Organization for Women: "Bill of Rights" adopted at NOW's First National Conference, Washington D.C. Copyright © 1976 by National Organization for Women.

Pogrebin, Letty: "Sex Education for Growing Up Free" from *Growing Up Free: Raising Your Kids in the 80's* by Letty Pogrebin. New York: McGraw-Hill, 1980. Reprinted with permission of McGraw-Hill.

Progressive, The. See *The Progressive.*

Raymond, Janice: "A Genealogy of Female Friendship," first published in *Trivia: A Journal of Ideas,* vol. 1, no. 1. Copyright © 1982. Reprinted by permission of the author.

Reed, Evelyn: "Women: Caste, Class or Oppressed Sex?" from *Problems of Women's Liberation* by Evelyn Reed. New York: Pathfinder Press, Inc., 1970, pp. 64–76. Copyright © 1970 by International Socialist Review. Reprinted by permission of Pathfinder Press, Inc.

INDEX OF
AUTHORS AND TITLES